Tokyo Bay and Airfields

Naka
Kuji
Utsunomiya
Iida
Mito
Omoi
Kima
Tone
Koizumi
Ishioka
Hyakurigahara
Tsukuba
Hokoda
Ara
Lake
Kasumigaura
Kashima
Mawatari
Konoike
Tone
Irumigawa
Tama
Shiroi
Imba
Katori
Tokorozawa
Tachikowa
Tokyo
Sagami
Chiba
Kawasaki
Yokohama
Mobara
Atsugi
Tokyo Bay
Ofuna
Kisarazu
Yoro
Yokosuka
Sagami Bay

0   20   40
miles

Kyushu

Hiro
Strait
Kure
Hiroshima
HONSHU
Korea
Inland Sea
SHIKOKU
Tsuiki
Usa
Sasebo
Beppu
Oita
Bungo Str.
KYUSHU
Saeki
Nagasaki
Yatsushiro
Izumi
Miyakazi
Kagoshima
Shibushu
Chiran
Kushima
Kanoya

0   60
miles

PACIFIC OCEAN

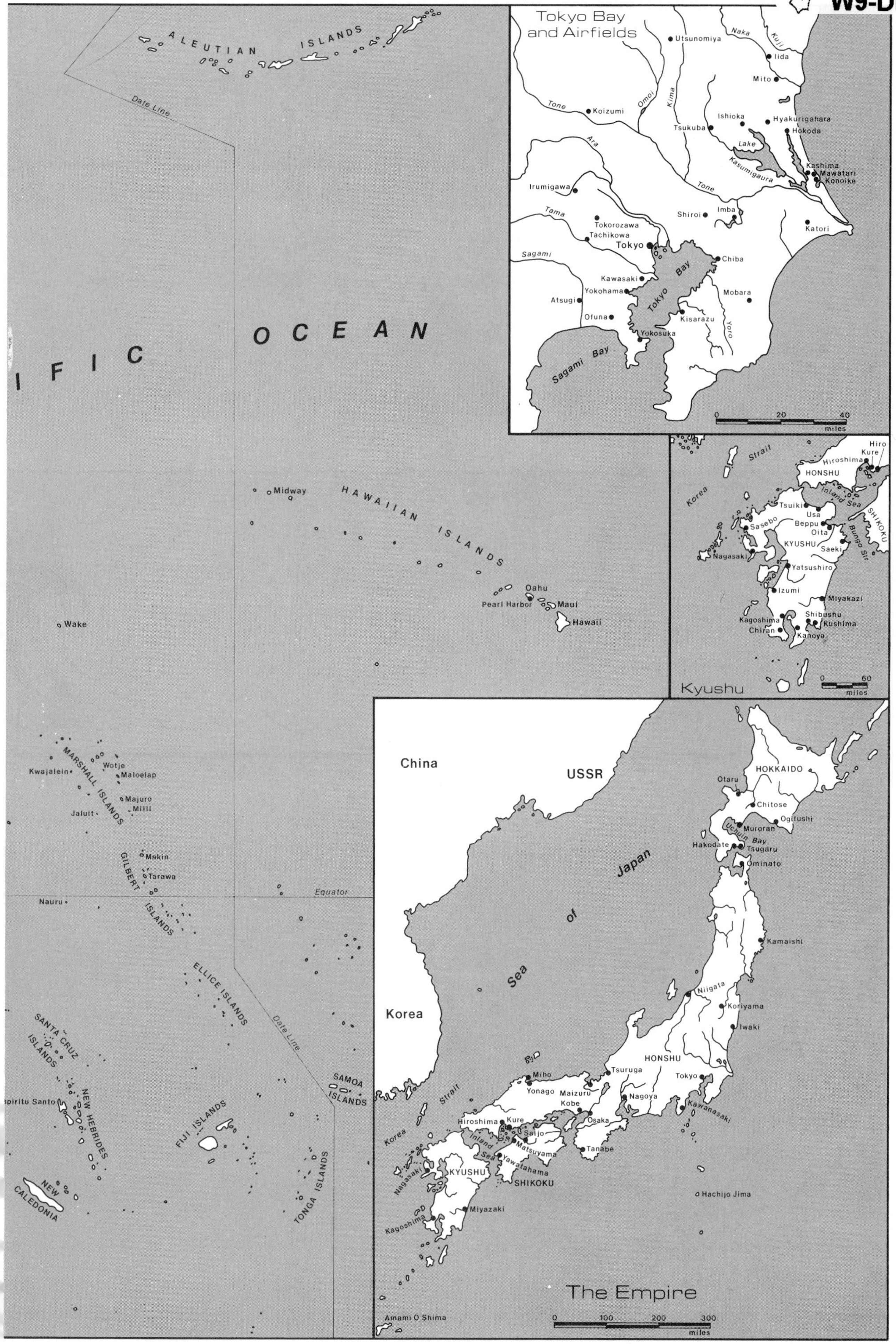

ALEUTIAN ISLANDS
Date Line

Midway
HAWAIIAN ISLANDS
Oahu
Pearl Harbor
Maui
Wake
Hawaii

MARSHALL ISLANDS
Wotje
Maloelap
Kwajalein
Majuro
Milli
Jaluit
GILBERT ISLANDS
Makin
Tarawa
Nauru
Equator
Date Line
SAMOA ISLANDS
SANTA CRUZ ISLANDS
Espiritu Santo
NEW HEBRIDES
FIJI ISLANDS
TONGA ISLANDS
NEW CALEDONIA

The Empire

China
USSR
HOKKAIDO
Otaru
Chitose
Ogilushi
Muroran
Uchiura Bay
Hakodate
Tsugaru
Ominato
Sea
of
Japan
Korea
Kamaishi
Niigata
Koriyama
Iwaki
Miho
Tsuruga
HONSHU
Tokyo
Yonago
Maizuru
Kobe
Nagoya
Hiroshima
Kure
Osaka
Kawanasaki
Korea
Saijo
Inland Sea
Matsuyama
Tanabe
Strait
Nagasaki
Yawatahama
KYUSHU
SHIKOKU
Hachijo Jima
Kagoshima
Miyazaki
Amami O Shima

0   100   200   300
miles

THE FIGHTING LADY

THE *NEW* YORKTOWN IN THE PACIFIC WAR
By **CLARK G. REYNOLDS**

PICTORIAL HISTORIES PUBLISHING CO.
MISSOULA, MONTANA

LIBRARY OF CONGRESS
CATALOG CARD NUMBER 86-61530

ISBN 0-933126-78-6

First Printing October 1986
Second Printing January 1989
Third Printing January 1993
Fourth Printing February 1998

Typography: Falcon Press
Layout: Stan Cohen
Cover Layout: Artmill, Inc.
Endcover Maps: Richard D. Kelly, Jr.

COVER PHOTO
The F6F-3 Hellcat of Jimmy Flatley stands poised on the flight deck of the new *Yorktown*
(CV-10) in 1943 before starting its engine. An airedale sits ready to remove the wheel
chocks as the well-populated island superstructure looms up in the background.
This photograph was taken by Lieutenant Charles W. Kerlee.

PICTORIAL HISTORIES PUBLISHING COMPANY
713 South Third West, Missoula, Montana 59801

Table of Contents

Unless otherwise noted, photographs are Official U.S. Navy Photos.

En route to attack Kwajalein in the Marshall Islands, December 1943.

To my Uncle Bob

F. ROBERT REYNOLDS
Ensign, USNR, U.S.S. *Yorktown* 1943-44
Lieutenant (jg), USNR, and Flag Lieutenant
to Rear Admiral J.J. Clark, 1944-45

who by his letters from the Fighting Lady
to his three-year-old nephew got me
started in naval history.

Jocko Clark and Bob Reynolds, March 1944

Illustrations

Most of the photographs, black-and-white and color, are official U.S. Navy photos. Lieutenant Charles W. Kerlee, USNR, took many of those from 1943 and early 1944; the rest were by Jeff Corey and other photographers mates. The color shots are extremely rare, having only recently been discovered by the Photographic Section of the Naval Historical Center. Most of these color photos, now deposited at the National Archives, are published here for the first time.

The oil paintings were done by Lieutenant William F. Draper, USNR, while assigned to the ship between March and May 1944. Though most have been reproduced elsewhere, this is the first time that all fourteen done on board the *Yorktown* have been assembled in the same book and with Draper's own titles for them. The originals hang at the White House, the Pentagon, the Pensacola Naval Aviation Museum and other facilities and are reproduced courtesy of the U.S. Navy Art Collection.

The cartoons, notably those of John A. Furlow,
were preserved by the men of the Fighting Lady.

NOTE:

ALL SALTY AND ROUGH LANGUAGE IN THIS
BOOK IS QUOTED DIRECTLY FROM PRIMARY
SOURCES AND RECOLLECTIONS OF THE
MEN OF "THE FIGHTING LADY"

Chapter I
Jocko's Ship, Jocko's Team

Guadalcanal, October 15,

1942. Two U.S. Navy F4F Wildcat fighter planes dived through a sky studded with anti-aircraft bursts to strafe six Japanese transports. "Our dives carried us below the mast tops and we observed numerous hits on three transports as we strafed them down the line, also hitting one large barge."

Lieutenant (junior grade) "Smokey" Stover was doing his part in trying to halt the Japanese onslaught in the South Pacific during those dark days of 1942. The handful of men who had donned uniforms before Pearl Harbor, Stover among them, had been buying time in the Pacific while America built her new fleet to win the war. Smokey recounted the events of this particular day in his action report.

"After I pulled out of the second run, I noted a seaplane coming down from the rear when we were at 7000 feet. I turned toward him and we approached each other for at least a half mile. He opened fire at extremely long range. His fire dribbled off to my right. I opened fire at 500 yards but was unable to observe any effect. Only 4 of my 6 guns were firing.

"We both continued in our head-on runs and delayed pull-out so long that we crashed in mid-air, my right wing hitting both of his right wings head-on. Finding that my plane was still controllable, I turned and saw the Jap plane below. I observed the Jap go off into a spin. I proceeded to Henderson Field and landed. I found pieces of fabric (including Rising Sun) on the leading edge of my plane."

Knocking down an enemy plane by colliding with it was the hard way, though Stover had already shot down three in the conventional manner. Either way, the superior aircraft of Grumman manufacture delivered the goods, and though Stover and his squadron mates of Fighting 5 didn't know it at the time, their heroic efforts were beginning to turn the tide of battle against Japan. But it was just the start of what promised to be a very long offensive in the Pacific.

That same afternoon Stover was evacuated by cargo plane with his squadron out of Guadalcanal and thence home for rest and reassignment to the new ships coming down the ways. The 22-year-old Elisha Terrill Stover received orders to one of them—the still-uncompleted *Yorktown*, namesake of the one American carrier lost at the Battle of Midway five months before.

Smokey had been at Midway on board the carrier *Hornet*, as had Lieutenant (senior grade) Edgar E. Stebbins, he at the controls of an SBD Dauntless dive bomber. Now, on October 26, 1942, in the Battle of the Santa Cruz Islands, the 26-year-old Stebbins dropped a 1000-pound bomb squarely onto the bridge of a Japanese cruiser, causing severe damage and heavy casualties. Turning for home, he encountered and shot down a Japanese fighter and a torpedo plane. But his home was no more, for Japanese planes had bombed and sunk the *Hornet*. The Navy lost no time in finding a new home for him on board another ship—the new *Yorktown*.

The *Hornet's* loss climaxed more than ten months of destruction of major U.S. warships by the Imperial Japanese Navy as it sought to rid the Pacific of challengers to its aggression. In order to complete the conquest of China, begun in 1937, and then turn against Soviet Russia for the domination of Asia, Japan had gone after the one navy to stand in its way. Japanese carriers had sunk the American battleships at Pearl Harbor on December 7, 1941. Japan had then pushed into the South Pacific to seal off Australia and had headed back toward Hawaii in a vain attempt to neutralize Pearl Harbor by capturing the airfield on Midway Island.

Although the Japanese lost four carriers in the

Battle of Midway in June 1942 and their bid to take the island, they had more success in their struggle to control the South Pacific waters around Guadalcanal. In several battles and submarine attacks, Japanese forces had eliminated America's carriers one by one: the *Lexington* in May, the old *Yorktown* at Midway, the *Wasp* in September and finally the *Hornet* in October, the same time that the *Enterprise* had to retire for repairs from battle damage. The *Saratoga* had been torpedoed and sent back to the yards on two separate occasions.

The American stand at Guadalcanal nevertheless blunted Japan's advance in the South Pacific and enabled the United States to build its new ships and train fresh crews and pilots in order to assume the offensive. Veterans like Ed Stebbins and Smokey Stover were key elements for the fleet then rebuilding.

Both Texans from the Dallas area and college-trained engineers, neither man was regular Navy. Steb had left S.M.U. in 1936 to fly for the Navy and briefly Braniff Airways. A shipmate described him as "dark-haired and slight, a friendly character with a funny gap between his two top front teeth that gives his smile a quizzical look." Smokey, nicknamed for the comic strip character, had graduated from North Texas State at age 19 in 1939. He was a gentle, lovable individual whom everyone liked but who as a pilot was merciless on airplanes. When asked how many he had destroyed, he replied, "Ten—four Japanese and six of our own!" His head-on collision was only the most dramatic example of just how much he demanded from his fighter.

These Reservists got their direction from respected regular Navy career aviators like James H. Flatley, Jr., a 1929 U.S. Naval Academy graduate and innovator in basic fighter plane tactics who became an "ace" by downing five enemy planes in the carrier battles of 1942. He commanded the "Grim Reapers" fighter squadron on the *Enterprise* at Guadalcanal, where he bumped into an old shipmate, Captain "Jocko" Clark. Clark made Flatley an inviting proposition. Having received orders to return home to take command of the new carrier *Yorktown*, Jocko wondered if Jimmy would like to join him as commander of the ship's new air group. Flatley accepted eagerly.

Joseph James Clark had been born a one-eighth Cherokee Indian in the Will Rogers neighborhood of Oklahoma before it became a state. On one of his first days at Annapolis, way back in 1913, Clark was standing in ranks when a classmate hollered out, "The Right Reverend J. Jonathan Jockey

"Jocko" Clark, skipper of the new *Yorktown*.

Clark!" The nickname stuck and added color to this rough-and-tumble character who graduated in 1917, saw convoy duty during World War I, and went on to take flight training at the relatively advanced age of 31 in 1925. He proved his mettle as a leader in the early 1930s while skipper of the crack Fighting Squadron 2 on the *Lexington*. Most of the squadron's pilots had been A.P.s—enlisted "Aviation Pilots"—but led by men like Clark and a young Jimmy Flatley. Both men again teamed up early in 1941, this time to open the new naval air training base at Jacksonville, Florida.

At Jax, the pilot trainees found an object of speculation in the gruff, 47-year-old pilot. Aside from his nickname, there were his physical features: a powerfully-set face with jowled cheeks, a high Indian-like humped nose, and protruding lower lip; light, blondish hair; a medium build with small hands; a scathingly loud bark and bite; and a peculiar limp in his gait. He had once tried to stop a loose-running anchor cable with his foot, only to have his leg snapped, causing compound fractures. He had talked the doctors out of amputation but was left with his limp, which turned out to be no handicap in the cockpit. A man who obviously knew his business, Clark lived—and commanded—by the motto, "Watch for every angle and fight for every inch."

In fact, Jocko Clark had only been an adequate peacetime naval officer who performed best in the cockpit, the nearest thing to combat. He was meant to be a fighting leader, not a desk officer or even a family man. His personal life had become something of a disaster, leading to unhappy divorce proceedings, though his energies were absorbed in the work of preparing the Navy's air arm for war. In May 1941 Clark transferred to the first carrier *Yorktown*, relieving a friend of many years as executive officer (second-in-command), Commander Arthur W. Radford. His captain was Elliott Buckmaster.

Clark chafed at the job. He regarded Buckmaster as too lax with the ship's department heads and downright unaggressive, although a good shiphandler. On the other hand, Clark himself hated administrative detail and tended to rely on his own small coterie of enlisted men, notably two, the chief master-at-arms and the exec's yeoman, rather than going through the proper officer channels. He was a hard-driving taskmaster, constantly pushing the crew to do its utmost.

Clark's impact on the men of the first *Yorktown* was mixed. The junior officers did not particularly care for him, whereas the sailors loved him. Morale on board had been at a low ebb due to Radford's general aloofness and strict adherence to "the book." Jocko identified with the men, showed concern for them, and as long as they did their work he was known to step right over an illegal crap game without saying a word. After the *Yorktown* raided the Japanese-held Gilbert Islands in January 1942, Clark was promoted to captain and detached from the ship, hell-bent on getting command of a ship of his own.

He was not disappointed. Selected to take charge of one of the first small escort carriers then under conversion from an oil tanker, the *Suwannee*, Captain Clark descended like a whirlwind on the Newport News Shipbuilding and Dry Dock Company in Virginia, where the ship was being completed. He endeared himself to the Navy high command and shipyard managers by cajoling, persuading and badgering workers and crewmen alike to finish the flattop in time to see action.

Without a day to spare, Clark managed to get the *Suwannee* completed and into the first offensive in the Atlantic—the landings at Casablanca, North Africa in November 1942. Then he took her to the South Pacific to beef up U.S. defenses there. So pleased was the Navy with Clark's performance that it issued him fresh orders to return to Newport News as prospective commanding officer of a big new carrier—the second *Yorktown*.

After enlisting Lieutenant Commander Jimmy Flatley as his air group commander, Jocko immediately requested—and got—Commander Raymond R. Waller for his executive officer. Softspoken, Tennessee-bred "Raöul" Waller, Annapolis '24, had twice served on the *Lexington*—with old Fighting 2 and as landing signal officer, waving the planes aboard. His new orders took him completely by surprise, however, simply because he knew Jocko Clark only by reputation and at that as a man with an exactly opposite personality than his own. But Clark knew Waller to be an absolutely meticulous and well-ordered administrator who insisted upon a neat and clean ship and who carefully attended to all details of shipboard management—all the things that Clark himself had failed to be as exec of the old *Yorktown*.

In short, the brusque Indian had recognized the need for a foil, a counterweight and cushion to his own fire-eating brand of leadership, and Waller would provide it.

As Clark headed cross-country to Newport News, he made a slight detour to visit his parents in Oklahoma, stopping off first at the Navy's sprawling air technical training center at Norman to obtain the use of a Navy car. On the evening he arrived, he could not pry a car from the duty officer, one Ensign F. Robert Reynolds, who was only following base regulations. At the "advanced" age of 27 for an ensign, Bob Reynolds had only just been commissioned out of "90-day-wonder school." As far as he was concerned, the rules of base commander Captain V.C. "You-all" Griffin were holy scripture. (The nickname came from Griffin's thick Alabama drawl; "I know you-all call me 'You-all Griffin' but don't you-all ever let *me* catch you saying it!") Whereupon Captain Clark went straight to his old friend Griffin (known to his friends as "Squash"), who called in Ensign Reynolds and chewed him out right in front of Clark.

When Griffin dismissed Reynolds, Captain Clark went out with him and laughed off the whole incident. Only then did the ensign realize that he had been "had." The whole scene had been staged at his expense.

As they talked, Reynolds could only think, "You bastard!" He had seen a puckish side of Jocko Clark that many others regarded as downright meanness. But not Reynolds. He saw the incident as a great joke, which it was, and he liked the guy for it.

"Where do you go from here, Captain?"

"I'm going to Newport News to take command of a big new carrier, take her out to the Pacific, and kick the hell out of the Japs!"

"Gee, I sure wish I could go with you."

"You really mean that?"

"You *know* I do!"

Jocko wrote down Reynolds' full name and serial number, took a Navy car and bade the ensign farewell. The latter thought nothing of it though, until two weeks later when he was greeted with orders transferring him from Norman to Newport News.

Jocko Clark had made a snap decision to use this eager young ensign because of the man's obviously quick mind and "clear eye." He could not know that Reynolds had graduated from Santa Barbara State Teachers College, had run his own trucking company before the war, and had even survived the disastrous Coconut Grove nightclub fire in Boston two months before. Clark knew only that he admired and needed men who wanted to fight; he'd find jobs for such fighters, whatever their qualifications.

A pal of Reynolds' at the Norman base just happened to have been a former shipmate of Jocko's— Joseph L. Tucker. Joe Tucker had enlisted in the Navy as a common seaman back in 1928 and had been a metalsmith servicing the Navy's aircraft ever since. The prewar generation of aviation officers, A.P.s and chief petty officers had been a closed circle, in which everyone knew each other; Joe Tucker had in fact served with Jocko on the "Old Yorky" during 1941-42.

Tucker agonized while that whole generation of his friends was decimated in the battles of 1942, including his own brother, shot down over Guadalcanal while flying with Smokey Stover. To make matters worse, the Navy had then given Tucker a commission as lieutenant, ending his carefree days as an enlisted man, and had sent him to Norman. The creation of such "mustang" officers was one of the Navy's ways of replacing its losses and manning new billets. Ere long, the easy-going Alabamian used Bob Reynolds to convince Jocko to order him also to the new *Yorktown*.

Jocko Clark was building his team from the survivors of the old Navy and from new young bloods who were still strangers to the old guard. Checking in first to the Bureau of Aeronautics in Washington, he ran into a former officer from the *Suwannee*, Lieutenant (jg) Herman S. Rosenblatt, the sharp younger brother of Jock's attorney who begged to return to sea with Jocko. Though a brilliant lawyer in his own right, Rosenblatt suffered from the anti-Semitism of the day, which shaped his personality as being aloof and obnoxious among his peers. But Jocko recognized the value of talent and absolute loyalty of someone like Rosenblatt whom, literally within hours, he shunted off to the air combat intelligence school at Quonset Point, Rhode Island, as preparation for duty on the *Yorktown*.

Clark also wanted bright lights who were on the way up in the Navy to join his team and provide the professional direction. Commander George W. Anderson, Jr., was such a person. Destined one day to become Chief of Naval Operations, the tall, handsome "Gorgeous George" had been a key planner for Admiral John H. Towers, Chief of the Bureau of Aeronautics early in the war. Now that Towers had taken command of the Pacific Fleet's air forces, he wanted Anderson out in Hawaii with him. First Anderson needed some sea time, however, so Jocko signed him on as navigator.

Captain Clark could not begin to select personally all the 125 officers for his ship; he could only hope that the bureaus of aeronautics and personnel would assign him competent leaders. Time would only tell whether they turned out to be the dynamos he wanted—or duds. Naval Academy regulars got the few senior posts on the new ship, but the majority of junior officers had joined up as Reserves only for the duration.

Aside from the same uniform and orders, then, little commonality could be found in the persons of George Anderson, Herman Rosenblatt, Joe Tucker, Bob Reynolds, Raóul Waller, Jimmy Flatley, Ed Stebbins and Smokey Stover. The force that would bind them together would be Captain Jocko Clark, as he gathered his team at Newport News.

"V" was (and is) the Navy's symbol for aircraft, "CV" for aircraft carrier, "VF" for fighter squadron and so forth. On December 1, 1941—six days before the Pearl Harbor attack—the keel of the Navy's tenth and newest carrier, designated CV-10, was laid down at the Newport News shipyard. The second of the new *Essex* (CV-9) class carriers, she had been authorized by Congress in July 1940 to the tune of $43,225,380 and was assigned the name of *Bon Homme Richard* after John Paul Jones' famous Revolutionary War frigate.

But the loss of the old *Yorktown* (CV-5) at Mid-

PLANK OWNERS' CERTIFICATE

TO ALL SAILORS AND AVIATORS
WHEREVER YE MAY BE — GREETINGS:
KNOW YE BY THESE PRESENTS THAT

Ens F.R. Reynolds

WAS A MEMBER OF THE ORIGINAL CREW WHICH COMMISSIONED THE
USS YORKTOWN AND IS THEREFOR ENTITLED TO ALL THE RIGHTS
AND PRIVILEGES OF A PLANK OWNER ON SAID SHIP INCLUDING A CLEAR
AND UNENCUMBERED TITLE TO ONE PLANK IN THE FLIGHT DECK.

DATE OF COMMISSIONING
April 15, 1943

J.J. Clark
CAPTAIN U.S. NAVY
COMMANDING

way led the Navy in September 1942 to assign the name of *Yorktown* to CV-10 in honor of the old gal. It was a name dear to the Navy, stretching back to the Revolution when, in 1781, the allied French fleet had defeated the British off Yorktown, Virginia (not far from Newport News) and forced Lord Cornwallis to surrender his army to General Washington at Yorktown, insuring American independence. In addition, a sailing sloop-of-war had carried the name *Yorktown* during the 1840s as had a turn-of-the-century gunboat.

The Newport News company, which had built the 19,900-ton first carrier *Yorktown* in the late 1930s, was the ideal choice to complete the job on the new 27,100-ton *Yorktown*. In the center of the yard stood a granite monument with a mounted plaque which epitomized the philosophy of Newport News and its dynamic president Homer L. Ferguson:

We shall build good ships here—
At a profit if we can,
At a loss if we must,
But always good ships.

Theoretically, the Navy gave the shipyard until September 15, 1944 to complete the *Yorktown*.

Realistically, the war would be lost by then if the new carrier and her sisters did not reach the Pacific long before that time. The old CV-5 had taken a leisurely 40 peacetime months to build, but the coming of the war led to unprecedentedly accelerated production schedules. Newport News finished the new *Essex*, first of her class, in a record 20 months and turned her over to the Navy on the last day of 1942. But even that was not fast enough.

One shortcut was to assign key prospective ship's officers and senior enlisted personnel to the shipyard during construction. So the *Yorktown's* chief engineer, Commander James A. McNally, reported in mid-1942, fresh from having reconditioned the engines of two battleships raised from the mud of Pearl Harbor. "Blackie" McNally—so nicknamed for his career in shipboard engineering "black gangs"—helped install the power plant over the keel: four big Westinghouse turbine engines, eight Babcock and Wilcox boilers, four turbo-generators for auxiliary power, and two emergency diesel generators. Superheated steam would feed power to the engines, then through four double reduction geared turbine units and to the four propeller shafts to provide 180,000 maximum horsepower. On a full load of fuel, the *Yorktown* was designed to cruise 20,000 miles at 15 knots or reach a maximum speed of 33 knots.

Hull number 393 was built around the engine plant, the length extending 855 feet along the main or hangar deck from bow to stern, and the beam (breadth) 93 feet 2 inches—the maximum allowable for a tight squeeze through the Panama Canal. "Gun tubs" of additional anti-aircraft guns would be installed once the ship reached the Pacific, increasing her beam to 101 feet. Superimposed over the hangar was the 872-foot-long, 147-foot, 6-inch-wide flight deck, while the draft, or depth in the water of the fully-loaded flattop, would be just over 28 feet.

Unlike the newest battleships with their 18-inch-thick armor belts, new carriers like the *Yorktown* were thinly armored in order to allow the stowage of a greater number of aircraft. The planes were supposed to prevent enemy planes from hitting the ship. Nevertheless, a modicum of armor was built into several decks: 0.1 inch of steel under the teakwood flight deck to shield the hangar from fires on the flight deck; 2.5 inches on the hangar deck to absorb a 1000-pound bomb before it could penetrate to the three decks of living and working spaces beneath it; and 1.5 inches at the fourth deck and a 4-inch belt of side armor at the waterline to protect the engines, oil tanks and ammunition magazines below. A triple bottom and transverse bulkheads (walls) would cushion underwater blasts from torpedo and mine hits. Splinter shields on the island superstructure towering over the flight deck did only that—protected personnel from small bomb fragments.

Newport News worked at such breakneck speed that it completed the hull and engines months ahead of schedule, enabling the date of launching to be fixed for January 21, 1943—only thirteen and a half months after the laying of the keel. This would put the ship in the water so that the outfitting could proceed over the ensuing five months, with formal commissioning set for June 21—more than one year ahead of the original timetable. Captain Clark, still en route from the Pacific, would not even arrive in time for the launching ceremonies, while Commander Waller reported in only two days before, on January 19, and officers and senior non-coms straggled in over many days.

And the Navy invited the First Lady of the land, Mrs. Eleanor Roosevelt, to christen the new ship, just as she had the Old Yorky back in 1936. She wasn't sure and wrote the Secretary of the Navy,

Frank Knox: "I wonder whether I should sponsor the new U.S.S. Yorktown inasmuch as the one I sponsored met such a sad fate? I know there are superstitions in the Navy, and would want to be sure that it was wise for me to do this before making any definite promise. Will you please be quite frank?" To which the Secretary responded, "Please banish any fears you may have in respect to your sponsoring the new YORKTOWN. Everyone in the Navy would love to have you do so." Perpetuating ships' names was an old Navy tradition. Whereupon she accepted.

Launching day arrived sunny but bitterly raw. Soldiers with submachine guns stood inside the barricade around Shipway No. 9, patrol boats cruised about in the James River and nearby Chesapeake Bay, and Navy fighters roared overhead. Among the dignitaries who arrived with Mrs. Roosevelt were Artemus L. Gates, Assistant Secretary of the Navy for Air, and Rear Admiral Buckmaster, last skipper of the first *Yorktown*.

The ceremony began and led to Admiral Buckmaster addressing remarks to the shipyard workers, "Your efforts to weld together the natural resources of America that go into the construction of such magnificent fighting craft is beyond praise. . . ."

Suddenly, at the word "praise," the great mass of steel before him quivered. Unaccountably, at 1237, seven minutes ahead of the appointed moment, the ship was starting to slip off its stocks, which sent a collective gasp through the old-timers on hand who imagined portents of bad luck for a ship launched without a formal christening. The massive weight of the vessel—2000 tons heavier than the yard had ever launched before—had simply created too great a strain on the "triggers" holding the ship in place.

But Mrs. Roosevelt jumped out of her seat, grabbed the bottle of champagne and swung it forward, only to have it hit the receding hull with a dull thud and bounce right back on its tethered ribbon, unbroken.

Eleanor caught it and gave it a solid swing. This time the bottle splattered on impact, spraying her and Admiral Buckmaster with champagne, while the *Yorktown* gained momentum. The carrier slid down the ways amidst the roar of approving shipyard workers and Navy men who now envisioned the ship as a great lady eager for battle.

Though now afloat, the unfinished carrier resembled little more than a hulk and was tied up alongside a pier for her "overboard" stage of outfitting. Captain Clark finally came aboard on February 15, inspected the ship, and went into a huddle with the assistant yard superintendent for outfitting, Douglas Petty. Petty had worked with Clark when the old *Yorktown* had been drydocked there and as key building supervisor on the *Suwannee*, Jocko's first command.

Jocko did not like the prospects. Though the date of commissioning of June 21, 1943 was now moved up even closer, to April 15, he knew that Navy ships just *weren't* commissioned on schedule, especially this one, now rated as only 73.8 percent completed. By contrast, a sister ship, the *Bunker Hill* (CV-17), had been launched six weeks ahead of the *Yorktown* at Bethlehem Steel in Quincy, Massachusetts; she was considered to be 85.2 percent complete. By pulling strings, Clark might be able to switch to command of the *Bunker Hill* instead of the *York* and get into the fighting earlier. He told Petty, "That ship is gonna go out first. I'd like to go with it."

"Captain," replied Petty, "if you stick with us, you'll go out first." Clark was not convinced. He approached company president Homer Ferguson for guarantees that the *Yorktown* would meet her commissioning date. It was a tall order, but Ferguson remembered their success with the *Suwannee* only months before, and he knew that with Clark's dynamic help it could be done. To E.F. Herd, general manager for the whole yard, and to Petty, Ferguson repeated his usual speech, "There's three ways to do a job: the right way, the wrong way, and my way. Let's do it my way." He persuaded the Navy not to divert any materials from the *Yorktown* to the *Bunker Hill* and gave Jocko carte blanche. The combined team of Ferguson, Eddie Herd, Doug Petty and Jocko Clark now got to work to set a record—eleven weeks "overboard" time from launching to commissioning, over three of which had already gone by!

Clark meant for his ship to be the Number One new carrier and to be the first of the *Essexes* into battle, which meant pushing ahead not only of the *Bunker Hill* but of the new *Lexington* (CV-16) as well, commissioned at Quincy on February 17. Way behind the *Essex*, already in commission, Jocko proclaimed he would beat them all into action by focusing on the *Essex*. "Beat the *Essex*!" became his battle cry. When asked in later years the source of all of this competition, Clark smiled, "I generated it."

Hard work alone could not beat the *Essex* and the other carriers, though it helped; what was needed were radical departures from traditional outfitting procedures, and Jocko made them. Cut corners, he said. If aluminum was needed but only steel was handy, use steel. Done. If hatches wouldn't close to keep out leaking fuel oil, coamings should be installed around them instead of rebuilding them. Done. In battle, shrapnel had hit gas lines leading up from the hangar to the flight deck; with no time to relocate them, casings should be put around them. Done. And when the Navy bureaucrats seemed sluggish, Clark or Waller would fly to Washington and just sit in the offending office until they got what they needed.

If material for these tasks was not available, Jocko said, it ought to be taken from sister flattops being built in the yard—the *Intrepid* (CV-11), the new *Hornet* (CV-12), *Franklin* (CV-13) and *Ticonderoga* (CV-14). And if more men were required to do the work on the *Yorktown*, they should be pulled off the other ships. Ferguson, Herd and Petty answered, "Go!" Jocko broke nearly every rule in the book. At one time he had over 4000 men of the yard's 31,000-man work force laboring on his ship alone.

It was a scramble, and as each department head and assistant head reported in they got it both barrels from the fiery Clark. Everywhere at once, so it seemed, he drove all officers relentlessly until they dreaded his coming. He was a taskmaster—a sundowner in Navy parlance—merciless, gruff, stern, loud, utterly humorless and totally uncompromising. "Goddammit," he roared at them, "If you can't run, walk. If you can't walk, crawl. But get the job done. And if you can't get the job done, get off my ship!"

Some men hated him for it and would be transferred by a displeased captain, but most of them didn't know any better. They had signed on to fight the Japs, and their captain must have been typical of all Navy skippers. Having no basis for comparison, these 90-day-wonders and kid sailors merely submitted to his tyranny without question. They worked to near exhaustion.

But none more so than Clark himself. An ulcer condition he had developed over recent years worsened to the point where he could eat only bland foods like tenderized chicken, creamed vegetables and goat's milk—a diet he would maintain for the duration. Yet, shipyard personnel marveled at his energy, admired his determination, and thus came to share his compulsion to make the *Yorktown* Number One. Jocko Clark was, in short, a LEADER.

Old Navy men and newcomers also appreciated the exec. Raöul Waller always seemed to be on the move to answer Jocko's every call. Scurrying briskly about, he tended to walk lightly on his toes, so that amused sailors referred to him as "Mr. Eggshells." Clark, preoccupied with finishing the ship, relied completely on Waller to organize his departments—Engineering, Navigation, Hull, Gunnery, Communications, Air, Supply, and Medical—and to assign the officers as they reported.

April came and with it the realization that Jocko and Petty might just make the desired commissioning date of the 15th. But the shipyard Trial Board first had to test everything—aircraft elevators, helm, machinery—which usually took a full week. Jocko told them to do it in a day—and they did! Then the Navy's Board of Inspection and Survey had to examine and approve *Yorktown's* readiness for acceptance into the Navy, and did so on April 9, six days before commissioning.

One of the inspecting officers was Captain Ralph E. Jennings. He couldn't believe what he saw. "Of the many new ships I inspected while on the Board," he said a year later, "she was in the best condition of them all as far as appearance and readiness for duty were concerned." So impressed was he, in fact, that he began to pull strings to get into line to relieve Clark as the second skipper of this fine ship. (He would succeed). The seven officers who comprised the Board began their report, "This vessel was in an excellent material condition. . . . Cleanliness was excellent." Many little things still needed to be done, but the Board recommended that commissioning proceed on schedule.

Jocko had done it. He had made the planned commissioning date of April 15, 1943—an unheard-of event. He had beaten the *Bunker Hill*, not yet in commission, though he had a long way to go to catch up with the new *Lexington* and especially the *Essex*. But nothing could now arrest the momentum of the *Yorktown*.

What was more, Jocko had showed how outfitting a carrier *should* be done. Not just his carrier, but *all* carriers. From this moment on, Doug Petty and Homer Ferguson and the other shipbuilding companies simply adopted the same methods of cutting corners to turn out their men-of-war. No formal decision was made. Everyone just knew how the *Yorktown* had been completed, and they just adopted its measures as precedents. Jocko Clark was ahead of the whole Navy! His ship had become Number One in its record completion, and Jocko

intended to make it Number One in the fleet.

The 2400 kids—"fresh from the cotton fields" in the words of Raöul Waller—came aboard all day the 14th after shipyard personnel moved the *Yorktown* over to the navy yard at Norfolk. Most had recently completed basic training at Great Lakes near Chicago, although Captain Clark had let them come aboard in large groups for general orientation over preceding days.

That evening, the captain gave his assembled officers the word: "This ship will reach the combat zone in record time and in complete combat readiness. Therefore any officer who remains aboard will grade his own fitness report a perfect 4.0, since I will tolerate nothing less!"

After the shipyard workers moved the ship to another pier at dawn on a cold and bitter April 15th, the V.I.P.s came aboard for the commissioning ceremony. In addition to Secretary Gates and five admirals, Clark had invited his Congressman and the chief of the Cherokees from Oklahoma, but ship's sponsor Eleanor Roosevelt had to cancel her appearance at the last minute. The ceremony could not begin until the ship's bandmaster, Lloyd A. Andermann, showed up; Commander Waller found "Bandy" wandering around the hangar deck, unable to find a ladder to the flight deck! These kids *were* green.

Finally, moments past the noon hour, Doug Petty presented the *Yorktown* to the Navy, and ship's chaplain Robert L. Alexander stepped forward. A tall, lanky Lincolnesque Presbyterian from Lumberton, North Carolina, the 40-year-old father of two nervously gave the invocation before the distinguished assemblage. Then Secretary Gates held forth, harkening back to the time when his Pilgrim forebears had landed on these shores. Next, Cherokee Jocko responded with the old Will Rogers line that *his* ancestors had been here to greet Gates', and the crew chuckled quietly as they watched Gates stiffen up at this crack.

Then Clark addressed the crew, and the new swabbies stood transfixed at his thunder. "We're all going to do our job and do it well, and we can all come out with flying colors. A chain is only as strong as the weakest link. I'm not going to put up with any weak links!" "Wow!" thought new fireman Wilbur Steg. Clark's voice rose: "Anybody who is dissatisfied and doesn't want to go to the Pacific with me, step forward and we'll transfer you now!" Of course no one did. None had the guts to.

After a banquet for the guests in the officers' wardroom, the ship was moved to a drydock, and next day Jocko made good his promises. He broke Navy Yard regulations by loading ammo in drydock and worked his crew to the bone taking on more guns, radar and general stores; the *Yorktown's* displacement would rise from 27,100 to 36,200 tons by the time she reached the Pacific. When the yard could not spare personnel to scrape down the hull for painting, Jocko had scaffolds lowered over the side and had his own crew—junior officers included!—do the job in one day with air-powered wire brushes. Yard workmen continued to add equipment, and more officers reported in.

As shipfitters installed pipes on the outside of the hull, chief engineer McNally noticed they had no expansion joints. He approached Captain Clark on the bridge, "You can't go to war without putting the expansions on! The pipes might carry away in a typhoon."

"How long's it gonna take?"

"About a month."

"To *hell* with it. If we get into a typhoon, we won't give a damn. We'll be too far out at sea. Don't put 'em on."

Blackie walked away, shaking his head and muttering, "Honest to God. This ship—I don't know. . . ."

One new officer who quickly won the affection of the crew was assistant medical officer Raymond F. Gard, a 42-year-old graduate of the University of Kansas Medical School who had joined up to do his part. In a letter to his teenage son he announced, "Sonny, who do you suppose is with us? The mighty ball pitcher George Earnshaw. If he gets a crack at a Jap with one of those fast inside curves, someone is going 'out.'" The 43-year-old 6-foot-4 "Moose" Earnshaw had been an ace right-hander over nine years in the big leagues, mostly with Connie Mack's world champion Philadelphia A's. Over loud protests of the Bureau of Naval Personnel that the athletic-specialist Lieutenant Commander Earnshaw would turn out to be a white elephant, baseball-loving Jocko Clark had sent him to Norfolk's anti-aircraft school to learn to be *Yorktown's* assistant gunnery officer.

On April 27 the drydock was flooded, and Jocko took the *Yorktown* out into the Chesapeake Bay for her sea trials in this enclosed sea secluded from German subs. The unseasoned swabs battled seasickness, and the officers on the bridge endured the wrath of the skipper as he put them through their paces, chasing them one-by-one from the bridge whenever they slipped up, which was usually every time they took the conn as officers-of-the-deck. Particularly disastrous was his attempt to maneuver alongside a fleet oiler, which repeatedly rammed into the carrier, causing minor damage.

But Clark's biggest concern was gunnery drill—practice firings by his twelve 5-inch/38 caliber, 32 40mm and 46 20mm guns at target sleeves towed behind planes from airfields ashore. He worked his gun crews mercilessly until they didn't dare miss. Back and forth, up and down the Chesapeake, the *Yorktown* steamed for days, working out the kinks and testing equipment and guns. Everything had to be in working order before the carrier could begin operating aircraft.

One day the preceding December, San Diego's naval air station bristled with the usual activity of many different types of planes, all with the same U.S. Navy markings. Few heads turned to watch just one more single-engine fighter roll down the runway and into the air. The pilot, Lieutenant Melvin C. "Boogie" Hoffman, could not help but wonder if his cross-country hop to the national capital would cause any sensation or even notice. For the plane, painted Navy blue with the regulation white stars on the wings and fuselage, was none other than a Japanese Zero. Captured virtually intact in the Aleutian Islands during the Midway operations, the enemy fighter had been sent to San Diego for tests. Hoffman was flying it to the East coast for further study.

Oddly enough, even in those jittery early days of the war, not one ground spotter or pilot reported the Zero on its long flight. Hoffman, an experienced test pilot, flew it to Florida for simulated dogfights against different types of American fighters. The data learned was rushed to the Grumman Aircraft Engineering Company's designers at Bethpage, Long Island, and then incorporated into the new fighter Grumman was developing to replace the F4F Wildcat and specifically to beat the Zero—the F6F Hellcat. Like the shipbuilders at Newport News, Grumman shattered peacetime records in completing the new plane—during the autumn. Then crack Navy test pilots like Boogie Hoffman took over ironing out the wrinkles before the plane could be assigned to the new carriers.

At the same time, new pilots were coming out of flight training at Pensacola and Jacksonville for assignment to squadrons then reorganizing after the battles of 1942 for deployment with the rebuilt fleet. Three squadrons were earmarked to comprise

Air Group Five on the *Yorktown*—fighters, dive bombers and torpedo-bombers. The Group was officially commissioned at the air station complex around Norfolk on February 15, 1943, even before Jimmy Flatley had returned from the Pacific to take command.

To lead the 36-plane fighter squadron, the Navy assigned a sensational test pilot, Lieutenant Commander Charles L. Crommelin, one of five brothers from Wetumpka, Alabama who had graduated from Annapolis (Charlie in 1931), four of them into naval aviation. Charlie had even married the daughter of Elliott Buckmaster, last skipper of the old *Yorktown*. Like Boogie Hoffman, whom he selected to go with him to the *York*, Crommelin found the F6F-3 to be a dream plane. And like Jocko, he wanted to get the first production Hellcats ahead of any other squadron. So one fine day in January 1943 Charlie took eight of his pilots to the Grumman plant in New York and finagled his friends there to give them the first Hellcats, earmarked though they were for the *Essex's* fighter squadron. Thus developed another aspect of the "Beat the *Essex*!" rivalry. The *Yorktown* fighters trained at the Oceana and Creeds airfields near Norfolk.

The 36-plane bombing squadron of *Yorktown's* air group was formed from two smaller units in California, 20 of these pilots flying to the Curtiss-Wright airplane factory in Columbus, Ohio also to receive a new airplane. The big, powerful SB2C Helldiver had been designed to replace the smaller but reliable Douglas SBD Dauntless. But when they returned to their West coast fields with the new plane, they discovered it to be plagued with mechanical difficulties. One malfunction claimed the life of one pilot, and the men soon nicknamed the SB2C "the Beast." When they received 36 new Helldivers after their arrival at Norfolk in April, they found these to be little better.

The 18-plane torpedo squadron flew the combat-proved TBF-1C Avenger, like the Hellcat built by Grumman. The bulky three-seat torpedo-bomber had made its debut at the Battle of Midway, flying from that island itself. One of Torpedo Squadron 5's aircrewmen, now 20-year-old Aviation Chief Radioman Harry H. Ferrier, had been the only enlisted man to survive the virtual annihilation of Torpedo 8 in that epic battle. The squadron skipper was tough, exacting Lieutenant Commander Richard Upson, who put his several senior lieutenants and green ensigns through rigorous drills at Pungo auxiliary airfield near Norfolk during the winter and spring of 1943.

The 446-man Air Group Five did not begin to function as a unit until the arrival of group commander Flatley late in March. He infused everyone with his marvelous *esprit*, telling his squadron commanders they had to be the best—or equal to the best—pilot in their squadrons. To the pilots, he stressed good flying, for, as the adage went, "There are two kinds of pilots—those who have accidents and those who are *going* to have them!" Jimmy warned his men, "A plane is treacherous. It throws you as soon as you lose respect for it." This was underscored in mid-April when two of his Hellcats collided at 15,000 feet and plunged into Dismal Swamp, killing both pilots.

Being one of the Navy's top fighter pilots and an ace, Flatley paid closest attention to Charlie Crommelin's fighter squadron. He was impressed with the new 2000-horsepower F6F with its speeds up to almost 400 mph and its ability to withstand violent turns to get inside of a Zero during a dogfight. With such maneuverability, the Hellcat pilots could use the defensive "Thach weave" which Flatley had helped Jimmy Thach develop: two two-plane sections scissoring for mutual protection when attacked by larger numbers of Zeros. But Jimmy stressed the offensive: each fighter pilot should seek deflection shots at an angle rather than stern approaches to the Zero; this way the Hellcat's six .50 cal. machine guns would have maximum effect on the highly inflammable Zero.

In particular, Flatley expected every one of his fighter jockeys to develop the instinct to kill, to let no Jap fighter escape. "The enemy who gets away today may be the one who will shoot you down tomorrow—or one of your comrades." A devout Catholic who believed in America's moral superiority over the Axis aggressors, Flatley nevertheless announced, "There is no chivalry in this war and there is no place for it."

After weeks of tactical squadron flying from their shore bases, each pilot of Air Group Five qualified for carrier landings by making eight landings and takeoffs on one of two escort carriers late in April. All that remained to be done was for the *Yorktown* to operate with her own planes, and this occurred on May 6. Jimmy Flatley in his F6F made the very first landing of any plane on the ship, followed by other planes on that and the succeeding eleven days, all within the confines of the Chesapeake Bay.

Finally, the *York* completed her sea trials on May 18 when the dive bombers and torpedo planes flew aboard to stay, and the ship docked at Norfolk, loading the fighters aboard by ship's crane next day.

The *Yorktown* was ready for her shakedown cruise to the Caribbean. Remarkably, in just a few days, the crew had begun to function as a team—2500 fairly green officers and men, plus 450 air group personnel, guided and taught by only ten senior regular line officers and four staff, eleven ex-enlisted mustang officers and half a dozen recent Annapolis grads, plus a handful of regular non-coms. Only nine of the pilots were regular Navy.

"Let's go get 'em!" was the universal feeling of the crew—an incredible spirit due primarily to the charismatic leadership of one man, Joseph James Clark. Loud as he might bellow and rant, the men knew that when the day of battle came their lives would be in his hands—and they were glad of it. "I've had three heroes in my life," Joe Tucker would say many years later, "Christ, Buddha and Jocko!"

First landing on the *Yorktown*, May 6, 1943, in the Chesapeake Bay, by Lieutenant Commander Flatley in his "Double Zero" F6F-3 Hellcat. Courtesy of Mrs. J.H. Flatley, Jr.

A Charlie Kerlee photo of Helldivers being spotted forward with wings folded during shakedown. Ship's radio antennas are in the horizontal down position.

Chapter II
To the Wars

Before any new warship could join the fighting fleet, it must first "shake down" in a practice cruise—for the *Yorktown* several weeks at Trinidad's Gulf of Paria in the Caribbean. After a brief return to Norfolk, the ship would then head for the Pacific via the Panama Canal. A short stop at San Francisco would lead to the final jump to Hawaii for training out of Pearl Harbor under simulated battle conditions—the final test before combat.

During shakedown and her early battles, the *Yorktown* would "act" in two motion pictures to publicize the Navy's new carriers; she had been selected by Captain Arthur Radford, innovative head of naval air training. Radford had commissioned America's greatest living photographer, Edward Steichen, to photograph the Navy's air war, beginning with the assignment of two of Steichen's best photographers to the *York*. Lieutenant Dwight S. Long took footage for a full-length documentary color movie that would eventually appear as "The Fighting Lady." Lieutenant Charles W. Kerlee manned the still cameras to produce some of the best black-and-white and color Steichen materials not only for the Navy but for posterity. A combat artist also came aboard with his easel.

Even more immediately, Commander Frank W. "Spig" Wead, pioneer naval aviator turned screenwriter after a crippling accident, offered Captain Clark the chance to use the *Yorktown* in a commercial film for Twentieth Century Fox—"Wing and a Prayer." Clark quickly agreed and welcomed aboard director Henry Hathaway and his cameramen to take background shots depicting a carrier in the early days of the war. Actors Dana Andrews, Don Ameche and Charles Bickford would do the screenplay back in Hollywood.

After a half-dozen engineers and mechanics from the Curtiss company came aboard to work on their troublesome SB2C dive bombers, Captain Clark eased the *Yorktown* away from the pier at Norfolk on the morning of May 21, 1943, destined for Trinidad. The crew mustered on deck, and Clark instructed the bugler to blow the proper calls to salute the admiral on board the *Iowa*, a brand new battleship docked nearby.

The bugler blew alright, but he timed it too early. Jocko pushed him away from the loudspeaker and yelled at him, "You dopey no good sonofabitch! What the hell did you do that for?" He railed on in a tirade, totally unaware that the mike was still open; his words went out over 3000 watts to the *Iowa*, whose sailors all doubled over with laughter. It sounded like Clark was calling their admiral a no-good s.o.b.! Needless to say, the crew of the *Yorktown* broke down in stitches.

Passing out into the rolling deep blue swells of the Atlantic, the ship was joined by three destroyers, equally new vessels. Two cruised in front, looking for U-boats as the entire formation zig-zagged to frustrate any sub's aim. The other stationed herself astern as plane guard, to pick up any fliers who might go into the sea.

Sitting in their air-conditioned squadron ready rooms, situated on the gallery deck one level beneath the flight deck, the men of Air Group Five watched a ticker tape message being projected on the screen at the front of each room. "SET CONDITION ELEVEN" said the order as transmitted from Air Plot high up in the island structure. It meant, be ready to launch aircraft. Presently, a verbal announcement came through the "squawk box" in each ready room: "Pilots, man your planes." Whereupon the fliers left their big leather chairs to make their way topside in a scene that would be repeated thousands of times in the life of the great carrier.

As each pilot settled into his cockpit, assisted by

his young enlisted "plane captain," he fixed his attention on the air officer, who looked down from "Pri Fly"—primary fly control. Lieutenant Commander Henry L. Dozier directed all air activity from Pri Fly. Though a career pilot and 1927 Annapolis classmate of navigator George Anderson, Dozier was unsure of his new heavy responsibilities. Nothing in the rush of wartime events had prepared him for the job, while his utterly humorless disposition made him a loner. He took Captain Clark's criticisms, which were plentiful, personally, and the junior officers called him "Hilarious Henry" behind his back.

operations took so long—time during which a U-boat could line up a shot. He vented his rage at everyone within reach, not least Commander Dozier, and continually chased inexperienced "deck" officers from the bridge. For four days on the run south Clark endured the malfunctioning SB2Cs and what he considered downright inept "respotting" of the planes—the yellow-shirted "airedales" pushing them forward to be parked during landing operations and then moved aft prior to launch.

Finally, on May 23, Clark erupted. He clambored down the ladder and emerged onto the flight deck.

Jocko Clark watches F6F Hellcats take off during shakedown. Courtesy of Richard C. Tripp

Dozier gave the order to start engines, the planes taxied into the launching "spot," and the launching officer waved them down the deck and into the sky. Jimmy Flatley took his boys out to sea and back on their first "group grope" of routine maneuvers. On the return, each plane circled the ship, then came "up the groove"—approaching astern and obeying the colored paddles of "Crash One," the landing signal officer, Lieutenant (jg) Edward N. "Red" Volz. Each plane's tail hook grabbed an arresting wire successfully and landed, except for one torpedo-bomber. Responding too slowly to a "wave-off" from Volz, the pilot could not stay clear of a wire, which caught the hook and sent the Avenger over the side. The plane guard destroyer quickly plucked the pilot and his two crewmen from the sea after the plane sank.

This kind of accident did nothing to relieve Jocko Clark's ulcers. He paced the bridge angry that flight

Hank Dozier was right behind him. Clark yelled at Dozier, "I'm gonna lock you up!" Then he bellowed at his Marine orderly, then at the airedales, "Get them planes moving!" Limping around with his usual gait, he took the unheard of move of directing traffic and showing the deck crew how to spot the planes properly.

"Bear a hand! Get the lead out!" he ordered, walking among the planes and helping to push one himself. The effect was electric. The young kids couldn't believe their eyes, nor could any of the old-timers—a 50-year-old four-striper down there, showing them the way. Then someone produced a *tree stump*(!) from God only knew where, which he mounted to lecture all hands on the art of spotting the deck. This totally unorthodox behavior humiliated Commander Dozier, especially as Dwight Long caught the whole thing on movie film.

The *Yorktown* passed through the submarine

TBF Avenger taking off in the Gulf of Paria, Trinidad, during shakedown, as the *Yorktown* plows through the water kicking up a large bow wave.

nets which guarded the Gulf of Paria at dawn on May 26 and dropped anchor near the brand new *Lexington,* also on shakedown. In the afternoon, Jocko took the *York* out into the 80-mile-long Gulf for flight operations, his planes being based at an airfield ashore. The SB2C "Beasts" performed so miserably—tail hooks falling off, wheel struts collapsing, hydraulics failing—that the Curtiss engineers could not repair them fast enough. One of the bombers even plummeted into the water; pilot and rearseat gunner rescued.

Though the Air Department had been laboring to speed up the spotting of the planes, Jocko again descended from the bridge, this time to challenge Lieutenant Hank Warren, flight deck officer in charge, to a contest directing the respotting. Warren, an old-pro mustang, had Joe Tucker clock the times and measure the parking intervals of his own respot and of Jocko's. At the conclusion, Tucker reported that Jocko had taken two minutes longer than Warren, and that Jocko's planes took up eight more feet of parking space than had Warren's. Whereupon Hank turned to Jocko and said, "Captain, I promise never to come up there and try to run that bridge if you leave me alone and let me spot the flight deck."

Jocko stared at him, ready to erupt, when a sly grin broke across the Indian's face and he said, "I promise."

Both Hank and Joe wanted to explode with laughter, but of course they couldn't even smile. It had been a severe test, Warren had known he was right, and he had stood up to old Jocko. Many times thereafter, Clark would boast, "Hank Warren is the best deck-spotter in the whole damned fleet!" And never again would he come down to the flight deck to try to run things.

Tucker now had a brainstorm which would enable the *Yorktown* to recover, respot and launch her planes faster than any other carrier in the fleet—which could provide the margin of survival when the ship came under air attack. Using two small tractors or "mules" which had been "appropriated" at Norfolk, he had them rigged with tow bars to pull each plane with the mules rather than relying on the muscle power of the tired airedales. The devices worked like charms, whereupon the *Yorktown* started acquiring more mules whenever it could and by whatever means. Over time, the technique became standard on all carriers, and Jocko had consciously to prevent other flattops from swiping away any of his mules until they could get their own through proper channels.

Such inventiveness merely followed on the heels of Jocko's example in the shipyard, and he left alone anyone who knew his business. One especially savvy Reserve officer was Lieutenant James J. Vonk, ship's aerologist or "weatherguesser." A talented, fun-loving Dutchman, Jim Vonk realized that Jocko understood absolutely nothing about meteorology, So when the tropical airs and rain squalls of Trinidad frustrated his flight schedules, Jocko ranted and raved at Vonk, even challenging his usually correct forecasts. The plain-talking Vonk simply set the captain straight, often by just wetting his index finger, holding it up in the wind and making a forecast!

One morning, threatening clouds led Jocko to ask Vonk, "What's your prognostication, Mr. Aerologist?"

"Captain," intoned the deep-voiced Vonk, "anybody who would send a plane off this ship today is just fucking Fate!"

"WHAT?!"

"Fucking Fate!"

Jocko roared with delight. Vonk was one of the few people who could out-fox the skipper and get away with it.

Clark's concern over accurate shooting by the ship's guns resulted in particular pressure on the gunnery officer, Commander Cecil L. "Stroke" Blackwell. When the 5-inchers, 40s and 20s opened fire on the target sleeve pulled by a plane, Jocko told Blackwell not just to aim at the sleeve but to sever the tow wire as well. When Blackwell protested that this would prevent them from retrieving the sleeve and measuring the hits, Clark snapped, "Shoot *down* the goddamned sock!" And they did, bringing cheers from all hands. Jocko even had the gunners shooting at Vonk's tiny weather balloons as they jerked and skittered aloft.

When the gunners missed, or took too long, Clark would summon Blackwell to the bridge. He did not believe in embarrassing his department heads by chewing them out in front of junior officers. So when Blackwell appeared, Jocko said nothing but took him into his own sea cabin adjacent to the bridge and shut the door so no one could hear. Then he would ream his ass, shouting so loud that *everyone* on the bridge could hear it.

Blackwell, a very tall, blond athletic-looking 1925 Annapolis graduate, endured Clark's merciless attacks for only so long. His gentlemanly Virginia manner kept him from doing otherwise, but one day it got to be too much, particularly since his gunners were showing marked improvement. He cut off Jocko, "I don't have to take this, and I'm not going to!" That stopped Clark, who actually respected Blackwell as a good "gun boss," and from then on he backed off.

By the time the cruise ended, three of the four 5"/38 twin mounts had won the battle efficiency "E" award—a remarkable achievement for such a new ship. The winning gun crews painted their "E"

"Mules" like Joe Tucker's pull Wildcat Fighters on another carrier.

Director Henry Hathaway supervises filming of "Wing and a Prayer" from the island structure during shakedown. Courtesy of Richard C. Tripp

on the side of the gun house, and each man received a $10-a-month bonus for his efforts. One of the closest students of Stroke Blackwell was his assistant, baseball pitcher George Earnshaw, who would eventually relieve him as gun boss.

The "Sunday punch" of the carrier was the air group, and the key links between ship and planes were two plotting rooms, Air Plot and Radar Plot, located up in the island near the bridge. Air Plot received and transmitted to the ready rooms weather, target and flight data. Radar Plot housed the very latest air-search radars for detecting approaching enemy planes and radios for "vectoring" the ship's fighters to intercept and destroy "bogeys." The science of fighter direction was in its infancy and untried, like so much else on the new carriers.

Captain Clark kept close watch on both places, essential as they were to the *Yorktown's* survival and effectiveness, and anything that went wrong fell on the shoulders of the overall "air boss," Commander Dozier. Air Plot functioned very well during shakedown, thanks to the expertise of its head, Lieutenant Commander Ed Stebbins, whose combat experience with the old *Hornet* paid off, and to his colorful assistant, Lieutenant Cooper Buck Bright.

A graduate of Rutgers University and businessman during the Depression, the bald, bespectacled Bright had actually followed his sister into the wartime Navy: Lieutenant Joy Bright Hancock, a "yeomanette" in World War I and a founder of the

newly-organized WAVES. Cooper had been a coordinator of land-based patrol planes against U-boats along the Atlantic seaboard before joining the *Yorktown.* Imbued with an outrageous sense of humor, "Skinhead" Bright amused the pilots by interspersing his ticker tape transmissions to the ready rooms with wisecracks and poems.

Radar Plot was another story altogether. "Off limits" to nearly everyone save for its occupants because of the secrecy of the new equipment, Radar Plot was officered by fighter directors selected for their skills in mathematics and statistics, men with

Lieutenant Cooper Buck "Skinhead" Bright in a pensive mood—and tie!

executive or legal backgrounds capable of coolly managing the complicated business of vectoring many fighters toward separate targets. One qualified pilot was included because he understood planes—Smokey Stover, fresh from Guadalcanal.

Unfortunately, from the outset the two senior officers there did not seem to understand their jobs or care, while Stover was only interested in getting back into the cockpit, spending most of his time in the ready rooms with the pilots or at Pri Fly helping Commander Dozier. One day Jocko caught Smokey out there and shouted, "What's this fellow doing out here? Get him out of here! I don't like him!" Hurt, Smokey retreated, only to be lambasted again a week later. And as Radar Plot made mistakes during shakedown, the captain got worse.

Two 90-day-wonders in the Air Department gradually got close to Jocko and became his confidants. As ship's senior air combat intelligence officer, Herman Rosenblatt spent much time with the captain, and like all ACIO's (each squadron had one as well), he was highly intelligent and able to give Jocko wise counsel. To the chagrin of his peers, though, he appeared to be a mere sycophant or ass-kisser; yet Jocko came to lean heavily on his advice.

Bob Reynolds, when brought in from the motor pool at Norman, Oklahoma, had had no assigned job until Captain Clark—completely dissatisfied with the lieutenant commander running airplane maintenance—turned aircraft material over to the very junior ensign, a most unorthodox recourse. Reynolds got to work streamlining the maintenance shop so well that his novel system of cataloging and arranging spare parts became standard on all carriers. But this man with the "clear eye" had both an ebullient and frank manner which the skipper appreciated. Soon, Reynolds became Jocko's "boy Friday" who also took upon himself the task of staying one step ahead of the captain in warning people targeted by Clark for a dressing down, a tip appreciated by the intended victims.

Complete opposites in personality and training who had no use for each other, Rosenblatt and Reynolds became key figures in the effectiveness of Jocko Clark on the *Yorktown* and later.

Rough though the captain was on his officers, he had absolute affection for the enlisted men. On one occasion, "right after reveille," remembered his Marine orderly, Bob Bender, "a short young sailor came up to me on the bridge, had his breakfast tray

Commander Raöul Waller checks with junior officers timing landing and takeoff intervals of the faulty SB2Cs during shakedown. Primary Fly Control is just beyond Waller.

with him, and asked to see the Captain. I figured anyone with that much guts should see Captain Clark. The Captain had just got up, was in his shorts, and said he would see him. The young sailor stood in front of the Captain and said, 'Sir, I cannot do a day's work on this kind of breakfast.' (It *was* sorry).

"Captain Clark looked at it, called his kitchen, and said, 'Son, what would you like for breakfast?'" The sailor ate breakfast with Captain Clark— "bacon, eggs, home fries, juice and coffee. Needless to say, Captain Clark had me bring the supply officer to him and what he said would be unprintable!"

The supply officer, Lieutenant Commander William L. Patten, a classmate of Waller's at Annapolis in '24, was still learning the ropes of how to feed the 2400 enlisted men on the big ship. The officers had less to grumble about, because they paid for their own wardroom mess, run by a University of Washington grad and restauranteur in civilian life, Lieutenant (jg) Lee Foster. The officers could chow-down at any time in the ward-

room. Bob Reynolds did it so often that Cooper Bright nicknamed him "Chow-chit."

Of the manifold headaches which fed the skipper's ulcers at Trinidad throughout late May and early June, however, none equaled the disastrous performance of the SB2C Helldivers. Their tail hooks pulled out of their wells so much that air maintenance officer Joe Tucker grounded half of the 36 "Beasts." So when several Congressmen came aboard to observe flight operations, Tucker refused Commander Dozier's call for a maximum launch. Enraged, Dozier ordered Tucker to have the malfunctioning Helldivers take part in the demonstration.

Sure enough, every one of the 17 bombers lost its tail hook on grabbing the arresting cables and piled into the wire crash barrier. Tucker's officers "were ready to kill me" because they now had to stay up all night working on the planes. Both furious and dejected, Tucker spilled out his woes to Bob Reynolds. "Chow-chit" had a suggestion: go directly to the captain. This meant going over

Bombing the target sled, 1500 yards astern, off Purvis Bay, Venezuela, June 12, 1943. Planes circle in the distance, avoiding one of Vonk's rain squalls. Courtesy of Raymond F. Gard

Pretty though this picture be of *Yorktown* and her new SB2C dive bombers during shakedown, the Helldivers had so many defects that Jocko had them replaced with the older SBDs.

the head of air boss Dozier, but Tucker agreed he had no other choice.

Jocko, seeing his old shipmate distressed, heard him out but could only reply, "Well, Joe, the SB2C is the dive bomber built for the new carrier program. If it doesn't work, we're in a helluva mess."

"We're in a helluva mess then," said Tucker, "because it's not gonna work until there are 200 or so modifications made that are all essential. It is not ready to go out there on carriers. The best thing in the world that could be done would be to return it to Curtiss-Wright and make them prove it before we put it on the new carriers."

Jocko eyed him, "If you were me, what would you do?"

Tucker thought a moment and figured he'd

crossed all his bridges; he was doomed. "Well, if I was you, Captain, I would sit right down and write a letter to BuAer and tell them—I wouldn't ask them; I'd *tell* them—to tell Curtiss-Wright to come and get their damned airplanes. And, I'd turn this ship right around and head back into Trinidad, and I'd put those SB2Cs ashore and *leave* 'em there!"

"What would you use in their place?"

"We're a lot better off with SBDs that'll fly than we are with SB2Cs that won't!"

Clark sat there, thought a few minutes, and said firmly, "You know, I agree with you." Then he yelled out the door, "Tell Commander Dozier to come up here! Andy, come in here!"

Navigator Anderson stuck his head in first, and

Jocko told him, "Set a course for Trinidad."

"What?"

"Set a course for Trinidad. Cease operations!"

"Aye, aye, sir!"

When Dozier arrived on the bridge, he was visibly shaken at the sight of Tucker with the captain. But Jocko had both men write a message informing the Bureau of Aeronautics that the *Yorktown* was returning to Norfolk prematurely and to request 36 brand new SBD-5 Dauntless dive bombers to replace the hapless "Beasts." Then Jocko rejected the entreaties of the Curtiss-Wright people to keep the planes, and he set course for Norfolk on June 13, escorted by three "tin cans," destroyers.

The ship's engines had yet to be given a full-power test run, so early on the 15th the captain turned over the ship to the chief engineer. Blackie McNally gradually increased her speed until she raced up to her maximum 33 knots. At 0800 he ordered full power, and the *York* surged ahead until its speed gauges registered 34.9 knots—a record for any carrier. The old hands chuckled, their teeth seeming to rattle as the ship kept it up for four straight hours. The speedy destroyers soon disappeared astern over the horizon, outrun by the *Yorktown*; even a lurking U-boat could not have lined up a shot at anything moving so fast.

Finally slowing down to allow the cans to catch up, a proud Jocko brought his fully shaken down carrier to Norfolk next day—but not before she had wandered around in a dense fog for three hours looking for the channel buoy marking the entrance to the Chesapeake. Captain Clark had every intention of shelving whatever official procedures were necessary for making certain his ship was in fighting trim. And if the regular Navy officers couldn't satisfy him, he'd replace them with Reservists, who were unfettered with traditions, protocol and the desire to get promoted. The *Yorktown* navy was becoming a civilian navy run by a sea dog.

The U.S. Navy had been officially "dry" ever since Jocko Clark had been a plebe at the Academy. This being so, movie director Hathaway now presented $2500 to Jimmy Flatley to buy liquor for the air group in gratitude for the pilots' help in providing scenes during the shooting of "Wing and a Prayer." When Jocko found out, he confiscated the money, reasoning that the ship's company deserved the credit. The medical officers therefore went ashore at Norfolk and purchased 2000 cases of beer and 200 cases of whiskey, to be broken out for a beer bust on some Pacific island at the appropriate time.

When Flatley reported the air group's loss to Henry Hathaway, the latter gave the pilots another $2500—which went for 3000 bottles of Four Roses, which found their way into each pilot's private on-board locker.

As the fliers resumed training ashore—the bombers with their new SBDs—the *Yorktown* docked at Portsmouth for repairs to its rudder. Captain Clark requested the Bureau of Ships to let him have 15 Army-type mobile 40mm guns to be kept in the hangar and hoisted by plane elevator to the flight deck during battle for additional protection. BuShips declined, saying such an extreme measure would foul flight operations, but it did agree to add 13 fixed 20mms to the ship's existing battery. These were now installed at Norfolk.

Jocko also learned that other ships were now having a new plastic coating sprayed onto their hulls to inhibit the growth of marine organisms and thus prolong operations before an overhaul in the yards would be necessary. BuShips informed Clark that the Navy Yard had not scheduled the *Yorktown* for the coating and could spare no personnel to do it, whereupon Jocko proclaimed that his crew would do it. On June 23 the ship went into drydock, and the captain told his men, "Clean the bottom, 'cause in two weeks I'm gonna leave to hit the Japs!"

The Hull Department superintended the monumental task. Its head, who wore two hats as first lieutenant and damage control officer, was a lovable New Hampshire Irishman, Commander Daniel J. Sweeney. Annapolis '26, Dan Sweeney had been wounded while exec of a gunboat when it was sunk by a U-boat. He liked Jocko's style, as did his two assistants. Lieutenant Eric C. Lambart was a well-traveled English-born American who had been stroke oar for Columbia University's crew team and a shipmate of Jocko's on the *Suwannee*. Lieutenant John W. Brady ran damage control. A classmate of Waller's at the Academy, "Diamond Jim" had left the Navy early but had returned for the duration. He was a vibrant and colorful fellow with a loud voice who did superlative work at his job.

The crew scraped down Sweeney's hull in the three days allotted, only to have the rains come, which meant the hull would need a week to dry out before the coating could be applied. "To hell with the rain!" bellowed Jocko, "Put on the stuff!" The shipyard workers obeyed, then were chagrined next to watch the coating peel off. The drydock was flooded anyway, and the *Yorktown* went back into the water without coating *or* paint. Barnacles and algae would eventually adhere to the hull so thickly that the ship's speed would be seriously slowed in the midst of the campaigning.

But no matter. Jocko was in a hurry. He had to beat the *Essex,* which had already reached Hawaii. Not that some of his fun-loving officers did not know how to use their Norfolk leave to advantage. The day the ship had returned from Trinidad, gregarious Bob Reynolds had telephoned Joe Tucker's girl friend, a Navy nurse in Norfolk, and proposed marriage on behalf of the bashful Tucker. The lady accepted, and after a rushed midnight ceremony the newlyweds rushed off to a Virginia Beach honeymoon—accompanied by ''Chow-chit,'' Diamond Jim Brady and mess manager Lee Foster! The four guys and a gal had a wonderful last fling.

Among new arrivals to the ship were two fighter director officers to beef up Radar Plot, both of them lieutenants (jg). Charles D. Ridgway III, a Princeton man of slight build, had come from 14 months on the *Saratoga* as one of the Navy's first FDOs.* Alexander Wilding, Jr., a robust University of Southern California athlete, had just graduated first in his FDO class of 65 at Norfolk. They turned out to be kindred souls, anxious to make *Yorktown's* Radar Plot the best organized and run operation in the fleet—a considerable challenge given its fouled-up condition following shakedown.

With a week left before sailing, Captain Clark showed off his ship out in the Chesapeake for visiting Assistant Secretary Gates. The first three days of July the bomber pilots qualified in carrier landings with their new SBDs. And Stroke Blackwell's 5-inch AA gun crews did such a fine job of shooting down more target sleeves that the same three twin mounts which had won battle efficiency E's at Trinidad repeated the feat, entitling them to add on a harsh mark next to the letter, since the new gunnery year had begun on July 1. The fact that a ship in commission for fewer than three months had won three gunnery E's with harsh marks for two gunnery years was downright remarkable. Jocko's pride swelled.

With departure time set for 1100 on July 6, 1943, Ed Stebbins rose early at his shoreside house, loaded the last case of whiskey bought with the movie money into his car, and reached the dock only an hour ahead of sailing time. He put a nickel in a pay phone before going on board and gave his wife Patsy a final cheerful farewell. When he hung up the phone, it went BONG! And some eight dollars worth of quarters came rolling out. He had hit the jackpot, which he considered a good omen, so he called up Patsy again to tell her about it.

Minutes after Steb climbed up the gangway, the ship he now referred to affectionately as the ''Old Yorkblow'' prepared to cast off the lines. The Pacific or bust! Actually, it seemed more like ''bust''—delays, rain and a malfunctioning propeller

---

*For U.S. Naval abbreviations and terms, see Appendix A.

FDO— Fighter Director Officer

Three early sparkplugs of the new *Yorktown* on the honeymoon of Lieutenant Joe Tucker (seated) and his bride Dawson, being snuggled by Lieutenant Commander Jim Brady. Ensign Bob Reynolds shares a smoke with the groom. Virginia Beach, June 1943. Courtesy of F. Robert Reynolds

shaft. Not until 1430 (2:30 p.m.) did the *Yorktown* pass through the submarine nets and speed southward past the waterfront hotels of Virginia Beach, ringed by landing craft, 16-inch coast defense guns and the hull of a torpedoed merchantman. Captain Clark rang up 27 knots, picked up three escorting cans and kept up the pace for three days—with good reason. The area was supposed to be crawling with U-boats; on the evening of the 7th an antisub TBF patrol reported spotting one.

Unknown to Jocko Clark, ten U-boats had begun to converge on Windward and Mona passages of the Caribbean in early July—coincidentally on a converging course with the *Yorktown*. On the 6th, one of them, the *U-759*, had sunk a Dutch merchantman in convoy off Jamaica. On the morning of the 8th it was sighted and attacked by a Navy patrol plane inside Windward Passage. Surface ships and planes were combing these very waters when the *York* and her three consorts hurried through at 30 knots that day. Five antisub searches from the ship encountered nothing but thunderheads. Just as the last patrollers were preparing to come aboard at twilight, the destroyer *Terry* flashed the alarm, "Torpedo on port side!"

Jocko grabbed the wheel from the helmsman and gave it a hard right. The *Yorktown* heeled sharply to starboard in a 100-degree pivot almost within the ship's length, and loose gear came crashing down as all hands hung on for dear life. The torpedo passed by harmlessly as the tin cans began dropping depth charges, but to no avail. In the mayhem on board, Jocko dispatched an orderly to find Chaplain Alexander and ask him to pray for the safety of the ship! The *U-759* laid low until two and a half weeks later when a Navy seaplane sent her to the bottom with depth bombs near the scene of her attack on the *Yorktown*.

The ship reached Colón at the Atlantic side of the Panama Canal on the morning of July 10, and Jocko gave the starboard watch section liberty that night. Between the pimps, whores and roughnecks in that filthy city, he was lucky to get everyone back alive. The night was so hot that many men slept under the moonlight on the flight deck. Suddenly, the quiet was broken when a very drunk airedale— Don Aitkenhead—let out a whoop and dashed across the flight deck and over the side! The junior officer-of- the-deck, Lieutenant (jg) Dick Tripp, standing his first watch, sounded the General Quarters alarm.

Battle stations! Horns and whistles blew as all hands fumbled around to repel some vague attack.

Searchlights on the beach scoured the night sky, guns at the ready, as pandemonium reigned. Captain Clark staggered down to the hangar in his one-piece knee-length night shirt, "What the hell's goin' on?! Who's the stupid sonofabitch who pushed the button?" Tripp turned off the alarm and dispatched a whaleboat, but moments later Aitkenhead was discovered on the dock, singing away. Jocko gave him coffee and told him to hit the sack. The men loved their captain for this kind of understanding—"no bullshit," as one of them put it. By the same token, however, Clark cancelled liberty for the port side section at Panama City on the Pacific side.

Next day the *Yorktown* squeezed through Gatun Locks, with assistant first lieutenant Rick Lambart trying to get his men to push on the inside of the hull so it wouldn't buckle! But they laughed too hard at the idea, and the ship went on through, eventually transiting Mira Florez Locks and anchoring at Panama City. The only other event of the day was the captain spotting a monkey jumping around on the flight deck; he ordered the stolen animal to be put ashore. Joe Tucker however had a real problem when he learned that much-needed spare parts earmarked for the *Yorktown's* F6F fighters had not arrived at Panama. A message from the Bureau of Aeronautics set his mind at ease; the parts could be picked up when the ship reached San Francisco.

When the *York* headed out into the Pacific on July 12, however, orders were received altering the ship's destination from Frisco to Hawaii. Hopefully, Tucker would find the spares for Fighting 5 there. Navigator Anderson set the initial ship's course at 287 degrees, aiming for the Great Circle Route to Pearl Harbor, 5000 miles away—a 13-day voyage. Now part of the Pacific Fleet, with its home port shifted from Norfolk to Puget Sound, Washington, the *Yorktown* instituted morning General Quarters.

"You should see me with my 'bonnet' on," radar repair officer Lieutenant (jg) Joe Hachet wrote to his family on July 15. "By bonnet I mean my steel helmet. It's so heavy I almost have to hold it on with my hands. In addition to that, my paraphernalia includes a life belt, a gas mask, a hunting knife and a .45. When we go to battle stations I'm really loaded down."

For two weeks Air Group Five flew constant tactical formations, and Stroke Blackwell's gun crews blasted away at target sleeves. Charlie Crommelin's Hellcats lived up to expectations as the weapon that would whip the Zero, and the bomber pilots were

Radar Plot during the voyage to Hawaii, July 1943. Lieutenant (jg) Alex Wilding sitting and (L to R) Lieutenants Ed Milholland (soon transferred) and Smokey Stover.

pleased to have the SBD instead of the beastly Helldiver. But not everything worked perfectly. Far from it. Despite the arrival of Charlie Ridgway and Alex Wilding, fighter direction in Radar Plot could not improve under the incumbent senior officers there. Cooper Bright of Air Plot planned to visit his sister's boy friend in Hawaii and try to get both senior FDOs transferred; the beau, Captain Ralph Ofstie, happened to be air officer to the commander-in-chief of the Pacific Fleet, Admiral Chester W. Nimitz.

Tension festered in Bombing 5 between the two groups of pilots which had been merged to form the squadron, one bunch resenting the other because the latter's leader had been given command—Lieutenant Commander Bob Milner. A torpedo-bomber and a fighter had engine failures and had to ditch in the sea, though the occupants were rescued. And one frightened pilot took six waveoffs from the LSO before finally making a correct approach to land. Ordered immediately to the bridge, he was dressed down by Captain Clark, "The ship is headed for Pearl Harbor, but we'll never get there by sailing east [into the prevailing winds, in order to recover planes] unless we go completely around the world!" Jocko had the man transferred.

At least the pilots appreciated the hokum of Cooper Bright in Air Plot. To get the young minds off their worries and their loved ones, the 33-year-old Skinhead would feed the ready room tickers with more than official data: "YOU YOUNG FELLOWS WOULDN'T UNDERSTAND WOMEN. I'M OLD AT THE GAME. WHEN I WAS YOUR AGE I WAS MARRIED FIVE TIMES. SIGNED BRIGHT, POAST 1/C—PACIFIC OCEAN AREA SEX TYPHOON FIRST CLASS." The readers whooped and groaned.

Finally, a live "target" presented itself as the *York* approached the Hawaiian Islands on July 23—the battleship *Washington*. But the TBF which sighted her erred in reporting her position, and the deckload launch of 45 planes went out 200 miles only to find nothing. When the *Washington* came over the horizon, Captain Clark signaled to her admiral that the *Yorktown* was reporting for duty. A historic moment, Charlie Ridgway reflected in his diary: "One year and almost two months after the sinking of the *Yorktown* at Midway the *Yorktown* returns to avenge itself. High words, these, but perhaps prophetic."

Nearing Hawaii next day, the *Yorktown* launched a predawn "strike" against Pearl Harbor, only to have her planes intercepted by Navy seaplanes and Army fighters. "Never got above them" fighter pilot Harry Harrison recorded, "and was shot down." Air Group Five then landed ashore at Naval Air Station Barbers Point. The ship herself endured several hours of "attacks" from Hawaii-based planes before entering the harbor shortly after the noon hour. The sight of the sunken battleships from the December 7th attack stunned all hands, a grim reminder of the task that lay ahead.

A signal flashed from Fleet commander Nimitz:

"The *Yorktown* carries a name already famous in the Pacific, and in welcoming you we anticipate that you will maintain the high reputation of your predecessor." To which Captain Clark replied, "Many thanks for your message. That's what we came here to do."

Other warships could be seen, some battle-scarred, some fresh from the States. The *Essex* was there, and the *Independence*, first of a new class of light carriers converted from cruiser hulls. As the *York* tied up at Ford Island's Pier Fox 9 in the middle of the harbor, the crew of the adjacent *Independence* gave the *Yorktown* three hearty cheers.

The war in the Pacific had reached a turning point. Japan's offensive had been stopped at Midway 13 months before and at Guadalcanal, which the Japanese had evacuated early in 1943. Land-based planes from both sides had slugged it out daily for supremacy in the South Pacific, with the Americans steadily gaining the upper hand. No carriers had seen real fighting in many months, since neither side dared risk the few they had left. The *Saratoga* was the only U.S. flattop in the South Pacific, and though the new carriers were starting to arrive in Hawaii their crews and fliers were utterly green.

Only weeks of training in Hawaiian waters could prepare the new carriers to spearhead the planned offensive for carrying the war back to Japan. American strategy called for a three-pronged push to begin during the late summer and autumn of 1943. Navy and Marines would sally forth from Guadalcanal up the chain of the Solomon Islands, while the Army drove up the coast of New Guinea. Both of these prongs were aimed at Rabaul, Japan's major base in the South Pacific. The third drive, Navy, Marines, and Army, would leave Hawaii to crack Japan's defenses in the Central Pacific—the Gilbert and Marshall island groups and the Japanese fleet anchorage at Truk in the Carolines.

The *Yorktown*, her sister ships and indeed most of the new warships belonged to this Central Pacific Force, or Fifth Fleet. The timetable called for the invasion of the Gilberts in November. Until that time, the ships would train in separate cruising formations, the pilots flying out from the air stations in Hawaii. Jocko Clark took pride in the fact that the *Yorktown* had beaten both the *Bunker Hill* and the *Lexington* out to Hawaii. The only goal left now was to go into battle ahead of the rival *Essex*.

Admiral Nimitz appreciated the *Yorktown's*

Admiral Chester W. Nimitz, Pacific Fleet commander, welcomes Jocko Clark and the *Yorktown* to Pearl Harbor, July 27, 1943. Courtesy of Raymond F. Gard

efficiency when he inspected her on July 27. He could not believe his eyes at the battle efficiency E's for two gunnery years on three of the 5-inch gun houses and asked Jocko if that was legal. "Admiral," Clark proudly answered, "I assure you it is legal." Following his visit, Nimitz complimented the *Yorktown* on its "high degree of cleanliness and the smart appearance of the officers and men."

The first order of business after the long voyage from Norfolk was liberty, indulged in whenever possible. Though martial law in the Islands forbade anyone from being on the streets after dark, the officers learned the usual haunts from their Old Navy shipmates—watering holes like La Hula Rhumba and Trader Vic's, which served the "Tortuga"—"British Guiana rums and fruit juices make this a potent and delightful drink. *Served with either crutches or a wheel chair.*" Or the "Pondo Snifter"—"They drink these to forget the heat in Borneo."

Three old hands stroll the flight deck before going ashore in Hawaii—Chief Bosun John Montgomery, Lieutenant (jg) Virg Irwin, and Bosun Dick "Junior" Meyer. Courtesy of Jesse Rodriguez

The most convenient bars were the officers clubs at Ford Island and NAS Barbers Point. Walking out of the former one day, Captain Clark sensed something amiss. He stopped abruptly and turned around, only to have his trusted Weatherguesser, Vonk, walk right into him! The suitably polluted Dutchman had been right behind Jocko, imitating his limp! "What the hell you doin'? Mocking me?" All that Vonk could do was give Jocko that shit-eating grin a drunk guy gives. But Clark, who respected his aerologist, gave him a ride back to the ship in a Navy car.

The pilots chased whatever ladies could be found, only to spend much of the time talking shop, "because," reflected a Fighting 5 pilot years later, "they want to live with it. In that way they'll live longer. The poor ones do it to impress pretty girls. And to make themselves believe they're indestructible." The deprived, faithful married men could only *talk* about sex, like Lieutenant Harry Harrison of the fighters. Deeply missing his wife "Squeeze" of two years, he wrote in his diary one Saturday night, "Every bush is rattling violently, and later the BOQ bedsprings rattled even louder. Wish I was with Squeeze, and I could do a right fair job of rattling myself."

Jimmy Flatley drilled the air group at night as well as daylight hours, sensitive to upcoming predawn launches against enemy targets. This activity proved dangerous for the young pilots: one dive bomber failed to return from a night hop out to sea, the two occupants lost forever; a fighter made a fatal

crash into some trees near the runaway; and two fighters collided while taxiing on the dark air strip at Barbers Point. But the old pros showed themselves to be very good indeed, like Boogie Hoffman who one day chased the famous Butch O'Hare all the way down in a "dogfight" over Maui. Still lacking however were the promised spare parts for the new F6F Hellcats; Joe Tucker could find none anywhere in the Islands.

After the *Yorktown* installed her last AA gun sponsons, she put to sea on July 29 with a cruiser and three cans for exercises, carrying her first admiral. Arthur Radford had been promoted to rear admiral, little knowing that *Yorktown* one day would carry him into many battles close to Japan. He admired the shooting of Stroke Blackwell's gunners but was less than enthusiastic about the smartness of the air group, which landed aboard in the afternoon—accompanied, incidentally, by about ten million mosquitoes. Next morning the ship ran out the bombing sled for the SBDs to attack with 500-pound bombs. Tragically, one SBD did not pull out its dive and smacked into the sea; both occupants went down with the wreckage. Morale plummeted in Bombing 5 after this second set of fatalities in days.

Flight deck operations, however, improved daily under the guiding hand of one of the grand "old men" of naval aviation, Lieutenant Verne W. "Pappy" Harshman. Now 41 (but looking 90), Pappy had lied about his age to enlist during World War I, had won his wings to become an A.P. in old

-26-

The *Yorktown's* first—and last—wartime admiral. Rear Admiral Arthur W. Radford enjoys a laugh with Captain Clark off Hawaii in July 1943. He would also be aboard on V-J Day. National Archives

VF-2 with Jocko and Raöul, and had been commissioned after the outbreak of war. As flight deck officer, Harshman headed the V-1 Division of the Air Department and oversaw Hank Warren's planepushing airedales, the aircraft and gassing gangs, and arresting gear and catapults. Admiral Radford rated the "handling of the flight deck good to excellent."

Shiphandling in these exercises was Jocko's responsibility, and he chased deck officers from the bridge so often that the senior watch officer had to be summoned repeatedly from his station at Damage Control Central, eleven decks down, to take over! This was Lieutenant George J. "Jiggs" Largess, Annapolis '39. Whenever a Naval Academy regular took the conn, Jocko criticized his every move, concluding with the observation, "What in hell *did* you learn at the Academy about responsibility?" And when a 90-day-wonder tried to handle the big carrier, Jocko finished his harangue with, "You Reserves ain't got no sense of responsibility." The bridge came to be known as the "can't

win room."

Tying up at Pearl Harbor's Pier B-22 late on July 31, the *Yorktown* faced an important personnel change. The crisis over leadership in Radar Plot had reached a head, news which Cooper Bright had conveyed to Captain Ofstie of Admiral Nimitz's staff. Consequently, a few days later the two inefficient senior lieutenants and an ensign were detached. Although this left Smokey Stover in charge, he preferred to let the experienced Charlie Ridgway run things, with Alex Wilding becoming intercept officer. In addition, Radar Plot was separated from Air Plot and its title changed to Combat Information Center—in battle the hectic scene within CIC would earn it the acronym "Christ, I'm Confused!" CIC would become the brain of the *Yorktown*, the defensive Hellcats its nerve endings.

Inept leadership also plagued the Medical Department, headed by a paper-shuffling doctor, Commander Clifton Aurelius Young. The ranking dentist, Commander Ralph W. Taylor, was senior to Young but subordinated to him on the ship. The resulting tension was compounded by the fact that battleship-weaned Taylor hated carrier duty. Young's assistant surgeon, Dr. Ray Gard, had found Young so insufferable that on August 3 Gard, in the presence of Chaplain Alexander, "told Aurelius Y. exactly what I thought of him and his conduct." In a letter to his wife, Gard explained, "For 15 minutes I let him have both barrels exactly between the eyes and he took it like a man. . . . Now the thing is running like a well oiled Studebaker and am I glad. I'm usually quite a gentle person, but I can get up on my hind legs too—if nothing else will do. I guess I held all the aces and the trumps too, for everything now is as sweet as apple pie."

On the hot, muggy and unusually windless morning of August 9 the *Yorktown* put to sea for its first exercise with another carrier, Admiral Radford again in command. Clearing the harbor, it was "attacked" by a flight from the incoming *Lexington* until two TBFs collided and crashed onto a bus ashore, killing 40 passengers along with the six fliers. *Yorktown* then launched her defensive Hellcats, which CIC vectored to a successful interception of the rest of the air group flying out from Barbers Point. Rejoiced Alex Wilding in his diary, "What a difference in our new CIC organization! All intercepts were consummated at maximum ranges, information was excellent, and the flow of information was excellent throughout the *Yorktown*" from CIC to the bridge, the gun directors and the ready rooms. "For the first time the radar plot of the *Yorktown* was functioning smoothly and competently.''

For three days flight operations continued, and not without humor. Landing signal officers Red Volz and Dick ''Dog'' Tripp masterfully waved the planes aboard, with the droll Tripp occasionally looking between his legs to see if each plane caught the wire. Amidst the general laughter, Jocko Clark would mutter, ''Goddamn, that's not a good attitude.''

Another time a roar went up from Pri Fly and the catwalks when fighter pilot Harry Harrison—a 1933 Yale man whom the boys called ''Stinky''—rolled down the deck with a lady's blond wig flowing from his head! ''Go give 'em hell!'' yelled the audience. ''Goddamn, that ain't funny!'' bellowed Jocko. ''Get him the hell out of there!'' Stinky had pulled a similar stunt wearing a Father Time white beard once when George Anderson had sent him off the old *Yorktown*. A high class gent, the diminutive Harrison had also flown Wildcats for Jocko off the *Suwannee*.

As if Jocko's ulcers didn't have enough cause for acting up, he was completely taken aback to spot a little gray dog dressed in a life jacket barking down on the flight deck! He yelled down, ''There's a goddamned dog barking on the deck! What the hell's goin' on here?''

''Captain,'' came the quick reply, ''we call him 'Jock.' ''

''Well, that's all right. He can stay.''

The pooch had been ''liberated'' at Pearl by a couple of airedales and given the name ''Scrapper Shrapnel''—''Scrappy'' for short, though some of the men just called him ''Bozo.'' As a mascot, he

proved ideal, since he seemed to love gunnery practice, when the deck shook and roared with thunderous claps. On the other hand, like any dog, he crapped all over the place, sorely testing Raöul Waller's penchant for a clean ship! Pilots Harry Harrison and Ed Owen once fooled Waller during an inspection by placing some artificial dog-doo under the desk in their room.

Perhaps Scrappy should have been named after the skipper. Years later, Harrison would buy a pet dog and let the whining pup sleep with him until one night it bit Harry in the fanny. Then Harrison named it ''Jocko'' because, he told his wife, Jocko Clark was always chewing everybody's asses!

On August 11 the light carrier *Independence* joined the exercise, and Rear Admiral Charles A. Pownall was flown aboard the *Yorktown* in a TBF to observe operations. Captain Clark instructed another torpedo jockey to fly ashore to bring out the Fleet's air commander, Vice Admiral Towers. He told the pilot, ''Now, you have a damned valuable cargo. You gotta be particularly careful.'' ''Captain,'' the man eyed the skipper, ''when I'm in that airplane, there's damned sure nothing more valuable than *I* am!''

Towers arrived safely just after sunup of the 12th, just before, in the words of Alex Wilding, ''a thousand planes attacked us continually all morning from Maui. We ran continual interceptions. Dead tired.'' But the same was repeated next day, at the end of which the ships returned to Ford Island.

Pearl Harbor now bristled with power, the most it had seen since the outbreak of war—the heavy carriers *Yorktown*, *Essex* and *Lexington*; three light carriers; a battleship; three cruisers and a host of

"Scrappy" wearing a life jacket and cloth helmet in the cockpit. Courtesy of Jesse Rodriguez

destroyers—but most untried in battle. Scuttlebutt was rampant as Admiral Pownall established his flag aboard for what appeared to be a major exercise. The arrival of some of Admirals Nimitz's and Towers' staff officers and no fewer than eight war correspondents on the 21st looked ominous. Alex Wilding told his diary, "Saw Op Plans and they call for only two days of gunnery, but that's just to throw spies off. . . . I'm a little afraid tonight—all it would take is just one bomb hit on top of the island, and I'd never see my loved ones again. I hope I can go to sleep quick tonight."

Of those on board, only Admiral Pownall and the Fleet staff officers on loan for the operation knew what was in store for the nervous crewmen and fliers. A "training exercise" was scheduled alright, but against a live target, a remote islet which only would be revealed en route in order to insure security. The savvy Joe Tucker figured something was afoot, and he desperately needed those spare parts for the fighters. When Captain Clark gave him carte blanche to solve the dilemma, Tucker turned to his fellow mustang officers, who came up with a daring plan.

After dark on August 20, leading Aviation Chief Machinist Louis T. Pisarski led a raiding party ashore to Ford Island. On its airfield sat over 100 brand new F6F Grumman Hellcats, which "Ski" and his partners-in-crime proceeded to field-strip of every removable piece of equipment. Then, for three hours, they loaded the stuff on board by ship's crane—tires, engine harnesses, tail hooks, carburators, fuel lines, etc. With much trepidation, Tucker had the captain awakened and told him to move the ship across the harbor ahead of schedule. Jocko understood and roused navigator Anderson to have the *York* push off at first light. By the time Tucker had stowed all this loot, cataloger Bob Reynolds discovered he had enough gear to repair Hellcats for a year and a half!

Jocko's team had merely followed his example, and the skipper protected them by ignoring frantic signal lights from the Ford Island tower and by posting "off limits" signs to visitors while the *Yorktown* took on fuel at Pearl's Number 1010 dock all day the 21st.

The great lady was ready for her first fight.

Captain Clark and Lieutenant Jim Bryan make a formal inspection of the air ordnance gang at Hawaii, August 14, 1943. Courtesy of Henry E. Bolden

Lieutenant Commander E.E. Stebbins, Air Plot Officer, Bombing 5, Air Group Five.

The View from Primary Fly Control ("Pri Fly") as an SBD Dauntless of Bombing 5 takes off. From the Steichen Collection, Nimitz Library, U.S. Naval Academy.

Chapter III
First Blood

"Now, station all special sea and line handling details!" boomed the *Yorktown's* loudspeaker.

"Hoist in all gangways and boat booms—the officer of the deck is shifting his watch to the pilot house and may be reached by dialing two-two-two."

By 0800 on this 22nd day of August 1943 a hot, bright Hawaiian sun shown down on the big ship, vibrating with engine power. Two and a half hours earlier the black gang had lighted (never "lit" in Navy parlance) fires under six of the eight boilers, then had gradually cut them into the main steam line.

Four yard tugs eased up against the hull and at 0821 pushed the *Yorktown* away from the dock. A Navy band on the dock played "Aloha Oe," answered by "Anchors Aweigh" from Bandy Andermann's musicians. The crewmen mustered at quarters on the flight deck to salute Admiral Nimitz's headquarters as the ship moved down the Pearl Harbor channel. Three destroyers led the *York* out to sea; the light carrier *Independence* and another can followed.

Ford Island's tower blinked out a last message of farewell, "You look good out there, honey!"

Ship's signalmen took it down and sent out *Yorktown* messages by light, flags and radio from the signal bridge and from "Main Comm" up in the island. Some of this traffic was in code and thus the personal concern of Lieutenant Commander James A. Morrison, head of the Communications Department. Because of the secret stuff, Morrison *"never* talks about anything at all," wrote Ray Gard. "He is very pleasant and everybody likes him, but except to eat he never opens his mouth."

Beyond the sight of land, more accurate shooting by Blackwell's and Earnshaw's gunners preceded bombing practice on the sled. As the SBDs made their runs, officers who had guessed the mission of this cruise wondered out loud. Dr. Gard, leaning on a railing, mused to leading Chief Bos'n W. J. Beaudette, "Frenchy, do you think the Japs know what we are doing?" The old salt sighed, "Jesus Christ, Doc, we're so fucked up we don't know ourselves what the hell is going on. How can the Japs know?"

Cooper Bright watched the planes from the catwalk outside Air Plot with the assistant air officer, Lieutenant Commander Raymond N. Sharp, an apt surname for a man who exuded calm, professional self-confidence. A 1930 Annapolis grad who had served with Clark and Waller in VF-2, "Red" Sharp commanded their respect and thus was a boon to his immediate superior, Hank Dozier.

With a perfectly straight face, Sharp remarked in a solemn tone to Bright, "I wonder how many of those fellows will be dead when we come back. There'll be a lot of blood on the flight deck! I'll bet you that some of us will be gone too!" Funnyman Coop looked at him wide-eyed, completely taken in by Sharp's leg pulling.

After the bombers landed, Fighting 5 tried to attack the ship but got mixed up. "What a bitched-up attack!" Stinky Harrison wrote in his diary after landing. "Hope when we get into a shooting scrape that things won't be as SNAFU!"—Situation Normal All Fouled (or otherwise!) Up.

The recovery of the two SBDs from late afternoon antisub patrol really fouled up. The first one's engine quit as it approached the carrier; pilot and gunner were rescued from the drink. Ensign Arthur W. Johnson was not as lucky. Turning too tightly to enter the groove, his plane spun slowly into the water, not 200 yards astern of the ship. Horrified, all hands topside watched the Dauntless hit and its depth charge explode, blowing to bits the plane, pilot Johnson and gunner Freeman Conner. Morale in Bombing 5 plummeted lower.

Next morning, the ocean began to fill up with ships, including a fleet oiler to refuel them and thus extend their range on what was sure to be a combat situation. The *Essex* joined the other two carriers, as did the battleship *Indiana,* two cruisers and ten brand new destroyers, all constituting Task Force 15. Rear Admiral "Baldy" Pownall commanded from the *Yorktown.*

After all ships had joined up, Pownall opened his sealed orders and showed them to Captain Clark. Commander Waller then assembled all available officers in the wardroom and projected a lantern slide of a triangular-shaped five-square-mile island. Its name was Marcus, Waller revealed, lying no fewer than 2700 nautical miles west of Pearl Harbor and less than 1000 miles from Japan itself! Planes from the task force would attack it all day August 31.

Since Marcus lay so deep inside enemy waters, Waller explained, any downed pilots in life rafts would have no chance of riding currents to friendly shores. And without a raft, the shark menace was real. At least for the day of the attack, however, a U.S. submarine would be standing by to rescue any survivors, a first in the Pacific war which had been arranged by Admiral Pownall.

The strategic importance of the raid on Marcus would be minuscule. Lying in the North Pacific, the island served as a weather station and airfield for perhaps half a dozen patrol planes. The main purpose of the attack was to gain battle experience for the new carrier crews and pilots. If the Japanese reacted by diverting forces from the South Pacific, so much the better, for Task Force 15 would escape before the enemy could respond in any strength. The only possibility of enemy interference might be planes from Wake to the southeast, Saipan to the southwest and Chichi Jima and Iwo Jima due west. So surprise was essential.

"We'll be in for a pack of trouble if we're detected before we reach Marcus," Alex Wilding observed in his diary that evening. "Radio silence is in effect and radar transmitter silence at night. From now on anything we pick up is enemy. Op plan is half-inch thick. This makes the first raid American forces have made in a year."

Should Japanese planes in fact attack the task force, it would have to maneuver defensively as one unit, the three carriers staying on station with the *Indiana* and the two cruisers inside the circular screen of destroyers in order to achieve maximum anti-aircraft fire coverage. Since no more than two

carriers had ever cruised within the same formation in the war, and carriers never with battleships, another purpose of the Marcus operation was to test this new cruising disposition. And every other day Admiral Pownall passed tactical command to Rear Admiral Alfred E. Montgomery, riding aboard the *Essex* as an observer. Both admirals and their staffs learned together.

Jocko Clark was no mean shiphandler himself, ever since his early years in destroyers. He now developed his "fishtail" method of bringing the *Yorktown* back inside the formation after launching or recovering planes outside the screen. He'd zip back between the destroyers at 25 knots with a sharp right then left turns which slowed the ship so that it ended up exactly on station.

The second day out, he executed this fishtail, dashing the *Yorktown* between two cans and by the *Essex* to resume his position perfectly—only to have Baldy Pownall come dashing up from the flag bridge to scold him: "*Clark! Clark!* Don't *ever* do that again!" For once in his life, Jocko was left speechless.

As for the plan of attack, Pownall relied heavily on Captains Herbert S. Duckworth and Wallace M. Beakley, loaned to him by Admiral Towers for the operation. Despite several days of opposition from Pownall and his staff, "Beak" argued that the repetitious Japanese had probably not changed their patrol plane patterns since U.S. carriers had raided Marcus early in 1942. Consequently, Task Force 15 should swing northwest to avoid enemy air searches from Wake, then turn south literally to follow the last afternoon Marcus air patrol back to its base on the 30th and be in position for a predawn launch next day. When Admiral Montgomery supported Beakley's thinking, the plan was adopted.

Following a suggestion from the *Independence,* Beakley decided to have radar-equipped TBFs lead the first wave of attacking planes through the darkness to the target. And he yielded to pressure from Jocko Clark that *Yorktown* planes be the ones to comprise that first flight. Consequently, Torpedo 5 skipper Dick Upson got the nod to lead it. Manning the radar set in Upson's plane would be an airborne radar specialist who had joined the squadron in Hawaii—Lieutenant (jg) Paul D. Searles, called "Blip" after his job.

To involve his pilots in the details of the air plan, Jimmy Flatley solicited ideas from them at squadron meetings. Otherwise, except for daily air patrols of a few planes, the pilots bided their time in the ready room, many endlessly playing acey-deucy—

the Navy's form of backgammon. The ship's junior officers, when off duty, played a more dangerous game—poker, at which they were usually clobbered at high stakes by the undisputed champion, Lieutenant (jg) Bernard J. Lally, ship's fire marshal. "Barney" Lally had come into the Navy directly from the New York City Fire Department.

The obvious nervousness of the novices over the approaching battle created opportunities for the old salts to have some fun with them. Chief Warrant Officer John E. Montgomery, an FBI agent in peacetime and now a fireman on the flight deck, swore George Earnshaw to secrecy and confided to him that Japanese spies had apparently planted bombs somewhere on the ship. When the old righthander went on watch, Montgomery switched the lightbulbs in Earnshaw's room with flashbulbs. Then he and his cronies lay in hiding when big George returned from watch. As Earnshaw flipped on his light switch, the bulbs went off like bomb flashes. George wheeled to flee, tripped and fell against the thin metal bulkhead, denting it and briefly knocking himself out. Angrier than hell at the obvious culprit, Earnshaw went looking for Montgomery for several days. But whenever Johnny saw him coming across the flight deck, he'd call a fire drill and drive Earnshaw back with a fire hose!

Real bombs appeared on the hangar deck on Wednesday morning, August 25—big 2000-pound "blockbusters" being loaded into the TBFs. Belly tanks were also installed on the fighters to extend their range on attack day. Arming of the planes was the responsibility of Lieutenant James T. Bryan, Jr., a zealous innovator who had streamlined the air ordnance crews and techniques much to the satisfaction of Jimmy Flatley. Rapid arming of the planes throughout the battle would enable all aircraft to keep hitting the target longer than in past battles.

"You can feel the tension growing a little tighter each day," Alex Wilding noted this day as his radar picked up a friendly search plane out of Midway long before the other big ships detected it. *Yorktown's* new CIC organization was working well, which only added to the confidence of the veterans. Wrote Flatley to his wife Dotty next day, "Sweetheart, we're out here for a training cruise, and it looks like it's going to be strenuous training. Well, we're fit. That's all I can say. Tojo is going to take an awful licking."

The *Yorktown* refueled from the oiler on the 27th, and next morning Captain Clark provided a demonstration of an anti-personnel "daisy cutter" fused bomb. A TBF, recorded Wilding, "cut loose a 2000 lb. daisy cutter astern so that all hands would have an idea of what one looked and acted like. Shrapnel flew 1000 yards in every direction. Hope we don't receive one of those amidships on the 31st. Only three more days now."

Just 900 miles from the Japanese coast, the task force used its radio direction finders to pick up transmissions from Tokyo, while a scouting submarine reported an enemy convoy, which included a carrier, south of Wake—fair game if it was close

Jimmy Flatley briefs bomber and fighter pilots in the wardroom before the Marcus strike. Harry Harrison stands second from right, Fred Bozard sits beneath him, hands folded.

to Marcus on "Dog Day," the 31st. But it wouldn't be. Flatley dashed off another letter to his wife, "Every day I go up and see Jock and each day he becomes more lovable and ostreperous. One thing is certain. We will never disappoint him."

Sunday, August 29, dawned cool, and the condition of the sea worsened in these northern latitudes. As all hands went to G.Q. wearing jackets and sweaters, Pearl Harbor informed the flagship of a weather front moving down from Alaska. Flatley and Weatherguesser Vonk calculated that the force could cover its approach to Marcus by maneuvering into the storm, a change of plan which Admiral Pownall's staff quickly adopted.

Heavily-attended church services in the hangar competed with revving airplane engines, the several congregations rotating all day long between Protestant Chaplain Bob Alexander and the new Catholic "Holy Joe," Father R.A.W. Farrell, a 40-year-old Dominican scholar who had recently completed a major four-volume work on theology. "By my orders," Captain Clark had told Admiral Nimitz, Lieutenants Alexander and Farrell "pray full speed all the time. We have the Lord on our side, and we will not miss!" They had additional help from lay Jewish leader Herm Rosenblatt and "Brother William" E. Davenport, a 21-year-old black steward's mate who conducted Southern Baptist revival meetings, highly-popular for their Negro spirituals.

The 29th was the last day of relative calm. The destroyers "topped off"—filled up their fuel tanks—with black gold hosed over from the carriers, and the tanker departed for Midway to stay clear of the battle area. The crew received orders to dye their white hats blue to ensure darkness at night. The entire air group took off for the final checkup of the planes, and everyone was treated to a turkey dinner with trimmings and chocolate sundaes. "Food continues to be very good," thought Alex Wilding, who was otherwise uncomfortable with a severe case of jock itch. "We're fast approaching zero hour. If we can get by tomorrow without being detected, all will be well. Tomorrow tells the tale." All hands were now invited to take out $10,000 life insurance policies!

After an evening serenade by ship's band at the base of the island, two *Essex* TBFs were forced to land aboard the *Yorktown* due to the deteriorating weather. Their pilots repaired to the Torpedo 5 ready room where the topic of conversation was survival gear, which the fliers were loading up on. To keep one's .38 revolver dry in a life raft, the *Essex* men suggested covering it with wax.

One pilot observed, "The Jap now protects most of his stuff in rubbers, and you know the kind I mean. Only they got all kinds of sizes—great big rubbers, little bitta rubbers, medium-sized rubbers—all kinds." Taking his cue, another pilot "enlarged" on the story: "Don't I know! We once found a dead Jap flier who had his automatic in a special rubber bag like that. We took the rubber—it must have been more'n a foot and a half long—and sent it back to a friend in the States. We wrote him: 'This will give you some idea of the men we are fighting.' "

Old salt Pappy Harshman regaled the young fliers with his experience in a raft over ten years before, after he had ditched at sea off Central America. Adrift five days, he had been rescued by a German merchantman which had immediately plied him with schnapps; near to starvation, he recalled that the brew "nearly blew my head off!" His singular experience, however, had led to the Navy's first practical steps toward supplying life rafts with emergency equipment and food.

Before dawn on August 30 the task force reached the northernmost point in its sweep around Wake Island toward Marcus, which now lay 550 miles to the south. Alex Wilding rejoiced that "today the gods are smiling on us for there is a complete overcast with occasional showers"—Vonk's weather front. At 0900 the ships turned south for the final run-in toward Marcus. Jocko had all available hands doing calisthenics on the flight deck, then informed the crew over the bullhorn that this operation marked the beginning of the Central Pacific offensive.

Commander Jim Morrison's radio listeners picked up transmissions from Marcus. Ensign Charles A. "Sandy" Sims, a Japanese language and radio intercept expert assigned to the operation, reported that the island seemed to be oblivious to the approaching danger and that a dozen Jap patrol planes had just landed there—"just 12 less for them when we get thru" sneered Stinky Harrison in his diary. Sims, who had spent his youth in Japan with his missionary-businessman father, tracked the enemy searches so well that Pownall's staff was able to pull in the escorts and avoid detection by Jap snoopers.

Last minute changes to the plan of attack for the morrow, however, caused some consternation. Air Group Five got the final approval to make the first strike, but this meant the launch and rendezvous of no fewer than 18 fighters, 12 bombers and all

18 "torpeckers" in total darkness, a tricky business, followed by navigating through the pitch black night. Alex Wilding "went over to Ready Room 1, VF 5, just as the announcement came over the squawk box. How they bitched."

But it also meant that the *Yorktown*, after months of pushing by Jocko Clark, would be the first of the new carriers to actually go into battle—"thus beating our rivals, the *Essex*, to a draw," reflected

are spread out under their planes on the flight deck.

"Excitement is beginning to be felt and the tension tightens. The Chaplain says, 'It's just like the night before Christmas.' The colored mess boys all have their life jackets on and are huddled in little groups talking. Pilots are all in Condition I," that is, ready to launch. "It's now 1530. The hangar deck is a bee hive of activity now as the bombs are being loaded into the SBDs. F6Fs are being checked

Greetings to the enemy from V-1-A air ordnance gang before the Marcus strike. In skull cap arming boss Jim Bryan faces his assistant John McCollow and Martin "Tadpole" Tauber.

pilot Harrison. "We've accomplished as much in six months as they have in a year and a half," the time in which *Essex's* Air Group Nine had been in commission.

Jim Bryan's arming crews loaded the TBF Avengers with blockbusters fused with daisy cutters, 500-pounders and clusters of incendiaries with which to light up the target during the first bombing run. The SBD Dauntlesses received 1000-pounders. In the afternoon, the skies cleared, the weather front moving ahead of the force toward Marcus—a perfect cover.

Prepared to spend 48 consecutive hours at his plotting boards in CIC, fighter intercept officer Wilding took a final stroll on the flight deck to witness the force now rushing southward.

"Speed now 25 kts. and *Indiana* is hard pressed to keep up. Cruiser *Mobile* is also smoking some. *York* lists 20 degrees on turns on our antisub zig zag plan. Gun crews are all standing by their guns with glasses and headphones on. The island structure is a mass of humanity with men at battle stations with headphones. Plane captains and crews

and rechecked. Every plane but one is in condition to go now."

Early in the evening the fliers gathered in the wardroom where Jimmy Flatley reviewed the attack plan. Teamwork would be essential—to maximize effectiveness and minimize losses. "If you get in a tough spot," he told his green pilots, "keep cool, outthink your enemy. You can meet any situation if you don't get excited and make the wrong move. Remember that all pilots get excited in their first combat. When the moment comes, say to yourself, 'Well, here it is and I'm getting excited.' Let it pass and make your first move."

Flatley quietly instructed his young charges: "Say your prayers tonight. We're out here fighting for Christian ideals established by our God. Ask Him for strength and courage to do your job well." Then, to battle: "You have the best equipment in the world. Use it effectively. Make the Jap pay through the nose with every bomb and every bullet where it will do the most good. We are the best Air Group on the best ship in the Navy. Let's prove it tomorrow!"

Squadron commanders Crommelin, Milner and Upson each said a few words, followed by Admiral Pownall. The pilots adjourned to cleanse themselves in a hot shower and to try to sleep. But even the veterans were restless. Harrison: "Could it be nervousness?" Typical was Hellcat jockey Lieutenant (jg) Jim Campbell, "I went to bed but sleep didn't come easily. I tossed and turned and woke up frequently. Apparently, later I did doze off."

As ship's officers came off watch, they gravitated to the dark, quiet flight deck with its first deckload of strike planes spotted aft. The sea had become absolutely calm, the atmosphere downright balmy. Stars studded the moonless sky, and the red planet Mars glowed in the direction on the target, an omen of the work ahead.

Dog Day for Marcus, August 31, 1943, began routinely enough at midnight as the officer-of-the-deck (OOD) noted in the log: speed 18 knots, all departments poised for battle in Material Condition Baker, Engineering Material Condition 32 and Condition Readiness III. Captain Clark had assigned his most experienced combat leaders to run the battle. The First Lieutenant, Dan Sweeney, was duty commander; Joe Tucker had the duty in the Air Department; and Charlie Ridgway was force fighter director.

Ridgway's radars picked up two bogeys in the direction of Marcus, one of which closed its distance to the task force to 50 miles before turning away and heading straight for home. Captain

Beakley had been correct; the Japs had not changed their search patterns since the beginning of the war! The force, as it were, just followed the snooper back to its base.

Air Department and air group were roused at 0200 for a battle breakfast of steak and eggs. Flight Quarters at 0300 summoned the aviators to their ready rooms. Half an hour after that general reveille awakened all hands, followed at 0400 by G.Q.: "General Quarters! General Quarters! All hands, man your battle stations!"

Air Plot fed the ticker tapes with the ship's position and speed; bearing and distance to the target; weather and sea and flying conditions—sea calm, temperatures in the 70's, ceiling unlimited, visibility eight to ten miles with light clouds; and distance to the nearest friendly land—"out of range!" The pilots took it all down on their portable navigating boards, while near panic struck Air Plot when Commander Waller walked in and ordered Ed Stebbins to have the head (bathroom) cleaned; a well-ordered ship had to look sharp if it was to function sharply. Steb made Cooper Bright supervise the task.

Air officer Hank Dozier fretted over the calm sea—hell, it was glassy! For the heavy-laden torpeckers to get airborne, they needed 30 to 40 knots of wind down the deck. The staff had assumed a minimum eight-knot wind, hoped for twelve, and got exactly none. So the three carriers rang up 28 knots.

Equally bad, with sunrise not due until 0652, the scattered clouds obscured the dark horizon, which

Battle breakfast of steak and eggs.

-36-

the pilots needed to see to avoid clearing the deck too low and hitting the water. Jocko Clark had a solution: each destroyer out on the screen should turn on one mast "truck" light to create an artificial horizon. Admiral Pownall turned him down, fearful of lurking Jap subs taking advantage of the lights to attack. Jocko persisted—no submerged six-knot boat could hope to hit ships moving at high speed, and his pilots needed that horizon. Pownall asked the advice of his staff officers, who agreed with Clark. Then Jocko went one step further by having Joe Tucker park his two mules at the forward end of the flight deck, headlights on.

Rear Admiral Charles A. "Baldy" Pownall on the flag bridge of the *Yorktown* during the Marcus raid. National Archives

At the sight of all the lights dotting the horizon, Admiral Pownall nervously paced the flag bridge, going through one cigarette after another. Though a heck of a nice guy and a superb peacetime officer, "Baldy" Pownall had come from a Stateside job and had yet to see action. Obviously rattled by his heavy responsibilities, he could not decide whether to launch and asked advice from everyone within earshot, including ensigns like Sandy Sims and his new flag lieutenant, Ernie Kelly. Assigned to the staff from the *Yorktown's* Communications Department, Kelly had been in action near other

admirals on the *Enterprise* in the South Pacific and had never seen them seek much advice. Pownall was a worrier. Finally, Captain Duckworth made the decision for him, and at 0415 the pilots emerged onto the flight deck. They felt the ship heeling over sharply to head into the wind, yet they couldn't see a thing, not even the big white stars painted on their planes. Airedales guided them to their aircraft, and soon they could make out the phosphorescent wakes of the other ships. As their eyes adjusted, the fliers could discern the artificial horizon Jocko had created for them.

Strapped into their cockpits by their plane captains, they waited. "Christ!" cursed one to himself. "The waiting is the worst of all. I wish I could take a leak. That goddamn pistol is sticking in my ribs. My goddamn foot is going to sleep. Jesus, it's dark. Going to be a bitch of a rendezvous. Black as a witch's teat. The air smells good this morning. . . ."

"Prepare to start engines!" blared the bullhorn at the air officer's order, and the pilots primed their engines. "Stand clear of propellers!" Plane captains patted their pilots on the head and jumped down. Airedales crouched by the wheels, ready to pull out the chocks.

"Start engines!" Ignition cartridges fired, engines coughed, props turned over—and over, until the *Yorktown's* flight deck reverberated with the deafening roar of some 48 piston engines.

Two rows of subdued white stud lights came on outlining the runway, and airedales with red and green handlights motioned the lead Hellcat into the launch spot. It was "Blue Leader," Charlie Crommelin, who now unfolded his wings and taxied into position. He looked up at the red light at Pri Fly which suddenly yielded to a green one: Launch Aircraft!

Hank Warren rotated a lighted green baton over his head as Charlie revved up his F6F and practically stood on his brake pedals. Warren then snapped his arm down, pointing the baton toward the bow. Crommelin roared down the deck and into the air, flipping on his lights to mark his position for the rendezvous. The time was 0423, seven minutes ahead of schedule and over an hour before the *Essex* would launch. Jocko Clark and the *Yorktown* had won the race!

The rest of Charlie's four-plane "Blue One" division took off, followed by Ed Owen's "Blue Five" then all of Dick Upson's torpeckers in three six-plane divisions. Fighters circled at 2000 feet on the port beam (left side of the ship), TBFs at 1000 off the starboard bow (right front). Division leaders displayed their brightest lights till all their planes had joined up, then switched to their dim running lights.

Now, trouble. Bob Milner taxied his SBD into the launch spot, only to have its engine quit. Fifteen precious minutes were lost while the plane was pushed aside and Milner pre-empted another pilot in order to lead this first mission. He rendezvoused O.K. with his own six-bomber division, but the second division assembled in the wrong sector. Then, on the deck, a Hellcat taxied into another one, fouling the launch of the last fighters. Jimmy Flatley was last off the deck, his "F6" equipped with three extra gas tanks to enable him to stay aloft longer and coordinate all attacks.

Dick Upson did not wait for Flatley or the messed-up bombers. Determined not to lose the element of surprise, at 0504 he headed off toward Marcus with his 18 torpedo-bombers, a decision Flatley now echoed. Charlie Crommelin gave up trying to coax the wayward bombing division into position and also departed for the target, as did Milner with his own six VB. But Captain Clark was livid at the botched-up rendezvous and put the blame on Milner.

Flight deck airedales silhouetted against the morning twilight off Marcus, August 31, 1943. Courtesy of Oliver Jensen

Battle dawn for Marcus as Run Two is spotted aft for launch. 20mm guns line the portside catwalk. One twin 5-incher points skyward.

Marcus Island lay 128 miles south-southwest, bearing 194 degrees True, and now navigator George Anderson turned the *Yorktown* in this direction to close the distance successive runs would have to fly throughout the day. An immense silence now engulfed the flight deck, creating a sense of emptiness, heightened by the half-light of the first rays of dawn. But Run Two—12 VF and 12 VB—soon came up the elevator and was spotted aft.

Run One stayed between 500 and 1000 feet off the water to keep under any Japanese radar beam on Marcus, and at 0534 the torpeckers sighted the lights of an enemy boat of some kind. Flatley decided to leave it for succeeding flights to hit. When fifty miles from the target, the planes climbed through a dark overcast to 8000 feet. The sea had begun to light up when at 0600 Commander Upson executed a prearranged right turn, and his radar set immediately picked up the island, 18 miles to the southeast. Five minutes after that, Upson blurted out over the radio, "There it is, boys, over on the left!"

Though half-obscured by clouds, the tiny triangle of land could be barely made out seven miles off to the southeast. Upson took his Avengers on a wide circle to the west of the island, while Milner's bombers climbed to "angels 9." All pilots were struck by the peacefulness of the place—only one light shown in the middle of it. Marcus had been caught completely by surprise.

As the three torpedo division leaders lined up their points of aim from different quarters, Upson had a brainstorm. He flicked on his lights to delude the enemy into thinking VT-5 was a flight of friendlies from Chichi Jima. He neglected to alert his other two divisions, which, in the dusk, figured Upson's planes *were* Japanese. Their turret gunners primed their .50 cal. machine guns before realizing their mistake.

At eight minutes past 0600 Upson executed his glide and released his payload. The two 500-pound bombs and six incendiary clusters hit amidst some airplane hangars, lighting up the area for the next five Avengers, which followed with their 2000-pound blockbusters. The other two TBF divisions had to guide on their radar sets because of the clouds and had to maneuver for better position. Then they too added to the general conflagration on the southern side of the island.

In the midst of the attack, puffs of anti-aircraft flak began to burst around the planes, sending burning smoke through the TBFs—a peculiar odor that make their occupants believe their planes to be on fire. Spotting first the fires on Marcus and then muzzle flashes from 3-inch AA guns, the initial fighters on the scene roared in, machine guns blazing away at the batteries. "Cousin" Ed Owen came in first with two ensigns, ignoring the flak bursting between 2000 and 3000 feet. Jimmy Flatley arrived with his wingman to direct the battle, and Charlie Crommelin's division was not far behind.

Pulling out, the torpeckers left five good-sized fires on Marcus, but the flak followed them out. Suddenly, division leader Pop Condit felt a "thump" and looked down between his feet to see a big hole in the fuselage. Flames spewed from the exhaust pipes in his engine cowling, and his oil pressure dropped. The shell had not only severed an oil line but had jammed open his bomb bay doors; the flow of air through them fanned the flames. Finding his gunner Ken Kalberg and radioman Gordy Marshall unhurt, Condit decided to try to make the *Yorktown*.

Moments after 0630 Crommelin's four Hellcats pressed home strafing runs on AA positions just as Milner's six SBDs peeled off in 70-degree dives from 9000 feet. The growing twilight provided good visibility for their 1000-pound bombs which plunged into fuel tanks and buildings. The bombers recovered and headed for home unscathed.

Flatley drew AA fire away from them by directing his fighters to keep up their low-level strafing runs. Ed Owen blew an ammo dump sky-high, but Ensign Clem Morgan took a hit. He radioed that his oil pressure was dropping, but no one actually saw him go down.

With the sky brightening, at 0640 Charlie Crommelin discerned seven long-range Mitsubishi 01 twin-engine medium bombers—"Bettys" to the Allies[*]—parked in line abreast 1000 feet apart on the north side of one leg of the airstrip. He and his division mates roared down, .50 calibers tearing into the craft and some 30 personnel running toward the first Betty. Predictably, the volatile Japanese planes burst into flames—"a beautiful sight" thought one of the strafers, Lieutenant (jg) Jim Pickard. No fewer than 16 passes were made at the Bettys and adjacent buildings by the four Hellcats, during which the sun rose to illuminate Marcus fully.

---

[*]For airplane names, see Appendix B.

"Blue Leader" Charlie now ordered his "blue chickens" to rendezvous. Pickard, whom the boys called "Izzy," wrote in his diary later, "We joined up at 0705 and departed for the ship grinning at each other from the cockpits. The tenseness was all gone by now. I think that was the happiest moment of my life. The first time is all over and it wasn't so bad." Seven pyres of black smoke which were once Bettys bore testimony to their well-earned badge of honor, their baptism under fire.

Mounting tension back on the *Yorktown* had broken the moment of Dick Upson's dramatic announcement. Sandy Sims, monitoring Marcus radio, heard the Japs receiving the weather forecast from Tokyo just as the torpeckers began their glides. The forecast kept coming in during the attack until finally at 0625 the exasperated radio operator on Marcus interrupted with a plain-language transmission to Tokyo, "Being attacked by four American planes!"

"You are crazy," Tokyo shouted back. "Get off the air until weather is broadcast!" The Japs never deviated.

All this got belly laughs from the crew of the *Yorktown* when Sims translated it over the bullhorn. Things got even funnier as radio Marcus now started talking to the *Yorktown*'s pilots, yelling orders to them in ridiculous broken English to change their target or return to base.

"Sector Able on the YE," Crommelin ordered, and the departing pilots moved their radio dials to pick up the coded dot-dash homing beacon for the flight home and flipped on their IFF (identification-friend-or-foe) signals. Jimmy Flatley kept orbiting at 12.000 feet while Run One headed back. Already, at 0628, Run Two had commenced taking off, its 12 fighters led by Harry Harrison and 12 bombers by Lieutenant Dan Harrington. This time daylight made the launch and rendezvous simple, and it was completed in a swift 12 minutes.

Meanwhile, one pilot trying to make it back was in trouble. Pop Condit's TBF gave out some 60 miles north of Marcus, and he made a "dead-stick" landing in the water. The impact knocked out gunner Kalberg, breaking his arm, but radioman Marshall pulled him free of the rapidly-sinking plane. Condit found the life raft stuck in the plane until he pulled the CO_2 toggle and the raft burst open, knocking him clear. He sank like a rock, with all his survival gear, but he finally managed to inflate half his Mae West life jacket and came up, gasping.

Kalberg and Marshall dragged Pop into the raft, then they just sat there, exhausted. Pop noticed a

Marcus Island under attack. Note pyres of seven burning Betty bombers on the left hand runway.

piece of flotsam floating by—a dime novel one of his men had been reading. He retrieved it and was startled to read the title: *I Killed Him at Last!* "To hell with that," and he tossed it back into the water.

Condit also noticed he was wounded—shrapnel had hit him in the leg and arm. He and Kalberg took some morphine to ease their pains, only to be rewarded with the dry heaves. Miserable, the three men just sat and waited—and watched.

Their squadron mates and Milner's bombers strafed and set afire the 150-ton Japanese cargo ship on their way home 45 miles northeast of Marcus. The late-arriving SBDs and F6Fs of Run One attacked the island at 0740, followed immediately by Run Two and by planes from the *Essex*—finally, the bombers diving out of the sun. As they retired to the north, Louie Richard of VB-5 spotted Condit's raft. He came in low—50 feet "off the deck"—and buzzed the three men, who waved frantically. Then Richard headed off to make a message drop on the *Yorktown* giving Pop's position.

By now, excitement filled the ship, the radars detecting a bogey 54 miles away at 0652. Then, Charlie Ridgway's CIC radios heard a pilot say a Betty had been shot down—incorrect. Admiral Pownall didn't know what to make of all this. Estimated flying time from the enemy airdromes at Chichi and Iwo Jima was four hours, so nobody expected Jap planes to arrive before 1000. Yet here seemed to be "bandits" (enemy planes).

Pownall asked advice of everyone, including, of all people, his flag lieutenant, young Ernie Kelly. What would Admirals Spruance or Halsey do in such a situation, he asked Kelly of his former fighting admirals on the *Enterprise*. Kelly quietly suggested sending out only two or three fighters to check on the "bogey"—unidentified plane or planes. Pownall agreed and dispatched three Hellcats, which found the bogeys to be TBFs without their IFFs turned on.

But now Pownall figured the entire Jap fleet might be coming, or at least enemy subs. So at 0711 he sent out nine TBFs from the *Independence* to the west to look for the former and an hour later an SBD antisub patrol. The latter had to be catapulted, since the ship was about to recover Run One.

A carrier was most vulnerable during recovery, and a worried Pownall took a walk. Jocko Clark and navigator George Anderson were at their posts on the bridge overlooking flight operations when Pownall suddenly appeared next to them. Putting his hands to his temples, the admiral moaned out loud, "Oh, why did I ever come to carriers?"

Clark and Anderson, stunned at this outburst, pretended not to hear him and said nothing. Presently Pownall descended the ladder back to the flag bridge. Clark turned to Anderson, "Did you hear what I heard? We don't need an admiral in the Navy with *that* attitude. We're here to *fight*!"

The returning pilots were full of fight as they came aboard and reported their hits to the ACIOs, laughing and jabbering. They also learned that Clem Morgan and Pop Condit were missing, but as soon as Louie Richard dropped his message of Pop's position in a small pouch onto the deck a float plane was catapulted from a cruiser to look for the raft. And *Essex* pilots over Marcus reported a man swimming amidst a large slick of green dye marker ten miles north of the island—no doubt Morgan.

Jimmy Flatley returned to refuel, while successive flights from all three carriers had no trouble locating the towering smoke over the battered isle. And on their return northward toward the task force, the planes all strafed the hapless, burning cargo ship.

Midmorning came and went with no Japanese counterattack by air from the Jimas, but at 1120 the Jap radio on Marcus resumed broadcasting— namely the position of the task force, located by radio direction finding. Jittery staff intelligence officers advised CIC intercept officer Alex Wilding that "we should be under attack from Yokosuka in three hours." That was from Japan itself, over 800 miles distant, a very long way away.

Ten minutes later Flatley took off with Run Five and heard a radio report of Jap Zero fighters over the target. This proved false, and the flight socked Marcus again. Only one TBF participated with the VF and VB this time around. "Jake" Kilrain released his 2000 pound daisy cutter from 2400 feet to hit a pile of lumber, which flew "all over hell."

But enemy ack-ack had found the mark on Kilrain's Avenger and two Hellcats strafing for him. Flak hit his left wing, not critically, but at the same moment it also struck the F6 flown by Ensign Lonnie Towns, who lost control. It rolled over on its back and went straight into the sea, exploding on impact. Another burst hit the left aileron of Fred Bozard's fighter, fragments breaking his canopy and wounding "The Buzzard" in the neck and head. But Bozard and Kilrain kept control of their machines.

Retiring VF-5 fliers now spotted Clem Morgan and circled him at 500 feet, frantically trying to raise the lifeguard sub *Snook* by radio. The *Snook*

Marcus Island burning during attacks by VT-5 Avengers. National Archives

Jimmy Flatley in Double Zero leads Air Group Five to Marcus, fighters equipped with belly tanks. The slashed line on the tail was the identification mark on *Yorktown* planes during 1943 and much of 1944.

responded and headed for the circling planes, which however had to break off at the last minute because of low fuel supplies. Morgan was never located. Though a strong swimmer and athlete at Oklahoma A & M before the war, Morgan succumbed to either a shark, wounds or exhaustion—or a combination.

Pop Condit had not been sighted after Louie Richard's flyover— no planes came near his raft— and the chances of rescue diminished each minute. For Task Force 15 was now heading north away from the target—146 miles by noon. The battle was going so well, however, that the captain of the *Indiana* wanted to head for Marcus to test his guns on it. Captain Clark and some of the admiral's staff wanted to return next day, continue the fight and locate Condit and possibly Morgan.

Baldy Pownall would have none of it. The enemy knew his position, and now the patrol submarine *Whale* reported a four-engine "Mavis" search plane 660 miles to the west. Then, when a returning plane jumped the wires and hit the barrier, Pownall concluded his pilots were tiring. It was time to leave, pronto.

Jocko Clark was incredulous. He recommended a special TBF search to find Condit, even if the entire task force had to turn around. Pownall turned this down as too hazardous. Several dispatches were exchanged between the flag bridge and the captain's bridge—a distance of about eight feet—until Pownall finally climbed up to discuss it with Clark. Except for George Anderson, the lookouts on the wings, and the captain's talker on the phones, they were alone. The talker, Charles Coburn, couldn't believe the way the old man treated the admiral about the downed fliers.

Clark: "We'll go back and get them in the morning."

Pownall: "No, I'm afraid they're expendable."

Jocko, sticking out his jaw, exploded right in Pownall's face: "You got the widest yellow streak up your back of any admiral I've ever seen in my life. Goddamnit, I don't care if when I get back to Pearl I don't have a ship and I don't have any command. You can make me a seaman second tomorrow, but this is my ship and these are my boys out there, and *I'm going* to send out a search for them! Do I have your permission?"

Pownall backed down. "All right. Send them out now, 75 miles."

"They're going out 125 miles!" Clark shot back, but before he calmed down he raised it to 160—all the way back to Marcus!

Eight torpeckers took off and fanned out, only one carrying bombs—four 500-pounders not discharged on the previous run. The pilot, Lieutenant Joe Kristufek, got separated during the search, came upon the unsinkable Jap ship, and bombed it to kingdom come; it blew up and sank. Then he pressed on to Marcus and searched around the island for half an hour. He almost strafed the *Snook,* until he saw the American flag waving over her conning tower. But Condit's raft was never sighted.

The loss of the five men cast something of a pall over the *Yorktown* as it retired at high speed from the target area. But Pownall, frantic to escape, was startled when in the midst of taking aboard the last planes in midafternoon, a destroyer in the screen reported an enemy sub 20 miles to the west. The orbiting fighters were vectored to the spot—false alarm. Several hours later another can saw something on the surface—a probable whale, as it turned out!

And so, in the words of Honolulu *Advertiser* war correspondent Laselle Gilman, Task Force 15 "races north into the wastes of the North Pacific at sunset, dodging through a lucky series of rain squalls and an astonishing forest of rainbows, and grimly prepared to repeal any belated aerial attack the furious enemy may attempt to launch in retaliation."

The only indication of possible Japanese retaliation came just before midnight as the force was executing its wide arc around air search tracks from Wake. Alex Wilding recorded that "a friendly submarine off Tokyo reports by radio that a large Japanese task force left Tokyo at noon heading in our direction." Whereupon Admiral Pownall changed course direct to Pearl—the quickest route to safety. No Japanese tried to pursue.

Captain Clark ordered "gedunks" (ice cream) for all hands while they took stock of their achievement. *Yorktown* planes had done most of the fighting and therefore inflicted more damage to the installations on Marcus than had *Essex* or the fewer *Independence* planes, including the destruction of all seven Betty bombers. Air Group Five had suffered the only losses. Jimmy Flatley told a United Press war correspondent, "Let's Marcus Tokyo" and then jotted off a letter to his wife: "My darling, I'm down, dog tired, but I'm not out. Tojo is. Serves him right for messing around with good old country boys. We don't really understand him. He says come on and fight. We fight. But, boy, he ain't no fighter. It's sort of brutal like. You knock him down, help him up, knock him down, help him up again, knock him down. Next time you can't even pick him up to knock him down. There just ain't nothing left. Breaks your heart, nice-like. . . ."

But another country boy, Lieutenant Raleigh A. "Country" Lancaster, assistant engineer on the *York,* had the proper perspective, "Attacking Marcus was like knocking a grain of sand off a mountain. We'll *never* get home!" The road to Tokyo would be a long one.

Up in CIC just before midnight a very tired Alex Wilding put out the last butt from two packs of Pall Malls he had smoked during the day, put down his earphones and descended the ladder. "At 2400 stood on the fore end of the flight deck and peered out into the lonely blackness and thought of those poor boys we left behind in the water and wondered if they would reach Marcus and if so how they would be treated. How lonely and lost they must feel in the water on a dark night like this."

That they did. Shortly after midnight, a light on the horizon had appeared to the three men in the raft. They fired a couple of flares from their Very pistol until they discovered it to be merely a star. Hope for rescue—by Americans—drained out of them.

For three days Lieutenant Condit and aircrewmen Marshall and Kalberg bobbed about in their raft, getting cooked by the Pacific sun. They fished with different sized hooks and bacon-rind bait from their survival kits but without success. They tried to snag fish under the raft—in vain. They even attempted shooting a sea gull with their pistols, but the pitching raft fouled their aim.

Then, on the fourth day, a Jap trawler came over

the horizon. The men voted 2-to-1 to try to get the boat's attention, but when they waved their arms frantically the Japs opened fire on them! Finally, the shooting stopped, and the boat came up, its crew of old men and boys probably as scared of the Americans as the reverse.

Hauled aboard, Pop, Gordy and Ken were stripped and searched and their pistols thrown into the sea. After Condit gestered to one captor not to drink from a can of orange dye marker, he and his mates were blindfolded and taken to Marcus. Put into separate cells, they were interrogated individually.

Pop gave only his name, rank and serial number. When Pop refused to give the name of his ship, his inquisitor said, "We're going to kill you," whereupon a guard put his gun to Pop's head and cocked it.

Figuring that they would kill him anyway, and that this would be the easy way out, saving him from certain torture, Pop replied, "Go ahead."

had to tell them something. They started by asking his hometown, which he told them, but they wanted more. The three men discovered that if the Japs figured you knew something, they would get it out of you, one way or another.

Bruised and bleeding, the tortured airmen were thrust into cells where they spent the night. Several days later they were tied up, blindfolded and thrown into a plane as if nothing more than sacks of grain. Heaped together near a hatch, they felt the cold air blowing through it when the plane took off; they figured they'd be pushed out. For maybe ten hours, the plane flew on, directly to Tokyo. There, still tied and blindfolded, Pop was taken off and pushed into the sidecar of a motorcycle. One of his crewmen was piled right on top of him, the man's foot scraping all the way down one of Pop's badly sunburned legs. The cycle took them to a streetcar, which delivered them to a train bound for Yokohama. Upon their arrival they were forced

Pop Condit hams it up with his crewmen (L to R) Gordy Marshall and Ken Kalberg and plane captain W.F. McMullen before the battle.
Courtesy of J.W. Condit

At this impudence, they knocked him off his seat and started beating him. More questions followed, and every time Pop answered they beat and kicked him. His intransigence only angered them further, especially when Pop tried to lie, not realizing that his information contradicted that given them separately by Marshall and Kalberg. The three men had never made plans for capture or gotten their stories straight.

Those working over Pop soon knocked out several of his teeth, and he quickly concluded he

to walk to the prison camp at Ofuna, where their blindfolds were finally removed.

The interrogation began that very same night by a particularly gruesome-looking English-speaking guard they would eventually come to know as "Handsome Harry." "I've got some bad news for you," he told Condit, "The *Enterprise* and *Saratoga* have been sunk."

"Too bad," grunted Pop.

"Now tell me all the carriers that you've got."

"I was on the *Yorktown.* Then there's the

Enterprise."

"What happened to it?"

"It's sunk!"

"How do you know it's sunk?"

"You told me."

"The *Saratoga?*"

"It's sunk."

"How do you know?"

"You told me."

"The *Ranger?*"

"It's been sunk."

"How do you know?"

"I saw in the paper that the Germans said it was sunk."

"Yes, I know. But what happened really?"

And so it went and would go on virtually every night of Condit's captivity—for weeks, months, years of torture, sickness, hard work and endless misery. A new war of survival began for the three men.

"Well, Buck," remarked Red Sharp to Cooper Buck Bright as the *Yorktown* sped back toward Hawaii, "did you get that blood off the flight deck?"

"What do you mean?" wondered Skinhead.

"Well, I told you there'd be a lot of blood on the flight deck," he laughed, "Did you get it cleaned up? Boy, I was giving it to you, watching you eat it up."

The prebattle fears did seem a bit absurd now, for the Marcus raid had achieved its prime objective. It had given the carriermen a taste of battle, and it had combat-tested the new air and cruising tactics, not to mention the brand new F6F Grumman Hellcat.

Beyond that, the one-day raid had little impact on the Pacific war. The Japanese commander of Marcus reported only 37 casualties out of his 1400-man garrison. The seven planes of his Yokohama naval air detachment were quickly replaced and the damaged facilities repaired. Radio Tokyo announced—which Sandy Sims translated—that the defenders had shot down 12 American planes in this "guerrilla air raid" and the rest of the American aircraft "repulsed."

"Repulsed my foot," Harry Harrison commented in his diary, "We started at 0530 and didn't stop wacking them until 1430. Propaganda's a great thing!"

Yet the Japanese also made a startling admission to their own people: "The enemy could have raided the homeland if he wanted to, so the people of Japan must further solidify the defense against the enemy."

The success of the Marcus operation confirmed the decision of Admiral Nimitz's Pacific Fleet planners to undertake similar raids with the *Yorktown* and other new ships, notably against Wake Island in October 1943. After that, the Pacific offensive would go into high gear with the initial landings in the Gilberts, supported by the new carriers.

Charlie Crommelin celebrates his promotion to full commander on the return from Marcus, September 1943. The Fighting 5 ready room is dominated by flight gear, data boards and teletype screen for messages from Air Plot. Harry Harrison smiles through his pipe. Mustachioed John Gray is in center.

"This war," Commander Flatley wrote his wife on the return trip to Pearl, "certainly separates the wheat from the chaff," meaning the fellows for whom he was writing citations. One of the best himself, Jimmy received orders to turn over command of the air group to Charlie Crommelin, now promoted to full commander, and to return Stateside to rest and be ready to assume an even more important job later in the offensive.

Harry Harrison also got orders home to bring out a new squadron, and Ed Owen was promoted to command of Fighting 5 in place of Crommelin. Bob Milner was issued walking orders by a dissatisfied Jocko Clark. Rather than select a new skipper from within the badly fragmented bombing squadron, Jocko chose an outsider—Ed Stebbins from Air Plot. Coop Bright "fleeted up" to direct Air Plot in Steb's place.

As for carrier skippers, the captain of the *Independence* would be relieved, he having become overwrought on Dog Day and unable to command effectively. Not the captain of the *Yorktown*. Old Jock had performed masterfully. His crew loved him for it and circulated a cartoon by radarman John Furlow showing Jocko scalping Japanese Premier Hideki Tojo. That the air group admired him was revealed when the planes took off for Barbers Point at sunup on September 7 and flew back over the ship in a formation spelling "J. J. C." Tears welled up in the eyes of Joseph James Clark.

In his diary, Alex Wilding noted the pride of his shipmates in the fact that "the *Yorktown* was the first of the new carriers to see action. Old Navy men say the *Yorktown* is destined to be the hottest ship in the fleet for a number of reasons. Her Captain wants to fight. The Air Group Commander, Jimmy Flatley, was written up in *Time* a couple of months ago as the best Navy air strategist. The whole personnel and ship have shaken down so that it doesn't resemble the ship that put into Pearl two months ago. Everyone ashore looks to her and speaks of her as the leader of all the carriers. It's true she's a taut ship now—but she was a heller three months ago."

Radarman John Furlow's cartoon of Cherokee Jocko Clark scalping General Hideki Tojo, Japanese premier.

As for Admiral Baldy Pownall's performance at Marcus, little could be said one way or the other. His nervousness in this first battle was understandable, and because he now had the only combat experience of any air admirals at Hawaii he would command future planned operations. Only time and events would tell whether he would measure up.

The *Yorktown* docked at Ford Island on the afternoon of the 7th, Bandy Andermann's orchestra serenading the mustered crew with "How Dry I Am" and "Roll Out the Barrel." To which the Navy band on the dock replied with "There'll Be a Hot Time in the Old Town Tonight."

But the "town" would not be Honolulu, for Captain Clark had just received a message for the *York, Essex* and four tin cans to make a high-speed "logistics" run to San Francisco to pick up men and equipment for transporting back to Hawaii.

Two days later the ships departed for Frisco, carrying over 900 veteran Army Air Force personnel and Marines, one of whom commented to Dr. Gard on the palatial life that carriermen led: "This ship is paradise—the first real food I've had for 15 months—imagine, all I can eat of turkey, ham, chicken, white bread, butter, ice cream, pie—My God, it can't be true."

The six vessels rang up 25 knots for 84 hours on a straight course for San Francisco Bay, which they entered on the 13th. Then Jocko Clark's Navy career nearly came to an end. Anchoring briefly just short of the Oakland bridge until a favorable tide could take them in to Alameda to dock, the ships were subjected to the tricky currents of the Bay. Just as the *Yorktown* weighed anchor, her forward motion combined with her sideways drift in the current to push her rapidly toward a concrete-steel bridge piling. If she didn't ram it, she would certainly lose her radio antennas, then in the extended horizontal position.

"Left full rudder!" hollered Jocko when he saw what was happening, "Raise starboard antennas!" With the ship just abreast of the piling, he called for right full rudder. The hull swung the other direction, missing the piling by just 15 feet. But two of the slowly rising antennas did not; the piling snapped them three feet from their tips, leaving them "hanging there," in the words of one ensign, "like limp pricks." Weatherguesser Jim Vonk, figuring a collision with the piling would have cost the captain his command, remarked to him, "You just avoided becoming Seaman First." A collision would also have finished navigator George Anderson, cutting short his destiny to become Chief of Naval Operations 18 years later.

While the crew enjoyed liberty in the Bay area, 2000 troops, 256 jeeps and trucks and some Army planes were brought aboard, and two days later the *Yorktown, Essex* and four destroyers departed at 25 knots for Hawaii. The run back was uneventful, except for the remark of an audacious Army "second looey" pilot to Clark, whose identity he did not know, "This is a fine fast transport." "Young man," snorted a galled Jocko, eying the lad coolly, lower lip stuck out more than usual, "this is a fighting attack carrier and *not* a goddamned transport!" To demonstrate, he held gunnery drills.

Actually, this transport mission paid off, for Joe Tucker's cumshaw artist Chief Pisarski carefully relieved the Marines on board of four of their jeeps, which he sequestered in the bowels of the ship and painted Navy gray for plane handling.

When the *York* entered Pearl on September 20, four battleships were present, the most since that infamous December Seventh when most of the prewar battleships had been sunk or disabled. But where were the carriers? That very day the *Lexington* and two light carriers were raiding Tarawa atoll in the Gilbert Islands, Admiral Pownall in command. When they returned to Pearl, all six carriers would sortie against Wake.

Two mornings later Captain Clark learned that Eleanor Roosevelt, the ship's sponsor, would come aboard in the afternoon. He accordingly ordered most of the crew to go over the starboard side with paint brushes to present a favorable appearance. They did it in a record four hours, only to have her approach from the port—unpainted—side in Admiral Towers' gig. "She really looked quite nice," noted Alex Wilding, "and gave a very appropriate and sensible talk—*sans* all flag waving." Dr. Gard found her "really very gracious" though looking "very old and quite tired."

While Air Group Five trained out of Barbers Point, especially Stebbins with new tactics for the bombers, the ship put to sea for more gunnery and to qualify the pilots of Air Group One. This new group, which would eventually relieve Five, lived aboard for the two days of training. Some *Yorktown*ers renewed Norfolk acquaintances, like Wilding. "Spent the evening talking over dear old Norfolk. At that we all agree that Norfolk isn't the ass-hole of creation—we unanimously award that to the Hawaiian Islands irrevocably. Someone does a mighty good job of publicity work selling these Islands to the States."

Mrs. Eleanor Roosevelt being piped aboard the ship at Pearl Harbor, September 22, 1943. Lieutenant Herman Rosenblatt salutes.

Jocko used the time to speed up not only respotting with his plane-pulling mules and stolen jeeps but arming the planes faster. Instead of taking 20 minutes to load bombs and torpedoes on their "skids" on the flight deck, the arming crews led by Jim Bryan did it in a record three to four minutes in the hangar. When the projectiles were hoisted by bomb elevator to the flight deck, the fuses were quickly installed and the ordnance mounted. These innovations gave the *Yorktown* 30 percent faster respots and launches than any other carrier, which was the equivalent of adding another carrier to the fleet. It also meant more missions and thus more work for the *York's* crew and fliers.

Air Group Five returned aboard, and the ship tied up at pier Fox 9 on September 26. Rear Admiral "Monty" Montgomery hoisted his flag on the *Essex,* this time in command of Task Force 14, and all hands made final preparations for the attack on Wake.

Among the farewells in the few days before sailing was Ensign Ken Hill of CIC to a young lady with whom he had fallen in love in Hawaii. She belonged to one of Hawaii's most prominent families, and her father had told Admiral Nimitz, "When you hit Wake, don't sink the dredge. My company owns it, and we get paid so much a day because it's been captured." When word of this outrageous request reached Cooper Bright, he went straight to Ed Stebbins, "You're a good bomber pilot, Ed. You *gotta* sink the dredge!" He would sure as hell try.

Task Force 14 sortied from Pearl Harbor on the afternoon of September 29, the largest American battle force *ever* assembled in the Pacific—six carriers—the heavies *Yorktown, Essex* and *Lexington* and the lights *Independence, Belleau Wood* and *Cowpens;* three heavy and four light cruisers; 24 destroyers, including one division under Charlie Crommelin's brother Henry; and two oilers, with the lifeguard submarine *Skate* heading to the target independently.

"Out again and going places," rejoiced Ray Gard in his diary, "gliding along over peaceful blue water. Rained hard for about 30 minutes and now a brilliant sun with huge cumulus clouds and a gorgeous rainbow reflected in the water."

Another diarist had just come aboard as the replacement pilot for Pop Condit—Ensign C. Roger Van Buren. "It really is wonderful to be at sea again. I can hardly believe that I have finally attained one of the big things that I have always wished for— being at sea on a large carrier, and headed for a little sport. All the years I've spent hoping for something like this were not spent in vain. It was well worth waiting for."

Rendezvous occurred southwest of Oahu on the 30th. "After chow," observed Van Buren," the boys all sat around bulling over the whole affair. There was a lot of bitching because we didn't have any battlewagons along; but that was soon lost in the rest of the discussion. It was very interesting to notice the train of the conversation. As I am new to it all, it was very evident to me. First everyone looked at maps and talked about distances, positions, etc. Then they started on the island defenses and the suicidal attempt it was going to be. Wake is one of the most heavily fortified Jap possessions especially against aircraft.

"From this they started joking at how they were going to get the hell in and get the hell out in a hurry. This naturally brought up a little talk about Marcus. Then they remembered what that was like and estimated what this raid would be like. The talk became more and more serious along these lines until it reached a point where everyone said, 'Oh, what the hell, there's no sense talking about it now.'

"From then on it was like walking into a different room. Some fellows started reading, others played cards, some went to bed, some just sat and seemed to be dreaming; and that's where I came in. I had more thoughts run through my mind that evening than any other evening in my life. Oh yes, and quite a few started to do a little drinking. Things were very quiet by 2200, and I got to bed. It was very warm in the bunk room."

The Junior Officers Bunk Room, near the bow of the ship, was affectionately known as "Boys Town," for here lived the young ensigns. The lieutenants shared two-man staterooms and pulled rank to get the better ones—like the time in Norfolk when Cooper Bright had asked Dan Sweeney to assign him a room "with a Southern exposure." The sly Irishman did it alright, putting Coop directly under the ship's crane with its loud, grinding motor. But ensigns had too little seniority to use—as the saying went, "Rank among ensigns is like virtue among whores."

At sea, Jim Morrison's radios picked up Tokyo Rose broadcasting her usual propaganda, which brought forth smiles. That is, until she reported the *Yorktown* sunk by a submarine, at which Jocko Clark stomped his feet in fury and used every foul word in the book to curse her. Chaplain Alexander, a witness to this outburst, quietly gave the skipper "my own special brand of Presbyterian absolution."

As the force headed due west on October 1, Roger Van Buren drank in the sight, "You can't imagine how beautiful and thrilling it is to see all these ships together. It's really the cream of the Pacific Fleet. Every one of the ships is almost brand new. The Task Force stays in pretty much the same formation all the time, but they have done a little switching. The oilers stay in the center, the carriers around them, the cruisers around the carriers, and the destroyers screening the outside. Most of the

destroyers stay in the same place, but a few dart in and out among all the ships. They really can move too. There are always anti-sub patrols being made by the TBF's. You can see six of them way off on the horizon most of the time."

At squadron briefings on the 2nd, Charlie Crommelin implored his men to "Pick your target intelligently, say to yourself 'that's mine'—then get it. No war machine yet invented can wreak the havoc and destruction in a short space of time as a determined carrier air group attack. We have the upper hand in this raid and we are going to make the most of it. Up and at 'em."

The chaplains were busy as usual on the last pre-battle Sunday, October 3. Noted Presbyterian Van Buren, who took communion, "It wasn't a very good service, but it was still church." And he poked fun at Father Farrell's full-speed worship: "The mackerels have a meeting every fifteen minutes it seems." So often, in fact, that Bob Alexander started scheduling more Protestant services just to keep up! At least the Protestants had more excitement when, as men knelt in prayer, a burst of machine gun fire roared over their heads! Three men fell wounded and one plane was hit when the tail gunner of a TBF had accidentally triggered his .50 cal. gun. Jocko broke the man in rank to seaman second class on the spot. OCTOBER 1943

On Monday the 4th the final run-in to the target began at high speed, 25 knots. Instead of Mars, the omen for the Marcus strike, amateur astronomer Ray Gard at 0400 observed the planet named for the goddess of love. "Venus was perfectly beautiful, huge, brilliant, casting a line of glistening silver across the water just as a baby moon would do."

Two snooping patrol planes were tracked by force radars during the day, the second closing to within 60 miles before turning away. Van Buren: "We were on the flight deck when this second alert was given. You should have seen things happen then!! In what seemed like seconds, they moved a group of fighters to the take off spot, and the fighter pilots were standing by in their ready room. They have jeeps and small trucks to tow the planes. They were running all over. Evidently we have not yet been sighted. It's now 1700 and there's a good chance it will be dark before we are sighted. They may not even sight us then. If they don't the raid may be a little of a surprise yet; but no one seems to think so." CIC thought so. Wilding: "We're very certain now that we're going to surprise them tomorrow morning."

Van Buren: "The spirit aboard is really good now.

Padre Bob Alexander conducts services in the hangar prior to the Wake raid, October 3, 1943. Sam Mandell's brass choir plays for Holy Communion.

Everyone seems to be happy and always joking. A few days ago they were biting each other's heads off at the least little thing; but now it's just the opposite." Nobody could believe it was so quiet and that the approach was so easy. It must be a trap. Some bolder fellows said, "Hell, let's jump ship and take the island ourselves."

At the final briefing this last night, Air Group commander Crommelin offered a bottle of Old Crow for the first pilot to shoot down a Jap plane. Then they all turned in, nervous as usual.

Except for the mid watch, the bakers were the first up on D-Day, October 5, 1943, to break out the groceries around 0200 in the humid storerooms and kitchens, fix breakfast for the fly-boys and make sandwiches and coffee for the ship's company; the ship would be buttoned up during the day and mess lines not practicable. Less than a square meal, these snacks earned the disdainful name from the sailors of "horse cock sandwiches."

In the ready rooms the pilots heard bad news from Vonk—overcast, scattered showers, ceiling a mere 1500 feet. Manning the planes, they found a flight deck darker and murkier than at Marcus; with twice as many carriers and air groups, six, the rendezvous would be sheer hell.

They were not disappointed. The first strike of a dozen Hellcats and half-dozen Avengers began rolling down the deck at 0445, as at Marcus guided by Upson's airborne radar toward Wake, 90 miles to the south. The weather caused a delay before the second predawn strike could get off at 0537—a full deckload of 18 VF, 24 VB and 11 VT. Boogie Hoffman led the first strike, Crommelin the second.

"Terrifying, almost horrifying" thought F6F pilot Jim Campbell as he went up into the night. It was so dark in fact that Bill Ruefle with the fourth TBF in line hit the Number One 5-inch mount and tumbled over the starboard bow, but pilot and crewmen managed to get clear to be rescued by a can. Si Satterfield's Hellcat turned left before clearing the deck and hit a gasoline strainer, damaging its landing gear, but was sent on anyway. And Crommelin's F6 sprang a leak in its main belly tank before takeoff, thus restricting the time he could spend over the target. "I can see now where this night carrier work is really dangerous," reflected Roger Van Buren back in the ready room, "You really have to keep right on the ball."

Ed Stebbins rolled down the deck with not only his 1000-pound bomb slung under his SBD but two smaller ones as well. "Why do you put so many bombs on your plane?" Coop Bright once asked. "In Texas," drawled Steb, "when we go out to fight, we go to win the war!" Now, his heavy-laden Dauntless dropped low off the bow, and everyone strained to see if he'd go in or gain altitude. He made it, barely, though air officer Hank Dozier later chewed him out, "Goddamnit, that's no way to do it. You scared us all to death!" Steb: "For Chrissake, what do you think *I* was doing down there? I was looking at the white caps going by!"

With the ceiling at 1500 feet, all planes from the

six carriers leveled off at about that altitude, instead of stacking by squadrons. "Every time I thought of a couple of hundred planes rendezvousing in that mess," Eddie Owen would recall, "my teeth chattered. I had to kick myself in the pants to get going—and I was fighter skipper!" Johnny Furstenberg's division of Hellcats encountered a large group of red and green lights—no planes, just lights—heading toward it on a collision course; they passed by, too close for comfort. VB-5 tried a new gimmick introduced by Stebbins—rearseat gunners of division and section leaders blinked Aldis lamps—but in the rain and murk these didn't help much. The planes simply had to pick their way through the clouds and rain squalls.

Thirty miles out, Joel Eshoo developed engine trouble in his SBD and turned back. Soon his engine failed altogether, and he and his gunner Alvin Golden braced themselves for ditching in a dark water landing. When the plane hit the water, Eshoo was knocked unconscious. Golden got out and struggled to free his pitot, but the plane sank too fast, taking Eshoo with it. A sickened and defeated Golden floated about in his life jacket until a destroyer picked him up later in the day.

The fighter sections climbed to 20,000 feet and at 0545 arrived over a dark, rain-soaked Wake. Visibility of the island was almost nil, except that at the sound of the planes the Japanese thought them friendlies and turned on the runway lights; "nice of them," everyone chuckled. Almost simultaneously, Alex Wilding in CIC picked up a bogey over Wake. "Yes, flying south from Wake (their morning patrol?)"—away from the incoming attack and the carriers. Another complete surprise!

Boogie Hoffman led the dozen fighters down in a low strafing run ahead of the Avengers. Alerted, the Japs turned two searchlights on the TBFs just as they released their bombs. Then the AA opened up. The fighters regained their altitude and circled the target until first light while the torpeckers headed for the rendezvous and flight home. The grey sky began to brighten.

Suddenly, at 0620, Boogie and wingman Bob Duncan made the long-awaited battle cry: "Tallyho!" Jap fighters were closing in on them from astern and at altitude, so they both rolled out to gain position for an angled deflection shot. The first dogfight!

Duncan maneuvered one of the Zeros into his gunsight and squeezed the firing button on his joystick. He watched his tracers tear straight into the Jap's cockpit, and the "Zeke" burst into an orange ball of flame. Bob eased back on his throttle, then winged around and climbed back into the fray. Having scored VF-5's first kill, he would get the prize fifth of whiskey.

As another Zero closed in on "Smiling Hugh" Kelley (the squadron sourpuss due to a bad ulcer), Duncan moved in. Seeing this, the Jap pulled up sharply, as only a Zero could, did a wingover and bored in on Duncan upside down, firing as he approached. Bob heard the bullets thumping into his plane behind the cockpit. Thank God—or Grumman engineers—that his seat was armored. The Jap pulled out of his pass and looped up into a chandelle, hanging at the top of it for a split second.

"Just there he turned," Duncan recalled, "I turned—I followed—I fired. He went spinning on fire. The pilot didn't bail out."

For his part, Kelley bored in on a third Jap fighter and got him in one burst. VF-5's shooting was pretty damn good, considering that the poor light had revealed only silhouettes. In fact, the broken overcast was so bad that Ed Owen and the second strike missed Wake altogether and had to come around and fly north again. Finally, the increasing daylight revealed the "V" shaped atoll ten miles ahead and to the right.

At 0640 Owen brought his 17 Hellcats onto the wild scene stacked by divisions at 20,000, 16,000 and 10,000 feet. They held their covering positions as the TBFs glided in and the SBDs dived from "angels 12." Heavy Jap ack-ack formed a curtain of fire through which all planes dropped, and some Zeros made runs on the TBFs. The flak startled fighter pilot "Jugbutt" Moore; "Those clowns down there are mad at us!"

The Hellcats highest up spotted Zeros just beneath them. Division leader Woody McVay dropped down after one, followed by his wingman Pruney Barton, second section leader Izzy Pickard and Shine Monaghan. The Jap moved away into a cloud, but another one winged over directly in front of the four F6s and Mac gave chase. They all roared down to 7000 feet. Pulling out, Izzy suddenly saw a Zero in his sights. He pressed his trigger, then—thump!

Pickard blacked out. A burst of flak had exploded under his plane, blowing off both his flaps and 14 inches of his left horizontal stabilizer (rear wing) and knocking out the radio and entire electrical system. When Pickard came to, he was cruising level at 12,000 feet. Looking over to his wingman, he noticed Shine grinning away at him as if to say, "You don't expect to land that thing, do you?"

McVay had flamed the one they had been chasing. Now another Zero appeared above but was quickly attacked by another Hellcat. Pickard motioned to Monaghan to head for the ship, and Shine led him off. Taking a last look at the battle, Pickard saw four parachutes floating down to the water.

While eager-beaver McVay had been Jap-hunting, Johnny Furstenberg's division witnessed four Zeros crossing in front of it to the east, outlined against the dawn. Jim Campbell picked out his tailend Charlie and fired at its cowling. The Jap's engine erupted in flame, but as the Jap headed westward into the receding darkness Campbell could not see it actually go down. Thus, he only rated a "probable" kill. Furstenberg destroyed two Zeros.

In another tussle, a cool, almost nerveless Rocky Aldrich saw a Zero climbing into a loop and followed him all the way through it—an incredible maneuver. Rocky won that one by flaming the Zeke handily.

Dick Newhafer, the squadron poet, was admiring the aesthetic qualities of a soft white cloud when suddenly a Zero darted out of the sun. "He came from four o'clock and above, but I saw him against the background of lazy cloud. I caught him with a 30 degree angle burst and blasted him 15,000 feet to the ocean beside Wake Island. He looked like a fiery rose as he tumbled earthward. We sent you more Japs, Major Devereux," remembering the Marine commander who—according to a tale-telling reporter—had asked only for more Japs before being forced to surrender Wake in 1941.

The fighters strafed when they were not dogfighting or covering the bombers, and as Hoffman and Duncan pulled up they caught sight of a Zero above them. Each gave it a burst before Duncan expended the last of his 2400 rounds of ammo. Boogie then nailed the Jap, only to spot another one 2000 feet above them and a mile away. The two gave chase, in and out of the clouds, until Boogie finally caught up with him and sent him down in flames.

As the fighters danced around each other overhead, Ed Stebbins and the bombers dived from a well-lit sky at 8000 feet through heavy small calibre fire. As they descended lower and lower, the sky grew darker and darker until at the drop altitude of 1500 feet they couldn't see anything and had to release their bombs blind! A little astronomy would have told them that the sunlight that brightened the skies at 8000 feet had not yet reached down to the deck.

The first sunlight to hit Wake revealed oil and water tanks, gun positions, revetments, barracks, magazines, radio installations, miscellaneous buildings and several parked Bettys, which the fighters strafed. Happily, everyone survived the action and dogfights, which ended about 0700.

The sun was shining brightly when at 0800 Charlie Crommelin and wingman Teddy Schofield arrived over the target. They strafed and burned three parked Bettys and some barges while flak peppered their planes, but the sturdy Grummans flew on. Both strikes returned to the ship safely, including Jim Pickard who made a perfect landing in his beaten-up F6, while Si Satterfield put his in the water near a can.

Exhilarated fighter pilots came up the groove, cockpits open, wind drying the sweat on their foreheads as they peered out to see the LSO's paddles. Catching the wire, each Hellcat jerked to a halt, and the pilot held up fingers denoting his number of kills. The excitement of aerial combat had everybody jabbering. Fighting 5 had destroyed eight Zeros of the two or three dozen airborne, the other carriers claiming the rest. No fighters or torpeckers had been lost, though Eshoo of the bombers was missing.

These and succeeding flights were longer than anticipated, the combat air patrols and antisub hops lasting three to four hours in the saddle, earning them the disdain of the pilots as "anus patrols." The fear of running out of gas was a big one; Ed Owen, catching the wire after a final four-hour hop, ran out of gas taxiing forward, which "scared the hell out of me!"

After their last debriefing, the exhausted pilots headed for "Dr." Joe DeWoskins' massage parlor near a flight deck catwalk to get their sore neck muscles and buttocks rubbed down, to hit the punching bag, and to work up a sweat exercising. A shower and a prescribed shot of medicinal Lejons brandy made them feel like new.

The ship stayed buttoned up all day, the AA gunners frustrated when bogeys approaching the force toward evening turned tail at the sight of Hellcat interceptors. During the day, the cruisers moved in close to Wake and shelled the island.

The alert vigil in CIC continued until after dark, for this task force was not running for home as at Marcus. Admiral Montgomery was made of different stuff than Pownall. Tough and steady, he also got downright mean whenever one of his migraine headaches hit him. From an early airplane crash and fire, he had permanently reddened facial skin which deepened whenever he got angry; the men called

Chuck Porter smiles at fellow bomber pilots as he marks down his hits on Wake Island for ACIO Bob Steiner. The cord around his neck holds the flashlight used in the cockpit. Also listening intently to the excited fliers, cigarette in hand, is Jim Vonk the Weatherguesser.

Rear Admiral Alfred E. Montgomery

him "Redneck" behind his back. His six carriers had easily won command of the air, so Task Force 14 lingered for a second day, moving north of the island.

But weatherguesser Vonk had more bad news for the morrow. "Scattered to broken cloudiness. Scattered showers. Ceiling unlimited lowering to 2000-3000 feet by late forenoon. Flying conditions average to undesirable in showers." Adding the predawn darkness, the morning of October 6 promised to be worse than that of the 5th.

And so it was; Vonk never missed. Thunderheads hung low over the sea, one huge storm blocking the course to the target 20 to 30 miles on each side. At least Air Group Five was not scheduled for Strike One, but it was on Strike Two, launching at 0515. Crommelin led them off, 17 VF, 27 VB, 8 VT, which circled the ship several times trying to rendezvous and avoid the clouds in a very disordered formation of two- and four-plane teams.

Fifteen minutes and 30 miles out, deep inside the squall, struggling pilots looked out in horror as one of their number suddenly dove out of a cloud from 2500 feet straight down, went into a spin at 500 feet and crashed into the sea. Others then witnessed a blinding explosion and fire in mid-air and two planes going down in flames, having collided in the murk. The first accident turned out to be Hellcat pilot "Coach" Crow, apparently the victim of vertigo. The next calamity's victims were SBD pilots Bob Byron and Bob Gregg with their gunners Tony Zanotti and Fred Marty. Other SBDs got hopelessly lost and milled around until finally ordered to jettison their bombs and land aboard.

Damned predawn launches. Fucking weather. SOB Montgomery for ordering predawn launches, raged the pilots. But the others pressed on, fighters paving the way.

Crommelin took the first planes from the *Yorktown* over the target at 0620 and led the fighters to altitude as cover. Immediately obvious to them was the fact that the enemy had no planes airborne, and Charlie radioed this news to Upson and Stebbins leading the torpeckers and bombers. His information helped to break the tension, so that the pilots of the attack planes could plan on lining up their runs without fear of interference. Still, Stebbins's nine SBDs got lost in the weather, but Steb radioed the lifeguard sub *Skate*, which flashed him the correct course by blinker light.

Chicago *Times* correspondent Keith Wheeler, riding in Bill Bogg's SBD, captured the scene in prose: "The sea was a rippled cobalt mirror im-

SBD pilot Ridge Radney prepares to drop his bomb on an already smoking Wake.

possibly far away under the flanks of the towered cloud castles and the morning was completely beautiful. We turned westward. A flight of Hellcats skittered across the face of the sea.

"'There's the island,' Lieutenant (jg) Bogg's voice crackled. The breath went out of me in a quick gasp. I twisted in the seat and saw it—and when I saw it the fear went out of me. I wasn't scared any more and it was like being born again." He admired the precision attack of the torpeckers at low altitude, "and as I watched a stick of bombs slashed across the clustered buildings there, black flaring mushrooms.

"'Here it is,' I thought, 'now it comes,' but strangely I didn't care. I looked at my watch, 7:05 a.m. The other dive bomber lifted a wing and peeled away as we came over the lip of a bit of high cloud. I glanced at the altimeter. It said 12,500 feet. I slipped the gun safety off and clutched the grips. . . .

"Something flashed past to port. There was a Hellcat 500 yards away, plunging straight down and its guns were flaming. Beneath it was another plane, also plunging down, but the lower plane seemed to be crumpling and thin white smoke wreathed the engine cowling and cockpit.

"There's a man dying; there's a Zero being shot down—but I didn't believe it.

"Then our nose tilted down suddenly and I jerked against the belt. We were diving, not steeply but with the engine wide open. The plane banked and twisted in its dive violently, throwing me around the cockpit. I had known this was coming—the high speed run-in before the bombing dive—but I hadn't known it would be so wild and berserk.

"Then quickly one wing jerked up, we rolled over and at the same second the diving flaps split open and the plane felt as though it had been seized and stopped in mid-air.

"The nose dropped almost straight down and we fell. There was no sense of flying. It was like falling, an interminable plunge that would never end. The island vaulted up at us.

"The air about us was full of darting red streaks that laced across our path, around the wings, above, beneath. Anti-aircraft I thought dimly. They're firing. They're firing but they can't hit us. Nothing can ever hit us. This was the greatest emotional thrill of a lifetime and it was going to last forever.

"The plane lurched. I suppose that was when we were hit, but I don't know.

"And then suddenly the nose came up, the flaps closed and we were twisting away, fishtailing, slipping, turning, still going down but now in a shallower dive.

"The red streaks were all around us now, chasing us, but still they seemed harmlesss. But I wanted to shoot back and tugged at the guns and tried to aim them at that fire-spouting beach now so close beneath us. But another violent lurch threw me down in the cockpit.

"Suddenly behind us on the point near the runway a mushroom of darkness and flame reared from the ground and smoke billowed up and grew and swelled and towered and suddenly I realized that that materializing genie was our work—Lieutenant Bogg's work, the SBD's work, the bomb's work—not mine at all, but I felt as though it was mine.

"It was then I noticed how slowly we crept, how agonizingly slow compared to the darting red stuff around us.

" 'The damned fool,' I thought. 'Why doesn't he hurry?'

"Panic came back and swelled my throat. The engine had stopped. We were going down, going to crash into the sea. I couldn't hear the engine. It had quit.

"I waited for the crash and swallowed and swallowing cleared the congestion of a 12,000 foot plunge from my ears—and then I could hear the engine. It was still singing its deep throated song. I could have kissed it." They made it back.

Charlie Crommelin pressed on with his strafing attack. A 5-inch shell burst 100 yards in front of him, damaging his plane, but he flew through the flak to set afire an oil tank and to photograph the island, even after the last fighters followed the bombers home at 0745. He stayed another ten minutes and on leaving spotted a man in a rubber boat. Dropping his dye marker near the guy, he circled him for ten minutes with his emergency IFF on and radioed the position to the sub.

Charlie Crommelin was one solid pilot and leader. His genius in the air was combined with an aggressive will to go in low, strafing to inflict the maximum damage and to obtain photos so vital for intelligence. He was absolutely fearless, though he had yet to kill a Jap in the air—which opportunity he badly wanted. His men worshipped him; said one, "That Crommelin is all man. I'd cut off my right arm for him."

Aside from patrols and searches, the *Yorktown* was not scheduled to send any more strikes against Wake. But since she had been launching and recovering planes in record time, Crommelin suggested another strike. Jocko Clark concurred, as did Admiral Montgomery. No Pownall, "Redneck" had seen with his own eyes what the *Yorktown* could do. Strike Three was ordered—13 VF, 15 VT, 19 VB from the *York,* Crommelin in command. Cooper Bright flashed the word to the ready rooms, finishing it with "GIVE EM HELL, BOYS—I'M GOING DOWN AND GET A STEAK SANDWICH!" Bright, you bastard!

Early in the afternoon, Crommelin's flight dived through the flak. But Hellcat pilot "Cotton" Boies took a burst in his port wing at 800 feet. The wing broke off, the plane burst into flames and turned on its back, crashing and exploding on a runway. Then Tim Tyler reported his oil pressure dropping, so Crommelin had him ditch near the *Skate*. Tyler executed a good water landing, dropped his green dye marker, and started swimming toward the sub. *Skate* came right up to him, and Charlie returned to the target.

The sub, on her very first war patrol, took her work seriously. While surfaced on the previous morning, she had been strafed by a Jap plane which had badly wounded one of her officers. His condi-

Charlie Crommelin puffs a cigar and with Woody McVay listens to pilots critique the battle.

tion apparently stable, *Skate* had stayed on line only to be taken under fire again on this morning, forcing her to submerge. Coming up, she retrieved one pilot then headed for an exhausted Tyler, when the enemy's coast artillery opened up. The *Skate* was only 5000 yards from the beach! A torpedoman jumped into the water with a life ring and kept Tim afloat until he was lifted aboard.

Tyler was far from safe, however, as a Jap "Val" dive bomber attacked while the *Skate* remained on the surface looking for a third aviator. She dove as a bomb hit near by, inflicting damage. With the wounded officer's condition suddenly worsening, Pearl Harbor ordered the *Skate* back to Midway at flank speed. But Admiral Montgomery had nine more fliers adrift around Wake by the end of the day. The *Skate* stayed, and the officer died the next morning—before the sub could have gotten him home anyway.

While Crommelin's fighters shot up 15 Val bombers parked on Wake, the SBDs, in Van Buren's words, "circled just out of range to get altitude. It was very ironical doing that. Those poor old Japs could see some 40 TBF's and SBD's just stalking the island, waiting to dive on it, and they couldn't do a thing about it. There were about 20 fighters along too. The *Essex* sent a similar group, so you can imagine what the sky looked like, and how the Japs felt."

Ed Stebbins now aimed for the dredge in the harbor—in absolute defiance of Admiral Nimitz's express orders to leave it alone. It was duck soup for the man who had bombed a twisting Jap cruiser a year before. He obliterated the dredge with his thousand-pound bomb. When news of this reached Nimitz, he ordered a full investigation as soon as the force returned to Pearl. But Cooper Bright was appointed to the investigating team; "You're safe, Ed," Coop told him. As for Ken Hill, whose girl friend's daddy lost the dredge, he'd lose the gal anyway to a rival.

Torpeckers then fighters roared in next, tearing up the island's installations so badly, recorded Van Buren, that it "looked like one big pile of smoke for awhile." So many pilots had ditched or parachuted after taking flak that their buddies condemned Admiral Montgomery for not sending a destroyer or float planes from the cruisers to rescue them.

No enemy planes approached the task force until late afternoon when Charlie Ridgway vectored Johnny Furstenberg's combat air patrol (CAP) division to intercept a bogey only 30 miles out.

"Tallyho. Single plane," Furstenberg announced—a twin-engine Mitsubishi 96 "Nell" medium bomber, hugging the water at 500 feet. The flight leader, with two Zero kills and an assist on the 5th, ordered his team to press in from 3000 feet and bracket the bogey. The Jap dove down to a scant 20 feet off the water, its turret gunner firing away at them.

Johnny executed a flat high side run from the port side of the Nell, aiming for a 60 degree deflection shot toward its engines, and fired a three-second burst. His wingman came up on the Nell's tail in a very flat low side run and got off a six-second 35 degree deflection burst at the tail. But it was Furstenberg's guns which struck home in a no-deflection four-second burst from astern. The Nell just blew up, plunging into the sea 300 yards away, 40 miles from the ship. "Splash one Nell," Furstenberg announced.

Task Force 14 retired from the area as a strike of Midway-based Navy PB4Y Liberator bombers arrived over Wake to cover the withdrawal. With 61 Japanese planes reported destroyed in the air and on the ground, the enemy made no attempt to give chase.

The Hellcat and its pilots had proved themselves in combat, and Bob Duncan—described as "a round, roly-poly, cigar-smoking, picturesque youngster who tells a good story"—received Crommelin's promised bottle of Old Crow for the first kill. At supper in the wardroom, the pilots continued to gesticulate about their dogfights. "You birds," remarked Skinhead Bright, "if you had to put your hands in your pockets, you'd never open your mouths!"

The two-day raid on Wake had been a resounding success. In spite of the losses, the new carriers had polished their previous performance at Marcus and were now ready to support the invasion of the Gilbert Islands.

And as after Marcus, pilots bloodied in their first engagement had been sobered by the experience. Reflected Roger Van Buren, "Well, I've found out one or two things on this cruise. First, this fleet game isn't half as glamorous as it is cracked up to be. It's one of those things you aren't too crazy about when you are doing it, but it's wonderful after it's over. Another is, it doesn't take much to get yourself bumped off, and if you want to be around after this is all over you really have to keep on the ball and be prepared for anything."

Chapter IV
Fire in the Gilberts

On October 12, 1943,
the day after the *Yorktown* tied up at Ford Island, Dr. Ray Gard took a stroll along the busy docks of Pearl Harbor. He committed his impressions to a diary he had started in order to supplement the less-secret contents of his long letters home: "The Jap is taking a beating. Something is coming. The activity is feverish. Ships and boats everywhere. Many going out the past few days. We are going some place soon. I'm going to be in the front row in a big show. I'm glad. If we don't do it now my son Howard may have to do it later, when it will be a bigger task.

"This is one of the peaks in one's life and by taking it in one's stride we can make it a profitable and valuable experience—one that will broaden our understanding and weld us more closely together. Our kiddies are finding that life is not just one happy song. It will help them to realize the necessity of understanding what is going on in the world and how essential it is for them to be aware of history and politics, both national and world wide."

What Gard witnessed was the sortie of warships to reinforce Allied attacks on Rabaul in the South Pacific and the gathering of the Central Pacific Force for the assault on the Gilberts in November. Vice Admiral Raymond A. Spruance, the victor of Midway, would command the Gilberts operation, which included the amphibious shipping and bombardment forces, Marine and Army assault troops, and what was now designated the Fast Carrier Task Force. These fast, 33-knot carriers had proliferated to eleven and were again commanded by Rear Admiral Pownall in the *Yorktown*. In addition, no fewer than six battleships were assigned to the Central Pacific Force to cruise alongside the carriers for additional anti-aircraft protection.

Starting with the Gilberts, this ever-growing fleet would drive across the Central Pacific all the way to the Philippines and the coast of China, there to link up with the forces from the South Pacific for a concerted push on Japan's home islands. The offensive would take years—how many was anybody's guess—and would undoubtedly lead to engagements with the Imperial Japanese battle fleet, rebuilding ever since its losses at Midway and Guadalcanal.

The mushrooming size and complexity of the Pacific Fleet brought new air groups into Barbers Point, which forced Air Group Five to relocate at NAS Puunene on Maui. The flow of new replacement units—including Harry Harrison's fighter squadron to the *Independence,* and the need for sound planning in all aspects of naval aviation meant that Vice Admiral Towers, Pacific Fleet air commander, required top talent on his staff to coordinate the forthcoming carrier war.

He had to look no further than the *Yorktown* for two key men. Already earmarked to be Towers' plans officer, Commander George Anderson was now transferred to the staff. He was replaced as the *York*'s navigator by Commander Red Sharp, assistant air boss, since Captain Clark preferred to use *Yorktown* men to fill vacancies rather than chance the Navy's bureaucracy giving him a lemon. Towers also took Jock's trusted executive officer, Raöul Waller, promoted to captain and moved to the staff to supervise the assignment of all air personnel in the Pacific Fleet.

The Navy assigned the new exec to the *York*—Commander Cameron Briggs, Annapolis '25, a loud, gruff, mustached spitting image of movie actor Wallace Beery. The senior officers welcomed him and bade Waller farewell with a cocktails-and-caviar party ashore, "followed by a lovely steak dinner aboard ship," in the words of Dr. Gard. "Jocko's speech was an embarrassed effort. He can fight better than he can speak." As for Briggs, "He has close cropped hair, two big fists and is plenty tough. Everyone likes him very much and so do I. Then there were cigars and much chatting. The nicest social affair we have had."

Chief Engineer Blackie McNally was also transferred and turned over his job to his assistant, Lieutenant Commander Walter T. "Bill" Hart, Jr. Senior dentist Ralph Taylor, left behind in San Francisco with a bad back, was now replaced by Lieutenant Commander John E. Krieger. The real live-wire in the "torture chamber," however, was the junior dentist, Frank J. Losey. Considering himself a Jekyll-and-Hyde character, Losey was a 1942 graduate of the U.S.C. School of Dentistry and collegiate trombonist, composer and bandleader who was consequently also made *Yorktown*'s entertainment officer.

leave CIC in favor of a cockpit with Fighting 5. To keep up his flight time, he flew small planes from shore bases while in Hawaii. Ken Hill kept badgering him for a "stunt ride in an SNJ" training plane, whereupon Stover took him up one day for "a few acrobatics" over Maui. What happened Smokey described in his diary.

"The last straw (or straws) were a couple of cartwheels following an Immelman with a split-Ess at the top (of a loop) followed by a slow roll. Hill gave his all and so completely that he was too weak to open the hood—making a fine mess on the floor of the cockpit. Threatened to make him clean it up but he got sick again when he climbed back in the cockpit after we landed, so while Ken collapsed on a nice lawn, an obliging chief hosed out the cockpit, getting rid of most of the evidence but still leaving

The crew of a quad 40mm Bofors anti-aircraft gun loads clips during gunnery drill.

Now, too, before the big push began, the ship received new enlisted men, but none more unique than a 4-foot, 11-inch, 99-pound platinum blond 17-year-old squirt runaway from Paducah, Kentucky named John Ezell. Lying about his age and still looking 13, he had stayed one step ahead of his mother's search before reaching the *Yorktown*. No-one knew what to do with him. Teased by officers and gobs alike, Ezell received the moniker "Cottontop" and "the Captain's scribe" and was turned over to George Earnshaw, who made him take a nap every day!

One man who begged Captain Clark for a transfer was Lieutenant Smokey Stover, who wanted to

that unmistakable odor. On the way back to Pearl Ken managed to open the hood and stick his head out in the slipstream when his time of agony came. He spent the rest of the day regretting the whole affair."

Successful though air operations had been on the Marcus and Wake raids, the *Yorktown*'s own guns had yet to open fire on an enemy plane. So a gunnery exercise was planned with the *Lexington* and five destroyers, and at the briefing in Admiral Nimitz's office Captain Clark rejected Nimitz's suggestion that the *Yorktown* fire first at the target drone. Intensely proud of Stroke Blackwell's gun crews, Jocko boasted, "Admiral, suppose the five

Jocko and Lieutenant Herman Rosenblatt share a laugh on the bridge.

destroyers fire at the drone first, then the *Lexington*, then I'll shoot it down!''

After the ships sortied October 15, the five cans and *Lex* fired away at the drone, then Admiral Pownall told Jocko to have a go at it, after which the *Lexington* could try again. ''Admiral,'' Jocko pronounced, ''if you allow us to shoot at the drone, there will be no drone left for the *Lexington* to shoot at.'' Pownall passed this off, whereupon the very first salvo from Blackwell's guns scored a direct hit, sending the drone flaming into the sea! Jocko jumped up and down, exclaiming, ''I told the sons of bitches! I told the sons of bitches I'd do it!'' He was so happy he felt like taking the whole crew ashore for a great drunk.

Air Group Five flew out to make night ''quals''— landing and taking off in the dark in order to avoid a repetition of the messed up predawn launches before Marcus and Wake. The ships then headed back into the harbor on the 17th.

Since a steady breeze pushed the *Yorktown* to the left toward shoal water as it approached pier Fox 9, the captain was glad when the tugboat *Mamo* came up to push the bow against the wind. But the tug bent her smokestack against the hull, and her skipper backed off. ''Tug *Mamo*, come alongside and push,'' *Yorktown* barked first over

the radio, then the bullhorn. *Mamo* only blew its whistle, the shoals got closer, and Jocko growled, ''I'm gonna blow these canucks out of the water if they don't pull me in far enough.''

Ensign ''Shack'' Moore, Junior O.O.D., handed a megaphone to Clark, who couldn't decide whether his lips went inside or outside of the mouthpiece. Finally he leaned over the bridge railing, waving the megaphone, and screamed out with his powerful voice, ''Goddamn you, *Mahoi* come alongside and push!!!'' He had even forgotten the name of the little boat, and the expletives rolled out across the water, ''*Mikki, Mikki,* move that tug! If you canucks can't do it, I'll get down there and pull it in myself. You sons of bitches!''

The crew of the *Yorktown* nearly died laughing during Jocko's ''little talk with one of the tug captains,'' as Dr. Gard put it. ''Some fun. A lesson in seamanlike cursing that I have never heard even remotely approached. It was a masterpiece of naval eloquence.'' Didn't do any good though. *Mamo* never did push, but other tugs did, and the *York* was finally eased into the pier.

That night a big poker game consumed the energies and pocketbooks of several officers who tried to beat the champ, Barney Lally. ''Well, I've done some foolish things in my life but this really capped the climax," moaned Smokey Stover in his diary afterward. Before the game ended at midnight, Smokey was out $500. "Poor old Lally seemed to feel bad about it. As he said, 'I'd be glad to win that from one of the cry-babies. . ., but you're a nice guy'—which is quite a compliment from a gambler like Barney who seems to have the Midas touch."

For the next three weeks, card games and Honolulu liberty offered brief diversions for the crew while the shipyard performed last minute maintenance, and supplies and ammo were loaded for the Gilberts operation. As loading lines passed food aboard, a separate, illegal line formed to siphon off chow to the enterprising sailors' own larders. Some of Jim Bryan's arming gang waylaid six cases of Admiral Pownall's beloved fruit cocktail from its route to the admiral's pantry, which led to a two-day search which finally located the stuff down in the bomb armory.

Neither was Captain Clark immune from such pilfering, a serious matter for his diet which depended on Avocet goat's milk. Marine Bob Bender recalled that Jocko "lined up his Marines and let us know we were stealing him blind in his kitchen, but would we stay away from his fresh milk. He needed that for his ulcers and stomach. We did."

Last letters were written before sailing, especially by Ray Gard whose correspondence was voluminous and detailed. Among other things, he discussed the forthcoming Presidential campaign of 1944. He noted Thomas Dewey's rise in the Republican camp and liked Wendell Willkie's intentions but doubted his abilities. "It is very certain I shall not vote for F.D.R. He is not safe."

Finally, on November 10, the *Yorktown* moved out with the bulk of the Central Pacific Force to attack the Gilberts. "The entire operation," reflected Charlie Ridgway in his notebook, was "on a scale of historic grandeur." Alex Wilding wrote in his diary, "Heard the *Essex* and *Bunker Hill* and *Independence* are hitting Rabaul, with the *Saratoga* this morning. They will finish and move over to take part in our operations. All lines away at 1530. We stood at G.Q. on the flight deck—just as we cleared the harbor the band played 'Farewell to Thee' and I wondered if it had any special significance.

"I really believe we will be torpedoed or bombed this time. I don't see how we can miss. For three weeks we will stand in range of 4 Jap air bases and take everything they can throw at us—they say the

John Furlow's caricature of Captain Clark looking for the Avocet goat's milk he drank for his ulcers. Courtesy of Raymond F. Gard

Japs have about 250 planes on these islands. Somehow I'm worried about this trip and don't feel the security I usually feel on these missions. I'm making all preparations to abandon ship at any time."

But when the ship rendezvoused with the rest of the sprawling fleet, Dr. Gard marvelled, "Rendezvous!!—and how! Never will I forget that marvelous sight. Are there any other ships anywhere? There is more of everything here than I've ever seen before and I have not the slightest fear or doubt about its successful ending. A splendid Captain, a good ship and the finest planes that have ever gone into the air."

This sense of optimism left all hands unprepared, psychologically or medically, when a young pharmacists mate being treated for "crabs" (lice), Ken Rayford, unexpectedly died a few days out. The men were stunned. And the doctors could not explain why he had expired during apparent recovery, shattering their record of no on-board fatalities. A sense of the immediacy of death came over the crew as it mustered on the flight deck for the November 17 funeral.

Alex Wilding's description fit many funerals which would follow over ensuing months: "Attended my first funeral at sea today. Officers' Call sounded at 0900. We assembled in the uniform of the day, officers front and center, forming in three ranks facing starboard. Adjutant's call was sounded and the word passed for all hands to bury the dead. The ensign was brought down to half-mast while the band played the Dirge. All hands were at parade rest. The band played 'Lead Kindly Light' and all

completed their salute and the firing squad fired three volleys. Taps were sounded, then retreat. The band played 'Onward Christian Soldiers' and the ensign was two-blocked. The *Yorktown* is a sad ship tonight."

Squadron briefings for targets were equally serious, so much so that Cooper Bright injected whatever levity he could to ease the tension. He particularly enjoyed poking fun at the pompous among his shipmates, not least Herman Rosenblatt. The latter concluded each air intelligence briefing by drawing a circle at the appropriate spot on the blackboard with the remark: "Here is the target!" So Coop carried a piece of chalk in his pocket, and

The first funeral at sea, November 17, 1943—corpsman Ken Rayford, who died from "crabs" (lice). Chaplain Alexander is in the center, Bandy Andermann conducts the orchestra, and Dwight Long (upper right) films the proceedings. Courtesy of Frank J. Losey

hands uncovered on the first note. The Marines were in formation at order arms.

"The body was brought on deck, sewed in a canvas bag, and placed on a large wooden slab that was on the edge of the flight deck and extending out over the sea. They draped an American flag over the body with the field of blue over the heart. Then Chaplain Alexander read a short service, all hands said the Lord's Prayer, and the Marine firing squad presented arms and all hands covered and the officers came to salute. The chaplain committed the body to the deep.

"The wooden slab was tilted up and the end of the flag was held and the body slid out from under the flag, over the side and into the waters below. A splash was heard, a few bubbles appeared as the blue waters closed over the body. The officers

when he encountered Rosenblatt he would draw a big circle on the deck and declare: "Here is the target!" The final blow came in the wardroom mess where Coop drew a circle on Herm's seat before he could sit down.

New Jerseyan Bright also liked to stoke the last fires of the smoldering Civil War by making jibes about Southern pilots in his ticker tape messages to the ready rooms. Alabamian Joe Tucker got even, though, when he fashioned a small Confederate flag from parachute scraps and replaced the launching officer's checkered flag with it. Yankee-born pilots shook their fists at the Stars and Bars, and Jocko summoned Tucker to the bridge for an explanation. "Why, Captain," smiled Joe, "it's only the state flag of Alabama." A laugh a minute.

Jocko Clark's *Yorktown* was a happy ship, the

supreme achievement for any vessel. Combined with respect, the good fun was what made the men love their skipper—and to go to any lengths to do as he asked.

The good feelings were no more important than on the flight deck, where ship's company and air group were in closest touch. Certain personnel changes simply improved what had become an unusually close relationship between crew and pilots. Gruff, lovable Pappy Harshman had moved up to Pri Fly as Hank Dozier's assistant, leaving Hank Warren to manage flight deck activities. Bos'n Dick Meyer stepped in as launching officer; "Junior" believed in always sending off the pilots with a smile. And when the well-liked Red Volz or Dick Tripp—"Crash One" and "Crash Two"—waved them back aboard, it was big-hearted Ensign Angie Peccianti, a former football star from U.S.C., who caught them in the arresting cables. *Yorktown's* flight deck was the envy of the fleet.

On November 13 Admiral Pownall informed his ships, "Good news! Rear Admiral Montgomery with

Dick Tripp gives a plane "the cut" to land. National Archives

his carriers destroyed 88 enemy planes" and damaged a number of warships at Rabaul two days before. "Most of [the] enemy planes were destroyed by fighter interception and ships' batteries. Four enemy attacks annihilated. This proves what *those* ships can do. Let's see what *these* ships can do!"

The chance came when the run-in toward the target commenced on the 17th. Miraculously, no Jap snoopers registered on the radars on the final approach next day, on which Commander Briggs cautioned the crew in his mimeographed Plan of the Day, "IF YOUR BATTLE STATION REQUIRES THAT YOU SHOULD WEAR YOUR HELMET, LIFE JACKET OR FLASH PROOF CLOTHING, WEAR IT OR HAVE IT IMMEDIATELY AVAILABLE, WHERE YOU CAN PUT IT ON IN A MATTER OF SECONDS. MINUTES WILL NOT BE AVAILABLE, IF WE ARE TO FIGHT THIS SHIP WITH 100% EFFECTIVENESS. ON YOUR TOES. LET'S GET ON THE BALL!"

On D minus One, November 19, 1943, Admiral Pownall interposed his own immediate task group—*Yorktown, Lexington* and light carrier *Cowpens,* plus escorts—between the targeted Gilberts and Japanese island airfields in the Marshalls to the north. The planes from these carriers would intercept any Marshalls-based Japanese planes from interfering with the landings at Tarawa and Makin, set for next day.

Unfortunately, more foul weather threatened *Yorktown's* predawn fighter sweep against Jaluit, 180 miles to the northwest, and the admiral worried that the six Hellcats and two Avengers might get lost and use up their fuel. Furthermore, strike leader Lieutenant John Gray—who was one hot pilot—delayed his departure from the rendezvous in order to arrive over Jaluit with sufficient sunlight.

Pownall need not have been concerned, for Gray reached the target just in time to see three big four-engine "Emily" flying boats taxiing into position to take off. Seeing no Zeros anywhere, he led his Hellcats in low, strafing, to ignite all three seaplanes. Gray himself went in so low that when he landed back aboard he had palm fronds sticking out of his machine guns!

In the meantime, Charlie Crommelin had taken off with 22 fighters and 15 torpeckers to strike Mille (pronounced "Millie") 80 miles to the north. Expecting to find many planes massed there, his boys were treated to but a handful of Bettys and Vals parked on the airstrip. They could not know

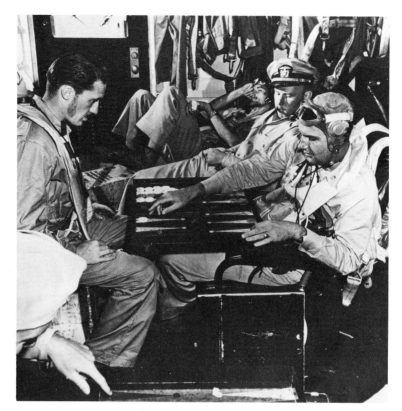

John Gray, growing sideburns, plays acey-deucy in the
VF-5 ready room with Jag Granger as Herb Gill looks on
and Whiskey Bill Dunn snoozes.

that Admiral Montgomery's attacks on Rabaul in the South Pacific had caused the Japanese to strip the Marshalls of defending planes.

Crommelin's fighters plunged through heavy AA fire to strafe the few targets. Woody McVay alone flamed a pair of Bettys. Johnny Furstenberg made a particularly low run and was hit. His plane immediately caught fire, rolled over on its back and crashed in flames into the lagoon—exploding on impact—"one of our most promising young pilots" lamented Charlie Ridgway later, "The fates have a strange process of selection." Johnny's three division mates, watching on in horror, joined up and headed back; in Jim Campbell's words, "we didn't feel like making any more runs." Johnny's wife was in her last month of pregnancy.

Furstenberg's other comrades finally silenced most of the guns, enabling the torpeckers to pick their way through the rain clouds for glide bombing runs from 6,000 to 3,000 feet to release at 1400. They flattened several buildings, blew up an ammo dump, started several oil fires and scored near-misses on two of several cargo ships in the lagoon.

The story was the same for succeeding strikes and throughout the day, although rain clouds occasionally obscured Mille, and Air Group Five

encountered no airborne opposition. Task force radios intercepted a Japanese report on the force's position and number of ships, which led to fears over a possible night attack on the formation. But it never came as *Yorktown's* task group headed south away from the Marshalls.

The rainy dawn of Dog Day, November 20, 1943 found the *York* and her group 69 miles due west of Makin atoll in company with Admiral Radford's task group of the freshly-overhauled *Enterprise* and two light carriers. The two task groups launched planes to cover the Army's landings on Makin, while two other task groups supported the Marines going ashore at Tarawa to the south. Charlie Crommelin's initial strike—19 VF, 19 VB, 8 VT— to Butaritari Island at Makin was armed to inflict casualties and destroy beach defenses: small bombs, Torpex depth charges and frag clusters.

Timing was essential for this first coordinated close air support of assaulting infantry. The flight was scheduled to begin its attack five minutes before H-Hour—when the landing boats were 800 yards from the beach and when the surface ship bombardment ceased—and to continue until 15 minutes after the first wave hit the beach. Air Group Five was assigned to strafe and bomb targets up to

100 yards inland of Beaches Red #1 and #2 and 500 yards on either end of said beaches. The signal to attack would be Very flares fired from the landing ships.

But the *Yorktown* performed too well. After making a record-time launch, Crommelin's strike arrived over the target at 0720, a full hour early, and a heavy rain squall sat right on top of it. Ordered to delay his attack, Charlie kept his planes in orbit while he tried to find worthwhile targets, but there didn't seem to be any. He was ordered to attack on schedule anyway.

Exactly at 0815 the signal flares burst above the landing craft. Hellcats peeled off and strafed the beach, followed by the bombing planes, all shooting at and bombing machine gun and mortar nests. But Charlie had been correct at the dearth of targets. In the words of Van Buren, "The troops didn't have too much opposition, and from what we hear now they have everything under control." Instead, the pilots simply enjoyed the scenery. "The trees were beautiful; we flew close enough to see the birds on the beaches and the coconuts in the trees. Circled over a small native village. It was really beautiful, just like in the movies."

Such was not the case over at Tarawa, where the planes of Admiral Montgomery's three carriers arrived late and then overestimated the amount of damage they inflicted. Resistance was brutal, and the Marines suffered accordingly.

Fearful that cargo ships left at Jaluit might try to reinforce Jap defenses in the Gilberts, Admiral Pownall at 1303 sent Crommelin with seven other F6s and six TBFs on a 201-mile mission northwest to Jaluit. Using skip bombing tactics for the first time, Dick Upson put a 500-pounder onto one ship's fantail; Ensign "Sully" O'Sullivan skipped two bombs into the vessel's side below the waterline; and a third TBF strafed crewmen scurrying about the deck. The ship quickly settled in the lagoon. The fighters went down to 100 feet to riddle eleven seaplanes, but only two ignited; the enemy was learning to degas his planes.

The threat of a major Japanese counterattack

Junior Meyer "tells" a Hellcat pilot to hold his brakes. Condensation forms a halo during launchings to attack the Gilberts, November 20, 1943. Note that the wartime censor has blocked out the fire control radar over the gun director at the top of the photo.

appeared when flagship radios intercepted, in Wilding's words, "a Jap message which ordered the Jap carrier fleet to put out from Truk to intercept us, also for every submarine to hurry to this area and for land-based bombers on Kwajalein to find us and attack as soon as possible."

The Japanese fleet never came, but Kwajalein's bombers did. At dusk, the gunners on the *Independence* in Montgomery's task group shot down six torpedo-bombers before another put a "fish" into her. She limped away to the south out of action. Then four *Yorktown* fighters on CAP were vectored to a bogey 50 miles out. It turned out to be a B-24. The four planes bracketed the Liberator, which trained its guns on the division leader as he wrote down its Bureau number. Later, the force learned that this B-24 had been shot down earlier in the Solomons and that the Japs were apparently using it to snoop the American fleet!

Three hours past midnight, November 21, force radars picked up three separate "raids" of snoopers totalling perhaps 20 planes, some of which came within nine miles of the screen before turning away. Lacking radar, they could see nothing, and Admiral Pownall slowed down all ships to a mere eight knots to reduce their bright wakes. The intrusion brought all ships to GQ two hours ahead of schedule. Then at dawn Smokey Stover directed a *Cowpens* fighter which destroyed a bogey 46 miles to the southeast.

Resuming its interceptor role to the north, the *Yorktown* sent off a deckload strike to bomb the airfield at Mille in the Marshalls, 120 miles away. Roger Van Buren recounted, "This raid turned out to pay for its efforts many times over. Later in the day two large groups of bogies were observed by radar plot to be circling the island. They retired to the northwest, probably to Kwajalein. This was proof of the job that was done on the field and it saved us from having to worry about air attacks from Mille."

Suspicious that some enemy planes might still try to use Mille, Pownall's staff told Charlie Crommelin to reconnoiter the island to see if another bombing strike should be sent. He was instructed not to attack. But when Charlie reached Mille with seven other Hellcats in the afternoon, he saw two planes taxiing to take off and could not resist the temptation. He made a lone strafing run which bagged a "Nell" and then recovered to go after a Betty.

Coming in at 350 feet, Charlie took a 20mm shell burst only inches in front of his cockpit. Shrapnel "frosted" his plexiglas greenhouse and windshield and peppered his body with over 200 wounds. Instinctively pulling back on his stick, he leveled off at 300 feet, but he was hurt badly—right wrist fractured; a bolt imbedded in one leg; one finger nipped off; several teeth chipped; penis, right shoulder and mouth bloodied; and eyes hit, leaving only partial vision in one.

But his mind was alert, and he broke his pencil in half and wedged part of it under the choke to keep gas feeding the engine. With his windshield shattered, he couldn't see forward, so he looked out the open side of his cockpit to stay alongside wingman Tim Tyler. Tyler coached Crommelin by radio and guided him the full 120 miles back to the ship. Remarkable though this feat was, Charlie still faced the challenge of landing.

"Clear the deck!" Jocko roared over the bullhorn, "Charlie's comin' aboard!" Luckily, the planes on the flight deck had already been respotted forward, but Pappy Harshman was thoroughly upset at Crommelin's plight and screamed over the Pri Fly bullhorn, "Get those airplanes spotted forward closer! The Air Group Commander's wounded! Get 'em up there!!"

LSO Dick Tripp faced the unusual phenomenon of two planes coming up the groove together, Crommelin heading for the deck, Tyler exactly on his wing to one side. At the precise moment, Tripp gave the "cut" and Tim yelled the order through his radio to Charlie. Charlie obeyed, dropped to the deck and caught the wire. He taxied out of it past the barrier and tried to climb out but had to be lifted. Trying to walk away, he finally collapsed.

Dr. Gard managed to save Crommelin's eyes, but, for the second time, Air Group Five had lost the services of its skipper. Jocko Clark could only think of one possible replacement. "Lieutenant Commander Stebbins, report to the bridge," beckoned the loudspeaker. The bombing squadron leader soon confronted the captain.

"Stebbins, can you fly a Hellcat?"

"Negative."

"O.K., you take off in one this afternoon."

Ed Owen immediately checked out Steb in an F6F, whereupon he took off, circled the ship a few times and made a perfect landing to gain the confidence of everyone. It was an unorthodox move. Normally, a more senior aviator should have been assigned by the Navy, but Jocko preferred *Yorktown*ers he knew and trusted. Flatley and Crommelin were tough acts to follow, but Steb laid down his guidelines that night. He would coordinate all air strikes and avoid dogfighting, while

Charlie Crommelin's windshield after taking an anti-aircraft burst in front of the cockpit. Crommelin landed aboard by looking out the side at another plane.

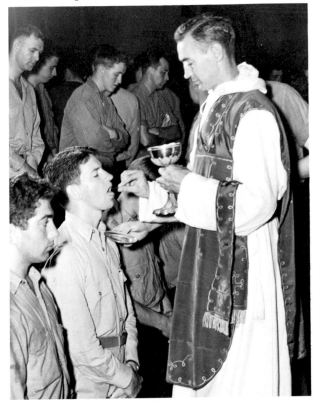

Bomber pilot Ed McCarten receives Holy Communion from Father Farrell before the Kwajalein raid, November 28, 1943. Courtesy of Edward J. McCarten

the fighter pilots must protect the bombing planes before dogfighting and strafing.

Stebbins also enjoyed the advantage in his close association with his roommate Cooper Bright, now running Air Plot. With so much very-high-frequency radio traffic making ship-to-plane communicating difficult, the two men now worked out a system whereby Steb would broadcast "blind" on high-frequency during the attack. Coop would switch over from VHF to HF on a simple Hallicrafters receiver they had purchased in Norfolk, enabling the *Yorktown* to get the news of the battle before any other ship. Ere long, Air Plot came to expect the familiar call-sign from Stebbins: "Skinhead, this is 99 Cairo. First report follows."

Preparing to hit Mille again on November 22, the task force was threatened by yet another menace—submarines. One was sighted at periscope depth but quickly submerged. "We know damn well," said sub-hunter Van Buren, "that these are Jap subs out there, but we can't seem to find them; or maybe they can't find us."

The admiral's staff ordered heavier antisub patrols, but when Cooper Bright in the flagship's Air Plot saw the order he found he hadn't enough planes for the already-scheduled large strikes and the increased antisub hops. He stepped out on to the bridge and informed the captain of his dilemma.

"Goddamn you!" Jocko roared, "I've got a job to do up here. You've got a job to do. The only thing I do is FIGHT THE JAPS! FIGHT THE JAPS!" He was now screaming. "To *hell* with the submarines. Fight the Japs! That's what we're here for. Get the hell outa here!"

So Cooper withdrew hastily and cancelled further *Yorktown* antisub patrols, putting the planes all over the target. Admiral Pownall called up Bright and asked what the hell he was doing. Coop answered, "I'm FIGHTIN' THE JAPS!"

Yorktown and *Lexington* bombers cratered Mille again on the 22nd in the face of heavy flak. On the flight back, Stebbins spotted a man in a life raft 23 miles south of the island. Ordering SBD pilot Tom Wiggins to circle the man, Steb sent back the rest of the strike and flew off to find the lifeguard sub *Plunger*. No more Pop Condits! For three hours Steb shuttled back and forth between the sub and the raft until Coop alerted him to approaching bogeys. Steb and Wiggins then returned to the ship, nearly out of gas, and learned that the sub had made the rescue in the face of enemy strafing which wounded several sailors.

Next morning, two hours before noon, force

radars registered a large bogey—many planes—85 miles to the northwest coming down from the Marshalls. Smokey Stover vectored *Lexington's* CAP to the intercept. *Yorktown* called for a "scramble"—22 fighters, at the time refueling topside. Even the bombing planes were manned in the hangar—"the worst place to be on a carrier in case of an attack," worried Roger Van Buren. "You can imagine how I felt just sitting there for what seemed like years and not knowing if and when the Japs would hit us."

By the time Fighting 5 arrived on the scene, *Lexington's* Hellcats had done all the work, shooting down 16 and five probables. Foul weather closed in at sunset, and all the carriers were unable to get their planes back aboard before nightfall. The *York* therefore agreed to take aboard five wayward Wildcat fighters from the escort carrier *Liscome Bay*, whose tiny flight deck was a tough base to light upon in the pitching seas now enshrouded in darkness.

Though the Wildcats still carried volatile belly tanks, the first three landed O.K., though one came in "hard," knocking off its wheels. The fourth approached too high and fast, so LSO Dog Tripp gave the pilot a waveoff. He ignored it and cut his throttle. All hands dived for cover. The plane caught an arresting cable, but the pilot panicked and gave it full throttle.

In the split second that the plane skipped over the crash barrier, flight deck fireman Johnny Montgomery started running forward and yelled to Junior Meyer, "Get the foam started!" The Wildcat then landed right on top of the plane in front, chewing to pieces airedale Joe Coppi who had been disarming it. The belly tanks of both planes exploded with a loud WHOOM and sent up a wall of flame. Meyer got the fire-retardant foam hoses going, with Montgomery and two kids taking one hose into the inferno.

Jocko Clark bellowed over the bullhorn, "Fire marshal and fire brigade, lay up to the flight deck on the double!" Fireman Barney Lally, supping in the wardroom, bolted to the scene. Jocko's thunder spurred the crew on: "Get the fire out! We can do it! We've done it before. We're not gonna lose another ship. You're not gonna let me lose this ship. It's all we've got!"

He sounded GQ, kept the helm into the wind to blow the flames away from the forwardmost parked planes, slowed speed from 20 to 18 knots, and headed for Air Plot to check on any enemy planes. The door to Air Plot, however, had been dogged shut for safety's sake, but his bark had the authority of Zeus: "Open the goddamned door!"

From the island, Jim Vonk could see men stretched out in the midst of the conflagration and yelled uncomprehendingly, "Get up, you dumb sonsofbitches! Get out of there! You're burning!" Chief Pisarski ran interference with a hose for Joe Tucker and an airedale who pulled a man free from the wreckage. But flight surgeon Doc McCaffrey, running up, took one look at the boy's liver—split open—and shook his head. Tucker jabbed a morphine hypo into the lad, who died with a smile on his face.

Commander Briggs, the exec, rushed down to direct firefighting up forward and saw a panic-stricken sailor drop his foamite hose which however continued to spew out foam until the stuff was three inches thick on the deck. Barney Lally had conventional water hosed on Montgomery and the others, just as strings of live machine gun shells in the planes started igniting from the heat. Their casings shot backwards, with only enough force to sting; Montgomery was hit by one in the butt.

The burning gas floated on top of the foam and began to pour into the elevator well and the hangar. Tucker ran down a ladder to get the foam going there, and someone with great presence of mind turned on the overhead sprinklers, saturating the hangar deck.

"Stand by to repel enemy attack off the port bow!" barked the bullhorn, and the ship heeled over in an evasive turn.

Alex Wilding, awakened from a nap, ran into "a solid wall of men unable to move" as he tried to get from the gallery deck up to the island. Someone produced a flashlight until Pappy Harshman growled in his gruff voice, "Turn out that goddamned flashlight! Do you want to give them a point to aim at?"

Wilding felt helpless, "just standing there with steel walls around you, the ship listing so heavily we were leaning against the bulkhead. Suddenly I became frightened, guns started firing, hell broke loose, I didn't want to just stand there and take it, I wanted a chance to fight the sea for my safety.

"But a solid mass of humanity was between me and three decks up. There was only one way—I yelled 'Gangway' in as an authoritative voice as I could and started forward—they separated for me and in the darkness never realized who it was. When I came to the ladders I bellowed, 'Move to starboard'—they did and I went right up to topside.

"My mind was all confused as to what was happening. I couldn't get a mental picture of the situation but had to immediately duck as bullets except that my heart was pounding so.

"I stepped out on the flag bridge to survey the situation but had to immediately duck as bullets splattered the bulkhead. But what I saw left me breathless. Our whole ship was afire amidships on the flight deck. Flames were shooting a hundred feet in the air—five planes were in flames with their gasoline tanks exploding."

The reported attacking Jap torpedo plane proved to be a false alarm, as did a submarine contact, but Captain Clark kept the *York* turning and twisting as its fires lit up the sea while Lally's firemen put them out.

Abruptly, the last flames flickered out—after only 16 minutes of a hell that had seemed an eternity. The wounded were gently moved to Sick Bay, where several expired. In addition to Joe Coppi, the dead included J.J. Martin, Gil Ray Howk, David S. Kasakow and "Wild Bill" Cody.

Smokey Stover knew the errant Wildcat pilot who had caused the calamity from Guadalcanal days, noting in his diary, "Foster Blair from old VF-5 was crashee." Blair had been nicknamed "Crud" for a skin rash, which gave Charlie Ridgway "some suspicion that his nickname is appropriate." Blair had recently been transferred out of Harry Harrison's squadron for failure to qualify in night carrier landings—a fear which had caught up with him. But it also underscored the need for proficiency in night flying.

Several planes damaged in the fire were cannibalized for their parts, then pushed overboard. The flight deck was cleaned up, leaving only two small scorched spots. The *Yorktown* had survived. She was a lucky ship.

The escort carrier *Liscome Bay* was not. Just before first light next morning, a submarine torpedo slammed into her side, starting a conflagration of her own. Flames pierced the inky sky for many miles; *Yorktown*'s lookouts could see it, well over the horizon. Charlie Crommelin's brother John, chief of staff to the *Liscome Bay*'s admiral, jumped overboard just before the stricken vessel sank with 644 of her 916 men. Fortunately, Captain Crommelin was eventually picked up.

After a hasty funeral for her own five fallen heroes after sunrise, the *Yorktown* sent off her CAP fighters under John Gray, who worried in his diary that the carriers were "just asking for trouble" by cruising in circles between Makin and Mille. Sure enough, at midday, the *Lexington*'s fighters intercepted some two dozen Japanese planes near Mille, and *Yorktown* scrambled her fighters. But again the *Lex* got all the gravy, destroying at least ten and chasing the rest back to Kwajalein with the loss of one pilot. Captain Clark radioed a message of congratulations to her skipper, "You've beat us out so far. I hope we have better luck next time."

With the success of putting out the big fire and for avoiding the fate of *Liscome Bay*, exec Cam Briggs spoke for all hands in the Plan of the Day for November 25: "TODAY IS THANKSGIVING DAY—WE HAVE PLENTY TO BE THANKFUL FOR!" The *Yorktown*'s task group pulled out of the line to refuel and enjoy a turkey day feast, with the *Enterprise* group filling in for it and coming under heavy air attack during the day.

Still, noted Alex Wilding, "tomorrow we'll be in the hot seat again and the closest group to the Jap bases. Looks as though they picked the right carrier for the job, as we've turned back every plane the Japs have sent."

Japan's Gilbert Island possessions of Makin and Tarawa had finally fallen to American ground forces, but the sinking of the *Liscome Bay* and the crippling of the *Independence* by enemy submarines and the growing number of air strikes from the Marshalls meant that neither the newly-won islands nor the supporting carriers were particularly safe and secure. At Pearl Harbor, Admiral Towers had insisted—and Admiral Nimitz concurred—that the fast carriers should run north and knock out enemy air and sub bases at Kwajalein once and for all.

Baldy Pownall did not want to go, using the feeble excuse that the occupied Gilberts could be covered by Army bombers from the South Pacific and the Hellcats of Fighting One, now shore-based at Tarawa. In fact, Pownall's behavior—increasingly erratic since the Marcus strike—had become suspect enough for Nimitz to assign an "observer" to the flagship. Rear Admiral J.L. "Reggie" Kauffman now reported aboard the *Yorktown* for the Kwajalein raid. Pownall regarded Kauffman as a "spy," which indeed he was.

The fact that the enemy was attacking increasingly at night was disconcerting not only to Pownall but to all hands, especially after sundown on November 26 when a bogey dropped two flares ten miles astern then attacked the *Essex* without success. Intercept officer Wilding lamented, "These night aerial attacks are terrible because you can't fight back. No planes to set on them, though the *Enterprise* has been experimenting with night fighters and declares it successful. The ships' batteries don't dare open up because the flash will give the enemy a point of aim and also draw every enemy plane and submarine in the vicinity. We just slow speed so we won't leave a wake and hug the blackness of the surface water and hope we're undetected—so far we've been lucky.''

Gun flashes over the horizon meant that Admiral Radford's *Enterprise* group was under attack. ''The Big E'' launched her specially-trained night team under the superb Butch O'Hare which shot down three Bettys and drove off the rest, but not before O'Hare was shot down by accident—a tragic loss and another grim reminder of the hazards of night operations.

Captain Clark immediately decided that he must organize similar teams to protect the *Yorktown*. At first he solicited volunteers to go up in the dark if necessary and then ditch ahead of the force if the *York* couldn't recover them should it be under attack. Several pilots came forward, but then Jocko thought better of it and organized two ''Bat teams'' to develop nighttime intercept procedures with CIC. Over the next several days the teams—each comprised of two fighters and a torpecker—drilled during late afternoons and into the dusk.

Two task groups departed Tarawa waters on the night of November 27/28 under the overall command of Rear Admiral Pownall. Pownall's immediate task group included the *York, Lexington* and *Cowpens*; four heavy cruisers; and a screen of the new anti-aircraft cruiser *Oakland* and six destroyers. Rear Admiral Montgomery had the *Enterprise, Essex* and *Belleau Wood.* ''Develops,'' said Charlie Ridgway in his diary, ''we're en route to make a strike on Kwajalein in the Marshall group—a singularly dangerous undertaking it would seem. We must pass literally under the guns of Wake, Maloelap, Wotje and Rongelap before even getting into position.''

During refueling on December 1 Admiral Montgomery was flown over to the *Yorktown* to finalize plans for the all-day attack on Kwajalein on the 4th. Captain Truman J. Hedding, Pownall's aggressive new chief of staff, and the air group commander from the *Lexington* argued for a two-day attack, beginning with a fighter sweep on the 3rd to eliminate the Zero menace, followed by full deckload strikes throughout the 4th. Montgomery argued forcibly against this idea as too risky, with which the mild-mannered Pownall agreed. Further-

more, radio silence was to be strictly maintained, with detailed messages between flagships to be dropped in pouches by planes.

The task force swung into a westward arc north of the Marshalls and commenced its final run-in on the morning of the 3rd. ''ON YOUR TOES, RAT EXTERMINATORS'' proclaimed the Plan of the Day, while word came in that Kwajalein was defended by some 250 aircraft against nearly 400 on the carriers. Shipping at Kwajalein was supposed to be plentiful, with seven cruisers, four cans and nine cargo ships—''marus.''

''Well, the impossible *has* happened!'' in the view of excited diarist John Gray. ''Tonight we are well within 300 miles of the Jap's main bastion of the entire Marshall-Gilbert area— Kwajalein Atoll. Two whole task forces united steamed right up their street, turned in at their driveway, right up to their front porch without being seen, and tomorrow we ring the front door bell—but punch it! And then listen to them scream!!''

December 3 ended as it had started, clear and beautiful, the sea bathed in bright moonlight—ideal conditions for a Jap night torpedo plane attack. A number of officers sat on the flight deck admiring the heavens; Dr. Gard picked out a number of Southern sky constellations he'd never seen before. Intercept officer Wilding and Weatherguesser Vonk discussed the impending battle. When they agreed it would be a rough day, Vonk exclaimed, ''Christ, I've got 6 quarts of whiskey in my safe. I'd better go down and drink the stuff!''

Unsnooped and unmolested during the night, the task force launched deckload strikes in the morning twilight of December 4. The *Yorktown's* 22 VF, 24 VB and 18 VT took off in very close 30-second intervals, breaking their record by clearing the deck in 31 minutes—best in the fleet.

Ed Stebbins led the flight to Kwajalein. The fighter divisions of Ed Owen, Boogie Hoffman and Woody McVay flew top cover up to angels 25 while John Gray's escorted the dive bombers and Herb Gill's the torpeckers. The flight took only 36 minutes to reach the target.

''Ships are there!'' Cooper Bright heard Steb announce over the Hallicrafters radio at 0750. While several Hellcats covered the *Lexington* bombers at Roi Island, Steb pressed on with most of Air Group Five to Kwajalein Island where some 30 merchantmen and only a couple of cruisers rode at anchor. Since none were underway to clear the confines of the lagoon and only a few planes were airborne, the Japanese had obviously been caught

Cook William E. Davenport prepares steaks for the officers during the Kwajalein operation. "Brother" Davenport also led prayer meetings for his fellow blacks as a Baptist lay preacher. Courtesy of Raymond F. Gard

by surprise.

But "big puffs of greenish smoke" greeted the SBDs as they screamed down in steep dives from 12,000 feet at 0835. J.J. Davidson and Louie Richard caused fatal damage to a 6,000-ton vessel with their thousand-pound bombs, with Chet Spray and Fred Joyce scoring direct hits on other ships. Then, on their pull-outs, they all had to jink violently—maneuvering wildly—to avoid the heavy flak.

One burst hit L.T. Gildea's bomber, knocking it into a spin, wounding the pilot in the left buttock and bending his .45 pistol out of shape. After regaining consciousness from a brief black-out, Gildea found himself in great pain and thought, "This is it. There is nothing more I can do—to hell with it." By Herculean efforts, though, he pulled the Dauntless out of the spin. But losing blood and fearing he might pass out, he called to his rearseat gunner, "Take her home."

Quiet 19-year-old George E. Kapotas took over the auxiliary controls and flew the plane while Gildea navigated and lowered his tail hook. Kapotas showed great pilot technique handling the bomber, and Gildea crash-landed her on the *Yorktown*.

The blockbuster-armed TBFs used the cloud cover to mask their attack from 12,000 feet. Ignoring the heavy flak, Roger Van Buren "picked the biggest damn ship I saw and really went for it. Still going down at full throttle and with well over 300 kts, I figured it was a cinch. I leveled off at about 200 ft. when I was about 200 yds. away. From there on in, I just sat and looked the harbor over. I could see Japs working like hell around those

3 inch guns on the bow and stern of the ship. Others were running helter skelter all over the superstructure. Both guns fired three or four times as I came in, and I could just see both of them converging on me. Many thoughts flash through your mind in a position of that nature in just a few seconds. At the first flashes I saw I thought to myself 'I bet you can't hit me you little bastards.' I knew they couldn't hit me because they couldn't swing those guns fast enough. . . . At the time I dropped I was so close to the stack I jerked back to make sure I didn't hit it. I really went over that tub a hellin'. She was an old freighter transport and looked rusty and in bad shape. No camouflage at all."

Unfortunately, his bomb missed that ship but landed so close to a smaller one that its bow was lifted out of the water. Van returned to the *York* "boiling mad about my beautiful miss. In fact, I never will feel right until I can get back at those little jerks for that." His squadron mates did better, leaving two ships on fire and two others settling by the stern.

Fighting 5 managed to avoid the airborne Jap fighters as it headed for many seaplanes parked on the ramp and in the lagoon near Ebeye Island. Someone called out over the air, "There's a Zero on your tail," whereupon every F6F turned over and dropped down—false alarm. Gill's and McVay's divisions burned perhaps 22 seaplanes before a burst of flak crippled Herb Gill's plane.

With no choice but to "hit the silk," Gill floated down into the lagoon about one mile east of Ebeye, toward which he swam to face capture—or worse. Boogie Hoffman and wingman Bob Duncan, seeing Japanese soldiers run toward Gill, tried to strafe, but there were too many. The two Hellcat pilots looked on in horror as the soldiers gunned down their buddy Gill.

Then a "Pete" float plane came into Boogie's view. He opened fire, only to have five of his six guns jam. Before Duncan could help him out, though, Boogie nailed the Pete with his one gun. It burst into flame, shooting the pilot out of the cockpit, then exploded. Duncan strafed an AA gun on a ship and managed to blow the entire vessel sky-high.

Directing the battle from high aloft, Ed Stebbins spotted a Betty, which he dropped down to intercept—in violation of his own rule to stick to target coordinating. Somewhat recklessly, he flew right up to the tail of the Betty—which should have blasted him—and gave it a point blank ten-foot no deflection burst. Betty went down in flames. Ed Owen, later marveling at Stebbins' achievement after only two weeks in the F6F, asked, "Steb, how the hell did you do that?" Came the answer: "I came up behind him and used the hose method. I just squirted him!"

Heading for the rendezvous, the Yorktown's fighters bumped into a swarm of Jap Zeros. Eighteen to 20 of them jumped Boogie Hoffman's division, coming out of the sun. The four Yanks immediately went into their defensive "Thach weave," the section of Hoffman and Bob Duncan scissoring back and forth with that of Si Satterfield and Den Merrill for mutual protection.

But these Japs showed themselves to be real pros by positioning six planes on each of the two sections, two Zeros always firing. As the VF-5 guys turned to counterattack, the two attackers pulled out in violent 60 degree turns and let two other planes close in, one on each side of the Hellcats. They fired on the outside of the bracketed Cats. These characters obviously knew how to beat the Thach weave.

The Yorktown fliers sweated each highside pass, especially Boogie, down to one operable gun. One Zero "stitched" Duncan's left wing with bullets all the way from the tip through the fuselage behind his armor-plated seat. Si Satterfield took a burst in his wing tanks. Instead of holding, the self-sealing tanks erupted in flames, which spread along the fuselage. Si dropped out of control, fighting desperately to pull out. But to no avail, and he crashed into the sea. Hoffman, Duncan and Merrill

managed to extricate themselves and get away.

Elsewhere, Ed Owen flamed a Zero chasing another F6, only to face three Zekes which came at him from inside a nearby cloud. They riddled his plane, knocking off an aileron and rendering his landing gear and flaps inoperable before breaking off their attack. While his division drove off ten Zeros, Cousin radioed the ship, "I got problems."

"We'll turn into the wind for you. Where *are* you?"

"I'm about five miles at 2000 feet. I got nuthin'!"

Moments later, his engine quit. Fearful of the high waves, he elected to bail out instead of ditch. Landing in the water, Owen inflated his Mae West and floated around until a destroyer loomed up and threw him a line. He was returned by high-line to the carrier later in the day.

The heavy fighting over Kwajalein convinced Admiral Pownall that counterattacks would come soon, confirmed when Commander Stebbins, departing from the target area, spotted a whole field full of Bettys—untouched! Fifty miles from the ship, he radioed the news. Alex Wilding took the call. Steb "recommended that another strike group be launched immediately. I advised Admiral Pownall and he said negative" and instead prepared to turn the task force "on a retirement course for Pearl Harbor."

The morning strikes had not done their job. In addition to the remaining planes, only four out of maybe 28 ships had been sunk, and no follow-up strike had been scheduled. But if those Bettys were not destroyed, they would surely attack the task force on the retirement that night. Ed Stebbins, Dick Upson and bomber skipper Dan Harrington each came to the bridge to urge Captain Clark to let them lead a second attack. He was ready, but Baldy Pownall was not interested.

Then, half an hour before noon, as a prearranged flight to hit Wotje was being spotted for launch, the Lexington's radar reported "many bogeys" 146 miles to the southwest and closing. Lookouts were cautioned to watch for low-flying planes trying to come in beneath the radar beam. At noon the strike began taking off—15 VF, 9 VB, 6 VT—with a few bombers and torpeckers standing by on the flight deck. Roger Van Buren was in one of these spares.

"As the planes started rolling down the deck, I noticed a lot of black puffs on the other side of the Lex, which was about 300 yards to our starboard. I had no flight gear and was not going to take off. I stood up in the cockpit to see what was up. No sooner had I focused my eyes on the scene, I saw a plane making a beam run on the *Lex*—then the damn thing burst into flames and dropped into the sea with a long path of smoke and fire. The sky was full of tracers. Another plane swooped into sight, and it really blew up. Just a big ball of black oily smoke filled with the most beautiful and intense red you could imagine. Out of this mass of smoke and flame dropped hundreds of small particles that had once been a plane and two men.

"It all happened so fast that for a second I couldn't think straight. At first I thought they were shooting our own planes. It never occurred to me that with all this might and power we had that Japs would ever attack us. With many planes maybe so—but not three planes. I didn't see the first one they got. One torpedo went astern of the *Lex* and didn't hit anything else. The whole attack was a suicide attempt; so some of those guys still have a little guts. That's the first time I've seen a Jap actually pressing home his attack since I've been out here."

"SCRAMBLE ALL PLANES!" yelled Hank Dozier at 1207. "All Hell broke loose," as Alex Wilding looked out from CIC. "Every ship opened up—another torpedo plane hit the water 40 yards astern the *Lex*. They had sneaked in undetected, coming in just skimming the water. Another one burst into flames and went down off our starboard quarter. Our CAP came screaming down from their high altitude. Torpedoes rushed by ahead of us and astern—all missed."

Yorktown's guns opened up, the 5-inchers firing to starboard, shaking the deck so badly that the remaining pilots doubted whether they could get off. "Once when I was on deck," in pilot Van Buren's words, "our 5-inch let loose and they damn near blew me overboard, to say nothing of the noise and pain in my ear drums. I have really learned to stay away from those babies."

Boogie Hoffman was taking off when the Jap planes came in, and as soon as he cleared the deck he just zoomed straight up in the air! As the Wotje-bound planes became airborne the pilots saw tracers (visible bullets—every third round) and bursts flying every which way and the three burning planes plunging into the sea—victims of the *Lexington's* guns. They were "Kates"—single-engine torpedo bombers.

"No one could believe what had happened," least of all Alex Wilding, the man responsible for intercepting them. "How could they have gotten in undetected? One officer said they must have been our planes, that's how impossible it seemed for the Japs to get in and surprise us. We had a circle of destroyers around us 8000 yards out. A circle of planes out 10 miles, and another circle out 20 miles, yet no one saw them."

The scramble cleared the deck of all planes—the Wotje strike plus six VB and two VT on standby—by 1217, by which time the firing had stopped. The *Yorktown* switched into the recovery mode and began landing its CAP fighters. As they taxiied forward and folded their wings, "every damned gun" in the formation opened up.

"Torpedo planes off the port beam!" announced the bullhorn—another surprise attack by many bandits. CAP fighters shot down all but four of them, which headed straight for the cruiser *San Francisco* on *Yorktown's* port beam. That ship turned hard left to avoid the torpedo of the first one, a Kate, and all ships in the formation turned into the direction of the attackers to "comb" the torpedoes—present their bows as the smallest possible target. Kate Number One splashed into the sea from the intense AA, her "fish" passing by the *Lex* harmlessly.

The other three torpedo planes had to climb over the *San Francisco* to execute their runs on the *Yorktown*. The second Kate passed along the cruiser's port side from bow to stern. Stroke Blackwell now ordered his 40mm and 20mm gun crews to open fire, but restrained the 5-inchers because of the *San Francisco* lying behind the attackers within 5-inch gun range. Kate Number Two burst into flames and went into the sea astern of the cruiser on *Yorktown's* port beam. The torpedo missed everything.

Yorktown's gunners now swung over to take the third Kate under fire, the boom-boom, boom-boom of the 40s and steady chatter of the 20s joined by the thuds of the 5-inchers set to local range. Kate came on, its rear gunner spraying the *San Francisco* as it crossed her bow, its fixed wing guns firing forward at the *Yorktown*. LSO Red Volz reported how these looked from his platform: "Eight of their 16-inch wing guns firing rapid order!"

Tracers and invisible bullets covered the skies to port engulfing the shiny black plane, which sported a yellow propeller hub. The nearly flat trajectory of the *Yorktown's* guns sent the bullets crashing all around the *San Francisco* beyond and then into her!

"Cease fire! Cease fire!" Admiral Pownall yelled up to Captain Clark. "You are firing on that cruiser!"

Incredulous, Jocko ignored him.

-72-

Band concert in the hangar, November 14, 1943, with dentist and ship's entertainment officer Frank Losey on trombone (far right). The perspiration gives some idea of the tropic heat, which played havoc with the reeds and drum heads. Courtesy of Frank J. Losey

Feelings of impending doom gripped the *Yorktown's* crew for the first time, with the Kate getting closer and closer on the port side. Dog Tripp, alongside Volz on the LSO platform, jumped from it in sheer terror to try to reach a hatch; he missed by three feet and tried to bury himself in the steel bulkhead. Chief P.P. Day ducked down behind an F6F spotted on the catapult, then realized what shielded him was the plane's belly tank full of high octane gas.

The Number Two 5-inch gun on the port bow followed Kate's approach all the way in, firing repeatedly. But on the adjacent Number Four, witnessed by gunner Jack Gazarian, a couple of scared gunners started to leave their gun. Their officer pulled out his pistol, "Get back there, or you'll get shot!"

At 300 yards, Kate took a shell from Number Two in its left wing root, and flames spurted out. Kate veered from the port to the starboard quarter, trying to crash the ship. It skimmed by the flight deck, not a hundred yards away, the heat singeing the beard of one of the gunners. The plane plunged into the sea nearby—100 yards close aboard—and exploded in a ball of smoke and flame.

Dick Tripp, finding himself on his hands and knees and feeling very stupid, now stood up on the LSO platform and raised his signal paddles in the horizontal position—meaning "R" for "perfect landing." Flight surgeon McCaffrey reported that the Kate was so close that he could see the pilot's mouth open; said Mac, "His teeth were defective

and his tonsils spotted!"

Al Cooperman's first photo in a sequence of four was so dramatic that it would be lauded as *Life* magazine's "Picture of the Week" and entitled "Flaming Kate" or "Burning Kate." Jocko Clark would have copies made for every man on the ship which he autographed. Dwight Long's color movie of the shoot-down was so good that it would find its way into nearly every World War II movie for the next hundred years!

The guns now trained on the fourth attacker, a Betty, which elected to withdraw quickly. She turned away, retiring at low altitude off the *San Francisco's* port quarter, only to be splashed by a CAP fighter. Wilding: "How long will our luck hold out? . . . They were on us before we knew it and only good alert gunnery was getting them."

The *San Francisco* reported one man killed and several wounded from the *Yorktown's* fire, but Admiral Pownall never mentioned his order to cease fire to Jocko, who had had no recourse but to protect his ship.

Pownall had been shaken by the attack. After discussing the situation with observer Admiral Kauffman, he signaled escort commander Rear Admiral "Ike" Giffen in the *Oakland* for another opinion. Came the response by signal light, "We better get out of here before we get our tail full of arrows." Giffen's reply fortified Pownall, who now gave the order for the task force to prepare to depart as soon as the Wotje strike was recovered.

A flabbergasted Jocko Clark several times during

"Flaming Kate" shot down by *Yorktown* gunners during the Kwajalein raid, December 4, 1943. The photographer was Al Cooperman: Jocko Clark signed a copy of the first shot in the sequence photo for each member of the crew and air group. Courtesy of J.S. Moore

the afternoon pounded navigator Red Sharp's chart table, "Goddamnit, you can't run away from airplanes with ships!" But orders were orders.

The last planes returned safely to the ships after having shot up Wotje, whereupon—at 1506—the flag ordered 25 knots full speed to try to escape Kwajalein waters. OOD Lieutenant (jg) Joe Hurley, being one of Jocko's best shiphandlers, was kept at the conn to begin his fourth straight four-hour watch.

High surface winds fed the waves, which now rolled up to the hangar deck level of the carriers and across the bows of the much lower destroyers, slowing their forward progress to 18 knots. Pownall had no recourse but to slow down the carriers to maintain position with their escorts. All ships girded for a night attack by the long-range Bettys.

Suddenly, in late afternoon, the bullhorn called out a dreaded announcement not heard since the drunken night in Panama: "Man overboard!" An airedale, Jim Blazejczak, had slipped on the flight deck into the catwalk, breaking his arm, only to be washed overboard by a high rolling wave. The fleeing task force could hardly slow down to look for one man, but Blazejczak was lucky. The destroyer *Nicholas* came right up to him and hauled him aboard after only eight minutes in the drink. After being returned by breeches buoy to the ship, Jocko summoned him to the bridge, asked if he had been treated well on the can, and then scolded him, "You picked a helluva time to go swimming. Now go below before you get courtmartialed!"

The sun set at 1809, and 36 minutes later *Lexington's* radar reported a bogey—one to several planes—48 miles at 160 degrees and closing rapidly, angels 3. A minute later another bogey appeared 66 miles out. The ship would remain at GQ and the pilots in their ready rooms. No sleep this night.

Roger Van Buren recorded events from VT-5's ready room: "They started out well behind us evidently misjudging our speed. They all got hotter and colder and much joking was going on. We knew that eventually they would find us and everyone was making bets on which group would spot us first. By the time we figured they spotted us, there were five or six groups out. It was a little after 2000 when they got in close enough to see us. Everything was with them—beautiful night, brightest moon I've ever seen, and all we could do was run, and run we did in all directions. Before long there must have been 20 or 30 planes flying all over trying to get in a good position to attack."

Admiral Montgomery's task group steamed seven and a half miles west of the *Yorktown* group. The *York* had one Bat team standing by, but Admiral Pownall did not want another Butch O'Hare incident. The planes remained secured, leaving the skies free for the hundreds of AA guns in the force to pierce. The Ridgway-Wilding CIC team would not be fighter directors, but AA directors.

Under the expert guidance of chief of staff Captain Hedding, Admiral Pownall ordered Admiral Giffen to station the *Oakland* astern of the *Yorktown* to protect the carriers, while cruiser *New Orleans* steamed ahead of the *York* as the formation guide. All orders were issued from the *Yorktown* by TBS voice radio.

Jocko Clark told Joe Hurley, "You stay between these cruisers. They're our best protection." More bogeys filled the radar screens, and the *New Orleans* began to make course changes in response to them every few minutes. Being larger than the cruisers, the carriers must make 27 to 28 knots to keep up with the sleek cruisers. But Hurley held the *Yorktown* right between them.

The very first snooper sighted Montgomery's group. Recorded Wilding: "We intercepted his radio message giving our longitude and latitude. In a half hour planes were coming into us from all directions. Groups of Jap planes 20 miles, 30, 40, 50, 70, 80 and 90 miles, all heading our way. We were going to be under a night torpedo plane attack—the most feared of all attacks, and in bright moonlight.

"This would be hot and heavy action for a few minutes and then it would all be over with—one way or the other. Here were 36 warships; which ones would they get?

"Everyone put their life jackets where they could get them easily. We watched them closing. The light cruiser *Oakland* was ordered back of us ten miles. She was to be the decoy and sacrificed, if necessary. She was to attract them to her. We dropped float lights from her to confuse the Japs. The *Oakland* was ordered to open fire when they were within 4000 yards of her. We hoped her firing would draw the Jap planes to her."

Some 30 Bettys of several bogeys combined into two general parts, one north, the other south for each task group, but they remained preoccupied with Montgomery's *Essex* group for a full hour. The bright moon hung in the western sky behind the planes, acting as a floodlight on the ships. For spotlights, the Bettys used parachute flares. Montgomery's guns drove them all away, splashing several.

A Furlow version of Jocko's response to Cooperman's best photograph. Courtesy of Jesse Rodriguez

The second group of planes orbited 25 miles to the west of the *Yorktown*, "playing with us it seemed like a cat plays with a mouse" believed Wilding. "They would start in to make their torpedo run and we'd make an emergency turn to throw our prow to them, then they'd turn and go back out. Another one would start in for our beam and we'd turn to meet him and he'd withdraw. A Jap would feint and we'd turn to meet him and a Jap seeing us turn to ward off the first Jap would come in."

After a full hour of this tense waiting, a snooper reported the position of the *Yorktown*. Radar showed him to be 18 miles out. Three minutes before 2100 Ridgway reported the large formation of Bettys orbiting to the west to be closing *Yorktown*'s formation in two groups. Jocko Clark was madder than hell as the enemy flights approached his ship—angry at the Japs, at Pownall for running, and at his own inability to retaliate with planes.

At 2105 Cooper Bright's teletype ticked off the Air Plot News to the ready rooms: "GROUP OF NINE PLANES CONVERGING ON OAK-LAND. . . . SHE HAS GIVEN THE ORDER TO FIRE. . . . OAKLAND IS LOCATED ASTERN OF YORKTOWN. . . . DO NOT LEAVE YOUR READY ROOMS. . . . DESTROYERS AND OAKLAND ARE FIRING. . . . PLANES SEEM TO BE COMPLETELY AROUND US. . . . FIRING ON PORT QUAR-TER. . . . SHIP IS SWINGING TO COURSE 270 DEG. TRUE."

Destroyer *Bullard* opened first, followed by the *Oakland*, as the ship turned and Joe Hurley rang up 26 knots. Hurley was running on sheer adrenalin as he started his *eighteenth* consecutive hour at the conn! With each fresh raid every few minutes, he changed course masterfully. Annapolis never produced a better shiphandler. The Reserves were winning this war.

The gunners on the cruisers and tin cans put up such an excellent and continuous curtain of ack-

ack that the attacking Bettys couldn't or wouldn't get close enough to the three flattops in Pownall's group for their gunners to get in a few licks. This luck—and good shooting—couldn't last forever, but it did for one hour, then another. All hands topside watched what Jim Bryan described as "by far the greatest 4th of July fireworks that I had ever seen," and everyone not needed inside the island lined the rails to watch. When at 2316 a Jap plane plummeted seaward in flames on the horizon near Montgomery's group, they all cheered jubilantly.

War correspondent Richard Haller of the INS admired Captain Hedding's maneuvering of the task force as it skipped from cloud shadow to cloud shadow to avoid the moonlight. During breaks in the action, Haller journeyed down to the engine rooms where he noted the temperature at 135 degrees as the engines kept up full speed.

At 2323 the *Yorktown* and surrounding waters and ships were suddenly bathed in artificial daylight. A string of four parachute flares burned brilliantly two miles off the port bow, slowly descending from 5000 feet and each outshining even the moon for over three minutes. The first plane had done its job lighting up the targets for his teammate. CIC tracked the latter from 8000 yards out, passing the word to Blackwell's gunners at intervals of every several hundred yards.

At 4000 yards Lieutenant Commander George Weiss' 5-inch gun directors got a reading on the plane, but since it lay in direct line with several escort ships the 5-inchers couldn't open fire. But the shorter range 40s could, and they pumped round after round at the attacker.

"3400 yards on the starboard bow," called off Wilding, then 3000.

Betty kept coming.

"Hard right!" bellowed Jocko to miss the anticipated torpedo, and the helmsman swung the great ship over to present her stern.

"2700 yards on the starboard bow."

At 2400 yards the 20mms opened up with their fusillade, their tracers co-mingling with the 40s across the moonlit water as the dim shape of the torpecker came closer at masthead level—2000 yards—1600—1400.

The *Yorktown* was still turning. Almost time to drop.

"1000 yards on the starboard bow."

Wilding: "Then you knew he was releasing the torpedo. Twenty seconds for it to reach you, 1, 2, 3, 4, 5, 6, 7, 8, 9, 10 you'd get a mental picture of it churning through the water at 40 miles an hour."

"Torpedo splash starboard bow!" yelled a lookout.

". . . 11, 12, 13, you'd start to get tense, you'd open your mouth to breathe easier, 14, 15, 16, now, 17, 18, now, 19, 20, 21 and suddenly you'd realize it had gone by and you'd forgotten to breathe for the past 10 seconds. Conversation would start again in Radar Plot."

Betty completed her two-minute run by passing not 50 feet directly over the flight deck in the light of the flares and tracers, and the 40s and 20s in the port side gun galleries took her under fire. Assistant gun boss George Earnshaw high up in Air Defense Aft reported proudly that his guys had hit the Betty, which crashed into the sea, burning some 1500 yards on the port quarter. Her torpedo had passed harmlessly by the bow. Air Plot News: "WE ARE HOLDING FIELD DAY: ANOTHER JAP DOWN."

But when will the damned moon hurry up and set?

Wilding: "For the first two hours, men were talkative, then they grew mad, because there was no way to fight back at night—all we could do was duck, and protect ourselves, try not to get hurt, we couldn't do anything to retaliate. The *Essex* group was firing again. Suddenly a ball of flame broke out in the sky and dropped toward the sea where it rested a minute on the surface and then disappeared."

Now Charlie Ridgway picked up a bogey at 9000 yards on the starboard bow over the screen, closing. Tracers licked up around her.

"Hard right rudder!"

Betty turned slightly at 5000 yards to the starboard beam, and again at 3000 to the starboard quarter out of line of the screen vessels. Radarman Third Class Marvin Wray picked him up on the *Yorktown's* scope, and Stroke Blackwell let all his 5-inchers open up. The forward and after turrets shook the ship as the flames spurted forth into the night. Betty released her fish, probably too early, then turned away to escape astern of the ship.

The fish missed, but also the gunners failed to bring down the plane. "Can't shoot perfect every time," thought one sailor, "we ain't Sergeant York!" Comparisons with the World War I marksman aside, *Yorktown's* gunners had at least kept Betty away. And Captain Clark executed four course changes in as many minutes afterward to throw off the Bettys.

Sweating it out in CIC, Alex Wilding tracked the

Japs as they came "from all directions and all distances, some were out 70 miles and heading for us. Others 50, 30, 20, 15, and many circling us at 10 miles. No clouds to hide under, no rain squalls; just plenty of moonlight. The *Oakland* was firing constantly, sending her red tracers heavenward in a continual stream.

"It was now 2330, 5 hours had gone by, was it to continue all night? The *Essex* was firing again now, again the ball of fire descending, only this time it didn't go out when it stopped on the horizon.

"Over TBS came the answer from the carrier *Enterprise*. 'Jap plane shot down, crashed on flight deck, flight deck on fire.' We watched the fire grow and then start to diminish, it was under control. In a few minutes the glow disappeared."

Down below, sailors in the engineering spaces heard and felt the concussions of the Jap torpedoes detonating harmlessly at the end of their runs. Except for one.

"Another run was coming in. Would our luck still hold? 5400 yards, 5000 yards, etc., then the plane shot over our deck, wing guns blazing, and disappeared into the night. Now the seconds, 1, 2, 3, 4, . . . 18, 19, 20, and the deep breath—when suddenly a terrific roar and flames leaped 200 feet in the air just 600 yards off our port quarter—the *Lexington*."

Yorktown's radios crackled in code names: "Hello, Stork. This is Hancock. Hit by torpedo. Have lost steering control. Over."

Yorktown replied: "This is Stork. Roger. Out. Alert, everybody. Hancock has lost steering control. Alert, everybody."

Wilding noted *Lex* was still making 18 knots, and "she still had a chance, though she couldn't turn her narrow beam to comb torpedoes anymore.

"Black smoke began to stream from her wound but that was quickly stopped. The *Lex* began to drop back now and out of formation. Then came an encouraging message from the *Lex*, 'Believe we can rig emergency steering in half hour.' We began to maneuver in every direction to keep the *Lex* in the center of us."

Lexington explained that a Betty had put a fish into her stern from her starboard quarter, disabling her steering engine, claiming several lives and jamming the rudder hard left. Pownall ordered the *New Orleans* and *Oakland* and destroyer *Chauncey* to stand by and passed the guide to the *Cowpens*. *Lexington* remained on the *Yorktown's* port quarter as Jocko stayed with her, following Pownall's order to cut his speed from 27 to 20 knots and to turn left.

As news of the *Lexington's* dilemma reached down below decks on the *Yorktown*, the men stationed over the *York's* propellers got nervous about the possibility of a similar fate for them. Then, at 2347, some 15 minutes after the *Lex* had been struck, Wilding reported, "Several bogeys starboard beam to starboard quarter. Closing 4 to 6 miles." Charlie Ridgway tracked them in, Jocko swung hard left, and *Yorktown's* guns opened fire. A Betty closed to 7000 yards then broke away. After one minute of shooting, the guns stopped.

More bogeys registered on the scopes but only circled. Their attack seemed to be over. At two minutes before midnight, *Lexington* informed the flag, "Stork, this is Hancock. Our steering engine room is flooded. We are going to put five submersible pumps to try to clean it out. There is no fire on the ship. The smoke comes from the smoke bombs aft, and we are going to fight our way out of this thing. Out."

"This is Stork," replied Captain Hedding of the staff, "Nice going. Nice going. We're with you. Stork out."

Wilding: "The *Oakland* was firing almost continuously—she had dodged every torpedo so far and was doing a wonderful job. Minutes passed slowly and then came the word that the *Lex* had an emergency steering gear rigged and while she zigzagged from 045 degrees to 130 degrees she made good an average course of 090 degrees. We placed her astern of the formation and gave her room to sail her unsteady course."

The *Yorktown* turned right to resume the base course and 25-knot speed as Skinhead Bright reported the good news to the ready rooms: "LEXINGTON HAS REGAINED STEERING CONTROL, EVERYTHING O.K., BUT AT PRESENT TIME AIR PLOT IS IN A STATE OF UTTER COLLAPSE."

Alex Wilding's CIC was not much better off. "The wind was blowing 40 knots and the sea was rough. The *York* was pitching and tossing, and sudden jerks from the heavy state of the sea would cause her to shiver all over at times. At first the men had talked much, kidding each other about digging fox holes, getting out from under the table, etc., then they became mad because of their inability to fight back, now with the attack going into its sixth hour they became silent." They were thinking of the *Lex*, torpedoes, the Jap planes still coming from all directions, the wind, the rough sea, the night, and the luck of the *Yorktown*. Maybe that luck wouldn't hold much longer. Then what?

"Men were all thinking and fear could be seen on faces. Some had been afraid from the start—not many, just three in my department—there had never been any normal reactions in their mind from the moment of the first attack—all officers—the enlisted men were marvelous. I'd rather be in a tight spot with the enlisted men than the average officer.

"I looked at the clock and it was 27 minutes to 1, Dec. 5th, and to myself I said, 'Happy Birthday Dear, it was just three years ago to this minute that you were born.' Then I thought of my family, home and in bed, all snug and peacefully sleeping. In the morning Holly would awaken and get her biggest thrill from a birthday. I wished them happiness.

"My thoughts were then diverted to the Japs again. The Jap flight leader had just radioed the Japs to gather in two groups on either side of the formation and attack simultaniously. Our radio intelligence officer [Sandy Sims] was doing a good job of intercepting messages.

"We watched them gather on the radar, about fifteen miles on either side of us in groups. Then they started in—our destroyer screen opened fire first, then our cruiser screen, and finally the *Cowpens* and *York* in the center opened. Half of the Japs turned back out, they couldn't face it, the rest came in to four thousand yards and veered off—none came in over the formation.

"They dropped their torpedoes far out and made them run two, three, and four miles—all missed. The firing ceased and for the first time more planes were leaving than closing on us. They were heading home to Maloelap, Wotje, Mille, Jaluit, Kwajalein, Wake and Eniwetok."

OOD Joe Hurley executed no fewer than·eight course changes during the first hour of December 5 to avoid the several groups of bogeys which approached, but the big event occurred at 0127 and was duly recorded in the quartermaster's log: "The moon has set—Thank God!"

The attacks continued out of the darkened sky, but the force now turned to base course of 080 degrees (T) at a reduced 20 knots—eastward toward home. At 0145 the last Jap made his run and missed—"seven hours from the first attack. The longest attack in history" reflected Wilding, who at 0200 reported to the flag that his radar screen was clear—"no enemy aircraft in sight."

The flag answered, "Thank God."

Then, at 0215, the bullhorn announced, "Secure from General Quarters. All gunners will sleep at their guns."

It was really over. Between 40 and 60 Bettys had been turned away or splashed during the long night.

But the two task groups were not out of the woods yet. The *Lexington*, steering by her engines, could not reverse course to turn into the wind for launching planes; Air Group Five and the *Yorktown* had to handle CAP for both carriers, this after a scant two hours of sleep. GQ at 0400 aroused the pilots for an eight-VT antisub hop and fighter CAP, all feeling like Joe Kristufek: "I'm probably more tired and nervous today than I have ever been."

Alex Wilding had had only an hour and a half of deep slumber. "We were putting up a large launch of pre-dawn fighters for we expected a dawn torpedo plane attack. We expected them to come back for the crippled *Lex*. The *Essex* group was still west of us 10 miles."

The fighters began the launch at 0555, followed by the torpeckers. At 0610 the sixth TBF—Jake Kilrain's—dipped its left wing enough to hit the deck as the ship suddenly rolled, causing the Avenger to plummet over the port side and hit the water just 30 feet from the ship. As Kilrain and his crewmen Don Wellman and Herb Smith climbed out to inflate their life raft, the plane's two 500-pound depth charges went off, triggered by their apparently defective hydrostatic bomb fuses. The blast exploded the plane's 400 gallons of gas and killed all three men.

The explosion lifted the shuddering ship out of the water, and as she settled back down, the men in the lower spaces—jarred by the blast—figured that a Jap fish had found its mark and feared that one of the ship's thousands of steam lines would break. With Arthur Kill were two machinists mates of the black gang and "one colored mess attendant who happened to be assigned to our station for GQ. All of a sudden the lights went out, and we soon felt the salt water at our feet.

"When the water reached up over our knees we figured that this was the end. The poor colored fellow started to pray and confessed out loud everything he must have done his whole life. At the time it wasn't very funny, but the lights came back on and were we relieved to find out that the salt water was coming from a split fire main and not the ocean."

Dr. Gard, at that moment dressing Charlie Crommelin's wounds in Sick Bay, remarked, "Was that a torpedo?"

"If you have to ask that," replied Charlie, "you can be sure it was not a fish."

The TBS radio alerted the task force: "*York* has

been torpedoed. Stand by to repel torpedo plane attack.'' But *York* the Stork quickly clarified the situation to the other ships.

As the ship quieted down, the normal vibration from the motors seemed to have stopped. The loudspeaker explained, ''Plane crashed on the port bow while taking off.'' ''That sure was tough luck,'' lamented torpecker Roger Van Buren in the ready room, ''But it's all in the game and just one of those things.''

The ship secured from GQ at 0644 as the sun rose and no Japs reappeared. Most crewmen collapsed into their bunks, and the morning passed quietly. In the early afternoon Charlie Ridgway vectored out the divisions of Bob Jones and Jim Campbell toward a bogey, Jones in command. Before long, the bogey faded and Ridgway ordered his ''chickens'' back. When the *Yorktown* pilots did not respond, Charlie frantically sent another flight higher up to try to raise them by radio. Nothing.

After the planes had gone well beyond the reported contact, Campbell found himself in a predicament. Jones, tired and angry at the Nips, charged out to 140 miles in hopes of shooting down some of the bastards. Campbell tried to raise him by radio but Jones kept on, silent and determined. Campbell, figuring they'd go all the way to Japan at this rate, finally flew up alongside Jones, patted himself on the head, and pointed back to the ship. As Campbell turned back with his division, Jones finally turned around and followed.

The pilots were drained, and some got sick from too much booze trying to unwind after landing. Jones could not explain his reckless action when he returned aboard. But Campbell's flight log told the story: in 16 days he himself had flown 71.6 combat hours, sometimes eight hours a day in three- to four-hour-long CAPs, including six pre-dawn takeoffs and 21 carrier landings, some after dark. Wrote Joe Kristufek in his diary, ''All the boys are tired, nervous and jittery now from all the strain we have been under, and most of us are sorry now that we ever became aviators. Peacetime flying is fun but this combat flying is HELL. If the Japs keep us awake again tonight we really will be in bad shape.''

Happily, the Japs could not find the force, which was now guiding on the *Yorktown*, though sudden rough weather did not endear a fatigued crew to Vonk the Weatherguesser. ''Pounding of the ship'' in these waves, noted Ridgway, ''often took on the reaction to an explosion which set the nerves on edge until sleep took over.''

By December 6 the carriers were out of ''Indian country,'' and word arrived that a Jap carrier had been sunk two days before by a U.S. sub in the enemy's backyard (the escort carrier *Chuyo* by the *Sailfish*). ''The *Liscome Bay* thus avenged,'' reflected Ridgway.

And the moon didn't look so bad to him this night as he watched the last destroyer complete taking on oil from the *Yorktown* and ''cast off in the moonlight—a lovely sight.''

Chapter V
Truk!

Yorktown *acted as rear* guard—closest to the action—on the uneventful withdrawal of the task force from Kwajalein toward Pearl. Uneventful, that is, until fighter pilot Dick "Lambchop" Newhafer out on dawn CAP called in, "Stork Base, this is Stork 42, I've got to come aboard. This is an emergency!"

"Wait," replied Air Plot, since the deck had to be respotted. Newhafer repeated his request, with greater urgency. Finally, the ship called him up. Silence. "Stork 42, do you read?"

"Stork Base, this is Stork 42. It's too late. I've already shit in my pants!"

A pause, then laughter in Air Plot. Skinhead Bright radioed back, "Don't get any shit on the flight deck!"

The "Prep Charlie" come-aboard flag was hoisted, and after Newhafer caught the wire and taxied forward, he shook his fist at Captain Clark up on the bridge. Jocko was laughing so hard that tears rolled out of his eyes. Lambchop dismounted from the plane, his pants cuffs tucked into his boots, and waddled to the showers.

The ship reached Pearl Harbor on December 9, 1943, with Air Group Five flying ashore to NAS Hilo on the big island of Hawaii. That evening at supper, Ray Gard recounted in a letter to his wife, "something very very lovely" occurred.

Engineer "Bill Hart speaking, as though I was not present, said to George Earnshaw, 'Charlie Crommelin said this morning before he went to the hospital, "Well, this is my third crash, the third time that doctors have pawed me over, the one really serious accident when I thought I might go out, and I'm here only because I have had the finest medical care that I've ever experienced. I didn't know that there were such doctors. Anything that Ray Gard says for me to do, I'll do. He's a perfect doctor." ' "

The assembled commanders and lieutenant commanders at the table applauded spontaneously. The speechless doctor fought back the tears, until "Socket-wrench Jim" Brady finally remarked, "Doc, I think you need a drink."

Yorktown's officers were delivering the goods, none moreso than the wild Indian at the helm. Jocko Clark had been selected for promotion to rear admiral, for the fleet needed such fighters, but Clark received the news with mixed feelings. Like every career officer, becoming as admiral was the pinnacle of success, but it meant he must leave his beloved *Yorktown*. At least the promotion process would take several weeks, so that Jocko could still lead his ship into one more operation.

The next objective in the Central Pacific offensive would be the seizure of Kwajalein and other islands in the Marshalls group. These airfields protected the eastern approaches to Japan's major advanced fleet base at Truk—pronounced "truck"—in the eastern Carolines. This fact led Admiral Nimitz and his planners to suspect that the Jap fleet might sally forth to contest the landings in the Marshalls, scheduled for the end of January 1944.

Such a prospect would require aggressive leadership. For one, Jocko Clark did not believe Admiral Baldy Pownall should be allowed to continue in command of the fast carriers. So Clark and his senior officers prepared a "white paper" condemning Pownall for his poor handling of the task force during the Gilberts campaign. They showed it to Admiral Towers and Towers' newly-appointed chief of staff Admiral Radford. Just to make sure the paper reached the very top, Clark sent Herman Rosenblatt home on leave to use his family connections and present the paper to President Roosevelt himself.

Though Rosenblatt carried out this extreme measure, it proved unnecessary, for Nimitz and Towers had reached the same conclusion when all the action reports of the Kwajalein raid were in. When Pownall left the *Yorktown* at Pearl, he left for good. Selected to replace him was one of the Navy's most veteran combat carriermen, Rear Admiral Marc A. Mitscher, then in a Stateside command, resting after his participation in the battles of Midway and around Guadalcanal.

During the respite between operations, the *York* and her sister ships exercised off Hawaii, while the men enjoyed liberty in the Islands—to their dismay. For the ship had been scheduled to return to the West coast to receive a new radar, meaning home for Christmas. But now the damaged *Lexington* had to go instead, for repairs. And the new carrier *Intrepid* had rammed the side of the locks coming through the Canal, requiring repair work which delayed her arrival in the war zone.

So the Pacific Fleet continued to rely heavily on the pacesetting *Yorktown*, which continued as flagship of the Fast Carrier Task Force, and Captain Clark used the time profitably to make personnel changes. He quietly transferred off five men caught engaging in homosexual activities. Equally troublesome was the arrival of a crop of draftees, regarded with disdain by the original crew, all volunteers. Fearing the old hands would tear apart the newcomers, the ship's "sheriff", Chief Master-at-Arms Leonard C. "Pop" Austin, led a delegation of chiefs to alert Joe Tucker. After a big discussion, the mustangs and senior non-coms decided to let the two groups settle it among themselves and not to bother the captain or exec about it. After a couple of free-for-alls, some black eyes and a few broken teeth, the veterans were satisfied, and the draftees became part of the team.

The *Yorktown* surreptitiously "stole" one of the Fleet's few photographic interpretation specialists from the Marines for its own Air Plot. At Ford Island, Cooper Bright ran across a very inebriated Lieutenant (jg) Robert W. Eaton, a slow-talking Texan who liked the offer of this "old bald-headed ignorant boy from New Jersey" to let him sleep in a clean bed instead of a foxhole. Then it turned out that Eaton had known Jocko's brother in Texas, so Clark took him aboard to assess target damage from aerial photos taken in combat. Eaton would also reveal himself to be as great a cut-up as his new boss Bright.

Air Group Five trained out of Hilo under Ed Stebbins. Charlie Crommelin went home to recuperate from his extensive wounds and then take over a new air group. Boogie Hoffman, with three kills to his credit, left Fighting 5 to train pilots in

Florida. He was replaced by Smokey Stover, who had at last gotten back into the cockpit. The night-flying Bat teams trained at Puunene on Maui, with Alex Wilding directing them by radio. These drills were a wasted effort, however, for Admiral Towers soon assigned a new night fighter team of four radar-equipped Hellcats to the *Yorktown*. Several replacement pilots reported in and were generally snubbed by the men whose fallen buddies they were replacing.

A new carrier admiral came aboard the ship to gain tactical experience—Rear Admiral J.W. "Black Jack" Reeves, Jr., fresh from commanding the air forces in the recent recovery of the Aleutian Islands in the North Pacific. Reeves took the *Yorktown* out on December 13 for three days of gunnery drills, qualifying new air groups in carrier landings, and simulated combat. The mock attacks became all too real, though, when a Hellcat accidentally strafed the port side, wounding three men!

Christmastime in Hawaii was a melancholy experience for all hands, so far from home. To make do, the crew set up a large pine Christmas tree on the hangar deck, and dentist Frank Losey orchestrated a Christmas Eve musical program. Afterward, the officers repaired to the wardroom to listen to Beethoven's Ninth Symphony on one of the three Magnavox phonographs donated by the manufacturer. But the *Yorktown* was anything but quiet that holy evening, as Ray Gard related in a poem to his family—

> 'Tis the night before Christmas and all
>   through the ship
> Air hammers and rivets are going full clip—
> With a boom, bang and batter—clink, clang
>   and clatter
> The disciples of Mars and children of Thor
> Are dressing a ship for her part in the war.

Christmas morning brought presents and 600 sacks of mail that Hank Bolden's mail clerks had sorted all night long. The junior officers spent the afternoon in their bunk room—Boys Town—polishing off Canadian Club whiskey before adjourning to a sumptuous Christmas dinner of turkey stuffed with oyster dressing. Newly-reported Ensign George A. Wille (pronounced "Willie") of the signal gang recorded in his diary that Vonk the Weatherguesser was "completely looped and having the life of his life" at the table. And the drinking went on into the night to the tune of teetotaler Cooper Bright singing, "Oh, let me hang my balls on your Christmas tree."

Christmas Eve program on the hangar deck, with Chaplain Alexander on the right. Courtesy of Raymond F. Gard

"It didn't take so long for Christmas to be forgotten and the business of training to perfection resumed," observed Ensign Wille as the *Yorktown* sortied the next morning for a four-day practice cruise. Passing into the narrow channel, however, steering control was lost, and the ship ran aground in the soft mud. "Jocko didn't know whether to jump through the bullhorn, or wrap his mouth around it" in calling back the tugs for help. Help they did, with Jocko bellowing, "Back it down! Back it down!" And by smart seamanship the skipper restored the steering, though not before his ulcers erupted after 'too much Christmas.' Between 0800 and noon he chased every watch officer off the bridge, and then started over at the top of the list!

In the last days of 1943 Air Group Five switched from Hilo to NAS Kaneohe on Oahu as the pilots took turns relaxing at "Chris Holmes' Rest Home"—the private garden mansion of the late Christian R. Holmes on Waikiki Beach. Dancing and singing with WAC gals from Fort Shafter, the fly-boys worked hard to 'survive' their five days there—with experimentally-spiked coconut milk punch "velvet hammers" for breakfast, beer and heavy booze in the afternoons and evenings.

Yorktown's enlisted men had it nearly as good at the Royal Hawaiian Hotel rest home at Waikiki, though El Jocko brought them back to snuff with morning calisthentics on the flight deck New Years Eve morning.

As the new year began, Julian Porter of the Gunnery Department took the first watch and fulfilled the time-honored Navy custom of making his January 1 0000 to 0400 "midwatch" entry in the ship's log entirely in verse. It was a masterpiece.

The U.S.S. *Yorktown* is moored starboard side to
Ford Island, Pearl Harbor at Pier Fox-2;
Three lines of manila are holding us fast
With help from six wires, as long as they last;
Generators we're using, are two, 1 and 4,
But in case they are needed, we still have two more.
1 and 8 are the boilers, we have on the line,
And so far they have suited our purpose just fine.
Now telephone service, the dock gives us free
The same as fresh water, the need you can see.
The SOP [Senior Officer Present] is at 2-Fox-2,
And the ship is dimmed out as we usually do.
The Gunnery department has set 23,
A condition of readiness, which is how we should be
There are many ships present, the sight's quite a treat,
All various units of the United States fleet.
This, then, is a new year, right here we'll record her
And to make it quite proper, we'll sign it—
    J.D. Porter
    Lt (jg)., U.S.N.R.

For every one-thousandth landing on a carrier, a frosted cake was presented to the lucky pilot. Smokey Stover got it for making the 7000th landing, January 10, 1944. Note Jocko has worn a tie for the occasion.

After another practice exercise for carrier quals Janauary 7 to 10—during which Smokey Stover executed *Yorktown*'s landing number 7000—shipboard activity accelerated for the pending sortie against the Marshall Islands. "Everyone is busy getting this and that aboard—rush-rush-rush," observed Dr. Gard. And damage controller Rick Lambart and Coop Bright supervised a final two-day party for the crew at Camp Andrews, Oahu.

The new fast carrier commander, Rear Admiral Marc Mitscher, was piped aboard the *Yorktown* on the 13th. As he reported to the quarterdeck, crewmen noticed a detective novel tucked under his arm—*Send Me Another Coffin*. For the Japs maybe. Short, bald, bantam-weight "Pete" Mitscher had been in naval aviation since the early days and carried with him the reputation of being "one part Ernie Pyle and two parts Connie Mack," that is, quiet and revered, seasoned and wise at his work. He and Jock Clark shared a mutual respect for each other.

A special passenger also arrived in the person of film maker Commander Spig Wead to observe operations and to advise Dwight Long in shooting his documentary film. Wead's old friend Jocko tried to get the crippled former pilot to use a pulley to get to the bridge. But after one try Wead would have none of it and used his powerful hands to climb the ladders to the bridge.

"What happens," asked Admiral Mitscher, "if he

has to abandon ship?"

Replied Jocko, "I don't expect to abandon ship; neither does he!"

Admiral Spruance's Central Pacific Force now turned to its numbered designation as its preferred title, the Fifth Fleet, and the fast carriers became Task Force 58, again divided into four task groups. Flagship *Yorktown* would cruise with TG 58.1, led by Black Jack Reeves and including not only the *Enterprise* and light carrier *Belleau Wood* but three battleships, three cruisers and 13 destroyers. With the nine other carriers plus escorts, Task Force 58 comprised the largest battle fleet ever assembled.

After Admirals Towers and Radford presented medals on January 15, three of the four task group commanders came aboard for a final conference with Mitscher. They were Reeves, Montgomery and S.P. "Cy" Ginder, another newcomer. Baldy Pownall even attended, he acting as an adviser to Spruance during the operation. The fourth group commander, F.C. "Ted" Sherman, was heading toward the Marshalls from the South Pacific where his carriers had been working over Rabaul.

The last details of the operation were hammered out, and the *Yorktown* settled down to her final night in port for many months to come. An "audacious fighting spirit" permeated the ship, reported an official observer to the admirals in Washington. "She is an exuberant ship, proud of all the records" thus far set, "proud to be the cleanest of all the carriers, proud that in every

Awards ceremony on the flight deck, January 15, 1944. (L to R) Captain J.J. Clark, Vice Admiral John H. Towers, and Rear Admiral Arthur W. Radford.

action she launched the fastest, flew the most, dropped the most bombs on the enemy.''

"I don't know where we are going and when we will be back," Coxswain Jesse Bradley wrote in his diary as the *Yorktown* put to sea midday, January 16, 1944. "I think we are going down in the Marshalls. If that's so it will sure be a hot time for about a month and a half."

Scuttlebutt—Navy rumor—had leaked this much information to the crew, whose hunches were confirmed once the ship was at sea. All hands knew for certain that this would be their last battle under Captain Clark, who roamed the bridge in absolute control. As the force headed southwest, the tropical sun beat down on Jocko's tender skin, forcing him to wear his short-brim hat and to cover his Indian hump nose and protruding lower lip with zinc ointment or the latter with a piece of cloth. He looked fearsome.

Yet, the men knew better. And someone had scrawled some graffitti in one of the heads:

"How does Jocko keep us on our toes?"

"He raises our urinals three inches!"

War or no war, the admirals had planned their approach to the Marshalls so that the force would cross the Equator and International Date Line simultaneously to enable the appropriate initiation ceremonies to be conducted. This meant that the 35 or so *Yorktown* "shellbacks" and "dragonbacks" who had crossed the Equator and the Line

respectively could now inflict the customary punishment on the 3000 "pollywogs" who hadn't, regardless of rank.

The initial planning meeting by the shellbacks in a mess area on the evening of the 20th was broken up by a gang of fire hose wielding pollywogs who flooded the compartment and soaked an enraged executive officer, Cam Briggs. Nevertheless, next day, following the usual gunnery exercises, "all work was knocked off and a watch posted all over the ship," recorded Alex Wilding, "and everyone goes to quarters on the flight deck while we welcome aboard the Royal Scribe, Davy Jones and party." All pollywogs dressed and acted outlandishly, as ordered by Mr. Jones' prior subpoena.

Jones—Frenchy Beaudette—ascended the bridge and read the indictment against the pollywogs for violating King Neptune's realm. Then the 110 fliers in full flight gear simulated a group takeoff and landing by running around on the flight deck and being tripped by the arresting wires—until John Gray led a counterattack of 40 fighter pilots "strafing" the shellbacks with handfuls of Navy beans.

"The horseplay," wrote Wilding, "continued all evening. At dinner we sat down to clam chowder, roast leg of lamb, green beans, mashed potatoes and gravy, cake with sauce—no knives, forks or spoons, we had to use our fingers."

Next morning, as the *Yorktown* crossed the two geographic lines, Davy Jones and his entourage stretched out a 30-foot target sleeve, two feet in

Night fighter Buck Dungan is seen "flying blind" during the crossing-the-line ceremonies, January 21, 1944.

Standing at Pri Fly, Davy Jones, the Royal Scribe (Frenchy Beaudette), reads the indictments against the *Yorktown's* assembled Pollywogs just prior to crossing the Equator and International Date Line. Commander Briggs stands behind him. Courtesy of Raymond F. Gard

Three senior Pollywogs on January 21, 1944: Country Lancaster holding salt-shaker binoculars, Skinhead Cooper Bright with the weather-reporting megaphone, and Joe Tucker with his headtop propeller. Lancaster and Tucker have their uniforms on backwards! Courtesy of Henry E. Bolden

Coming out of the "torture" sleeve, January 22, 1944. Note the paddle held by the man on right—canvas packed tightly with paper soaked in sand and hardened overnight. Ouch! Courtesy of Raymond F. Gard

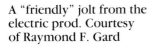

A "friendly" jolt from the electric prod. Courtesy of Raymond F. Gard

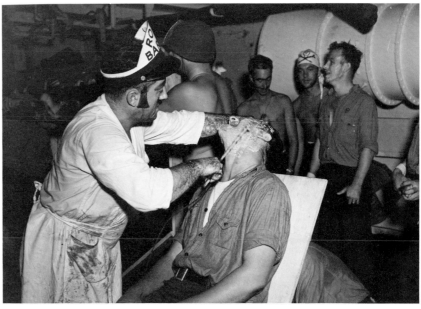

diameter, through which each pollywog crawled at top speed. As each fanny bulged out, shellbacks whacked it with two-foot paddles of canvas tightly packed with bits of paper, soaked in sand and hardened overnight. Pollywogs caught with padding inside their trousers were locked in stocks and swatted mercilessly. This painful indignity was followed by each man rolling over inside a coffin filled with "seasoned" week-old garbage; a charge from an electric prod; a shampoo of grease and graphite or a "haircut" by indiscriminate whacking; a drink of croatan oil and milk; a face-painting with oil; running a gauntlet of rubber fire hose paddles; and crawling back through another target sleeve of swattings. Fire hoses then swept them along the deck like fallen leaves.

"Now I'm a Shellback and a member of the court of the Royal Dragon," sighed a battered Wilding, "not to mention a butt full of large welts, raw sore, and hot—there'll be no sitting down for some time." Unpopular Marine Lieutenant "Moe" Sadler required six stitches in his rearend, while shellback Smokey Stover told his diary later that his roommate Vonk "had some nice purple splotches, but Jim Bryan, next door, outdid them all. Being skinny with no hips at all, he didn't have any fat to take up the shock so he has been sleeping on his stomach for several nights."

The agonies of play succumbed quickly to the realities of the approaching battle, which called for Air Group Five to hit Taroa atoll at Maloelap the first day, January 29, neutralize Kwajalein Island on the second, and cover the landings there the next two.

"Some program!" John Gray confided to his diary, "And each is being hit the favorite Navy way—strike after strike from dawn till dark so that all aircraft are destroyed and the field and facilities put completely out of action." These islands' airfields could then be kept neutralized by "roving carrier forces. Japan's beautifully situated staging bases will be knocked out at one fell swoop, making any further air defense of the Marshalls a virtual impossibility. The one road left open to them is the one we would like to see them use—carriers. If they *will* risk their CVs we can shorten the war tremendously right here and now—but I think they are smart enough to realize that the odds are against them."

In spite of continuous hops over the week preceding the attack and the fact that the *Enterprise* fighters would get all the gravy by making the first sweep, *Yorktown's* fliers were excited, none moreso than Smokey Stover. "Will be my first offensive flying with this VF-5. Haven't fired a gun at a Jap since that memorable day of October 15, 1942 [when he crashed midair with the float Zero]. My 'strike' is actually a combat air patrol which might accidentally develop into something."

Anticipating Japanese air attacks on the final run-in, exec Briggs wrote in the Plan of the Day on January 28: "IT NOW TAKES THIS SHIP APPROXIMATELY FIVE MINUTES TO GET TO GENERAL QUARTERS. THIS IS NOT BAD; HOWEVER,—LOW FLYING, ATTACKING TORPEDO PLANES REQUIRE ONLY SIX MINUTES TO FLY IN FROM THE CONTACT POSITION TO THE DROPPING POSITION. WE CAN AND MUST GET TO GENERAL QUARTERS QUICKER!"

The same day Stover reflected that he "would give a lot to get a Jap or two tomorrow or during our stay around here. It would not only be an enormous satisfaction to me but would show that my switch in jobs is worthwhile. Whatever the outcome, I'm not sorry for the change from the very safe seat in Radar Plot to an always hazardous seat in a fighter. Believe I could even take a life-raft ride now with good grace, at least I shouldn't have any reason to complain, having 'asked for it.' " Little did he know that just such a fate lay in his future.

John Gray this night appreciated the beauty of his fighting lady: "We have started our high speed run in to the target, and the old girl has picked up her skirts, and the 25 knots is swishing the white foam of her petticoats up around her knees."

A couple of hours after midnight, Admiral Mitscher appeared on the flag bridge and asked Vonk what the weather was going to be like. "Shitty, Admiral, perfectly shitty," blurted out the blunt Dutchman, as others nearly dropped their rocks at such plain talking. But Mitscher liked it; Vonk was his kind of guy.

A dismally rainy, black night—ceiling 700 feet—confronted the force, the kind of conditions which invited disaster during launch. The fighters and bombers would go at daylight in a later strike, but VT-5 was scheduled for the predawn strike, escorted by fighters from the *Enterprise*. When Captain Clark recommended to Admiral Reeves that the launch be postponed till first light, Reeves turned him down, fearful that the enemy would get the jump on them. Jocko shouted loud curses at this refusal; Black Jack was living up to a reputation as a hardheaded customer.

The TBFs were manned and their engines fired in a driving rain squall. The pilots and rear-seat gunners sat in their open cockpits getting drenched. At 0520 Dick Upson went off first, though unable to see the truck lights of the screening vessels. Four more followed. No-one could see anything, except a blinding flash somewhere ahead of the ship. Apparently it was two TBFs colliding, for the two crews never reached the target; missing forever were Willie Meehan and his crew, Bob Olds and George Haigh, and Si Simenson and crewmen Bob Parks and Phil Atwater.

Jocko held the rest of the torpeckers until the squall passed, yet the rain slackened only slightly, and the Avengers took off at irregular intervals—until the one flown by Sully O'Sullivan went into the drink. He and his crew were rescued by a can, but the other TBFs were kept on board. Only the six which were airborne proceeded to the target, Taroa-Maloelap. The flights from the other flattops fared no better. Damned weather! Damned Black Jack Reeves. "I hope the bastard is satisfied," grumbled John Gray in his diary later.

Worse, heavy AA fire greeted the attackers, who made uneven bomb runs into the thick of it. Flak struck five of Bombing 5's 22 SBDs on the next flight but none fatally. No enemy planes seemed to be airborne, so the only opposition was the flak. Woody McVay and the fighters escorted bombers from other ships and strafed some 45 parked planes at Taroa, but McVay followed a bomber so closely that when its bomb exploded, a six-foot log flew up and wedged in Woody's wing. Flak hit two fighters and ripped off part of Tom McGrath's TBF; it crashed into the lagoon, killing the pilot and crewmen Dick Robinson and Ed Haselgard.

Joe Kristufek developed an electrical failure inside his Avenger and had to hand-crank his wheels down on the return flight. When his tail hook did not respond, he got Jocko's permission to make a crash-landing on the ship. He touched down O.K. but slammed on his brakes so hard that his wheels burned. Just as they crossed an arresting wire, he recalled, "an alert operator flipped up the wire with split-second timing and caught it in the tail wheel." The plane jerked to a stop, safely.

"What is the name and rate of that barrier man?" Captain Clark yelled down from the bridge.

"Casey, Aviation Machinists Mate, Second Class," came the reply.

"Tell Casey that he is now an Aviation Machinists Mate, *First* Class!"

This was one of the captain's rare spot promotions, though Casey shared honors with the arresting gear officer who had trained him, Angie Peccianti, and with Joe Kristufek for his part.

Continuous hops all day—some pilots spent over eight hours in the saddle—discovered how weak Jap air defenses in the Marshalls were, with only occasional Bettys and Kates snooping the carriers. While Woody McVay's division covered the cruisers bombarding Wotje atoll, they spotted a Kate taking off and gave chase. Woody eventually caught up with the torpecker and flamed it with one burst—to the delight of his teammates.

Suddenly, late in the afternoon, a flight of ten bogeys appeared low on the horizon, approaching from out of the sun in a classic torpedo attack formation. The battleships and destroyers opened fire, and Hellcats from the *Enterprise* shot up two of them. *Yorktown's* closed in until—to their horror—the pilots saw white stars painted on the fuselages. Army B-25s! Their crews had erred in behaving like Jap torpeckers, and the Navy had erred in faulty recognition.

One of the stricken B-25s made a good water landing, five of its six men being rescued by a can. The other crash-landed later near Tarawa with no losses. "A sad incident," commented Charlie Ridgeway. "No excuse for such stupidity," wrote a less-charitable Stover.

The day thus ended with "a bad taste" in everyone's mouths. Torpedo 5 had lost nine men and four planes, while 14 of VF-5's 37 Hellcats required major repairs from battle damage. Admiral Reeves admitted his error in ordering the predawn launch and switched the plan for the morrow to a twilight launch. "So now," a pissed-off Gray noted, "after this has happened, we will launch at dawn tomorrow with some light! This suits me fine, since I'm the first off the deck for the early CAP, but it burns me to think this morning's debacle could have been prevented."

The weather on Dog minus One, January 30, was equally foul, and the planes were held even longer. They found the target, Kwajalein, quite clear and executed skillful attacks following a bombardment by the battleships. The fighters spotted Japanese landing craft ferrying troops between islands to reinforce the larger ones.

Jim Pickard of McVay's division picked out "a large landing barge filled with Jap soldiers about 50 yards from shore. The four of us made 6 runs apiece on the barge and sunk it just as it reached shore and the occupants tried to run up the beach to the reefs but we shot them as fast as they started running. A large red spot on the white sand could be seen where each man fell.

"An hour later the water was red with blood for 200 ft. around the sunken barge. Photographs showed 50-60 dead Japs and not a one was seen to get away. This was the most fun I've ever had. We then strafed 6 small boats in the lagoon with unobserved results. I made a total of 15 runs—2400 rounds of 50 cal. ammo—and had a hell of a good time." The strafing F6Fs and SBDs sank more barges in the lagoon, their heavy-laden troops drowning under the weight of their equipment.

"This afternoon was a heydey," rejoiced John Gray. "The island was pretty well creamed. Pretty well, Hell! It looked completely dead! The United States has come a long way from the sad days of the Philippines." Stover: "A real picnic. Dunc sank one small boat and we strafed a couple underway, probably getting some Japs. The island looks pretty well blasted but will probably still do plenty of shooting tomorrow. Seven hours today, 8 1/2 yesterday—and am I sore?!!"

Coxswain Jesse Bradley sat idle at his 40mm gun. "The Japs said they was going to get this task force, but I don't believe they will make the grade." Life on the *Yorktown* all day was "very uneventful and dull," complained Alex Wilding, while "the Japs are getting the living Hell kicked out of them."

January 31, D-Day. "TODAY OUR MISSION IS TO SUPPORT THE ARMY LANDINGS OPERATIONS ON TWO SMALL ISLANDS (Ennylabegan and Enubuj), WHICH ISLANDS WILL BE USED AS BASES FOR ASSAULTING AND TAKING THE BASE AT KWAJALEIN."

Ed Stebbins led the first air support strike, which dropped smoke bombs to blind the enemy and then swept in just ahead of the landing craft to bomb and strafe targets assigned them over the radio. So close and accurate were the SBDs that the barges warily slowed down, unused to such precision. Indeed, over succeeding days, the fighters would strafe so close to the advancing troops that their empty cartridge cases would fall within friendly lines!

Beyond that, however, the planes had little to do, and the fliers bitched at Admiral Reeves for subjecting them to such long "anus patrols." John Gray found his two hops "a killing pace. It isn't too bad when you're hopped up doing something—strafing, fighting, or just escorting, but to sit on your duff in one position strapped in for nine hours is a pace no one can stand for long." Smokey Stover agreed: "8 3/4 hours today, two hops CAP!!! Saw some natives on Libi Is. from the air, including a dark-toned damsel in grass skirt and nothing else languidly waving at us as we zoomed by." Joe Kristufek dropped the natives cigarettes.

The Marshalls invasion was turning out to be a pushover. The smaller islands fell easily during the day, and the Army had no trouble at all in over-running Kwajalein and the Marines taking Roi and Namur over the next four days. The airmen had little more to do than admire the aggressive work of the victorious ground forces, while flight deck crews were treated to a new sight—an F4U Corsair night fighter landed on *York* by mistake, a first for the ship.

Ed Stebbins made two particularly low and dangerous photo runs on D-Day which drew the praise of John Gray—"sixteen-inch shells, ricochets, were sizzling around his ears, and his neck was out a mile." On landing back aboard, however, Steb discovered something to be terribly amiss and made a bee-line for Air Plot with his camera.

"Buddy boy," he confronted his old compatriot Cooper Bright with the squinty-eyed look he had when he was displeased, "I've got a few things to report to you."

"What is it, Steb?"

Plopping the camera down on the chart table, he made his report, "I went in at 200 feet. My wing's got holes in it. I didn't get wounded, but my gas line was leakin'. Well, I'll do anything for Uncle Sam, anything for the old *Yorkblow*. But, Skinhead, I come back, opened up the camera—ain't no goddamned film in it!"

Somebody had goofed, and Jocko, in the words of Gray, "nearly had apoplexy." Admiral Reeves as well.

The only other noteworthy event of the day was a 50-foot, two-masted boat with four or five AA barrels sunk by *Yorktown* planes. Recorded Smokey Stover, in on the attack, "On returning to the ship. . .the captain called us up to the bridge to congratulate us! Some feat, sinking a Japanese man-o'-war like that!"

Next day TBF pilot Andy Lett spotted a 25-foot motor sailboat trying to escape Kwajalein, but when he and three other Avengers lined up to strafe it four frantic Japanese crewmen on board waved their hands in surrender. The torpeckers orbited their unique capture until the destroyer *Knapp* came up and took off the prisoners, then sank the prize.

The crew was transferred to the *Yorktown's* brig—an officer, two sailors and a "pathetic looking" Korean laborer, in the view of Roger Van Buren; "the other three looked like they would slit your throat without thinking twice." Interpreter Sandy Sims began interrogating the officer and civilian in English, but they only looked puzzled. "Don't kid me that you don't understand English," Sandy scoffed in English, "You probably went to UCLA or Southern Cal." They only jabbered away to each other in Japanese until Sims joined in on the conversation in their native tongue! After doing a double-take, the two prisoners talked to him like a couple of magpies and in flawless English.

The possibility of enemy air attacks from Truk and outlying Marshalls bases plus several false submarine contacts kept the ship "buttoned up" at GQ each day. This meant men could not pass between compartments without "undogging" watertight doors and rebolting them after passing through. In the weather office this created a problem, since the enlisted men had locked the door to the head, in order to keep it clean for inspections, or so they explained to their boss, Lieutenant Jim Vonk. He accepted their reasoning, even though he had to undog doors to relieve himself in another head.

Over several days Vonk noticed a foul odor which seemed to be emanating from inside the locked head, though the men denied smelling anything unusual. One day, however, the Weatherguesser *had* to take a leak and demanded that Aerologists Mate Second Robert M. Drew give him the key to the head. Drew couldn't find it. "Goddamnit," the loud Vonk demanded, his Dutch temper rising, "it's around here somewhere. You find it!"

Crestfallen, Drew produced it and reluctantly handed it to Vonk. Opening the door to the head, the Weatherguesser was nearly knocked over by the stench that greeted him. His enterprising swabs, behind his back, had turned the head into a still! Using everything they could find—raisins, apples, oranges—and drawing the necessary chemicals from the pharmacy, they had been fermenting it all into raw alcohol.

"Those dirty bastards!" was all Vonk could think as he took his pee. Slamming the door behind him, he exploded: "You have until midnight to clean up this whole mess. I want this head spotless!"

Come midnight the head was clean as a proverbial whistle, but Vonk also heard a commotion in his office and went to investigate. There he found a sight he would never to his dying days forget. The men were having a party, straining off the alcohol and dipping their cups into the raw stuff. Stone drunk, they were puking all over the place, creating a stench which, along with the stinking residue of the fermented fruits, made the weather center almost uninhabitable for days.

The door to the head would never be locked again.

So obvious was the defeat of the Japanese in the Marshalls that *Yorktown* actually passed within view of Kwajalein on February 2, enabling the crew to witness gun flashes and tall columns of smoke arising from the "shredded" atoll. John Gray saw it from the air next day as the cruisers shelled "the luckless islands. And they looked luckless! On that first attack on December 4, they looked lush and green and peaceful with the indolence of Nordhoff and Hall Pacific islets, and now—like pictures of no-man's land churned by four years of war in 1918."

Amid rumors that Task Force 58 would next visit the South Pacific to help take Rabaul and then attack Truk, the *Yorktown* departed Kwajalein waters on February 3. Pilot Gray reflected that, since the Gilberts had been a British possession, the capture of the Marshalls had special significance. "We have our own way now in the first Jap territory to be conquered since the beginning of the war. And this is just the start. Wait till we start hitting the Jap mainland—then listen to the yellow monkeys scream!"

The following day the ship led the task force into the sprawling lagoon of newly-captured Majuro atoll, 200 miles to the east of Kwajalein, though Captain Clark and navigator Red Sharp sweated the tight entrance passage between the jagged coral reefs. Charlie Ridgway marveled that the *Yorktown* dropped its anchor "along with 9/10s

of the U.S. Pacific Fleet quite as casually as [if] we'd come to rest in Pearl Harbor instead of practically inside the Japs' back yard." He identified no fewer than nine fast carriers, four escort carriers, eleven battleships, eight cruisers, countless destroyers, maybe a dozen fleet tankers and even tugboats. "No Pacific harbor has ever held such a concentration of warships outside of Pearl."

The sight took on an aura of almost mystical glory when John Gray strode onto the flight deck on the 5th "as the first light of dawn came out of the sea to the east behind the palms and thatched huts. It was one of the most impressive sights I have ever witnessed! Here was pictured in soft Technicolor the might of a free people! This morning the red glow pastel of what had been a week ago the Jap rising sun was now softening the grim, battle blue gray of the mightiest U.S: Fleet that ever rode at anchor in a foreign port! The magnifying power of morning twilight exaggerated the size of the giant carriers."

Dr. Gard reassured his family in a letter, "More 'stuff' arrives daily—power is accumulating, more than the world has ever before seen in one mass. This war here is going to be a naval 'blitzkrieg'— an obliteration of all opposition in areas, one at a time, at far removed places keeping the Jap off balance, wondering where the next blow will be. And all the time new battleships—*Missouri*—new carriers, *Franklin* and *Hancock,* and new cruisers and destroyers are being put into commission. The defeat of Japan is inevitable and the 'how' becomes more clear each day."

The enlisted swabs were less generous in their regard for Majuro. Jesse Bradley recorded the first night that "a Jap plane flew overhead late tonight. If this finds us in this place somebody is going to get hurt. This place is about eighty miles from two Jap airfields, Mili and Jaluit. I guess we are going to form another task force and hit something else. Maybe Truk."

But first, rest and reflection. Captain Clark broke out the liquor from the " Wing and a Prayer" movie gift, and shore parties on Majuro atoll chilled the beer with CO_2 fire extinguishers for three mornings of beach parties. The officers devoured the whiskey there during the afternoons. Chaplains Farrell and Alexander were kept busy meeting the spiritual needs of the sailors, with Alexander sharing long hours with the popular Smokey Stover discussing infinite matters as they gazed out across the lagoon.

The curious incongruity of tropical lushness and

Swimming off the ship at Majuro, February 8, 1944. Between the ship and the atoll can be seen a nest of three destroyers. Courtesy of Raymond F. Gard

machines of war struck the more reflective of the officers, not least John Gray, whose brilliance in the cockpit was matched by a talented pen. Wandering forward to the forecastle, he leaned over a 40mm gun mount parapet to enjoy a lovely evening—"a night for dreaming dreams not even repressed by the fringe of warship shapes, silent, but with restless blinking eyes at anchor in this small paradise. The Moon is full, and the thin chiffon skirts of cloud swirl gently around the legs of Night. There is a glisten, too, to her silver slippers on the floor of the lagoon, as there is a twinkling sparkle from the stars of her tiara. And in her hair she wears a single huge moon-shaped gardenia set in tresses so black they seem dark blue. And the breath of Her is hushed with promise and soft, like a lover's should be, with inaudible sounds learned eons ago.

"As she pirouettes about the floor, I am struck with the sense that this has happened before—that I have stood before like this watching Night dance, and thought the same thoughts, and yielded to the same pressure of imagining things that have no basis in thought—things brought suddenly to me without ever having entered my consciousness. Mystic imagery called up by some mystic dance—perhaps such a one as the Owled Nails dance for their men, but yet without the beat of that desire.

"And I wonder how varied the dancing repertoire of Night. To what tempo can she not dance? Of what romantic waltz and wild voodoo is she not equally mistress? Night knows a myriad dances, and I have seen the scope of her varied programme. Oh, She is versatile, and fickle, and not always friendly—not loyal. She was a lovely French refugee in the heavy perfume of Nassau, but she was a dangerous bitch, a wicked jealous strumpet north of Kwajalein on December 4th, who kicked at the shins of the carriers with Jap torpedoes, and danced around lighting torches for the bombers to point out their intended victims.

"And she reveled in the fireworks of the frantic gunfire, speeded up the tempo of her dance, plucked at the tight strings of men's nerves already drawn to snapping pitch until she found that none would break. Gradually she used up her torches, tired of the dance, and sleepily pulled the covers over her head as if she were ashamed of having treated us so badly, and would frown her darkest on our rival for her favor.

"All this, and more, I remember, as the syrupy caresses stroke the decks of the carriers, and think, 'you beautiful, gorgeous, inconstant creature! You lovely body without a soul, mistress of the art of love, traitress to its meaning! Never will I trust you; never watch you dance without knowing of the pearl handled wicked little derringer you carry in your sequined evening bag—knowing you would turn on me if the whim moved you. I have seen you, Night, and love you; but in loving, never trusting.''

The thoughts of Jocko Clark were less poetic. He had received his final orders instructing him to put on his rear admiral's stars and turn over the *Yorktown* to his relief as soon as that individual arrived. Jocko hoped the man would not report in before the next battle but was disappointed when on the afternoon of February 8 a big flying boat landed alongside bringing the new skipper.

Captain Ralph E. Jennings, the same who had inspected the ship prior to her commissioning, had hastened to Majuro all the way from New York, anxious to assume command. As Clark and Jennings inspected the ship all next day, the crew reacted adversely. Charlie Ridgway wrote, "We feel unhappy about changing skippers at such an important moment." The men worried, reflected Jim Bryan, "about changing horses in mid-stream." John Gray: "Captain Clark is a rough, tough old S.O.B., but the pilots have a lot of confidence in him. Old Jocko can lead me into a fight anytime."

What the men could not know was that Clark would lead them again—and soon. Because he was so valuable a combat leader, Clark was being retained in the war zone by Admiral Mitscher instead of being rotated Stateside for the usual indoctrination period for a new admiral. He would command a task group, and thus he tried to transfer as many of his best *Yorktown* officers to his staff as Captain Jennings would release. Bob Reynolds and Herman Rosenblatt would go immediately to be his flag lieutenant and flag secretary respectively, along with his Marine orderlies and Filipino mess boys. Over the ensuing months, he would also get gun boss Stroke Blackwell, navigator Red Sharp, fighter director Charlie Ridgway and pilot Douglas A. "Tex" McCrary of Torpedo 5.

On the morning of the 10th, after packing his sea bag, Clark said farewell to all his department heads and assistant heads in his cabin. "Tough old Jocko," noted Ray Gard, "almost broke down." Then he faced the entire crew, mustered on the flight deck. He read his orders into the mike, his voice cracking a couple of times, and then, for the first time that anyone could remember, choked—at a complete loss for words. His puffed-up lower lip was visibly shaking as he finally, with thick voice, blurted out, "This is the best group of fighting men in the Navy. You have never missed a schedule."

The band struck up "Aloho Oe" as Jocko crossed the flight deck, picked up his belongings, and descended to the hangar. There he was startled to find about two-thirds of the crew lined up all across the hangar deck as sideboys, officers in front. It was a spontaneous final gesture of affection by men who had known him as their only captain. Jesse Bradley: "Nobody wanted to see him leave because he sure was a good man." Each officer shook hands with Clark as he made his way through the throng

Captain Ralph E. Jennings reads his orders taking command of the *Yorktown*, as Jocko Clark sadly looks out on his crew, February 10, 1944. Cameron Briggs stands behind them. Jocko's deck is neatly spotted—as usual.

toward the gangway, tears streaming down his face and the faces of many of the crew, Chaplain Alexander among them.

Saluting the ensign and accompanied by his aides, Rear Admiral Clark was piped over the side.

Throughout the Marshalls operation Lieutenant John Gray had guessed that the next campaign would be fought over the big Japanese bastion of Rabaul in the South Pacific. Then, on February 4, he had changed his projection. "I predict a blow at Truk itself soon—one smashing raid, I should say, not an attempt to take the place, for we are not yet ready to do that—may only hit it to prove that the Japs can't use it, and then go around."

At almost the same time, Admiral Nimitz back at Pearl Harbor had reached the same conclusion. The crushing victories at Kwajalein and in the South Pacific meant that the Fifth Fleet could now bypass Japan's "unsinkable aircraft carriers" of Milli, Jaluit, Maloelap and Wotje in the Marshalls and even Rabaul itself. Occasional air raids by the carriers and daily bombings by land-based planes would render these island airdromes impotent and make invasion unnecessary. The fast carriers could now concentrate on Truk.

Whereas the once-dreaded Rabaul had often been pronounced "Raa-bool" and Navy men had kidded "only a fool would go to Raa-bool," they joked

A tearful Jocko Clark relinquishes command to Captain "Al" Jennings beneath, appropriately, an "efficiency" E.

Expressions of admiration, respect, even love grace the faces of Jocko's assistant department heads bidding him farewell; (L to R) George Weiss (gunnery), Country Lancaster (engineering), Ray Gard (medical), Jim Brady (damage control), and chief engineer Bill Hart. Flag secretary Herman Rosenblatt stands at the right facing the O.O.D., Ensign Tony Capriotti. Courtesy of Raymond F. Gard

To Lieutenant H.S. Roseblatt USN *[signature inscription]* 1 with sincere regards and in ... a modern soldier in the ... 1 USS YORKTOWN 1944 *[signature]* USNavy

"Fuck Truk" of that feared stronghold, spoken of only "in a whisper" during 1942-43. "The name itself had a death-doom sound," pilot Dick Newhafer would recall, "foreboding as a midnight shadow on a graveyard wall. To the men of the fleet it brought forth the crawling fear of the unknown. It was a place known only by circles on a map. . . painted to awesome images by fables and ignorance. . . . A stronghold so powerful and impregnable it had never been spoken of as a target except in jest."

"Truk," Alex Wilding confided to his diary when he got the word on the 5th, "Everyone is scared to death of what is going to happen. Truk is just like our Pearl Harbor and we know the defense Pearl could put up. We're not going to enjoy this one. Five days from now we'll be sitting in a hot seat."

The initial plans of Task Force 58 to sortie from Majuro on the 10th were delayed two more days, however, so Fifth Fleet commander Spruance, a battleship-weaned admiral, could accompany the carriers. "So the whole scheme was delayed," observed a sarcastic Charlie Ridgway, "while he ran over from Kwajalein to contribute his genius." The recent glories had already endeared the men of TF 58 to Mitscher, their leader. John Gray: "Admiral Spruance, in whom nobody seems to feel confidence, that is, the confidence he would feel if

Admiral Mitscher were in complete command as was the original arrangement, is to be in command of this deal."

Alex Wilding worried that the two-day delay of the bold plan "doesn't look so good. The element of surprise is wearing off and the Japs will undoubtedly get their fleet out and planes in, which will make it rough on us. Saw the pictures of Truk today. Shows four airfields with 300 to 400 airplanes on the runways with possibly many more underground. Two aircraft carriers are anchored in the harbor, cruisers, destroyers, and about 60 large ships. Looks very formidable. We will have 16 subs outside the entrance to Truk anchorage to pick off any ships that try to escape. We expect a major fleet engagement. Wish I were home—it's a little bit scarry."

Task group commanders Reeves, Montgomery and Sherman met with Mitscher on the *York* on the 9th, and two days after that all air group and squadron commanders worked out the air plan on board the *Enterprise*. The two-day attack on Truk would commence with a fighter sweep of six dozen Hellcats on the morning of February 16. *Yorktown's* contribution would be the divisions of Ed Owen, Stover and Gray.

"This all adds up to a gorgeous possibility!" thought Gray, "Barring unforeseen difficulties, this should give us a wonderful chance to knock down a lot of planes and knock out a lot on the ground— so that there would never be a chance of a repetition of a fiasco that VF-9 pulled on Kwajalein that first raid when all those Bettys were undamaged and left operational to come out and plaster us with that 7 1/2 hour torpedo attack that night.

"Fighting Five has done more strafing than any other squadron and done a better job before. We will again! It will be a real fight, but a lot of the Jap air force will end up out of commission. With the set-up as it is, it will be another sad day for the Emperor's batmen!" Each of the nine carriers would launch six strikes per day of fighters and bombers.

The sheer power of the force and self-confidence of the carriermen led the more knowledgeable to disparage Admiral Spruance's battle plan—"a real War College array" in Charlie Ridgway's opinion which unrealistically anticipated a gunnery duel between the battleships, something which Spruance had indeed studied in three prewar tours of duty at the Naval War College. The hard-hitting carriers were replacing the big gun ships.

All hands got the word soon after the task force put to sea on February 12. "We've hated this place

FEB '44

for years," wrote pilot Jim Pickard, "no white man has seen it in 20 years. It's big game now." George Wille: "In midshipman days, this was known as the equivalent to comitting honorable suicide." Excited though the pilots were, all had their doubts, like Smokey Stover, "However unprepared we may find the Japanese, it seems pretty sure that our flight deck won't be so crowded going back as it is now." And "Glow-dome" Bright held forth on the Air Plot News to the ready rooms: "DON'T BE AFRAID OF GETTING SHOT DOWN, BOYS, I HEAR THE ISLAND'S ENTIRELY INHABITED BY WOMEN."

The horrors of Truk could well be imagined by pilots fearful of getting shot down and taken prisoner. Well-known were Jap atrocities in China before the war and at Bataan, Corregidor and Guadalcanal early in the fighting. Unknown were the agonies that Pop Condit was experiencing in the prison camp at Ofuna, while the Japs at Truk had executed 127 American prisoners since the summer and during January and February were performing "medical experiments" on American POWs there.

Captain Jennings took the *Yorktown* northeast at high speed in an ocean "rough as hell." The flagship again teamed up with the *Enterprise* and *Belleau Wood* in Reeves' task group. A mild-mannered gentleman, "Al" Jennings had gained experience as a shiphandler over the preceding year while in command of an escort carrier delivering planes to the forward areas. But he was totally unprepared when O.O.D. Shack Moore roared the ship back into the formation at 32 knots in Jocko's "fishtail" maneuver after recovering the CAP at sunset.

Standing out on the wing of the bridge, Jennings cradled his head in his arms and cried "Oh, no!" when Moore made his first turn to slow the ship. Then, when the *York* fishtailed the second time, the captain cried out again and hung on for dear life.

At that moment Captain Hedding, Admiral Mitscher's chief of staff, appeared on the bridge. Jennings thought Hedding had come up to question the maneuver and launched into a long—and inaccurate—explanation of what was going on. "Oh?" remarked Hedding, "I hadn't noticed. I just brought you the Admiral's night orders." The ship ended up on station, as usual, but Jennings ordered no more fishtails. For future admiral Shack Moore, all shiphandling compared to Jocko's was "minor leagues." Having qualled top watch with Jocko, the next 29 years were smooth sailing down hill.

Daily briefings about Truk's defenses increased the anxiety of pilots and crew alike. The possibility of a night air attack on the way in made them appreciate the presence of the four new radar-equipped Hellcat night fighters, now spotted on the catapults for immediate possible launch: Detachment B of VF(N)-76, led by Lieutenant Russell L. Reiserer.

The first bogey contact occurred during daylight hours, however. In the midst of refueling on the 14th, a *Belleau Wood* fighter splashed a Betty—most likely out of Truk—only 35 miles north of the task group. It had probably *not* seen the ships. Alex Wilding: "If we're spotted on the way in this time there will be a fight." But the *York* was ready, spurred on by its new captain, who concluded a pep talk over the bullhorn next day with the war cry, "Let the yellow bellied bastards remember their own Pearl Harbor!"

"An air of tension over the ship" became apparent to Dr. Gard. "A few more hours and night will cover us and we will be in again without being seen. This is a tremendous sight—all these ships steaming at flank speed with no zig zag, straight toward our objective, hoping to destroy the place and all it contains.

"This ship is spick and span from stem to fantail. Two days of 'field day'—there is no dirt, trash or anything left unsecured. The planes are fully armed, fully tested and polished to the brilliance of a new car. Our new Captain is splendid and I'm sure he is going to do a good job.

"Everyone off watch has 'sacked in' expecting to be up for 2 days and nights after the launching hour. Everyone has his life belt, his helmet and first aid kit as ready as possible. In the sick bay are only 3 patients. The appendix is doing very well, a pneumonia and a fracture.

"I'm going to 'crap out' for a few hours. The sun is down—sky overcast—no evidence of having been sighted. The moon comes up about 0100."

Little nuisances added to the general apprehension, like the lack of the customary steak and eggs. Bemoaned John Gray: "Having been out so long, the stores on board are being reduced to sad excuses for food. Oh, nobody will get scurvy, and the general health isn't to be compared to what Columbus's men had to put up with, but *they* probably had indigestion to start with! If it only weren't for these rubber eggs! They date from Norfolk and taste like it!"

The pilots quietly prepared for the big day, discussing final details. Smokey Stover put over $700 of poker winnings in a letter to his parents.

The plotting board chart of Truk carried in each plane
during the strikes of February 16-17, 1944. It measured
eight inches square.

His wingman Bob Duncan dropped by Smokey's room to chat just before turning in. He spotted a brand new pair of shoes Smokey had set out with his flight suit. "What are you going to do with them?" he asked.

"I'm going to wear them tomorrow!"

"What do you want to wear those for? You're going to get oil all over them."

"When I get shot down," Smokey replied, "the Japanese aren't going to give me any shoes."

On the other hand, Smokey had often told his friends, "They'll never take me alive." And when Jim Bryan poked his head in the door after reveille, he found Smokey busily waterproofing his pistol. The idea of getting shot down seemed to have become an obsession with him.

Sleep did not come easily for the fliers. "I was scared chicken," confessed Roger Van Buren later. "That was the first time I have ever felt like that; I had a solid case of the jitters—didn't sleep a wink."

Instead of the usual "ungodly" Flight Quarters call at 0230 or 0300, the pilots were not beckoned on strike day, the 16th, until 0545, which "felt like a gentleman's way to run a war," in John Gray's opinion. "Except that we know better! This was no gentleman's war."

Sixty minutes later Gray, Stover and Owen took off with their divisions as part of the sweep, followed immediately by the first bombing strike of 15 VB, 9 VT and 8 VF. Ed Owen led the 100-mile flight, staying under Truk's radar most of the way, and then circled the lagoon making certain no Zeros were aloft. Finding none, at 0810 he ordered the three divisions to drop down and strafe.

Suddenly tracers whizzed by Owen's wingman, Chuck Stephens, who turned to see a float Zero zoom by him and up into a cloud.

"Tallyho!" announced Owen, who took his dozen Hellcats up toward angels 8. Through the clouds, they now saw Jap fighters all over the place—Zekes, Rufes, Hamps and Tonys—perhaps three or four dozen. "It was like flushing quail," Owen would say later, "I didn't know which one to shoot first! Like duck soup."

More Japs took off from Truk's island airstrips, only to be boxed in by VF-5 and other low-flying Hellcats like Harry Harrison's squadron from the *Intrepid*. Up high, *Essex's* Phil Torrey of Air Group Nine, target coordinator and friend of Owen's, radioed down to "Cousin", "What's goin' on? What's goin' on?" The Japs couldn't get much higher than 8000 feet. It was Fighting 5's turn in the barrel.

The ack ack opened up, more accurate and more deadly than ever before, but the fighters ignored it. Tom McClelland spotted a Zero closing on a section of Hellcats, dove down and opened fire. The Zero started to burn as it passed into a cloud. Bob Duncan took a hit in his engine as his wingman Smokey Stover made a run on a float Zero but missed it. Duncan retired to the carrier leaking oil.

Smokey winged over through the flak and downward to look for Jap warships, followed by division mates Den Merrill and D.O. Kenney. He sighted ships and radioed the *Yorktown*—"Three or four light cruisers or destroyers and a merchant ship" underway toward North Pass to escape the attack. Even their main batteries were belching occasional rounds at the planes.

Just then a burst of flak shook Smokey's plane. He pulled up, trying for some altitude and distance away from Truk, but Merrill flew alongside and radioed, "You're hit, badly!" His plane burning, Smokey had no choice now but to jump. His chute put him into the water some three miles north-northeast of the barrier reef, where he inflated his rubber life raft, climbed in and waved both arms to Merrill circling overhead. He was in serious trouble, for the prevailing winds were blowing him toward North Pass, the very break in the reef into which those Jap warships were heading.

As the bombing planes approached Truk in the dawn, Roger Van Buren thought "the tops of the clouds looked like dreamy castles with endless circling staircases" until "every ship in the harbor broke loose with all the fire they had." Aside from the few reported cruisers and cans, these vessels proved to be merchantmen; the battleships and carriers had obviously already escaped to safer waters. The bombers and torpedo planes pushed through the flak and dropped their payloads. Some hit their marks.

Those Jap warships present and Smokey Stover's raft were heading toward North Pass from different directions, and Den Merrill frantically tried to raise the lifeguard submarine *Searaven*, patrolling 30 miles north of Truk, for help. The heavy radio traffic made this impossible, so Merrill had to leave Smokey and return to the *Yorktown* with Smokey's position. The *Yorktown* then tried to raise the lifeguard sub *Darter*, but that boat was patrolling south of Truk and could do nothing if it had heard the transmission. But it didn't, while *Searaven* had to stay submerged all morning because of so many Jap planes in the area.

Dogfights filled the skies over Truk as successive flights of Hellcats came onto the scene and kept the growing numbers of Jap fighters busy, allowing the bombers to deliver their wares. Ed Stebbins relieved Phil Torrey as target coordinator at 0910 and soon saw the five enemy warships clearing North Pass. He reported this and some 25 marus and tankers at the Dublon-Eten anchorage. The *Yorktown* launched a strike at 1000 to go after the warships, though some of the pilots, fearful of those ships' heavy flak, chose to go after the merchantmen instead.

Stebbins directed all the planes until he retired at 1130, having failed, as had many of his pilots, to spot Stover on the reef or to raise the *Searaven* by radio. Indeed, just at 1130, the sub surfaced 30 miles north of the island—27 miles from the reef—only to sight two of Admiral Spruance's battleships and escorts roaring toward it aiming to sink the Jap ships. So *Searaven* got out of the way by diving again—and staying down for three hours!

The *York* sent off another strike to hit the warships. Torpecker Van Buren carried six 100-pound bombs on this second mission of the day for him. "There were 9 of us with 6 SBDs and fighter cover. Our flight approached the ships at 12,000 feet. They were about 15 miles off the atoll. The dive bombers went in first with not a hit. The ships maneuvered violently, turning in all directions.

"When we went down, I saw one of our planes get a direct hit on a large cruiser. It practically left the ship dead in the water. There were several

A Jap destroyer twists and turns in a high-speed attempt to avoid an attacking TBF Avenger north of Truk. It is following the wake and oil slick from another ship.

A Hellcat strafes an already-burning Japanese can at Truk, February 16, 1944.

damaging misses on the same ship. I was closest to a destroyer, so I went after it. Before I was down to 8000 feet, he had maneuvered out of position for me. I held my altitude to start again. After making three such starts, I decided to wait and let him get himself in position for me, instead of my trying to jockey around him.

"Sure enough, he brought his bow around and started turning. He was just where I wanted him. I dove from 8000 feet. There wasn't much AA before this; but that one can sure filled the sky with it then. I led the can plenty as it was making good

speed. Dropped and pulled out at 1500. The tracers were flying past so fast I couldn't begin to count them. I heard my gunner on the ICS—'you hit it.'

"As I turned, the can was covered with spray and smoke. My first two bombs hit close to the bow and the third just forward of the turret. It didn't seem to have any apparent damage. Previous to this the can had received many damaging misses. Two bombs straddled its stern. They must have sprung the plates badly.

"I still had one bomb left and circled for altitude to make another pass. While I was doing this, the can lost speed and soon was dead in the water. Smoke and steam were pouring from the stacks. I could see that she was in a bad way. I started another pass, but couldn't get enough speed, so I got out in a hurry. They fired several times but didn't come close. My last pass was started too low, and I gave up when they started firing. I dropped the bomb when I pulled up, hoping to throw it at them, but I was too far away. On that sixth pass, I decided to leave well enough alone.''

The light cruiser *Katori* had fallen victim to direct hits by "Boris" Thurston, Alex Rapp and Bennie Benson of Torpedo 5, and the other ships were taking hits as Admiral Spruance's battle line closed in just past the noon hour. As the big gun ships pounded four of the five already-clobbered ships until they sank, the next *Yorktown* bombing strike went after the shipping inside the lagoon, covered by 16 VF-5 Hellcats.

Bob Duncan, watching John Gray's division strafing, abruptly barked out over the air, "Tallyho! Bandits at Angels 20! Get up here fast, we have more than we can handle!''

Ten to 15 Zekes were diving out of the sun, and Duncan's section began its defensive Thach weave with Den Merrill's. A Zeke came down on the first section for a high-side run at ten o'clock but instead showed off his acrobatic skills by flipping over on his back and shooting upside down. His burst hit the plane of Duncan's wingman, but old pro Duncan turned in and under Zeke for a long burst at four o'clock as the Jap recovered ahead and above, then burst into flames.

Then another Jap recovered in front of Duncan after missing everybody, and Bob squeezed his trigger but missed. The Zero turned on Duncan and passed by, whereupon Dunc also turned and set him afire with a short burst.

As Gray's and Teddy Schofield's eight Hellcats raced at full speed to altitude and started to work on these interlopers, Duncan engaged a third Zero which attacked from above. They twisted and turned to avoid each other's bursts until the Jap broke off and headed down for the clouds at 5000 feet. Bob gave chase and flamed him in the tail at 8000. Duncan blacked out from his dive but came to at 4000 and climbed again.

Schofield shot down one Zero and chased another all the way down to the deck, blazing away at its tail. The Jap, electing to land, made a wild disjointed approach. His wing touched first, setting the plane afire and cartwheeling it through a row of parked Bettys, igniting three of them before coming to rest in front of a big Emily four-engine flying boat. Teddy watched the four planes burn but as he recovered he lamented that he had missed the Emily.

Duncan meanwhile encountered another Zeke diving on him from 300 feet above him at one o'clock. They flew head-on, the Jap giving off a short burst, and Duncan replied, but found only his starboard guns working. Seconds before they were about to collide, Zeke rolled over on his back, and Bob pulled up and banked just as the Jap spiraled earthward. Duncan's brief fire had apparently killed the pilot, and the plane crashed into Dublon Island—Dunc's fourth kill for the day.

Ed Stebbins returned in the afternoon to direct more attacks, observe the final sinking of the *Katori* by Spruance's battle line and to keep looking for Stover and the *Searaven*. Four bandits jumped his division over Tol Island, but Steb sent one Zeke down in flames. Another flew head-on into Jim Campbell's gunsight. After a long burst with all six guns, Campbell watched the Zero blossom in flame and then had to swerve to avoid it.

Zeros poured lead into several of Dick Upson's eight TBFs and exchanged slugs with their turret gunners. Two Tonys scissored through a dozen passes at Ensign Benson's Avenger, one of them hitting the turret, which showered glass and metal, wounding gunner Bill Moak. Benny dove for the deck, spewing Moak's .50 cal. ammo out of its boxes, but Moak fed the gun with one hand and fired with the other. Radioman Jack Hancock manned the .30 cal. stinger gun in the plane's underbelly until a Tony blew a hole in the fuselage, badly wounding Hancock and starting a fire.

Bill Moak shot down one of the attackers and three times climbed down from his perch to fight the fire. When the Tonys broke off their attack, the bleeding Moak jettisoned all the burning materials through the hole in the fuselage. Reaching the carrier, pilot Benson found his tail hook to be inoperative, so he crash-landed handily. Medical corpsmen rushed both wounded aircrewmen to Sick Bay, but Hancock died on the way.

More crippled planes managed to crash aboard, one accidentally discharging its guns and slightly wounding seven men, but the wreckage was cleared away and the deck quickly respotted. Admiral Mitscher interviewed Jim Campbell about conditions over Truk, then paid a visit to Captain Jennings to compliment the crew: "This is the best flight deck I ever saw!'' *Yorktown* was Number One in the eyes of Pete Mitscher.

Fighting 5 added luster to the reputation of the ship by shooting down 29 bandits during the day, or almost half of Task Force 58's total score. Bob Duncan had gotten most with four kills, which, added to his previous two, made him the squadron's first ace. Tom McClelland, "Dapper" Nelson and Harry Hill each nailed three, and Ed Owen, John Gray, Den Merrill, Chuck Stephens and Jim Schiller had two apiece.

"If Smokey was picked up by sub," wrote Charlie Ridgway, "this was a perfect day." But Stover was in fact missing; his greatest fears had been realized.

Radio interpreter Sims passed on enemy broadcast news to an amused crew that evening, leading Gray to comment, "The Japs say that their army and navy forces are still beating back all waves of American planes that are trying to attack, and here I am writing this in my room as the old girl lifts up her skirts and strides haughtily away from the sound of such nonsense! The vaunted Pearl Harbor of the Jap Central Pacific is now just a badly dented and beaten up chip in the Greater East Asia Co-Prosperity Sphere. There is nothing prosperous about it!! The 16th of February, 1944, will go down in history, I am confident, as one of the greatest aerial battles ever won!"

Shortly after 2000 GQ sounded as the radars registered the first of seven single-plane bogeys. Al Jennings ordered eleven emergency turns over the ensuing two hours while AA fire from the screen drove away the interlopers. The moonlight was the same as that hairy night off Kwajalein, but Admiral Mitscher did not order night fighter Russ Reiserer to be catapulted from the *Yorktown* until the last bogey retired at 2320; he had preferred to rely on ships' guns.

Then, just after midnight, the *Enterprise* tracked a fresh bogey and vectored Reiserer to the intercept. Unfortunately, his airborne radar was not in tune, and he could not prevent the plane—a Jill—from making a determined torpedo run on the *Intrepid*, steaming on the *York's* port quarter (left astern). No ships opened fire, for fear of hitting Reiserer, and the Jill's fish slammed into the *Intrepid* near the rudder, the very same fate of the *Lexington* off Kwajalein. The Jill escaped, but Reiserer stayed aloft for two more hours to deter other snoopers and allow the *Intrepid* to regain steerage and retire.

The *Yorktown* stayed at GQ all night and suffered a freak casualty when Commander Bill Patten, ship's supply officer, fell into a plane elevator well from the dark flight deck and badly injured himself.

Only flak greeted the carrier planes when they returned to Truk on the 17th, but the flak was heavy indeed. Sully O'Sullivan's TBF suffered a severed oil line and ditched seven miles northeast of the reef. Dick Upson sent the others home and circled O'Sullivan for three hours—in spite of a broken gas gauge! Tom Page finally relieved him and guided the *Searaven* to the rescue of O'Sullivan and his crew. Grateful for his comrades' vigilance, Sully rejected a substantial "survivor's leave" to remain in combat with them.

Ed Stebbins coordinated a midmorning bombing attack on the shipping at Truk, during which a burst of flak wounded dive bomber jockey Jim Mackie in the right leg. Despite the loss of blood, Mackie flew back and made an excellent *wheels-up* landing.

Steb remained over the target for two hours taking pictures—this time *with* film, looking in vain along the reef for Smokey Stover and assessing damage. Finally, he radioed Admiral Mitscher his opinion that the remaining targets were "not worth the risk involved in keeping the force in the vicinity any longer." Mitscher concurred and at noon ordered high speed set to the northeast for, in bomber pilot Ridge Radney's words, "that very important naval maneuver called 'getting the hell out of there.'"

"TRUK HAS FELT THE MIGHTY AX," a poetic Cooper Bright opined from Air Plot, "THE YORKTOWN FEELS IT CAN RELAX." The fast carriers had destroyed perhaps 200 planes, most of them on the ground, and sunk nearly 150,000 tons of Jap shipping, including two cruisers, four cans and two dozen marus loaded with equipment, in addition to inflicting enormous damage to other ships and planes and shore installations.

Yet, Jim Pickard spoke for all the fliers when he penned his diary entry, "I'm glad that's over." No U.S. ships had been lost, though the *Intrepid* had been put out of action for months of repairs. Seventeen carrier planes had gone down and 29 airmen with them. *Yorktown* had lost Jack Hancock and Smokey Stover, for whom squadronmate Dick Newhafer composed a final tribute that evening:

> The call came
>   On metal-fashioned wings,
> And echoed til it spent;
>   He bade farewell
> To all the well-loved things
>   And then he went.
> A fresh wind
>   Bore him away tonight,
> The world is sad,
>   He gave his mirth
> For all the world's delight,
>   T'was all he had.

Smokey was listed as missing in action, though postwar interrogations of friend and foe would complete the story of his probable fate, along with six other American aviators. The Japs brought in seven from the reef—on which their rafts had stranded them—and beat and tortured them. On the afternoon of the 17th, after the mighty American aerial armada had withdrawn, the seven luckless pilots were lined up near a beach. Two Japanese naval officers drew long samurai swords and, one by one, struck off the heads of their prisoners.

"Pilot morale continues to be at a high state," Ed Stebbins concluded his action report as the carriers retired on February 18. In spite of their many battles, Steb attributed the airmen's enthusiasm "in no small measure to the expectancy of relief and rehabilitation at an early date." Meaning, rotation Stateside for leave and reassignment.

Hardly had he written these words, however, when several announcements jarred even the most complacent listeners. "About 1730 this afternoon," as Alex Wilding recorded it, "news started to break fast. . .We are going back to the Marianas and hit Saipan and Tinian in Japan's own back yard and much too close to Tokyo for peace of mind and a long life. Appears we're getting a little bit too cocky." After hitting the Marianas, deep inside "Indian country," Captain Jennings informed his crew that the fast carriers would retire briefly to Majuro, then head to the South Pacific and possibly send a follow-up strike against Truk! "The Golden Gate in '48," lamented his listeners.

The Marianas—Saipan, Tinian and Guam—far to the north and west of Truk, constituted the administrative heart of Japan's entire defense system in the Pacific Ocean. This hastily conceived raid was designed to keep the Japs off balance. But the exaggerated fears over Truk made this new prospect seem anticlimactic. When the tankers hove into view, Radar Fire Controlman Second Joe Chambliss boasted in his diary of refueling at sea "in the midst of Japs' defense perimeter. They are slipping!" These replenishment ships enabled Task Force 58 to continue driving westward to places like the Marianas without having to return to Pearl Harbor.

The one problem which plagued Admiral Mitscher was how to deal with Jap air attacks at night. *Yorktown's* lone night fighter had failed to prevent the torpedoing of the *Intrepid* but had kept Pappy Harshman's flight deck crews up most of the night respotting the deck. Now, in the predawn of February 19, two snoopers approached from the direction of Truk. One of them dropped a fish which missed a destroyer, only to be splashed by ack ack from the screen. The second dropped six bombs—all duds—near a cruiser and escaped after being chased 90 miles by an *Enterprise* night fighter. CIC boss Charlie Ridgway lamented, "It was a sad blow that he did not shoot the Jap down as Mitscher is the more strongly against using Night VF now."

Lieutenant Charlie Ridgway directs fighters in CIC (Combat Information Center). This photo was actually taken on the *Hornet*, where Ridgway had joined Admiral Clark's staff. Courtesy of Charles D. Ridgway III

After sun-up Mitscher passed the word from the *Yorktown*, "February 22 is Washington's Birthday and I cannot tell a lie. On that date we strike Saipan." In addition to a Betty bomber base and fighter training field there, intelligence revealed that an enemy carrier would deliver planes to Saipan on the morning of the attack.

Admiral Spruance returned to Majuro, leaving Mitscher in command of two task groups for the mission. Monty Montgomery led TG 58.2—*Yorktown, Essex* and *Belleau Wood*. In the afternoon Mitscher designated Alex Wilding as fighter director for the entire force—"final word rests with me, a helluva responsibility, but I'm going on the axiom of shoot first and ask questions later." But a distant bogey didn't even bother old Pete as the carriers charged northward. "The plane that had been snooping us this afternoon is lost," he announced to the ships that evening, "He is asking for homing [from Wake]. Happy days!"

Turning west at high speed on the 20th, the force went undetected until late the next day when Wilding vectored *Essex's* CAP toward a fleeing snooper. "I chased him with fighters but couldn't catch him; he'd duck in heavy clouds and hide, ceiling 1000 feet. Finally, an SBD [flown by *Yorktown's* C.F. Avery] caught him coming out of a cloud and chased him 90 miles, a Betty, killed his rear gunner, but couldn't down the Betty. At 1900 he radioed our position to Tokyo."

The crew was watching a Hopalong Cassidy Western when a message from Mitscher interrupted at 1937: "Our position has been reported: Target alerted. Stand by for a fight to the finish."

Wilding: "Everyone is ordered to sleep by their guns tonight. We are sort of caught in a trap. Truk is 500 miles southeast of us. Chichi Jima 500 miles north of us, Marcus and Wake behind us, and Japan in front of us. The only answer is to fight our way out. I feel as though tomorrow will really be a day when I'll need all the prayers from home. I don't feel so secure this time, maybe it's because our force is only half the size that hit Truk. We have only 3 big carriers. By tomorrow night we'll know the answer to this war."

The first bogeys from the Marianas registered on the radars after dark at 2116, making single-plane runs as usual, and the screen promptly shot down two. Captain Jennings had ACIO Jim Sutton broadcast all the action over the loudspeaker to keep all hands informed, while everyone "who could leave stations were on deck somewhere to see the show," said John Gray, "and it was some show!"

Four groups of Bettys filled the scopes an hour before midnight, and, noted Gray, every time one "would get within six miles the ships would open fire, mostly radar controlled; of course the targets could never be sighted. As the Admiral tried to keep the force turned away from the nearest attack, most of the firing was astern.

"The ships were just great dark things in the night, illuminated only by starlight and the flash of their own guns. At times *Essex* could be discerned as a great hulk a shade darker than the horizon, but the rest of the force could not even be seen, only

Amidst parked Hellcats in the after hangar bay ordnancemen service 1000-pound bombs while off-duty sailors watch a movie.

felt. At least some 3000 men on the *Yorktown* could sense them there, and the radar plot officers and men straining over the plotting tables could 'see' them there. . . .

"In radar plot the battle lights reflected in sweat the strain of officers as they traced the paths of the Emperor's henchmen as they maneuvered for attack outside gun range. The fresco of radio speakers, transmitters, receivers, intercommunications boxes and phones, myriads of indicator lights and signals, headphones and microphones with coil after coil of wire snaking around underfoot made the place seem a temple of chaos.

"Far from it! Outside of secondary conn we could hear the talkers relaying radar plot's information on bearing and distances of enemy planes to the fire directors of the quadruple 40mm mounts.

"'Raid at 180 degrees—20 miles closing.'

"'Roger.'

"'Now at 180-17, coming in.'

"'Raid at 175-15, still closing.'

"'175-10, start your motors.' This to the gun captain of the quadruple mount to start the electric motors that train the guns. The motors would hum, making it necessary to strain to hear the talkers' directions. Then suddenly a tracer would dive for the sky from one of the screaming ships astern.

"One, then a few scattered ones feeling out the range, then a can would open up with all its guns, another can and another until the sky astern was a filigree of pink-gold tracer. And then one of the AA cruisers would open up! A sight like nothing anyone ever saw before! Just as if her magazines had blown up! The sky would volcano a mountain of fire covering the cruiser, and seconds later the shells would burst in the air with huge 1/2 second oranges.

"By this time the fire control would have the target well in range, and that stern half of the screen would open up with everything down to the 20mm. Then would come suddenly a huge, ugly, dirty red torch to fall what seemed a few feet to the water where the gasoline of the Jap bomber would go up in flame and black smoke, making a setting sun on the surface of the sea, marking for a quarter hour or so the grave of another six of the Emperor's 'heaven sent' sons.

"During this action, the carriers themselves, the nests which must be protected to launch our attack at dawn, never fired. They would have if the Bettys had ever penetrated beyond the screen, but they never did. Fourteen went down trying, and more are thought to have made their final hop that

night." For four hours the ship maneuvered smartly to avoid the Bettys, all hands topside cheering wildly as each bogey fell meteorlike out of the sky in full view.

Jim Bryan: "I saw sixteen Jap planes burst into flame and crash in the water in the vicinity of our ship. . . . At one time during the night when things were hottest, we had three Bettys burning on the water on both sides and astern of us. Not over 1000 yards away. The new battleships, especially *South Dakota,* did a marvelous job with their AA guns. However, why the Japs didn't hit any of the ships is beyond me."

The last attackers were shot down minutes after 0300 on February 22, leaving precious little time for sleep. The enemy didn't help either, for at 0530 another attack, recorded Charlie Ridgway, "woke us up after a 2 hour nap—drugged slumber that— proved to be 5 planes coming up from the southwest in perfect scouting line. One passed too close to the screen for our trigger happy boys, and they let loose with all and everything.

"Immediately all the others discontinued their steady course and commenced circling. Peculiarly enough only one pressed home an attack or two, retiring each time he was fired on. Apparently this is the prelude to a more concerted attack at dawn." Sunrise was due at 0834.

Air officer Hank Dozier called the pilots to their planes in the midst of the action but held them. Bryan: "We were afraid to start the engines for fear of lighting the ship up due to the exhaust. Everyone from Admiral Mitscher on down was plenty anxious about loading the bombs and having the loaded planes sitting on deck while Jap planes were circling and crashing all around the force."

Mitscher decided to play his ace, and at 0710, just as the bogeys started to open their distance from the force, he had two night fighters catapulted from the *Yorktown* in hopes of chasing away the interlopers long enough to get off the regular launch. While Russ Reiserer circled and attempted to find the Japs on his radar, VF-5 started its engines. But when a bogey closed in, the engines were cut. Ridgway: "The Jap was coming in for his attack so Russ was forced to retire before he could get close enough to fire. The Jap continued to close until he was within gun range." Whereupon the screen drove it away.

The 12 fighters for the sweep restarted their motors. At 0813, just as the screen was shooting at a fresh Betty, the *Yorktown* began sending off the sweep. The bombing strike—12 VF, 12 VB, 9

VT—lined up ready to follow.

With the coming of dawn, wrote Wilding, "we could see the torpedo planes coming at us skimming over the water." He and Ridgway tried manfully to vector the eight *Belleau Wood* fighters on CAP to the many contacts north and south. Ridgway: "What between hysterical demands from the Chief of Staff [Captain Hedding] and the Operations Officer [Commander Don Griffin] that we get fighters on 'those Japs to the south of us' and efforts on our part to hit the raid at 280 degrees little constructive resulted.

"We did not have enough fighters on Combat Air Patrol, and no amount of effort seemed to avail getting more launched. Meanwhile also our strike planes, with pilots ready, sat on the deck awaiting a chance to get free of the maelstrom."

Dick Upson's strike planes managed to clear the deck just as a flood of bogeys appeared over the screen—Bettys, Val dive bombers, and bomb-laden Nick and Tony fighters. George Wille stepped out of his radio shack to a nearby gun gallery just in time to see a Betty "get the treatment. By this time, the sunrise was in all its glory, and on the western

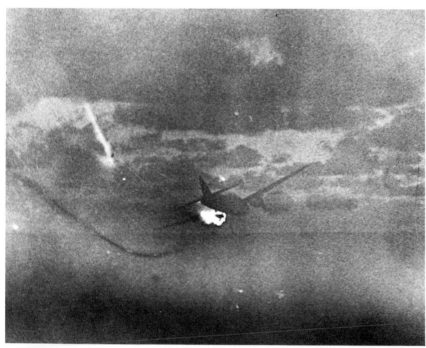

A Betty torpedo bomber is knocked down by ship's fire on the morning of February 22, 1944 as Task Force 58 approaches the Marianas. Seen from the *Yorktown*. Courtesy of Oliver Jensen

horizon a twin-engine plane was cruising very low on the water. He mosied around out there for quite awhile and flew around until he was about northeast of us and then headed in.'' Soon after the screen and heavy ships took him under fire, ''he headed for the water, streaming smoke. He hit with a nice 'phoom' with much flame.''

Ridgway: ''This will remain as one of the most spectacular sights of the war. Two Bettys loomed out of a rose colored cloud, black and lumbering in the early morning light. Then suddenly on them in a flash were 3 specks—our fighters. One fighter made a prolonged firing run on the nearest Betty, then turned to join his comrades on the second. The first, left to itself, dove leisurely towards the water, pulled up as if in preparation for a low torpedo run, then crashed into the sea in a billowing froth of smoke and flame.

''Meanwhile the fighters—all three—were making darting, stabbing passes at the second Betty which wallowed onward in an attempt to get into position for a torpedo run from our port quarter. Ages seemed to pass, then the Betty went into a slow left bank with one engine smoking. He never recovered, crashing as his brother, in the same awesome gush of flame and grey smoke.

''Three black columns of smoke were now silhouetted against the sun's early rays. However, after a sleepless and nerve-wracking night, profound fatigue dulled the brilliance of the scene.''

As quiet finally enveloped the formation and Upson led his orbiting flight off to hit Saipan, 119 miles to the west, 16 VF, 17 VB and 10 VT were brought up from the hangar and spotted aft for another hasty launch as the second strike.

John Gray: ''Just as we had strapped ourselves in the cockpits, started engines, and were waiting to take off, here came a Betty—low on the water, as fast as she could make it, headed right for the *Belleau Wood*. Everything in the force opened up, and in a few seconds—that familiar dirty red flower of flame as she hit. And here came another! The same fate. And another from the bow—same end. And then one that appeared to be flying almost *under* water!

''I have never seen a plane fly that low! Actually about four feet off the water—straight at us. She got past the screen, zig-zagging a bit, but coming straight on, the hundreds of guns having no more effect than streams of water played on a gasoline fire. She turned just before she got to the *Belleau Wood*, dropped her fish, and headed straight for that ship.

''It seemed impossible that anything could survive that hail of searing steel and flame, but still she came! Until just before it seemed she must crash the ship, she feathered a flame, pulled up over the *Belleau Wood's* bow and crashed in a shower of exploding gasoline between us and them. There was an instant of silence when the guns eased, as dead as the crew of the Jap bomber, then a shout of triumph exploded the tense, pent-up emotions of the crews of each ship.

''That exultation didn't last long, however, for at that moment a bomb exploded just off the stern of the *Essex,* dropped by a dive bomber which had come down on us unseen and unchallenged. Every eye in the thousands in the force had been turned on the drama being enacted on the surface and ten feet above it, and no one had seen the dive bomber coming. Fortunately he missed, but he also got away.

''Immediately every eye was turned up and every neck craned against high attack, and sure enough, here came a twin-engine bomber like a hellion right for our stern where the attack group was waiting, engines turning over, completely at the mercy of whatever dropped from the skies. A few incendiary bullets spraying that flight deck could cause a mass cremation such as we had not yet inflicted on the Japs in all our attacks on them.

''A bomb would have been even worse—45-50 planes jampacked in a space 100 feet by 400 feet all full of gas and bombs and crews! Nobody I ever saw wanted to be cremated! Not that is, until he had been good and respectably dead for the accepted amenities to have been performed.

''This was just too damn good a chance to have it happen all at once—and in what order wouldn't matter—the effect would be the same. The same thought must have occurred to everybody at the same time, for the pilots of Air Group Five, Fearless Fighting Men of the Navy, collectively and individually shrank behind their armor plate to the size of a colony of midgets.''

Like many of the enemy planes this morning, this one dived out of the sun, making it hard to identify. It was a Tony fighter or was it a Val bomber? Diving through a hole in the clouds at 3500 feet, Tony was accompanied by a Nick fighter, both astern for 5000 yards, the Tony releasing its small bomb and passing off the port beam. The bomb fell across the ship and hit the water just 150 yards ahead and 100 yards off the starboard bow, followed closely by the plane itself, splashed at 1500 yards. The Nick, now strafing the stern, veered off and escaped into

A Betty goes in ahead of the *Yorktown*, the victim of her guns. Seen from the *Essex*, astern of the *York*.

the clouds.

George Wille in the radio shack "didn't see any of this, but the whole ship reverberated, rattled and shook from the jarring crashes of the main batteries, the sharp barks of the 40's and chattering of the 20's as hundreds of projectiles were laid at the elusive target." To be exact, 14 rounds of 5-inch, 702 of 40mm and 5,046 of 20mm! It had been the *Yorktown's* first encounter with dive bombing planes.

The screen splashed a few more snoopers until the attack dissipated at 0945. Admiral Mitscher ordered the sweating pilots of the second strike to stand down to await the results of the first, and the flagship remained buttoned up so tightly that the midday meal was scratched in favor of horsecock and gedunk—sandwiches and ice cream.

Dick Upson needed Blip Searles' radar to guide the first strike through heavy rain squalls beyond Saipan to a Jap carrier reported damaged by a sub. The planes found only the stern afloat of what in fact was only a large cargo ship; they bombed and strafed it and several small boats. "Those Hellcats," approved Roger Van Buren when three of them blew up a boat, "really have the original sting of death when they beat out their tunes on those six 50's."

Fighting 5 remembered Smokey Stover, Herb Gill and their other lost buddies when they sighted what Van described as "several large rafts that held numerous survivors. The fighters worked them over with their remaining ammo. It was a pleasure to see those Japs jumping into the water. I would imagine that about half of them never got back to the rafts after we left."

Other planes dropped through the rain to sock Saipan and Tinian and were pleasantly surprised to find dozens of Jap planes parked wing-to-wing at both places. Woody McVay brought his division over Saipan, Jim Cole flying wing, with Izzy Jim Pickard leading Art Davis in the second section.

Pickard: "Davis and I went in to strafe the field,

while Mac and Cole came in later to strafe the seaplane base. Just before strafing I saw 2 Zeros in a hole over the field about 1500 ft. above Davis and I. In order to stay behind them we climbed through some thin clouds. Davis was never seen again. Later a man in a life jacket was spotted just off shore who might have been Davis. If so he was probably taken prisoner. "I circled above the clouds hunting for him and then went down under them but could not locate him. I then joined on another team and strafed four twin-engined bombers and burned two of them. AA fire was light and no Zeros were seen. One parachute came by me and hit on the island."

McVay went down to 300 feet in the murk to strafe the seaplanes, and he too was never seen again. Some pilots reported seeing a second parachute and swimmer and postulated that McVay and Davis had collided inside a cloud. The fighters blew up a torpedo boat, and the bombers claimed two marus, but the VF-5 pilots headed for home with spirits equal to the overcast sky. None felt more miserable than Jim Pickard. "This is the worst day of my life. McVay and Davis, my team leader and wingman, both gone on one hop. I guess it's just luck or fate. It's a hell of a life. I'd almost like to quit flying."

As in the case of Stover, neither man was ever heard of again, and the lifeguard sub could not be raised on the radio.

Bombers and fighters burned shipping and buildings, but as they pulled out they noted many still-undamaged parked planes. Admiral Mitscher therefore ordered another strike to be led by Stebbins. In midafternoon these planes ravaged the airfields at Saipan, Tinian and Guam. A few airborne Zeros appeared, but their flying merely revealed the poor quality of the pilots, who were easily eliminated by the F6s.

Jim Campbell saw four Zeros "go down in flames" before he could get to them, and then he headed down, "for parked on the runway at Tinian were over 70 planes, lined up as if for inspection.

It seemed as if the air was full of Hellcats boring in from every angle at the juicy targets on the ground and we had a field day. I don't know how many runs I made but I got my share of the planes, which were twin-engined bombers. We really hit them a lick and our bombers were very effective also."

Steb and Dick Rubner of VT-5 brought back hundreds of excellent photos needed for the eventual invasion of the Marianas, after which Task Force 58 turned eastward for Majuro.

"We bombed the hell out of Saipan and Tinian," concluded an amazed Alex Wilding, whose fears were finally starting to subside, "Completely wrecked the two places." The two task groups claimed 168 Jap planes destroyed against six of their own; Air Group Five had demolished 34 of these on the ground and three Zeros in the air. "We were lucky—not a single ship hit—seems unbelievable."

After debriefing, the pilots collapsed in their bunks. In John Gray's words, "The expenditure of nervous energy on a raid like that is terrific, and you don't realize it until it is over. Then you get that by now familiar feeling—that of a tired, sandy wet bathing suit kicked into the bathroom corner."

"Somehow, Fighting Five has a jinx," concluded Charlie Ridgway. "One at least of its crack pilots is lost on every raid. Towns and Morgan at Marcus; Crow and Boies at Wake—sub picked up Tim Tyler; Johnny Furstenberg at Mille; Herb Gill and Si Satterfield at Kwajalein December 4th; Smokey at Truk; and McVay and Davis at Saipan."

Jinx or not, the fliers from the *Yorktown* had made history. The achievement of Task Force 58 at Truk and the Marianas had changed the whole complexion of the Pacific war by exposing the fundamental weakness of Japanese defenses in the Central Pacific. Allied strategists now decided that an invasion of once-mighty Truk was unnecessary. Like Rabaul and most of the Marshalls, it too would be allowed to wither and die on the vine.

Feb 16, 17 TRUK
Feb. 22 SAIPAN

Chapter VI

Just One More Raid

Oh, it's one more operation,
tho' the Air Group grows impatient,
And the *Yorktown* in elation awaits the President's
citation;
But before this thing is over, let it once for all be
said,
The mighty *Yorktown* will fight on, till all the Air
Group's dead.
—Anonymous

Air Group Five wanted only one thing—to go home, and medals be damned. Commander Stebbins again recommended it in his action report of the Marianas raid, strongly endorsed by Captain Jennings: "They should be relieved by another air group unless there is a definite 'Rose Bowl' operation in the immediate offing."

Indeed there was. To keep pace with the Central Pacific drive toward the Philippines and China, General Douglas MacArthur was pushing along the north coast of New Guinea from the Southwest Pacific. He needed the carriers to cover his seaward flank by eliminating enemy air strength from that quarter and to support his landings at Hollandia, New Guinea in April 1944.

Carriers already on hand would therefore raid more enemy island airfields, support the assault, then return to Majuro and head south to operate out of Espiritu Santo in the New Hebrides. The pilots of Air Group Five knew that Air Group One was waiting back in Hawaii to relieve them, but the *Yorktown* was not scheduled to return there until the completion of this " 'Rose Bowl' operation."

This word was received soon after the *York* reached Majuro on February 26, 1944—along with the news that the air groups on the *Essex* and *Bunker Hill* were going home immediately. "The air group is pissed off about it," wrote a critical Alex Wilding on March 1. "These boys don't want to have another thing to do with the Navy; they're all ready to turn in their wings."

"I hate to put this in writing but our aviators are not pressing home their attack. They're playing safe and pulling out of their dives too high to get hits—they're afraid to come down and release because they want to be sure to get home. Consequently we get damn few hits. For the number of bombers and bombs going in over a target we're not getting 40% of the damage and results that we should. The way they feel now they won't go near a target.

"It is a rotten deal but at the same time they're getting damn close to being classified as Yellow. That's not our air group alone but also the air groups from other carriers. . . .

"This war is not being fought—it's being stumbled through to Victory—but someday it's going to cost the fleet plenty. Luck will not always save us as it did on our first attack on Kwajalein and Saipan and Tinian. We have been so lucky to date. I don't want to be around when that luck runs out.

"I wish I could tell the American public the truth of what is going on out here. Those decrepid, ignorant, moth-eaten old admirals have a brain that's been undermined by termites and a complete lack of background. The Navy needs a young man with some guts and an aggressive spirit."

Whereupon Wilding went ashore at Majuro with "a boatload of officers, many cases of beer, Scotch, bourbon, Rum, Ice, 4 bartenders—with but one purpose, get tight as hell. Most succeeded.

"Hamm, *Life* photographer, was 'Life Goes to a Party' in reverse. Got so tight he went in circles, tried to piss, fell flat on his back, continued to piss just spraying himself. Fell in the drink getting aboard [the launch] with all his cameras. From the island back to the ship we had to keep fishing them out of the drink as fast as they would fall overboard. It accomplished its purpose—to give everyone a let down and some recreation."

The heat and homesickness accentuated the

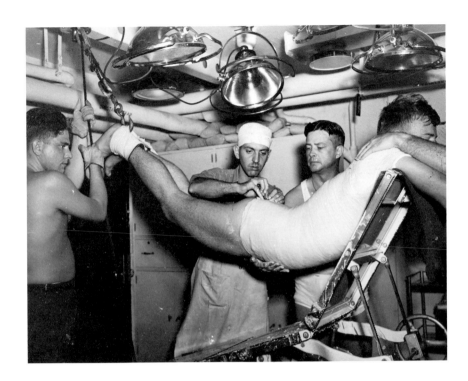

Doc Gard works in the heat—in his underwear—while corpsmen Wildermuth and Turner assist him in putting a hypertension cast on a sailor who had fallen asleep and fallen off his turret to fracture his lumbar vertebrae. He was sent ashore. *Yorktown's* Sick Bay could do just about anything. Courtesy of Raymond F. Gard

aggravation. "This is the first time," wrote Dr. Gard, "I've felt so completely isolated and out of touch with what is going on. No mail—no papers—nothing to let me know what goes on." That was the crux of the problem—no mail after just one batch. After seeing a seven-year-old movie which had snow in it, Gard complained to his diary, "I'm getting tired of sweating 24 hours each day."

At least good news came for two VF-5 pilots, recorded John Gray: "Two of the boys, Harry Hill and Duncan, became fathers this last trip! Life does go on—we lost two pilots and came back to find that babies have been born to two others. Lose two—gain two. It's really hardly like gaining two *pilots* for those two lost, but it all adds up in Nature's book anyway. And then, the boys may not be killed at that—only prisoners. I hope so, even if I would certainly almost as soon be dead as a Jap prisoner of war for the duration."

The liberty parties ashore gave the crew another chance to observe Micronesians. Wilding: "When the Japs left here they took all the native men and women from 17 to 35. The men were put in labor battalions and the women in whore houses on other islands for Jap soldiers. Navy gave the king and queen a party ashore, greatly pleasing the natives."

At least the pilots and crew were learning to appreciate their new skipper, Al Jennings, who now gave his first formal address. "In Pearl, on the coast and in Washington before reporting on board, I heard that the Lucky Y was the best, and what I have seen since taking over is proof enough that

she is still out in front. . . . The ship which attains the highest level of performance sets the standard for the others, and the role of the carrier in this war is so important that the length of the war can very well depend upon the performance of the pacesetters. We intend to keep the *Yorktown* out in front and make her the most successful and famous empire wrecker of them all."

The crew had already discovered, in the words of Chaplain Alexander, "that Captain Jennings was all-the-way-up, and all-the-way-down, and all-the-way-across different from his predecessor, and that, with one or two exceptions, any resemblance between the two was coincidental." Indeed, with the coming of Jennings, all the tension that Jocko Clark had generated disappeared.

Under Jennings, the crew took a fling at journalism by printing a ship's newspaper, or rather an irregular periodical to be issued whenever conditions allowed the time for it. Entitled SEA-V-TEN, it contained stories about the ship, anecdotes and much hokum. The enlisted men did most of the work on the eight-page effort, though under the censoring eye of the exec, Commander Briggs.

The *Yorktown* received a new admiral at Majuro. Pete Mitscher shifted his flag to the newly-repaired *Lexington* and assigned task group commander Cy Ginder to the *York*. Unfortunately, Ginder from the start displayed little knack for command. Trying to endear himself to the men, he referred to his ships as the "Tally Acker Squadron" and issued pronouncements under the cornball title of "Tally Ho

Volume I   No. 1   **U. S. S. YORKTOWN**   **March 15, 1944**

A Furlow rendition of the exec, Cam Briggs. Courtesy of Jesse Rodriguez

Ack Ack." The crew would wince whenever these were read over the loudspeaker.

The ship weighed anchor on March 8 to the tune of "Tally Ho Ack Ack Number 31" which announced the South Pacific destination—"old hunting grounds for many of us, virgin territory for others, but the virgins are scarce." "Good Lord!" groaned Alex Wilding in his diary, "Once a day from now on—why, oh why, oh why!"

After a fierce equatorial storm on the 9th, the force entered the equatorial doldrums and an indescribably beautiful sea and sky; at sundown the captain invited all hands who could be spared to come topside to enjoy it. Dr. Gard took a stab at explaining the glassy scenery. "All the ships in sight are riding atop their reflections. The great cumulus clouds are mirrored in the water. One cannot see an horizon. We are as if suspended within a globe. Then the sun goes down and such a display of color I shall never see again. It would have faulted even Turner."

The lazy sunbathing and volleyball games had no appeal for Lieutenant Joe Tucker, who dropped in on Air Plot to hear the latest scuttlebutt about where the next operation would be. He had a habit of reading all the dispatches there, which he was not supposed to do, and then go below and make bets with the scuttlebutters.

Coop Bright, irritated at this, made a decision: "We gonna fix Tucker." Skinhead rigged up a phony dispatch: "CANCEL MOVE SOUTH. REARM AT SEA FOR OPERATION SUNSET. STRIKING TRUK ISLAND. YORKTOWN, BELLEAU WOOD," etc.

Presently, Tucker ambled up to Air Plot, "Any new dope?"

"Not much. Just some stuff about the next operation."

Joe eagerly read it, went below and placed his bets with all takers. He nearly lost his shirt!

Bright nearly did not have the last laugh, for a couple of days later a real dispatch did arrive, ordering a change in plan to strike another target, though not Truk. Bright and his cohorts in Air Plot figured they had caused the dispatch to occur! But the next day this order was cancelled.

The *Yorktown* joined many units of the fleet at steamy Espiritu Santo harbor on March 13 and received several new personnel. A big-framed, big-voiced Commander William E. Moring reported as the new supply officer, replacing the injured Patten. Tall, handsome Commander Arthur Stephen "Ben" Born, a football star at Navy, '27, relieved his classmate Hank Dozier as air officer. Commander Jim Morrison turned over the Communications Department to his assistant, Jim Tippey; Dr. John T. Smith relieved Dr. Young in Medical; and Ed Owen handed over command of Fighting 5 to Lieutenant Bob Jones.

Among the transfers off the ship, the most awkward was that of air officer Hank Dozier. "Hilarious Henry" had had hardly a friend on

Ogling the actresses of the Ray Milland USO company, Admiral Ginder (seated right) and his staff prepare to host luncheon in the flag mess.

board, and virtually everyone avoided saying good-bye to him. His final demise would be tragic. Assigned to an admiral's staff on another carrier during the autumn. Dozier would disappear one dark night without a trace. He either fell overboard or was pushed.

Yorktown's visual record continued as cameraman Dwight Long returned to Hollywood to complete his documentary movie about the ship, and a combat artist, Lieutenant William F. Draper, reported aboard. Not only a damned good painter, he fell in with the Torpedo 5 crowd and turned out to be an accomplished piano player and right good drinker whom Weatherguesser Vonk nicknamed "Draper the Raper."

Liberty ashore at Espiritu was enhanced by two USO shows led by actors Ray Milland and Allen Jenkins which included three starlets and several gal hoofers. The actresses were brought out to the *Yorktown,* where Admiral Ginder monopolized them. For a party at San Juan Hill, the Army officers club, Chaplain Alexander could round up only six Army nurses plus the USO dancers, all of whom were worn ragged on the dance floor by the scores of fliers and ship's officers. Pilot Dick Newhafer did better on a visit to a hospital ship, dancing on deck with a Navy nurse under a tropical moon.

Fresh movies from home raised morale, except those starring teenage heartthrob Frank Sinatra. Dr. Gard teased his bobbysoxer daughter in a letter, "Ginny, we had one of Sinatra's pictures on the ship. You should have heard these 2500 sailor boys give him the Bronx cheers. They weren't in the mood for such saccharine croonings and were not restrained in their comments by the presence of any of the gentler sex. They practically took the picture to pieces and heaved it over the side. If that boy expects a future he had better get into some sort of a uniform."

Booze was on the minds of most officers, several of whom swapped *Yorktown* steaks and eggs with the Army doctors and nurses for the only available whiskey, a vile spirit known as "Australian death." Photo interpreter Bob Eaton "done found the mother lode," he told Stebbins, when, after plying an Army general with six big fillets, he arranged to clean out a warehouse of no fewer than 138 cases of Australian death! He and a torpecker pilot "borrowed" three Army trucks by hot-wiring them to move the hooch to the beach. With two fifths they bribed a coxswain to take it out to the ship in his barge and with two more bribed a bosun to lower a cargo net during movies. Then he sold it to the

thirsty pilots on board. Eaton's reputation as a "bootlegger" spread throughout the fleet!

The respite finally ended on March 23 when the *York* sortied from Espiritu to participate in another raid—the neutralization of Jap air forces on the Palau Islands of the western Carolines prior to MacArthur's invasion at Hollandia. "This meant practically nothing to us" pilots, noted Roger Van Buren, "as we had never heard of them before. It wasn't long before we all had the dope on these places. It turned out that Palau was only 500 miles from the Philippines. Naturally that put a little excitement in the air." "Another humdinger" in Charlie Ridgway's view.

On the morning of the 27th, Mitscher—just promoted to vice admiral—convened a planning conference of key staff officers on board the *Lexington.* Dick Rubner carried Commander Ken Averill, Admiral Ginder's chief of staff, to it in his TBF. After the meeting, the *Lex* catapulted Rubner's Avenger, which suddenly lost air speed and plunged into the water. The impact stunned Rubner and Averill, but the pilot and his crewman were able to struggle free. Averill just sat there with a glazed expression and went down with the plane—a tragic mishap.

Mitscher sent over Captain Hedding as temporary chief of staff to Ginder, who now directed a reorganized TG 58.3 of the *York* and *Lex,* light carriers *Princeton* and *Langley,* four battleships, five cruisers and 16 cans. Admirals Montgomery and Reeves had seven flattops between them, and familiar verbal tirades over the radio announced the presence of another rear admiral. Jocko Clark was riding as an observer aboard the new *Hornet.* – CV/12

In the midst of another muggy, still day with a mirrorlike sea, John Gray boasted how Task Force 58 was proceeding "westward between Truk and Rabaul right into the lion's mouth, or rat's mouth as you choose. Such a short time ago Truk and Rabaul were names feared and respected by units of the U.S. Fleet. Now we openly thumb our noses!! And what a fleet! From the flight deck I could count 85 warships at one time! And at that, I couldn't quite see them all.

"This is truly the pride of the U.S. Fleet and could take on *anything* that the Japs could send against us, including their whole Imperial Fleet! And they are all *fighting* ships—not an auxiliary, not one antique, not one that can't steam at 30 knots and pull her own weight in a knock-down, drag-out fight! So—let the Japs come! If they send out their fleet, so much the better—it will do more than any other single blow to shorten the war and pave the road to Tokyo.

The high-speed run-in commenced this day, the 28th, and at noon—to use George Wille's understatement—the task force "was visited by several emissaries of the opposition." CAP fighters from other carriers shot down no fewer than eleven snoopers, one only 25 miles from the *York*, but one got away. Remarked Admiral Ginder to *Newsweek* correspondent William Hipple, "They know we are coming. Now we'll see what they do about it."

Whereupon he issued Tally Ho Ack Ack No. 41: "TOMORROW IS THE DAY . . . . OUR FIGHTER PILOTS ARE SNORTIN LIKE BULLS IN A PEN. THEY ARE READY—NO FOOLIN—WITH BLOOD IN THEIR EYES, TO POUNCE UPON, JUMP UPON NIPPON'S LITTLE MEN."

As the day ended, the gunners prepared for the night attacks, and an idle Coop Bright decided to engage in a little friendly grabass with Marine Major Jeff Overstreet—whom he called "Overshoe"—a quiet Mississippian in charge of the Marine batteries at Air Defense Forward. Skinhead knew his Civil War: "The greatest thing that ever came out of the South was The Free State of Jones. Did you ever hear of Newt Knight? There was a good old man. He stood up against those damn rebels down there and declared The Free State of Jones in Mississippi. They had to go in there and try to capture him, but they couldn't. He stayed with Old Glory!" (Knight in fact had been nothing more than a Confederate deserter.)

"Now just a minute here," drawled Overshoe. "You're talkin' about something I know something about!"

Soon the two men were refighting the last war between gentlemen in earnest—until George Earnshaw bellowed out from his post nearby, "Attack coming in on the starboard beam!"

Bright: "Now you take Vicksburg."

Overshoe: "Let me tell you about Vicksburg!"

Nothing was being relayed to the Marine gunners, whereupon Earnshaw fired a blast at the Blue and the Gray: "Alright, goddamn both of you, the next time you get fightin' that Civil War, get *the hell* out of here and fight *this* war! Planes comin' in!"

Overshoe: "Every time I get with him I get in trouble."

Earnshaw: "Put those damned phones on and start talking to those batteries. To hell with him."

A nearly first quarter moon hung high in the western sky after sundown as six bogeys appeared to the southeast at 28 miles on *Yorktown's* radars. The ships in the screen let loose and within five minutes took under fire an unseen bogey making a low torpedo run on the starboard beam. *Newsweek's* Hipple observed that "from the firing you could tell just about where it was. Still it moved nearer through that hail of fire. Then there was a flash of brilliant white over the water . . . the plane . . . smearing flames over a large patch.

" 'Yowee!' bellowed a bluejacket. 'One down and more to come. That's only the beginning, folks, only the beginning.' "

From the opposite side of the ship a second bomber came on to drop a flare. As it pressed its attack toward the stern, recorded Gray, "the entire screen opened up with one of the most thrilling displays of night fireworks I have ever seen! The climax was a huge explosion in mid-air as what appeared to be a 40mm incendiary shell hit the plane's gas tanks, and the whole burning mass fell inside the screen just a few hundred yards off our port quarter."

The firing continued as several more snoopers closed the force, but none closer than 30 miles to the *Yorktown*. It was all over—unbelievably—after only two short hours.

John Gray decided to "turn in and sweat that pre-attack sweat that has a fear-smell all its own. Maybe it isn't exactly fear, but at least the nervous sweat that accompanies the highly keyed-up nervous tension of everyone who realizes that tomorrow he faces the possibility of death and hopes he can stare it down.

"Animals can smell fear, they say, and I believe it, because the personal odor of healthy perspiration from physical work does not even smell the same to my obtuse nostrils as the heavy rancid odor of my own flying suit after a flight in the air. Any man who says he isn't afraid either is a liar or a fool, and I am neither, but I take a kind of pride in realizing that I am afraid to start with, and overcome it to perform with credit to myself and my service. It's a solid, good feeling."

King Day, March 30, 1944, began with three night fighters being catapulted at 0501 as CAP. The ship's new air officer, Commander Ben Born, had scheduled a predawn fighter sweep to clear the air of Zeros and six strikes throughout the day.

Because of the suspected presence of Japanese heavy ships at Palau, the torpedo planes were armed with torpedoes for the first time in VT-5's combat career. The TBF pilots figured this would be their last operation, so they hoped to score some hits with these fish. Unfortunately, several of the torpedoes were discovered to be drained of their alcohol for drinking purposes and had to be refilled at the last minute. The culprit, an old chief torpedoman who had joined the ship at Espiritu, would be bounced off the ship when it returned to Majuro.

At 0615, due north of Palau, the *Yorktown* went to GQ, and war correspondent Hipple watched as 12 Hellcat pilots, "laughing and shoving, piled out of the room onto the flight deck." Led by the new fighter skipper, Bob Jones, the sweep took off in the dark and arrived over a clouded, rainy Palau at 0745, just before sunup. A quick look around revealed no Jap fleet—only a cruiser, a destroyer, some cargo ships and a few parked planes. But Zeros were airborne, so the fighters took them on.

Jones' division, including Pickard, Cole and Lew Cobb, scored quickly with a kill for each man except Pickard. As they strafed Bettys parked on the airfield, Pickard saw "a Betty and what I thought were two Jap dive bombers approaching the field very low with their wheels down for a landing.

"I took a head shot at the Betty, did a wingover and came back at it on its starboard quarter just as it reached the edge of the field. I fired and it went down in the area between the runways in a cloud of smoke. On the pull out I ran head on into one of the two Zeros, Cole having chased the other one out to sea.

"As he came in for another landing, I fired but only had ammunition remaining in one gun. I made two more head on attacks on him very low over the field without being able to hit him with my one gun. AA from the field was shooting at us both as we would cross over it at about 100 ft. He pulled up his wheels just after he had gone under me for the third time and whipped around on my tail.

"For the first time I was sure he was a Zero and not a Val as I had at first thought. We did a couple of tight turns with him gaining on me in the turns, but he did not shoot. I tried to evade him by twisting and turning. I didn't dare head out and run straight away because I thought sure he'd get me on a level shot. He was so close I could look over my shoulder and see the guns in his wings staring at me. We hedgehopped over the trees, and I screamed for somebody to please get him off my tail, but nobody was around. I decided to run for it as all my ammo was gone by this time. Boy, was I scared!

"I rolled out of the turn, and he crossed under my tail and pulled up on my wing. I gave it all the power she had, said a prayer, and headed for home

leaving that Jap behind like he was sitting still. He surely must have been out of ammunition as I was, but then I should never have played with him with only one gun that close to the ground."

"Smiling Hugh" Kelley noticed new Oscar fighters trying to lure the Hellcats into the heavy flak over Peleliu and chased one to within 100 feet, where he fired a burst which apparently killed the pilot and sent the plane spinning down crazily. While strafing low, J.J. Brosnahan nailed another just taking off, only to be hit by flak. As he pulled up to 1500 feet, Teddy Schofield close behind, Brosnahan's Hellcat burst into flames. "Bail out! Bail out!" yelled Teddy into this throat mike, but no response. Brosnahan stayed with his plane and went smoking into the sea, where the F6F seemed to break into a million pieces, spewing burning gas over the water.

Fighting 5's ten kills paved the way for Ed Stebbins and the first bombing strike. Steb ordered Dick Upson's 12 torpedo-bombers, 12 SBDs and 12 Hellcats to attack the Jap destroyer—its name was *Wakatake*—attempting to flee the anchorage. The fighters strafed, after which one or two dive bombers scored direct hits on the can, starting a fire on her stern and dramatically slowing her speed as she turned.

The torpeckers held the ace. Instead of lining up in a conventional torpedo run from one direction and "leading" the target by one-half to three ship lengths, Upson surrounded the *Wakatake* with his TBFs from 12 different positions. One by one, the "turkeys" swung off "in long, lazy circles" for their simultaneous attack, their hapless victim maneuvering frantically, its gunners blasting away at VT-5.

Roger Van Buren thought "the can looked helpless as we approached, and I was wondering just what was going on aboard her, and just what they were thinking. She didn't have a chance and everyone knew it. Our 12 plane net drew closer and closer. As I approached the dropping point, I realized I had a bad shot, so I didn't drop. Two other planes also kept their fish. The others dropped almost simultaneously."

Upson watched the fish splash together and converge on the *Wakatake*. He prayed to himself, "Just one hit—just one."

Joe Kristufek: "I was determined to make a perfect drop (since I expected it to be my last one) so I did everything according to 'the book.' My release was at 600' and I aimed just back of the bow. I had to fly directly over the ship with my bombbay doors open and really expected to get hit.

When I looked over the side, it seemed that all of the gunners were shooting at our torpedoes. After passing over the ship, I closed the bombbay doors and dove toward the water to pick up speed and be a smaller target.

"There was no explosion so I assumed that we had all missed."

Van Buren: "As there was no AA, I passed very close to the ship about 50 yds. I had lots of speed so I pulled up to get away from the other planes and also to observe the torpedo runs. It was absolutely breath taking. You could see the torpedo wakes headed straight for the doomed ship. The wakes looked like long fingers running through the deep, blue water. They all seemed to say 'you' as they pointed and continued to get closer. It seemed ages before they struck. I almost felt like getting down there and pushing them along; although the fish were running at 35 kts.

"It was all over in a second. Four fish seemed to be fighting it out to see which would strike first. There was no first. It was a dead heat with all four torpedoes exploding at once. What followed was the most awe filling sight I have ever seen. A red flame, the color of which I have never seen, extending from stem to stern, leaped into the air a thousand feet. Everything went at once, the 4 fish, the ship's boilers and her magazines. The black, grey smoke that shrouded the scene lasted about 15 seconds. As it cleared, the last remaining section of the can made its final plunge. No one had seen it sink except for this one piece. Everything had

taken place in the midst of that smoking, burning inferno.

"A second later another torpedo made its run over the boiling water. It exploded when it hit some wreckage. There was a huge geyser of water. Our fighters then began making strafing runs over the oil and wreckage covered water just to make sure there were no survivors. That wasn't necessary. Superman himself couldn't have escaped the destruction of that day.

"I couldn't take my eyes off that spot for some time. When I did look around, I saw the four remaining fish with their trailing wakes streaking through the water. One of them had a bad run. It was dancing crazily over the long swells like a lost jitterbug. The others just ran until they expended their propulsion power."

Van Buren, Frank Fondren and Bennie Benson still had their torpedoes and broke off from the others to attack a 5000-ton maru in the harbor, ignoring its one 3-inch gun popping away at them. Van, "determined to get a hit," had his radioman call out the ranges "all the way in. I had the plane at the correct speed and altitude. When we passed the dropping range of 1000 yds. I continued in just to make sure. I dropped at 700 yds. or less. I felt sure it was going to be a good run. Sure enough when I turned and watched the wake it was on a dead run. The other one was right beside mine, but a little behind. The third was a bad run, as it went shooting down the lagoon . . . .

"Again it seemed as though the fish would never

Five torpedoes find their marks—four on the ship, one on wreckage—in VT-5's perfectly executed attack from all sides to literally blow up the Japanese destroyer *Wakatake* west of Palau, March 30, 1944. The can has trailed oil up to the location of her demise. Three torpedo tracks are clearly visible in the water as two TBFs fly over. Courtesy of Joseph R. Kristufek

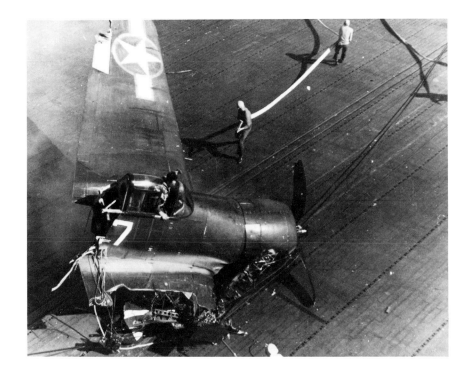

Ensign Bob Black comes back from Palau, his plane shot up with flak, March 30, 1944. In a spectacular crash landing, he comes aboard and splits his Hellcat into four pieces by ramming a 5-inch gun turret. But he walks away from it!

get to the ship, but I had no fear as I could see it was running dead on. I just sat waiting. When she hit it took the whole forecastle deck away including the gun and crew that was firing at us. A second later, the other torpedo ran right over the spot where the bow had been. It exploded a few 100 yds. on the other side of the ship when it hit a coral head.

"The ship settled rapidly, but not like the can. It never did sink, because the water was too shallow. It did go down until its decks were practically awash. I really felt good about this. My first fish and one ship to show for it. That's the reason I wanted to be a VT pilot. At last I had done what I wanted to do. It wasn't a combat ship, but nevertheless it was a ship and just one more ship the Japs will never use.

"We joined up and continued down to take a look at the rest of the island. Smoke was rising from 100 places. A huge oil fire was burning up in the hills. It was evidently their main fuel storage. The airfield and seaplane base were blasted. We could see some 25 ships now. Many were smoking."

John Gray's fighters caused much of the damage by strafing, with "Gooch" McCutchen blowing an ammunition ship sky-high while only trying to shoot out its bridge. When a Red Cross-painted "hospital ship" threw up AA fire in flagrant violation of international law, the fighters needed only five minutes to explode it too!

Returning to the *York,* Ensign Bob Black radioed that his brand-new F6F had had its hydraulics shot away by flak, so he couldn't operate his landing flaps. Told to crash aboard anyway, he skewed to the right. As he caught the wire, his tail hook pulled out, which sent the plane smashing against the Number Seven 5-inch gun mount and breaking up the F6F into four parts—tail assembly, one wing, trunk and the front section from the armor plate forward. The latter spun up the deck and came to a stop next to the island. The dazed Black, his scalp only slightly cut, sat there a moment, then climbed out from what Charlie Ridgway labeled the "most spectacular crash of the year." Ship's moviemen caught the whole thing on film.

On the second strike, Dan Harrington's bombers scored three direct hits on a large merchantman, which settled on the bottom, while planes from the other carriers obliterated the Jap aircraft parked on Peleliu. The destruction was so complete that Admiral Mitscher diverted *Yorktown's* third strike to look for possible Japanese fleet units escaping westward. All that the flight encountered was apparently "an enemy destroyer taking typical Japanese evasive action." Torpecker Tex Cooper scored a near-miss with his bomb before Sully O'Sullivan noticed the target to be a lifeguard sub, the *Tunny.*

The poor recognition resulted in sufficient damage to require the *Tunny* to cut short her war patrol, but not before she completed her lifesaving role, though the only pilot she rescued turned out to be a Jap! The *Yorktown* received welcome news from the sub *Gar,* its rescue being J.J. Brosnahan, who had gotten out of his burning Hellcat after all.

Literally surrounded by enemy island airfields, TF 58 began dealing with bogeys in late-afternoon. At dark, four Saipan-based Bettys picked out the *York*. Ridge Radney of VB-5 was among the spectators on deck: "The night sky was suddenly split by the red-hot shells from the AA batteries of our screen, and all observers thought the fun was about to begin. Why the possibility of being blown sky high in the middle of the night should be considered fun is somewhat hard to understand; nevertheless the boys seemed to enjoy the sight of the 40mm shells feeling for the incoming torpedo plane."

As one Betty got past the screen, the *Lexington* took her under fire, and the *York's* gunners got ready. George Wille watched from the signal bridge. "As the plane got close we could see the various lines of tracers intersecting, and it was in this way that we could determine the approximate position of the target. The plane came closer and all of a sudden every 20 and 40mm battery on the starboard side opened up, and what a noise and flashing of light resulted!

"The din was terrific and the glare from the streams of tracers was dazzling. The Jap passed right between the *Yorktown* and *Lexington* on a parallel course. He was lucky to get through. Had a momentary glimpse of the plane—just a blur in the night. He was close enough that the roar of his engines could be heard."

Remarkably, all four planes kept right on, surviving the AA, dropped nothing and escaped into the night. Ginder's task group had no more business, and the waters off Palau fell quiet an hour before midnight.

"ROUND TWO COMING UP!" Cam Briggs announced in the Plan of the Day for March 31. "Things really started off with a bang this morning" in the words of gunner Jesse Bradley when Ed Stebbins' 50-plane fighter sweep from four carriers ran into a swarm of Zeke, Hamp and Tony fighters near Peleliu. The Jap pilots behaved as if they were as new as their planes.

Gray: "They were bright and shiny, as though they had come right out of the factory, and we were over Palau a little over an hour chasing those bastards around. The hardest part of the fight was to beat some other Hellcat to getting a Zero. I'd beat on the cowl with my fists, shouting to myself, 'Let that guy alone! He's mine.'"

But John did well enough. He chased down five separate bandits, shooting down three for certain, one probably, and assisting in another kill. Dapper Nelson, Fred Bozard and "Whiskey Bill" Dunn got two apiece. Gray and Nelson were now aces. Untypically, several Jap pilots tried to escape by bailing out, only to be machine-gunned in their parachutes by the men of Fighting 5 who gave an eye-for-an-eye with the fanatical Jap.

The Japs played by no rule book, as Bill Dunn learned when he coasted into the drink with a severed oil line. He ditched so close to the lifeguard sub *Gar* that he was able to walk out onto his wing and into the sub's life raft without even getting wet. While his rescue was underway, recorded Alex Wilding, "Japs tried to shoot him up but our fighters saw the Jap and sent him down in flames and stood guard over the survivor until the sub got him."

Dunn joined J.J. Brosnahan and eventually six fliers from other carriers on the *Gar,* which radioed the task force: "Forming airedale club in forward battery. Everybody crowded but happy."

Among the very effective bombing of Palau's ships and facilities was Roger Van Buren's low attack over the crest of a ridge against a maru anchored close to the shore. Braving intense AA fire, he missed the crest by only 25 feet. "It was only a matter of 3 or 4 seconds after we cleared the island till I dropped my four 500 lb. bombs. I waited until I couldn't miss. As we pulled out we ran into another hail storm of tracers coming from the nearby seaplane base. The only hit was on the stinger gun. It blew the camera away and knocked the gun out of my radioman's hands. The bombs had 5 second delay fuses. We were well clear of the ship and jinking over the bay when my gunner yelled that we hit it. When we were well clear of all AA, I turned to see the ship settling to the bottom. All four bombs hit on the stern and just blew it away."

The exuberance of the returning pilots was not shared by the task group commander. Unfortunately, Admiral Ginder had developed a bad case of the jitters, far worse than even Baldy Pownall had experienced in the early battles. Suddenly, in the midst of air operations, he had cracked, gone completely to pieces, a quivering mass of nerves.

Captain Hedding stretched him out on the deck, applying cold compresses to his head and trying to console him, while uncomprehending enlisted men and junior officers looked on, thinking "Jesus Christ, this is the head man. What's going on?" No one ever said that war was easy, and the sudden, heavy responsibilities of combat command for an unseasoned admiral could not have been anticipated

Commander Briggs (center) chats with Captain Jennings, while the Tallyho Acker Admiral Cy Ginder sits pensively at dinner after the return from Palau, his brief combat career over. The "flowers" are made from carrots and turnips. Courtesy of Raymond F. Gard

until the shooting started. Cy Ginder was unfit to lead in battle and would have to be relieved.

At least the Palau operation was nearly over. Admiral Mitscher cancelled the last strike of the day and on the next used only a sweep and one strike to pound tiny, insignificant Woleai. No bogeys got closer than 30 miles during the withdrawal, and the task force re-entered Majuro lagoon on April 6 in the midst of a four-day howling rain. Rear Admiral Ginder was transferred, and the Tally Ho Ack Ack bulletin ceased. Neither he nor it would be missed.

As per General MacArthur's request, the airdromes at Palau had been silenced long enough for him to proceed with the Hollandia assault on the north coast of New Guinea, supported by Task Force 58. On the retirement, most *Yorktown*ers had chosen to forget this projected operation. Ridgway: "Speculation is rife as to whether the *Mighty* Y will get to the States or not or if we'll be sent on 'just one more operation.' Seems fairly certain that the Air Group will go back." Van Buren: "Scuttlebutt was flying thick and fast. By the time we reached Majuro, everyone practically talked himself into believing he was already home. What a disappointment it was when we found out we were to go out again. Morale dropped 100%."

Ship's journalists produced the second issue of SEA-V-TEN, dated April 15—*Yorktown*'s first birthday—but including a fictional account of the *sixth* anniversary on April 15, 1949, when "we find the poor old *Yorktown* still cruising around

awaiting orders for the next attack. Uncle Sam forgot to notify us that the war is over."

Beer parties ashore, general relaxation and a moving Easter sunrise service on the flight deck were climaxed by a first anniversary smoker on the 12th organized by dentist-entertainment officer Frank Losey, who composed a song for the occasion entitled "Just One More Raid." The production, a phony radio show, was a real morale boost of skits developed by Photographers Mate and future television star Jeff Corey; jitterbug exhibitions by airedale Joe Sharkey; boxing matches highlighted by 1942 Chicago Golden Gloves welterweight champ Gunners Mate Bob Johnson; and the whole show built around the title "The Gonzales Gedunk Hour" for the "sponsor," "Weelie" Gonzales, ship's soda jerk.

Another morale booster of a different sort was the elevation of Rear Admiral Jocko Clark to task group command in place of Ginder. Though Clark kept his flag on the *Hornet,* he sent its Air Department people over to the *York* to learn the ropes, and he visited his old ship to raid it for staff officers. In return, he transferred over Lieutenant Commander Myron T. Evans of his staff. Wrote Dr. Ray Gard of Clark, "His heart is still here." Jocko commanded TG 58.1, Montgomery 58.2 and Reeves 58.3. For the first time, the *Yorktown* had no admiral aboard.

Lieutenant (jg) Oliver Jensen reported aboard at Majuro. A prewar staff writer for *Life* magazine and a veteran destroyerman in the Atlantic, Jensen became a *Yorktown* ACIO to gather material for

Weelie Gonzales holds up hands while Jeff Corey reads the script and Frank Losey laughs along. Note cue-card to the left. Courtesy of Frank J. Losey

"Ten-Hand Working Party"—Pete Volsomy —and emcee Frank Losey at the ship's first anniversary smoker, April 12, 1944. Courtesy of Frank J. Losey

Front row brass have a good laugh at Losey's skit. L to R—navigator Red Sharp: behind him VT-5 skipper Dick Upson: chief engineer Bill Hart: behind him assistant dam con boss Diamond Jim Brady: supply boss Bill Moring: behind him assistant first lieutenant Eric Lambart: damage controller Dan Sweeney: Captain Al Jennings and exec Cam Briggs.

a Navy-sponsored book about the carriers. After renewing acquaintances with Jim Bryan from their days together at Yale, Jensen paid his respects to Captain Jennings. "I can see he isn't going to communicate any startling facts to me. But the main purpose of this is to see what happens for myself."

This he began as he stood on the bridge with cigar-chomping Cam Briggs watching Task Force 58 steam out of Majuro lagoon on a hot April 13, 1944. "This," remarked Briggs, "is the biggest, goddamndest thing I ever saw." "A steady, warm northeast trade wind," in Jensen's words, "whipped out the ensigns and vertical rows of flapping signal flags" as the carriers and their consorts fell into column one by one.

"Talk about ruling the waves," snorted Briggs as he gestured at the flagship *Lexington*, "these babies can go anywhere *he* pleases, and the Japs can't do anything about it!" The "he" was of course Pete Mitscher.

Once at sea, Captain Jennings announced the destination—support for MacArthur's April 22 assault on Hollandia, New Guinea. Somehow the crew was unimpressed. Gunner Jesse Bradley reflected, "Myself, I don't think that there will be much to it. But you can never tell about them Japs." And Oliver Jensen couldn't coax the veteran fliers to exhibit any excitement. When he kidded Ed Stebbins about the reporters who were surely going to swarm around him at the end of the cruise, Steb drawled, "All I can think to tell them is that crack the guy makes in this book I've been reading, *Shore Leave*: 'It was nothing, really. Any man with a genius for flying and unlimited courage could have done as well.' "

The ACIOs poured over recent charts and recon photos of the targets, while newly-reported photo interpreter Dave Gibson fashioned a bas-relief model of the area in plaster and clay. Although intelligence estimates claimed over 300 Jap planes to be in the target area, the biggest concern seemed to be losing a day when the force shifted to East Longitude time on April 15—or 16th, always confusing—but "a disturbing matter personally" to Oliver Jensen, "since it happened to be my birthday." His 30th at that. A kind of euphoria throughout the ship led the exec to warn next day: "I'VE NOTICED A SLACKENING OF EFFORT AND AN ATTITUDE THAT THIS OPERATION IS PRACTICALLY IN THE BAG. I CAN TELL YOU RIGHT NOW THAT IT ISN'T."

The *Yorktown* steamed through heavy seas in TG 58.2 with the *Bunker Hill,* light carriers *Monterey* and *Cowpens,* two battleships, six cruisers and 16 tin cans. Two snoopers from Truk probably spotted the force during refueling on April 19 before they were splashed by CAP fighters. On the 20th, while topping off the destroyers, the carriers were definitely reported by a snooper.

The run-in to the target then commenced, with the pilots getting one final briefing for next day's attack. ACIO Ned Magowan showed the fighter pilots slides of Hollandia and slipped in a few he had borrowed from the crew showing bare-breasted native girls. This, of course, brought down the house; "always try to put on a show," Earthquake Ned told Jensen. Alex Wilding, drolly: "Talked to the fighter pilots and saw nudes."

Reveille at 0400 April 21 occurred in the midst of a violent storm buffeting the ship. The predawn fighter sweep had to stand down until it could accompany the first bombing mission in daylight. Visibility, kidded one officer, was down to "a little below zero." ("They should see the Atlantic," mused former convoyer Jensen.)

As the gray, dreary dawn reluctantly showed itself, the wind abruptly died, and an anxious Al Jennings rang up more speed. "The bridge is crowded," observed Jensen—"The Captain, very tense and worried; Exec, smiling and munching a cigar; Air Officer Born tears around (He's the guy who invented a lot of airborne radar equipment); the AGC, 'Steb' Stebbins, big hero of Scouting 8 [at Guadalcanal]; the Assistant Air Officer, a sour [actor] Ned Sparks-ish lieutenant [Pappy Harshman]; the Air Plot Officer, Lt. Cooper Bright, signalmen, Marine orderlies, ass't j.o.'s, etc."

The dawn strike took off to hit Wakde Island, which it found devoid of airborne defenders but populated by a great many parked planes as sitting ducks. Jim Pickard couldn't "figure out why they let us catch their planes on the ground all the time." But the attackers had difficulty setting them afire, since their gas tanks had obviously been drained.

Pickings were so meager that the *Yorktown's* second strike was diverted to hit the shipping at Humboldt Bay and the four airfields around Hollandia, where planes aplenty were parked, some apparently dummies. To Ed Stebbins, two of the fields "presented the appearance of a salvage dump, with plane parts strewn all over them," wreckage, it was later learned, caused by heavy attacks by MacArthur's own land-based air forces.

The ack ack was especially light for a change,

much to the relief of pilots like Jim Campbell who were glad they might not have to ditch in Lake Sentani with its "log-like objects around the edge" later diagnosed as crocodiles! Air Group Five dropped over 82 tons of bombs on Wakde and Hollandia throughout the day which accounted for but a portion of TF 58's absolute plastering of the target.

Alex Wilding: "This was the quietest, most uninteresting and uneventful attack we have ever made. So dull." Dr. Ray Gard: "When will those slant eyes learn! Everything went perfectly—little opposition." Photographs taken of the landing beaches were flown—still wet—over to the *Bunker Hill* for Admiral Montgomery's perusal. He could see that the enemy's defenses had been thoroughly wrecked, which would make MacArthur's assault an easy task.

Neither did enemy planes ever bother the force, although John Gray had some excitement on a late afternoon hop over Hollandia. When he recounted the story in the wardroom that evening, Gray was so excited that, according to Jensen, "his eyes glistened, his hands jerked quickly, his chin quivered."

Overhearing another pilot's call of bogeys somewhere near the coast, Gray had gone looking and found two twin-engine Sally bombers flying "along the water, hugging the shore. I went down, down like this [expressive sweep of the palm] and came up under their tails. They were in formation like this [two-hand gesture, in tandem], the one in back had a smoking port engine. I hit his other engine and he went in.

"I pulled up right over him and went for the other. He didn't just fill my [gun] sights, he filled the whole windshield. He wasn't more than 100 feet away and I riddled him. He was burning everywhere—not an explosion. Bounced on the water once, twice, and then turned in like this [sweep of the hand] and sank. The gas burned for quite a while. I know I killed the pilots."

"How does it feel?" he answered Jensen, "Like the first time you get a girl in bed. You just feel you're goddamned good."

Jensen asked the pilots about many subjects during this wardroom bull session. When the discussion turned to admirals, only Mitscher had the approval of the airmen. They roundly criticized Pownall for running from Kwajalein, and Montgomery for condoning it. Also, "Montgomery is 'runner-up' to Black Jack Reeves for killing more Naval aviators than the Japs, mostly by stubbornly insisting on pre-dawn take-offs. In pre-dawn take-offs, there is one advantage put forward: SURPRISE."

The principal objections revolved around collisions in the dark during the rendezvous and confusion between air groups on the flight, not to mention trying to see the target adequately. The topic was a sore one, for a very early predawn launch had been scheduled by Montgomery for next morning, the 22nd.

Nineteen-year-old Ensign Owen J. Ramey of

Nineteen-year-old Owen Ramey (center) and his crewmen Jim Russell and Doyle Parker in front of their TBF Avenger. Courtesy of Carness F. Ramey

VT-5, the youngest pilot on the *Yorktown* since reporting in December, turned in just as his chessmate George Wille, who occupied the adjoining bunk in Boys Town, was about to go on watch. Wille chided Ramey about Ramey losing their last two games of chess. Replied the always-smiling Hoosier, "I'll stake my life against yours, Wille, that I can beat you."

Ramey's plane was the first Avenger spotted for launch behind the fighters when the pilots manned their aircraft in a dark, cloudy night that showed only a few stars and no horizon at all. Even the dim red truck lights of the escort ships were difficult to see. Jensen: "At 0445, according to schedule, the first strike is launched into stygian darkness. No light until 0630! Air personnel curses softly. I stand on the bridge watching. First are the F6F fighters, then the TBF torpedo planes . . . .

"A half dozen carriers are launching in this area in hopeless confusion—and planes circle for an hour in vain efforts to effect their rendezvous. Suddenly float lights appear astern of the *Bunker Hill*. The damned idiots are racing us to get their group airborne first, and a pilot taking off into the slipstream of air left by the next ahead (a tricky torque of whirling air) has gone into the sea. The lights are thrown over by shipmates to guide rescuers.

"Then, tragedy strikes us. A TBF . . . leaves our bow and struggles for altitude ahead of us. People with better sight than I possess claim they can see his form rising—toward the cruiser *New Orleans,* some 20 degrees Relative on our starboard bow. His bulk blanks out her truck light. Then suddenly there is a fire, a crash and a bright, horrible blaze on the water, falling gradually astern of the cruiser.

"We steam slowly by it, but there is a great deal of doubt who it is—or even whether it is our own plane. Stebbins says it can't be—that plane must have crashed from high altitude. Some lookout saw it come from the *Cabot*. No visual signals (too dark), no radio messages (radio silence). We wait. The ship buzzes with excitement. Aviators curse in the ready rooms."

Dropping toward the water on takeoff at 0516, the plane had struggled for altitude in the 1700 yards between the *Yorktown* and the *New Orleans*. Ensign Dave Evans, following it off the deck in his torpecker, also struggled for altitude, guiding on its exhaust flames. Veering to the right, this lead TBF #10 flew into the radar mast and starboard yardarm of the cruiser, knocking off its left wing and careening across the forecastle and into the sea.

It killed one sailor in the process, and all that was recovered of the plane's crewmen were bits of a flight jacket and life jacket, part of a man's skull and some human flesh.

The explosion nearly blinded Evans in the next torpecker, who just missed the *New Orleans* himself. "My knees shook all the way to the target and I was soaked with perspiration."

But who was it?

Weatherguesser Jim Vonk, sickened over the tragedy, took it personally, though the weather was hardly his fault, later got himself plastered and tore apart the wardroom in rage—breaking furniture, phonographs and even his favorite classical records.

The remaining eleven Avengers, fighters and bombers reached the landing beaches just after a leaden sunrise and attacked only 500 yards in front of the amphibious craft. Ed Stebbins and Dick Upson brought in the second strike in midmorning, with VT-5 ACIO Harvey "Judge" Reynolds in Upson's plane assigning targets by grid coordinates.

When the first flight returned aboard, a head count was taken to ascertain the identity of the crashed TBF crew. It was Owen Ramey, with gunner Doyle Parker and radioman Jim Russell. When the sad details of the tragedy were transmitted from the *New Orleans,* the message was passed around the bridge. No one spoke. George Wille couldn't believe his chess games with Ramey were over. Even Chaplain Alexander found himself doubting his faith.

Oliver Jensen went down to the Torpedo 5 ready room, "a gloomy place, quiet at first as the pilots talk about Ramey, then suddenly indignant at admirals who launch predawn hops for 'surprise' when no surprise can possibly exist.

"It is nothing, however, to the indignation later, in the evening, when another predawn launch is ordered for tomorrow. 'What the hell is that son of a bitch trying to do—kill all of us? He's got half of our original group already.' Talk veers to whether these 'flying' admirals would make predawn hops themselves (or whether they could even fly any of our modern carrier planes), and I drift out. I heard that before from B-24 pilots in England."

"Every time I hear a radio announcer report in his cheery way that 'only one' or 'only two' of our planes are missing," one pilot summed it up, "I get mad as hell."

MacArthur's assaulting troops quickly discovered that most of Hollandia's defenders had departed days before, while those remaining had no stomach for a fight. Nevertheless, insurance flights from the *York* on the 23rd socked Hollandia and Wakde-Sawar before more foul weather closed in. These strikes turned out to be milk runs, enabling Captain Jennings to greet Fred Bozard after he made the ship's 10,000th landing, while another outrageously beautiful sunset drew a large audience topside.

And that was it for Hollandia. "This operation was a cinch," in the mind of Jim Pickard, as indeed it had been. But the pilots and crew were in an ugly mood during refueling on the 24th. "Our admirals are figuring out what to do next," opined Alex Wilding. "Speculation says Halmahera or Mindanao in the Philippines—makes no difference to me if they go straight to Tokyo. . . .

"Everyone sick and tired of all this and wanting to go home to the States. VT boys are so soured they stayed up all night bitching and drinking and some didn't go to bed at all. They got pretty drunk. If the ship doesn't soon go home the men are going to crack—they don't give a damn anymore and only half do their work. Morale is so low there just isn't any. . . . No one gives a good God-damn."

Torpedo 5's cold, abrupt skipper, Dick Upson, who had often risked his own neck to save his squadronmates, was so exhausted that one day he passed out in the ready room. Harboring a severe cold and an inner ear infection, he had to promise Doc McCaffrey he would ease off. But he didn't—he had to lead and set an example for his disgruntled pilots.

The pilots' chief hate remained, of course, the Japs, four snoopers being shot down on the 26th. Charlie Ridgway, directing Bob Duncan's *Yorktown* CAP, learned that "Duncan overheard *Cowpens* VF discussing a Betty they had shot down. 3 survivors in water. Pilots were eager to dispose of them but were instructed to preserve them until a [destroyer] could pick them up." Wilding: "One of our planes dropped them a life raft and a destroyer went and picked them up—but only because we wanted some information from them. Another Jap got out of his plane and was clinging to a tire in the water—we left him there though we could have rescued him."

Now, electrifying good news: Air Group Five finally got the word—it was going home.

The bad news: it would hit Truk again en route. Wilding: "We are ordered to leave the area tomorrow, proceed East, refuel, take on ammunition and replacement aircraft, and then hit and bombard Truk, Satawan and Ponape and return to Majuro. After Majuro, we lead an invasion force into the Marianas (Saipan, Tinian, and Guam)." The pilots and 500 crewmen of the air group would go home before the Marianas but not the rest.

Pickard: "Now they tell us we'll have to attack Truk for 2 days before we can go home. Damn, I'm getting tired of this war. Haven't had a hop in three months that wasn't in Jap territory."

Jim Campbell: "The Admiral thought he would give us the honor of a second lick—an honor that we'd just as soon pass up. Our last target! Would anyone be lost on the last strike? We didn't discuss it much, but it was on everyone's mind. We had

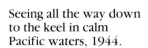

Seeing all the way down to the keel in calm Pacific waters, 1944.

mauled Truk once and we would do it again.''

Wilding: ''The wrath of the pilots is increasing and is bound to draw a reaction soon. At dinner tonight the pilots said, 'Let the Japs sink the whole fucking Navy—and if I'm up when they come I'll help them do it.' And they weren't just kidding.

''Their attitude is reflected everywhere. On the flight deck when the starter gives them the flag they delay in taking off; or they'll give their plane a down for some trivial reason. On one day 5 of 6 TBFs took a down. It's too bad the Navy over-looks morale. Without it a ship loses 80 percent of its efficiency.''

Of course the Navy was *very* sensitive to morale, but the threat of a Jap air buildup at Truk had to be eliminated in order to cover MacArthur's toehold at Hollandia and to neutralize Truk once and for all before the landings at Saipan, scheduled for June. Snoopers continued to be shot down, while several Jap subs in the area were being depth-charged.

On April 27, as the task force headed due east away from Hollandia, gunner Bradley noted that the *Yorktown* was now ''One hundred days out of Pearl Harbor. In four more days we will break the record of the old *Yorktown*.'' Refueling 400 miles south-southwest of Truk, each carrier got its target assignments. Air Group Five would hit the bomber strip at Dublon and the fighter field at Eten, both tough targets already familiar to the fliers, who therefore required little prebriefing.

The fatigue and apprehension on board the *Yorktown* combined with the daily Radio News to affect Oliver Jensen on the 28th. He suddenly burst forth with a brief cynical essay in his diary entitled ''HOW TO STOP BEING A FREE REPUBLIC''— ideas he would never entertain in later years as editor of *American Heritage* magazine.

'Just one day's news: The Army (particularly MacA) as usual claiming credit for everything, from Germany to Hollandia. More pussyfooting about the 2nd Front—'it had already begun with air attacks'—Single Armed Forces Scheme proposed by Stimson—'Big Navy to defend our shores' poppycock for after the war from Senator Overton who believes in Peace & Security with a 37-ocean Navy—Hershey adding fuel to the flames for Universal Compulsory Post War Military Training—Quarrel with Sweden— MacArthur runs second to Dewey in Pa.—and Roosevelt 3rd in the G.O.P. primary—U.S. govt (FDR) sends Army to seize a man's factory (Montgomery Ward) because it won't accede to Communists in Administration and C.I.O.—Romanism in Boston—General Patton

shoots off his mouth about Anglo-U.S.-USSR ruling the post-war world—his critics snap and bark in Washington—King says U.S. Navy will exceed all others combined before end of war. Dig in that pocketbook, boy.''

As Task Force 58 re-entered the West Longitude time zone, it repeated the date of April 29, 1944. On the first one, the destroyers were topped off and nine replacement planes flown aboard the *Yorktown* from an escort carrier. The ship received 85 rain-soaked sacks of mail; pilot Joe Kristufek got five letters, two Easter cards and a Christmas present. The force then commenced its run-in to the launch point for its initial strikes on Truk on the second April 29. Admiral Mitscher proclaimed, ''THE NEXT OPERATION IS OUR PET HATE. PLASTER IT WITH EVERYTHING YOU HAVE, INCLUDING EMPTY BEER BOTTLES IF YOU HAVE ANY. WE HAVEN'T.''

Commander Briggs added his own war cry, ''WE PLAN TO DELIVER THE KNOCK-OUT PUNCH THIS TIME. WHEN THE BELL SOUNDS COME OUT FIGHTING!'' After the predawn fighter sweep, a long succession of bombing strikes from all the carriers would attempt to finish off Truk as an operating base for the Japanese naval air forces— just as the February raid had driven out major shipping for good. Each carrier was enjoined to use up all the ammunition still on board; no point in taking it back to Pearl.

The fighters were told to expect over 200 enemy planes at Truk, with perhaps another 120 staging in from the Marianas. ''Upon discovery,'' noted Oliver Jensen, ''we expect a heavy dive-bombing attack on our task force, as the Japs can track our VF sweep back. Gunners are pleased at that prospect.''

Among several bogeys detected during the morning, one Betty closed to within 40 miles before a *Bunker Hill* fighter shot it down. In midafternoon Alex Wilding learned that ''the Japs reported a carrier task force 150 miles to the west of us—our CVEs [escort carriers] escorting convoy—good news for us 'cause Japs will think we can't reach Truk by the morning. At 1600 set course 020 degrees speed 20 kts. Truk is 320 miles away now. Will be in position to launch against Truk an hour before dawn tomorrow. Should give Tojo a real surprise.''

In the evening, fighter skipper Bob Jones worked up the flight schedule for the sweep and left off the high-scorers—notably Gray (8 kills), Duncan (7) and Dapper Nelson (5)—in order to let the others get a few scores. Jones was spreading the wealth.

The print shop mimeographed and distributed the Plan of the Day, highlighted by the exec's announcement, "TODAY IS SATURDAY, 29 APRIL, AGAIN. TODAY WE START A TWO DAY RETURN ENGAGEMENT AT THAT POPULAR THEATER WHICH WAS SO RECEPTIVE ON OUR LAST VISIT. THIS TIME WE INTEND TO KNOCK THEM COMPLETELY OFF THEIR FEET WITH OUR PERFORMANCE."

Worsening visibility due to rain showers led Admiral Montgomery to delay the launch of the sweep 25 minutes until 0655, at which time launching "starter" Junior Meyer waved the 16 Hellcats down the deck in record 18-second intervals. Truk lay 78 miles to the northeast. Bob Jones took Fighting 5 to angels 15, with another 68 fighters arrayed above and below them. Then at 0730 Ed Stebbins led off the first strike of Air Group Five's last battle—14 VF, 15 VB, 9 VT.

The 0743 sunrise illuminated what bomber pilot Radney described as "the musky, slow rising clouds with their grey, streaming rain squalls"—just as Admiral Mitscher was informing the sweep that his night fighters and the lifeguard sub *Tang* had reported enemy planes taking off from Truk. Fifteen minutes later force radars picked up a large group of bogeys at 5000 feet 60 miles out and closing.

The flagship ordered Stebbins to climb to angels 18 and continue to the target, leaving *Bunker Hill's* CAP to make the interception. But these Hellcats missed making contact in the clouds and overshot the bogeys by 15 miles. *Bunker Hill's* fighters doubled back and gave chase, finally overtaking 15 Zeros 30 miles out and screaming for help.

Commander Born at Pri Fly poked his head into Air Plot where the four voice radios chattered with messages, all being assimilated by Buck Bright and his crew. "What is the situation over the target?"

Bright: "Can't hear the planes clearly. The enemy's jamming this circuit."

Message from Mitscher: "An order has been intercepted from Japs at Truk: Send subs after American Task Force."

Then the CIC squawk box blared news from Charlie Ridgway: "Bogeys closing in 150 degrees 30 miles. Over."

Bright: "Roger, CIC." Into another squawk box: "Ready One, Two, Four. Stand by for a scramble. Bogeys closing in."

Captain Jennings: "Sound General Quarters."

The gongs rang out, and the bugler blew a fast battle call.

An Air Plot radio: "All Cairo from 99 Cairo. I've got many Zeros above clouds." Stebbins had reached the target and orbited at angels 12 to direct the attack. Some 15 Zeros had left their strike force and followed the U.S. bombers back to Truk. The flak was extremely heavy.

CIC: "Bogeys low. Low bogey—3 to 5 planes—at 3 o'clock." They were coming in on the starboard bow, directly out of the newly-risen sun, making about 220 knots.

Oliver Jensen was at Primary Fly. George Wille stepped out of his radio shack to watch. Joe Chambliss was in Air Plot. Time: 0816.

Jensen: "There is a roar from our starboard side. First the cans and then battleships of the screen have opened fire on low-flying Jap planes coming in from the northeast. *One Jap* is splitting off north—looks like he will pass ahead of us. *Jap Two* is boring right in through the most terrific blanket of fire from all sizes of guns I have ever seen. *Jap Two* comes closer and closer. . . ."

There were four of them, Jill torpedo planes plus many more being attacked by Hellcats.

Radio: "Combat Air Patrol has splashed a Zeke."

While *Jap One* and *Jap Two*, as Jensen labeled them, headed straight for the *Yorktown*, *Jap Three* and *Jap Four* turned more toward the *Belleau Wood* on the *Yorktown's* port bow. Both carriers were directly screened by the battleship *Iowa*, cruisers *San Francisco* and *Boston* and many destroyers. The attackers flew just 50 feet off the water, coming straight in and not jinking.

Jensen: "Out on deck I see a Jap torpedo bomber (*Jap Three*) coming in on a cruiser. Cruiser and *Iowa* open fire. The Jap drops his torpedo, but must miss. There is no explosion. . . ."

Chambliss: "A can and a cruiser took the left hand [*Jap Three*] coming in on a cruiser. Cruiser and *Iowa* open fire. The Jap drops his torpedo, but must miss. There is no explosion. . . ."

Chambliss: "A can and a cruiser took the left hand plane [*Jap Three*] under fire and with a heavy double concentration of all of their A.A. batteries, the Jill promptly exploded and burned in the water." in a position to bear effectively with her batteries. The *Boston* promptly fired at the flight and with the aid of our 40mm mount #2 knocked down one Jill [*Jap Four*], which made a lovely fire on the water" 4700 yards on the port bow.

Jensen: "On the other side *Jap One* and *Jap Two* are getting in range of us now. Our starboard five-inch main battery opens up and the whole ship shakes. (Our planes are spotted aft.)''

Wille: "The two planes made a beautifully coordinated attack, starting on the starboard bow and coming right on in.''

Lieutenant (jg) Bill Bowie of the signal gang rooted with many others as if at a ball game—but for the visiting team! "Put 'er right in there, boy! Put 'er right in there!'' All they wanted was a little torpedo hit that would force the *Yorktown* to be sent back to Bremerton for repairs—and their longed-for leave. Admittedly, in Bowie's words, they had all gone "a little Asiatic.''

But George Earnshaw thundered at his gun crews on the island: "Shoot him down! Shoot him down!'' His fearless image inspired the frightened sailors, as did that of the calm Captain Al Jennings, who walked around from the starboard to the port side of the bridge facing the strafing Jills as they came in. He stayed directly in harm's way.

Lieutenant (jg) R.K. "Stu'' Stuart of Communications stood rooted on a starboard catwalk, his gaze fixed on the torpedoes hanging under both Jills, wondering if they would explode or drop. *Jap One* bore 35 degrees Relative (to the bow), *Jap Two* 50 degrees.

Chambliss: "Our five-40-20 batteries were working the two over. They continued to fly their chosen path and seemed determined to successfully complete their mission of death and destruction. By this time, our gunners could plainly see the two large torpedoes slung beneath the planes. This was like a 'shot in the arm'—the volume and accuracy of fire increased with tracers and bursts all about the two Jills.

Wilding: "The screen was late opening fire and their fire was meager—only a few five-inch bursts were observed. Their range was soon fouled and it was all up to the *Yorktown*—fortunately [the Jills] arrived at the *York* 30 seconds apart so our fire could be concentrated. [*Jap One*] received little fire until the guns of the *York* were brought to bear on him and then not until he was within range of the 20's.

"His run was perfect and I watched and waited for him to drop his torpedo, it was hanging long and narrow under his belly, he couldn't have missed us—we were broadside to him—no effort was made to maneuver the ship to meet the attack. For some reason that will always remain unanswered, he never dropped. He crossed our bow.''

Chambliss: "They began to smoke with occasional licks of flame from the motors. They closed within good torpedo range but failed to release their

fish which undoubtedly would have hit our starboard bow had they done so. It is believed the pilots were either killed or wounded. They both flew over our flight deck and the rear-seat men were observed to one side as if dead.''

Jensen: "Now *Jap One* has apparently fired his torpedo at us and swings around across in front of our bow. We let him have everything we have. (Why in hell doesn't Captain Jennings turn *into* the attack—later I find that at the last minute he ordered full right rudder).''

Wille: "The first Jap had [a torpedo] secured under the fuselage and it stuck out like a sore thumb when he crossed over. Both planes crossed within a few seconds of each other and were caught in the cross fire of the 40mm and 20mm batteries on the port side.''

Jensen: '*Jap One* now has passed a few hundred feet in front of us, bursts into flames, turns and dives into the water. [500 yards] on our port bow. I am just staring at this when with a roar *Jap Two* crosses about 40 to 60 feet over my head, still apparently undamaged. A dozen cameras grind—every gun fires in an ear-splitting roar.

"*Jap Two* is a greenish khaki—a single-engine torpedo plane. Great shining orange balls on each wing, one on his fuselage. [Wille: "It was the first time I had ever seen a 'meatball.''] A little flame bursts out of his port side, just aft of the shiny 'greenhouse.' Tracers are all around him like rain drops. He pulls up about 100 feet beyond the deck, wobbles a moment. One wheel drops down (His hydraulic system punctured, probably—same happened to other.)

"MEANWHILE we are waiting for his torpedo to hit. No one here ever saw a more beautiful torpedo [plane] run. All over the deck and bridge people crouch and brace themselves, pulling their tin hats into position. I am suddenly aware that if anything shatters, the island, radar, gun platforms, yardarm and everything will light on my head, and I pull back against the bulkhead.'' Other sailors flop to the deck, bracing for the impact.

"Now 200 feet away [from the port side] you can see the Jap is hit badly. He starts to dive, bursts into the brightest sheets of flame I ever saw and dives into the water on one wing on our port beam, 200 yards. No one bails out.''

Chambliss: "By this time they were burning and out of control, for the planes began their next dives into the ocean. Both exploded as they hit and burned furiously on the water with loud applause and sigh of relief from all hands.''

In one of the most dramatic photo sequences of the war, Japanese Jill "Number One" seems to lead a charmed life as she bores in through the *Yorktown's* withering fire with a torpedo slung under her belly, then failing to drop it rises up over the ship and goes down on the other side. The Lucky Y has done it again, en route to Truk for the second time, April 29, 1944.

Jesse Bradley, at his quad 40: "I fired 64 shots at one that came in at me. When he passed about 50 feet from me he had a fire started in the body of the plane. He flew for about 100 yards then he blew up and hit the water about 30 seconds later. Two more hit the water beside me. I believe [that in] the one I fired at the pilot was dead before he got to the ship because he never did drop his 'Tin Fish' and he sure had plenty of time. If he had, I'm sure he would have hit us."

The official Anti-Aircraft Action Report noted that four 5-inch guns had fired 32 rounds, seven 40mm mounts had fired 635, and no fewer than 57 20mms had unleashed 3537 rounds to get both Jills and an assist on the other. The one Jill was estimated to have hit the water 500 yards on the port bow and the other 700 yards on the port beam.

Dr. Gard: "Boy Oh Boy—The good Lord had his hand over us this time."

Jensen: "Now there are three pyres of flaming gasoline on the water, each one sending up a column of black smoke.

"Still no torpedo explosion. Only later, from the photographs, do we discover that the Jap never fired his torpedo. It is still slung to his underside. So was the fish in *Jap One*. Evidently the pilots got rattled, their controls jammed, or they were killed before launching."

All this action had taken place inside of three minutes, 0816-0818, and in the midst of a general aerial battle around the formation between the CAP and the screen's guns on the one hand and incoming Zekes and Kates on the other. In the ensuing half-hour the former knocked down seven of the latter.

One near-casualty went unreported. Shipfitter Eugene Murphy, having stashed away two cans of beer in the CO_2 shack, had made his way there during the height of the attack to imbibe while everyone else was preoccupied. Shutting the door, he let go a CO_2 bottle to cool the beer. But the room had become airtight, and the carbon dioxide sucked up all the oxygen. Murphy dropped to the deck, suffocating. He could hear the guns firing as he figured he was about to die. What a way to go. Finally, he got the door open and gasped in the air. Murphy would never go near beer again.

At 0906 air boss Ben Born finally received word from Stebbins that the attack on Truk was "progressing favorably." Fighting 5 engaged some 15 Zeros doing their usual fancy aerobatics and effortlessly swept them aside. Tom McClelland and Harry Hill each flamed two to become aces. Among the other kills, Bob Duncan pumped lead into one until smoke burst forth and the pilot bailed out.

The festering rage of Duncan's long fights and lost buddies welled up in him. He came around at the dangling pilot and opened fire. The Jap "wriggled and doubled his knee up to his chin, then fell apart." Other Americans strafed other parachuting Japs. The Orientals had again succeeded in bringing the Occidentals down to their level. Remember Pearl Harbor.

An incensed war correspondent later accosted Duncan. "Don't you have any moral sense? Don't you know about the Geneva convention? How did you feel, strafing that guy?"

"Well," reflected an angry Dunc, "when I saw his body move, I knew I was hitting him. It made me feel real good."

Stebbins found an opening in the clouds over Truk for the bombers and torpeckers to pass through to bomb their assigned targets on Eten Island. With a mere 3500 feet of ceiling, the dive bombers pushed over toward the grey-green forbidding Eten and into the teeth of its flak. The same old story—planes versus AA—with the same results: a bludgeoned airfield and a few bullet-holed *Yorktown* aircraft. Losses: radioman J.L. Villareal took a piece of shrapnel in his left butt.

The fighters went in strafing and came out with the bombers for the rendezvous; Stebbins himself setting fire to a large coastal vessel. Every building seemed to have a Red Cross painted on it, though the men knew better. Jugbutt Moore carried a big bomb on his F6 to drop on his assigned target—a causeway used by Japanese troops. He bored in, let the bomb go and scored a direct hit. Though pleased with himself, he would discover after the war—while helping to map Truk as part of a geological survey—that his bomb had also blown the roof off a little abandoned Catholic church next to the causeway. A postwar convert to Catholicism, Jug would help to rebuild the church.

Air and arming bosses Ben Born and Jim Bryan now collaborated on cleaning out the *Yorktown's* magazines. With the force closing to within 45 miles due south of the center of Truk atoll by noon, Born reduced the normal four-hour sorties to 2 1/2 hours and ordered all planes to return to base pronto so they could be rearmed and relaunched in record time in five more strikes during a banner day of 224 individual sorties. The intervals of the planes averaged 18 seconds to launch, 27.2 to be landed.

Ridge Radney: "Eten-Dublon-Dublon-Eten-Eten-

Dublon, bomb-strafe-bomb-strafe, smash-Smash-SMASH! Destroy the airfields, the planes, the town, the ammunition, the hangars, the docks, the guns, the installations, the morale, the people. Scar it, sear it, burn it, dig it out and blow it up, cobble the dirty soil with steel bullets! Color it red with Japanese blood!''

And they did—with 29 2000-pound blockbusters, 65 1000-pound semi-armor-piercing and general purpose bombs, 99 500-pounders, 104 250-pound GPs, eleven 350-pound depth bombs, 27 140-pound incendiary bombs, 14 130-pound fragmentation clusters, and 59 100-pound GP bombs. Total—104.3 tons, a new high for the *Yorktown,* plus 80,960 rounds of .50 cal. machine

the Japs reported the position of the force, but little good it did them. Everything was so easy that in midafternoon Cam Briggs released some of the crew to lay below to visit Weelie Gonzales for a refreshing gedunk break.

As the last strike of the day visited Truk at 1800, the perfect clockwork finally hit a snag. Just after Jim Pickard planted his 1000-pounder in the middle of Eten's runway, Harry Hill came in behind him strafing when a burst of flak set Hill's Hellcat on fire. Harry headed away from the lagoon to the southeast in the direction of the force, his buddies close behind. Three miles out, his engine quit and Hill ditched.

When the word was flashed back to the ship, the

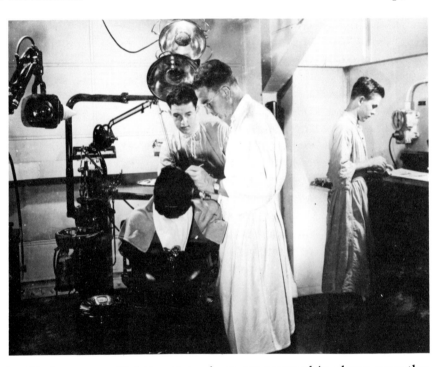

Dentist Frank Losey at work on the *Yorktown.* This photo adorned the cover of *Our Navy* magazine in June 1944. Courtesy of Frank J. Losey

gun ammo and 13,065 of .30. And the *York* was only one of five big carriers, along with seven lights.

In the midst of it all, a TBF returned aboard still carrying a 100-pound bomb that the pilot had been unable to release. His bomb bay doors were open when he hit the wire, and the bomb suddenly released and skipped forward down the deck from the plane's momentum. The bomb came to rest not far from Jim Bryan and the Bomb Farm by the island. Without hesitating to see if it had armed itself or not, Bryan ran up to the bomb, picked it up, carried it to the side, and threw it overboard. Such heroism had become commonplace on this fighting lady.

Charlie Ridgway's radars picked up a few bogeys around midday, but they either faded or were chased away by the CAP from the *Monterey.* Twice

Fighting 5 ready room erupted in alarm over the fate of the cheerful blond new papa. Wilding: ''He's 3 miles on upwind side of Northwest Passage and drifting towards reef. He's in his Mae West and apparently unhurt. Falstaff [submarine *Tang*] is 35 miles away on the other side of the island and cannot reach him.''

With the prevailing wind conditions, it looked like Harry would drift back onto the reef and face capture. Smokey Stover all over again. Each pilot in all three ready rooms volunteered to go to Hill's rescue, while several planes already circled him— Bob Jones who transmitted information to the ship, Jug Moore who raised the *Tang* on his radio, Unc Avery of the bombers who dropped his life raft, and torpecker Joe Kristufek who dropped not only his raft but lights, food, cigarettes, matches, and a note telling him to hang on, all in tennis ball bags. But Hill never got them.

Captain Jennings and the *Yorktown* bombarded Admiral Montgomery on the *Bunker Hill* with messages in a two-hour drama recorded by Alex Wilding.

"1804—We asked Admiral Montgomery to send a seaplane to rescue Harry.

"1805—Admiral Montgomery refused. Said Falstaff could rescue. At the same time Admiral Reeves sent a seaplane from his task group to rescue one of his pilots.

"1810—Again we requested Montgomery to dispatch seaplane.

"1811—Again, 'no.' The sea is too rough—he says.

"1830—Requested Admiral Montogmery to allow us to launch a torpedo plane with a survivors kit and a fighter to accompany.

"1831—Admiral Montogomery replies, 'Affirmative' if they return by sunset (Sunset is 2000 tonight and Harry is only 39 miles away.)

"1855—Admiral Montgomery said negative to launching torpedo plane and fighter now as they couldn't get back by sundown. The TBF [Andy Lett] was already turning up on the catapult and before the catapult officer [Bill May] got the word the TBF had been launched, the fighter [Burt Taylor] was immediately launched. (There is every evidence that this message was deliberately delayed in reaching the catapult officer.) We never acknowledged to Admiral Montgomery that we had received his message.

"1905—TBF and VF catapulted [Blip Searles navigating with the TBF's radar]. They were given 35 Falstaff 110 [degrees] as a better bearing and distance.

"1920—Lt. Jones and division still guarding Harry, and Lt. Lett was now in communication with Lt. Jones. He was still 3 miles outside reef and not drifting toward reef anymore.

"1925—Lt. Lett and Taylor now rendezvoused with Lt. Jones.

"1927—Lt. Lett now has visual contact with Harry.

"1933—Kit now dropped to Harry," who must swim over to it.

"1940—Lt. Jones left Harry to return to the ship.

"1945—Lt (jg) Taylor turned on his emergency lights as he circled tightly over Harry and we took a radar fix on Harry's position [from Blip's radar]. He bore 002 degrees True from us, distance 39 miles.

"1947—Lett and Taylor were ordered to return to base.

"1948—Lt (jg) Taylor was ordered to broadcast '25 Falstaff 120 degrees' all the way home. He did so and received an acknowledgement from the submarine.

"1950—Lt. Jones landed aboard.

"1951—Submarine *Tang* acknowledged three times for '25 Falstaff 120 degrees.'

"1958—Lett and Taylor now over base.

"2000—Lett and Taylor landed aboard.

"2000—Sunset. (Note: a destroyer could have been detached by Admiral Montgomery when word was received that Harry was down and returned to the force with Harry before sunset if the Admiral had desired—he failed to take action)."

A very lonesome, wet and frightened Harry Hill paddled in Lett's raft as long as his strength allowed in the heavy seas to get away from Truk's reef, though he was not far from the *Tang*. Lieutenant Commander Richard H. O'Kane of that vessel zigzagged all night to the south of Truk and had a green Very flare fired every 15 minutes, hoping to attract the attention of several aviators reported to be down in his area. Hill saw the flares but elected not to fire his own, lest the Japs on shore spot him. He battled fatigue and seasickness as he waited for the dawn.

Wilding: "Morale of the pilots is very low tonight and it is fortunate for Montgomery's ego that he cannot hear the things being said about him."

In the VF-5 ready room Bob Jones assembled Hill's pals in a council of war. The squadron, by God, was not going to lose another pilot on this, its last battle. They decided that on the morning fighter sweep they would dispatch any airborne bandits—probably none left—and then form a 16-plane scouting line to fly at low altitude in line abreast and look for Hill. If and when they found him, they would circle until the sub arrived.

Their plan flew in the face of Commander Born's continued timetable of 2 1/2 hour sorties with maximum ordnance and no belly tanks, but they were determined to do it, even if it meant court-martial for insubordination.

Heavy weather returned to Truk and the task force during the night, and Admiral Montgomery at 0530 on April 30 ordered the fighter sweep for 0720 delayed until the wind and rain died down. At the same time Dick O'Kane brought the *Tang* to the surface ten miles south of Truk to look for Hill and other fliers in the water. As his lookouts scanned the surface with their binoculars, they instead spotted a submarine conning tower which forced O'Kane to dive immediately. It was an RO class Jap sub, which also dived.

Much as he wanted to stay and hunt for the boat—*RO-45*—O'Kane's mission was rescue, so he headed away and reported the position of the Jap, which was heading for the carriers, notably the *Yorktown* group. And at 0632 the *Bunker Hill* reported a surface contact 17 miles to the north of the formation. Montgomery dispatched two destroyers which depth-charged the *RO-45* until she exploded—proved when debris and "large chunks of human bodies" came to the surface.

Meanwhile, Admiral Montgomery cancelled the fighter sweep. Flying conditions were so poor that even two bogeys on the radars could not locate the force. When the skies finally cleared at 0827 the first strike group got off, escorted by the fighter sweep, for concentrated attacks on Dublon. Only flak greeted them, save for one Kate or Jill taking off being blasted into oblivion by Jugbutt Moore and John Gray.

The attacks completed, the flight turned for home and a scheduled 1100 recovery, except for eleven rebellious F6F pilots. Led by Bob Duncan, they broke away from the formation and went into their prearranged scouting line to look for Harry Hill. In the meantime, the *Tang* and float planes from the battleships moved into the offshore waters and began picking up survivors.

At 0940, Alex Wilding recorded happy news: "11 Cairo, Lt. John Gray, reports sighting Harry Hill midway between Moen and Kuop Islands. Friendly sub given his new range and bearing. Three divisions of fighters led by Lt (jg) Schofield, Lt (jg) Duncan and Lt. Gray now orbiting Harry. He is OK.

"I asked permission of Air Plot to request Admiral Montgomery to send seaplane for Harry. Air Plot said, 'Wait.'"

Dick Upson now began to pester Captain Jennings to let him go look for Hill. Upson had grounded himself with his cold on Doc McCaffrey's orders, but a downed pilot had always been his special concern. Jennings finally agreed, and Upson told Jim Bryan, "Load her up with some bombs. I might as well have them in case I find something to hit while looking for Hill." After this, his 30th and last combat flight, Upson hoped to take his tired TBF—the very same plane he had flown ever since Marcus—back to the Grumman factory to show the workers how their handiwork had survived all its battles.

At 1020 Ed Stebbins took off with the second bombing strike, afterwhich the deck was readied for the recovery of the first. Ben Born was then alarmed to count only one returning division of fighters with the bombing planes, since he needed to respot the deck for another launch. When Born called Duncan on the radio and ordered him to return immediately, the feisty ace practically told Born where to go! Charlie Ridgway noted a growing hysteria over this insubordination and that Born and Jennings were turning 'rather purple with rage," especially after Admiral Montgomery ordered the fighters back at 1112 and they refused to hear him.

As the pilots covered the area over Hill, they spotted two Jap scout planes, Kates or Jills, and Duncan and Ensign Kenney chased one into a cloud. The two men positioned themselves on either side of the cloud, and when the Jap came out on the right side Kenney gave him a burst, sending him down in flames. It was Fighting 5's 93rd and last kill.

Duncan buzzed the exhausted and seasick Hill and dropped him a parachute laden with provisions and a bottle of Old Crow. The package hit just ten feet from Hill's raft, but Harry was so weak he could not paddle over and retrieve it. Duncan had the most gas so he sent the other two divisions back and did not leave Hill himself until Tom McClelland's division arrived to relieve him on the vigil. The insubordinate fighters were all back aboard by 1150.

After they were in the ready room, noted Wilding, "Air Plot called them up and gave them Hell but they didn't care. No one gave a damn—morale at a low ebb—they would screw Montgomery if he didn't rescue Hill. Admiral Montgomery was already two hours behind his schedule. Serves him right—pilots would all enjoy the pleasure of strafing him.

"1200—Admiral Reeves launched 2 seaplanes from the *North Carolina* to pick up *Enterprise* pilots near Hill. (Montgomery still does nothing and our Capt. Jennings has still made no formal request to Admiral Montgomery.)"

The noon strike from the *Yorktown* finally got spotted after the return of Hill's guardians and was altered to include three TBFs carrying more survival gear for Hill. Dick Upson decided to fly the lead Turkey with radar officer Searles as navigator. Just as the planes prepared to take off, however, the rescue mission was scrubbed as Hill seemed about to be picked up. Upson nevertheless accompanied the strike to Truk in order to unload his bombs.

"1300—Cairo (Capt. Jennings) to Stagehand (Admiral Montgomery). . .request seaplane rescue for Hill, sea conditions reported satisfactory at his position.

"1301—'Roger, wait' from Montgomery.

"1314—Visual message received from Admiral Montgomery, 'Negative. Do not consider conditions suitable for seaplane rescue of Lt. Hill.'

"1326—Ens. Black, Lt (jg) Tyler, and Ens. Newhafer now orbiting Hill.

"1330—They were ordered to return to base immediately.''

While planes picked their way through thickening clouds to hit Truk, Jim Cole developed engine trouble in his F6 and had to ditch. He settled his fighter into the water two miles beyond the reef just a few miles from Harry Hill's raft. Cole, however, couldn't get his raft out and was left to swim about in his Mae West until a plane dropped him a rubber boat. By this time, he had swallowed a good bit of the Pacific Ocean and got too sick to hoist himself into the boat. He climbed only half way and hung over its side, inadvertantly making the lower half of his body into a sea anchor which arrested his progress toward the reef.

Ed Stebbins, orbiting overhead, observed that low clouds had covered the tops of the atoll's mountains and that the rain was reducing visibility, thus making further bombing and strafing runs hazardous. He broadcasted this information 'blind' on high frequency to the ship and recommended that operations cease and no more groups be sent. Admiral Mitscher concurred, and Steb ordered all planes to return to base.

Stebbins saw some torpeckers lining up for low-level glide runs. He figured it was Dick Upson and personally radioed to him, "Abort your attack. It's too risky and not worth it."

Upson replied, "I've already commenced my run," and finding a small hole in the overcast dived through it, although his division mates were unable to see enough to follow him through. Upson was just as aggressive in the last battle as in the first—the mark of a real pro.

Dick O'Kane meanwhile had moved the *Tang* into the bay between Truk and Kuop atolls under the cover of strafing Hellcats which kept down the Jap gunners on the shore. The *Tang's* crew executed a simple man-overboard drill and hauled Harry Hill aboard, transmitting word of it to the *Yorktown* at 1526. Then the sub turned south, sped five miles to the eastern reef where Tom McClelland

had shifted his vigil from Hill to Cole, and half an hour later edged in nearly to the coral to drag aboard a waterlogged Jim Cole.

By now the last strike planes had returned to the *York*. All, that is, but one—Dick Upson, by 1600 long overdue. Alex Wilding tried repeatedly to raise him on the fighter director net but only got silence. Being a man of few words, maybe Upson just wasn't talking. Ben Born took the transmitter, "Acknowledge. This is an order!"

Silence.

The other torpecker pilots told Born they saw their skipper dive through a cloud but never come out. One reported he saw a TBF crash into a clouded mountain top.

But if Upson was down, subs, seaplanes and destroyers were there to find him—in spite of the weather. When Dick O'Kane picked up his last pilot, he had 22 airmen aboard, squeezed in among his crew of 80. Pretty heads-up rescue work, unlike the first visit to Truk. But Dick Upson was not among those rescued.

On the bridge of the *Yorktown,* several pilots stood quietly, their eyes searching in the direction of Truk. Finally, someone said, "Well, he's reached his gas limit now."

They drifted below, though Alex Wilding kept transmitting. Upson had obviously gone down, taking Blip Searles and gunner Dick Wertman with him. The weather negated sending a seaplane, but the ship launched fighters Fred Bozard and Nick Carman at 1815 to look for Upson and to assist the *Tang*. No luck, and the two landed back aboard after dark.

"Missing in action,"noted the OOD. Upson and his crew were never heard from again. The finality of war.

"There was no sunset over Truk on April 30th," Ridge Radney recalled soon afterward, "just gray clouds and blackest night—Death's colors. Then and only then did we begin to withdraw, tired, grim, but satisfied. We weren't 'getting the Hell out of there' this time—rather we were proudly leaving the scene of recent victory, unhurried, unsullied, inwardly smiling."

Some unfinished business involved the young rebels of VF-5, whom Commander Born had put on report and now assembled during the evening for a severe tongue-lashing. "It isn't your responsibility to assume the rescue of Hill. We have rescue units assigned to that task." Sunshine Kelley responded, "I thought that was what we were supposed to do!" Squadron skipper Bob Jones staunchly defended the actions of his men, but Born put four of them in hack and turned the case over to Captain Jennings. When the *Tang* sent a message to the *Yorktown* thanking the fighters for directing it to Hill, Jennings let the men out of their confinement.

Within hours the captain made his ruling: "It is my view that these pilots have been in continuous combat for too extended a period of time, almost eleven months, and as a result are suffering from pilot fatigue which has affected their judgement. The report is dismissed." A happy solution—and a correct one.

But while Hill and Cole were safe, Upson, Searles and Wertman were gone, and the men of VT-5—joined by the man whose radio had failed to raise Upson, Alex Wilding—got good and drunk during the evening.

The completeness of the victory at Truk became immediately evident when not one snooper bothered the carriers during their retirement that night. Truk had indeed been knocked out as an airdrome. Not only would it not be assaulted, but Task Force 58 would never again have to pay it a visit; Truk would be kept neutralized by American planes operating from captured islands.

The *Yorktown* sailed away from its latest success with eager anticipation. Minutes after morning GQ was sounded on May 1, the loudspeaker beckoned all ears: "This is the Captain speaking. We're going to Majuro and then Pearl Harbor. The Air Group will be relieved. The ship may or may not go to the States for overhaul. That is all."

"All? What more be said?" exulted Radney of the bombers. "Manna from Heaven." Home—that magical word, that magical place. During refueling next day, the ship's orchestra struck up "California, Here I Come," which, noted Wilding, "brought down the house—everyone started to sing with much gusto."

Upon arrival at Majuro on May 4, the *York* received nine Japanese prisoners picked up from the waters around Truk for transportation to the stockade in Hawaii. The crew had mixed feelings toward them and their ultimate fate. Oliver Jensen recorded the "Marine guards theory: 'We ought to chase 'em over the fantail.' My theory: Treat them well now, get them in a clean, healthy P.O.W. camp, and start 'selling' them the so-called American Way of life."

On the 4th Alex Wilding set down the latest 'word' in his diary, a sad notice indeed: "News is out that we're included in the op plan for the

Marianas. We go to Pearl, exchange air groups, and return immediately. I hope it's wrong." And next day executive officer Briggs warned in the daily Plan: "KEEPING A DIARY IS, AND HAS BEEN SINCE THE VERY START OF THE WAR, A DIRECT VIOLATION OF NAVY CENSORSHIP REGULATIONS," whereupon all the dedicated diarists made fresh entries into their personal notebooks.

The SBDs were flown ashore at Majuro for delivery to the Marines; the rugged Dauntless left the *Yorktown* for good, to be replaced by an improved version of the SB2C Helldiver. Then, on May 6, this fighting lady departed for Hawaii amid riotous parties in the ready rooms.

Two members of the *Yorktown* team came out of battle in the forward torpedo room of a sub, Harry Hill and Jim Cole on the *Tang*. The most senior aviator of the 22 aboard the sub was Commander A. R. Matter, air group commander from the light carrier *Bataan*. After the *Tang* remained off Truk for several more days on patrol, Matter asked skipper Dick O'Kane to radio Admiral Mitscher to please rendezvous the task force with the sub so that the 22 pilots could "effect their return to parent air groups." This would mean having *Tang* ordered to Majuro.

But O'Kane was no fool; he knew jolly well that, except for Matter, these men "neither wanted nor deserved rest on the sandpit of a flat atoll. They wanted to go to our rest camp, the Royal Hawaiian Hotel at Waikiki, and I meant to get them there." He handed Matter's dispatch to one of the junior aviators who was standing coding watch and asked him to take care of it. This worthy took one look at the proposed communication, muttered "That sonofabitch," and promptly pocketed it—as O'Kane had intended all along. *Tang* headed straight for Hawaii, arriving on the 11th, the same day as the *Yorktown*.

Captain Jennings had a broom hoisted to the masthead meaning "Clean sweep" for the ship's triumphant entry into Pearl Harbor after 116 days out. Alex Wilding "went ashore for a milk shake. Found out we get Air Group 1 and go back for the Marianas—no States. Went to the O Club and got drunk." Commander Briggs' disappointment in his Plan for May 12 went undisguised. Downgrading what he had previously termed the $64 and $128 question, he announced, without capital letters, "The $2.00 question has been answered. Just once more! Anyhow, this is better than waiting around in the Sleepy Lagoon." Meaning Majuro.

The pilots made a presentation before leaving—

an "Anti-Glare Shield" to Skinhead Bright "to reduce the glare of the sun off his head from blinding the pilots when landing aboard." He accepted graciously since "you all know I am undisputed holder of the title 'Pacific Ocean Area Sex Typhoon' because I possess *the* greatest expanse of kissable face. You—being younger and with insufficient experience and maturity in the love game, and possessed of luxuriant hair—you know in your hearts it is impossible to unseat me from this love throne."

"Old group leaves—everybody gloomy, dismal," a dejected Dr. Gard wrote in his diary. "Damn. Not getting what we want!—and how." Navigator Red Sharp transferred to Admiral Clark's staff and was replaced by Commander "Dick" Matter, the very same just rescued by the *Tang*. Commander Dan Sweeney passed the duties of first lieutenant and damage control officer to Socket-wrench Brady and

left the ship. Reluctantly, lovable old salts Joe Tucker and John Montgomery departed the *York*. And that peerless Weatherguesser, Jim Vonk, was tapped by Admiral Mitscher himself to become aerologist for all of Task Force 58. "He's pissed off," recorded Wilding.

"So it is not the same ship at all," lamented Ray Gard, "so many men (over 500) are leaving this ship for other duty." Three hundred of these boarded a Liberty ship for passage to San Francisco, only to have its inebriated captain run it aground on the Faralon Islands just short of the Golden Gate. All hands were rescued by small boats, but it "seemed anti-climatic" to Ed Stebbins' plane captain Jack Loughran "that after surviving battle that these people would be shipwrecked some 30 miles from home!"

The fortunes of war.

Lieutenant Joe Kristufek of Torpedo 5 pays a visit to Shirley Temple in Hollywood after returning home from his year on the *Yorktown*. Courtesy of Joseph R. Kristufek

At Majuro *Yorktown* shows off her new "razzle dazzle" camouflage paint job, June 5, 1944. Courtesy of Raymond F. Gard

Chapter VII
The Big Battle

"Here I am!" a jubilant
Lieutenant (jg) Chuck Ambellan scribbled in his diary as Air Group One reported aboard at Pearl in mid-May 1944. "We've finally gotten a carrier and it's a honey! The *Yorktown* is just about the best of them all and we couldn't want for anything better. Guess that we'll see about four months of sea duty and then go home!" Unfortunately, he was in his ninth day of hack for having given a bomber pilot a ride in his Hellcat, sitting on his lap! Walking aboard was the cruelest punishment, "watching the boys operate off the carrier and me not being able to. Gee I love to fly!"

Air Group One's eagerness to join the ship compared with Air Group Five's desire to leave it. The three squadrons had been split up for much of the preceding year and thus had reason to celebrate their first anniversary on May 9—"Here we go again," cheered Bombing 1, "booze and food, smooth or crude, dressed or nude, let's get stewed."

Though the pilots had twice qualified for carrier landings aboard the *York,* and Commander Jim Peters had taken command, late in 1943, the squadrons had been shunted around the Pacific to fill in holes. Fighting 1 had spent the two months after the Gilberts landings flying CAP out of captured Tarawa, getting exactly one kill but many sleepless nights between the stench of rotting corpses and the noise from trigger-happy Marines as well as dengue fever and dysentary. Their miserable New Years Eve had been spent sitting in foxholes to deter a Jap landing that never occurred and singing their own "Italian love song"—

Pisonia, pisonia, pisonia.
In Italian it means I love you.
If I had my way,
I'd pisonia all day.
Pisonia, pisonia, pisonia.

Bombing 1 and Torpedo 1 had trained and fought

the "armored gnats" at Hilo before moving to Kaneohe at year's end. In January all the torpecker fliers were dispersed as ferry pilots to the fast carriers, some to fly missions from them, including the *Yorktown*. The fighters and torpeckers rejoined the bombers at Kaneohe in the spring to train endlessly and battle the blues associated with it. They all seemed to enjoy liberty in Hawaii, although as one fighter pilot wrote to a cousin, "genuine companionship is scarce, and nobody has had a piece [!] since California."

When the *York* returned to Hawaii, their attitudes improved overnight. Wrote Lieutenant (jg) Bob Frink of VF-1 to his parents: "Thank God my morale is no longer at ebb tide. We're finally back on the first team again, and it certainly feels good for a change. See you in the newsreels. Don't fret if you shouldn't hear from me for quite a length of time. Ole Bob's skin is foremost in ole Bob's mind!"

The *Yorktown* sortied from Pearl on May 14 to give its new group three days of refreshers. "Boy, are they hot," thought Jesse Bradley, "If we can't get to the States we sure can give the Japs hell with this outfit." Air boss Ben Born was less impressed, a concern shared by Alex Wilding in CIC, "This new group is pretty green and needs a lot of work—not in a class with our old air group, Five. They better improve fast, for the coming operation is a heller."

That "heller" was known to nearly everybody in the Pacific Fleet—the invasion of the three principal islands of the Marianas group, beginning with Saipan in mid-June 1944 and followed with Tinian and Guam. Equally important was the long-anticipated first major naval battle with the Japanese fleet since Midway two years before.

The *Yorktown* received another admiral for the refresher cruise and the Marianas operation: Rear

Admiral Ralph E. Davison, who would observe in a "make-you-learn" capacity before getting his own task group command. His chief of staff was another Crommelin, Captain John, formerly of the sunken *Liscome Bay* and who, in Ray Gard's estimation, "looks, speaks and acts like his brother Charles."

After the maneuvers, the *Yorktown* spent ten days of "availability" in the shipyard at Pearl getting minor repairs and a complete new "razzle dazzle" camouflage paint job to give her the appearance of a battleship at a distance. This would hopefully discourage any attacking plane from facing the heavy AA of a battlewagon—an interesting concept which probably never worked. Air Group One spent the time at Kaneohe going through carrier "bounce drills" at night with ship's "Crash Two," Dick Tripp. Assistant engineer Country Lancaster swore he would never again allow himself to get close to any of these pilots; he had lost too many friends in Air Group Five.

The torpedo pilots loaded up the bomb-bays of several Avengers with all the liquor they could find—one carried 25 cases of whiskey, champagne, the works—and landed aboard the *York* without incident after she cleared Pearl Harbor on May 29. Destination—the Sleepy Lagoon, Majuro.

"The whole ship is spotless," observed Dr. Gard, whose Sick Bay had "almost no patients. Everyone well and eager to get a job done. This *is* the best ship in the Fleet and we are all hoping for a ship Presidential citation some of these days." To show the Allied Royal Navy just how such a smooth-running carrier did things, Vice Admiral Towers had assigned British naval aviator Commander Richard M. Smeeton to the *York* for the operation.

The most important new addition to ship's company was Lieutenant Thomas Jefferson Patterson. The transfer of Stroke Blackwell had left ex-pitcher George Earnshaw as gunnery officer and gun control boss George Weiss as his assistant, neither of whom were professionals in the art of shooting. The big, fun-loving "Tiny" or "Pat" Patterson was. A marksman from childhood in Texas, he had gone to Canada during World War I and lied about his age—13!—to enlist there, because "I didn't want to fight alongside the goddamn Yankees!" After picking off Germans on the Western front, he had returned to Waco to become a state medalist for the National Rifle Association. Attending 90-day-wonder school at Dartmouth College, he had pounded several worthies of Northern extraction with his fists for laughing at his accent. Patterson became the brains of the Gunnery Department and

the nemesis of Yankee Bright.

When the ship's guns weren't shooting at sleeves on the trip to Majuro, the planes operated. Air Group One *was* a crack outfit. In addition to the 36 F6F Hellcat fighters, it was comprised of 36 improved SB2C Helldiver dive bombers—still a "beast" in many ways but faster than the SBD and with twice the bomb load—and 18 TBM Avengers, the General Motors version but only slightly different from the original Grumman TBF. A new night fighter detachment had also been assigned to the ship.

Although group skipper Jim Peters inspired no particular following, each of his squadron commanders did. Newly-reporting replacement pilot Ensign Ed Buickerood told his diary that Fighting 1 "is very much on the ball with a very strict and efficient skipper." This was Lieutenant Commander Bernard M. Strean. Strean had been nicknamed "Smoke" at Annapolis because of the rhyme with "smoke screen." A taskmaster, he had whipped his guys into flying shape with precision tactics to carry on the traditions of VF-1 as the "High-Hatters", the Navy's oldest fighter squadron. Lieutenant Commander Joseph W. Runyan had been a dive bomber pilot most of his career since graduating from Southern Cal and had proved to be as strict a disciplinarian as Strean at the head of Bombing 1. The kindly Lieutenant Commander Walter F. Henry

Lieutenant Commander Walt Henry of Torpedo 1.

of Torpedo 1 had two Navy Crosses from the battles of 1942 and was a man of few words who said only one thing when a pilot missed a target: "Goddamnit, we came out here to kill Japs, not fish!"

Captain Jennings' announcement of the operation plan drew exclamations from crewmen and airmen alike. Jesse Bradley: "This ship is going to hit Guam and Rota Islands. From there we go to some island 511 miles from Japan itself. Boy, is this going to be hot." Or as pilot Chuck Ambellan put it, "seems that after a hit at the Marianas we strike the Bonin Islands only 500 miles from Tokyo. Hmmm—." Specifically, these were Iwo Jima and Chichi Jima, airdromes which had to be neutralized before the Japanese could stage planes through them to interfere with the landings at Saipan, set for June 15.

In Ready Four ACIO Jim Barker informed Bombing 1 that it had been designated to fly a three-section search during the operation, flights which would take the planes within only 250 miles of Japan itself. Questions abounded, including the usual wisecracks. "Where will the rescue subs be?" "How many hundred cruisers will we have to protect us?" Or, as Bennie "the Bum" Rato said, "I'm not yellow—I'm just turnin'."

Alex Wilding, however, didn't think "we'll have much trouble. Our forces will be too powerful." Admiral Spruance's sprawling Fifth Fleet amphibious and bombardment forces would be spearheaded by no fewer than 15 fast carriers of Vice Admiral Mitscher's Task Force 58. They were organized into four task groups under Rear Admirals Clark, Montgomery, Reeves and W. Keen Harrill, another newcomer.

Jocko Clark had already become Pete Mitscher's ace task group commander but had so irritated the officers of his flagship *Hornet* by remarking "We didn't do it that way on the *Yorktown*" that they refused to say the name *Yorktown* in his presence. It was the "Nameless," which naturally enraged him.

When the "Nameless" arrived at Majuro on June 3, according to a story in *The Saturday Evening Post*, Clark "draped himself over the bridge, drinking in the sight, his lower lip stuck out like a platform. 'That's a wonderful ship,' he kept saying over and over again in a husky voice."

Happily for Jocko, the *Yorktown* was assigned to his task group, 58.1, as the other large carrier with *Hornet*, along with light carriers *Belleau Wood* and *Bataan*, five cruisers and 14 tin cans. Clark was glad to have Ralph Davison available for

advice on the *York*. An intellectual who had graduated third in his class at Navy, Davison confounded his staff with word games and his general erudition. The only real flaws in his character, which affected his professional performance not at all, was a tendency to go on extended drunks off duty, with attendant misdeeds.

At Majuro, Admiral Clark claimed his last staff officer from the *York* in the person of Charlie Ridgway to be task group fighter director on the *Hornet*. Alex Wilding fleeted up to the fighter director job on the *Yorktown*, enabling him to coordinate closely the air defense of the group with Charlie by radio. Alex was especially pleased when Admiral Davison called him in for advice. "Davison seems like a good guy. I like him. He is no 'know-it-all' and realizes his shortcomings in CIC matters. And I think he has confidence in me now."

Chuck Ambellan, as hot a fighter pilot and as acute an observer as John Gray had been, reflected in his diary at Majuro that the *Yorktown* was "a helluva big team striving for clockword efficiency, and they usually get it. We all know that we're in something big this time and on the best carrier in the fleet." Which Ed Buickerood seconded, "The Japs are in for one hell of a pasting in just a few days."

"HERE WE GO AGAIN!" a rejuvenated Cameron Briggs proclaimed to his "RAT EXTERMINATORS" as the task force sortied on June 6, 1944. His exuberance mirrored the sentiments of crewmen like Joe Chambliss in Air Plot, "Our new air group aboard is raring to go and so is the ship after learning that 'Jocko' Clark is going to be the Task Group Commander. We are out for a grand prize and it is generally believed and felt that the Japs will resist in force in the defense of this all important point in their island defense perimeter." Wilding: "All ship's company expects this to be a big operation—and a show down with the Jap fleet. I hope so. The guessing game is that the Jap fleet will show up the end of the second week."

A sense of victory could be felt when a concise bulletin was read over the bullhorn that evening: "FRANCE INVADED." D-Day at Normandy!

As Task Force 58 headed south and west toward the Marianas, the pilots attended briefings "nearly every hour of the day," in the view of Lieutenant (jg) Norm Duberstein of the fighters. Captain Crommelin dropped in on the bombers and told them their dive bombing "had better be good because the Jap fleet couldn't duck much longer. And he didn't seem to think that they were a pushover," according to the VB-1 historian.

Sure enough, word began to trickle in on the 7th. Wilding: "Intelligence told me today that the Jap Fleet was getting restless—starting to move around a bit." And next day, "Adm. Davison states flatly to me that there will be an engagement with the Jap Fleet during this operation—he's on the inside position and should know."

The blissful optimism of all hands was shaken on the 8th when an airedale, Seaman First Jimmy Schreck, slipped under the wheel of a fighter being towed, killing him; within hours, his body was committed to the deep. Tension heightened as the force passed 500 miles north of Truk on the 10th and a bogey passed 70 miles ahead. It proved to be a Betty, spotted by an Army B-24, and had probably not seen the ships.

But Admiral Mitscher could not be certain. Wanting to preserve the element of surprise, he advanced the initial fighter sweep by one day from dawn of June 12 to the afternoon of the 11th. Captain Jennings passed the word over the loudspeaker

that night of the 10th, "Tomorrow we'll mow 'em down."

Next morning Alex Wilding commented that the "new tactic looks great on paper. This afternoon at 1300, while we are still 250 miles from the Marianas, we will launch 209 fighters from the Task Force to go in and clean out all Jap aircraft.

"This should be an added preventive measure to decrease any attacks on the Task Force. But we will give away the element of surprise in our strikes tomorrow. Can't win them all! Our VF will return to land before sundown. We then will start our hispeed run in to the target. A great tactical move on the part of Adm. Mitscher."

As the task group turned into the wind for the predawn launch of the CAP, Admiral Clark on the *Hornet* got out of the sack early to compare the rates of the launch between the two big carriers. His surprise was duly reported over the *Hornet's* Air Plot ticker: "THE YORKTOWN TOOK OVER 6 MINUTES LONGER, AND THE ADMIRAL, APPEARING ON THE BRIDGE IN LOVELY GREEN

Fighter pilots surround Captain John Crommelin of Admiral Davison's staff for the latest intelligence during the approach to the Marianas: (clockwise, from bottom left) Dube Duberstein, Booby Baysinger, Pablo Henderson, Tank Schroeder, John LeBoutillier, Bill Tukey, George Staeheli and Morris Wilmot. Courtesy of Arthur Abramson

Commander B.M. "Smoke" Strean of Fighting 1.

PAJAMAS, WAS HEARD TO REMARK, 'I'LL BE DAMNED IF I KNOW WHAT SHIP THAT IS, SURE CAN'T BE THE YORKTOWN.'''

While Smoke Strean agonized over which pilots to send up on additional CAPs and which to go on the sweep, task group radars registered a Truk-based bogey 60 miles to the northwest at 0817. Alex Wilding vectored out *Bataan* fighters which splashed the snooper, a twin-engine Helen medium bomber. For this achievement, Admiral Davison personally brought Alex a box of Panatella cigars, "Thanks for keeping the Task Force undetected."

"Everyone was on edge and keyed up," recorded Bob Frink of the fighters who didn't altogether appreciate the bombing and torpecker pilots lining the island as they took off. The spectators waved and held up five fingers, meaning, "Get five. Become an ace!" ("To hell with that," one Hellcat jockey had already told them, "I might run into a Jap who's looking for *his* fifth one!")

At noon, Wilding vectored one CAP division to intercept a big Emily four-engine flying boat 70 miles out and closing. Arthur "Cherrybutt" Payton polished her off within minutes; two of her crew managed to get out of the wreckage and were retrieved by a destroyer on forward picket station. Moments later, Wilding directed another division to a second Emily 50 miles to the northwest which George Staeheli and Bill Tukey chased and shot down. At the same time Charlie Ridgway on the

Hornet directed Ed Martin in the destruction of a twin-engine snooper 30 miles to the south. *Hornet* fighters bagged another Emily to end the threat. Jocko Clark signaled his old ship, "Your CAP has turned in the usual and expected top-notch *Yorktown* performance. Congratulations."

"PILOTS, MAN YOUR PLANES," Coop Bright's ticker flashed to Ready One for the 1300 fighter sweep to Guam, 192 miles due west. An excited Smoke Strean bolted from the room without his parachute harness, with which someone had to chase him all the way to his plane. He, Jimmy Peters and 13 other fighters took off with the bombers of Joe Runyan and "Whiskey Stew" Roberts, these carrying rescue equipment should any fighters have to ditch. After clearing the skies over Guam, each Hellcat would drop a 500-pound bomb and then strafe parked planes on the island.

On their arrival, the pilots of Fighting 1 saw no airborne enemy planes, so they worked over Guam against only AA fire until, south of the island, Strean spotted five Zeros heading southwest. Smoke led two divisions in a 2000-foot climb toward them, which Bob Frink described later, "Just as we got near them, they turned and attacked. One or two came in over our heads just in the overcast about 12 or 13,000', but could not get their guns to bear upon us. One came right through the captain's [Strean's] division and head on at us." Frink was glad to be in company with two of the best pilots in the squadron, division leader Lieutenant Richard T. Eastmond, a prewar swimming star at the University of Utah, and Lieutenant (jg) John LeBoutillier, Long Island childhood chum of Jim Bryan's and ex-Yale man.

"Eastmond gave [the Zeke] a short no deflection shot in the port wing root, and the Jap was smoking when he went by on my port side. The next I remember was taking a burst at one ahead of me traveling 90 degrees to my course headed north, losing altitude, and flames were coming from his starboard wing root. I turned into him as I fired. No one was chasing him, and I had a notion to chase him for a sure kill, but decided to stay with the division. This was no time to be caught alone!

"The next I remember was making a 180 degree turn to the port, and Eastmond, LeBout, and I all three pouring a withering fire into a Jap almost astern, though he was in a slight, falling right turn. He was smoking, and flames were emitting from beneath his wing at short intervals.

"That night, when we were interviewed, it amazed me as to how hazy the whole thing was

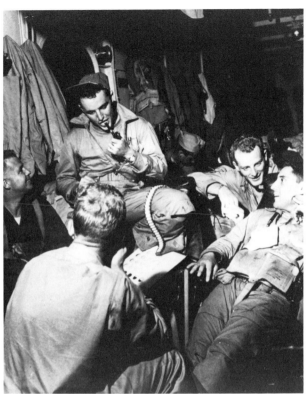

Excited VF-1 pilots recount the strikes on Guam, June 11, 1944, in the ready room. (L to R) Pablo Henderson, Artie Ward, Red Wangberg and Norm Duberstein

in my mind and how many different stories popped up concerning those brief moments of excitement. Eastmond was credited with the first plane, and LeBout and I were forced to toss for the other. I lost, but we agreed that I should get the next one."

Fighting 1 headed back to the task force with the rest of the sweep, having eliminated the feeble airborne opposition. "We caught the Nippos as usual," commented Dr. Gard, while Admiral Clark informed the task group: "DAMN WELL DONE. UPWARDS OF 30 ENEMY AIRCRAFT DESTROYED AGAINST ONE OF OURS SHOT DOWN"—more than a third of TF 58's total score. More snoopers were splashed during the day, although force radios intercepted a transmission from one reporting the position of the carriers to Tokyo. But none of the bogeys seen on the radars during the night closed.

Adding a fresh tactical wrinkle to his bag of tricks, Admiral Mitscher launched all four *Yorktown* night fighters of Detachment B, VF(N)-77, under skipper Lieutenant Tony Benjes at 0230 on June 12 to "heckle" Guam's two airfields, Orote and Agana. They strafed these fields from 0319 to 0530, keeping the Japs awake and off balance for the first incoming strike. And Alex Wilding vectored *Bataan's* predawn CAP to successful kills of a Betty and a Judy at 0525 and 0600.

Towering cumulus clouds and scattered squalls greeted the launch of the *Yorktown's* 21-plane fighter sweep and bombing strike of 14 VB and 9 VT half an hour before dawn. The fighters again carried 500-pound bombs and for the first time the torpeckers added rockets to their usual bomb load.

Again Japanese fighters were waiting, and again VF-1 brushed them aside. Lieutenants 'Mo" Moseley and "Booby" Baysinger each splashed a Zero, then joined their mates for strafing runs on both airfields. "Guam was just another pretty green island" to one Helldiver pilot, "but we soon found that the black puffs all around us spoiled the view." Radioman Horace N. Harris, the peacetime minister known as "The Reverend" in Lieutenant (jg) Bob Kimbrel's Avenger, "didn't see how it was humanly possible for a plane to go through the barrage without being hit. I said my most fervent prayers right. It worked—we came through without a scratch, while nearly every plane in the formation was hit."

Cherrybutt Payton took a burst of flak in his Hellcat and crashed into the sea 25 miles west of the island. He sank with his plane. Lieutenant Norm Merrell took a hit in his TBM but pressed his attack, dropped his incendiaries squarely on his assigned target buildings even as he trailed smoke and flame, and pulled out engulfed in fire. The popular pilot ditched but perished with his two crewmen, Harold Mongraw and Stan Carr, a loss the squadron felt keenly. "From that day on," in the words of its historian, Torpedo 1 "never once asked for quarter or gave it. Its attacks were effective, cold and vicious." Merrell's loss at least solved one problem—his marriages to *three* willing ladies on his way to the wars, which the Navy had only recently discovered.

The SB2Cs worked over the gun emplacements and reported them knocked out, "only to come back the next hop and still find them shooting." As one pilot put it, "It seemed to me that the Japs were having a lot more fun than we were. We'd have to go down pretty low to get a decent drop, and then there was that curtain of small stuff to get through. If we learned nothing else that day we learned how to jink—and in a hell of a hurry. Some of us nearly jinked our gunners right out of their cockpits."

Lieutenant Dick James, leading the second bombing strike, took a hit at 7000 feet during his dive, and his wing bomb slowly eased into his prop until the blades quit. He completed his dive, however, released the bomb at the proper altitude and pulled out to the east, gliding over Apra Harbor, "his engine so silent that he could hear the Jap guns shooting at him." His rearseat gunner, Dave Smith, instead of jettisoning his guns as prescribed by doctrine, fired back at the AA emplacements. James just managed to glide 100 yards beyond the reef, flaps gone and bomb bay doors open, for a water landing. They rigged a sail in their life raft and took five agonizing hours to navigate eight miles to the rescue sub *Stingray*.

Several '2Cs searched west of Guam for possible enemy shipping. Larry Liffner—the real life subject of Frederic Wakeman's fictional "Andy Crewson" in *Shore Leave*—and three division mates of "Liffner's Loafers" ducked into clouds to avoid a dozen Zeros. Two of the bombers strafed and burned a sampan, while Liff reported a small convoy of three enemy destroyers and three marus before breaking off due to low fuel. The powerful but hydraulically-temperamental Beasts had proved effective for the sortie. As for the return leg, "You don't worry about navigation," in the words of pilot "Silent John" Kilgariff, "—just follow the trail of hydraulic fluid back!"

"Sherman was right—," wrote Norm Duberstein of the fighters after six hours in the cockpit, "WAR IS HELL." But the Japanese suffered the most, for Admiral Mitscher gave them the same treatment on Dog Minus Two—June 13: night fighters dropping bombs and flares, a predawn fighter sweep, and five regular strikes against Guam and the other islands. No planes had survived to oppose the bombers, though flak struck many *Yorktown* aircraft, none fatally.

Two of the radar-equipped night fighters guided Smoke Strean with 15 bomb-carrying *York* Hellcats and six from the *Hornet* to their extreme range of 300 miles to hit Liffner's convoy. The excited pilots dodged the flak to claim many hits on the six vessels, but their inexperience in glide bombing resulted in damage to only one ship. A late afternoon search-strike by Torpedo 1 missed finding the convoy due to faulty navigation.

"Tokyo Rose," screen commander Captain W.K. "Sol" Phillips signaled Admiral Clark, "has just announced on the radio that all our ships are sunk." Replied Jocko, for all hands to see, "Do not believe Tokyo Rose. When the rising sun goes down she will sing a different tune."

The sun had set on scores of Japanese planes in the Marianas, most of them on the ground, by the close of the day, June 13, thus freeing two of Mitscher's task groups to head north for the planned treatment of the staging bases at Iwo and Chichi Jima.

Unfortunately, neither task group commander wanted to make the trip. During refueling on the 14th, Admiral Clark protested to Mitscher that he might miss the big battle with the enemy fleet, especially since, in midafternoon, the Jap fleet was reported to be on the move. Mitscher's amused staff appealed to Jocko's vanity by suggesting the danger and difficulty of the mission might indeed be too great. Jocko rose to the bait and shot back a message that he would go north at high speed, clobber the Japs up there, and be back in time for the battle.

Admiral Keen Harrill, on the other hand, considered the task to be exceedingly hazardous, what with typhoons reported to be raging around the Jimas. And the Japs surely knew they were coming, because of a snooping Betty shot down during the morning. Harrill notified Clark he wouldn't accompany him. Flabbergasted at Harrill's reluctance and remembering the timid Pownall at Marcus and Kwajalein, Clark had himself flown over to the *Essex*, Harrill's flagship, in a TBM to persuade Harrill. Only when Clark threatened to carry out the raid with his task group alone did Harrill agree to participate.

That night the seven carriers headed north. Dr. Gard caught the mood on the *Yorktown*: "We change course and shove it into high. The old girl quivers and shudders as her 160,000 horses shove her headlong thru the sea—rolling and pitching—worse and worse as the night wears on."

En route, orders came in from Admiral Mitscher for the two task groups to limit their attacks to one day, the 16th, and to use the 17th instead to rejoin the other carriers off Saipan. For the Japanese fleet had indeed been reported on the move, and Mitscher expected the naval battle to take place on the 18th.

Jocko Clark still wanted two days to work over the Jimas airfields and pushed TG 58.1 to full speed in order to launch a strike one day early, on the afternoon of the 15th. "GET THE SHOOTIN' IRONS READY AND MAINTAIN A KEEN LOOKOUT," Cam Briggs told the *Yorktown* that morning. "THESE ARE THE CLOSEST BASES TO JAPAN PROPER EVER ATTACKED BY NAVAL AIRCRAFT"—511 miles distant. Just how close this was was demonstrated when the task group came upon a transport and sampan in midmorning. Two destroyers sank them both and recovered only 100 survivors—civilian workers returning from Truk.

Moderate to rough seas and "a solid, thick blanket" of rain squalls and heavy broken clouds

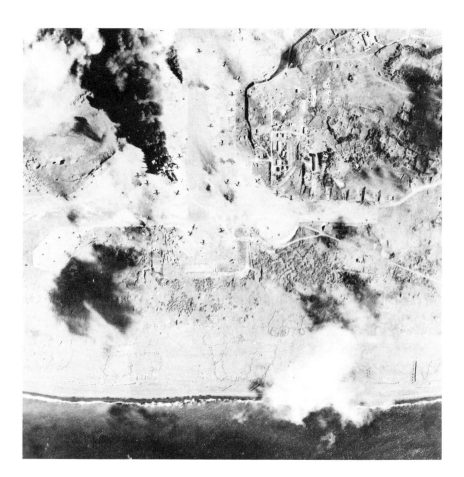

The great airdrome at Iwo Jima is surprised with most of its planes still on the deck during the June 1944 strikes. Courtesy of Arthur Abramson

weighed heavily on the nervous Admiral Harrill over whether to contribute to the 200-fighter sweep. An astute war correspondent on the *Essex* observed him carefully: "He had an almost harrowing [pun intended!] difficulty making that decision. It was plain to any eye that he had lived a life of conciliation, of reasoned compromise. He was almost incapable, temperamentally, of uttering a simple yes or no. In the end, other men really made the decision for him." Namely, Jocko and Harrill's own staff.

Taking off at 1330, Smoke Strean led the entire flight, including 15 *Yorktown* planes as part of the sweep 155 miles to Iwo and eight with the sweep 192 miles to Chichi, followed by the attack planes to Chichi—from the *York* 15 VB, 15 VT, 9 VF. Each fighter carried one 130-pound fragmentation cluster.

Battling the weather all the way, Fighting 1 roared down on Iwo at 1445 in four divisions led by Strean and Lieutenants Eastmond, Dick Shireman and "Pablo" Henderson, bombing and strafing. The surprised Japanese—for what damned fools would fly in this soup?—scurried across the field for their planes, only to have Eastmond's Hellcats cut them down and flame several parked or taxiing Zeros and Bettys. Smoke and Easty rendezvoused south of Iwo

at angels 8, then turned eastward.

"Tallyho!"

Three Zeros suddenly dropped out of the sky on to Strean's division. Hank Hankins turned inside one to destroy it in the starboard wing, while "Mad Dog" Tomme gave another the same treatment and watched it plunge straight into the water. Eastmond exploded the third with a steep highside attack and a long close-range burst. Four more Zeros weaved in behind Smoke's boys until Beck Bechtol flamed one. Shireman's division now entered the fray, Pablo Henderson's going after another bevy of bandits, and the general melee was on. Fighting 1 had obviously stirred up a hornet's nest.

At first, Zekes seemed to be everywhere. Photographic runs by Mike "The Mad Greek" Alexatos and Bob Garman were interrupted by interceptors, six of which chased lone Alex 35 miles out to sea until he dived away to elude them. Shireman hit a Zero flying above him in the cockpit just as another came at him head-on. Dick plugged this one in the cowling and watched him roll over in flames, then dispatched a third in like manner. A fourth got on Shireman's tail until George Staeheli pumped tracers into its cowling and it "fell off blazing in a falling leaf."

Bill Tukey chased one Zero off an F6F's tail then

-144-

watched it do a "sick wingover" into the sea. After rescuing another pal, he was jumped by two more Zeros. Pulling up, Tuke rolled sharply to get away. Down to 200 feet, he fired his only two functioning guns at a Zero almost out of range and exploded its starboard wing for the kill. Fearing engine failure, he jettisoned his bomb and limped back to the carrier.

Jack Hogue made his bombing run but took a fatal burst of flak in his starboard wing, outboard of the root. As the fire grew, Hogue jumped clear and parachuted a half mile off shore. An *Essex* fighter who saw him enter the water and start drifting toward the shore radioed his position to the rescue sub, full well realizing that the boat was not scheduled to arrive for another day. Hogue was never seen again.

"There they are. Let's get 'em!" yelled Pablo Henderson, whose three F6's came right up behind the three Zeros heading northwest and flamed all three with no-deflection tail shots—port to starboard, "Silas" Morner, Henderson and Johnny Meharg. Then, suddenly, 25 more Zekes came up out of the clouds behind the three in flames. The three *Yorktown* pilots took them on.

After the first pass, Meharg pursued one Zero into a mass of debris—apparently two Zeros had collided! Another one entered his gun sight long enough for Johnny to destroy him with a long burst. Yet another appeared dead ahead; as Meharg fired on it, the pilot bailed out right before his eyes. A third Zeke made an overhead run on Johnny, but missed, and Johnny chased it all the way down to the water shooting and watched it blow up under the right wing.

"It was just like the movies," according to Meharg. "I made all the mistakes in the book, and I can't remember what all happened, but I got four of 'em. I musta made 12 passes. One blew up right in front of me and I practically flew through his plane. I had to chase one clear down to the water and I only had one gun firin'. Forgot I even had a frag bomb on till I was out of ammunition. I dropped it from an altitude of 3000 feet and headed for home."

Henderson and Morner had moved after other targets. Pablo easily knocked two out of the sky and watched one of the pilots bail out. Silas ripped pieces off another Zeke, causing its wheels to drop before it entered a cloud. Down at angels 3, both men radioed for help as they each flamed another from behind then together chased a Zero down in such a steep dive that this foe smacked into the sea.

Pulling up at 1500 feet, they wanted to help Tukey and Hogue, but when the aggressive Pablo raced over toward them, three Zekes got on Morner's tail and Silas called Henderson back. Pablo turned around and charged in, announcing over his radio, "I've already got four, and I've got thirty more cornered."

Morner—nephew of movie actor Dennis Morgan (whose real name was Morner)—quickly jettisoned his bomb but forgot his belly tank; as he turned to port the Zeros boresighted him and pumped 20mm and 7.7mm slugs into his starboard wing and fuselage. The shrapnel knocked out most of his instruments, wounded him in the left foot and leg, and severed an oil line which caused oil to shower the cockpit. The same nest of Zeros bored in on Pablo and shot him down—a terrible blow to the squadron.

Silas pushed over into a vertical dive from 6000 feet and did not level off until only 100 feet off the water. "I was jinking, trying to shake them before I headed into a rain cloud and lost two of them. By then, I couldn't see anything, there was oil all over my face and over the cockpit." He navigated toward the ship with his few remaining instruments, only to have a Zero fall in behind him. For 20 miles he jinked violently and had his prop wash rip off his goggles as he watched his pursuer.

"I guess I must have looked like a cold kill because this third Zeke just turned into a beautiful slow roll and disappeared." Apparently out of ammo, the Zero wigwagged a farewell gesture as he left. Morner finally joined up on an antisub patrol, but could get his tail hook down only by violently rolling his wings. With one wheel jammed, his arm ached as he used stick pressure to keep up the damaged starboard wing. After one waveoff, his view obscured by the oil on the windshield, he made a belly landing on the carrier. The airedales just pushed the beat-up plane overboard.

Instead of Zeros, a small typhoon greeted the Chichi Jima strike. The fighters shot up barges full of troops while the bombing planes worked over transports at anchor. Jap AA gunners aimed at the holes in the clouds through which the planes must dive. Flak struck many, including the TBM of Lieutenant (jg) Johnny Keeler. The popular pilot had to make a water landing 50 miles south of Chichi where he, radioman "Bonzai" Webster and gunner "Armor Piercing" Normandin climbed into their raft amidst a 40-knot gale and heavy seas. "Will" Wilmanns dropped them his own raft, and skipper

Walt Henry ordered Charlie Nelson and "Kimo" Crenshaw to circle while they tried to raise the nonexistent lifeguard sub by radio.

The two pilots dropped their life rafts, shipwreck kits and a radio transmitter and leaned out their carburetors to conserve fuel until their engines sputtered. The men in the water and those in the air waved at each other for half an hour, gas gauges dropping and nighttime approaching.

Nelson to Crenshaw: "Kimo, how much gas have you got?"

"Charlie, I've got exactly 90 gallons."

"You'd better go home."

"Naw, I'm not going to do that. We'll go home together."

Silence, then Crenshaw, figuring Nelson would follow him, said, "Charlie, I've got just enough gas to get back. I'm going home."

Silence again as Crenshaw turned to go. Then he turned again and came back. Nelson called, "I told you to go on home, Kimo."

"I'm not going without you, Charlie."

More silence, then Nelson: "I've got more gas than you, Kimo. I'm going to gain altitude and see if I can see the sub. I can get back. Now go on home!"

Crenshaw doubted whether he had the gas to make it, but he obeyed. Nelson followed him ten minutes later. The last rays of daylight disappeared as the planes trickled in to the *Yorktown*. Wilmanns landed and ran out of gas while taxiing up the deck. Crenshaw landed with but four gallons, and Nelson came aboard another carrier closer to him, his tanks empty as he rolled to a stop.

Johnny Keeler and his crew never made it home.

Ensign John Delmore brought his bomber back low on fuel, only to get two waveoffs. His third approach was OK, except that his fuel quit and he flopped into the drink just off the stern. The big waves stunned him as the plane went in by the nose, but his quick-thinking gunnner Larry Flanaghan scurried to the cockpit when the nose bobbed up again, pulled Delmore out, unbuckled his parachute, and inflated his Mae West jacket. Destroyer *Izard* picked them up.

The day's score for the *Yorktown's* air group was 20 Zeros shot down plus three probables over Iwo; five had gotten away. Four more and ten bombers had been destroyed on the ground, with three seaplanes shot up and three cargo ships devastated in Chichi's harbor, but at the cost of five men. The other air groups scored, and suffered, equally.

Chichi Jima's typhoon moved over the carriers, making deck operations hazardous for the big carriers and well-nigh impossible for the badly-pitching light carriers. The *Belleau Wood* erupted in flames as a plane jumped the barrier and crashed into others parked forward. The crew overpowered the conflagration while eight of that ship's fighters landed on the *York*. At least the wind and rain were insurance against a night attack, and the pilots sacked out early. But sleep eluded the likes of Chuck Ambellan "in the middle of a typhoon all nite that made this baby rock and shake like a can."

In the predawn of June 16, Torpedo 1 suffered a freak casualty when skipper Walt Henry ran toward his plane in a torrential downpour and fell into the forward elevator well. Instead of breaking his neck, he only suffered a sprained ankle and severe bruises but could hardly move and had to be grounded for several days.

Eight-foot swells brought green water over the flight decks and convinced Admiral Clark to make a welcome decision, which Skinhead Bright relayed to the ready rooms: "SCHEDULED COVERAGE BY PLANES OF THIS FORCE THIS MORNING IS CANCELLED. IN OTHER WORDS, NO FLIGHTS. WE INTEND TO GET BACK IN THE SACK AFTER GQ. AIR PLOT WILL NOT BE OPEN FOR BUSINESS. SECURE FROM GENERAL QUARTERS. OH WHAT A BEAUTIFUL MORNING? TO RETIRE ONCE AGAIN TO THE SACK!!!"

Jocko Clark, determined to hit Iwo again before heading south to rejoin Mitscher off Saipan, came up with a brilliant idea. In the words of diarist Joe Chambliss in *Yorktown's* Air Plot, "We attempted the unbelievable today in refueling destroyers during the typhoon. The cans pitched very heavily but other than a few parted lines and hoses the feat was accomplished without casualty which readied us for immediate operations upon clearing of the weather. [Admiral Clark] tried a fast one in running East into clear weather, launching his strikes and then seeking cover in the bad weather where detection was impossible. This worked swell for the Japs never expected an attack during such weather."

The 15-plane afternoon fighter sweep and two composite strike groups from the *Yorktown* plus sorties from the other carriers expected, in Chuck Ambellan's words, "to spend the next few hours fighting Zeros by the score, but we never saw a G.D. one!!" The enemy had been caught flatfooted, planes all parked.

From clear skies, Smoke Strean led the strafers down to tear up the helpless Zeros amid only moderate AA. Ensign Jim Spivey however did not recover from his run, and between attacks his pals searched for him but found nothing. Flak ripped into "Mad Russian" Cal Kalousek's torpecker, and he flew home complaining that "one of my wings is missing." Squadronmate "Needlepoint" Cusick—whose bombing accuracy was likened to threading a needle—radioed the ship from over Iwo, "Planes are blowing up all over the place. Whoom, they go, and then in a minute or so, whoom!"

A particularly aggressive Lieutenant "Woodie" Wood made the rendezvous after his bomb run only to discover that two of his 500 pounders had not released. Whereupon he broke off and returned to Iwo—unescorted and alone. He dropped them into a bevy of parked planes, after which he circled the entire island at tree-top level and shot at targets of opportunity. The ACIOs estimated that 63 planes were destroyed by the *York's* fliers.

During the afternoon, recorded Norm Duberstein in the VF-1 ready room, "Captain Crommelin told us of the B-29's going over Japan, and the Army steals the headlines again. He also said we would see the Jap fleet in a day or two, and it sure scares me." Alex Wilding had received the news earlier in the day: "Our subs report Jap fleet heading for the Marianas...Fleet consists of 3 CVs, 2 BBs, 6 CAs, and DDs. Fleet appears to be rendezvousing with other Jap fleet units on the way. They are just clearing the San Bernardino Straits in the northern Philippines."

In the evening the two task groups turned southward then southeast to rejoin Mitscher off Saipan and next day sent out long 687-mile round-trip air searches to the west looking for the approaching enemy fleet. They found nothing in the five-hour hops, but Mike Alexatos with another fighter and two bombers got lost on the return leg. Alex Wilding sent a *Bataan* fighter out to radio them, which it did. The four pilots fired off all their bullets and jettisoned everything that wasn't nailed down to lighten the load on their engines. Then they homed in on the *York's* signal. When Mike finally landed aboard, he had five gallons of gas remaining. His hop had lasted seven and a half hours!

Continuing southward the remainder of June 17, the two carrier groups got the word, which Commander Briggs wrote out in his Plan of the Day for the 18th: "MAJOR UNITS OF THE JAPANESE FLEET HAVE BEEN RELIABLY REPORTED TO BE RENDEZVOUSING AT SEA IN THIS AREA. OPPOSITION TO OUR OCCUPATION OF THE MARIANAS IS DEFINITELY INDICATED. THE

NUMBER ONE BATTLE OF NAVAL HISTORY MIGHT BE JUST AROUND THE CORNER. BE READY TO COME OUT FIGHTING!"

As June 18, 1944 dawned, Alex Wilding in *Yorktown's* CIC noted its red-letter significance for him personally, "It's my birthday today. Happy birthday to me. I am 36 today—and feel every year of it."

During the morning a submarine reported seeing the approaching Japanese fleet units. But they were out of range of the carrier planes, so the four task groups left their positions west of Guam and headed for a new rendezvous to the eastward. The pilots in the ready rooms, wrote Chuck Ambellan, were "excited about meeting the Jap fleet. The tension sure grew, and the teletype was going a mile a minute." This sentiment was shared by the crew. Dr. Gard: "The Jap Fleet is out and we are to intercept it. *Damn!* Everybody excited and telling one another how glad we are that we finally are getting a crack at it. I wonder how glad each one really is?"

"ALL PILOTS STAND BY FOR STRIKE ON JAP FLEET" ordered Air Plot shortly after the noon hour, but the order was cancelled when the cause of the alarm proved to be only those ubiquitous snoopers. "The place is alive with them," said Wilding, "They are all around us. They pop up into our radar for 1 or 2 hits and then disappear below the radar horizon....1614—Our position was turned into the Japs by a snooper."

Ambellan: "Then we got the entire dope on the Jap Fleet. It's amazing how we can keep track of them. 9 CVs altogether, and a helluva mess of BBs etc., on down the line." Duberstein: "We are closing every minute and we all feel this is the decisive battle of the Pacific war. I hope we knock the hell out of them—we will."

Finally, TG 58.1 swung smartly back into formation with the rest of Task Force 58. "*Speed, speed,*" admired Ray Gard, "—these ships were built for it and Jocco [*sic*] drives like Jehu. That is the reason the old---made us fuel in a storm! On and on—rendezvous. Lord, what a bunch of ships— where are the Nippos?"

No one knew for sure as June 18 drew to a close, except that the Japanese fleet was approaching through that part of the western Pacific known as the Philippine Sea. At 2030, birthday boy Wilding was surprised to learn that, instead of heading westward toward the enemy, Fifth Fleet commander Admiral Spruance directed Task Force 58

CV - Aircraft Carrier   DD - Destroyer
BB - Battleship
CA - Heavy Cruiser

to continue eastward in order to protect the amphibious troops now battling ashore on Saipan. Soon, however, Wilding took heart when he intercepted a voice transmission from Admiral Mitscher to Spruance asking to shape a westward course during the night in order to close with the Japanese fleet, wherever it might be.

"A long wait," noted Wilding, "and then Admiral Spruance replied, 'Negative, I am afraid of an end run—set course 080 degrees (T) Speed 18 knots.'

bother Admiral Mitscher, but Spruance had assumed tactical command in fear of an "end run" by the Jap fleet around his own carriers. Mitscher and his airmen knew they could never be outflanked, since they could send their planes over 200 miles in any direction. The carriermen knew that Spruance had missed his big chance to sink the whole damned Jap fleet by heading west for a search-strike at dawn.

With the carriers retiring to the eastward, they would be within sight of Tinian by sunup, where

Waiting in the Fighting 1 ready room are (L to R) Dick Shireman and Dick Eastmond in the front row, George Staeheli and John LeBoutillier in the second, and Ed Martin and Bill Tukey in the third—suited up and ready to go. Courtesy of Richard T. Eastmond

"I don't believe it—I'm absolutely stunned. We have the greatest fleet the world has ever assembled—all trained, experienced and ready, and we put our tail between our legs and slink off in the dark of night. The Navy brass have been pounding their chest for a long time and screaming for a chance to close with the Jap fleet. Now they turned Yellow—no fight—no guts.

"Every man aboard ship is thinking his own thoughts tonight—if he expresses them he could be court martialed. Spruance branded every Navy man in TF 58 a coward tonight. I hope historians fry him in oil. What a birthday present for me!"

As Spruance's disappointing message was being received, the *Yorktown* launched a night fighter in pursuit of one of two snoopers, which escaped, probably to report Task Force 58. This did not

the planes of the Jap fleet would surely hit them. The enemy's carriers would stay well to the west beyond the range of Mitscher's planes and launch long hops to Guam to land, refuel and return—attacking TF 58 coming and going, *if* they survived Mitscher's 450 defending Hellcats to land at all!

"WE STILL DON'T KNOW EXACTLY WHERE THE LITTLE SO-AND-SO'S ARE," Briggs' June 19 Plan of the Day declared, "BUT, UNLESS THEY'VE SET OFF IN THE DIRECTION OF THE SETTING SUN, WE SHOULD CONTACT THEM TODAY." Another snooper visited the screen just before the 0600 sunrise and was promptly shot down by a can.

Belleau Wood launched the initial CAP into a fair sky of excellent flying conditions, and *Yorktown*— call sign "Coal"—sent off four SB2Cs and four F6Fs on two-plane search sectors southeast to Guam, hopefully to report any enemy carrier planes shuttling in from the west.

Pilots and aircrewmen anxiously watched their ready room teletype screens for Coop Bright's hot dope on the Japs.

At 0628 Wilding detected a bogey 100 miles due south and called Charlie Ridgway over on the *Hornet* for confirmation. Charlie saw it too and told Alex to send a division of *Belleau Wood's* CAP to intercept it.

Needing amplification of this suspicious bogey, Wilding consulted his other radars "and discovered it was right over Guam. . .growing rapidly in size."

Now the bald-headed Pete Mitscher called Wilding, "Coal, this is Bald Eagle. Send help to Guam."

Wilding acknowledged and vectored two more *Belleau Wood* divisions toward Guam as reinforcements.

"Tallyho! Tallyho! 20 to 25 Zekes and more taking off from Guam."

"The Japs had sneaked the planes into Guam during the night!" Wilding decided, correctly. "The *Belleau Wood* fighters fought for their lives, being greatly outnumbered, so I ordered them to disengage and return to base." He informed Ridgway and Admiral Davison "of the surprising conditions over Guam," whereupon Admiral Jocko Clark ordered a 24-plane fighter sweep to Guam. At 0704, Wilding noted, "One helluva big bogey over Guam now but they appear to be leaving and flying north."

The battle had begun, phase one to be labeled later in the day by one pilot as the "Marianas Turkey Shoot," the whole action dubbed by historians as the Battle of the Philippine Sea. As *Belleau Wood's* Hellcats were shooting down ten Japs, *Yorktown's* teletype addressed eight men of Fighting 1: "PILOTS MAN YOUR PLANES ON THE DOUBLE." It was 0744 and Cooper Buck Bright went on to explain that the *York* and TG7 58.1 were the furthest west of the four task groups and closest to any incoming attack. Entirely to Jocko's liking!

Eight minutes later Air Group One commander Jim Peters led five of the initial fighters aloft to join others from the *Hornet* and *Belleau Wood* on the flight to Guam. But by the time they got there, most of the excitement was over, the surviving bandits having fled northward. The Hellcats chased a few but failed to catch up, whereupon Admiral Clark instructed this flight to strafe Guam and Rota.

At 0850 fighter director Wilding intercepted a transmission to the fleet which had been delayed by atmospheric interference until the sender, a PBM seaplane, landed—over seven hours later! "He reports sighting the Jap fleet at Lat. 13 degrees 28' west of us. . . . If we had not been ordered to a course of 080 degrees by Admiral Spruance last night we would have been in good striking distance now and in one big decisive battle."

He vectored *Bataan's* CAP in the destruction of a Rufe float plane half an hour later and watched several bogeys register on his radars to the north which faded. "They're out there but they are staying out there."

Now the planes over Guam turned for home, only to run into several bandits. Anxious to try out the 20mm wing guns of his SB2C, "Fearless Fred" Cuneo filled his sights with a big Emily flying boat, only to have a Hellcat suddenly swoop in and shoot it down. Bomber "Moose" Mulvihill and Jim "Cess" Pool didn't even try but gave vectors and advice to their F6F partners Lyle Clark and Jim Pfister, who splashed two planes each—a Zeke, a Kate torpecker and two Jake float planes.

At 0942 a large group of enemy planes registered on the radars 115 miles due west, and 16 minutes later another incoming bunch appeared at the edge of the search radar: the first notice of incoming attacks from the Japanese carriers. Admiral Clark ordered the *York* to launch all available fighters; Charlie Ridgway was amazed that Jocko gave this order without prior clearance from Admiral Mitscher, but this was precisely why Mitscher had Clark up front.

Captain Jennings rang up 20 knots, while air officer Born gave Cooper Bright fresh orders for the teletype: "FIGHTER PILOTS MAN YOUR PLANES ON THE DOUBLE, TEN PILOTS VF. . .1010. . .LARGE BOGEY AT 265-105 MILES ON COURSE 090 AT ESTIMATED ANGELS 24." Smoke Strean and nine charges raced up the ladder and across the flight deck to their waiting Cats. In four fast minutes Junior Meyer sent them off.

Alex Wilding made a new entry in his log at 1017, "We hold a large bogey. Estimated 40 aircraft. Bearing 250 degrees—106 miles and closing. The battle is on and the Japs are striking first." He vectored 17 *Yorktown* and *Bataan* fighters to intercept this bogey at 20,000 feet. And the rest of the task force joined in the fray in like manner.

"SCRAMBLE ALL READY ROOMS. . .DISENGAGED SIDE IS TO THE EAST. . .TIME 1020. . .SCRAMBLE FOR PLANES ON THE FLIGHT DECK ONLY. . .NIGHT FIGHTER PILOTS MAN YOUR PLANES ON THE HANGAR DECK IN CASE

Dick "Junior" Meyer is all smiles, as are his assistants, as he holds a VF-1 "High-hatter" (see emblem) Hellcat with belly tank in the takeoff spot at the height of the great Turkey Shoot. Junior believed in always sending the nervous pilots off with a smile. National Archives

WE WANT TO BRING YOU UP AND LAUNCH YOU." All bombers and torpeckers were sent off to free the decks for handling fighters only for the air battle.

"The force went into V-5 [anti-aircraft defense] formation," recorded Joe Chambliss in Air Plot, "and a tight Condition Affirm was set throughout the ship. We really expected the worst. Our air officers directed all of the TBFs and SB2Cs to form and strike the fields at Guam and Tinian—similar instructions were given to the air groups on the other carriers. These planes were loaded with everything—APs-depth charges-incendiary-frag-mentations-rockets-GPs and SAP—all of this should really make the Japs at Guam uncomfortable in a big way.

"When our decks were cleared, all patrols and searches were landed and immediately re-serviced and re-launched against the additional bogey groups that appeared on the radar screen." Only a few pilots remained in the ready rooms to share the mounting tension with the crew.

"BOGEY NOW AT 260-95 MILES...BOGEY NOW AT 255-90...WE HAVE FRIENDLIES AT 280-45 AND 265-35...BOGEY NOW AT 260-85...ESTIMATED SPEED OF BOGEY 200 [mph] ON COURSE 080...BOGEY NOW AT 255-75..."

"Tallyho!!" It was 1034, and the call was from *Princeton's* fighters 68 miles to the west. "30 to 40 bandits, nine o'clock low, angels 16 to 23."

"RAID ONE AT 265-60 AND ANOTHER BOGEY AT 330-57...THIS LAST BOGEY HAS FADED. ESTIMATED AS SIX TO EIGHT PLANES...OUR FRIENDLIES ARE NOW WITHIN 15 MILES OF BOGEY...RAID TWO NOW AT 340-50...RAID ONE IS ESTIMATED AT 40 PLANES...'

Of all the *Yorktown* planes heading out, Smoke Strean's ten were now closing on the approaching foe. He took them up to 25,000 feet at first, then got a new order, "Go down to 5000." They dived down, only to receive yet another directive: "Now go back to 25."

The pilots strained to pick out unfriendly planes. "Do you see anything now?" someone asked over the radio once they reached altitude and the expected point of tallyho.

A pause, then another voice gasped, "My God, the sky is black with several hundred coming in!"

"Tallyho! Tallyho! Bogeys dead ahead. Low." It was Smoke Strean talking—but thinking at the same time, "Gee whiz! 400 of them, ten of us. We won't last very long." As he reported to the ship, he started climbing with his ten to get above the many bandits. Suddenly, F6F Hellcats from many carriers started pouring in from all sides to break up the enemy formation. Of the two divisions en route to join Strean, Wilding recalled one to orbit "as a safeguard" against planes which might break through at low altitude, undetected by radar. This left 13 VF-1 Hellcats to engage.

Strean's and Dick Shireman's divisions started the dogfights. "Excited as a kid" was Chuck Ambellan. "We wheeled over to meet them," dropping down

-150-

from 25,000 feet. "We peeled off on runs. I and most of us thought it was the bombers and were looking up for the fighter cover, but as it turned out, these were the fighters themselves and the bombers were below in still a larger formation." And getting worked over by other squadrons.

Strean himself knocked down a Tony and a Zeke, both from dead astern, while wingman Beck Bechtol flamed a Tony head-on, then a Zeke from above. In the second section, Hank Hankins zoomed between angels 10 and 18 to blow up two Zekes, his wingman Mad Dog Tomme disintegrating a third.

Dick Eastmond dropped down to 17,000 feet where he tore apart a Zero from behind, then counted 17 burning planes in the sky. Breaking out of a loop, he killed the pilot of another Zeke and narrowly missed colliding with him. With parachutes blossoming from the general dogfight, Easty turned to starboard at 7000 feet and fired a long semi-deflection burst at the stern of his third Zeke, fatally igniting its starboard wing root. Climbing to 11,000 feet, he pumped about 250 rounds into a Tony from the rear until it exploded, pieces flying back to hit his own plane. Along with single scores at Tarawa and Iwo, Eastmond had now become an ace.

Chuck Ambellan finally got what he had wanted so badly. "As I began my run and knowing no one was behind me, I kept looking over my shoulder and spotted two Zeros making a run on me! I turned back up into them and was surprised to see them turn away. Shot a rather long burst into the tail of the trailing Zeke which didn't seem to do much good, and then as I was closing, they each pulled apart and violently back to catch me in a weave so I just got the hell out of there as fast as 2000 horsepower could get me.

"Lost them and again made a run on the formation, this time picking out a single plane. Gave him a burst and as I was really going, passed him. As I looked back, he was smoking badly and suddenly burst into a beautiful orange flame. Then closed another one who after some maneuvering suddenly just seemed to lose all control and just went straight on down into the water.

"Made some more unsuccessful attacks, and finally, when they were all pretty much dispersed, chased a Zeke all the way to the water and spent quite a while trying to get him. He would go tearing along at about 10 ft. over the waves until I got within range, then turn inside of me and go shooting off in the opposite direction. Finally after

about three or four times like that, I got him on one of his pull ups. He burst into flames and went crashing into the water."

Bob "Stinky" Frink ignored the slow rolls of a tail-end Tony to flame it at angels 18, then nailed a Zeke at 17, even as another F6 was blasting a Zero off Frink's tail. At 12,000 feet Frink caught a lone Zero at the top of a loop and sprayed fuselage and wings with a full deflection shot until the Zeke dived seaward smoking, followed by a probable on a Tony at 8000.

Dick Shireman's division roared down from angels 20. Shireman sent a Zeke spinning into the sea, with wingman George Staeheli knocking the cowling off a Tony at 5000 feet—results fatal for the pilot. "Tuke" Tukey made a glide stern run for a 90 degree portside deflection shot which tore apart two Zekes.

Rudy Matz ignited a Tony into a solid sheet of flame in a head-on run, feeling the heat as he passed by. Then he dived on a Zeke with a 30 degree deflection shot from the port side until the gas tank exploded and Zeke went down. Two more Zekes and a Tony now closed in on Matz at 10,000, but two Hellcats drove off the Zekes, leaving the Tony to roll over on him from above for a head-on attack. Rudy opened fire, hitting the engine, which he watched smoke as he passed 25 to 50 feet under his victim. Down to 6000, he made a high side run on a Zeke and succeeded in setting him afire. Unfortunately, Matz did not see the latter two planes actually crash, so he only got "probables" for them.

"TEN TO FIFTEEN ZEKES HAVE BEEN SPLASHED SO FAR. BOGEY AT 345-45 DESIGNATED AS RAID SIX...ALL READY ROOMS: PILOTS BE STANDING BY TO MAN THESE [recovered] PLANES AS SOON AS THEY ARE GASSED...RAISE LAST SPLASH FIGURE TO 15 TO 20 ZEKES SPLASHED...."The Japs broke through to attack Harrill's task group. "ESSEX IS UNDER ATTACK. CLOSEST BOGEY ON SCREEN IS 260-30 BUT ESSEX GROUP IS FIRING, SO LOW FLYING PLANES ARE PROBABLY IN THE VICINITY...WE HAVE TWO MORE BOGEYS AT 190-40 AND 225-36...RAID SEVEN 130-15 MILES...SHIPS ARE FIRING ON STARBOARD QUARTER..."

Dube Duberstein: "It was a great melee next and looked just like the movies. I was on CAP at 10,000 and I could see everything, the dogfights, the torpedo bombers coming in, the fleet zigzagging, the ships shooting their big guns. It was an awe inspiring sight."

A Hellcat brings down one of some 400 Japanese planes shot down during the Marianas Turkey Shoot, June 19, 1944.

With the shooting getting so close to the *Yorktown,* Ben Born prepared to launch his remaining fighters and set Condition Affirm for the other pilots—dispersing them throughout the ship to avoid a mass slaughter should a bomb strike a ready room.

"ALL READY ROOMS: IF PILOTS ARE SENT TO THE DISPERSAL AREAS, LEAVE THE READY ROOMS EQUIPPED TO MAN PLANES FROM THE DISPERSAL AREAS. CALL AIR PLOT ON THE SHIPS SERVICE [phone] AS SOON AS THE FIRST PILOT GETS IN THE DISPERSAL AREA IF YOU ARE SENT."

Wilding noted that at 1100 Strean reported the area of the battle "clear of all Japs." None had gotten closer than 55 miles. Round One to the U.S. Fleet.

"MANY SPLASHES ARE BEING HEARD OVER THE RADIO. APPARENTLY OUR BOYS ARE DOING A GOOD JOB. . .TEN VF AND FIVE VFN

WILL BE CAP OVER FORCE. . .THESE FIGHTERS WILL FORM A CAP OVER THE SHIP FOR PROTECTION OF THE GROUP. . .WE HAVE BOGEY AT 310-40 MILES. . .THIS LAST BOGEY CONSISTS OF TWO OR THREE PLANES. . .HOWEVER, WE HAVE FRIENDLIES IN THE AREA AND THEY MAY BE OURS. . .HORNET REPORTS BOGEY AT 250-130 CLOSING. . .THEY ARE FIRING OFF OUR STARBOARD QUARTER. . ."

Time to get the last fighters up in to the air. "PILOTS MAN YOUR FIGHTERS ON THE AFTER END OF THE FLIGHT DECK. ALSO MAN TWO FIGHTERS ON THE HANGAR DECK. . ." At 1115 the ship turned into the wind. "BOGEY OF MANY PLANES AND DESIGNATED AS RAID EIGHT BEARS 249-120. . .BOGEY NOW AT 250-116 MILES. . .FIGHTERS NOW BEING LAUNCHED GOING TO ACT AS CAP OVER FORCE UNTIL VB AND VT NOW ON THE SHIP ARE LAUNCHED TO GO TO GUAM. . .THESE FIGHTERS WILL THEN

VF-1 pilots prepare to leave the ready room to join in the Marianas Turkey Shoot, June 19, 1944. Abe Abramson in the foreground, George Staeheli and Ralph Wines stand, and Mad Dog Tomme is in the background. Courtesy of Arthur Abramson

BE YOUR ESCORT INTO GUAM...

"FIFTY TO SIXTY PLANES IN RAID EIGHT WHICH IS NOW AT 250-100 MILES...WE ALREADY HAVE VF OUT AROUND 60 MILES AND FDO WILL BE IN YORKTOWN...BOGEY AT 250-90. ALL VF CONTROLLED BY YORKTOWN HAVE BEEN VECTORED 250...RAID EIGHT NOW AT 257-90..."

The fighters took off, but not to go to Guam. "NEXT LAUNCH WILL CONSIST OF 1 VF, 6 VT, 12 VB...RAID EIGHT NOW AT 258-85...VT LOADED WITH TORPEDOES WILL NOT BE SENT ON THIS STRIKE. HOWEVER AN ATTEMPT IS BEING MADE TO HAVE THEM LOADED WITH BOMBS...THERE MAY BE SOME CHANCE OF FRIENDLY WARSHIPS IN AREA ABOUT GUAM...LOOK TO YOUR IDENTIFICATION... RAID EIGHT AT 258-70 MILES...RAID EIGHT NOW 260-63...BOMBER PILOTS MAN YOUR PLANES ON THE FLIGHT DECK..."

While FDO Wilding sent his fresh 17 fighters to angels 25 over the ship, Born launched 9 SB2Cs and 3 TBMs to hit Guam. By 1130 the *Yorktown* was stripped of practically all of her planes. Climbing to altitude toward the estimated incoming 50 to 60 Jap planes, the interceptors made the tallyho at 1139—about 60 bogeys, mostly bombers.

"1143...ANOTHER BOGEY AT 000-90... COAL ONE JUST TALLYHOED ESTIMATED 20 TO 25 JILLS, ANGELS TEN, NO BEARING GIVEN...." Commander Peters's division arrived in this second phase of the morning dogfights in time to see two Zekes crashing into the sea. As another flew past Peters, he filled its cockpit and wing root with slugs until it exploded. As he pulled out, a second Zeke entered his sights, and he shot it down with a no-deflection blast. Section mates Booby Baysinger and Boyd York Weber each set afire a Zeke at angels 11.

At 20,000 feet Mo Moseley exploded the gas tanks of one Zeke and tore away at the engine of another until it began squirting flames and plunged toward the water. Maneuvering for a third attack, Moseley saw a Zeke come at him, make a flipper turn onto Mo's tail, and pour 7.7mm and 20mm hits into Mo's tail and fuselage. Other F6Fs drove this one away, while Moseley chased his original prey down smoking into the water for a probable. After landing aboard the *Hornet,* his well-holed Grumman had to be jettisoned. Ensign Bob Garman was never seen again after the initial tallyho, undoubtedly shot down.

"TORPEDO PILOTS MAN YOUR PLANES ON THE FLIGHT DECK...TWENTY PLANES HAVE JUST BEEN REPORTED BREAKING

THROUGH..." Alex Wilding released his two "backstop" CAP divisions overhead to stop them. "COAL FOUR HAVE BEEN VECTORED OUT TO SEARCH FOR ENEMY FISH LOW ON THE WATER...PLANES WHICH BROKE THRU HAVE BEEN TALLYHOED BY COAL FOUR AT 245-35...TORPEDO PLANES ARE ATTACKING 58.3 WHICH IS FIFTEEN MILES FROM US."

The excitement on board remained at fever pitch. "PILOTS MANNING BOMBERS ON HANGAR DECK RETURN TO YOUR READY ROOMS... ANY PILOT BEING LOW ON GAS OR HAVING TROUBLE CAN LAND ON ANY DECK...58.3 IS FIRING...RAID NINE HAS CLOSED TO 330-48, SMALL BOGEY...LOOKOUTS HAVE REPORTED FOUR SPLASHES OFF OUR STARBOARD QUARTER...ANOTHER JAP HAS JUST GONE TO VISIT HIS ANCESTORS OFF THE STBD QUARTER...PILOTS GO TO DISPERSAL AREA..."

While Wilding's backup Hellcats engaged most of these 20 Jill torpeckers at 1152, eight of them eluded the fighters to pick out any ships as targets. "Of all things," observed Joe Chambliss, these bandits headed not for the carriers but toward the battleships, "composed of the heaviest AA batteries in the world." Sending up a wall of flak, "the BBs really enjoyed this attack" by shooting down all eight planes.

Meanwhile, recorded Wilding, "A large bogey appeared on the radar. All ships in the fleet held it. Fighters were started out and then it was evaluated as a spurious signal—cloud return. VF CAP was returned to station. We're getting trigger happy!"

In the meantime, the bombing scramble to Guam had split up after taking off, the nine torpeckers armed with fish under VT-1 exec Joe Spengler on a long and fruitless search for the enemy fleet, the 15 dive bombers following Lieutenant Stew Roberts to bomb Guam. Directed to hit Agana, they did so against heavy AA, one burst hitting the SB2C flown by "Diz" Diem, severing the cable which lowered the landing gear and wounding gunner "Steve" Stevens in the leg. The tall crewman nevertheless removed his ammo cans, lowered himself to the floor of the cockpit, forced his big frame through the opening into the bomb bay, located the severed wire, wrapped the loose end tightly around a screwdriver, and manually lowered the hook!

After "Roberts' Rangers" rendezvoused, Stew got an urge to make a strafing attack on the Orote field. This unauthorized initiative, however, cost him his life, as flak brought him crashing down in flames on Guam. His gunner, Walt Warmoth, perished with him.

Joe Runyan led the second bombing strike to plaster Guam at 1140, and did so, using depth charges to obliterate parked planes there. But John Delmore did not recover from his dive, and he and gunner Larry Flanagan—the man who had saved him from the water landing only days before—went to their deaths.

Joe Chambliss reported in his diary: "Our bombers and TBFs were really having a field day at Guam and Tinian. They unloaded over the grounded planes in fine fashion. The depth charges did wonders against unprotected planes. The SB2Cs had incendiary 20mm ammunition that also spread great destruction.

"The Japanese tactics in so far as sending their planes to Guam and Tinian for re-service were sound as was the fact that they stayed outside of our striking range, but their tactics in so far as coordinated attacks and putting their planes to the best use were in the least very hard to understand. The many groups of 30 to forty planes were very soft meat for our approximately 400 fighters that were in the air for interception at any point.

"These small groups continued to come in all during the early afternoon and they as their forerunners were promptly splashed. There was no escape for any Jap. First he encountered a steel wall of F6Fs (who got practically every plane in the air), second, if by chance the Jap got by this wall, he had to attack a very heavily gunned task group almost by himself and if successful in not getting shot down yet, he could land at Guam which was under constant attack by our bombers, or he would have to land in the water because of lack of fuel. He could not turn back for his ship was over 300 miles away.

"I personally would hate like Hell to have been a Jap pilot today of all days!"

Half of VF-1 had landed aboard for rearming, regassing, sandwiches and coffee, and a leak—and much happy gab, while at 1242 Wilding vectored the CAP from *Hornet* to intercept another raid. Making the tallyho at 1303, *Hornet's* Hellcats destroyed 15 of 16 Zekes, the other one breaking through for a run on the *Essex* until a *Yorktown* fighter got him. At that moment, Charlie Ridgway on the *Hornet* directed *Yorktown* day and night fighters in the destruction of seven more incoming Zeros 100 miles out. Unfortunately, however, one of these shot down night fighter W.F. Wolf.

Since late morning the *York* and TG 58.1 had been steaming steadily into the wind, eastward,

In the midst of the Turkey Shoot, Lieutenant Harry "Mule" Mueller burns out his tires as he heads for the wire barrier. Airedales duck on the catwalk, lest an arresting wire snap, but nothing happens. National Archives

toward Rota Island while continuously operating planes. The island was only 45 miles away, so close that the CAP fighters were ordered to strafe it. By steaming east, however, TF 58 was going away from the direction of the Japanese carriers, which Admiral Mitscher wanted to locate and attack. At 1330 he sent off a *Yorktown* search-strike of fighters and bombers to the extreme range of 315 miles, but it would find nothing.

More incoming raids were destroyed by planes from other carriers, except for one "raid." "THE BOGEY AT 145-38 HAS NOT MOVED AND IS BELIEVED TO BE GUAM!" Thanks, Skinhead. Then, good news from a can: "GRIDLEY REPORTS ENSIGN WOLF, PILOT OF VFN 5, PICKED UP IN GOOD CONDITION. . . ." By midafternoon, the Japanese attack seemed to be spent. Then, alumni news: "NIGHT FIGHTER REISERER OF HORNET JUST SHOT DOWN FIVE PLANES OVER GUAM. . . ." Wrote Reiserer in his diary, simply: "Shot down five Vals when Jap [carrier] air group. . .tried to land at Guam."

Intermittent tallies were announced over the bullhorn throughout the day, and an excited Dr. Ray Gard smoked more cigarettes than usual as he jotted them down for posterity: "'18 Zeros shot down'—'23 Zeros shot down'—'76 Zeros shot down'—Bettys, Nells, Kates—-down, down, down. Hot damn! All day long, the score 163—186—210—252—275—300—on and on. All day long the scores come in. . . .

"310 planes shot down. 325 planes. Cruisers shot down 5 planes, Midafternoon—score 368 enemy planes shot down, others destroyed at Guam by our bombers. It is over, can it be possible? We go on. The reports are confirmed. None of our ships damaged to any extent. Everyone happy."

The Turkey Shoot was indeed over. Boasted a pleased though tired Alex Wilding, "Fighter direction made history today. Preliminary reports indicated 402 Japs were splashed today, and only about 15 got close enough all day to see our fleet." Fighting 1 had shot down 37 Jap planes plus six probables and lost one, Garman.

Joe Chambliss: "The various commanders published their gratifications and words of praise to all concerned—and in particular to the air groups. We now want to do a bit of attacking on our own—probably tomorrow. The Japs have lost their airborne striking and defensive forces and should be easy prey for our attack groups tomorrow. Anyway, we shall see!"

"WE STILL DON'T KNOW EXACTLY WHERE THE LITTLE SO-AND-SO'S ARE," Commander Briggs wrote in the new Plan of the Day, "BUT WE DO KNOW THAT THERE ARE A LOT LESS OF THEM THERE!"

Admiral Spruance, finally convinced that no enemy force was lurking for an "end run" around

whitewashed."

At least one of the "big brass" would not escape punishment for inept performance. Admiral Keen Harrill, leading TG 58.4 in the *Essex,* had neglected to refuel his destroyers and requested permission to stay behind—the last straw in his lackluster performance since the beginning of the operation. His

The long fruitless search for the Japanese fleet on June 19, 1944 ends as the planes, here a VF-1 Hellcat, land at sunset, 1800. Somewhere in the direction of the setting sun lie the ships of the Rising Sun.

Task Force 58, returned tactical command to Admiral Mitscher. But instead of heading west to locate, attack and sink the fleeing Japanese fleet, the carriers consumed more precious time milling around 30 miles west of Rota to land their last planes. Finally, at 2000, they reshaped their course to 260 degrees at 17 knots. But disappointment was keen from Mitscher on the *Lexington* and Jocko Clark on the *Hornet* down to fighter director Wilding on the *Yorktown.*

"Our course is finally westward tonight. The horse is out of the barn—a golden opportunity to end the war early has been wasted—we'll never catch them now. All day long we've been on the defensive and we haven't been in a tactical position where we could launch an offensive weapon. Why, bets are being laid as to whether we'll ever see the Jap fleet. Looks like the Academy boys are trying to make a career out of this war." Ed Buickerood of VF-1: "If we had caught the fleet the whole war outlook would have changed."

Wilding: "The fuel in our DDs is getting low—we can't continue the chase more than one more day. I hope the true facts will be published someday—but you can bet the big brass will be

group withdrew from the battle to refuel. A sudden case of appendicitus for Harrill ten days hence would give Mitscher a convenient excuse for getting rid of him.

The thought of missing a possible fleet engagement greatly concerned Jocko Clark, who, upon hearing Harrill's request, signaled, to Mitscher, "Would greatly appreciate remaining with you. We have plenty of fuel."

Mitscher shot back, "You will remain with us all right until the battle is over." Furthermore, as usual, Clark's TG 58.1 was in the van, closest to the expected action.

Details for the anticipated battle reached the ready rooms as June 19 drew to a close. "AFTER LAST RESPOT PLACE [three] VICTOR FOX NAN [VFN] IN CONDITION ELEVEN [ready for launch] UNTIL SUNRISE. BE PREPARED TO LOAD WITH BOMBS ON SHORT NOTICE." If the Jap fleet could be located on the 20th, "STRIKE LEADER TO BE FROM HORNET AND YORKTOWN IN THAT ORDER, BEGINNING WITH INTERCEPTING VF CAP. CVL WILL TAKE FORMATION PATROLS... THE BOGEY LOCKER IS CLOSING...SECURE FROM GENERAL QUARTERS...WE ARE TO BE

PREPARED TO LAUNCH A STRIKE GROUP OF 16 VF 9 VT 12 VB AT 0530 WHICH IS TO PROCEED DOWN THE MEDIAN OF THE SECTOR BEING SEARCHED BY THE HORNET."

Air officer Born counted 27 F6F, 24 SB2C, 15 TBM and three night F6F available for the morrow. Jim Bryan's ordnancemen armed each strike fighter with a 500-pound general purpose bomb; each bomber with a 1000-pounder, G.P. or semi-armor-piercing, plus two 250s; and four of the torpeckers with four 500-pounders each, the other five with torpedoes.

Now, the waiting.

Jim Tippey's radio listeners spent the night glued to their receivers for the vital news. At 2245 they got something: during the day a sub reported that it had scored "three positive hits on a Jap 29,000-ton carrier" then had endured 105 depth charges. "Sub believed CV destroyed." The position helped to pinpoint the earlier whereabouts of the Jap Fleet. In fact, the report by the sub *Cavalla* was correct. It had sent the big carrier *Shokaku* to the bottom. Not only that, but the sub *Albacore* had similarly 'done in' Japan's newest big carrier, the *Taiho*. That left seven enemy flattops.

At half an hour into June 20, 1944, a surface radar contact report from a PBM seaplane caused the fleet's course to be shifted from 260 degrees to 320 degrees (True), due west to northwest, but the contact was lost minutes later and the former course resumed. Too bad, since the new bearing happened to be the correct one.

Joe Chambliss arose with the crew before dawn, expressing its general mood: "We all look forward today for some more excitement, but this time our boys will carry the ball. Thus far they have never let us down so 'all hands' are resting in the utmost confidence—those boys are really swell! It's really wonderful to know how exacting they are—a bogey contact—a vector—a tallyho—and then a Jap splashed!"

At 0524 Captain Jennings turned the *York* into the wind for launching the first searches, and Air Plot News resumed: "LAT 13-35. LONG 141-00. PT OPTION CUS 250 DEG T SPD 15 KTS...WEATHER, SUR WIND 104 DEG VEL 11 KTS...LOW SCATTERED TO BROKEN CLOUDS...FREQUENT SHOWERS AND SQUALLS...CEILING: UNLIMITED LOWERING TO 1000' WITH PASSING LOW CLOUDS... VISIBILITY: 10 MILES REDUCED TO 1-3 IN SHOWERS...FLYING CONDITIONS: AVERAGE... PILOTS FOR ALL PLANES SPOTTED ON THE FLIGHT DECK WILL BE KEPT IN CONDITION 11 UNTIL RETURN OF [*HORNET*] SEARCH...EIGHT VF PILOTS MAN YOUR PLANES FOR ENGINE WARMUP ON THE FLIGHT DECK—0555."

These took off searching to the northwest, the strike group remaining in Condition Eleven, ready to be launched the instant the Jap fleet was sighted.

At 0650 *Yorktown's* search intercepted and splashed a Rufe—a single-engine float plane—almost due north, probably from a battleship or cruiser, then at 0755 another Rufe met the same fate further to the northwest. The Japs were trying to see how close Mitscher was getting to them. Their ships were out there—somewhere.

The coming of dawn caused the force to commence zigzagging to avoid possible enemy submarine attacks. These movements required reduced speeds, 16 or 18 knots, and kept taking the task force off its 260 degrees heading.

From the occasional snooper contacts Admiral Mitscher decided that the enemy fleet was not due west but retiring to the northwest, and at six minutes before the noon hour he ordered a major course change from 260 degrees to 330 degrees. The decision would prove to be a wise one, as confirmed by the northwest searches which now encountered and splashed three separate single-engine snoopers, "which means," in Wilding's words, "there must be a Jap carrier around some place in the vicinity." Still, he lamented that the chance for actually finding any enemy flattops "looks pretty bleak." The afternoon dragged on.

Suddenly, at 1545, a Morse code message was picked up by *Yorktown's* communicators on a frequency of 6740. It was from an *Enterprise* search plane: "00V24 V 47V24. Enemy fleet sighted. Time: 1540. Latitude 15 degrees-00'. Longitude: 135 degrees-25'. Course: 270 degrees (T) Speed: 20 knots. Three groups of ships. Correction on longitude and latitude. Latitude 15 degrees-35' North. Longitude 134 degrees-35' East."

All radio ears in the force fixed on this sighting report, a textbook account in its completeness: "Northern group—[carrier] *Zuikaku* and 4 battleships, 5 heavy cruisers, 8 destroyers. These ships are now changing their course to 000 degrees True. Southern group—2 small carriers, 2 oilers, 10 destroyers. Western group—one large carrier, battleships, cruisers and destroyers. This group is 60 miles west of the other two groups. The north and south groups are within ten miles of each other. Weather over target is good, ceiling 2000." (To which add three more carriers.)

"Like an electric shock," in Dr. Gard's words, the sighting report stirred the entire task force.

A quick computation placed the sprawling Japanese fleet 270 miles west of Task Force 58. Admiral Mitscher and his staff took only minutes to discuss the hazards of such a long flight. Very little daylight would be left for the attack. The return and recovery would be in the dark—though this should present no difficulty for Air Group One, which had trained at night. This might be the only chance they'd ever have for a crack at Tojo's armada.

Jocko Clark anticipated Mitscher's decision; at 1552 he ordered the *Yorktown* to prepare to launch the deckload strike it had had spotted since dawn. One minute later, Mitscher's order was received: "Expect to launch everything we have, probably have to recover at night." This meant that a second deckload must be readied for an immediate follow-up punch.

Ben Born telephoned the pilots in the wardroom, "Report to your ready rooms," and at 1600 Lieutenant (jg) Bill Ray, one of the *Yorktown's* steadiest OODs, took the conn for the long and hazardous operation. "Get the Carriers!" signaled Mitscher. At 1608 the task force increased speed from 16 to 23 knots. Two minutes after that the carriers swung into the wind, and in another six minutes they rang up 25 knots. Get 'em off!

Task Force 58 was sending 216 planes to try to sink the Jap fleet, all behind Lieutenant Commander Strean, who would also lead VF-1. *Yorktown's* flight leader was Air Group Commander Peters, Joe Runyan had the bombers and Charlie Nelson the torpeckers: 16 VF, 15 VB, 9 VT. At 1610 the airmen bolted from their ready rooms, chart boards in their teeth as they snapped on their gear. Revving up their engines, however, the bomber pilots received a sudden piece of bad news, held up on blackboards by airedales on the noisy deck: the enemy fleet lay 60 miles further than first reported, or just beyond the round-trip fuel range of the SB2C. That meant a return flight in the dark and then a water landing. Much of the excitement now turned to more sobering thoughts of that fate.

Yorktown began her ten-minute launch at 1620, during which Jocko Clark signaled to "Ramshackle," Captain Phillips leading the screen in the *Oakland,* "Ramshackle, tell Tokyo Rose to stand by for a ram."

"Good luck. Ram where it will do the most good!"

The planes rendezvoused quickly and began climbing slowly at about 135 knots, fighters in the lead, Smoke Strean in front. With the corrected position report, Admiral Mitscher now cancelled the second strike, and *Yorktown* respotted her remaining planes just as the force heard Radio Tokyo boast of sinking two U.S. carriers and destroying 300 carrier planes in the previous day's fighting. Listeners could only hoot.

Captain Jennings resumed the *York's* course of 300 degrees toward the enemy. Then, at 1647, task group radars picked up a bogey 30 miles due north—000 degrees—closing on course 180 degrees. The *Bataan* vectored out its CAP but recalled it three minutes later, evaluating the bogey as friendly—probably returning planes with missing engines.

But as the bogey pressed on toward the screen, Alex Wilding grabbed the CAP fighters back from *Bataan* and commenced the intercept again. The skipper rang GQ, and George Earnshaw's gunners raced to their guns. It was a Nell, at which the screen now opened fire. The Nell turned away to the north in view of the CAP and escaped, and the *Yorktown* recovered four of its strike planes with engine trouble—one VF, one VT and two VB.

For nearly two and a half anxious hours and almost 300 miles they droned on, fighters reaching 20,000 feet, the others 15,000. The clouds looked deceptively like ships in front of the setting sun.

At 1840 they made contact. The *Yorktown* pilots counted four separate groups of ships, but their leaders told them to go after only the two (actually three) with the carriers. Visibility was an excellent 25 miles, with scattered cumulus clouds down to 2500 feet. But less than half an hour of daylight remained, with the sun touching the cloudy horizon. Fighting 1 encountered none of the 75 bandits which dared contest the strike.

The waning daylight meant that coordinated bombing attacks would only waste precious minutes, so the bombing sections went into immediate, individual dives. "Pretty yellow and purple puffs" of flak licked up at the Helldivers as they peeled off, the bursts following them all the way down. Commander Peters orbited overhead to observe the attacks on the enemy ships, which maneuvered violently to evade the bombs.

At 15,000 feet the bombers and torpeckers followed Charlie Nelson's TBM between and away from two Jap carrier forces steaming some 15 miles apart and flew towards a large towering cumulus cloud. Near it, Nelson executed a sharp left 360 degree turn, diving steeply around and through the cloud, followed by the four other planes of his division, all loaded with fish.

The five Avengers headed toward a group of three flattops, whose names—which the airmen could not know—were the light carrier *Ryuho* and the mediums *Junyo* and *Hiyo* (or *Hayataka*).

In Nelson's abrupt maneuver, three bomb-laden torpeckers led by Bob Mahoney got separated but soon followed Nelson's five toward the same group of ships. So did Smoke Strean's 15 bomb-carrying Hellcats. Joe Runyan, on the other hand, turned right with his 13 Beasts and headed northward toward a *Shokaku*-class heavy carrier and three cruisers. It was the *Zuikaku*, last surviving carrier of the attack on Pearl Harbor.

Planes from other carriers also attacked these two formations and the third group of three light carriers and several battleships to the southwest, plus the fourth group, tankers to the south.

Closest to the attacking *Yorktown*ers, the *Zuikaku* made a tight turn to starboard as Runyan's Onions approached at high speed from 15,000 feet and at 1850 pushed over in steep dives at 12,000. The carrier, cruisers and seven escorting tin cans threw up an intense curtain of flak, and a Jap fighter plane closed in until deterred by the fire of a rearseat gunner. The SB2Cs made excellent dives and one by one released their bombs from between 2000 and 1000 feet.

They pulled out amidst the continuous multicolored ack ack. One bomb struck near the base of the carrier's island superstructure, and at least two more hit aft on the flight deck, leaving "a large hole, rimmed with fire apparently emanating from the hangar deck below," in the words of the VB-1 historian.

The smoke which billowed up obscured subsequent results, but Bombing 1 got perhaps another hit or two· and some near misses. In fact, the *Zuikaku* was taking such a beating that the last two pilots changed to a different target, a nearby cruiser, on which both claimed probable hits. Burt MacKenzie recovered next to a heavy cruiser and flew right alongside it, "afraid to jig into AA which was bursting both above and below him." Bill MacLean lifted a wing in fear of hitting the mast of a destroyer. As he looked down he could actually see Jap sailors "crouched behind their guns, blazing away."

Meanwhile, Charlie Nelson—with his gunner Lyle Young and radioman Conrad Lantron—emerged from the big cloud at 2500 feet, dropped down to 350 feet for his torpedo run on the light carrier *Ryuho*, and cut his air speed to 220 knots. Three TBMs followed him, and the fourth came down at some distance behind these.

Charlie braved the flak and held his fish until just 1000 yards from the CVL, then he released. The torpedo made a straight run, while Nelson pulled up over the ship. The ack ack followed him, hitting the exposed Turkey in the belly until it burst into flames, rolled over on its back and crashed into the sea, killing all three men.

The others pressed on. Kimo Crenshaw "looked down and saw the carrier below, the biggest damn thing I'd ever seen." With puffs of flak all about him, he dropped successfully and recovered over the *Ryuho* as its gunners peppered both his wings. The next three also dropped—with unknown effect. The four surviving TBMs pulled out to observe the results of their handiwork, when enemy fighters jumped them, only to be driven off by the rearseat gunners and the timely arrival of an F6F. The torpeckers later claimed to have seen two hits on the carrier and a destroyer blowing up. Sad to say, however, their eyes either misled them or they were looking at the carrier *Hiyo* shuddering from torpedo hits by *Belleau Wood* planes. And no destroyer actually took any hit in the confused and exciting action.

Bob Mahoney's three torpeckers then made glide bombing runs from 10,000 feet on a carrier, either the *Hiyo* or *Junyo*. Mahoney and Bob "Long John" Kimbrel released their sticks of four 500-pound bombs from 2500 feet, each scoring a hit or near-miss, but Bob Carlson was unable to release before a burst of flak hit his plane, sending it down in flames. His gunner "Rick" O'Shea and radioman "Trouser" Trau died with him. As Kimbrel recovered, "The Reverend" Horace Harris in the turret sprayed the carrier's deck, and radioman Bob Yount "could see seven distinct columns of smoke rising up"—though some of these were probably fire from the ship's guns.

Smoke Strean took the fighters into their bombing runs. Eleven of the Hellcats released from about 2200 feet over the same flattop, *Junyo* or *Hiyo*, while another shifted over to a light cruiser. Between them, they claimed three direct hits and five near-misses on the carrier and a probable hit or near-miss on the cruiser. But Commander Peters, trying to observe results from far overhead, tended to discount all these claims, though both carriers did in fact receive damage from some planes. On the pullout, Ensign "Whitey" Reinert engaged a Val bomber head-on but missed it.

This sight over the Philippine Sea greets Air Group One in the final minutes of daylight as the Japanese carrier *Zuikaku* maneuvers amidst her escorts in the center of the picture, June 20, 1944. This photograph, taken from a *Yorktown* plane, is reproduced here for the first time. Naval Historical Center

As Air Group One finished its runs in the fading light, it turned for home at about 1919 but without bothering to effect any rendezvous. "There wasn't much of a chance to get all the boys together again with the gas problem what it was," the VB-1 historian recalled. "They came home singly and in pairs, their props and mixture controls way down in manual. They were so gas conscious that they were even afraid to bend the throttle getting out of there. Lou Ruzicka, for one, went through the enemy cruiser screen at 30 inches. This stinginess got the Onions back to the force that night, though, and we liked that." The alternative of recovering straight over the Jap fleet and AA was to go around it and out—too expensive in fuel consumption. So

they took the direct route, and its flak.

TBMs faced the same dilemma and with the SB2Cs climbed slowly to conserve gas, while the general confusion prevented the F6Fs from finding their own pals. So planes indiscriminately joined up on other planes. Meanwhile, at 1900, Commander Peters had radioed the *Yorktown*: "Believe both attacks completed. Two CV, one unknown, one *Shokaku* smoking."

In the Fighting 1 ready room, someone jotted a hasty poem on the blackboard:

> Roses are red
> Violets are blue
> Sink one Shokaku
> And another Maru!

Peters' report was correct. Two carriers were smoking. The *Hiyo,* gutted from torpedo hits, finally rolled over and sank, but the *Shokaku*-class *Zuikaku* survived its seven bomb hits by heads-up damage control parties which managed to extinguish the raging fires. Three other flattops had been damaged in the action (plus the two others sunk the previous day by subs). Otherwise, only two oilers were scuttled and 65 planes shot down as a result of TF 58's attack.

Darkness fell quickly over the Philippine Sea, and the two-hour return flight encountered only thin wisps of clouds playing tag with brilliant stars in the moonless sky. Exhausted though they were, however, Air Group One's pilots now profitted from their night-flying drills in Hawaii.

But it wouldn't be easy, this flight, and its leader, Smoke Strean, wasn't the only one who must navigate all the way home. Over the hypnotic drone of their vibrating engines, throats craving "a long, cold drink of water," sweat making their clothes into a second layer of skin, hands gripping the stick, and tense legs and feet carefully balancing the pedals, the pilots glued their eyes to that one vital lighted gauge on the instrument panel—the artificial horizon.

The young rearseatmen in the bombers strained to detect signs of lights on the water. They saw the exhausts of other planes, and they saw stars. Some of them also saw flashes of light in the direction of the task force, and their pilots turned toward these. But it was only lightning in a rain squall, and when force radars showed planes heading toward the flashes several night fighters took off to find them and bring them in.

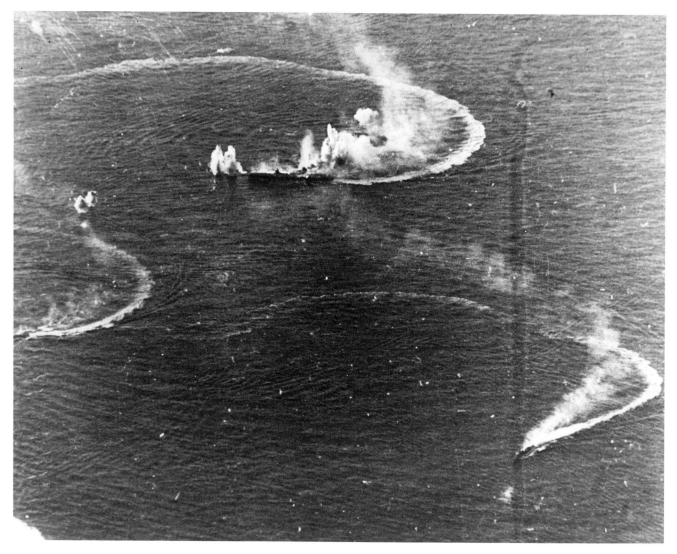

The heavy carrier *Zuikaku*, last survivor of the attack on Pearl Harbor, takes several bomb hits from Air Group One and other groups in this final phase of the Battle of the Philippine Sea. Two destroyers twist with her to avoid the attacking planes. In spite of the damage, *Zuikaku* would survive until sunk at Leyte four months later. National Archives

The bomber pilots continued to fly on a dangerously lean fuel mixture, so dangerous it threatened to burn out the engines, and white sparks were the first warning, then a sputtering motor. Feeding in more fuel until their exhausts cooled, the fliers leaned out the mixture again, all the while listening for that familiar radio homing beam to guide them home. The first pilots picked it up some 60 miles from the force.

Captain Jennings turned over tracking of the flight to his expert fighter director Wilding, while navigator Dick Matter and OOD Bill Ray kept the ship on station. The task force was spread out, ready for their return, task groups 15 miles apart. Course was 315 degrees True, northwest, speed 19 knots, when the returning planes were picked up by force radars on 307 degrees and heading toward

Clark's and Montgomery's task groups. Admiral Reeves told his ships to be ready to throw float lights in the water to mark planes if they went in.

Jocko Clark was the first to act. At three minutes before 2000, he ordered TG 58.1 to turn into the wind preparatory to landing planes. Al Jennings brought the *Yorktown* sharply around to course 100 degrees, ringing up 25 knots as he did so, and the screws whirred up from 161 to 193 R.P.M. Each ship in the formation turned on its two dim truck lights and each carrier a dim glow light and tiny, hooded runway bulbs—standard procedure for night operations, though these lights allowed for no individual recognition and could only be seen from a fairly close proximity.

At 2001, *Yorktown's* radios heard the crackle of flight leader Stream: "Coal Base, this is Double

Zero."

Wilding acknowledged and asked, "How much fuel do you have left?"

"Several hours," Smoke kidded.

"OO, orbit base and I will take you aboard last. I want to get those low on fuel aboard first."

"Wilco. Expedite recovery, as many aircraft are very low on fuel. Some have landed in the water along the track from the target."

Admiral Clark was startled by this news and immediately, at 2003, ordered some of his destroyers to make smoke to help announce the position of the force and at 2012 reversed course to the northwest to gain a few more precious miles for the fuel-starved bombers.

All ears topside and in the ready rooms now listened in silence for the first sound of returning planes. "There was no acey-deucy that night" for Bombing 1's waiting fliers. "As pancake time approached we were all in Ready 3 and Ready 4 sweating them in. Finally we heard engines and some of us crawled out on the catwalk to take a look. One look sufficed. It was as if all the worst nightmares of Hilo night flying had been telescoped into this one moment."

The first planes were racing to get in the groove as Clark bought the *Hornet*, *Yorktown*, *Belleau Wood* and *Bataan* into the wind again at 2020. In spite of the truck lights, the pilots could not identify their own carriers and told Alex Wilding so: "Coal Base, give me a vector to the ship."

"Land on any base. All are recovering."

Well and good, except that each *Yorktown* pilot wanted his own Dick Tripp to wave him aboard: he "knew" Tripp's style, and it was the Dog who had drilled them at Hilo. In blind panic, planes competed in trying to find the first friendly flight deck before their fuel went, edging each other out of the landing circles, ignoring waveoffs, and piling into arresting wires and barriers.

Wilding: "The Fighter Director net now carries one announcement after another from the carriers, 'Our flight deck is fouled.' Planes crashing on all flight decks. Planes dropping in the ocean all around us. CAP and Strike frequencies loaded with Mayday messages. This is a catastrophe."

Flight deck officer Hank Warren climbed up to Pri Fly and told Pappy Harshman, "We should have cargo lights." Pappy quietly got to work rigging one under Pri Fly in case it was called for.

Captain Jennings turned to Coop Bright, "Are our planes coming back?"

"There's no way to count 'em. They're landing on any ship."

"I'm interested in getting information from you on *our* planes. Are they safe?"

Bright hurried back into Air Plot to listen on the radio and direct Air Group One. He told Lieutenant (jg) Ben Tate, "Tate, you get the hell out of there, and you go up there with a pair of glasses and start looking for airplanes coming in. Keep me advised of anything that you think might be worthwhile."

Tate went out on the bridge, where there was much yelling and screaming at the unfolding calamity. "At this point," Al Jennings recalled, "hundreds of us on deck were wracking our brains for the change that would get the landing operation off dead center. Something different, an innovation was needed. I stepped off from the bridge to Fly Control and found the answer."

Pappy Harshman spoke to him: "I have rigged a cargo light under Fly Control here and recommend that it be turned on."

"That means we'll have to light ship."

"That's right, by God! We'll get those planes out of there."

"It did not take long to decide to light up the landing area," Jennings remarked, "I really had no choice. Exchange of messages would have taken precious time, while an order to dowse the light would not be long in coming." He ordered the light trained on the deck, and no order came from Clark on the *Hornet* to turn it off.

As the flight deck was bathed in light, Coop Bright—amazed that Jennings had ordered it—broadcasted to the fliers: "*Yorktown* is lit up."

It was 2030 when Jocko went one better and ordered the *Hornet* and *Yorktown* to turn on their 24-inch carbon arc searchlights and the cruisers *Canberra* and *Boston* to fire star shells to aid the planes in homing.

A Hellcat touched down on the *Yorktown* at 2034, and one minute later the cruisers raised their main batteries to an elevation of 65 degrees and started shooting starshells at several minute intervals. At 2040 *Belleau Wood* and *Bataan* lighted up, and two *Yorktown* planes landed on the latter, the second, Bob Frink's Hellcat, crashing into the barrier. These were the only planes to land on *Bataan* this entire hectic night. Frantic pilots now rushed for the *Yorktown* and *Hornet*, and the lights had to be switched off until decks were clear of just-landed planes.

Bomber pilot Burt MacKenzie was off to the south at 2029 when a formation of ships beneath him turned on its truck lights. He responded to

Wilding's order to land on any carrier by entering the landing circle of a big, dark carrier. As he came up the groove at 2035 the flattop turned on its runway lights, and within seconds he grabbed the wire. It was the *Wasp* in Montgomery's group. He was the first plane aboard her; three minutes later, the nearby *Bunker Hill* took aboard her first pigeon.

The popularity of Jocko Clark's task group was understandable. It was the only illuminated group, but as its lights went off the pilots yelled for help from Wilding. "So many transmissions coming into me from planes—they don't even give their call signs—just press their transmitter button and say their message—as 'I'm out of gas and going in the water'—'I got a hit on a carrier, that's about all.'— then silence.

"A hysterical voice came in, 'Take me aboard, take me aboard. I'm going in the drink—God damn you sons of bitches. All I can say is that you're losing a God damned good pilot.'"

Thankfully, returning planes were finally arriving over Reeves' task group where Admiral Mitscher rode on the *Lexington*, and Old Pete immediately understood the situation. At 2040 he transmitted an order to all three task group commanders: "Have one DD in each group turn searchlight on as nearly vertical as practicable in forward part of your disposition."

Just as this order was being acknowledged, however, two planes crash-landed in close succession on the *Yorktown*, and the cargo light was switched off. Jennings called the *Bataan* for help at 2043: "I've just landed two and both cracked up. I can't take any more. They'll put me out of commission. Can you get your planes over your ship?"

Bataan replied: "They're mixed up which carrier is which. We can't take them into landing circle. Our planes are in someone's landing circle, I don't know whose."

One minute later, at 2044, Mitscher ordered all three groups to change course into the wind to land planes. Clark and Montgomery had done this many minutes before, and now finally Reeves followed suit.

At 2045 Mitscher again instructed each task group, "Turn on one searchlight...to assist pilots in homing." Then, "Land on any base." These orders were really only for Reeves' group, affirming what Clark and Montgomery were already doing.

Now all of Task Force 58 lighted up. Not only the carriers but the other vessels as well, and more cruisers fired starshells to illuminate the entire formation. The *Yorktown* again lighted up at 2048.

"The 24-inch carbon arc lights were pointed up straight in the air" in the words of junior signal officer George Wille, "The light they projected looked like two great white pillars sticking into the night," making a display "quite spectacular, and that plus innumberable running lights of the planes made the scene as bright as a Christmas fete."

Wilding: "The *Yorktown* starts sending 'Charley' on the 24-inch searchlight, beamed up into the sky. Our flight deck is clear. Our DDs are firing starshells. We advise our pilots. We are now sweeping our flight deck with searchlights. To Hell with Jap subs. Now our aircraft are landing aboard without crashing."

While Dog Tripp brought them in—sometimes with two or three planes responding to his signals for one—Angie Peccianti and his crew got the planes out of the wires in "super fast" time. Suddenly Tripp told his talker to inform Angie's talker, "Hey, I've got two planes coming in. I'll try to put the first one on Number 8 or Number 9 wire—you try to get him out as quickly as possible—and I'll try to put the other one on Number One or Number Two wire."

The two planes did it, SB2Cs, to the cheering of all hands not needed below who had come topside to witness the spectacle. These pilots were *Yorktown*ers, Joe Runyan and Bob Carmichael, who dragged themselves into the ready room. "The Skipper and the Hawse came in grey and soaked with sweat and they confirmed our judgment" about the nightmare outside, said the VB-1 historian. "Carmichael's rendition sounded like something out of Marco Polo. We eyed the ready room door for more of our warriors. None came."

At 2050 a plane ditched off the *Yorktown*'s starboard quarter, and the helm had to steer the ship clear of the plane. In four fast minutes the destroyer *McCall* came alongside the plane to easily retrieve survivors. When the carriers dodged the ditchers, they lost the wind.

"The World's Fair" some called the excitement, but no midway amusement ride ever equaled the sheer terror of night water landings or deck crashes. The bombers and torpeckers crowded each other for groove positions, "like trying to get a drink at the Kaneohe bar at 1800"—closing time. Long John Kimbrel in his TBM took so many waveoffs from one carrier that he changed traffic circles in frustration and landed aboard the *Enterprise* in Reeves' group.

Chuck Ambellan, who had waited all four hours in the ready room for the strike group's return, now witnessed the debacle. "It was pathetic watching planes taking waveoffs with only five gallons of gas. In the few minutes I watched, one beast came in and was lucky enough to get a cut and make it just as he ran out of gas. Planes were plunking in the water all over."

Time was running out for the bombers and torpeckers. Three Bombing 1 and two Torpedo 1 planes made it safely to other carriers, but no such luck for their comrades. On the *York*, "Nitro" Kalousek went down to his room, got on his knees, and prayed out loud for his missing pals; others followed his example.

The hapless, fuelless pilots alerted their crewmen, strapped themselves in tight and slowed their speed as much as possible as they lost altitude. Gazes fixed on their artificial horizons and airspeed indicators—their only guides—they braced for the impact. And they prayed—that the plane would not flip over on impact, that the canopy would not freeze shut and entomb them, that they would not be dragged under. Then there was Lou Ruzicka, who couldn't swim!

Thoughts and emotions filled them all, only to be suddenly crowded out by the shudder of the fuselage as it bounced off the water and then slammed to a halt—and started sinking.

Into the rafts they clambered, out came the flashlights and their .38 revolvers, which they fired, the tracer cartridges marking their positions for the destroyers which darted in and out among the carriers to pick them up.

The cruisers were not to be outdone by the cans. At the very same moment, 2130, two of them, the *Canberra* and *San Juan*, stopped their engines and picked up bomber pilots Cash Regester and Dave Wilson with their gunners. All four men were unhurt. *Canberra* treated Regie well; they "liquored him up, swiping most of his flight gear. The hospitality was high class throughout the Force that night except for the souvenir hunters."

Many downed fliers would bob around for hours waiting to be picked up. When two rafts floated close to one another, one occupant yelled out, "Hey, you!"

"Who, me?" came the laconic response.

Smoke Strean continued to orbit in his F6, while his VF-1 comrades sought out flight decks. Artie Ward landed on the first flattop he could find and asked, "What ship am I on?"

"The *Yorktown*!" was the welcome reply.

Booby Baysinger, Boyd Weber and Tank Schroeder flew all the way back together, and Baysinger landed first—on the *Yorktown*. Weber took his turn in the landing circle and followed him in, only to discover he had landed on another ship, the *Lexington*!

Schroeder followed Weber in, thinking also it was the *York*. He landed, taxied forward, climbed out and walked away—only to have the next plane crash through the barrier into his plane. Tank and a chief raced back through the burning Hellcats and rescued valuable film he had taken of the Japanese fleet. They then went into the island, where the chief took the films to be processed.

Schroeder opened the door of the ready room, only to be greeted by a sea of strange faces. He now learned that he too was on the *Lex*. The flight surgeon gave him three or four bottles of medicinal Lejons brandy—he lost track—and an hour later he was summoned to the flag bridge to discuss the photos with Admiral Mitscher. By this time, Tank was six sheets to the wind, but he could appreciate how tired Mitscher was. The admiral put his arm around Tank's shoulder and talked about the Jap carriers and battleships, but Tank was weaving back and forth. Finally, Mitscher remarked to one of his staff, "You know, I think this young man could stand a cup of coffee!"

At 2150 Mad Dog Tomme found the *Yorktown* and brought aboard his Hellcat for a perfect landing. As Tommy taxied forward, a young panic-stricken ensign flying a *Hornet* F6F forgot to lower his tail hook, ignored Dick Tripp's frantic waveoff, missed the barrier and landed right on top of Tomme, killing him instantly, and careened forward into the parked planes. "To say nothing," Chuck Ambellan agonized over this "most horrible thing, of messing up the deck so thoroughly that many more were forced into the water with no place to land."

Ben Born pulled the master switch on Pri Fly's light panel, and the *Yorktown* went dark again. Crash crews rushed forward and sprayed foamite on the dead plane, and corpsmen dragged Tomme's body from the wreckage. The cherrypicker hauled the plane to the side, where airedales pushed it over. After five agonizing minutes, the light returned.

Dick Tripp's arms were heavy. The electric wires weighted down the 24-inch aluminum wands, and with them he must wave off plane after plane while letting aboard one at a time. The loss of Tomme made Tripp's whole body heavier.

Soon, another plane belonging to another carrier came up the groove. Dog extended his arms while a spotlight was played on the plane's undercarriage.

Its wheels were up, no doubt locked. Tripp waved him off, but the plane came on and splatted down on the *Yorktown*. Born again darkened ship to warn off other planes, but this mess took twenty long minutes to clean up.

Tripp rested his arms and gazed out on the scene. Planes pushed and shoved their way into landing circles and grooves, pilots momentarily blinded by the bursting starshells and searchlight beams. "And through the confusion," according to one account, "flickered the lights of the planes themselves, red and green and white and yellow, swarming through the air bobbing and weaving and crisscrossing like neon confetti in a whirlwind." Tin cans and cruisers rushed between carriers to get at burning flares and flashlights in the water, and fires erupted from other flight decks as planes crashed aboard.

"We have planes from practically every carrier in the fleet aboard—we hope they have ours," reflected Alex Wilding. By the time the last plane came aboard—an *Enterprise* SBD—*Yorktown's* flight deck was jammed with planes—four VF-1 Hellcats, six from the *Bataan*, four from the *Hornet* and one each from the *Bunker Hill, Lexington*, and *Belleau Wood,* plus a torpecker from *Hornet*, two SBDs from the Big E and two VB-1 SB2Cs.

In Ready 3 and 4, "At 2200, when even the optimists admitted that Beasts just couldn't stay up that long, we retired reluctantly to our rooms. A few bitter words were said but we were really too stunned for much talking. The boys just took a good stiff drink (if they were able to get hold of one) and turned in."

Chuck Ambellan of VF-1, sick with grief, penned in his diary back in his room, "We have only a paltry few fighters back, only two bombers out of twelve [thirteen], and no torpedo planes out of sixteen [eight]! Of course a few may be on other ships, just as we have pilots from other ships aboard here, but I hate to think of taking the total roll tomorrow—I hope and pray for those guys—."

As the drama wound down, the TBS radio crackled: "There's a plane with red balls on his wing flying over my bow." Then another—"a plane with red balls on his wings is flashing 'Love' with is red turtle-back light in my landing circle." At 2222 the *San Jacinto* in Reeves' group called Reeves, "I believe there is a Jap plane over *San Jacinto*. Over." Then: "The plane with the bright red light over formation appears to be a Zeke dead ahead of me now."

Three mintues later *San Jacinto* asked the flag if it had gotten the message. Replied Reeves from the *Enterprise*: "We're looking it over now. Is it the one that just passed us with bright light? Over."

"That is the one. Over."

San Jacinto, again: "That plane passed low over us and his red circles were quite discernible on his lower wing. Over."

Reeves: "Roger, out."

Destroyer *Caperton*: "That plane flying over has red balls. He is a Val. He went close enough to our searchlights to see those balls."

Reeves ordered his group to open fire on the Val at 2227 but delayed it six minutes later when an *Enterprise* night fighter approached to investigate.

By now the bogey had left Reeves' air space and headed toward Jocko Clark's. Ben Tate came rushing into *Yorktown's* Air Plot. "Commander, I think there's a Japanese plane—a Zero—in the air!"

Coop Bright, doubtful, yelled at him, "Get the hell back up there. Where are *our* planes?"

Then Skinhead went over to see Ben Born at Pri Fly. They watched a plane coming in to land which suddenly zoomed off. Born shouted, "Jesus Christ! It's a Zero!" In disbelief, the men on the island plainly saw the red meatballs on the wings. Born to Bright: "What the hell would we have done if we had landed that thing?"

The two men rushed into CIC and told Alex Wilding, "Track that thing!" Born went to the skipper, "Captain, there's a Zero!" Jennings retorted, "Get the hell out of here. I have other problems!"

Wilding: "One Jap plane is in our landing circle and hovering over us, evidently followed our planes back to us—he's not attacking or menacing—appears to just want to land on one of our carriers—prefers that to the cold dark and forbidding sea. All carriers wave him off.

"More pathetic transmissions from pilots—one after another—no intermissions. Frantic voice called—no call sign—message: 'Where shall I go into the drink?' I told him to go into the drink 200 years ahead of one of our destroyers and I would alert the screen—also advised him to have his flashlight ready for use as soon as he cleared the plane. His reply: 'Haw, Haw! I haven't got a flashlight. Goodbye.'"

Another transmission was heard: "Today the Navy is losing one of its best fighter pilots. I am now going in. Out!"

And another: "Switch to Channel Able, fellows; God's got that channel!"

Wilding: "The sea around us is alive with downed aviators—if the Japanese only knew how costly our attack on them had been in operational losses.

"2300—we finally landed our last plane—or at least I thought we had. I had been wearing split ear phones with the Primary Strike Control on one ear phone—Primary CAP frequency on the other—headset only partially covering my ears so I could receive the Primary Fighter Director frequency set on speaker over my head and the Primary TBS #1, also on speaker. With the last plane landed I switched my headset to overhead speakers and took off the headset and closed my eyes and let myself go limp—what an emotional day.

"I took a couple of deep breaths, and then the Primary Strike Control speaker was being keyed—and the message came in loud and clear, 'This is OO. May I please land now?'

"My God! Smoke Strean—I had told him to orbit and I would take him aboard last. I had forgotten all about him during the melee. I grabbed the mike and trying to make my voice sound as non-chalantly as possible I gave him a 'Charley' and told him he was clear to land now. (I tried to make my message sound like: OK, Smoke, I knew you were up there drilling holes in the sky all the time and I was just waiting for the opportune moment to bring you aboard.) I'll hate to face Smoke in the morning—for I know he isn't going to buy my story."

Just as Strean made his landing, however, at 2301 the hovering bogey sent the *Yorktown* to GQ. "There goes General Quarters," Chuck Ambellan jotted in his diary. "Looks like another nite attack. God Damn it." On reflex, he hustled up the ladders toward the ready room, "then thought, what the hell, and came. back down and hit the sack."

Coop Bright confirmed his decision: "ALL PILOTS IN READY ROOM SECURE TO HIT SACK. DO NOT REPORT FOR GENERAL QUARTERS DURING THE NIGHT."

"2315—Screen is clear," Wilding recorded, "except for one Jap bogey opening from the Task Force on course 270 degrees—nobody wants him. He opens out to 55 miles and then disappears from the radar screen. Did he go in the drink? Or just over the radar horizon? After being over the force all night there's just no way he can have enough fuel to reach the Jap carrier force—so he's destined for a watery grave."

The *York* remained at GQ until 2349, then secured while the brass faced the two immense problems before them: the rescue of many downed airmen and the pursuit of the Jap fleet. Cam Briggs began his brief Plan for the next day: "A TOAST TO THE JAPANESE NAVY:—'BOTTOMS UP!'" And at 2330 TF 58 turned west, 280 degrees to give chase. But, as Wilding lamented, "We wasted so much time tonight landing into the wind...that I doubt we will ever see the Jap again during this operation."

At 0152 on the new day, June 21, as Bryan's ordnancemen armed the next deckload strike, one of them dropped a parachute flare he was installing on a night fighter. Hitting the deck, it ignited in flames. Pandemonium broke out. An exhausted airedale, Ralph Kendrick, sleeping near the edge of the flight deck, awoke with a start, jumped up, grabbed his blanket and leaped for the catwalk—but missed and went overboard. Shipmates threw him an electric float light and life jacket, and a destroyer moved in, but he went under.

Meanwhile, the brilliant flare, burning at one million candle power, aroused others sleeping under the planes, notably Seaman First Don Aitkenhead, who grabbed a bomb hoist and tried to beat out the fire with it. Fire hoses and CO_2 extinguishers were turned on the flare but only served to push it underneath the full belly tank of the plane. Trying not to look directly into the blinding light, Aitkenhead kicked the flare and noticed that the arming wires loose on the end of the flare were not burning.

He grabbed these and dragged the flare from under the plane, while the firefighters played water on him. With a mighty hammer throw Aitkenhead flung the conflagration over the side, thus preventing a potential disaster. But the brilliance of the flare blinded him for the next half hour. Captain Jennings rewarded the hero with a spot promotion to aviation ordnanceman third class.

Several carriers launched searches over the ensuing hour, and at 0600 the entire force sent off its deckload search-strikes out to 300 miles, *Yorktown*'s flight included. Dube Duberstein: "Left at 0600 to continue search for Jap fleet and found nothing but survivors and wreckage and many oil slicks. This was our golden opportunity as we had demolished all their air cover and they were at our mercy; but due to fueling difficulties we couldn't catch them. We are still chasing them on 270 degrees and may still do some good tomorrow.

"We have caused major damage to their fleet and if we follow it up we might knock them out. At present we are nearing Formosa and the Philippines. It scares me!" At 0700 Alex Wilding picked up a detailed contact report of the enemy's fleet which he quickly plotted. It "places the Jap fleet 360 miles west of us and north of us. They are out of range, so they will escape."

The Battle of the Philippine Sea was over. A lot of "turkeys" had been shot out of the sky over the Marianas, but only three Jap carriers out of nine had been sunk—and only one of these by carrier planes, the other two by subs. A victory, to be sure, but not nearly the one that could have been. If anyone was to blame for the missed opportunity, it was Spruance. As for Mitscher and Task Force 58, however, given their tremendous score of kills, it had been their finest hour.

During the morning of June 21 the *Yorktown* launched its visiting planes to return to their own carriers and received back its own wayward pigeons—all of the fighters and several bombing planes. It buried Mad Dog Tomme at sea while passing over the very spot where the late afternoon attack on the Jap fleet had taken place. Airmen were being plucked up by seaplanes from Saipan, by float planes from the cruisers, and by destroyers and four lifeguard subs. Although eight *Yorktown* dive bombers and three torpeckers had ditched, thankfully all their crews were rescued and transferred back to the *York*. Overall, TF 58 had lost exactly 100 planes, but after the rescues its personnel losses were reduced to 55 men. Chaplain Alexander conducted a thanksgiving service when the final count was in.

When the last of the VT-1 guys had returned aboard several days later, their soft-spoken skipper Walt Henry gave his men his second speech in the life of the squadron: "I'm sure glad to have you boys back. I never told you what I thought of you because I wanted to wait and let you prove it to yourselves. You've done that now, and I'm proud of you—each and everyone of you. You're good—damn good!"

On the evening of the 21st Task Force 58 broke off its fruitless chase and turned eastward again. Among the letterwriters, John LeBoutillier of VF-1 recorded the recent exciting events for the folks back home "because some people think our life is easy, and the above was only 3 weeks of action. We lost 1/5 of our squadron, fellows I have eaten and drunk and lived with for over a year. Fellows who hurt [me] to see go. Fellows who died nonchalantly and who never would have admitted they were brave.

"But this is an extraordinary group. There have been others all these years, in all the theaters of war, in all branches, who have done and are doing the same thing, day in and day out. My turn to go may

be next—if so, that is the end of it or, as a psalm says, I will have shaken my earthly cares away."

For the moment, though, victory. Administrative officer Jim Sparks of VT-1: "Once I boarded this fine fighting ship, I got the feeling for the first time that it was all over with for the Japs, and after the magnificent Marianas Turkey Shoot during the Battle of the Philippine Sea, I knew I was right. That big red meatball on the side of all those Zeros and Bettys and Kates was finally sinking over the horizon—and fast."

M.M. "Mad Dog" Tomme is laid to rest in a hasty funeral the morning of June 21, 1944, as Chaplain Alexander reads the last rites. The pilots are in their flight gear in the event the Jap fleet is again sighted.

Chapter VIII
Marianas Dirty Work

The landing of three

divisions of Army and Marines on Saipan meant simply that Task Force 58 now had to keep the Marianas protected from further Japanese attempts to save their garrisons at Guam, Rota and Tinian. This required carrier strikes to neutralize the air staging bases to the north: Pagan in the northern Marianas, Iwo Jima in the Volcanos and Chichi Jima in the Bonins. And the planned landings at Guam and Tinian must be supported.

So on June 23, 1944, Admiral Mitscher ordered Jocko Clark to strike Pagan before following the rest of TF 58 to its new anchorage at Eniwetok in the Marshalls. Clark, though happy to do so, wanted to finish his earlier job on the Jimas and thus obtained Mitscher's permission to do so. But hitting Pagan and Iwo after so many aircraft losses and damage was going to be rough. During a morning stroll, Alex Wilding found the hangar deck of the *Yorktown* absolutely devoid of planes and the after flight deck down to a short spot—the ship was 41 planes shy of the normal complement of 90—"but thank God," he told his diary, "we have the pilots."

At 1240 this June 23rd the *Yorktown* launched all 26 of its fighters, its remaining 14 bombers and six of its ten torpeckers to hit Pagan. The heavy ack ack peppered the fighters as Smoke Strean took them down in dangerously low strafing runs against sampans and a handful of parked planes. Smoke's own F6 erupted in flame but only briefly. His wingman Roy Bechtol was not as lucky. An AA shell knocked off the tail of his fighter, which plummeted in flames into the island.

"It's a damn shame," wrote Chuck Ambellan afterward. "Beck and Tomme were the last two to go—the best of buddies since they were kids, and their wives were living together back in the states."

Late in the afternoon Wilding directed *Bataan's* CAP in the destruction of five Zeros and a Betty.

But the biggest excitement followed a dream that Tex McCrary of Admiral Clark's staff had that a good friend of his, Lieutenant Commander Bob Price of the *Cowpens*, shot down eleven days before, was still out there—alive! Jocko Clark took no chances and sent out eight planes to search the area, only to have the destroyer *Boyd* actually sight the raft and rescue the sunburned but happy Price. It was a miracle, yet the sea does not give up its victims graciously. Months later, Price would be washed overboard during a typhoon and lost forever.

"Operation Jocko" unfolded near the Jimas and in their familiar heavy seas and rain squalls. With his usual tenacity, Clark launched a fighter sweep of 51 planes against Iwo at dawn of June 24. Fighting 1 contributed 16 Hellcats, each armed with a bomb, led by Harry Mueller and including "virgin" pilots still seeking their first dogfight. At the end of a 235-mile flight, the sweep ran into "a slew of Zeros."

Norm Duberstein "saw about 40 Zeros, so we turned into them and tried to disperse them. God, it was a melee!! Planes were smoking, burning or exploding all over the sky. I saw at least three guys in parachutes and I'm sure there were plenty more around. The Zero is a marvelous airplane for maneuverability." As the Hellcats jettisoned their bombs and split up between angels 11 and 12, it quickly became apparent that these Jap pilots were the most skillful that VF-1 had yet encountered— in fact, a well-trained bunch led by the legendary Saburo Sakai. They immediately shot down and killed Whitey Reinert—"One swell fellow," reflected Ed Buickerood.

One Zeke did an aggressive wingover at Mueller, but the Mule evaded him and came up behind an Oscar at 7500 feet. Both dived, and Mueller set its engine afire with a no-deflection stern shot which

Ben Born and Empty Evans at Pri Fly watching planes landing and being taxied forward and spotted off the Marianas.

sent it spinning into the sea. When a second Oscar whipped past, Mueller swung in behind and above for a second identical kill. His wingman Barrie Canfield chased a Zeke upstairs, firing in a 45 degree deflection shot until he hit the pilot and the plane plummeted to a watery grave.

In Mueller's second section, Abe Abramson dived on a Zeke a thousand feet off the water and ignited its right wing root, which sent Zeke into the sea. Abe pulled out to the right just as another Zeke passed directly over him. He nosed up and surprised the Jap with a burst into its right wing root also; this Zeke exploded in flames. Wingman Artie Ward brought smoke from a Zeke directly in front of him but the Jap pulled up in a steep wingover and then a spin—a probable.

Don Kerlin fired a no-deflection shot into a Zero which pulled up in front of him, then followed it until it plunged straight into the water. Another Zeke flew toward Red Wangberg until Red disintegrated its tail and watched it plop into the sea and sink. "True" Place came up behind an unsuspecting Zero from dead astern and flamed it easily.

Booby Baysinger's division was red hot, with Booby himself getting one kill and a probable. In less than five minutes Tank Schroeder destroyed three bandits. He exploded one from behind, just as the second crossed above and in front of him.

Tank pulled up to ignite its wing root, the fire spreading over the whole plane. In an identical pass, he nailed his third victim, which fell into the sea without exploding. Mike Alexatos, the Mad Greek, flamed a Zero head-on and gave a second one a burst at point-blank range. The pilot jerked back in his seat, then slumped forward, and the plane spiraled into the ocean.

Lyle Clark's division was no less successful, with Duberstein knocking two out of the sky after they had riddled his Hellcat with 30 slugs. Bob Hansen got directly behind a Zero at 4000 feet and shot into its engine until it started smoking and plunged seaward, whereupon another one zipped in front of him. Hansen opened up, saw no flame or smoke, but watched the Zeke pull up in a sharp bank, then fall off and spin down to its doom. About to rendezvous, Hansen quickly set another Jap fighter afire.

This second string of VF-1 jockeys had shot down 18 Nippos plus five probables, possibly a third of the Force's total score. "With all the virgins taking part," Chuck Ambellan approved, "now most of them are no longer virgins." But five Hellcats from other carriers, plus Reinert, did not return.

No sooner had the fighters landed back aboard than the Japs sent another attack. At 1000 Alex Wilding responded to a large bogey on his radar. "I vectored our [*Hornet*] CAP out and they tallyhoed 12 Jap torpedo planes and shot 11 of

Commander Born goes over flight patterns with fighter pilot Jack Chilton, using the blackboard at Pri Fly, during Marianas operations.

them down. Some of the Jap pilots parachuted. Lt. Russ Reiserer, leader of the fighters, was asked by his wingman if they could strafe them. Russ replied, 'You can if you want to. I don't have the stomach for it.'

"The wingman started a run on the Japs and someone else in the flight keyed his transmitter and said, 'Cut it out, you Goddamned sonofabitch, or I'll shoot you down.'

"I then made a blind transmission, using the Admiral's voice call and told all CAP pilots they were authorized to shoot any Jap in the silk. Silence."

Of the eleven of these single-engine Kates shot down by the *Hornet's* CAP, three of their pilots "hit the silk." Angry *Hornet* fliers riddled their chutes so thoroughly that they did not open, and the slugs ripped their bodies to shreds as they plummeted; a destroyer found one in the water all mangled.

Charlie Ridgway in *Hornet* and Wilding in *Yorktown* kept tracking individual snoopers and larger bogeys during the busy day and directed the CAP to four more kills before noon. And when one bogey roared down at the cruiser *Oakland*, Admiral Jocko himself got on the radio and bellowed to Captain Phillips of that ship: "Ramshackle, there's a plane coming at you. Have you got him?"

Reply: "I've got the sonofabitch." And *Oakland's* gunners duly shot it down.

In midafternoon Wilding spent an hour and a half fruitlessly trying to vector *Hornet* fighters against a snooper which "was evidently smart to radar. . . . He would change course 90 degrees every 10 minutes and change altitude. He used cloud cover to his maximum advantage. I was tracking him constantly while the *Hornet* was trying to intercept and I discerned a pattern in his tactics.

"When the *Hornet* CAP was getting low on fuel I called Charley Ridgway on the *Hornet* and asked him to give me a division of *Bataan* CAP and let me have a crack at him. Charley said OK and added, 'I'll give you a bottle of Scotch if you get him.'

"I sent the division of *Bataan* fighters on a climbing vector to 20,000 and placed them astern of the bogey. Two minutes before I thought the Jap would make a 90 degree turn I ordered the CAP to a cut-off vector to starboard, gambling that he would make a starboard turn—he did—the CAP tallyhoed him and before he could make the next cloud the CAP splashed him—1 Jill. He fell in flames 20 miles ahead of us, the lookouts confirming.

"Adm. Davison came to Radar Plot and personally congratulated me. Adm. Clark sent a message 'Well Done.' I'll bet I'll never see that bottle of Scotch!" (But he would—a bottle of Chivas Regal at Christmastime seven years later!)

Shortly afterward, at 1624, Alex vectored two divisions of *Bataan* fighters to intercept a dozen

Zeros and six Judys 80 miles out. They shot down four and three respectively, but not before the Japs killed the *Bataan's* fighter skipper. "Somehow," lamented Wilding, "when I have CAP under my control and when one of our CAP is shot down I feel responsible for it. It always has an effect upon me."

This bogey and another one led Captain Jennings to put four more divisions of fighters into the air to back up the *Hornet's* guys. From 65 miles out came the tallyho. Bob Frink and True Place each claimed a Zeke and Willie Wilmot a Kate torpecker—his preferred prey. But *Hornet's* fighters had gotten the gravy—twelve kills.

Though able to destroy many planes in the air, Task Group 58.1 had not been able at attack the airdromes at Iwo. With the weather still bad, and replacement planes, fuel and ammo sorely needed, Admiral Clark decided to go on to Eniwetok as scheduled and hopefully to return again after a short rest. In the evening, in the words of VF-1 pilot Duberstein, "We made out an action report but I didn't flower it so I guess I won't get any medals. Some of the guys really threw it [the bull] like professionals."

A sad postscript was added during next morning's CAP when Ensign Ivan Schug, a new replacement pilot, suffered a malfunctioning fuel pump and came up the groove for an emergency landing only to have his engine conk out before he could reach the deck. As he ditched close aboard, the plane cartwheeled. Still, he managed to climb out of the cockpit but apparently was dragged under and drowned. "Another swell fellow gone," wrote Ed Buickerood, "He was married." "Boy," noted Ambellan, "we're averaging almost one a day."

On the retirement to Eniwetok, the word was passed of new and immediate transfers, with *Yorktown* veterans usually fleeting up to fill in the vacated posts. So Commander-made-Captain Cameron Briggs could be relieved as executive officer by Ben Born and Born in turn replaced as air officer by Commander M.T. Evans. And when the ship dropped the hook at Eniwetok on the 26th, Dr. Ray Gard spotted the battleship *Pennsylvania*, his next assignment.

"*There* she is," he wrote in his diary. "This is where I get off. I feverishly pack my trunk and box and bag, bid my friends adieu and early in the morning leave the ship that has been my home for more than 14 mos. I hate to go. She is a good ship and I've many friends aboard. I hope my new ship will be as interesting and as fine. Goodbye Earnshaw, Krieger, Lambart, Losey, [Corpsman Pinky] Sites and all the others."

"It has been a wonderful experience on this ship," he then wrote to his family. "I think that maybe I can be a better doctor for having been here. It is giving me a better understanding of men than ever I've had before." Just past midnight he wrote his last diary entry, "Good night now—It has not been easy saying goodbye to all these men—for I suppose most of them I'll never see again." True, at least until he attended a reunion with some of them in 1983—at age 81!

The victory over the Japanese Fleet and the pending fall of the Marianas with their subsequent development into B-29 bomber bases allowed for much shifting of ships and personnel. TG 58.1 now consisted of the *Yorktown*, *Hornet* and *Bataan*, with several carriers and personnel rotating home throughout the summer. The first flattop to depart was the good old *Intrepid*, due for more repairs at Pearl. "'The Increpid'!" Alex Wilding called her, "She's a 4F carrier." Admiral Ralph Davison now left the *Yorktown* to assume command of his own task group.

At Eniwetok Admiral Clark convinced Mitscher to allow him to return to the Jimas and finish the neutralization of the airfields there, with Davison's group to accompany him. Then both groups would rejoin the other two to soften up Guam and Tinian preparatory to the landings on both islands late in July.

After a brief respite of drinking, visiting and trying to rest at the muggy atoll, the *Yorktown* weighed anchor on June 30 and set course straight for the Bonins. Duberstein: "We are definitely going to Iwo Jima. Should be fun but it scares me. Scuttlebutt has it that we'll be home in about a month. I've got my fingers X'ed." This third visit to the Jimas led Admiral Clark to issue mock shares in the "Jocko Jima Development Corporation," and the pilots were briefed on the afternoon of July 2. Dube, again: "The ack ack has me worried!! That's one thing the Japs have the word on. Saw 'Tarzan's New York Adventure' tonite in ready room, a stinker from way back—."

Cooper Bright used the idle time of the pilots en route for grabass. He liked to stick his head in the door of the VF-1 ready room and yell, "You goddamned rotten sonsofbitches!" Then he'd slam it and run, leaving a roomful of cursing fliers.

The pilots took this insolence just so long, until Mike Alexatos organized a counterattack. One day Coop threw open the door as usual, only to be seized immediately by the pilots lying in wait. They wrestled him into a ready room chair and tied him up. In all the ruckus, no-one heard the call for pilots to man planes.

Finally they heard it and ran out, locking the door behind them and leaving Skinhead well tied. Within moments the bullhorn beckoned, "Lieutenant Commander Bright, dial 2-2-2." It was the bridge. After some ten minutes, someone happened along and untied him.

Skinhead had made himself into a delightful personal aggravation for photo interpreter Bob Eaton and assistant gun boss Pat Patterson, both Texans. When in the evenings they'd sit around "and bullshit about Texas" others would gather and listen. Whenever anyone said anything derogatory about the Lone Star state, big tears rolled down Pat's big, round face. And of course that "New Jersey sonofabitch" Bright loved to tease them both, his way of helping to ease the tension on the eve of battle.

In spite of some unexplained power and speed loss in the engines (later discovered to be marine organisms clinging to the hull), this fighting lady

"Tiny" or "Pat"—Lieutenant Commander T.J. Patterson, assistant gun boss from Texas, seen in his anti-flash clothing. Courtesy of Thomas J. Patterson

pushed north for the next action. Reveille at 0400 on July 3 began the final run-in for the Fourth of July strikes on Iwo, Chichi, Haha and Muko Jima. But a snooper contact after sunup caused Admiral Clark to speed up his timetable, as he had during the first visit in June.

"1200—All plans changed," Wilding recorded. "Jocko has decided to kick off a fighter sweep this afternoon. 60 VF to hit Iwo Jima." Two hours later Smoke Strean took off with his first string on the 315-mile flight. But if the Japs knew of the approaching carriers they also probably figured on the usual dawn strike. As Chuck Ambellan observed later, "We must have taken the Japs by surprise because no planes were up to meet us, and they were just taking off like mad."

John LeBoutillier, his head aching from a malfunctioning oxygen mask, was with Dick Eastmond's division: "Easty and I got separated and made attacks on about 12 groups of them and it lasted for an hour. He started into a cloud and I followed. When I broke through, I could not see him and there was one Zero.

"We scissored and he was on my tail in a steep circle in no time. I purposely stalled towards him and went straight for the runway in a right spiral. I didn't give much of a damn about AA as long as he was following. At 6 to 4000, he gave up the chase." Easty bagged three Zeros and told Ambellan "he saw 2 of mine hit the water."

Ambellan was with Mueller, Abramson and Duberstein: "Our division went down to get some of them out low on the water. We picked two of them. Mule took one and Abe and I the other. He burned and since Abe started on him first, I let him have the credit. Then we climbed up again and [had] a few skirmishes and then I got one.

"Boy, he flamed beautifully and the best view I've ever had of a Zeke is when I pulled away and alongside to avoid parts flying off and there was the Jap pilot getting out. I couldn't have been over 50 ft. away and saw him clearly with his black suit and helmet. Then his plane rolled over and I saw the chute billow out while the plane exploded and went in.

"Chased a few more, and then got on one's tail and followed him through a verticle [sic] slow roll and got him smoking. He split s'ed and I thought he was going in, but somehow he got out of it, and when I went after him again, I was beat to it by a couple of *Hornet* fighters. Abe was with me then. Mule had already headed back with Dube who was shot up. Abe and I headed back 'cause we were both

"Ole" Chuck Ambellan, showing two kills from the Turkey Shoot. Courtesy of Arthur Abramson

low on gas and ammo.''

Duberstein: "I was shot up pretty badly, the main trouble being a 20 millimeter in the port wing knocking out the hydraulic system. It was impossible to lower wheels so I landed with them up. Not a bad job either. Ward didn't get back,'' having been jumped and shot down by three Zeros. Artie Ward turned out to be the only VF-1 loss.

The sweep had engaged some 30 Zekes in the air and destroyed them all—Fighting 1 eleven for sure plus two probables, with *Hornet* and *Bataan* planes getting the rest. Perhaps 50 other planes, mostly bombers, were observed to be on the ground, some being strafed while fuel permitted. Several cargo ships were also seen in the harbor.

That the damage sustained by the "Jocko Jimas'' during the three visits by their new "owner" had been great was borne out by the fact that no snoopers even challenged the force during the night as it closed to within 66 miles of the islands in good weather.

In the pitch predawn blackness of America's Independence Day, the *Yorktown* catapulted the

night fighters of Buck Dungan and Johnny Dear to heckle Chichi Jima. Though they each shot down at least one Rufe float fighter, both Hellcats were silhouetted against the morning twilight for Chichi's alert AA gunners, and the flak prevented them from attacking ground targets. Finally, Dungan took a 7.7mm armor piercing bullet in his shoulder, breaking his collar bone, but he made it back to the ship.

The *York* sent off her first of six bombing strikes of the day at 0450, led by air group commander Jim Peters. Arriving over Chichi, Peters was surprised to find that the Jap ships had not fled during the night. A convoy of two small destroyers and two cargo ships now attempted to escape, but 13 other merchantmen were stuck in the harbor. Literally stuck, as events proved, for the Japs, unable to escape, had opened the sea cocks of their marus to let them settle on the shallow bottom rather than have any torpedoes or bombs puncture their hulls and cause irrevocable damage.

In spite of "ideal dive bombing weather—unlimited ceilings and negligible winds'' and few airborne enemy planes, heavy flak greeted the attackers. Worse, after the Helldivers made their perfect drops, they recovered beneath the level of Chichi's high cliffs where many AA batteries masked in caves caught them in deadly crossfires. Kenny Wright took a burst, and his beast exploded in flame. A parachute blossomed forth, either Wright or his gunner Fred Pryor. The jumper landed in the harbor but was never heard from again.

One by one the bombers ran the gauntlet, and one by one the gun emplacements worked them over. Owen Hintz was shot down over Little Ani Jima, but his gunner Lloyd Woellof parachuted safely. Jack Drysdale and gunner Bruce Dalton were also destroyed in the action. The rest of Bombing 1 escaped "eerie Chichi'' and did not hang around to strafe as at Guam.

Next came Torpedo 1, led by its aggressive skipper Walt Henry. Glide-bombing perilously low, Henry dropped his four delayed action bombs squarely on top of a medium maru, which blew up. He recovered just 300 feet off the water and braved the flak successfully—which inspired his men to follow him in and out, with splendid results and no losses.

The fighters on the third strike strafed the fleeing convoy with telling effect. Their .50s detonated the depth charges on one destroyer, which exploded violently, and set the second afire, while *Hornet, Wasp* and *Franklin* planes combined to polish off the two merchantmen.

The fourth strike included fighters John LeBoutillier, Mo Moseley, Tank Schroeder and Bill Tukey. LeBoot: "We dropped on a large AK [merchantman]. We made a second run strafing a Betty and Zeke. Mose was on my right and his belly tank caught on fire; he pulled up over the bay and jumped just as his tail broke off." Schroeder: "I heard someone say, 'you're on fire.' I saw him come between the mountains, his ship burning, and the ack ack flying at him from both sides. He pulled up to 1000 feet and we saw him bail out and land in the water. We saw him splashing in the water and another plane dropped him a liferaft." Tukey: "We came at each other at a 90 degree angle and I just missed him, and he jumped. The chute opened okay. We watched him try to swim for a life raft we'd dropped and then the chute pulled him down and he was gone."

The bombers claimed 13 hits, three probables and 15 near-misses. Recorded their historian, "we also killed a lot of fish and blasted tons of rock off the steep slopes down into the harbor." "Eager John" Beling ignited an ammunition ship, then later knocked the stern off another ship. The first blast "came right up in the Prussian's [Dave Kinzer's] face, conveniently blowing him over to a secondary target." One flight also worked over Haha Jima, but "failed to see the joke" there.

The torpeckers sank two marus and severely damaged seven others and obliterated two villages, two radio stations and two fuel dumps, while Bob Kimbrel flew a photo hop over Muko Jima where he exchanged fire with a machine gun protecting a radio shack. Three bullets hit his TBM, as gunner Yount "shot at anything I could see."

Airplanes, seaplanes and a "country club" according to True Place got worked over at Chichi by all squadrons, but Torpedo 1 almost lost Nitro Kalousek. While in his dive a heavy AA shell blew a large, gaping hole in his starboard wing, tearing off parts of the wing covering and buckling the wing. He pulled out of his dive "as gently as he could" and called his crewmen to check the underside of the wing for damage.

"First hole I'd ever seen!" gunner Jimmy Coumatos noted on this, his 22nd combat hop. "I wanted to land on the water and the radioman wanted to bail out." Both insisted the wing was in "terrible shape" and that the Turkey would never stay airborne. Then they got into a heated argument over which course of action to take.

Nitro couldn't get a word in edgewise, so he joined up on Jim Thorburn, signaling him to have a look-see at the starboard wing. He signaled back a 4.0 hand signal—"You're in good shape. Everything OK."

With this foul-up, and his two crewmen chattering away on the intercom, Nitro stayed in character. He barked at them, "Shut up! I'll get her back." He flew a mile or so away from the formation "in a wild rage" and ignored the others all the way home, landing back aboard smartly.

Of the heavy damage to Chichi's planes, ships and facilities, *Yorktown's* air group claimed two cans and six marus sunk, with damage to more ships and aircraft shared by her sister carriers. But it hardly seemed worth the price—for *Yorktown* alone five pilots and three aircrewmen.

Just how deadly Chichi was only gunner Lloyd Woellof, who had jumped, discovered first hand. Wounded in the leg and shoulder by shrapnel, the medium-built 18-year-old rearseat man had struggled loose from his parachute in Ani Jima's harbor and swum toward shore, determined to give the Japs a fight to the finish. As he approached the beach, he saw three Jap soldiers waiting for him, rifles at the ready with their long bayonets fixed. Touching the sand, Woellof whipped out his knife and lunged fiercely at them—frightening all three, as postwar interrogations of the Japanese would reveal. But he was felled by a bayonet rammed into his wounded shoulder.

His captors took him directly to Army headquarters on Chichi Jima and tied him to a tree until an interpreter could be found. Finally, an English-speaking cadet arrived, and Woellof was untied and brought before a Jap major named Horie. Matted with dirt and blood from his ordeal, he was allowed to sit in a chair while being interrogated for half an hour. His captors could only pronounce his name as "Wolf," and they learned he was from the carrier *Yorktown,* but he revealed little else.

A surgeon treated his leg and shoulder wounds, he was brought fresh water and biscuits, and he refused the cigarette offered him. The Japanese found him thin, exhausted and "not very handsome" and allowed him to wash and shave. Then they placed him in a garage near the headquarters building and provided him only with the customary Nipponese mat to sleep on. Because of his wounds and great pain from them, he was not tied again.

Lloyd Woellof was questioned over the next three days but could not and would not reveal any special information, and he spent the next several weeks in and about his makeshift jail, slowly recovering. The day after his arrival an Army B-24 pilot joined him, the sole survivor of a Liberator shot down by the deadly Jap flak. Major Horie protected them both from others who wanted to finish them off and had Woellof teach him some English. Eventually, the U.S. Army lieutenant and Major Horie were flown out to Japan, leaving the helpless Navy gunner to his fate—whatever that might be.

Admirals Clark and Davison turned their task groups south to join in the pre-landing bombing of Guam and Tinian. At least one *Yorktown* sailor looked forward to the liberation of Guam—F.G. Alig, the "Captain's Boy," born on Saipan but raised at Guam where his family still lived under Jap rule.

On July 5 the *Yorktown* registered her 100,000th mile of cruising and 13,000th landing aboard. Yet, "the main topic of conversation these days," noted Chuck Ambellan, "is when the hell we are going home. Scuttlebutt is thick and fast—maybe three weeks, maybe three months. I'm ready anytime." Duberstein: "I'm getting to the point where I don't give a damn if I never get shot at anymore—Yep, the novelty has worn off."

During refueling 150 miles northeast of Saipan on the 6th, John LeBoutillier jotted a short V-mail note to his sister, congratulating her on her new baby boy. "I have been having what you would call a time but it is funny how one gets to take almost anything as a commonplace affair. I would like very much to see ice and snow again, to feel a relaxed tiredness from physical work, to be able to stay awake later than nine o'clock, to get married and make babies."

Wonderful as the little things of life in the future meant to these men at war, they were not to be for LeBoot. For that very afternoon the *Yorktown* sent him and 19 other Hellcats as part of a 60-plane sweep to Rota, where they faced only ack ack in destroying exactly one plane on the ground plus some buildings. As Dick Eastmond prepared to lead his division in a strafing run, he called back to wingman LeBoot, who seemed to be lingering over Rota, "Have you got a problem?" "No." "Close up. We're getting ready to go down." The four peeled off, but only three recovered. LeBoot was missing. "He just seemed to disappear," noted Ed Buickerood. The Mule searched for his plane, but found no trace. LeBoot would never see ice and snow again.

"God Damn it, it's getting me mad!" was Chuck Ambellan's reaction. "We lost one of the swellest guys I've known, today. LeBoot. I don't know what the jinx is but we've certainly got a black cloud following us. That makes the 12th one out of an original 44. LeBoot left a big and favorable impression on many fellows. Wish I could leave as good a one when I go—." Dube: "This survival race is getting down to a select few now."

That morning Jocko Clark and Ralph Davison had conferred in person with Admiral Mitscher on the *Lexington* to map out the Guam-Tinian operations. Their two task groups were to trade off striking Guam and Rota, the latter to be neutralized to prevent staging in by enemy planes. Guam-Rota-Guam-rest, then repeat, with the other groups under Rear Admirals Montgomery and Gerald F. Bogan rejoining in a week. Task Force 58 would then support the landings on Guam on July 21 and Tinian on the 24th until both islands were secured.

Routine. Never had this oft-uttered Navy word applied more than now. The flak would be as dangerous as ever, bandits from the Jimas could be expected, and men would still die in action and in accidents. But it would all be done routinely—with no sense of urgency or fear of a lurking Jap fleet. The sheer excitement and victory at the Battle of the Philippine Sea made all this seem anticlimactic.

That evening, while Captain Jennings' old ship, the escort carrier *Copahee,* sent over replacement aircraft to the *Yorktown,* crewmen like Alex Wilding admired a "beautiful moon tonight, full and bright. We're not far from Pagan—could this be the Pagan moon Bing Crosby sings about?"

At midday on July 7 33 planes from the *York* struck gun emplacements on Guam, and that night enemy snoopers counterattacked. When Charlie Ridgway missed vectoring *Hornet* night fighters on the closest bogey, he turned over pilot Bill Levering to Wilding, who had worked with Levering when the detachment had been on the *Yorktown.*

Wilding "vectored Bill on the tail of one of the bogeys and brought him in on bogey's course and speed and 1 mile astern. Bill made immediate AIA [radar] contact, then he reported that he was in bogey's slipstream, and then he saw him visually, with flames coming out of his exhaust.

"Bill gave the Jap a burst and after a two minute dog fight splashed one Betty in flames [at 2023]. All hands on the flight deck saw the Betty fall in flames into the sea from 14,000 feet. To my knowledge that's the first night interception ever made in this task force by VF under positive control. Adm. Clark sent a message of 'Well Done.'

"Bill Levering was happy as Hell and just before

The "crash team" of (L to R) landing signal officers Dick "Dog" Tripp, Red Volz and Jim "Hazy" Cozzens and arresting gear officer Angie Peccianti, standing on the LSO platform.

landing radioed that the interception was absolutely perfect. He was so happy, just like a kid—it was the first Jap he has shot down, day or night. Just before he touched down on the *Hornet* he radioed, 'Goodnight Alex.' He landed at 2300.''

Only one other Betty pressed on toward the formation, whereupon Ridgway put Russ Reiserer's *Hornet* night fighter on it. Wilding: "Russ fired him at 12,000 feet, but he was burning in only one wing, so he dropped down slowly, finally hitting the sea and exploding as all hands watched. Cheers went up, like a touchdown at a football game. Night and day the Jap losses mount now. With night fighter direction perfected we can now feel a higher degree of security from night attacks.''

After dawn this July 8, a life raft with five Japs was sighted off the starboard bow, survivors of Reiserer's Betty. The destroyer *Helm* dispatched a launch to rescue them, but they paddled away and resisted capture. Finally, Jocko lost his patience and bellowed over the TBS radio, "Hit them over the head with a shillelagh and drag them aboard!'' Finally subdued, the Japs were taken aboard the can along with an official mail bag chock full of documents and charts.

In the afternoon 32 *Yorktown* planes bludgeoned Rota with incendiary bombs. Ambellan: "The town was lit up like a Christmas tree with incendiaries and beautiful bomb hits by VB.'' The airfield was rendered non-operational, and the flak was so light that Norm Duberstein thought "they've got something up their sleeve.''

Next morning, July 9, 32 more *York* planes struck the airfield at Agana and other targets on Guam, the TBMs carrying 5-inch rockets, which required long, flat approaches dangerously exposing the torpeckers. Sure enough a burst of flak hit Carl Sanborn's Avenger, which exploded and crashed, killing Sandy and crewmen "Steff" Steffen and "Buck" Buchanan. "The inventorying of pilot personal effects,'' wrote Duberstein in his diary this same day, "is a nasty job, but one that must be done.''

The 10th brought respite for the ship, and Dr. Jack Smith released Buck Dungan from Sick Bay with his mending broken collar bone and shoulder wounds, and he was assigned to share Alex Wilding's room. Obviously unable to climb into the top bunk, Buck was given the bottom one by Alex, who climbed up top to sleep.

At 0150 of the new day, July 11, Wilding was deep in slumber when his phone rang. "I was still three quarters asleep as I rolled over on my side to crawl out of the bunk, and lowering my feet, expecting them to touch the steel deck, as they have for 15 months. I forgot I was sleeping in the top bunk and I fell the full distance flat on my face on the steel deck.

"Buck turned on the light and found me out cold on the deck, and my head lying in a pool of blood. He revived me, and my face was a mess—two big eggs over each eye, blood running down my face from an abrasion across my forehead.

"I finally answered the phone—a Jap bogey, closing. I splashed water over me, wrapped a wet towel around my head and headed for Radar Plot.

Two separate Jap planes appeared to be heading for Guam. We launched two night fighters—sending one to fly CAP over Rota and one to fly CAP over Guam. They found nothing."

Wilding stayed at his battle station with his injury and got more business at 0312: "Single Jap bogey 285 degrees—35 miles, closing. We launched another night fighter. I put the night VF on the bogey's tail, [and he] got an AIA radar contact immediately. At 0337 splash 1 Betty." All in full view of the ship; said Jesse Bradley, "He sure made a nice fire."

At first light, 0600, this 11th of July, the ship launched 33 planes to bomb and rocket Guam, though several rockets malfunctioned and had to be carried back to the ship. On catching the wire, the rocket-laden planes provided some fresh excitement when several of the projectiles broke loose, arming themselves as they bounced down the flight deck. Nervy airedales had to run out, pick them up and throw them overboard before they detonated. So a cargo net was quickly rigged with two sailors manning it to snare the loose rockets and dispose of them that much more quickly.

One of the new replacement pilots, Ensign Leon Cyphers, came up the groove but lost engine speed and was given a waveoff by LSO Red Volz. The excited youngster ignored it, tried to land but spun in close aboard. The Hellcat sank, and Cyphers did not get out. Duberstein: "That makes thirteen guys so far. He had 2 kids and was expecting a third."

After refueling, *Yorktown* planes struck Rota on the 12th and Guam on the 13th in what were regarded as easy milk runs. The constant sorties and dives gave the pilots a chance to analyze each other's performances until "a spirit of healthy competition started," in the words of Commander Peters, "that almost made them forget that Japs were shooting at them while they were working." The achievements of the better pilots were announced over the bullhorn each evening by the navigator, Commander Dick Matter.

After rest on a stormy July 14 just off Rota, during which the crew could actually see *Hornet's* bombs hitting the island, the *York's* radar picked up a bogey before dawn of the 15th. The ship launched night fighter Joe Rohde into the soup, and Alex Wilding took control. *Cabot* also sent up a CAP of four day fighters.

"The bogey started to open and I started the night fighter in pursuit. The nite VF was out to 65 miles at 220 degrees and right on the tail of the bogey when he radioed to me, 'I am in trouble.'

He also disappeared from the radar screen at that instant. That was the last I saw or heard from him—Ens. Rohde. The *Cabot* started their division of airborne CAP out to investigate. The CAP went through a cloud 20 miles southwest of us, but only 3 of the division came out on the other side of the cloud—nothing seen or heard of him again either—Weird!"

The strange phenomenon of disappearing planes would gain notice after the war, but surely these losses could be explained by the erratic weather conditions. Morning searches for both planes took off at 0758 but had to be recalled an hour later when the weather worsened. No trace of either plane. Like the man said, weird.

Jocko Clark never let foul weather stop him from getting at the Japs, so the *Yorktown* launched 33-plane strikes against Guam on the afternoon of the 15th and Rota next morning. On the latter, bomber pilot Paul "Moon" Mullen had the aileron cable of his Beast break while in his dive and could not regain control. He and gunner Nick Boutas parachuted safely, but when the cans arrived soon afterward to pick them up the ships found that Boutas had drowned and that the sharks had already gotten to Moon; they retrieved only his flight jacket and lungs.

The gloom over VB-1 from Mullen's loss was compounded on July 17. On the 30-plane noon strike Diz Diem's SB2C was hit over shallow water off Agana, and either he or gunner Stevens was seen to jump—but too low for the chute to open. The Beast crashed in the water. Then an explosive AA shell blew the tail off the 2C of Joe McCall, who rode it down in the flames to his death along with rearseat man Frank Metzenbauer. The black cloud shadowing VF-1 had moved to the bombers.

The 18th was the first of three intensive pre-landing strike days against Guam, coordinated with the amphibious forces. Using a grid, the planes bombed and strafed guns and pillboxes on the target beaches. Read Coop Bright's Air Plot ticker: "IT MAY BE OF INTEREST TO KNOW THAT HORNET PLANES REPORTED THEY WERE UNABLE TO GET THROUGH TO THE TARGET. JOCKO'S REPLY WAS THAT YORKTOWN'S DID—YOU GET IN THERE. AFTER MANY ATTEMPTS THEY DID SUCCEED." Added the Skinhead, "ALL PILOTS OF THE ASP [antisub patrol] AND CAP, WE THANK YOU FOR RETURNING TO THE SHIP ON TIME. THANKS KALOUSEK—NO HAIR FELL OUT. YOU SHOULD LEAD IT ALL THE TIME."

This ho-hum routine was shattered on July 20

when torpecker Woodie Wood failed to return from his mission. Lost with him were not only his crewmen Ed Donahue and Al Sabol but special photographer Owen Smith. At least Bombing 1 could herald the return of pilot Dick James and gunner Dave Smith. Shot down over Guam a month before, they had endured Jap shore batteries and a fire on board the lifeguard sub *Stingray* while on patrol before reaching Majuro on July 10. James had even stood decoding watches and enjoyed the benefits of steak at midnight whenever hunger called.

While the *Yorktown* completed topping off a destroyer between strikes on the 20th, the can's skipper signaled, "Thanks. Have a good time in the States." Later the same day a copy of a dispatch came in: Bureau of Ships to Navy Yard Bremerton, "Have SM radar ready to install on the *Yorktown.*"

The news spread like proverbial wildfire. "Glory be," Alex Wilding joined in the general approbation, "we are going back to the States soon—to Bremerton—and we'll get the height-finding SM radar. We're really going home—when?"

Not yet, for on "William Day," July 21, 1944, Air Group One ripped apart Guam's defenses ahead of the infantry. "A beautiful pattern" of bombs was laid down on Beaches Green and Blue by the Beasts accompanying the strafing Hellcats, "not a bomb landing in the water," noted the Bombing 1 historian, "and we had really helped the Marines out." A cumulative 35.7 tons of bombs from *Yorktown* planes helped pave the way inland for

Marines and Army, "a thrilling sight to watch, the landing boats in formation going into the beach," thought Dube Duberstein. "On my second dive a bullet hit my windshield but didn't penetrate the bullet proof glass, thank God."

Suddenly, by noon, it was all over. The three morning strikes, recorded Jesse Bradley, "finished up our bombing for a while. We haven't got any left. The last strike was carrying bomb skids and just about anything they could find to drop on the Jap." The lightly-opposed troops were moving over the beach and no longer needed the *Yorktown.*

"Guess that finishes up our connection with the Marianas," speculated Ole Chuck. "Tomorrow, we load up with bombs at Saipan. The next day, we get refueled and plane replacements, and then go hit somewhere—Palau? Yap? Philippines?" Scuttlebutt sounded good as the *York* anchored at Saipan. The bombers, said their history, "talked about Stateside with all its lonely women, and once again we got that Old Feeling. We sought confirmation by eavesdropping in the heads and intercepting despatches."

The ship's anchorage, just eight miles from enemy-held Tinian, afforded the crew a ringside seat for the cruisers and destroyers shelling that island, though all hands had to endure an attack by "land based flies. They were fat and lazy and easy to kill but they came in swarms, making sunbathing impossible." Coxswain Ted Rohrbough recalled that the flies "covered the entire fleet, and the Admiral was concerned about the entire task

Avengers of Torpedo 1 fly in close formation over landing boats circling prior to assaulting Guam behind strafing and bombing planes, July 21, 1944.

"That Old Feeling" rendered by John Furlow.

force coming down with some disease. They were burning Jap bodies in long trenches at that time,'' accounting for the bugs. The smell of the corpses even floated out to the ship.

On the afternoon of July 21 Jocko Clark's TG 58.1 of *Yorktown*, *Hornet* and *Cabot* set course southwest to hit atolls in the western Carolines, while other groups supported the troops on Guam and Tinian (assaulted on the 24th) and attacked the Palaus. For four days beginning July 25 Clark's planes shot up virtually defenseless Yap and Ngulu, the only crisis being over a Helldiver stricken by flak on the third day.

As the VB history told it, "Eager John Beling got nailed right over the airfield. A lot of the boys saw it—a trail of smoke, then as he zoomed for altitude, a tongue of flame. One parachute blossomed, and there was a big explosion as the plane crashed on the fringe of the reef. Cess [Pool] and the Prussian [Kinzer] spotted the chute and went right on down to look.

"It was John all right, up to his hips in the pale green water and looking very disconsolate. They dropped him their life rafts, and so did about ten other people. In fact, we scored a couple of near misses on John himself. He looked kind of sore

Bombing One Helldivers approach in the upper landing circle after the Yap strikes, July 26, 1944.

about it. The area was scoured for [rearseat gunner Curt] Wright, but all that was seen was a slick of dye marker near the wreckage. It is believed that Wright might have jumped and that his parachute failed to open.

"The Kingfishers came in [from the cruiser *Biloxi*] and despite gunfire from shore [silenced by *Yorktown* fighters] got Eager John out of there." He however suffered from second degree burns. Dube: "Everyone thought he was a goner for sure."

Back on the ship, noted Alex Wilding, "Everybody pedaling their own scuttlebutt edition of when we're going to the States—it's rampant throughout the *Yorktown*. You can hear what you want to hear—one edition from each man on the *Yorktown*." This time, however, the rumors were true; Air Group One flew its last strikes on the 28th.

"WE'RE GOING HOME!!!" pilot Chuck Ambellan announced in his diary during the evening of July

28. "Official as hell, as the captain of the ship announced it tonight. Hot dawgs, only 7000 miles to go—." The crew was going too; as gunner Jesse Bradley rejoiced: "I have just heard the best news I have heard in over a year. The Captain told us at 1900 that we were going back to the good old U.S.A. His words were: THIS SHIP WILL BE AVAILABLE FOR TRANSPORTATION TO THE EAST STARTING TOMORROW MORNING. I am still about 13,000 miles from home but at least I'm on my way back. Boy, I never seen such a happy bunch of sailors in all my life, including myself."

Wilding: "On July 30 the *Yorktown* is detached from Pacific duty to return to the States.—HOORAY! 20 days of leave authorized for each man—with those going to the East coast getting the first leave period." Visual message from Jocko: "As always the *Yorktown* is a first class fighting ship. Well done, good luck and hurry back. Admiral Clark."

Next day, the 29th, homeward-bound passengers came aboard and enjoyed the general spirit—except for one young ensign who was relieved of duty and confined to his quarters for "conduct unbecoming an officer and gentleman"—and his room was placed strictly off limits until he could be transferred. The agony of being different from other men had again raised its head on the ship.

As the *Yorktown* and escorting cans pulled out on the 30th for the two-day run to Eniwetok, the amphibious forces were winning the battles on Guam and Tinian. Had the ship been kept in the force another week, it would have seen more action, for on August 4-5 Clark and Montgomery struck the Jimas again with six carriers before heading for the barn, from which both battle-worn admirals would then head home on leave.

"The longest sustained carrier operation to date" thus came to an end, recorded Russ Reiserer in his diary on board the *Hornet*. "From the food we've been getting lately, I can realize what [this] means." Then he mused, "Sure feel sorry for the poor damn Japs in a peculiar sort of way. Don't especially want to show them any pity. Still I feel that they should be pitied for their stupidity."

The Jap felt no pity for his enemy, as Aviation Radioman Second Class Lloyd R. Woellof of VB-1 discovered. A prisoner on Chichi Jima since July 4, he was moved into the hills during the devastating carrier attacks on August 4, then brought back to Army headquarters next day where he was joined by a B-24 pilot just shot down. The Japs, infuriated at the heavy damage and losses incurred during this attack, bayoneted Woellof and the pilot mercilessly until they died. Then an officer beheaded both bodies, which were buried on the spot. It was the first of several atrocities which would be committed in the Jimas before these islands could be invaded.

Woelloff was the last of Air Group One's heavy casualties: 31 planes in combat along with 46 men in them, of which 25 had been pilots downed by flak. Lauding the courage of his men, Commander Jim Peters concluded his final action report: "Some few pilots fight because they like it. Most of them do not come back. Some few pilots will not fight. They must be carried along until they can be sent back. The great majority fight because of their sense of duty and for the respect of the other people with them." Among the best were VF-1's two aces, Dick Eastmond with nine kills (plus three he "gave" to buddies who had helped him) and the late Mo Moseley with six.

During the stopover at Eniwetok the crew was exceptionally jovial and the pilots stewed, and

when the *Yorktown* pulled the hook on August 4 some joker hoisted a pair of "silk step-ins" from the mainmast! En route to Hawaii, ship's journalists produced another issue of SEA-V-TEN, Chuck Ambellan beat Jim Peters to become air group acey-deucy champ, and one of the doctors gave all hands "a sex lecture—anticipating liberty in Pearl."

Ignoring a mock predawn air attack by *Intrepid* planes early on August 10, the *Yorktown* pulled into Pearl. But after officers and men had gathered at the gangways, the bullhorn announced, "No liberty. We sail for Bremerton at 0700 in the morning." So the sex lecture had been a waste. Then hospital cots were erected in the hangar and 372 wounded soldiers and Marines brought aboard. "A sad and heartbreaking sight," thought Wilding, "as you see the nice looking young men in such sad shape. I had to turn away from watching them after awhile."

That evening, the crew was treated to a sneak preview of a new movie. Lieutenant Commander Dwight Long came aboard with it, the documentary he had made on board the *York* through the spring and filled out with some flight deck footage from several other flattops. From 60,000 feet of 16mm Kodachrome film, Long had cut it down to 800 for a one-hour epic and then had battled Navy red tape and a disinterested Twentieth Century Fox mogul Darryl F. Zanuck to get it cleared and produced.

Zanuck changed his mind after he finally viewed Long's footage and then ordered the magnificent documentary completed in record time—typical of *Yorktown*'s style. Producer Louis deRochemont talked Zanuck out of the title "The Fighting Wench"—an utterly graceless signature—in favor of "The Fighting Lady." He brought in John Stuart Martin to write a superb script, narrated by actor Robert Taylor (himself a wartime naval aviator) and backed by Alfred Newman's fine musical score. The final product, ready for public viewing by the end of the year in order to compete in the 1944 Academy Awards, promised to be a blockbuster. For this, Long's boss, the eminent photographer Edward Steichen, paid the ultimate tribute in *U.S. Camera:* "Without Dwight Long, 'The Fighting Lady' would have been impossible." Equally important, the completed movie finally provided the *Yorktown* with a nickname for the ages: The Fighting Lady.

Before she would fight again, however, it was home, rest and overhaul. The *York* weighed anchor on the morning of August 11 to the tune of "California, Here I Come," since Bremerton,

Washington, had no song. Alex Wilding plotted the ship's changing latitude relative to the U.S. west coast. August 12: same as Mexico City, "getting colder all the time." 13th: San Diego, "cooler each day." 14th: Santa Barbara, "Wonderful." 15th: Northern California, "Cold now." 16th: "Cold and feels great. Slept with a blanket last night—first time in 16 months. Went into Blues today—no more khakis till we go back to Pearl."

Air Group One, noting it would reach the States on the 17th, one year to the day after it had left, as a final farewell tribute presented Skinhead Bright with a comb with no teeth and a bottle of engine lubrication oil as a restorative. He had given them enough grabass for memories that would last a lifetime.

Prior to the last movie before entering port, Father Farrell lectured the entire crew at great length about the evils which would tempt them ashore. He warned them that any individual who practiced sexual promiscuity would be rejecting his faith, his mother and what-have-you. The men listened in hushed silence, but when the padre finished, the crew gave him a big cheer and yelled, "Let's have the movie!" After a year and a half of deployment—thanks but no thanks.

Farrell was not stiffnecked. He had a good sense of humor and was greatly respected by the men. But the fighting had taken its toll on his constitution; the eminent theologian would not long survive the war.

On the afternoon of the 17th the ship discharged its passengers and the first leave party at the entrance of the Bremerton Navy Yard and next day moved right into the drydock. Noted George Wille later, "The fellows on the ship were in high spirits, and a number of female yard workers who were watching our entrance were cheered uproariously. What a gay time the next 50 days turned out to be! A fine O-Club, a big city close at hand, plenty of liberty, the admiral's daughter—ah, it was wonderful!"

Wrote one of the *Yorktowners*:

Here's to an hour of sweet repose,
Belly to belly, and toes to toes,
And after a moment of sweet delight,
It's fanny-to-fanny for the rest of the night.

While the first half of the crew rushed home for 20 days, the second turned to the immense task of helping the shipyard preen the *Yorktown* for her second war cruise. As the water drained out of the drydock, the sight of the bottom was something to behold. It looked "like a sea of redwoods" hanging from the underside; seaweed hung down, with huge barnacles encrusted on it. So here was the answer to the ship's reduced speed in the water. The bottom was again scraped and sprayed, much to the relief of the first lieutenant, Diamond Jim Brady.

Internally, the big change reflected the organizational streamlining of the Air Department. With the air boss, now M.T. Evans, so busy with keeping the aircraft maintained and in briefing pilots, he had gradually turned over air control operations—air strikes, CAPs, ACIOs, weather—to Air Plot and fighter direction to CIC. So now Air Plot officer Cooper Bright was redesignated air operations officer, and both his office and CIC were given more personnel and moved out of the island and down to enlarged spaces on the gallery deck. Equipment-wise, it meant new radar arrays on the island—notably the SM height-finding fire control radar, the SP for night fighter direction, and transponders (radar beacons). Exec Ben Born, an acknowledged specialist in the new electronics, would begin to spend more time in these new spaces.

To increase the ship's protection, the yard added seven more quad 40mm mounts on three new sponsons to the existing ten quad 40s and increased the number of 20s from 55 to 61. Among the multitude of lesser changes were two barber chairs illegally added to the one already on the ship on the orders of supply boss Bill Moring and which began months of fruitless correspondence by an irate Bureau of Ships.

After the first 20 days in the shipyard, the first leave section returned and the second departed. Bremerton itself proved to be a pretty dismal liberty port, so two ship's dances were held at the Puget Sound Navy Yard recreation center, the printed invitations inaugurating the new name, "The Fighting Lady."

Even in a fairly dead port, enterprising officers could make their own sport—like assistant gun boss Tiny Patterson. At a nightclub one evening Pat got into an argument with a chaplain from another ship because the latter had "taken" hundreds of dollars from the enlisted men in poker games. When the padre went into the men's room, he left his uniform coat at the table—and his poker winnings with Tiny for safekeeping. Pat, who took a dim view of this ill-begotten money, switched coats, went up to the bandstand and grabbed the microphone. Everyone thought he was a chaplain.

"I have been observin' this sin," the big Texan proclaimed, "an' my heart jus' cries for you people in here. I want you girls [prostitutes] to know that if you want to go home an' lead the right kind of life, I'll buy your ticket."

Somebody started playing the piano, and 'Padre Pat' called for the B-girls to come forward. Here they came. Tiny looked down at them, "You can't go to heaven, sisters, in high-heeled shoes." Off came the shoes as the girls kicked them everywhere. And Pat took out the real chaplain's bankroll and started peeling off the bills—to the tune of over $900! Just as he finished, the Holy Joe returned from the restroom, enraged. But justice had been done, Texas-style.

Personnel transfers continued at Bremerton, starting at the top. Like Jocko Clark, Captain Al Jennings had been selected for rear admiral. He had worked mightily to meet everyone's needs for liberty, and the crew saved an honored spot for him in their cruise book. His leadership they lauded as "an inspiration to the officers and men working with him. His leaving brought to many a sense of personal loss. He had created a happy ship."

Jennings' relief was Captain Thomas S. Combs, Annapolis 1920, who had flown fighters and bombers throughout his career before commanding a seaplane tender in the Aleutians campaign, where he had proved himself to have an uncanny seaman's eye as a shiphandler. He had spent two years with MacArthur in the Southwest Pacific in the temporary rank of commodore. An immensely popular officer, he went by the nickname "Theda" for an occasion when as a midshipman en route to a shower clad in only a towel he was greeted by a classmate, "There goes Theda Bara than ever!" But Theda Combs would no more be a sexy 'silent' film star than would be the Fighting Lady; the crew would soon become accustomed to his yelling at them from the bridge.

In spite of more than 50 men absent-over-leave by the end of the second leave period, the overhauled and spruced up Fighting Lady could not wait to return to the wars; the absentees would have to hop westward-bound ships to catch up with her. On September 29 Captain Combs formally relieved Al Jennings and next day took the *York* out to sea for a trial run. The new navigator, Commander Elliott L. James, Jr., Annapolis '33, a happy, though shy sort of a fellow who had relieved the austere Dick Matter, steered her out, while the new chief engineer, Lieutenant Commander George A. Crawford, gave her full power to reach 31.4 knots.

She performed as usual, wrote George Wille, in "stately fashion."

After two more days of test runs through Puget Sound, the ship received aboard two squadrons as passengers—the old arch rivals from *Essex*, Fighting 9 and Bombing 9. Although Admiral Monty Montgomery hoisted his flag aboard, Alex Wilding was happy to learn that Rear Admiral Arthur Radford had been reassigned to the carriers. "I'm glad to see him come out to the Pacific Fleet for he has a good reputation in Navy circles."

Departing Bremerton finally on the 9th for San Francisco, the *Yorktown* came under "attack" next day by land-based torpeckers from Astoria, Oregon; they belonged to Charlie Crommelin's new air group. A Navy blimp then bucked strong winds to touch down on the flight deck, transfer mail and pick up a passenger. The ship reached Frisco and tied up at Alameda on the 11th for two days of loading cargo and more passengers, including Army planes and VT-9, for transit to Pearl.

As the loading was being completed, Socket-wrench Brady called up radio officer Lieutenant Peter Joers, "Hey Pete, there's a gig over there. You want me to swipe it for you?" "Sure," answered the radio boss, and the crew hoisted aboard a beautiful new white motor launch.

The Fighting Lady cast off at 1359 on a gray October 13 to "a noisy symphony of horns and claxons and cheering crowds on the Golden Gate Bridge" for a thoroughly uneventful run to Hawaii. "I tell you," lamented Jesse Bradley in his diary, "it sure was a sad feeling to pull away from that dock and know you are leaving the good old U.S.A. for quite a while to come. We are sailing on Friday the 13th. I wonder if there is any bad luck in store for us."

Escorting destroyers swung into position, and once the land dropped below the horizon Jim Brady got Pete Joers to the hangar to look at the immaculate all-white gig they had heisted. As he removed the protective tarpaulin, Joers stood back agog at the sight of a four-star emblem mounted on the boat. This exquisite admiral's barge was obviously earmarked for Admiral Nimitz in Hawaii. Too late to return it ashore, the guilty officers had the insignia and ruffles removed and the gig repainted a dull battleship gray.

After a swift five-day voyage punctuated only by heavy seas and a couple of gunnery exercises, the *Yorktown* reached the Islands on the 18th. Air Group Nine immediately left the ship, being still undertrained for carrier duty, and reported to

NASKA (Naval Air Station Kahului) on Maui. The ship moved to the navy yard on the 21st for some last-minute alterations.

Though the *Yorktown* had departed from the States, she left behind an unusually widespread visual and literary record, although the censors did not always allow her to be identified by name. She graced the cover of *Flying* magazine in October, the same month that Bill Draper's paintings of life on board appeared in *National Geographic*. Dentist Frank Losey and his assistants made the June cover of *Our Navy,* and Max Miller's book *Daybreak for Our Carrier,* written on board the year before, was out. "Wing and a Prayer" was showing at theaters across the land, with "The Fighting Lady" about to appear.

The real Fighting Lady sortied from Pearl Harbor on October 24, 1944, to rejoin the fight.

A toast to success on the *Yorktown*, October 4, 1944, as Captain "Al" Jennings (L) turns her over to Captain "Theda" Combs at Bremerton.

Dick "Dog" Tripp waves one aboard.

Chapter IX

Philippine Storms

The long jump from the
Marianas to the Philippines during the last four months of 1944 called for sustained operations by the Fast Carrier Task Force to support and protect the landing forces against Japanese counterattacks. While the *Yorktown* had been at Bremerton, the Marines had landed in the Palaus, and in October MacArthur and the Army went ashore at Leyte in the Philippines. The mission of the *Yorktown* was now to help defend that beachhead and fend off a new menace—the kamikaze suicide plane.

Thanks to energetic lobbying by Commander Macpherson B. Williams, his Air Group Three was assigned to be the *York's* new main battery. A "gentlemanly" leader known affectionately to his pilots as "the Colonel," Mac Williams had been launching officer on the old *Yorktown* before the war and had commanded VB-9 on the *Essex* through the Marcus raid. At the helm of Air Group Three for a full year, he stressed group tactics over individual squadron operations, turning in his beloved bomber for a fighter in the process.

Like Williams, a 1930 Naval Academy graduate, all three squadron lieutenant commanders were "trade-school boys." The youngest, William L. Lamberson, '38, led Fighting 3; an aggressive hard-charger, his pilots referred to him as "the Iron Major." John T. "Jigger" Lowe, '34, had flown in combat from two carriers before taking over Bombing 3. Charles H. Turner, '35, of Torpedo 3, "the Little Liberators," had been a plankowner of the Old Yorky and in action from another flattop.

Exuberant, these fliers made their way to the flight line at Maui's NASKA on the forenoon of October 24, 1944, applauded by the local Seabee brass band and a cheering section of air station personnel. "Go get the yellow bastards!" shouted the fans, and the pilots answered by whipping out their .38s and .45s and firing over their heads cowboy

style. Then the entire air group paraded over the field in a fine display of showmanship. "Their glorious departure from Maui," the VF-3 historian remembered caustically, "was soon offset by the cool reception they received from the gallant but business-like Fighting Lady."

Dog Tripp, now senior LSO, waved them aboard one by one for an hour and 32 minutes, unusually long by CV-10 standards. Congratulating themselves in the ready room on what they thought had been some pretty damned good landings, the pilots were brought up short by air boss "Empty" Evans, who lectured them on "the do's and don'ts and how to fly the carrier way." The aircrewmen of VT-3 also grumbled when Captain Combs confiscated a large supply of booze they had tried to smuggle aboard.

This being the *York's* third air group in six months, close friendships between crew and aviators had become impossible. Thus the ship's veterans made no attempt whatsoever even to learn the names of the new airmen, an attitude from which the newcomers took their cue. Mused Tim Sullivan of the bombers, "I am now a member of a section, of a division, of a squadron, of an air group, of a ship of a group of a force of a fleet of a Navy—a small potato indeed." And so they all were.

For nearly two months the *Yorktown's* sisters had hammered away at enemy air forces protecting Japan's inner line of defenses in the Philippines and at Formosa. They were led by Admiral William F. "Bull" Halsey, Jr., who had relieved Admiral Spruance, now planning subsequent operations. Fifth Fleet had been renumbered Third Fleet, and Task Force 58 was now TF 38. With MacArthur's army ashore at Leyte, the Jap fleet counterattacked on this very day, October 24, and the next, in the momentous Battle of Leyte Gulf. The American fleet won this engagement and sank the *Zuikaku* and three other flattops but at the cost of the light carrier *Princeton* and several smaller warships.

The fanatical Japanese, stripped of experienced navy pilots, committed their new special corps of kamikaze ("Divine Wind") suicide planes during the battle. Over succeeding days these human-guided missiles damaged the luckless *Intrepid*, the *Franklin* and the *Belleau Wood*. Such savage resistance exhausted ships' crews and pilots so quickly that replacement carriers and air groups had to be rushed forward ahead of schedule.

Hence the *Yorktown* and her planes made haste toward Eniwetok—not even bothering to initiate pollywogs at the Date Line—and conducted gunnery exercises and night Bat team fighter direction drills, simulated attacks, and bombed the sled. And tragedy struck early when one of VF-3's most popular pilots, Lieutenant Bob Overmier, lost his entire tail assembly in a strafing dive and plunged to his death.

At least the fly-boys had a patron saint in Dr. Frank Voris, a most colorful flight surgeon. A big, robust Dutchman who relished giving innoculations and performing appendectomies and tonsilectomies on the sailors, he had been a Park Avenue eye-ear-nose-and-throat specialist in civilian life and now took a special interest in the men's diets. He'd stand in the messing compartment, inspect each man's tray, and serve up the vegetables himself. "Hey!" he'd stop a man, "You need more carrots—good for your night vision, you know." Or he'd splat potatoes down on the tray, "Keep some fat on your ribs!"

The *Yorktown*'s good chow pleased the airmen, except that supply officer Moring was giving them beans for breakfast. When they'd get up about 16,000 feet, they would bloat up like footballs. Then—boom! And someone in a TBM would roar over the intercom, "Who shit?!" After three or four flights loud protests resulted in Voris getting the menu changed.

Anchoring at Eniwetok on October 31 only long enough to refuel, the *Yorktown* made a bee-line next day for the recently-occupied Ulithi atoll in the western Carolines—a superb lagoon which had become the new forward base of the fleet. As the *York* dropped the hook at this hot and sticky refuge on November 3, she was greeted by an amazing message: "Congratulations! Tokyo Rose reports you've just been sunk." Then, a follow-up from the *Enterprise*: "Don't worry about it. We've been sunk three or four times." But one look at the kamikaze-stricken *Franklin* and *Belleau Wood* buried any

humor in it.

Going ashore at Mog Mog island for some suds at "Crowley's Bar," the pilots listened to stories about the fighting from friends in other squadrons and kidded each other about which one would win the $50 war bond. Back in February while training at Whidbey Island near Seattle, Ensign "Pee Wee" Spaulding had died in an operational mishap. Whereupon his mother had offered the bond for the first of her late son's buddies to bag a Jap plane. Then she had enlisted in the Army as a buck private.

The ship sortied from Ulithi with three other carriers and many escorts on the 5th to join Task Force 38 off the Philippines. Admiral Mitscher had just gone back to Pearl to help Spruance plan future operations and had been replaced by Vice Admiral John S. McCain, an old sea dog like Halsey. News from the carriers then striking Luzon in the northern Philippines was good. Alex Wilding marveled at the dearth of snoopers bothering the force over three days of strikes which destroyed 400 Jap planes on the ground.

But bad news too. Force flagship *Lexington* was hit by a kamikaze, and Admiral McCain shifted his flag from the *Lex* to the *Wasp*, which now took him back to Ulithi.

"Why?" Wilding asked himself. "This leaves [Admiral F.C.] Sherman as TF 38 Commander, while McCain was gone. I can't see Mitscher ever leaving his fleet in command of another admiral." *Wasp's* permature return to Ulithi was for a new air group, but Wilding was correct about "Slew" McCain; he could not compare with Mitscher as a leader. Sloppy and careless, though well-liked, McCain acted as little more than a rubber stamp for Halsey. "The Bull" called all the shots.

The *Yorktown* joined Admiral Montgomery's Task Group 38.1 on the afternoon of November 7. It included old friend *Hornet* and the *Cowpens*, two battleships, two cruisers and 17 tin cans. *Wasp* would join up later. As the group headed toward the coast of Samar near Leyte to rendezvous with Sherman's and Davison's task groups, the weather worsened into a typhoon which forced the ships to slow down and ride out the edge of it.

Commander Jigger Lowe of the bombers recorded on the 8th, "Everybody listening for election results but not surprised on what comes in." FDR for the fourth time. "Nobody knows where we are going," complained Jesse Bradley in his diary, "Everybody sure is down in the dumps."

On the 9th Montgomery shifted his flag from the *Hornet* to the *Yorktown* and ordered Wilding to his staff as task group fighter director. A reluctant Alex found this admiral whom Air Group Five had hated so much for his fatal predawn launches to be "very curt and formal. He has the personality of a dead fish."

That he did. As his staff officers described him, "When things were quiet he was somewhat irascible and impatient, but in combat operations he was calm, quiet, always thinking, and came up with more effective decisions." He coupled sarcasm with occasional humor, but continual migraine headaches under the tensions of combat "made him difficult to work with."

Word of the mission—to support the Leyte beachhead—was passed to all hands on the 10th as the task group made its final run-in. When searches from other carriers sighted a Jap troop convoy heading for Ormoc Bay on the west side of Leyte, Air Group Three received orders to hit it next day. It would go into action with a newly-implemented organization to improve anti-kamikaze defenses. Several dive bombers had been traded in for fighters, giving the unit 45 instead of 36 F6F day fighters, four night Hellcats, 24 instead of 36 Helldivers, and 17 TBMs. In addition, whenever possible the fighters would henceforth be catapulted to hasten the speed of launch, with the heavy-laden bombing planes making the usual powered takeoffs.

Armistice Day 1944. Reveille 0510. GQ 0525. Sunrise 0620. Point Option: 126 miles northeast of Samar, the island adjacent to Leyte in the central Philippines. After twenty fighters formed a CAP umbrella aloft, a full deckload strike took off to attack the convoy, now reported to be comprised of four troopships, three destroyers and two light cruisers. The 20 fighters carried rockets, the 23 bombers three bombs each, and most of the dozen TBMs torpedoes. They flew in the rear of the 292 planes from Montgomery's task group.

Last to arrive over the western side of Ormoc Bay, the *Yorktown* strike spotted tall columns of smoke from two large troopships already sunk, but five destroyers and a destroyer escort were still afloat (no cruisers present). Mac Williams acted as target coordinator, but since no enemy fighters were present, Jigger Lowe's four divisions of bombers could line up for clean runs. In addition to Lowe, the three lieutenants were all combat veterans: Raymond S. "Gus" Osterhoudt; John "Mary Lou" Clifford, Navy Cross recipient for Midway; and Chris Fink, Silver Star winner at the Battle of the Eastern Solomons.

Picking out three destroyers, all on different

headings trying to escape, Lowe led the dives from 11,000 feet. The three cans maneuvered at high speed—all could make more than 35 knots—and threw up thick flak from their many 5-inch/50 cal. and 25mm guns. Lowe himself selected the largest one, probably the brand new 3500-ton *Wakasuki*, which with its size and eight 3.9-inch guns made it almost a light cruiser, hence the earlier report. The second man in Lowe's division, John C. Smith, planted a thousand-pounder squarely onto her bow, while his mates scored near-misses and possible hits until the victim stopped almost dead in the water.

One of the fleeing destroyers may well have been the equally new 39.9-knot *Shimakaze*, fastest of the six vessels under attack. Joe Vercelli of Osterhoudt's division put his bomb onto her bow, slowing her down and sending her circling out of control. Aerial photos would show her bow blown off. About half of Bombing 3 went after the third can and hit it twice to arrest its progress too.

"Goodtime Charlie" Turner brought in six of his eight fish-laden torpeckers behind the bombers from angels 11 for a textbook attack on the *Wakasuki*: average drop approach from 11,000 yards, drop altitude 580 feet, speed 230 knots, angles of attack from 40 degrees to 70 degrees on the starboard bow of the slow moving target. At least three of the tin fish hit, and the *Wakasuki* blew sky-high and sank.

The two other torpedoes, fired at the *Shimakaze,* may have hit her, as might also several of the bombs from two of the bomb-carrying TBMs of VT-3. The fighters covered the bombing planes and swept in raking the decks of all six targets with rockets and machine guns, though some of the rockets failed to release.

In addition to the *Wakasuki* and *Shimakaze* were two one-year-old sister ships, the *Hamanami* and *Naganami*; the *Akishimo*, commissioned only eight days before (!); and the 13-year-old but fast (38-knot) *Akebono*. All but the latter two were sunk during this battle by Air Group Three and groups from other carriers. Also, all four transports went down, drowning nearly all of their 10,000 troops on board.

A good day's hunting, especially for the group's very first action, but trouble developed on the return flight when Ray Coleman's fighter engine quit, forcing him to ditch in Maqueda Bay just off Samar. Bill Lamberson and R.C. Van Ness reported this and circled him, though air officer Evans ordered them to return to base. They refused and watched Coleman start paddling toward a village on the coast, confident that it was in American hands because of "Dugout Doug" MacArthur's communiques to that effect. One of several native Filipino canoes offshore intercepted him to reveal that the Japs still held the place. The natives took custody of Coleman, allowing Lambo and Van to leave.

Empty Evans, remembering also Harry Hill's agonizing rescue off Truk, gathered the entire squadron in the ready room to give the two orbiters and everyone else "a bad time for orbiting a downed pilot and fouling up his deck, but all hands listened in stony silence and their policy never changed." As for Ray Coleman, the natives delivered him to the Navy in good shape within a week for eventual repatriation.

During topping off of destroyers in midafternoon, Seaman First Joe Soccaccio—"one of my buddies," wrote Jesse Bradley—was climbing the ladder from his 40mm gun mount to the flight deck when he missed the last rung and fell backwards over the side, hitting the life lines as he fell. He struck the water on his back and struggled to stay afloat while two life jackets were thrown to him and a flare fired to mark the spot. He soon lost the battle, though, and passed from sight.

After refueling on the 12th, Task Force 38 headed north to prevent more troopships and planes at Manila from reinforcing the defenders at Leyte. For the first time from the *Yorktown*, a new weapon would be employed—napalm, jellied gasoline carried in the belly tanks of the fighters and a headache for the ship's new arming officer, Lieutenant John G. McCollow.

Air Group Three roared over Manila Bay at dawn of November 13 and attacked several of the 25 to 30 enemy ships there. Though torpedoes from the TBMs were detonated by defensive torpedo nets, Joe Sanders hit one maru amidships; it settled on the bottom. Bomber pilots "Jenk" Jenkinson and G.R. Day scored direct hits on a freighter and a tanker, while bomber Russ Hummel and four torpeckers destroyed the old captured drydock at Cavite.

After strafing with machine guns and rockets in the morning, thirteen VF-3 Hellcats took off at noon equipped with napalm-filled belly tanks to escort the bombers. Near the outskirts of Manila they dove down at high speed—340 knots—in two lines abreast, seven in front, six of them half a mile behind, for simultaneous drops on the piers, warehouses and other port facilities. Leveling off only 125 feet over the housetops—and looking *up* at the church spires (!)—they fired short machine

gun bursts at their targets and the batteries and ships firing at them. Omar "Chee Chee" Menoher, Gilbert "Pappy" Joynt and Johnny Schell planned to release their tanks of napalm "just as their picked targets disappeared under the nose of the plane" to set afire Manila's waterfront.

Experimental tactics these were, for which VF-3 paid dearly. Some pilots tried manual release, others electrical, but only four of the first wave worked, and a burst of flak knocked off Joynt's bomb, and a bullet wounded him in the head. Perhaps three fires were started, and the second wave braved the AA. But a burst hit Leonard "Mo" Row's plane directly, and he plunged into the streets, plane and napalm exploding on impact in a ball of fire.

The bombers then dived on the shipping, two of them scoring fatal hits on at least one maru but suffering much damage from the heavy flak. E.F. Andersen had to ditch offshore and was plucked up by the destroyer *Maddox*. When the torpeckers took their turns, George McDow and F.C. Dull used 500-pound bombs to sink a medium-size freighter.

No bogeys visited the force until midafternoon, when radar-equipped destroyers on a forward picket line took over directing the CAP fighters. The *Maddox* vectored Clyde "Willie" Williams' division overhead to the intercept of a bomb-and/or belly tank-laden Zero—surely a kamikaze. Just as Williams and wingman Art "Chico" Leach dropped down to bracket the Zeke, the second section of Bill Kitchell and Dick Ridle saw four more Jap planes come out of a cloud above them. They climbed up in pursuit.

VF-3 waded into its first dogfight. Willie's burst tore off pieces of metal from the bandit, which maneuvered away brilliantly with both Hellcats close behind—only to have another F6 come from nowhere and knock down their prey.

As Kitchell and Ridle closed in on the other four suiciders, these jettisoned their bombs and turned to flee. Kitch blasted two of them from the sky in 20 quick seconds and using only 175 of his 2400 rounds from three guns. It happened so fast that Ridle complained he didn't have time even to trigger. Ironically, just before the dogfight, Kitch had reported his other three guns not functioning and had requested permission to return to the *Yorktown*. Instead, he ended up with Pee Wee Spaulding's mom's $50 war bond prize.

More bogeys threatened before and after sundown, keeping the crew at GQ awaiting an expected Betty attack. Joe Chambliss, now commissioned an ensign, observed everything from the radar plotting room of the gun directors. "Business picked up a little but still not the fire works that we expected. We put up 2 night fighters which chased the bogeys for quite some time. These Japs must have some dope on night fighters now. They used very radical evasive maneuvers to throw them off—had several merged plots but not splashed. One bogey decided to go home and actually outran an F6F by miles! (something new has been added.)."

Reinforced by the *Wasp* during the night, *Yorktown*, *Hornet* and *Cowpens* rearmed their planes for another day of working over Manila, but without the unpredictable napalm. Air officer Empty Evans had only one constant word of advice to all pilots: "Get lower!" And exec Ben Born announced in the Plan of the Day for the 14th, "TODAY WE TAKE ANOTHER SLAP AT THE YAPPING JAPS, STRIKING AT SHIPPING AND AIR-FIELD TARGETS. EVERYONE BE ALERT and on the job so we don't get caught napping. Let's be prepared to fight the 'Fighting Lady' with 4.0 efficiency." The new nickname was taking hold.

At daylight, Jigger Lowe's 12 Helldivers pummeled one hapless maru with three direct hits, causing it to settle by the stern, but targets were otherwise scarce. As John "Pappy" Dayton in Pleasant Victor Miller's TBM (some name!) noted in his diary, "Harbor is a huge graveyard of sunken ships." So the bombers worked over the wharf area at Cavite.

Among the fighters, Ensign James M. "Big Jake" Jones—6-foot-3 hunk of peacetime property of the Chicago White Sox—bagged a Zeke just taking off from Grace Park, wheels still down. A fighter search to the south discovered a convoy off western Mindoro and called for help. Freshly-launched *Yorktown* Hellcats carrying 500-pound bombs were dispatched under the control of division leaders Pappy Joynt and George H. Smith. The boys called Smith "Super" for having survived 21 days in a life raft in the Solomons after being forced down in heavy weather.

The Hellcats caught the convoy by surprise—an oiler and freighter escorted on both sides by four patrol craft. Diving out of the sun and down to masthead level, the fighters dropped their bombs—and missed, as fighters usually did. But they came around in strafing runs from 1500 feet and quickly set both marus afire and witnessed white jacketed sailors trying to douse the flames on the tanker.

Meanwhile, back on the ship, the print shop's radio news was being circulated to the crew; it included a bulletin from MacArthur's headquarters re-counting the operations around Leyte and Ormoc on the 11th. Joe Chambliss: "Old 'Dougout' Doug MacArthur has a few words to say about us. Generally the boys came back with the retort of serving in MacArthur's Navy. Some advance the reason for our being in the Philippines as due to the fact that 'he couldn't dig his regulation fox hole of 90 ft.—only got down to 70 ft. and hit rock so he brought in "his navy" to protect him.' Some say that 'he uses a periscope in his 70 ft fox hole.' Others maintain that 'he wears a parachute while climbing in and out of his fox hole so if he falls he can save himself with the chute.' Anyway, it makes good conversation."

Having disposed of the two marus which would have helped MacArthur's opponents on Leyte, Admiral Montgomery now ordered the next fighter strike to finish those four patrol craft so they would escort no more convoys to Ormoc. Nineteen *Yorktown* Hellcats took off at noon with skipper Lamberson in the lead, each armed with 500-pounders. They found the four boats in a tight anti-aircraft formation, so Lambo ordered a strafing run first to silence their guns.

After the first Cat whizzed by unopposed, the four craft unleashed a withering AA barrage. It blew off the tail of Van Ness' F6 which spun dizzily down to the water, the bomb exploding on impact and leaving no visible debris. The young ensign had joined the squadron only a month before. At this loss, Lamberson called out, "OK, boys, we'll polish them off one at a time. Don't let any get away."

The others came around strafing and bombing. Dick "Maidenswoon" (!) English made a masthead attack on the southernmost boat, his bomb hitting squarely at the waterline and passing clean through it to explode on the other side. Bill McLeroy blew the stern off the eastern vessel in a low-level run, but flak hit the wing tanks of "Gorgeous George" Martin's Cat, blowing off a wing and sending him cartwheeling across the water until his bomb disintegrated the plane. Lambo thereupon instructed the others to attack from higher altitudes, but in so doing they missed everything. Nevertheless, the sternless victim dropped back and ran into the beach, where McLeroy strafed the sailors trying to get overboard.

In spite of several lost pilots and crews, Task Force 38 had done well. The two surviving destroyers from Ormoc, *Akebono* and *Akishimo*, had been sunk, along with two other cans, a light cruiser, seven marus and the one patrol boat. One can and one oiler were severely damaged, along with much of Manila's waterfront area.

During the retirement and refueling over succeeding days, Cooper Bright diverted the gloom of the tired pilots with some of his choice humor over the Air Plot ticker. One such barb invoked the image of well-known fighter pilot Commander "Jumpin' Joe" Clifton of the *Saratoga*.

> WE MAKE NO ATTEMPT TO BE LEWD
>   BUT KEEP IN MIND, THE SITUATION IS
>   FLUID...
> LAMB THE SKIPPER OF FIGHTER THREE,
>   MANY CAUSTIC REMARKS HAS MADE TO
>   ME,
> SUCH AS 'HELLO BALDY' AND 'PUT OUT
> THAT LITE'
>   JUST INSULTING THE HEAD OF COMDR.
>   BRIGHT.
>
> NOW WE OF AIR PLOT ARE MEN TO FEAR,
>   SO HARKEN, HEED, AND LEND AN EAR,
> NOW WE'RE RESTING FROM THESE
> QUARRELS,
>   'CAUSE THE GREAT H.P. LAMBO
>   BURNED OUT HIS BARRELS.
> IT SOUNDS TO US LIKE A JOE CLIFTON
> TRICK
>   THAT CAN ONLY BE DONE BY SOME
>   SORT OF A PRICK...

Fighting 3 rose to the occasion with a riposte from Lamberson and his boys.

> NOW SKINHEAD BRIGHT HAS A SCALP
> LIKE GLASS
>   THAT CAN HARDLY BE TOLD FROM A
>   JUVENILE'S ASS,
> AND HE MAKES LOUD ADO TWEEN ME
> AND YOU,
>   IT LOOKS LIKE A LAWN WITHOUT
>   GRASS.
>
> HE THINKS IT A CRIME
>   TO PUT INTO RHYME,
>   HIS DEFECTS SO VARIED AND MANY,
> BUT FREE SHOW IS HIS FORTE,
>   AND BEING A SPORT,
>   HE SPENDS NOT SO MUCH AS A
>   PENNY.
>
> BUT EAT AS HE MAY,
>   THERE'LL SOON COME A DAY,
>   WHEN THAT SHINING BALD PATE OF
>   OLD BRIGHT,
> WILL BOAST OF A GROWTH,
>   AND TICKLE US BOTH,
>   EVEN THO HE REMOVE IT AT NIGHT
>
>   SHAKESPEARE...

Aside from his outrageous humor, Bright impressed many with his seeming genius at coordinating air ops so well, although he was known to make mistakes. As he explained it, "The only genius I have is that I've been out here so damned long; all the mistakes have been made at least forty times. I can almost *smell* what's going on." He could even pick out *Yorktown*'s planes in a returning flight. In fact, it was time for Coop to be transferred ashore. Captain Combs had promised to let him go after 30 days. But by now the 30 days were up, and Combs followed Al Jennings' advice to keep him aboard because of his long experience.

This operation was a difficult one to plan, simply because General MacArthur's foothold at Leyte had to be defended by the fast carriers, with plans worked up on a day-to-day basis as needs arose. Wrote Jesse Bradley on November 17, "Nothing much is going on. We are running around in a circle. We will be around here for a few days patroling. We are 300 miles east of Samar operating in an area 50 miles wide and 150 long."

A reshuffled TG 38.1 of *Yorktown*, *Wasp* and *Cowpens* found no airborne enemy fighters before or during November 19 strikes on Manila's two airfields at Mabalacat and a third at Tarlac. But the flak was deadly as ever, destroying the Hellcats flown by "Speedy" Bacchus and N.A. Lotz. Noted Ensign Dwight Horner in his diary, "This makes the fifth to be killed out of the J.O. Bunk Room." Then Tom "Jeeter" Lindsey's engine quit, forcing him to ditch and swim around in the heavy seas until one of several life rafts dropped bumped him in the back of the head, and he climbed in. His mates kept orbiting, thus fouling Empty Evans' flight deck respot, until a destroyer literally happened along. Lindsey was picked up, suffering only from a "a good sunburn, and the Air Officer could finally respot his nice little carrier deck," recorded the VF-3 historian sarcastically.

Because the Japanese had carefully camouflaged their parked planes around Manila, results of the attacks were meager and difficult to assess. So Montgomery's 38.1 and Davison's 38.4 were ordered to return to Ulithi, with ships' guns and night fighters breaking up several raids of Bettys and new Frances twin-engine bombers that night. Their inauspicious conclusion to supporting the Leyte operation was not shared by Bogan's 38.2 and Sherman's 38.3, which were both clobbered on November 25 by kamikazes even as their strikes tangled with bandits over Luzon. Suiciders and/or bombs plunged into the *Hancock, Essex, Cabot* and

Intrepid; the old "Decrepid" suffered so heavily that she would yet again have to return to the States for major repairs. The *Yorktown* had again enjoyed her luck in missing all this.

During the retirement Captain Combs held gunnery practice "to keep in shape," in the words of Gunner's Mate First Edward N. Wallace, another new diarist. George Earnshaw's boys proved themselves sharp as ever, the 5-inchers knocking down three of the four target sleeves. The reward was a sumptuous Thanksgiving dinner on the 23rd for all hands.

Less pleasing to Admiral Montgomery was Alex Wilding's CIC operation. "Redneck" chewed out Alex for not reporting each radar blip of every bogey mile-by-mile—a useless exercise. "If the Adm. was that stupid I'd compound his stupidity and make him the laughing stock of his staff," confided Wilding to his diary, which he did by having his talker to the flag fake non-existent night fighter blips by guesswork. "Of course no one in Flag Plot will have a true picture of the tactical situation as it exists but it will keep the dumb son-of-a-bitch off our backs." Sure enough, the next night Alex tracked a bogey and night fighter until the former faded, calling bogus plots to the flag each mile. Afterwards the admiral summoned Wilding.

"See," Montgomery told his fighter director, "I knew you could do it if you really tried—that's the way I want to see all the plots here in the future." When the admiral turned away, Wilding "looked at the Chief of Staff [Captain John B. Moss] and he had a half-amused grin on his face—he knew." Returning to CIC, Alex gave his talker a well done, "and everyone in CIC had our little laugh."

When the *York* dropped the hook at Ulithi on November 24 a tired Father Farrell transferred off the ship as the new Catholic chaplain reported aboard. Every bit the peacetime scholar that Farrell had been, Father Joseph N. Moody was forty years old, had a Ph.D. in French history from Fordham University, and had left his chairmanship of the history and political science department of Notre Dame of New York to join the Navy. Convincing Captain Combs to let him give the several daily news broadcasts over the bullhorn, the tall, stately priest quickly won the affection of the crew.

A new enlisted man, Radarman First Edward A. Brand, reported to CIC after several months on the *Bunker Hill* and two weeks on the *Essex*. He soon found the *Yorktown* to be "the cleanest ship I was ever on," and he told his diary, "These fellows are really lucky; they have everything in their canteen.

George Wright and Joe Moody, Protestant and Catholic chaplains respectively.

We really have a nice CIC. Most of the fellows in the division are still pretty green, but they will be O.K. after they find out what they need to know."

Ulithi provided the usual suds and rest, though the new junior dentist and diarist George Franklin Smith found it "an attractive island much as Hollywood would picture it. Saw former articles of Jap habitation and grave of nineteen year old princess killed by our gunfire in going ashore. All but the very young and old were taken by the Japs as slaves and prostitutes."

The respite provided Task Force 38 commander Admiral McCain and his staff the opportunity to devise new defenses against the kamikazes. General MacArthur had his own planes ashore at Leyte, releasing the fast carriers to support his next landings at Mindoro and Lingayen Gulf in December. This would place them on the *west* side of the Philippines, between kamikaze bases on Luzon, Formosa, China and Indochina. McCain's tacticians now came up with special CAPs, airborne radar pickets, more picket destroyers and a continuous "big blue blanket" of fighters over the target, including hecklers at night.

To stop the hordes of anticipated suicide planes, the admirals in Washington, Hawaii and Ulithi agreed that the answer lay in many more defensive fighters. So now the air groups were reshuffled, more bombers and torpeckers being traded in for additional fighters. Squadron morale plummeted as Bombing 3 was further reduced from 24 to 15 SB2Cs and Torpedo 3 from 18 to 15 TBMs. Conversely, Fighting 3 swelled from 54 to 73 F6Fs, with 17 fresh pilots reporting in. All were organized into "new-fangled combat teams," one of which received the immediate nickanme of "The Notre Dame Backfield." They were Beaumont, Strombotne, Zelenski and Kozlowski (shades of Knute Rockne's four horsemen Layden, Stuhldreher, Miller and Crowley). Unfortunately, most of these "pool pilots" had not flown an airplane in six weeks and gave Empty Evans gray hair with their ragged landings.

Ulithi provided more anxiety than actual rest, thanks to the Japs. Four midget subs penetrated the lagoon and sank a tanker carrying much of the *York's* Christmas mail and packages, while enemy bombers struck Saipan, and snoopers visited Ulithi. Jesse Bradley reported, "The Japs say they are going to bomb this place, so they got us standing four [hours] on and four off [watch]." Half the *York's* guns were manned all the while at Ulithi. Then, heavy Luzon-based enemy air attacks on MacArthur's forces on Leyte caused the fast carriers to be recalled to Ulithi just hours after they had sortied on December 1 for the Mindoro landings—now postponed.

So the tense boredom returned for another ten days, relieved on the *Yorktown* only by a smoker for the crew on December 9. This was the work of the new Protestant chaplain, George A. Wright, 31-year-old former car salesman, caterer, nightclub musician, headwaiter and emcee-turned-Evangelical minister and the logical successor to Frank Losey as ship's entertainment officer. Cherubic and fun-loving, Wright stood in marked contrast to the magisterial Father Joe Moody.

Exec Ben Born and damage controller Jim Brady studied a report from the damaged *Intrepid* on the art of fighting fires from kamikaze hits, while gun bosses George Earnshaw and Pat Patterson advised their men, "Automatic weapons [40mm and 20mm] can set fire to suicide divers at short range but it takes 5" to tear up and demolish the plane and prevent success of the kamikaze." That meant if the fighters and the 5-inchers let one get through, then it wouldn't much matter if the lighter guns hit it;

it would crash into the ship at least as flaming wreckage. Oh, boy. . . .

The air group received "some good looking patches for aviators to wear on their flight jackets," wrote Alex Wilding—CBI patches denoting their Allied status in the China-Burma-India theater. Each also received a large American flag emblem with Chinese writing to carry with them; "that tells us something." In addition, they were issued "pointee talkers" to help them communicate with Chinese, Formosans or Filipinos if shot down, along with Philippine money, cloth maps of ocean currents and U.S. flags.

Before the carriers would send planes over Japanese-occupied China or Formosa, however, they had first to neutralize enemy airfields on Luzon before and during MacArthur's assault at Mindoro on December 15. Consequently, Task Group 38.1 left Ulithi on the 10th with Admiral Montgomery in the *Yorktown* and McCain in the *Wasp*, accompanied by *Cowpens* and *Monterey*, two battleships, five cruisers and 16 tin cans. They rendezvoused with Bogan's TG 38.2 and Sherman's 38.3 en route. "Funny," observed Wilding, "we used to fear these waters—now we own them."

"WE STRIKE THE JAPS TODAY," announced the Gunnery Department's Plan of the Day for December 14, 1944. "Vigilance is the best defense against 'zoot suiters'. Be mentally and physically alert at all times. Be a Gunner, not a Goner." The green- and yellow-colored suicide planes had been nicknamed for the wildly-attired teenage zootsuiters of wartime America. The Fighting Lady would have a wild time of her own during Mindoro.

"WE STRIKE and STRIKE OFTEN TODAY," Commander Born's battle cry declared, "WE HIT ALL THE AIR FIELDS AROUND THE MANILA AREA! ALL HANDS BE ALERT." Any hope for surprise was lost before dawn when an Emily flying boat spotted the carriers, only to be knocked down by an *Independence* night fighter.

The first strike was launched from the black, rain-swept deck of the *Yorktown* at 0634 from 250 miles northeast of the target, led by Mac Williams. The planes bombed, rocketed and strafed parked planes at Nichols Field, but only Jake Jones encountered any airborne opposition. Taking on three Zeros singlehandedly, he splashed one and scattered the others.

Succeeding strikes encountered only flak as the *Yorktown* shuttled fighters to and from this "Target

Bomb magazine of the *Yorktown* and 1000-pound bombs.

CAP." Dwight Horner lost eight inches of his port wing to flak on his first hop, "landed aboard at 0935, ate some ice cream and manned my plane at 1010 for a 5 hour CAP over Manila. We looked around all airfields for a good target. Ended up at Grace Park A/F [airfield] where I dropped my bomb (500# GP) on an aircraft dispersal area and felt sure of some damage although no smoke was seen.

"Climbed back up to 6000 feet and made a strafing run first on gun implacements and next on the dispersal area. On my recovery or pull out small caliber AA hit my oil line in front of the fire wall, covering my windshield completely with oil and was smoking badly. I regained a little altitude, blew up my IFF gear [so it would not be captured], and prepared to go over the side.

"My division leader, Lt. John Schell, came alongside and told me to join up on him, which I did. My oil pressure dropped from a normal 80 pounds/sq.in. to 20 before I got to the mountains on Eastern Luzon. I dropped my belly tank and tried to jettison my hood, but everything in the cockpit was covered with oil.

"Since I couldn't see forward Schell led me around the mountains and we reached the Eastern shore of Luzon at 7000 ft. at 1217. My engine was making so much noise that Schell had to contact the rescue picket destroyer. My engine went into full low pitch (3770 RPM) and burnt out at 9000 ft. I proceeded on course on my let down and prepared for water landing.

"I hit the water at 1239, making a good water landing. I got clear of the plane and inflated my rubber life raft. The plane stayed afloat for a long time for a F6F (40 seconds). I swam around and picked up loose gear and lashed it to the raft. At this moment I remembered the many pictures I had seen in training for this moment, so I plotted my position, threw out the sea anchor, covered my face with sunburn ointment, bailed out the raft, etc.

"I got sick at first but felt better after I vomited. A bird lit on my knee and later on my head. All this time Schell circled my position and I saw several strike groups high and headed for Manila. I hit the water about 15 miles to East of Luzon but still 130 miles to west of rescue destroyer.

"The destroyer (DD #731 the USS *Maddox*— code call 'Goodspeed') picked me up at 1833 after six hours in water and was I glad to see them. They treated me like a king. I slept in the captain's cabin, etc. I sat and talked with the officers and men the rest of the day."

On the next flight, flak hit Billy Commons' Hellcat in its dive at 1000 feet and blew off the right wing. Commons spun to his death into Nichols airfield; it was his first and last combat flight.

For Uncle Day, the 15th, assault day at Mindoro, the officers and crew went to chow early. Cooper Bright noticed the new flight deck boss, Lieutenant Commander Paul Hesch—nervous, always in a hurry—gobbling down his food. "You know, you ought to slow down," Coop remarked, "Enjoy your food. Take it with you." But when Flight Quarters sounded at 0540 Hesch dashed off, leaving most of his breakfast uneaten.

The weather was excellent, though the night very dark with no moon. Fighting 3's twenty Grummans coughed and whirred as their big propellers roared to life, and they began taking off. Suddenly, in the midst of it, tragedy. Paul Hesch stumbled back from the wash of a whirling prop into another. Its blades sliced off his right arm at the shoulder and his right ankle, fractured his skull and split open his stomach. Flight surgeon Voris took one look and reported, "He's O.K.," meaning he had died instantly—thank God. But the launch had to continue, uninterrupted.

As the troops stormed ashore at Mindoro, the carrier planes repeated their previous day's work over Manila without incident, keeping the zootsuiters on the deck. Joe Mayer scored a direct hit on a large oiler, and *Yorktown* planes destroyed 13 "sitting ducks" on the airfields. Unfortunately, on landing, Bob Glaisyer's Cat crashed into the barrier, causing the pilot head injuries which proved fatal next day.

Repetitious strike schedules led Air Group Three's mild-mannered skipper Mac Williams to complain bitterly to Admiral Montgomery's operations officer "about the fixed schedule of our daily operations. I pointed out that we did the same thing, at the same time, every day of our three day strike and joked that the Japanese were setting their clocks by our attacks. He convinced me that [the staff] couldn't do a new operation order every day but told me that after we had hit our assigned targets I was on my own."

Having made two flights the day before, a tired Williams decided to make only one on the 10th— Strike One Able at 0505, strafing and bombing three airfields around Manila. This accomplished, he reported later, "we had forty minutes to spare. I released the three section leaders to browse on their own and to join me here, over Laguna de Bey, in thirty minutes." He and wingman Jake Jones headed north up the Pasig River to Marikina airfield to strafe five planes in revetments. After the first pass, the Japanese gunners had figured out the American tactics, and in the second pull-out the flak scored two hits, one punching a big hole in Jones' starboard wing.

The other burst hit the Air Group Commander's F6 on the starboard side of its engine. Flames spurted out momentarily then flared up again and spread completely around the cowling. Williams turned eastward toward the hills east of Manila and supposedly friendly natives there, climbing to 1000 feet. It was no use; his plane was fatally stricken.

Four miles from the airfield Mac pulled up the nose of the smoking plane, banked sharply to starboard, and bailed out.

"I had been mentally rehearsing this first parachute jump for fifteen years, ever since I started flying. When it came, I did it all wrong. I abandoned my aircraft at low altitude, high speed, and out of the wrong side. I jumped through an envelope of flame, escaped the empennage, pulled the rip cord, the chute brought me up with a jerk. I hit the ground hard and fell on my backside."

He had hung in the air fewer than 30 seconds, with Bert Larsen circling him at 2000 feet. The Swede did not zoom Williams for fear of indicating his position to the Japs, but watched the plane crash from some distance away, then headed home, leaving Williams to his fate.

"Here I was, a lone fellow in enemy territory, more seriously burned than I realized, with my emergency pack, my deployed parachute, and my gun. I abandoned the parachute and started toward the hills, just to the east. I burst through some underbrush and right into a Filipino lad who was plowing his fields.

"With much poor Spanish and some gun display I tried to entice him into helping me evade the Japanese. He was completely noncommital, so I left him and started running towards the hills again. I stopped, exhausted, and turned to see my 'rescuer' hot footing it toward Manila. Apparently he was terrified of the Japanese and wanted no part of me. When I [later] saw my thoroughly singed visage in a mirror I understood his reaction much more clearly.

"As I slumped in the high grass, catching my breath, I was suddenly surrounded. People sprang up all around me. I had my gun and six bullets and little else. Fortunately they were friends. In the van of this surrounding throng was a good looking young teen age boy and directly behind him was Captain Fury. I really had no choice so I capitulated, praying that they were really friends.

"Captain Fury informed me that I was with friends, that he was in charge of the rescue party, that they had observed my jump from my burning plane, that they kept every American attack in their area under observation and that they did everything in their power to succor surviving U.S. aviators. I sighed with relief.

"We marched away to the home of an elderly Filipino couple where I met Madam 'C' who was deeply involved in the guerrilla movement. She gave me first aid, coffee and sympathy and soon departed to the east where this band had an outlying command post. We learned later that we left this house about twenty minutes before the Japanese arrived. In some way, from lost pilot reports, or from markings on my plane, or otherwise, the Japanese had discovered I was the air group commander and they were most interested in my whereabouts."

Meanwhile, two more *Yorktown* strikes visited Manila during the morning, and in the exchange of gunfire Bud Hopp's Hellcat took flak in the engine over Nichols Field. Luckily, the engine conked out over lake Laguna de Bey, into which he was able to make a deadstick landing. Climbing out, he inflated his life raft and waved to several native outrigger canoes approaching him. As two comrades buzzed overhead, one of the boats took Hopp aboard.

"I was picked up in a sail canoe with eight friendly Filipino men aboard. We headed north along the west shore of Talim Island and after a few minutes had gone by, another boat (*banca*) came alongside; a boy about twenty-two years of age came aboard and asked in English if he could accompany us to their village (*barrio*). He explained that he was Lt. Oliva of the guerrilla forces and knew of a safe place for me to hide. I had no choice other than to say yes, so we went to a small barrio where I was hidden for the remainder of the day."

As the Filipinos spirited Williams and Hopp out from under the noses of the hated Japs, Air Group Three went Jap-hunting. Ed Hauser strafed a military truck five miles out of Manila, killing about half of the two dozen green-uniformed riflemen inside as the truck flipped over its side and burned. Later in the day Joe Mayer's division spotted a troop and tank convoy north of Manila. Flathatting down to treetop level, the fighters strafed the long line of vehicles, which began to disperse under the trees and into civilian residential areas. Fearful of hitting innocent Filipinos and their homes, Mayer had to let them go.

Willie Williams silenced a battery of 8 to 10 light AA guns near the road, while Pappy Joynt's division gave chase to a lone staff car, racing away at 80 per. Using full deflection leads, Bayard Carlson blew out a tire which sent the auto spinning off the road. And as several Jap "brass hats" stumbled out and headed for the woods, Dick Noel cut them all down in a strafing run.

At the end of the full day of strikes on Manila's defenses, the *Yorktown* retired with the task force. Halsey's three-day operation had successfully protected the northern flak of the Mindoro beachhead and destroyed perhaps 200 planes on and over Luzon. Worsening weather covered the withdrawal to refuel next day.

The storm grew during the night, forcing the crew of the *Yorktown* to labor all night long in double and triple lashing down of everything movable and heavy, especially aircraft and flight deck mules. On the planes, tires and shock absorbers were "bled" and tanks degassed. Exposed watertight doors and hatches were closed and dogged down and all hands warned not to loiter in danger areas like the fo'c'sle where the raging sea could dash a man against the anchor machinery or bulkheads or even dump him overboard.

At daylight of December 17 wildly-blowing wind churned the seas into mountainous crests, but the *York* still managed to get off her morning CAP and antisub patrols. The oiler *Chikaskia* manfully maneuvered alongside but only passed 100,000 gallons—half the required amount—before the hoses parted. The destroyer *Buchanan* moved up to take on twelve VF-3 pilots for transfer to the escort carrier *Altamaha* to receive replacement aircraft.

Bob Rice was one of them; all got a thorough dunking as they were transferred over to the can by breeches buoy. Upon arrival on board the "Buck," as her crew called her, Rice decided "a destroyer must be so-called because it does its utmost to destroy human happiness, comfort and health!" The badly-pitching *Buchanan* rolled so dangerously close to the jeep carrier that the pilots' transfer had to be postponed for another day.

"We drew alongside a tanker to refuel our desperately low supply of fuel oil, which also acts as ballast in stormy seas. Once again the non-pacific Pacific thwarted our plans; in fact, its violence severed the oil hoses, discharged enuf oil over us and our ship to supply all American automobiles with sufficient petrol to carry them to the race tracks and back!"

Another can came alongside the *Yorktown* to top off with precious ballast. Coxswain Ted Rohrbaugh was among those who held their breaths as the can maneuvered on the starboard side by the number one crane. "A swell raised the destroyer as high as the flight deck, and then the destroyer went completely out of sight except for the top of the mast.

"Finally, after expert ship handling, a hose was passed to the destroyer and hooked up, by two men who were above decks on the destroyer, when a large swell came between the two ships, hitting the

Photographed from the *Yorktown*, an escorting can lifts her bow completely out of the churning green water of the great December 1944 typhoon.

superstructure of the destroyer. It killed both men and washed them overboard. It also broke the fuel hose and other lines."

Needless to say, all refueling attempts had to be stopped, in spite of the fact that the destroyers lacked stability without the vital ballasting oil. Visibility during the day dropped from twelve to six miles, and at noon the storm was finally diagnosed as a typhoon.

Typhoon! The word has a foreboding ring to it, enhanced by eons of seamen's tales recounting the sheer terror of such force. "Typhoons were very spectacular and very interesting to me," reflected signal officer George Wille, "who had always wanted to see a northeasterner from the shore. This was it with a double vengeance! Visibility during these storms is greatly reduced, both by low-hanging clouds and driving rain. The ocean is whipped up to a wild, plunging, watery waste, with great hilly fields of water moving before the wind, their crests breaking and the spindrift driving over the surface like so much sleet."

The ceiling dropped to 1000 feet, and the patrolling planes were given a Charlie to land. No easy task, as the deck was pitching badly. Ensign Al Wolters came up the groove but got a last-minute waveoff from Dick Tripp. He pulled up, but so did the bow,

to rip off one wheel. As Wolters regained the air, Empty Evans concluded that the 38-knot wind and now a 500-foot ceiling would make a crash landing difficult and advised him to bail out.

Wolters stood up in his cockpit but released his parachute too soon and the slipstream wrenched him by the chute out of the cockpit and into the tail of the plane. If this didn't kill him, he perished soon after as the chute blossomed only momentarily before his body hit the water on the downswing. A destroyer rushed up but could not recover him.

Fortunately, the rest of the planes successfully negotiated the rolling deck to come aboard, whereupon they were immediately secured. Captain Theda Combs sent the crew to GQ, reduced speed to six knots, and held the rudder at 30 degrees to keep the ship on course.

Diarist Rice and his eleven compatriots lamented their exile on a destroyer for the ordeal, "And my 24th birthday coming up the next day! I felt over 35 that night! Our stomachs took on that giddy feeling around dinner time, and one Spam sandwich was more than enuf for each of us—even the ship's officers who were already comparing this storm with a hurricane they had weathered for 36 hours off of Palau. Came sack time, and we all were temporarily assigned to enlisted men's bunks, or cots placed in the wardroom, as was my case. That nite was indescribable, and I daresay not one of us got over an hour's sleep, including the skipper. My cot toppled over once and I rolled downhill for ten feet along the wardroom floor before an overturned chair stopped me. The 'tin can' pitched and tossed like a wild horse all night, but the worst was yet to come.''

Commander Robert W. Curtis saw no point in telling his guests just how dangerous their predicament was on his 'cork on a wave' destroyer. The *Buchanan's* generators blew, making the ship uncomfortably hot, the gyro went, and as she heaved and crashed she once rolled 54 degrees to port but without turning turtle.

At this, recorded the VF-3 historian, ''Billy McLeroy was pitched out of his bunk and across the passageway, but the next roll brought him back. Jack Lyons caught a wardroom chair as it sailed thru the air, an incident which resulted in all chairs being secured to the table. C. Wall [nicknamed "Seawall"], Ikey Hart, and Ensign Howie Parker took over the skipper's cabin and, when Hart and Parker stepped into the wardroom the evening of the 18th for their K rations, a lot of the ship's officers wondered if survivors had been brought aboard.'' All the others finally lashed themselves into their bunks.

Many officers in the fleet wondered what the hell Admirals Halsey and McCain were trying to do by not maneuvering the force away from the approaching center of the storm, but both these men refused to believe it was a typhoon at all!

Admiral Montgomery on the *Yorktown* damned well knew the meteorological situation, because Alex Wilding was tracking the storm on his radar. "The radar shows," noted *Yorktown's* CIC officer during the rough night, a "very heavy weather front north-east of us. The weather is so heavy on the scope that I doubt a target could be detected through the weather, except on the 'A' scope.

"The *Yorktown* was shuddering all night. It was as if some giant was up at the prow and periodically placing his hand on it and stopping the *Yorktown* dead in her tracks. Slowly he would release her and the shuddering would cease.

"About midnight I went up to CIC, and I could hardly pick my way along the passageways. The enlisted men were sleeping on the steel passageways and in every nook and cranny inside the island superstructure topside. They were all over the hangar deck. They didn't want to go down below with the ship being battered around in the high seas.''

Some sailors, like Ted Rohrbaugh, however, bunked regularly above the hangar deck level. "Our division living compartment was midship forward right over the forecastle, and right under the flight deck. We found out what it must be like to sleep on a destroyer during normal times. All during the typhoon, the mess cooks couldn't set up the chow tables as they were flying all over. When we ate we sat on the deck, leaning against the bulkhead, sitting the tray on our lap.''

The sleepless night proved only to be a harbinger of worse things to come, especially for some of the cans. Bob Rice on the *Buchanan*: "Came dawn, which was really no dawn at all, but rather 'a grey mist on the sea's face.' The wind acquired a hellish howl. For breakfast we had coffee, toast and marmalade—that is, for the few who dared try it. China was breaking right and left of us, and the gallon can of marmalade was drifting from one end of the table to the other. Sugar, cream and coffee were all over the rug. Once no one was at the end of the table to catch the marmalade, so off it sailed into the lap of a pilot sitting on a plush leather couch. It took half an hour to clean up. Everything was shattering all around us.

"I would go topside into the driving rain just to get some fresh air and to keep from erping, and in this way I was able to hold on to my cookies thruout the whole ordeal. While holding onto the railing I would see the waves rush up to me as the ship listed over to my side—at times I was looking straight down at the water, just a few feet below me. I looked aft at three men lashing rope into place and one was swept overboard; the other two men continued at their task realizing rescue was impossible.

"Inside the hatchway where I stood were 6 parachute bags, each filled with two parachutes which contained emergency life rafts, so I was prepared at all times to make a grab for one of the bags if and when the ship went down. Later I learned that the idea had never struck any of the other pilots in my group—they were all down in the wardroom or in the enlisted bunk sections heaving or otherwise feeling miserable. True, I was taking the greater chance being out on the weather deck, and holding onto the railing for dear life, but I can truthfully say I never felt ill. As scared as I was, I nevertheless sensed a vicarious thrill about the whole affair, thinking that I was experiencing what probably few other men had ever encountered or would encounter.''

"It was a silent crew at General Quarters this morning" on the *Yorktown*, recorded Alex Wilding. "There are mountainous seas out there. Green water is spraying over the bow. After GQ I stepped out on the flight deck and looked around at our Task Group.

"One minute I could see the destroyers, and the next they would completely disappear in a sea trough. Green water breaking over them—even the CVLs were taking water over the flight decks. As I watched one destroyer bobbing up and down like a cork, he never came back up. Just disappeared. I couldn't believe it.

"I went back to CIC and on the radar scope was a perfect crescent, 60 miles from us, the eye of the typhoon. I reported the center of the eye to Adm. Montgomery and Capt. Combs—and we started tracking it. In 5 minutes we had a good course and speed on it—and it was closing us on a collision course. I advised Adm. Montgomery.

"From then on we kept a good track on it—set a Condition I watch in CIC [at 1000] so that Adm. Montgomery and Capt. Combs would have a continuous up-to-minute track on the typhoon. The radar picture was beautiful, so clear, and the eye of the typhoon was so well formed on the radar. And we were closing on a collision course. There was no doubt about it. The seas were terrific now—the typhoon was only 15-20 miles from us."

Montgomery, however, elected not to inform McCain or Halsey, for he logically assumed they had the same or even better data on it. But they did not, and throughout the morning visibility dropped to a quarter of a mile, ceiling under 200 feet, average winds 33 knots but going to 65 and periodic gusts of 75. Joe Chambliss in the gunnery plotting room: "The ship rolled and pitched quite heavily. Blinding rains and spray made visibility practically zero. Waves rose to mountainous proportions.'"

The seas were separating the ships of the task force, and when one of his radar operators showed the waves on the PPI radar to Captain Combs, Combs said, "Are you sure those aren't ships?"

"No, sir, we've been watching them roll right through."

Skipper Curtis wisely chose to maneuver the *Buchanan* independently to keep her from foundering, sweating out the fact that he had only twelve hours of fuel left. Rice: "The wind increased in violence, reaching 80, then 115 miles per hour

Typhoon! A big roller breaks over the bow and flight deck as the *Yorktown* heads into it and sailors watch behind a protective barrier, December 1944.

before our anenometer broke (understand it hit 132 mph at its severest). Waves 40 feet high crashed resoundingly over the Buck's second deck. Metal, rags, and pieces of wood were flying every which-way. The National Ensign ripped off. SOS's were coming in faintly over our static-y [sic] radio, announcing that men were being washed off of other ships."

The *Yorktown* received the first "Man Over-board" alarm at 0816, when a *Baltimore* sailor was reported by a can to be in the water 300 yards on the starboard quarter. *Yorktown* dropped a smoke float to mark his position, but (Wilding) "nothing could be done about it—there just wasn't any way you could rescue a man out of those wild waters."

It was not easy to maintain formation, and Captain Combs had to heave to and assume independent courses most likely to cause a minimum of strain on the ship's structures. Still, the armor plate at the fifth deck aft suffered an eight-foot-long crack, and a beam at the bow snapped. Such maneuvering, including backing engines, caused a roll, but at least it eliminated the pounding.

As the noon hour approached, noted dentist George Smith, the *Yorktown* "was tossed about heavily and creaked and groaned under the terrific strain. Mountainous waves, higher than the flight deck, gave her quite a beating," and she took eight inches of water in the bilges. "At one time," George Wille recalled, "we were maintaining steerage only with the help of the engines."

Wilding: "Reports started coming in on the TBS. Planes were loose on the flight decks of the *Cowpens* and *Monterey*—they were hitting other planes, going over the side and fires were being started. Catwalks were being bent up by the force of the waves. The *Langley* was taking green water over the flight deck and her catwalks were being bent and twisted. Now planes were loose on the hangar deck on the *Monterey*. More fires.

"The radar says we are in the center (or very close to it) of the typhoon at noon. It has quieted down a little—but as we come out the other side all Hell breaks loose again.

"They can't say that this task group didn't have beautiful information on this typhoon. Our main display board shows a perfect track from 65 miles out to right over us. I'm having the track transferred to the DRT so we will have a true geographic picture of the whole thing—just in case there is ever any questions."

Of course questions would come, and Montgomery and the *Yorktown* would be clear of responsibility. "Bull" Halsey never asked their advice; he was not that kind of admiral. Only at noon did he finally decide he could not meet his fueling schedule and that he had to face up to the realities of the typhoon.

But it was too late. In the 45 minutes before noon, three of his 250-man destroyers turned over and sank, taking with them all hands save 62 from the *Hull*, 24 from the *Spence* and a paltry six from the *Monaghan*.

"Our own '*Buck*'," recorded Bob Rice, "being without ballast, pitched so violently that all hands were ordered first to starboard, then to the port side of the ship to try somehow to even up the ship. A list of 45 degrees is considered dangerous for a ship; ours reached 47, then 54 (and later I understood it to have hit an unbelievable 63 degrees) list. That was when we were given a General Quarters alarm, ready to abandon ship. For ten hours the storm thus continued, with papers flying all over the place, lights all out, glass shattering, chairs automatically righting themselves from fallen position, etc. I doubt Cecil B. DeMille could have depicted the scene as we saw it. And here I was, celebrating my 24th birthday."

Wreckage and men in rafts and lifejackets passed by the *Yorktown* all day, while the forward single 5-inch gun mount was torn loose and moved back three feet. The typhoon scattered the ships throughout the afternoon until, "when the storm broke at four P.M.," in the words of dentist Smith, "and the mist lifted, only one cruiser and two destroyers were in sight."

Wilding: "The typhoon opens from us and disappears from the SK radar at 70 miles. It is still a wild sea. The men in CIC are going to sleep in CIC tonight—they have my permission. I never want to go through a storm like that again. Fortunately, the *Yorktown* came through in relatively good shape."

With no possibility of topping off the tin cans in the churning sea, the scheduled return to hit Luzon naturally had to be postponed, and while some ships looked for survivors, others were finally refueled. In the evening the force turned west toward Luzon—the men still sleeping topside—and spotted survivors in lifejackets and rafts. Searchlights were turned on them while the ships circled.

On December 19 and 20 the *Yorktown* took on oil and kept her air patrols aloft searching as much for survivors as for bogeys. Dr. Smith echoed the incredulity of all hands as the disaster was pieced together on the 20th: "Damage to our task force amounted to millions of dollars and over a thousand lives [a gross exaggeration]. We were in the center of the storm. We knew of the storm from the radar, etc., and could have changed course to miss it. Why this wasn't done is a question in all minds; Admiral Halsey was on the *New Jersey*!!''

The hero of Guadalcanal had revealed his feet of clay. Veterans of the Leyte Gulf battle, in which Halsey had been lured away from the beachhead by the clever Japs, had already begun to question Halsey's abilities, and the *Yorktown's* crew joined in the general criticism of him. Even now, with the task force battered, he headed back into battle for more strikes on the 21st—until that morning when he learned that the typhoon had socked in Luzon, so the ships shaped course for Ulithi.

Yorktown lookouts sighted more sailors adrift on the 21st, and the ship directed their rescue. The force refueled again during the day amidst floating wreckage, the metalsmiths welded the cracked armor plate, and the general gloom engulfed the exhausted crew.

Taking stock of the low morale, Coop Bright went to work on the Air Plot teletype to divert everyone's spirits. His subject was a regulation calling for new grey uniforms to be issued to the fleet: ''NOTICE TO ALL READY ROOMS: MEMORANDUM ON PURCHASE OF SET OF GREY UNIFORMS: THE FACT THAT I HAVE BEEN FORCED TO PURCHASE A SET OF GREYS IN NO WAY SIGNIFIES THAT I RECOGNIZE THE LOST CAUSE OF THE CONFEDERACY. I AM STILL DEDICATED TO STOMPING THE STARS AND BARS OF JEFF DAVIS TO THE DUST. TO PROVE THIS STATEMENT, I'LL LICK LT. WILLIE WILLIAMS OF VF-3 ANYTIME.'' Williams hailed from Alabama.

Not allowing the dust to settle, Skinhead went on about a new policy for pilots to take classwork and exams in their 'spare time': ''EVEN IF YOUR LOGGED TIME RUNS INTO THE THOUSANDS OF HOURS, YOU'RE *NOT* A QUALIFIED COMBAT PILOT UNLESS YOU CAN ANSWER THESE QUESTIONS IN THE AFFIRMATIVE: 1) CAN YOU SPLICE A CONTROL CABLE WITH THE TOES OF YOUR LEFT FOOT IN THE EVENT THAT THE CABLE IS SHOT OFF ALONG WITH YOUR RIGHT FOOT? 2) DO YOU FULLY UNDERSTAND THE USE AND LOCATION OF THE PEE-TUBE RESET BUTTON? 3) CAN YOU TRANSMIT MESSAGES IN CODE BY MEANS OF THE RECTUM IN CASE YOU LOSE CONTROL OF YOUR VOICE?. . . .''

Bright's outrageousness had its desired effect, and his confreres took up the challenge. Radio boss Pete Joers turned out an essay lamenting the dissension that had broken out on this ''otherwise fine ship'' because of ''the ugly fact that there is a professional Texas-baiter on this ship. Now Buck Bright is a baldish, bespectacled mild-looking chap who is the oldest officer in point of service as a *Yorktown* officer, and is tending gracefully toward middle age. He is the last man in the world one would expect of trying to stir up trouble with Texans, because he has the appearance of wholesome intelligence. But his conversation, when within the hearing of Texans, runs somewhat along these lines:

'' 'I can lick any damned Confederate in the Ready Room. I can lick them, and I will. You Texans can't do any good with guns and you never will. I know just what you Southerners are good for, because I went down to Staunton Military Academy in Virginia when I was a boy, to school, and got the Confederate point of view. I went down to find out what was wrong with the South, and I found out. The first thing we need to do when

The last battle of the Civil War? Skinhead Bright (center) and Tiny Patterson about to settle their differences, with Empty Evans counting off the seconds. Courtesy of Thomas J. Patterson

this war is over is to go down and reconstruct the South again. I'll do it if I have to do it myself with my bare fists'. . . .

"Skilled as he is in the art of verbal abuse and epithet, Bright has, as might be expected of Texans, an adequate opponent in the person of T.J. ('Tiny') Patterson, a drawling six-footer, as bald-headed as Bright, lovable by nature and quick to anger. He describes himself modestly as an ignorant cuss who can't read and write and who has an inferiority complex, but these are just Texas exaggerations."

Joers allegedly quoted Patterson, "I wouldn't want you to think that I'm prejudiced in favor of Texas, however, to the exclusion of all Yankees. There are good Yankees, I suppose. Take Commander Evans, for instance. He is not a bad fellow at all. You know he has one secret desire. He dreams of being sometime a Texan. And I told him that at the end of this cruise if he does good work I'll have the governor of Texas grant him an honorary birth certificate stating that he was born in Texas."

Joers went on: "Consultation with Commander Evans indicates that there is very little substance to this story. On being asked about it he passed immediately into a blind rage and spluttered incoherently.

"I have found it necessary," Patterson continued according to Joers, "to tell some Northerners around here that if any more insults are cast on my native state I would use my political influence and sway Texas to sign a separate peace with Japan and Germany, who have been making unsuccessful peace overtures to Texas for the last two years. I need not dwell upon the foreseeable results of such an action. The whole military structure of the Allies would collapse, naturally, if we called all Texans home."

Joers: "This is merely another Texas exaggeration, of course. Everybody knows that as long as there is a fight going on, no matter how far away from home, no Texan would willingly drop out of it. Especially if, while fighting, he could occasionally turn aside and insult a nearby Northerner."

There was no cheer for Father Moody, however, who on the 22nd slipped while jumping from the Number One aircraft elevator and fell on his right wrist, breaking it. In no way, however, did the agony deter this great man from organizing the choir and planning Christmas services.

Reaching Ulithi at noon of Christmas Eve, *Yorktown's* crewmen unwound with torpedo juice, raw alcohol from a still in the engine room, or Schenley's "Black Death." Pilot Bob Rice and his roomies opened their little bunk room to "every celebratee aboard the *Yorktown.*" Eight fifths of whiskey—"virtually the entire pre-Christmas Eve stock aboard ship"—were consumed by the host and guests from Padre Wright "to eight mess attendants who serenaded us with 'Straighten Up and Fly Right' umpteen times . . . . Carols were really slaughtered, so our hoarse voices took up 'One Ball Riley', 'Redwing', 'Bell Bottom Trousers', etc., which are more notorious for their words than for their music." Pilot Dwight Horner found officers country "one big drunken party."

In Coop Bright's and Bob Eaton's room a big gang of officers were downing the stuff when Eaton got up to go to the quarterdeck to assume the duty as OOD. Being that he was smashed, some Annapolis men warned him against standing watch in that condition. The short Texan responded in a slurred drawl, "You damned Regulars *can't* drink before going on duty!" Skinhead backed him: "Hell, any Reserve can do better drunk than you Regulars can when you're sober."

After Eaton made his exit, Regular Navy Joers decided to get even with him for these unkind remarks by building on a dispatch that had come in telling of Admiral Nimitz's presence at Ulithi to inspect typhoon damage. After a while, Pete called up the quarterdeck and babbled away *in Spanish* that Nimitz might be coming on board for a visit this night.

Texan Eaton, drunk or sober, knew enough Spanish to figure out the message. He panicked. First of all, Nimitz had just been promoted to the new five-star rank of fleet admiral, and the *Yorktown* had no five-star flag to break at the yardarm. Second, Admiral Montgomery and Captain Combs were having a big party and were in no shape to receive the Pacific Fleet commander. And third, the whole ship seemed to be in a drunken stupor.

But Eaton dutifully informed his superiors of Nimitz's pending arrival, and pandemonium ensued. One senior officer had to fish his false teeth out of his highball. All the brass gargled frantically to try to erase their telltale breaths. Empty Evans charged down to the quaterdeck and lined up the Marines. And Redneck Montgomery told Eaton to inform him the minute Nimitz's barge was to arrive. Everyone just stood there, looking at the OOD, "M.T." getting angrier and angrier.

After a long hiatus, during which heads were spinning, Eaton got nervous and called up the Main

Comm shack. The men on duty there knew of no such message. Eaton then had to tell the admiral, whose neck got good and red as he demanded to know who had originated the message. When Joers was found out, Captain Combs put him in hack. The story spread throughout the fleet!

Father Moody's midnight mass also proved exceptional, for he borrowed the black stewards' quartet which Protestant George Wright normally used. The four Negroes—who often harmonized in the popular style of the Ink Spots—started by singing "Silent Night." After a few bars the beat picked up, and soon the whole hangar deck was jumping! Moody had great difficulty holding confessions, but then, the men had few sins to confess out there in the middle of the ocean anyway.

Cooper Bright was feeling blue in CIC as he fiddled the dial of the trusty Hallicrafters radio to see what he could pick up. Everyone was standing around, each man alone in his own thoughts, when suddenly the voice of Bing Crosby came out of the radio, crystal clear from San Francisco, singing "White Christmas." Der Bingle went through it

twice, then the signal was lost.

Good as it sounded, this touch of home did nothing to change anyone's mood. Coop walked out to Pri Fly, where Pappy Harshman, "looking like an old dog," was sitting on his perch. Said Pappy, "What's wrong? What's wrong?"

"It's Christmas Eve, and there's not going to be any Santa Claus tonight."

"What do you want, Buck?"

"Pappy, give me a word for Christmas. I need something to pick me up." For Pappy always had a bag of stories for any occasion, including this one. Looking out to sea, he reached into his bag for a variation from Rudyard Kipling:

'Twas the night before Christmas, within the prison walls.
The warden said, "Merry Christmas, men," and the prisoners hollered, "Balls!"
"Just for that," the warden shouted, "You'll get no Christmas pudding."
Up spoke a prisoner in a voice as rough as brass;
He said, "Take your Christmas pudding, And ram it up your ass!"

A Yorktown V-Christmas card of 1944, drawn by Furlow. Courtesy of Richard C. Tripp

"That's fantastic!" Coop roared and then put it on the ticker for the pilots to enjoy.

And, lo and behold, Santa Claus made it to the *Yorktown* at Ulithi during the night, for come Christmas morn the forward end of the hangar was heaped with several hundred sacks of Christmas mail and packages. The gifts brought on a curious mixture of joy and homesickness, and as carols were played over the loudspeaker all day the men tore into their presents.

Bob Rice watched his roommate Bob Barclay open "up a present from his married sister; it's a 'Christmas Wallet,' designed to hold as many greenbacks as the sender wants to enclose. A card reads: 'Here is something a fellow can always use; So spend it in any way you choose.' Deep down in the recesses of the billfold Bob found, not a ten dollar bill, but a snow-white condom."

A Christmas dinner of turkey and Virginia baked ham laid on by supply boss Bill Moring brought kudos from all hands, not least Alex Wilding: "The *Yorktown* is still the best feeding carrier in the fleet."

It was not so for ex-*Yorktown* torpecker pilot Pop Condit and his crewmen Gordy Marshall and Ken Kalberg. The three prisoners had languished at the secret Japanese Ofuna "naval interrogation center"—until October 1944 when they had been separated, Pop going to Omuri.

The Japs did not call them prisoners of war but "captives," so that the International Red Cross did not have to be told of the camp's existence, much less that the men were even alive, and these captives would not have privileges. Instead, they received no clothes and only three-quarters of the normal POW food ration—300 calories per day: one bowl of barley for breakfast and supper, and soup at noon, with an occasional "all dumpo" of leftovers for the evening meal—a far cry from the sumptuous cuisine of the *Yorktown*.

Pop and his men could never figure out why the Japs thought they—a lowly torpecker crew—knew anything, but the prison guards nevertheless beat them, sometimes nightly, in efforts to learn more about the American navy. The guards especially liked to humiliate the officers, but the younger the officer the more he could take from the baseball bat-size clubs. No-one dared cry out. They only moaned.

The guards were the dregs of the Jap navy, spoke no English and thus never knew the English-language names given them by the prisoners, names befitting their appearance and demeanor. These were "The Slugger" for his brutality, and the blank-look "Flange Face," also "Metal Mouth" and "Indian Joe" who resembled a cigar-store wooden Indian. And "Shit-head" and "Piss-ass," but also "Little Lester," one of four friendly college-age boys. "Swivel Neck" made them bow low to go to the head. One of the goons even got three nicknames for his notoriety—"Blinky," "The Pest" and "The Snake."

Yet, among these misfits was one interrogator, "Handsome Harry," who treated the Americans with relative civility. He even seemed to be more American than Japanese, and small wonder. Though Japanese born, this James Kunichi Sasaki had graduated from the University of California and been secretary to the Japanese naval attaché in Washington at the time of Pearl Harbor. He had been interned in West Virginia prior to repatriation in 1942. Even so, Handsome Harry ordered at least one fatal beating that would earn him a sentence of 18 years at hard labor in war crimes trials later.

Typical of Japanese everywhere, the Ofuna camp appeared to be spotlessly clean, and the prisoners were kept at work to insure this. Following international law, the Japs had to pay the men for their labors according to rank. So Lieutenant Condit received 122 yen (50 cents) everyday, but the Japs took it right back next day to deposit in postal savings which would indeed be given them at the end of the war. Each man also got one day off a week from his labors and received tobacco for working into smoking shape. Pop smoked a pipe.

In all, it was sheer hell. Pop once had to stand at attention for 72 hours, spent time in solitary confinement, and had to endure the Japs stealing clothes and Red Cross supplies from him. With the reduced food ration, they all lost a lot of weight, and sleep did not come easy with only one blanket—and that infested with bed bugs. Then, when mail finally began to come through via the Red Cross, the Japs cut it off out of sheer cruelty.

A warrant officer commanded the camp, but the actual power was wielded by the sadistic camp pharmacist. He tried to stop the inevitable dysentary but used the same needle on everyone, which only helped to spread this and other diseases. Between illnesses, the diet, and the beatings, the men suffered—and died.

Regimentation ruled, and the Americans were not allowed to converse on the prison grounds, but the utter boredom of their existence led them to see the joke in whatever they could. For instance, they marveled at a crippled duck they called "Gaga" who limped in formation with the prisoners every morning. Not only that, but he bowed his head in the direction of the Emperor's palace just like the guards!

Another "Pappy" at Ofuna was Major Greg Boyington, Marine Corps fighter ace with whom Condit had flown off the old *Yorktown* before the war. One day, as the men made their separate rounds in silence, Boyington whispered over to Condit as they passed near to each other, "Junior"—Pop's prewar nickname— "I'll bet you a case of whiskey that the war won't end until years from now." As they came around again on the next circuit, Condit whispered back, "Greg, 1945." At least it was something to do—speculate.

And a few weeks after the end of the hostilities, at his home in Washington late in 1945, Pop would get a phone call. It was Boyington: "Junior, I've got a present for you." A man of his word, Boyington personally then delivered the promised case of whiskey to Pop's doorstep.

The biggest war news came first-hand on Thanksgiving Day 1944 when big, very-long-range B-29 Superfortress bombers flew over the camps en route to bomb military targets inside Japan. Originally based in China, these strategic bombers had just begun to operate from newly-completed airfields in the Marianas. The war was getting closer to the home islands.

Christmas brought food packages from the Red Cross, and though the Japs took back the new blankets as soon as the Red Cross officals left, the prisoners joined in singing Christmas carols since the end of the war seemed so much closer. January brought more B-29s. And at home, as the Navy released "The Fighting Lady" for public viewing, a thoughtful officer telephoned MaeBelle Condit to tell her that her husband could be seen in the film.

But the beatings, near-starvation and hard life continued unabated at Omuri at the hands of the enraged Japs, made worse by the winter weather. Scurvy, beri-beri and ulcers afflicted the prisoners, who walked around the compound in the snow just to keep warm. And in February the Japs allowed Pop to write a short note home through the Red Cross: "I am in good health and spirits...."

Lieutenant (jg) Bob Rice, VF-3

Chapter X
Formosa to Saigon

The day after Christmas

1944 Alex Wilding had the forenoon watch and saw Admiral Montgomery over the side of the *Yorktown* into his barge to visit another carrier at Ulithi. While disembarking from the gig to step onto that ship's ramp, the admiral "slipped and fell down between the two—he was caught there as the swells pushed the barge against the ramp and he was injured— the full extent of which is not yet known" by midday. In fact, some ribs were broken. The Marines there drolly figured the coxswain had jerked the gig away on purpose.

By evening, Wilding and others who had run afoul of the disliked "Redneck" could rejoice: "Looks as though Montgomery has been put out of action. Scuttlebutt is rampant—will Radford or Jocko Clark relieve him? The best rationale is that it won't be Clark because he was skipper of the *Yorktown* and it would be embarrassing to Capt. Combs to have Jocko aboard in a flag capacity. I go along with that reasoning."

Admiral Nimitz followed the same logic, and two days later Arthur Radford came aboard. He lost no time in assigning Wilding additional duty as task group fighter director officer. On the 29th, "Adm. Radford called me to his quarters and we had a nice two hour chat. We seemed to hit it off together and I am going to enjoy working for him. He's a real gentleman, suave, smooth and intelligent. I briefed him completely on CIC operations. He said he had heard many complimentary things about me and that he would give me a free hand in CIC and back me 100 percent." "Raddy" knew very well that a successful Combat Information Center meant the survival of the task group against the kamikazes.

That same day Air Group Three—now commanded by bomber skipper Jigger Lowe as the downed Mac Williams was still dodging Jap patrols somewhere on Luzon—put on a novelty show. The songwriters passed out sheets for a community sing of some favorite popular songs but with brand new special lyrics, notably "I Have Returned," a spoof on the Navy's unfavorite general and his promise to return to the Philippines. It included references to the "pig-boat" subs and to Admiral Thomas C. Kinkaid, Seventh Fleet commander in the Philippine landings, and was sung to the old Civil War tune, "When Johnny Comes Marching Home."

> When Doug MacArthur at last went back,
> "I have returned."
> He followed the fox-hunting, pig-boating track,
> "I have returned."
> Oh, the carrier planes were overhead
> And the battleship turrets spouted lead
> So the general could go ashore, it's said, singing
> "I have returned."
>
> Cincpoa* divisions were at his side,
> "I have returned."
> And Phibspacfor** provided the ride,
> "I have returned."
> Oh, the subs went up to the sea of Japan,
> And the carriers ranged from Saipan to Bataan,
> So the general could land, according to plan, singing
> "I have returned."
>
> MacArthur petitioned God by prayer,
> "I have returned."
> But God decided He couldn't be there,
> "I have returned."
> But to help. . .God went to the utmost limits,
> For God sent Kinkaid, Halsey and Nimitz
> And MacArthur went along to kibitz. . . singing
> "I HAVE RETURNED."

---

*Commander-in-Chief, Pacific Ocean Areas (Adm. Nimitz)
**Amphibious Forces Pacific Fleet

MacArthur had indeed returned to the Philippines—first at Leyte in October, then Mindoro in December, with the next stop Lingayen Gulf on the west side of Luzon, landings now scheduled for January 9, 1945. The Third Fleet would again provide a big blue blanket of fighters over Japanese airfields. Recorded dentist George Smith, "Very heavy opposition expected. We will be subjected to attack by land based planes. Japs are known to be able to throw 1800 planes per day against us from Formosa. Our task force contains approximately 1500 planes."

The fast carriers weighed anchor at Ulithi on December 30 amid continuous briefings. Gunner Jesse Bradley wrote, "This force has been assigned targets on the northwestern part of the island, there three important ones, Taihoku [or Taipei] the capital and the two naval bases of Tansui and Kiirun. The island of Formosa is about 90 miles wide and about 250 miles long. The east side has very high mountains. All factories and industries are on the west, S.W. and N.W. parts of the island. Our objective is to destroy all planes and knock out the airfields."

get a slight idea of what it's like to have every gun open up simultaneously—and trying to sleep thru it all. So it was over to the machine shop, all shook up. Then came some rowing-machine workout, followed by some punching bag exercises. And they say the whole year is just like the first day!"

That was a sentiment shared by Bull Halsey. Still in tactical command of Third Fleet, but with Vice Admiral McCain passing down the Admiral's orders to Task Force 38, Halsey was out for blood and planned to hit the Japs every day until they threw in the towel. After striking Formosa and Luzon in support of the landings at Lingayen Gulf on the 9th, he then wanted to head into the South China Sea to hunt for two battleships-with-flight-decks which had escaped him at the Battle of Leyte Gulf, the *Ise* and *Hyuga*. Then north again to strike Okinawa and hopefully even Tokyo.

It was a tall order, but Halsey was determined to do it all, kamikazes notwithstanding. McCain did not appear equal to the task, issuing obnoxious war cries and imprecise refueling directives—beginning on January 2. On the TG 38.1 flagship *Yorktown*, Alex Wilding reflected, "Once again with Halsey

Admiral Radford (L) chats with Captain Combs.

New Year's Day of 1945 brought gunnery exercises, aptly described by pilot Rice of Fighting 3: "If you can put together at one time an earthquake, a clap of thunder, a cat being wooed just outside your window at midnite, a Wagnerian finale, the chimes of Big Ben and a locomotive plowing into the rear end of a freight car full of chickens, pigs and ammunition boxes, you might

and McCain we are going to have to launch our first strike while still 140 miles from the target. (Spruance and Mitscher would have had us in around 100 miles from the target.)" In fact, by launch time, Point Option would be 210 miles out!

Assuming, however, that all went well, that the Lingayen assault was successful, and that the Luzon Straits would then be blocked to enemy shipping, then the South China Sea and oil-rich East Indies would be sealed off from the Empire, thus beginning the blockade of Japan. Radford's TG 38.1—one of four task groups—included the *Yorktown, Wasp, Cabot* and *Belleau Wood*, two battleships, four cruisers and the usual destroyer screen. The ACIOs of Air Group Three warned the pilots about Formosa. Weatherwise, the big island was said to average one clear day each January; *Yorktown's* fliers would not find it. The briefing on "escape and survival" was just that—brief; the natives were not friendly.

The aviators wore their CBI shoulder patches as well as two small silk flags—one U.S. and one China—with messages in Chinese and Burmese sewed on the backs of their flight jackets should they come down in enemy territory. Each man received two packets of counterfeit money— Japanese and Chinese—"More folding money in evidence than at any time since 'Dirty' Deavitt cleaned house in a game of galloping dominoes," noted the VF-3 historian. An announcement of the meager exchange rate quickly cooled off wide-eyed speculators.

The run north to colder climes brought welcome relief to a heat-rash-beleaguered crew, and reveille on the 3rd found brisk temperatures "like autumn in New England" in the opinion of gunner Ed Wallace. The 0547 fighter sweep launch—two hours before sunrise—was executed in indescribably bad weather: solid overcast, of which the VF-3 historian said, "A self-respecting homing pigeon would have remained sack-borne, but the first strike was launched predawn, with Lambo leading, to feel its way to a rendezvous and to the target through rain, clouds, and a ceiling which varied from zero to 300 feet." The weather, in short, was fit "only for groundhogs and submarines."

By skillful navigating, Commander Lamberson reached northern Formosa's coastal airfields, only to find them completely socked in. With no Japs airborne, Lambo took his three divisions in under the cloud cover seeking targets of opportunity. Instead of airstrips, however, they found railroad trains!

Fighting 3 tallyhoed a long military train approaching a high bridge over the Tansui River south of Taihoku and pressed home its attacks just as the train reached the bridge. Charlie Lee planted his bomb squarely on the bridge, while the others rocketed the span and several box cars, severing bridge and train alike. The cars stopped dead, some

hanging over the edge, though the locomotive escaped on ahead.

The devastation of these first runs was not without its price. Division leaders Ed Gage and Walt McNeil made low passes to avoid the flak and score bomb hits, but the explosions caused both planes to disintegrate in midair—an unforeseen hazard of bombing trains on bridges. The remaining ten fighters hit Tansui seaplane base, where they strafed several planes on the ground and ramp, and Lambo himself placed a bomb squarely on the fo'c'sle of a 5000-ton freighter at Kiirun harbor. "The bow was completely blown off," he later told the ACIO, "but the screws kept turning and the momentum carried the ship under within two minutes for a confirmed sinking."

While planes from the other carriers ranged across Formosa, Okinawa, the Sakishima and Pescadores islands, and B-29s pounded the coast of occupied China, Air Group Three worked over its same targets all day. The fighters found three more trains southwest of Taihoku and blew up the boilers of all three engines, and bombers Gus Osterhoudt and B.E. Hackett scored bomb hits on two large freighters at Kiirun. The torpeckers visited Okaseki airfield, where Ensign Zeke Zegler radioed skipper Charlie Turner, "Bandit, eleven o'clock."

"To a torpedo pilot without fighter cover," recalled Turner, "this is not a heart-warming call. It turned out to be a twin-engine type about two miles away headed in the direction of Formosa. We turned towards it, saw it was a transport [a Topsy] instead of a bomber type, and poured on the coal. Zeke tried to fire but his guns were jammed. I put the throttle to the fire wall [floorboard of the TBM], flew in on his tail, and watched with great excitement my .50 calibers, one in each wing, set his engines afire and then enflame the entire aircraft. It splashed a la Hollywood." The boys nicknamed him "Topsy" Turner for his achievement.

Hellcats and Helldivers—the latter using their 20mm cannons—destroyed four patrol boats off Sancho Point by strafing, and 15 fighters led by Bill McLeroy shot up parked planes at Matsuyama airfield and obliterated two more locomotives. Worsening weather caused everyone to head for home "on constant lookout for rock-lined clouds."

The miserable overcast led to a delayed launch on January 4 and only one break in the clouds over Tansui, where the fighters were able to shoot up installations. Bombing 3 could see absolutely nothing at Kiirun and simply jettisoned its bomb loads at random. Whereupon the task group

The Air Group Three staff. Standing (L to R)—Ferd Fletcher, ACIO; Pete Grace, admin officer; Jigger Lowe, air group commander; and Doc Voris, flight surgeon. Kneeling—Chief Photographer Robert E. Jones and Chief Yeoman David B. Price

withdrew to refuel next day and resume strikes on targets around Manila on the 6th. But again the weather fouled up everything.

The high winds caused two deck crashes by planes coming aboard and made takeoffs equally hazardous—as Bob Rice explained in his diary: "Shortly after finishing a letter in which I described a premonition of death shortly, I hopped in my plane and started warming the engine up. Suddenly I noticed hunks of metal flying over in my direction, some penetrating the thin skin, some going clear thru the entire fuselage and coming out the other side. What happened was the plane to my right [Joe Mayer] in warming up had edged its chocks forward along the greasy deck, so that its propeller came into contact with the tail of the plane in front of it. The prop was chewing up pieces of rudder, elevator, and the tail hook, hurling it all right at me, even tho the pilot had by this time cut his engine.

"It seemed to take forever and a day for his propeller to stop windmilling; all the while I was ducking like an ostrich after closing the hood, praying that the side of the plane would stop all the flying metal. When his propeller finally shot its wad, I started to assess the damage; a chunk of tail hook had gone clear thru both legs of my mechanic [Seaman First Joe Lehr], who died within five minutes from the loss of blood; another had sailed completely thru the fuselage about two feet behind my head; a third had passed thru my belly tank, which was belching gasolene out both sides."

Admiral Halsey had hoped to head north to hit Formosa again, but the sudden appearance of kamikazes over the Lingayen invasion armada caused him to keep working over their fields on Luzon.

Rice: "The next morning twenty of us took off at 0515 for Manila. Since it was dark, and extremely cloudy, it was very difficult to rendezvous with your own four-plane division unless you had the fellow ahead of you in your sights at all times. The plane I joined up on was being piloted by a new member of our squadron, Ensign [Garold] Brass, fresh out of training in the States. He had 'lost' his own division so had joined our group. I had no alternative but to fly wing on him until he became better oriented and could spot his own division.

"I noticed as we climbed to 14,000 feet that his plane quite often went into violent skids, and on several occasions he almost 'spun' me in, because he wrapped up his plane at critical angles in trying to stick to the three planes ahead. He was obviously suffering from vertigo. I had to leave him just to save my skin, so ducked away into a thick cloud and struck out for Manila alone. That was the last that anyone saw of Brass, who undoubtedly spun on into the ground from three miles up. It could well have happened to me, for a wingman puts his life in the hands of his leader since the wingman isn't supposed to refer to his instruments too much, but actually follow the leader.

"I skirted a massive, ominous-looking cloud formation, and half an hour later came out over Manila, and not one of the 20 who started for that target was there. I circled just east of the city for almost twenty minutes, drawing a terrific amount of anti-aircraft fire, since a single plane, silhouetted against the clouds above and idling along at 125 miles per hour to conserve fuel, is a sitting duck for ground gunners. Then I heard our strike leader announce that his division was going to make one more pass at Clark Field, then go home, so I headed in the direction of Clark Field.

"Just as I neared the area I heard the leader open up again: 'Tally Ho! One bogey 12 o'clock, same level'—meaning me! He naturally presumed me to be a Jap plane, since I was single, and all of our fighter planes fly at least in pairs. I scanned the skies and finally saw four planes bearing down on me from an 8 o'clock position. When they were within firing distance I executed a slow turn broadsides so that they could see my belly tank which characterized American planes. The leader immediately ordered 'Hold your fire', and I soon joined up. [Nine] of us, it turned out, were the only ones out of the twenty who had reached Manila. My original division ended up 150 miles south of Manila in trying to avoid the really thick cloud formations.

"On the way back I found myself in need of the pee-tube. No sooner had I started to fire way than we entered the thickest, blackest and roughest cloud ever. I lost my leader and not knowing how close I might be to him or if I was on an intercept course, I immediately had to throttle back. One hand on the stick, one hand controlling the tube AND needing one hand to bring back the throttle. When one's life is at stake, discomfort takes a back seat, so down fell the tube, and it wasn't just sweat which soaked my flight suit!"

Pissing all over the joy-stick was a minor problem compared to what some other pilots experienced on this nightmarish January 7. Vertigo had already claimed one pilot, Brass, while intense St. Elmo's fire danced on the wings as ice began to form on them at 16,000 feet. Partial clearing enabled Jigger Lowe to take his bombers against Clark and Grace Park fields, where heavy flak claimed Del Landry's TBM. He had his two crewmen bail out over land. Happily, all three were rescued by the Huks—Filipino Hukbalahop guerrillas—and taken into the hills. For two weeks their rescuers cleared out a crude airstrip, upon which an Army L-5 landed and took them out under P-38 fighter cover. They would rejoin VT-3 before the month was out.

Other fliers were less fortunate during the continuous flight operations. Fred Foss' torpecker spun in off the bow directly ahead of the ship which ran over it before Foss and radioman Andy Park could get clear. Gunner B.C. "Pappy" Blair just made it though and was quickly plucked up by a destroyer. When the SB2Cs pushed over in their dives on Clark Field, flak hit Karl Baertschy's, which erupted in flames at 5000 feet. A chute opened before the plane crashed into the field. Whether the survivor was Baertschy or gunner Morgan Edmonson mattered not, for he must suffer the usual fate of captured aviators at the hands of the enraged

Japanese. Neither man was ever heard of again.

Bayard Carlson and Pappy Joynt shot down a Jill kamikaze, and Willie Williams' eight Hellcats made dangerously low strafing and rocket runs at Grace Park to destroy kamikazes hidden in the woods. That they succeeded was affirmed by Williams' oblique photos, by leaves and branches in the rocket racks of Ensign Rolan Powell, and by *mud* on Ensign John Rodgers' windshield!

After refueling on the 8th, Radford's group returned to its targeted northern Formosa airfields and Kiirun harbor—and their damned weather conditions—during the Lingayen assault on January 9. "One more day of instrument time" sneered the fighter pilots who searched "diligently for a way in through the soup." As air group admin officer Pete Grace put it, the weather was "'undesirable' which is a refined aerological term for stinking." Aside from sinking some picket boats and luggers, the pilots could see nothing, including the *Yorktown* on their return. They had to dive from 10,000 feet into solid stratus clouds, breaking out below 200 feet—remarkable flying in what the VF-3 historian called "by far the most exhausting and harrowing flight the greater majority of the pilots and crewmen had ever encountered."

A sudden bogey contact early in the afternoon was seen by all hands topside—a twin-engine Dinah bomber, in the words of gunner Ed Wallace, "coming out of the clouds and in plain sight of everyone on the starboard side forward. Four fighters were on his tail." It "zoomed directly over the ship startling everybody," and climbed, trying to escape into the clouds. Van Vanderhoof and Ray Coleman followed in hot pursuit, most of the ship's guns not even yet manned for a shot. All the destroyers fired but missed. Then Coleman set Dinah's engines on fire, and she crashed into the sea eleven miles from the *York*. The thrilled eyewitnesses would talk about it for days. "Close shave!" penned dentist Smith.

The afternoon strike to Kiirun harbor stayed under the clouds to locate the target easily. The low ceiling, under 500 feet and below the surrounding mountains, created a suicide situation for an attack into heavy AA. Nevertheless, Lieutenant "Fearless" Frank Frazier lived up to his reputation by taking his six torpeckers low and slow into Kiirun.

Absolutely withering flak broke up the attack. A burst knocked out Frazier's oil pressure, forcing him to ditch offshore, with other planes being holed. Undaunted, Ensign R.C. Jensen glided his bombs squarely into a cargo ship, which broke in two and sank. "Suicide Sam" Berrey—so nicknamed because of his terrible carrier landings—put his bombs into a chemical factory ashore as shown by the colorful explosion and debris. They all saw Fearless Frank and his crewmen Murl Dain and Gene Weeks floating in their life raft, a fact reported to the lifeguard sub. But its search was in vain; the three men were never heard from again.

The rest of the Cats, Beasts and Turkeys went after a destroyer escort just north of the harbor breakwater. "It was murder," but this time for the Japs. In the words of the VF-3 historian, "Carlson's fighters hit first and stopped most of the AA, from then on it was a mad rat race of VF, VB, and VT strafing under a 300 ft. ceiling, dropping delayed action bombs, and dodging each other in the clouds."

F.S. "Fox" Johnson cascaded his three Turkey eggs into the bow of the DE, with the others doing complementary damage. "The enemy put up a gallant fight but he never had a chance. As fast as one bomb set him on fire another near miss would swamp him with water and douse the fire. Finally, minus a bow and burning furiously from the well placed hit by Johnson, he went down struggling."

Picket boats were then strafed and burned as this fourth strike group turned back toward the *York*, where the crew was still shaking from a second visitor—a Helen which, described by Pete Grace, had suddenly come "scooting out of the clouds—almost close enough to hit with a well aimed pistol shot." It got clean away.

By the time January 9 ended it had been wild indeed at Lingayen Gulf, where the Army had stormed ashore successfully, visited by only a few kamikazes. Japanese air defenses on Luzon had obviously been shattered, indeed all but annihilated by the carriers and land-based Army planes. Finally, after two and a half months since the Leyte landings, Task Force 38 was released from protecting MacArthur's beachheads in the Philippines.

Admiral Halsey at last had the opportunity to go after half-battleships *Ise* and *Hyuga*, suspected to be in the South China Sea, which Third Fleet would enter during the night—the first time that American warships would visit these waters. To the *Yorktown* went the honor of leading in the whole fleet as flagship of Admiral Radford's task group. Under cover of the foul weather, Commander Elliott "Jesse" James skillfully navigated first the ship and then the Fleet into the shallow (six fathoms deep) and treacherous Bashi Channel an hour before midnight of January 9/10, 1945.

The ships had to go through single file, which produced a beautiful image on the radar screens—and great anxiety among the crew. But they made it—undetected. En route, Alex Wilding in CIC wrote, "Intercepted radio traffic reporting a large Jap convoy east of us. No sign of our changing course in that direction—we are still heading South." Halsey decided to ignore this vulnerable juicy target of 20 cargo ships and five escorts, reasoning that an attack on it would betray his position and jeopardize his avowed primary mission to sink the two battleships, which intelligence claimed to be at Camranh Bay, French Indochina (Vietnam). Admiral Jocko Clark, riding on the *Hornet*, shared the incredulity of many men over Halsey's decision to pass up the convoy. The Jap fleet was dead anyway; why worry about it? Get those marus! But Halsey intended to hit Camranh Bay and nearby Saigon on the 12th. He maintained course and let the big game get away.

Night fighters from the night carrier *Independence* splashed three snoopers in view of the ships just before dawn of the 10th as the *Yorktown*'s men reflected on their arrival in "this baliwick of the Sons of Heaven." According to Pete Grace, "the water looked the same and weather did not change. For the multitudes who serve aboard a carrier, lost in its innards, the China Sea is no different than Chesapeake Bay except that you can't visit Main Street every other weekend and get 'blotto.'" Jesse Bradley detected one dissimilarity: "The water…has a greenish color, where the Pacific Ocean is a deep blue."

Dawn searches to an extreme 450 miles failed to sight those illusive Jap fleet units: "the only results of these six hour hops were paralysis of the butt." Then, to everyone's chagrin, the radio crackled with a clear Yankee voice from somewhere aloft: "Man, lookut all them ships down there—hope they're friendly."

"Yeah—gee," said another, "look at 'em. Must be the Third Fleet."

As one gawked, he proceeded to give a short lecture on ship recognition by picking out some of the major vessels by name! The Fleet's secrecy had been blown sky high by a couple of patrolling planes from the escort carriers off Lingayen Gulf. Tokyo Rose must have been most grateful.

Whether or not the Jap heavies were found, the pilots were briefed on mainland targets—occupied French Indochina, notably the naval facilities at

Camranh Bay and Cape St. Jacques and adjacent airfields; British Hong Kong; Portuguese Canton and Chinese Swatow; and Hainan Island in the Gulf of Tonkin. "This trip," a smug Alex Wilding guffawed during refueling on the 11th when still no Japs interfered, "is like a boat ride in Central Park."

Encouraged by a reported Jap battleship, cruiser and destroyers near the Indochinese coast, Halsey launched a fighter sweep and bombing strike simultaneously at dawn of January 12, the former to Saigon, the latter to Cape St. Jacques, 200 miles distant. The weather, unbelievably, was perfect.

"Tallyho!" Marvel of marvels, bandits were airborne, and others taxiing around on the ground to boot, all well-gassed—another break from the tedium of searching the woods for hidden, degassed planes. Bill Lamberson spotted the first one, a Tojo taking off from Tan Son Nhut field and climbing to 800 feet. There Lambo gave him a short burst from astern then swung around with a full deflection burst into the cockpit. As Tojo erupted in flames, the pilot bailed out, but his chute never opened.

Climbing, Lambo entered the general fray which had enveloped Saigon's skies. Strangely, the enemy pilots didn't seem to be fighting but rather just trying to run. It soon became apparent that the airborne Japs had been up on morning training hops to get in some flight time and had been taken by complete surprise. In taking them on, Lambo and his pals did not even bother to jettison their belly tanks or ordnance.

Lambo sprayed his second Tojo at 3000 feet and watched another chuteless pilot jump. An Oscar roared past Charlie Lee, who fell in astern to flame it. Another Oscar came straight toward Jim Scott, R.G. "Tool" Armstead and Ken Hansen who obliged by tearing it apart with their .50s. A Tony came at Johnny Schell, who flamed it before maneuvering to blow up a Hamp in a no deflection burst. All the Japs were painted that nauseous greenish brown except for one silver Tony which was double-teamed by Super Smith and John Robbins. Vanderhoof and Ed Baumann each shot down a Val, and Sherman Olsen needed several runs to polish off a Helen.

What a motley array of airplane types, and Fighting 3's eleven kills were only four short of TF 38's entire bag for the day. In addition, Lambo took his strike down to work over the taxiing and parked planes at Tan Son Nhut and Thu Dan Mot airfields and Cat Lai seaplane base. This time, the targets burned handily. VF-3 claimed 18 destroyed on the

ground (plus a runway steam roller!), perhaps a fourth of the force's claims for the day.

Flushed with victory, the Iron Major's charges still carried their belly tanks, bombs and rockets and followed their leader in 50-degree dives from 6000 feet against Jap shipping anchored in the Saigon River. Lambo himself placed his bomb on the fantail of a maru, which started to burn, and Jeeter Lindsey, Dwight Horner and Charlie Lee each scored direct hits with bombs and rockets on other merchantmen. Fires were also started on the docks.

The surprise fighter sweep had enabled VF-3 to do its work against light and inaccurate AA fire—a luxury not afforded the bombing mission to St. Jacques, where anchored ships joined gun emplacements on shore in throwing up a mass of ugly flak.

Gus Osterhoudt took in the Helldivers first. Tim Sullivan scored a direct 1000-pound bomb hit on a large freighter, and Fox Johnson and W.J. Swearingen dropped theirs onto a destroyer escort which sank in five quick minutes. A few near-misses added to the damage, the VB attack setting up the torpeckers for their runs.

Each TBM carried a string of four 500-pounders. Joe Sanders led three other planes against the maru burning from Sullivan's hit; they scored enough near-misses to send her to the bottom. Chief Austin dropped on top of another cargo ship apparently laden with ammo, for it exploded with a blast that rocked Mike Arthurs' torpecker on his approach, breaking the nose of his radioman John Lindsay against his gun. One of Arthurs' bombs hit a patrol craft squarely, sinking it. Three down, many more to go.

John Dayton, P.V. Miller's TBM gunner, told his diary, "Ships loaded with aviation gas were a beautiful sight when they blew up and sank. Killed thousands of Japs today. Every plane planted their bombs and rockets in at 1000 ft. pullout. Ships exploding everywhere in huge balls of red flame and black smoke. Pure slaughter. The cloud of black smoke travelled down the coast for a hundred miles. I strafed a burning cargo ship. Our bombs scored a near miss on 7000 ton ship which heeled over and was sinking when last seen."

The torpeckers braved the flak all the way in and out. One piece of flak pierced Sanders' right shoe on the inside at the ankle, slit his shin for two inches, continued on up inside the pants leg and came out at the knee level, finally nicking him in the ear. Lucky Joe survived, as did everyone else, although extensive damage to many planes kept the

Three VB-3 Helldivers and a VF-3 Hellcat from the *Yorktown* pass over the burning French cruiser *LaMotte Piquet* off Point Vinay, French Indochina (Vietnam), during strikes on Saigon, January 12, 1945.

airplane mechanics up all night long making repairs. En route home, Dick Noel scratched a Nell low on the water, and all the planes strafed the convoy they had passed on the way in.

Strike One Baker circled the burning city of Saigon, selecting objectives and taking advantage of the smoking wreckage to screen their runs. Beast pilot Russ Hummel sighted a heavy warship anchored four miles east of the main river. It turned out to be the French light cruiser *LaMotte Piquet*, which Hummel could only assume was in Japanese hands (Vichy France had signed an armistice with

Nazi Germany) and seemed to be under repair by them. In his first dive he put his 1000-pounder close aboard, then climbed again and scored a direct hit with his second bomb. After burning four merchantmen and one tanker, his compatriots joined him. Jack Smith hit the cruiser, and as they all strafed her she began to develop a list.

The torpeckers added to the conflagration, with skipper Turner himself setting fire to one maru with a 500-pound bomb and others causing fires in warehouses and at the Cat Lai seaplane base. But a burst of AA knocked a wing off Hal Skinner's plane, which he and crewmen Moe Skidmore and Bill Garner rode down to their deaths. Despite the carnage to the *LaMotte Piquet,* however, she did not sink, but the Japanese had never used her anyway—and the damage to her did not please the French.

While Strike One Charlie—six VB and five VT escorted by eleven VF—ranged 270 miles up the Vietnamese coast to attack shipping at Tourane Bay in the early afternoon, Lamberson led a dozen fighters south toward Saigon until worsening skies caused him instead to scour the coast between Cape St. Jacques and Camranh Bay. He came upon a crippled convoy, to which his boys added more damage to beached and burning patrol craft. Jake Jones put three rockets into a fairly healthy maru, joined by others strafing and making near bomb hits until the ship settled by the stern.

The bombing planes bypassed a coastal convoy to press on to Tourane, but the thickening overcast caused them to miss it altogether. So they backtracked to the convoy, which they found near Cape Sa Hoi, severely battered by attacks from other air groups, with several freighters and tankers beached. One intrepid destroyer escort was still underway, however, and skippered by a very talented Nip, who managed to elude every bomb dropped at him, except for one put onto the fantail by Bill Runnels in an F6F. Four of the torpeckers were carrying fish, but some of these hooked and broached to no effect. The DE received an unhealthy amount of strafing, as did the cripples, but it finally escaped—the only ship to do so.

The last strike from the *York*—six fighters led by Bill McLeroy in midafternoon—worked over Saigon's shipping and Tan Son Nhut airfield. McLeroy and Bob Thienes teamed up to go after an unscathed freighter. "Just as Mac was getting set," according to Thienes (pronounced Tee-nis), "there were two bursts of AA about 500 yards astern to us. I cocked up my port wing and looked down to starboard, trying to spot it. No luck. Then I looked down to port, and that's the last thing I remember.

"I never felt the shell hit me, and when I became conscious again I didn't feel any pain—only a kind of numbness all over. But I knew I'd been hit, all right. I couldn't see the instrument panel. I took my left hand off the throttle and waved it in front of my eyes. I couldn't see that either. I couldn't even tell whether it was daylight or dark. I thought, 'This can't happen to me! I'm blind!'"

A 37mm shell had exploded inside Thienes' port

wing, not only damaging the plane, but the shell's fuse cap had pierced the cockpit and hit Thienes in the back of the head, fracturing his skull and coming to rest against his brain. The crippled Hellcat and pilot spun out of control toward the earth.

"I was sitting there, panicky, when all of a sudden I realized that the plane was spinning down. Instinct or Navy training or something made me check the rudder controls. The left pedal was out, so I kicked it and pushed the stick forward. Then I realized I didn't know how long I'd been unconscious or how far the plane had fallen. I couldn't see the ground. For all I knew, it was only a foot in front of me. I jerked the stick as hard as I could and waited for the crash." Blacking out again, he went into a second spin, came to, and again recovered. For 15 minutes he flew aimlessly about in Saigon's skies.

"When I came to for the second time, the plane was climbing. The Lord had taken care of me in that dive, and I was absolutely sure He'd stand by me from then on. Right there my eyes cleared a little. I still couldn't read the instruments, but I could tell earth from sky. I called Mac and told him I'd been hit and was heading for open water. I knew I'd have to land before I became unconscious again, and a water landing was my best chance.

"Mac asked, 'What's your course?' I reached for the instrument panel and felt my way to the compass and focused on it. The figures were fading in and out and jumping all around, but I thought I could read them. I told him, 'One-four-zero.'

"Then he asked, 'Where are you?'

"I didn't know. I saw something that looked like Cape St. Jacques, but I was too sick to tell. My mind was all fuzzy. I couldn't think of the words to explain it. I guess I never answered him at all. . . ."

But McLeroy couldn't find him and called out over the air, "All planes in Saigon area, this is Seven-One Cobra. Have wingman wounded. Has anyone seen an F6F circling or making a water landing?"

"Seven-One Cobra," came an answer a few moments later, "this is One-Oh-Nine Stymie. An F6F is circling below me ten miles north of Cape St. Jacques."

As several "Stymie" SB2Cs joined up on him waiting for McLeroy to arrive, Thienes felt all over his body for the wound. "Then I happened to run my hand over the back of my helmet. It felt wet, and when I looked at my fingers, I could make out that they were red. I put my hand back there again. This time my fingers went into a hole.

"I opened my first-aid kit and fumbled around. The first thing I hit on was a tube of ammonia, I took a couple of whiffs. It helped clear up the daze a little, and I began to see enough to spell out 'SULFA' on a big package. I dumped some of the powder into my hand and smeared it into the hole."

When McLeroy came roaring up, he saw holes in Thienes' port side and "a big blob of blood on the canopy behind his head, and more blood around a rip in the back of his helmet. Bob himself looked stunned. His head was rolling on his neck and he kept blinking his eyes. I wasn't sure he saw me until he called me and said, 'Mac, let's go as fast as we can for Camranh Bay.'" Thienes wanted to make a water landing there, but McLeroy figured he would never survive it in his condition. They argued over the radio, especially when Thienes suggested giving himself a shot of morphine. In the meantime they passed beyond Camranh Bay, and McLeroy assured his wingman, "You're O.K., pal. You're doing fine! Stick tight and hold what you've got and we'll be home in a few minutes"—though he didn't let on that the *Yorktown* lay 260 miles away.

As they droned on, McLeroy kept talking and arguing with Thienes in order to keep him awake and in the air. Thienes thought of his new bride, and when he desperately wanted to ditch McLeroy said he'd go down with him to help him in the drink. Recalled Thienes, "The idea of Mac's being willing to make such a terrific sacrifice for my sake put new heart into me." McLeroy said later, "Bob had always been a smooth, tight wingman. But now his plane was all over the sky, dipping and swerving and weaving around. He keep lagging slower and slower, until we weren't making more than 150 knots." McLeroy advised the ship of the situation.

Captain Combs swung the *Yorktown* into the wind, Empty Evans alerted the crash crews, and Dr. Voris positioned his stretcher bearers near the island. Radford's whole damned Task Group 38.1 was getting ready for one pilot, rooting for him all the way. But Thienes "was getting weaker and sicker and I knew I couldn't hold out much longer." Then he saw the task formation. "The fact that I still had a landing to make never entered my mind. I was home!"

McLeroy: "Right after we crossed the destroyer screen, I told Bob to lower his wheels and flaps and tail hook and I'd check them for him. He didn't show a sign of hearing me, and that's when I really got worried. Here he was, wounded and half blind, going in like he was making a strafing run instead of a landing. He was on his downwind leg when I saw his wheels go down, and then his flaps and tail hook. Brother!"

Thienes: "I saw the LSO only off and on. Sometimes he melted into the canvas screen behind him. Once he seemed to be waving 16 flags in each hand. I blinked, and when I looked again, he had vanished completely. If I answered his signals, it must have been by instinct. I don't remember anything about the landing." He closed one eye and got a better fix on Dick Tripp.

The Dog was signaling him that he was coming up the groove "a little fast." His approach was short, and Thienes overshot the groove, then snapped the plane back into it, but overcorrecting until he couldn't see Tripp. Then Tripp gave him the cut, Thienes wavered, cut his engines and dropped to the deck, catching the third wire. "Better than average," admired Tripp.

Doc Voris jumped up on the starboard wing and located a metal fragment sticking out of Thienes' head, which he hastily dressed. Corpsmen maneuvered Thienes into a stretcher on the wing and took him down to Sick Bay where X-rays showed the piece of metal to be an inch in diameter and more than half an inch thick. It had driven two inches into his brain tissue in the area of the visual centers. "The slightest additional pressure would have pushed it straight through his brain," said Voris later. "I have strong doubts that he could have survived a water landing. It's providential that Mac was there to talk him out of it."

Voris got the fragment out in short, successful order, and Thienes began a long, slow recovery. ACIO Ernie Stewart wrote it all up in the action report as "one of the most striking examples in the war of the miracles that can be accomplished by good training, good instincts, and guts."

"Today, we had our biggest victory in months," dentist George Smith reflected on the day's work. In addition to over 40 ships totalling more than 130,000 tons sunk and 100-plus planes destroyed, "fuel dumps and oil tanks were set ablaze at Saigon by our planes. This is a vital region for the Japs. They obtain their rubber and much rice, etc. here. This was a costly day for the 'Rising Sun.'"

Bull Halsey, however, dissatisfied at not finding the two Jap half-battleships, scheduled a 420-mile round-trip dawn search for next day, January 13, which began in rain-blown darkness. Bomber pilot Russ Hummel, relatively new to the squadron, turned up in the fighter ready room by mistake. No matter, except that he did not know the geography

Returning from his attack on Saigon, a badly wounded Bob Thienes overcomes the effects from a shell fragment embedded in his skull to land aboard. Doc Voris jumps up on the wing to help him out of the cockpit. January 12, 1945. Courtesy of Robert L. Thienes

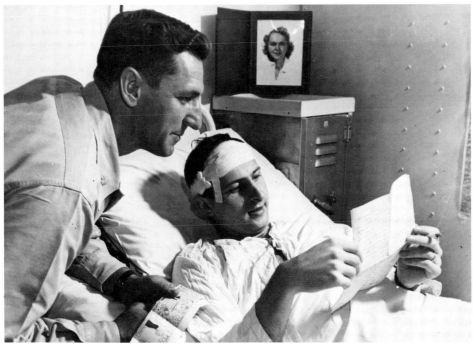

In Sick Bay, Doc Voris helps a recuperating Thienes read a letter from home and shares a "Blondie" cartoon strip. Courtesy of Robert L. Thienes

of the ship. So when the order came to man planes he exited the passageway onto the catwalk to go to the flight deck, but instead of turning to the ladder he turned the wrong way—and fell overboard. No one saw him fall in the rain and darkness. The pilots climbed into their cockpits and sat there in the rain until the launch was called off because of the storm. One pilot had not reported, and when he did not return to his ready room, the tragedy was pieced together. Hummel was gone forever.

The seas churned so badly that the carriers could not refuel from their tankers. "Maybe another typhoon?" suggested Alex Wilding. No, but it was bad enough and lasted into the next day. Long searches on both days failed to find the elusive half-battleships, forcing Halsey to give up the hunt and turn the fleet northward toward Hainan Island, Hong Kong, Canton and dear old Formosa.

The carriers reached the northern end of the South China Sea and Point Option just before dawn on January 15. Executive officer Born proclaimed to the crew of the *York:* "Today we spread our destructive strength from China to Formosa. These days are history-making days. Do your share—all anyone can ask is that you do your best. If you do, 'The Fighting Lady' will be justly honored."

Despite the usual meteorological situation—lousy—the *Yorktown* contributed fighters to separate sweeps to Hong Kong and northern Formosa and a composite deck load against shipping at Takao on the southern Formosa coast. The sheer complexity of this multi-faceted attack taxed the well-honed practices of Coop Bright of *Yorktown's* air ops and Alex Wilding, ship and task group FDO. They argued over their respective responsibilities until even Admiral Radford had to intercede—in favor of Wilding.

The incident did not affect the success of the several missions. Bill Lamberson's fighters pressed down through sudden breaks in the clouds to strafe, rocket and bomb parked planes at Tien Ho and Whampoa airfields at Hong Kong, with Rip Miller shooting down a Tojo fighter. Turning on Hong Kong's harbor installations, the fighters braved the flak, which however ignited Joe Scordo's belly tank as he planted a bomb into a picket boat. He jettisoned the tank, but the fire had spread, forcing him to ditch in Kowloon harbor; he apparently went down with his plane.

The clouds protected most of northern Formosa, though the Hellcats were able to attack shipping in Kiirun harbor with unknown effect. An oddity was the flak—small parachute projectiles which burst between 400 and 700 feet, scattering two or three objects suspended from little sky-blue chutes which exploded in a white burst a few minutes later. They proved harmless. A Jake float plane tried to intercept Bill McLeroy, but wingman Walt Gamboni came up 200 feet behind it to explode one pontoon and the plane, revealing that the pontoons must have been filled with gas.

The same overcast and ack ack were the case at Takao harbor in the south, where barrage balloons were seen among the clouds—another anti-aircraft device new to Air Group Three. When Jenk Jenkinson saw a break in the clouds over Takao, he pushed his SB2C through it, followed by Joe Vercelli. The Jap gunners concentrated on the hole, though, making "the bursting shells as thick as the clouds." The flak apparently destroyed Jenk and gunner John Scrafford and badly damaged Vercelli's tail section.

When a sister carrier's fighter exploded directly in front of the flight, VB-3 and VT-3 decided to jettison their bombs from above the clouds. But fighters Jim Harms and Joe Mayer were able to blast a factory north of Takao, causing many explosions

and clouds of red dust. Had to be a ceramic plant.

"Just for the record," the VF-3 historian observed, "the 'Rover Division' got five men launched for this strike." Every air group had them—the goldbricks who did everything possible to avoid fighting. "All made it to the picket can, but the strain was too great and the division leader plus two escorts returned to base."

One of them, Kelly Davis, was a buddy of Bob Rice, who explained in his diary, "He's now what we call a 'Rover', i.e., a pilot who finds himself suddenly grounded just when he is about to go on an important strike due to a cold or something else. Kelly's been offered 10 bucks for the secret of his rovering success. His system: Just don't be around when they ask for volunteers or when they need you for anything. Instead, go to the head, or rack up, or even report in to Sick Bay. I left my last six fifths with Kelly for storage in his room safe, since I have none, and three of them were stolen when he left the latch unfastened one day. I'm going to keep mine close to me from now on; Kelly's given his to the 'Doc' to be kept with his 'medicinal supplies.' "

Yielding to the hopeless weather, Admiral Halsey kept the fleet operating south of the Luzon Strait for devastating strikes on the Canton-Hong Kong area throughout January 16. Not even AA fire contested the planes at Canton, but Hong Kong was another story, with nine warships sending up a withering fire. The strafers and bombers struck several of them, but as John Lavender pulled out, a burst hit his Beast while the bomb bay was still open, killing him, but gunner Jean Balch bailed out and was taken prisoner.

Steaming northeast on the 17th, the Third Fleet, recorded dentist Smith, was "scheduled to leave the South China seas tonight through the four-mile wide strait between Formosa and Luzon; however, since our entrance the Japs have mined the channel and have torpedo boats, etc., ready for our night run. Due to these facts our task force is continuing south in order to cross over into the Pacific."

"The ship is rocking so severely right now" from another storm, noted diarist Rice, "that I have to pause between every other word in order to write on the level." Refueling had to be postponed, but Halsey launched still more 420-mile searches to the southwest looking for the Jap "task force"—"if there is one," doubted Dwight Horner. Then intelligence was received that the hybrid *Ise* and *Hyuga* were safely in hiding near Singapore. The pilots raced back to the ship with yet another storm close behind.

With further flight operations cancelled, the king of grabass, Skinhead Bright, used the slack time to have some fun with the idled fighter jockeys. He picked on Super Smith by manufacturing a bulletin to the effect that a blessed event had just occurred in Smith's life. Fighting 3 bought the story, and for several hours Smith felt the full weight of jibes from his pals as Coop kept the teletype busy: "WHY GEORGE, HOW COME YOU NEVER LET US IN ON THIS, SO THAT CONGRATULATIONS WOULD BE IN ORDER?" And, "GEORGE'S NEW THEME SONG: 'HAVE I BEEN AWAY THAT LONG?' AND 'DID SMITH FILLER, OR SOMEONE ELSE??'" Bob Rice reflected, "I am told she wouldn't rate a second glance, but nevertheless George brought her to one of our dances at NAS Kahalui." This "made everyone surmise just one thing."

In the thick of the storm, Halsey headed south away from its center on the 18th, planning to slip through the central Philippines to the open Pacific until Admiral Nimitz ordered him to leave the South China Sea the way he had entered—through Luzon Strait. So the carriers turned north again toward Balingtang Channel for a dusk transit on the 20th, ignoring Tokyo Rose's warnings not to try it. For some strange reason, this winsome-sounding lass seemed to enjoy singling out the *Yorktown*, and now she declared the Fighting Lady would never get out of the South China Sea. Captain Combs could only guffaw at this one. The *Y* had been the first carrier into this Sea and, according to the op plan, would be the very last one to leave! Come and get us, you yellow bitch.

"Don't be surprised at anything," Seaman First repairman Kenny Parkinson heard the announcement over the bullhorn early on January 20, with everything from mines and subs to zootsuiter kamikazes expected. "Japs all around us," he told his diary, and the first one closed at 0935. GQ, and within minutes the bogey passed directly overhead, but very high up—a George fighter. A *Lexington* fighter gave chase and shot it down with ease. Sadly, though, a *Yorktown* CAP fighter flown by Howie Parker developed engine trouble and spun in on trying to make the *Wasp*, pilot going down with the wreckage.

Late in the afternoon, several bogeys tried to penetrate the formation but were splashed, and as the Fleet began to enter the narrow channel just after sunset the Japs pressed home more attacks. As the carriers passed up the center of Balingtang, the destroyers squeezed into tight screening positions in the four miles breadth of deep water. Bogeys filled the radars, and George Earnshaw's gunners got set for their first night action of their second war cruise.

At 1915 the screen opened fire in the tight quarters on two bogeys, shrapnel from their bursts falling onto the *Yorktown*'s flight deck. Now the *Wasp* let go with her 20mms—the *Wasp*, in the words of radio officer George Wille, looking like "a Fourth of July 'flowerpot.'" Its shells also burst over the *Yorktown* and struck the destroyer *Stockham*, wounding several men. At 1932, as the bogey—a Betty—closed the *Yorktown*'s bow to 1000 yards, then turned around to starboard, George Earnshaw told his forward 20s to commence firing, and they held forth for a full minute, but did not score. The bogey escaped. Night fighters rose up to chase off the bandits that the ack ack missed. In all, the force shot down perhaps eleven planes.

Yorktown, bringing up the rear of Task Force 38, transited Balingtang Channel two hours before midnight. Alex Wilding—having matured into a sharp critic of the Halsey regime—noted: "We are out of the South China Sea—that was a waste of time and energy."

Perhaps so. The two old Jap battleships were hardly worth the effort to try to sink, and even the many cargo ships sunk in the foray were being rendered useless anyway by the closing of the Luzon supply bottleneck. The additional protection provided to MacArthur's seaward flank at Lingayen Gulf no doubt had helped the Army, but as matters had turned out the weather had helped even moreso. Yet, men had been lost—probably needlessly—in the South China Sea.

The real threat remained Formosa, toward which beclouded bastion Halsey again now turned his mighty fleet. Formosa. "Damn it!" responded Dwight Horner. "What again?" kidded the pilots grimly. "Why, I can hit the place without even navigation; just follow the blackest clouds." Which was precisely why Air Group Three was again selected to return to Taihoku and Takao—its familiarity with them. The other carriers would strike the Pescadores and Sakishima Gunto as well as Formosa.

The tedium was getting everyone down. And the whiskey was about all gone now, meaning that the well-guarded raw alcohol for the torpedoes became the object of desire for many men, while several gunners got plastered drinking the alcohol used for cleaning the gun sights. Holy Joe George Wright begged some of the hooch from gun boss George Earnshaw, who countered, "I can't give you any of this alcohol. Why don't you try the sacramental wine?" Said Wright, "I polished that off last night!"

Yorktown's planes revisited Matsuyama and Taien airfields in northern Formosa and Takao in the south throughout January 21, battling the usual clouds and flak in the process. George Kapell shot down a lone Dinah near Takao's Koshun field, where Hellcat pilot Rolan Powell was brought down by AA. Though he lost his life raft, a TBM dropped him another which he climbed into. Orbited by several planes, Powell was picked up three hours later by a can. The bombers struck several vessels, W.J. Swearingen scoring a direct hit on the stern of a tanker, which started to settle in the water.

A second morning fighter sweep found "the inevitable train at Taihoku." Charlie Wall stopped the locomotive with two well-placed rockets, whereupon Pappy Joynt and Chico Leach blew it to smithereens. But on returning near the ship, the flight was advised to stay clear by Alex Wilding since the formation was under attack by kamikazes. Ensign Gerry Nichols, however, tallyhoed a Zero being chased by the *Cowpens* CAP and eagerly went low and right up behind the Zeke to nail him. Nichols was too close, though, as the explosion of the Jap fighter consumed Nichols' plane, which took its pilot into the sea.

As another strike was being readied, the "Divine Wind" of suiciders made its most dramatic appearance in two months. Around the noon hour the kamikazes and conventional bombers began attacking Sherman's and Bogan's task groups, causing heavy damage and loss of life to the *Ticonderoga, Langley* and two destroyers at the cost of fifteen attackers. Formosa was obviously the source of these attacks, so the Fighting Lady sent off an afternoon strike which worked over the airfields and shipping around Kiirun. "The Baron," Art Chambers, chased and exploded a lone Dinah after it took off from Matsuyama, while fighters and bombers clobbered more marus riding at anchor. But no kamikazes were found in northern Formosa.

Turning northeast at the end of the day toward brand new hunting grounds, the Ryukyus and Okinawa, the force detected a Betty heading in. Joe Chambliss' *Yorktown* gun directors locked on to it just after dark. In the words of gunner Ed Wallace,

batteries "6 and 8—my new battle station, opened fire with the 5 inch and I saw an enemy plane go down in flames and we kept firing as did most of the ships in the task force. The concussion wrecked two planes on the flight deck and at times spectators on the flight deck interfered with the firing." Two cruisers claimed the honors, but, noted Chambliss, "We got credit for a kill when the Nip disappeared from the screen." Eight 5-inch guns had participated in the three-minute battle, firing a total of 117 rounds.

After the force brought down two more attackers, the *Yorktown* secured from GQ, and exec Born added a note to the new Plan of the Day, "It was a good feeling to see our guns bark again—the shoot down places another [Jap] flag on Air Defense Forward. Remember we survived this only because we are a team—Always work together for the destruction of our enemy."

The team had one more immediate task— Okinawa—and Empty Evans had several Hellcats loaded down with photographic equipment so that intelligence could be gathered for the anticipated landings there in April. The skies over the Ryukyus were clearing. "Beautiful weather. Sea calm as glass," noted John Dayton, welcome news for the 0544 predawn fighter sweep of Commander Lamberson on January 22 to neutralize Okinawa's biggest airfield, at Naha.

"The Japs seem to be asleep," radioed Lambo to his charges over Naha, whereupon ground flashes, tracers and aerial bursts suddenly punctuated the gray dawn to announce the beginning of a heavy barrage. Fighting 3 pushed through it however, and after finding no airborne targets strafed the field and fired one small vessel. Two composite strikes followed during the bright clear morning, fighters strafing ahead of bombers and torpeckers, all raining destruction on parked planes and installations.

The last of seven strikes of the day was another fighter sweep, Lambo leading as usual and in his typical cocky and ruthless manner. While four Hellcats photographed and bombed Miyako Jima, the other 16 executed steep dives at Naha's airfield and north of it looking for targets of opportunity. Super Smith put at least four of his six rockets squarely into a picket boat in Naha harbor; it exploded and began to sink.

Several fighters concentrated on what appeared to be a big industrial plant north of Naha which they duly obliterated with bombs and rockets. Ed Baumann, the "Bronx Navy pilot," landed back aboard very excited about his role in this achievement, only to discover the target had been a silkworm experimental station!

While several F6s worked over luggers, pickets and fishing boats, Lambo and wingman Van Vanderhoof discovered a 60-foot lugger anchored in a cove to the north. Lambo made his customary low and close strafing run on it. Just as he passed over it at 100 feet, the lugger blew sky-high, disintegrating and doing the same to Lambo's plane. Van and Smith's division search frantically for Lambo but all they saw in the water was the belly tank and some debris. The boat must have been loaded with ammo.

The Iron Major was gone. "He was, to my notion," wrote Dwight Horner, "one of the best qualified men I know. A graduate of Annapolis with more 'guts' than anyone I have ever known. The squadron will feel this loss badly. That was the only incident to mar the beauty of the day."

"An odd trick of war" for so intelligent and aggressive a fighter pilot to go in this way, lamented his comrades. "The squadron felt sad at the loss of a friend and topnotch fighter pilot who loved to plan and lead a hop and get in and slug it out with the enemy. Wherever all good airmen pass, Lambo must be there planning new ways to do lower slow rolls and insisting that air discipline be maintained."

"I think," Admiral Halsey signaled to Admiral McCain during the retirement from Okinawa to Ulithi, "that all hands except the Nips can rejoice over the results produced by this team of old poops, young squirts and lieutenant commanders."

Among the "old poops" who had scored high during the cruise in the estimation of all *Yorktown* hands was Captain Theda Combs. Interviewing Combs for the next issue of SEA-V-TEN, Chief Journalist Davey Price "looked into a pair of very friendly, tired and tolerant eyes that were so hypnotic that I almost failed to observe that his scalp, for the most part, was naked. I could not help imagining him in a business suit on the beach."

All in all, the crew was pooped. "This is the first day we had it easy," wrote plankowning airedale Joel Connell in his diary on January 24. "We had one patrol and a movie. Crapped out the rest of the day. Headed for Ulithi." Scuttlebutt abounded, with Air Group Three's pilots especially anxious. Noted Bob Rice the same day, "Since the gossip at Mary Lou Clifford's cocktail party centered around the exact date and place we're expected to arrive back in the States, how about letting us birds in on the great big secret? Seems as if the order of letting things out of the bag runs something like this: Chet Nimitz; Chet's confidential secretaries; Navy wives; Enlisted men; Ship's officers and lastly, the pilots themselves. At least that's the way the 'word' gets around here."

One "word" all hands got when the *York* entered Ulithi lagoon on the morning of the 26th was the sight of the *Ticonderoga*, riding at anchor, her flight deck charred and torn from the kamikaze which had struck her. The men of the Fighting Lady could only wonder if such a fate lay in store for them.

Adding Air Group Three's recent scores to those of Five and One on February 1, 1945. The "sitting ducks" in the lower left represent parked planes destroyed. Courtesy of Larry Raymond

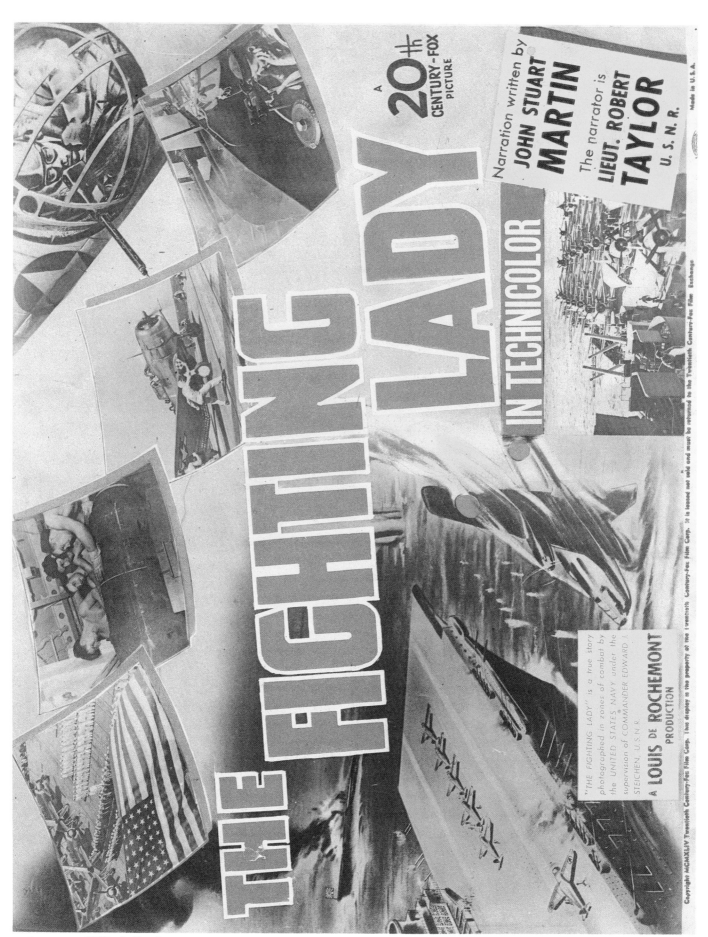

Courtesy of Billy L. South

Chapter XI

Thirty Minutes Over Tokyo

"ARE WE RIGHT?" **Father**
Joe Moody asked in the third issue of SEA-V-TEN, due out in March 1945. "This seems like an idle question when we consider the evil wrought by our enemies. Their whole philosophy is wrong, and their acts are in keeping with their ideas. It seems safe to say with conviction that America is on the right side of this war."

Just as Moody's words of reassurance never failed to lift the morale of the battle-weary crew, so did Chaplain George Wright's good works keep the men jumping on board and at Ulithi's Mog Mog atoll. On February 2 Wright staged a big smoker of music, skits, boxing matches, a pie-eating contest, and a community sing which concluded with a ditty Wright himself wrote especially for the occasion, "Beautiful Mog Mog."

> Beautiful, beautiful Mog Mog!
> Down where the Sea breezes Blow.
> We're proud of Crowley's Tavern,
> Where the beer and whiskey flow.
> You may know of a cozier atoll,
> But you ain't seen no atoll at all,
> Till you've seen beautiful Mog Mog!
> Most beautiful atoll of all!

Mog Mog offered one last respite as the carriers prepared for their most important operation yet— an attack on Tokyo itself while the Marines stormed ashore at Iwo Jima. This tightening of the noose around the Japanese Empire would be conducted by Admirals Spruance and Mitscher, who now relieved Halsey and McCain in command of the redesignated Fifth Fleet and Task Force 58. Rear Admiral Jocko Clark resumed command of Task Group 58.1, with his *Yorktown*-weaned staff now headed by Captain Raoul Waller. Former *Yorktown*ers Jimmy Flatley and Jim Vonk ran Mitscher's air operations and weatherguessing; no

typhoons would slip up on these gentlemen.

Just how much of an impact the *Yorktown* had made on the fleet became apparent the evening of February 5 when a large throng of admirals and invited guests from the ships at Ulithi attended the "Fleet premier" of the great movie on board the *York*. Great it was, for "The Fighting Lady" would soon win the Academy Award as the best documentary film of 1944, to the universal appeal of the critics. Lieutenant Commander Dwight Long, who had done most of the filming, presented a print to the ship in a ceremony at which several of the "stars" took bows.

Cooper Bright got just three seconds on camera, but everyone recognized him, and he was mobbed afterward in the wardroom. "You were marvelous! Never saw such a performance in my life! One minute you had me crying, the next minute I was rolling in the aisle. And that scene where she brings in the baby and shows you the resemblance, how it's bald, just like you—kid, you knocked me out of my seat!"

Among the visitors at the fleet premier, the crew was most interested in the impressions of a very special war correspondent in the audience—Ernie Pyle. This much-loved reporter who had trudged across North Africa and Europe told a SEA-V-TEN reporter: "The *Yorktown* as far as I'm concerned is THE QUEEN OF THE FLEET, and in years to come, grateful men and women will look up to her and say, 'THE FIGHTING LADY!'"

Then, on an inspection of the ship, Pyle discovered a gun tub whose occupants gave out with the worst (or best) combination of profanity and sex terms he had ever encountered in the military— "masterpieces," he called them. Another *Yorktown* distinction!

Unfortunately, the movie included some scenes inserted from a few other carriers, notably the

Ticonderoga, which led the Navy in Washington to identify the ship in "The Fighting Lady" as in fact "The Big T." This press release caused a near-mutiny on the *Yorktown* when word of it reached the crew. The vessel's publicists quickly corrected the Navy Department, which then admitted that 75 percent of the film had been made on the *Yorktown*, 15 percent on the *Hornet* and ten percent on the *Ticonderoga* (with at least one scene from the *Bunker Hill*).

Ashore, the sailors relaxed with Budweiser and "Black Death" whiskey. Admiral Radford threw a party on Asor Island for Ernie Pyle on the 7th, at which Ernie sang "Lili Marlene" over and over, though no-one really listened; he missed Europe. Pilot Bob Rice "sauntered over to the one and only crap table on the island. It was well hidden by a solid mass of bodies four or five persons deep. Altho I could see nothing from the fifth tier, I could nevertheless hear the familiar crackle of the dice, and oh's and ah's and a frequent 'sonovabitch,' so I knew I had stumbled upon a crap game. Having had a couple of short snorts under my belt, I drew out a sawbuck, weaved my arm thru four or so bodies, dropped the tenner on what I presumed to be the table and yelled: 'Ten with him!' Some high effeminate voice piped up with, 'I've got you!' with a questionable inflection on the 'you,' and from then on it was a game by ear only—I never saw the dice in action once! 'Five's the point.' 'C'mon little fever.' 'Now, now, baby, up a freckle.' 'Ten to five no five.' 'You're on' (from the fairy again). 'Keee-ryst, Keee-rap!' There went my ten-spot, so back I went to the bar to re-fortify myself."

On board ship, fun-loving padre George Wright showed Cooper Bright some new tricks. Working the entire flight deck, Wright would engage a sailor in conversation, while a confederate sneaked up behind the guy, fingers in a glass of water, let out a sneeze and splashed water on the unsuspecting sailor's neck. "Goddamn you!" the swab would roar, wheeling around on the sneezer, then try to catch his language in front of the good reverend. When the guy realized he was the brunt of a gag he almost busted Wright in the nose. But nobody ever hit a chaplain.

"Everybody is working hard to get this ship loaded," observed Jesse Bradley on January 28, "Big things are coming up." Ed Brand, next day: "My men and I started to work at 4 a.m. and got off at 10 p.m. We were on AK 69 [cargo ship *Virgo*]. Boy, we really worked." Then a breather on Wednesday the 30th for most men to celebrate the tradi-tional occasional day of loafing called "Rope-yarn Sunday." But not for one man—Shipfitter Third E.B. Pierce who was electrocuted when he hit a live wire while welding outside the hull. His body fell into the lagoon and sank, bobbing up three days later.

Admiral Radford welcomed aboard his regular staff officers to replace those whom he had inherited from Admiral Montgomery. "Raddy" had won the respect of the crew in his month of combat with the *Yorktown*. Quiet, calm and tough-minded, he gazed directly at a person when he spoke, his keen mind always gathering information for the decisions he made with seeming ease. Radford had tolerance for just about any short-comings, except when he regarded a person as both stupid *and* pretentious. Also, importantly, he had developed a very human touch with the enlisted men.

Captain Frederick M. Trapnell, the chief of staff, "found it was very trying to keep up with the Admiral—Ideally the Chief of Staff should be smarter!" The operations officer, Commander Andrew McB. Jackson, Jr., tried to be, having been top man at the Naval Academy in the class of 1930 (following three years' head start at LSU!). Both future admirals themselves, Trapnell and Jackson represented the kind of high-calibre talent with which Radford surrounded himself. "Trap" had been a pioneer test and carrier pilot since his graduation from Annapolis in '23, whereas "Andy" lived by the code of advancement through key jobs to the top, beginning at the Academy as a member of the secret "Green Bowl Society" (to which Ben Born had also belonged) and going through graduate work at Cal Tech and heading the design section for the F6F at the Bureau of Aeronautics. He was exciteable and impatient with Reserve officers and a thoroughly disorganized person.

Aware that the key to survival in the kamikaze war lay in expert fighter direction, a discipline unknown in the prewar career Navy, Admiral Radford had no qualms about choosing a Reservist to be his staff FDO, namely Alex Wilding. "Hooray," Wilding told his diary on January 27. "Am I happy to receive these orders. Adm. Radford called me to his quarters and expressed his pleasure at getting me assigned to his Staff. He asked me to join his mess and also he wanted me to have breakfast with him in his sea cabin just off Flag Plot each morning we were in the operating area. Purpose: to discuss operating strategy for that day. This is going to be great."

A few days of flag chow opened Wilding's eyes: "This Adm. Mess is something. I thought the food was excellent in the wardroom of the *Yorktown*, but the Admiral's Mess is terrific. When the reefer [refrigerator] ships come in, the Admirals get the first choice. Meats are hand selected. They get the frozen strawberries and fruits—also the frozen vegetables—and the fresh vegetables. I weigh 245 pounds now—20 pounds over my 'fighting weight.'"

Wilding's pending replacement as *Yorktown* CIC officer also reported aboard and was also assigned as temporary CIC officer to Radford's staff: Commander Carl Ballinger. Ballinger had all the necessary credentials—rank and training, that is, Academy '39, naval aviator and fighter director school grad. What he lacked in experience he must learn from Wilding; it would not be easy. But Coop Bright found the tall, skinny Regular a delight, with an infectious laugh and great sense of humor. With Ballinger's eyes set close together, Cooper nicknamed him "Cyclops."

Coop found another adversary one day while briefing the pilots over the ticker for a group grope: 'I CALL ON ALL THE LOYAL UNION PILOTS TO STRIKE THE ENEMY AND STRIKE HARD. I WILL GUARANTEE THE SAFETY OF THIS SHIP BECAUSE ALL THE BOMB LOADS ON AIRPLANES FLOWN BY CONFEDERATES ARE BEING REDUCED SO THAT NO CONFEDERATE PILOT CAN COME BACK AND BOMB THIS SHIP IN THE NAME OF JEFFERSON DAVIS." Then he gave the flight data.

Ere long, a towering form appeared at the door of Air Plot, roaring, "Where's the goddamn Yank in here who put that stuff in the message?"

"Why?" said Coop, looking up.

"I gotta meet you. I'm from Richmond, Virginia. Suh, I'm a Southern colonel. My grandpappy served with Mosby's raiders in the war," and on and on.

Laughing, Bright thought to himself, "This guy's a character!" And thus began a new campaign of the Civil War—and a lifelong friendship.

Lieutenant Commander Joseph Bryan, III, had been assigned as a special press officer to Radford's staff. Forty years old, Joe Bryan was even more ancient than Bright and had been an editor at the *Saturday Evening Post* before the war. As an ACIO he had served with Captain Combs in the Southwest Pacific and with Mitscher during the Turkey Shoot. He had come to the *Yorktown* to write a book about the carrier war.

But none of this impressed Bright, who learned that Bryan had graduated from Princeton, of which Rutgers man Bright took a dim view. Worse, one of Bryan's forebears had been a Confederate balloon aeronaut in the 1862 battles around Yorktown, Virginia. At New Georgia in the Solomons, Bryan had "organized" a Confederate command of Navy and Marine personnel to wage war on Yankees, the Army and the Japs—in that order. Had Cooper Bright met his match?

One day Bryan introduced Bright to Radford's flag secretary and fellow Princetonian, Lieutenant Commander Wellington S. Henderson.

"Wellington Henderson!" Coop blurted out.

"Yes," said the slightly startled individual.

"You know," Coop offered, "with that name, you could go out and sell Blue Sky stock and make a fortune. You'd walk into a room and say, 'Wellington Henderson', and they'd buy anything!"

Henderson didn't know how to react to this, but Joe Bryan roared with delight. Before long, however, Henderson realized the point of Coop's fun-loving grabass, which was good because "Hendy" occasionally had to be the Admiral's watchdog in CIC to make certain Bright did not overrule flag FDO Wilding in the complicated air operations of the task group.

One night down in the wardroom everyone was sitting around talking when Skinhead suddenly remarked, "You know, Wellington, I've been thinking about that name, and I've got another use for it."

"Oh, God, no!"

"Yes. You know, I could picture you in a great movie. You'll walk across the ballroom when everybody is standing around, and the girls are all in long dresses. You'll have on a stovepipe hat, a clawhammer coat, white gloves, carrying a cane. When you get to the middle of the floor, they're going to announce, 'Wellington Henderson!' And all the girls will go into a catastrophic swoon!"

"Goddamn you, Skinhead," Henderson bellowed above the laughter, "I thought I had a good name. Now I laugh all the time at it!"

Joe Bryan's diary was that of a professional writer. February 6: "This morning our hangar deck looks like a country store after a tornado. We're loading supplies...[Commander] Stew Lindsay [a flag communications officer] tells me that the *Washington* and the *North Carolina* will be in our task group on the coming operation. I like that news. I've got a feeling we're going to need every gun we can beg or borrow.

"On the flight deck, painters are outlining false

elevators in red. Even if the kamikazes are deceived into hitting them, I don't know how much we'll save by it."

Next day, "All the pilots and crewmen in our air group, AG 3, were called to the wardroom this morning for a lecture on survival, by a Marine captain. He didn't say so flatly, but his implication was unmistakable: our next target is Tokyo.

"As soon as it became evident, there was a flurry of whispers and nudges, then the men's faces sobered down. When they left the wardroom, they didn't laugh and jostle, as they usually do."

The blockade of Japan was about to begin. With Manila and its airfields in American hands, Japan's sea lanes between the Empire and East Indies had been severed. The Jap fleet was pretty well spent, but the kamikazes promised to make the Pacific Fleet pay dearly for its scheduled attempts to take Iwo Jima and then Okinawa, both to become airfields and the latter a forward naval base for the eventual invasion of Japan. The big B-29s were now regularly pounding the home islands from airdromes in the Marianas, and Task Force 58 prepared to initiate carrier strikes right at Tokyo to take the heat off the assault forces at Iwo.

Air Group Three—whose markings were changed from the white diagonal stripe Yorktown's planes had always used to white wedges on the tail and a 14-inch stripe around the cowling—was reorganized on February 1 to accommodate the creation of a new squadron. The 72-plane VF-3 was split in two, one half becoming VBF-3 for bombing-fighting or fighter-bombing. The change was mostly administrative, for the Hellcats of both squadrons performed identical functions.

Thus the new bombing-fighter pilots were irritated by the "B" in their label. Although, their historian attested, "they carried no more and no fewer bombs or rockets and they flew no fewer and no more CAP's and shared the same F6F's, the B implied a distinction, a step in the wrong direction, toward mere explosive-lugging and bomb-dumping, which they secretly resented."

Jigger Lowe remained group commander, and both Hellcat squadrons got new C.O.s—Lieutenant Commanders Edward H. "Bugsy" Bayers replacing Lamberson in Fighting 3 and F.E. "Fritz" Wolf in Bombing-Fighting 3, he a former Flying Tiger in China. And Bud Hopp rejoined VF-3 after having been spirited out of Luzon by the natives after eluding the Japanese. So had Commander Mac Williams, but he was sent home to recoup from his wounds.

For a solid week the pilots were briefed on targets for Iwo Jima by close air support experts, culminating with the official announcement by Captain Combs over the bullhorn on Feburary 9: Target Tokyo! "When I learned of our destination," admitted Yeoman Davey Price, "I admit that I looked longingly at the plane elevators, wondering if I could fall gracefully from the flight to the hangar deck and escape with small enough a fracture to get me a hospital ship."

Fighter pilot Joe Mayer, "The Great Kid," reputed to "eat anything, drink anything, fly anything, or fight anything, and no questions asked," commented to Joe Bryan as they looked at the scoreboard of splashed planes and sunken ships, "When this operation is over, there'll be a lot more of 'em up there on the island—if we have an island. Me, I take a dim view of those kamikazes, dim in spades."

Heading into the ready room for another briefing, neither Mayer, Bryan nor Bill McLeroy could find a seat. "Never mind," said Mac, "Plenty of seats after this operation. We'll have some drinkin' whiskey too."

"How's that?" asked a curious Bryan.

"We're bound to lose a lot of pilots, and when a man's shot down, we always raffle off any liquor he leaves, and I always win the raffle. I've won three so far. I'm just a lucky son of a bitch."

Mayer: "In spades. This bastard could fall into a cesspool and come up with the Russian crown jewels. Don't ever gamble with him. He'll win your hat, ass and overcoat!"

After the briefing, McLeroy engaged Bryan in gin rummy, Joe having ignored Mayer's sage advice. After Mac won each hand until he had six bucks, he exulted, "Hot damn, old lady Mitchell!"

The ready room bulletin boards displayed a memo from Admiral Mitscher, "The coming raid on Tokyo will produce the greatest air victory of the war for carrier aviation. . . . The battle will be primarily a fighter combat. The enemy will be forced to come up to protect the capitol of his empire. He will be aggressive and eager to display his ability to his people on the ground. In his eagerness and inexperience will he meet his downfall in great numbers but only if you keep your heads and apply your teamwork to the utmost. . . ."

History-conscious vets reflected that the strike days, February 16 and 17, marked the first anniversary of another momentous air battle—the first Truk strike.

Last minute issues included heavy clothing for

the northern climate, first-aid kits, anti-bomb flash clothing and ointment, and gas masks—that still-unneeded grim holdover from the last war.

Next morning, February 10, 1945, the sortie began. Said the key line on the Plan of the Day: "0830. Underway for Indian Country." Author Joe Bryan took it all in, "The first destroyer moves out, then another, and another. The *Essex*, on our starboard beam, seems to be sliding backward. No, it's the *Yorktown* that is moving. Somehow, I had expected her to start with a jerk, like a railroad train."

No fewer than eighteen destroyers comprised TG 58.4's screen and led the heavy ships out through Ulithi's torpedo net to the ocean. "At 0900, the gong and the bos'n's pipe call us to General Quarters. A few minutes later we pass through the net and head for the open sea. Our three carriers [*Randolph, Langley, Cabot*] fall into line astern of us. Two battleships [*Washington, North Carolina*] follow them, and the light cruisers [*Santa Fe, Biloxi, San Diego*] take station on our flanks. Their camouflage is excellent. Near as the cruisers are, it's impossible to tell whether they're opening or closing the distance."

As usual, Admiral Mitscher had Jock Clark's TG 58.1 in the van. Following behind Radford's 58.4 came Davison's 58.2, Sherman's 58.3 and M.B. Gardner's all-night-fighting 58.5.

"As we steady onto our course, the sun glares from the huge, freshly-painted '10' on the forward end of our flight deck. A sharp breeze is blowing. There are rainbows in the spray. Big red flying fish curvet across our bows. A battery of 20mm guns is just below the starboard side of flag bridge. One of the gunners is singing, 'We're off to see the Wizard, the wonderful Wizard of Oz!'"

"This operation we are now on," Commander Born proclaimed for the next day, the 11th, "will require EVERY MAN TO DO HIS BEST not only on strike days but *NOW*. Don't hitch your wagon to a false star and gauge your efforts by a weak link. Don't be satisfied with your first results—constantly *improve—improve*."

Alex Wilding's fighter direction gang went to GQ on the double, dressed for work—men in dungarees, officers in khakis, all in short sleeves—and settled into place "when the door opened and an apparition stepped into CIC. All the officers and men looked up—and it was Ballinger," Cyclops, the newly-reported fun-loving FDO, for his first GQ.

Wilding "couldn't believe what I saw—I wanted to laugh, and yet I didn't dare—and every man had the same reaction. Ballinger looked like a man from

Mars. He had flash clothing on, including a baseball cap pulled down low on his forehead, his gas mask case was over his left shoulder, but the gas mask was hanging down from around his neck. His First Aid Kit was over his right shoulder. He had a two-edged 12-inch knife in a scabbard hanging from his belt. He was wearing a Mae West. His .45 service revolver was strapped down to his right leg. Extra .45 clips were attached to his belt. His pant legs were tied with string around the bottoms. And he carried a brown paper bag.

"I couldn't resist my curiosity, I just had to ask him what was in that brown paper bag. Answer: food. God bless those men—not one cracked a smile—but it took a lot of self control."

The day being Sunday, in addition to the regular Protestant and Catholic gatherings, services were held for Mormons and Christian Scientists as well. Chaplain George Wright stopped himself in the midst of the Protestant service, "What's the matter with you men? Your faces are so long this morning, you could eat oatmeal out of an 8-inch pipe!"

It was the prospect of Tokyo, but married man Joe Bryan had to chuckle when his prayer book happened to fall open to the 63rd Psalm: "I remember thee upon my bed and meditate on thee in the night watches."

"Still," he reflected in his diary, "there's this to be said for fleet duty: you never pick up a glass and find its rim smeared with lipstick."

The air group took off into crisp morning skies on February 12 150 miles northeast of Guam in the Marianas for strafing runs on a sled towed behind the *Biloxi*. Splinters flew as VF-3 and VBF-3 blasted away, each Hellcat peeling off in smart order until tragedy struck veteran "Swampy" Creel and his newly-arrived wingman Norman Schmitz. According to Dwight Horner, "Schmitz had passed Creel up in his dive when someone hit Schmitz's tail with a rocket and it just disintegrated. He went straight on in. Part of Schmitz's plane hit Creel, tearing off his port aileron. Since he could not control it under 160 knots, Creel decided to parachute in front of the force. He rolled the plane over on its back at 3,000 feet but the nose fell through and he didn't get clear of the plane in time for his parachute to open. His body sank a few minutes before a destroyer came to the scene." Neither did the can find a trace of Smitty, who "was married and had a baby he never saw." Wreckage and green dye marker served as brief headstones.

After all planes were recovered, George Earnshaw and Pat Patterson turned their gunners loose on a sleeve towed by a torpecker. The 5-inchers rattled Joe Bryan's teeth on the flag bridge. "You don't mind it so much when they're firing at an enemy plane; your excitement and anxiety insulate you. But when it's nothing but target practice, your attention wraps itself right around the gun barrels, and you feel every concussion to its uttermost erg." He retreated to his stateroom, only to be driven back out of there by the acrid smoke of the 40s and 20s being sucked through the ship's ventilating system.

"WE ARE HEADING FOR TOKYO," Ben Born repeated in his Plan of the next day. "We are getting back into cold weather. All hands are directed to take care of themselves, and prevent colds. All men feeling cold coming on report to Sick Bay for medical attention."

The tanker *Cacapon* hove into view for two days of pre-battle refueling. Though the sea was glassy, long rolling swells kept this activity as exciting as ever—and *Yorktown*'s hose handlers amused themselves watching the *Cacapon*'s mascot fox terrier chase and bark at each high wave.

In the afternoon Joe Bryan visited the torpedo ready room for coffee. A pilot remarked, "You know, I think all this coffee is keeping me awake."

"Not me," replied another. "It's not the jamoke. What's keeping *me* awake is Tokyo!"

At sundown on the 14th course was set at 340 degrees for the run-in north under a solid overcast. "WON'T HIROHITO BE SURPRISED?" Born chided in the Plan of the Day, "TOKYO HERE WE COME."

In the typically beclouded dawn of Formosan latitudes on the 15th, destroyers in the screen exploded a floating mine and sank a 50-foot fishing boat in full view of the Fighting Lady. "My first surface engagement," acknowledged Ed Brand— "really something to see." A can rescued a lone survivor who had subsisted on raw fish for many days, giving him, in the words of Admiral Radford, "a built-in fragrance even after a thorough washing." Davey Price "saw him in Sick Bay, and he looked like a scared kid. From that day I wondered about the futility of war."

Staff Japanese language officer Lieutenant (jg) Bill Kluss learned just how impersonal it was for the enemy when he interrogated this 17-year-old boy named Sadao Watanabe. The kid, relating how his boat had been adrift for three weeks with a dead motor, believed his shipmates had been killed by planes flown by the *Chinese!*

"Do you think Japan will win the war?" Kluss asked as the near-starved kid wolfed down his first square meal in weeks.

"Certainly. China is big, but she is weak."

"Look Sadao. Where do you think you are now?"

"I don't know. All I know is that I am with friends."

Told the truth, he responded that he would enlist in the U.S. Navy and spend the rest of his days with his new friends.

Repeating this conversation to Joe Bryan, Kluss wondered, "How the hell can you dope out people like that?" The fun-loving pilots knew; they taught the POW to say, smilingly, "Tojo eats shit!"

At noon, the CAP spotted a bogey. Ensigns Paul E. King—"Peking"—and D.C. Conlan of the bombers sighted a Betty 25 miles southwest of the group, gave chase, and sent it down in flames before it could get off a contact report to Tokyo. Surprise, essential to success, was preserved.

With the greatest carrier air raid of the war about to unfold, and everyone thinking of home, all hands eagerly devoured a fresh communique from radio officer Pete Joers which bore the imprimateur of the Chief of Naval Personnel, subject "Rotation of Personnel—Pacific Ocean Area." According to its Article 1763, "Homesickness and Nostalgia," all enlisted men and officers, in order to be eligible for rotation Stateside, "must have spent seven years or more in the Pacific Ocean Area, at least four of which were in areas west of the Philippine Islands." What the hell!? In addition, they "must have at least three broken limbs"—no strains, sprains or ruptures; "the break must be clean."

Crap! More grabass. Also, Joers went on, graduate degrees from at least four accredited universities were required, along with a minimum of three major medals, such as the British Order of the Knight of the Bath or the Order of the Soviet Union. Diseases like athlete's foot, scurvy, housemaid's knee, B.O. [body order] or halitosis [bad breath] wouldn't count for rotation, nor would duty in Hawaii or Ulithi. Exceptions, however, might be made for anyone with 12 years service "in either the Panama jungles, Tibet, Burma, Majuro Atoll, or Norfolk, Virginia"—all regarded as "Uncivilized Habitats."

During the day Tokyo Rose added her two cents in a bona fide intercepted message, noting that the *Yorktown* was on its way to Tokyo and that it would be sent to the bottom before the morrow was over.

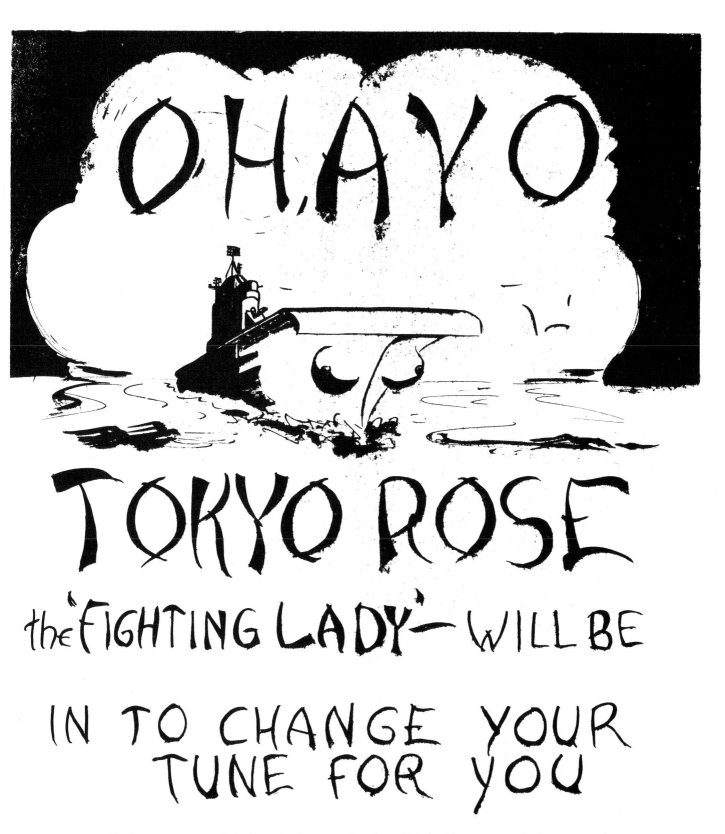

Yorktown propaganda leaflets for the Rose of Tokyo. "OHAYO" is Japanese for "Greetings!'

Under cold and clammy conditions, Task Force 58 began its final high-speed run-in late on February 15. In a final briefing before supper, the pilots were ordered to strafe, rocket-blast and napalm the Emperor's palace and the 10,000 tinder-box houses on the grounds around it. No sooner was supper finished when another important briefing was called: "Do *not* go near the Emperor's palace or imperial grounds!" A wise decision, for the killing of Hirohito would no doubt stiffen the enemy's resistance to fight on forever. To the people, the Emperor was a god.

That he was to be well-defended was conveyed to the pilots. Dwight Horner: "Latest intelligence reports 2,500 planes from 47 percent of Tokyo area depicted by photo coverage. More than we planned for. I figure tomorrow will be the biggest day of my life with the first fighter strikes over the Empire."

The ACIOs delivered boxes of propaganda leaflets to the bombing and torpedo squadrons for delivery over Tokyo. Charlie Turner of VT-3 was furious at this added chore, since his guys must also drop "window"—foil strips to foul up Jap radar readings—in addition to their bombs. He told his pilots, "Drop the pamphlets still in the box but only after the window has offloaded from the airplane." A pilot interrupted, "By the time we drop all the bombs and window, the flight will be over the ocean on our return to the ship." Snapped Topsy Turner, "To hell with where the pamphlets land!"

Come reveille on the 16th, an almost business-as-usual attitude prevailed in the ready rooms—upon which Joe Bryan commented to Bill McLeroy. "Hell," retorted Mac, "it's too late to get excited now. The time to get excited is just before you join the Navy." Ben Born's Plan of the Day was deceptively brief but summed up the general feeling: "WE HAVE FINALLY ARRIVED. LET'S GIVE THEM OUR COLLECTIVE HELL."

"FROM CAPTAIN COMBS—" Air Plot ticked off a final call to battle. "THIS IS THE DAY WE HAVE BEEN WAITING FOR. YOU ALL KNOW YOUR JOB AND I KNOW YOU WILL DO IT WITH THE SAME OUTSTANDING RESULTS YOU HAVE OBTAINED IN THE PAST. STICK TOGETHER, TEAM, AND GIVE THEM THE WORKS. WE WILL KEEP THE FIGHTING LADY READY FOR YOUR RETURN."

But air officer Empty Evans had unhappy news for the pilots: "FLYING CONDITIONS UNDESIRABLE." Which meant, according to one pilot's sarcasm, "the ceiling is below the waterline." Hopefully, it would be better over Tokyo.

"0500," recorded Alex Wilding, "We are at our launch position—120 miles from Tokyo and 60 miles from the southern tip of Japan. I had breakfast with Adm. Radford at 0400. He asked me how I was going to deploy my CAP since the weather was so bad. Cloudy, overcast, with solid overcast from 5000 to 12,000 feet. I had decided to hold all of my CAP at bottoms (5000 feet), and disperse all except one division on a bearing toward the expected direction of attack—from the Jap mainland. One division I would keep overhead at 5000 ft. for low flyers and Jap snoopers.

"Adm. Radford said he would like to see two divisions on top of the solid overcast at 15,000 feet in case of a high level radar bombing attack. I told the Admiral I didn't think the Japs had bombing radars yet, and if they did they would be ineffective bombing through a solid overcast of 15,000 feet. But of course I complied with his expressed desires.

"The first CAP launch came from the *Randolph* and I ordered their Air Controller to send two divisions to be stationed bearing 345 degrees, 15 miles, angels 15, and one division to be stationed overhead, angels 5. When the two divisions were ordered by their controller to climb to angels 15 they radioed they couldn't get through the 7000-foot solid overcast and refused to go up.

"When their Air Controller advised me over the Primary Air Control net, I repeated my order for them to go to angels 15. Again they refused to go up. I had no recourse but to advise Adm. Radford. He grabbed the TBS, called the commanding officer of the *Randolph* [Captain Felix L. Baker] and gave him the order, with instructions to report to him after the operation.

"Needless to say, in about 3 minutes the two divisions of CAP received personal orders from the Captain on the Primary Air Control net (the message went out, 'This is the Captain speaking') to take angels 15. This time they went through the soup and reported on top and on station."

An inauspicious beginning for *Randolph's* Air Group 12, commanded by Charlie Crommelin, though Radford, for his part, was overcautious in his own right.

"PILOTS, MAN YOUR AIR BUGGIES," ticked out Bright's order, and the task group turned into the wind and a wet uncomfortable twilight. Complained Dwight Horner, one of 20 F6Fs launched at first light, "I had on heavy flight gear and the cockpit heater was on, but I still froze. The plane iced up coming through the clouds." Worse, the overcast prevented planes of any carrier from even finding the coast of Japan!

As they headed back, a second sweep had better luck. Fritz Wolf led 15 Hellcat fighter-bombers over Konoike and Hokoda airfields, where the flight was pleased to see the clouds break open, the AA fire only light, and airborne opposition totally ineffective.

Crossing over the coast of Honshu, Japan's main island, related Bob Rice, "we were in a 'Thach weave,' so any section/division leader could technically claim he was 'the first Navy pilot over Japanese soil in WW II' (I naturally felt my section was first!). Caught aircraft on ground, neatly parked in rows. No return fire except from small-calibre arms fire in corner of airstrip. Made 3 very successful passes, setting fire to many 'sitting ducks.' Couldn't believe our eyes; thot [sic] it a possible 'Jap trick.' One plane tried to take off, but was shot down before it reached end of runway. We returned to CV-10 hardly believing our good luck."

Seven or eight bandits tried to intercept the Hellcats as they strafed the parked planes at Konoike, but did little more than fancy acrobatics and hardly any shooting. Rider Moore destroyed a Hamp with bursts into the fuselage below the cockpit, and Del Lundberg polished off a Tojo as it pestered some Randolph fighters. Jim Harms and Bob Eastham sent a Dinah bomber flaming into Lake Kasumigaura. Big-butt Bettys and many biplanes—biplanes, no less!—lined Konoike and Hokoda airfields and were easily burned. During the withdrawal Moore and Joe Smith exploded another Dinah just offshore.

Tokyo had been surprised and Jap fighter tactics found to be singularly unimpressive. But Yorktown's next sweep was jumped by 15 or more aggressive Nips while strafing Mawatari airfield. The Japs seemed to lack any kind of leadership and displayed their usual aerobatics, some not even bothering to open fire when VBF-3 soared up into them. Willie Williams had to dodge one determined "anti-social" Zeke three times as it apparently tried to ram him, but on the fourth head-on pass Williams fired at 200 yards and observed hits. Still Zeke pressed on, and Willie had to break sharply down and to the left to avoid the collision—the last Williams saw of him.

Bill Kitchell chased an Oscar, which fell off in a steep dive, and a parachute blossomed. Kitchell was distracted by the chute until he realized it was a dummy thrown from the plane, which now pulled out of its dive and started to climb. Bill

stayed with it, firing until the engine burst into flame and Oscar hit the ground, pilot and all. Leo Krupp had a similar experience with another Oscar later, "and the pilot jumped out with no chute. Son of a bitch hit the ground and *bounced,* so help my Christ! I was so busy watching him, I didn't watch the Oscar, and goddamn if it didn't make a shallow turn and pull straight up into me. I fired, and it crashed and burst into pieces." The Jap pilot which had bounced was another dummy.

The Japs kept coming on, but so did "Dirty" Red Deavitt's flight when it saw these same attackers taking on Charlie Crommelin's *Randolph* fighters. Deavitt and wingman "Ubangi" Urbano zoomed head-on toward a Tojo and exploded it in mid-air as they passed over. Ubangi gave chase to a Zeke which crossed in front of him, firing at extreme range until he witnessed smoke in Zeke's left wing root. Pursuer and pursued were now far inland. Fortunately, Deavitt had stayed with Urbano, for an Oscar suddenly appeared, dropped its wheels so as not to overshoot, and began a run on Ubangi. But Deavitt shot first and destroyed him, then saw Ubangi's Oscar flip over on its back and crash.

The general melee over Mawatari became wild and woolly—the first big aerial battle for *Yorktown* fighters since the Marianas. A Tojo recovered directly in front of Clay Beck, who smoked him with a quick burst. Jim Graham was lured away by a Nate, only to be jumped by a group of Oscars. He drew black smoke from one for a probable and damaged another, but in the head-on pass took a hit in his own engine. As he trailed out blue smoke, Sea Wall came to Graham's assistance, but Graham headed back into the fray until his engine quit and he had to ditch offshore, where a can just happened to be waiting.

Now Wall saw two Tojos bearing down. As one passed, Wall followed him and got in a good stern burst which hit a hydraulic line, causing one wheel to drop, and Tojo crashed in flames. Wingman Chico Leach also fell in behind the second Tojo as it overran him. He knocked pieces off Tojo's fuselage and wings. This Tojo also plummeted down, and Seawall and Chico combined for another probable.

Before the sweep could rendezvous, Bill Runnels knocked the right wing off a Zeke at low altitude, and A.T. Miles and Paul Lorah bracketed an attacking Zeke which jinked violently and executed slow rolls before doing a handy split-S at 500 feet to escape. When they last saw him, he was smoking from both wing roots—a probable kill.

These midmorning activities claimed five Zekes, four Tojos, two Oscars, and one Nate, while Bud Hopp's CAP destroyed a Tony and a Jill over the force.

Just before noon Super George Smith led more devastating rocket runs on many sitting ducks at Konoike. Spotting a pair of airborne Franks, Jeeter Lindsey and John Robbins excitedly peeled off to go after them, only to have their wings collide. Both damaged planes were thrown into dives, but the pilots leveled off, Robbins luckily missing being hit by a poor-shooting Zeke. Smith and his wingman let the Franks go in order to escort their crippled pals back to the ship.

John Banks exploded the right wing tank of a Tony at angels 12, then blew off the wing itself with a second burst. Though the pilot bailed out, his chute failed to open. Wingman Sherman Brent hit a Tojo, though another F6 finished it, but Brent got on the tail of a second Tojo to flame it. Lining up on yet another Tojo, Brent was again frustrated as Johnny Schell swooped in from above to smoke it. Van Vanderhoof blasted a Pete, and Dwight Horner scored a full deflection shot to kill a Zeke bothering some strafing Hellcats.

It was a bad day for Japan, whose air forces could not even get a suitable counterattack on Mitscher's carriers, which kept their "blue blanket" of fighters over Tokyo's airdromes through the noon hour. While Commander Lowe acted as target coordinator for one more sweep, VF-3 skipper Bugsy Bayers led the strafing attack on Mito South airfield. Jim Scott, "the little fat man," tore apart a Judy after a long chase, and Charlie Lee pursued a Frank, firing until it crashed in flames.

Six to eight Zekes and Tonys suddenly roared down on Bayers' division. But Buggsy came up under a Tony and burned it in one burst. Then Scott flew over to catch a Zero as it pulled out of an overhead run. When Zeke began a split-S, Scott killed him with a 60-degree deflection shot; Zeke flipped over on its back and crashed. Wingman Tool Armstead got another one from astern.

As Jigger Lowe, with Rolan Powell on wing, cruised overhead selecting targets for future attacks, he spotted two Georges—a new and much superior Jap fighter to the Zeke. The two men pushed over, one George got away, but the other charged straight at Powell, who pressed on. The George swerved away just in time to avoid a head-on collision, whereupon Powell kicked his Cat around, followed George in a long dive, and caught him with a long burst less than 500 feet off the deck. The George

erupted in flame and hit the earth in an inverted dive.

Two Zekes attempted to frustrate this dogfight, but Jake Jones intercepted and destroyed both of them. Heading over to Mito South, Jones and wingman Tony Stroeder encountered a third Zeke at low altitude, pumped tracers into him, and watched him roll over and into the ground. Nine kills for *Yorktown's* last sweep of the day.

Now, in midafternoon, the only composite strike took off, Fritz Wolf's 18 fighter-bombers escorting VB-3 and *Randolph* Helldivers against the assembly and repair plant at Kasumigaura airfield 25 miles north of Tokyo. Jap interceptors greeted them with a new tactic—one plane attacked while another followed at perhaps 200 yards hoping to catch a Hellcat chasing the first one. VBF-3 was so careful, however, that only one Hellcat received any damage from this. Art Chambers fell in behind a Jack, and when a Tony came up behind him, Fritz was there to blast the Tony's engine and cockpit.

At one point a Tony headed straight toward Wolf, who opened fire at 700 feet, whereupon Tony broke off and tossed out a bogus jumper and parachute. "At no time in this run," reported Wolf, "did the Tony fire, although he was in a position to do so. The impression given was of an inexperienced pilot in a state approaching panic."

When one fighter-bomber developed engine trouble, it was escorted homeward by Bill McLean. Passing over the radar picket line, McLean spotted a Jill just off the water heading toward the carriers, made a flat side run and sent Jill into the sea with a long burst of fire.

Bombing skipper Gus Osterhoudt led his SB2Cs in bomb runs on the Kasumigaura plant, which also received 13,500 propaganda leaflets. On the pullout, they were intercepted by eight Jap fighters of various types. Hellcats were there too, though, shot down an Oscar and chased away others, with no small help from three rearseat gunners in this final action of the day.

The total bag for *Yorktown's* pilots on this first carrier raid against Tokyo was 39 kills in the air, three probables, and 21 damaged, with similar figures on the ground. Jake Jones was high scorer with three Zekes. Not one *Yorktown* flier had been lost—"a new record for 'The Fighting Lady,' " Dwight Horner celebrated. Other air groups were not as fortunate, several inexperienced pilots allowing themselves to be lured out of formation and destroyed—60 in all! But Mitscher's airmen destroyed more than 300 airborne Japs.

Still, the Japs had not put up nearly as many planes as expected, nor were their pilots very good. "I guess in general the Japs have been doping off all day," wrote Jesse Bradley. A wry Lieutenant Jay Smith, assistant air ops officer on Radford's staff, suggested to Joe Bryan that "The Jap high command is exactly like ours. The closer you get to headquarters, the harder it is to get anything done. You have to go through channels. . . . If we'd been attacking an island outpost today, a tough Reserve lieutenant would have seen us coming and thrown all his planes into the air, and there'd have been one hell of a fight. But headquarters doesn't do things that way. The order to intercept us is probably waiting for some admiral's signature right now, and the admiral's out playing golf."

At least some observers on the ground were overjoyed at the sight of the American planes. When Pop Condit and his fellow POWs at Omuri heard the bombs falling on Yokosuka, they knew that the Philippines must be securely in American hands. Their guards ordered them into their cells and to stay away from the windows. But they refused to miss the excitement and watched the slaughter even though they were beaten for looking on.

The prisoners—and their captors—realized the obvious from this great air raid of February 16, 1945: the end was near for the Japanese Empire. Some guards started to treat the prisoners a little differently, and the POWs now began to steal food from under the noses of their guards. The bad news was that more fliers arrived, shot down over Tokyo.

Several weeks later Condit and most of the oldtimers would be moved to Sumidagawa on Tokyo Bay to unload soybeans and rice from railroad cars. There they received better food and fewer beatings, except that the nightly B-29 raids deprived them of sleep, and as "captives" rather than official POWs they were not allowed in the bomb shelters.

With the raging battles throughout the spring and the ground shuddering from the bombloads of the Superforts, the American prisoners were astounded by the generosity and nerve of Japanese civilians who smuggled them pocketfulls of roasted soybeans, so much did the people hate the military. Then the men were assigned to dig caves for supplies and as shelters in preparation for the eventual American invasion.

As Task Force 58 prepared for Round Two, Tokyo Rose returned to the airwaves with the sub-

dued news, as Ken Parkinson jotted it down, that "a few carriers hit Tokyo today and caused small fires." Said Ben Born's Plan for the 17th, "It is difficult to predict what action we will see today. You can believe this, however, the Japs had no picnic yesterday and they may be out in force today. So heads up and be ready." George Earnshaw's gunners remained at their guns through the cold, rainy night, so jumpy that when one bright star peaked through the low cloud cover, the Number 3 5-inch crew trained the gun on it.

At dawn Fritz Wolf and Willie Williams took fighter sweeps back to Tokyo to strafe and bomb Ishioka airfield. "Meatballs all over the sky," noted Bob Rice of Wolf's flight. Since none of the enemy planes seemed eager to attack, Yorktown's guys took the initiative. Carl Carlson and Dick Noel went after a Zeke and a Jill, Carlson scissoring with the latter until he put a burst into the cockpit, sending it down in flames. Noel knocked down the Zero in his first pass. Over Hyakarigahara field, Jake Jones made quick work of the first of two Hamps, but in so doing found the second one maneuvering in behind him. Before this Hamp could open fire, Tony Stroeder shot it down. Both Jap pilots parachuted. Shifting to Hokoda airfield, each man flamed an Oscar, one pilot jumping to safety. With his three kills of the day before, Jake Jones became Air Group Three's first ace.

The pilots took in the scenery, admiring Mt. Fujiyama but likening Tokyo to a bigger but "browner" Hong Kong, so brown and devoid of tall buildings that they thought it might be camouflaged. "All the reservoirs were frozen," said one flier back on the ship, "and there was snow everywhere. I'd hate like hell to go down in that country!"

The second sweep encountered a half-hearted flight of Nips over Utsonomiya airfield, where Emmet Blackburn knocked down one Zeke. After the F6s strafed some 50 degassed planes—none of them burned—they were met by a fresh swarm of bandits. "My wingman and I," Bob Rice, that is, "spotted a Frank at about 12,000 feet, caught him from behind and set him afire. As he dove groundward I followed him for wing camera evidence, and also to verify if he wasn't pulling a trick. In the middle of my dive I heard over the air: 'Watch out, Cobra in dive. Two bandits on your tail!'

"Too late! I felt the controls stiffen as I tried to pull out of my dive. Had to effect pullout by hydraulic tabs, rather than by the stick, so I knew that I'd been hit. Was 2000' passing seaward off the coast of Japan, with elevator forcing me slightly downward in spite of trim tabs set for ascent. I knew that 3 rescue submarines lay 10 miles off the coast, and that the Task Force was about 60 miles offshore.

"Decided not to ditch near rescue 'fish', but would try to land aboard the nearest CV, which happened to be the *Hornet.* Got O.K. to make emergency there. My plane was somewhat controllable and descent not too serious at the moment. Rough landing aboard *Hornet.* Inspected plane; several gaping holes in both rudder and elevator."

As Rice escaped from the Frank on his tail, Herm Lyons and Dick Kerr teamed up to shoot down the assailant. *Yorktown's* planes headed back to the ship over the worsening weather, boasting 12 airborne kills and three probables, against no losses—a good score.

Unfortunately, though, the heavy demands for fighters reduced the required 32 Hellcats to a mere eight for *Yorktown's* contribution to a 100-plane composite strike from TG 58.4 in midmorning. Handicapped by severe cold, sleet, rain and nearly zero visibility, Radford's planes managed to reach the coast, where they broke into the clear and were dazzled by the sight of hundreds of carrier planes filling the sky.

The primary target, the Tachikawa aircraft engine plant, one of Tokyo's largest, lay just 16 miles from the Imperial palace on the north side of the city, 90 miles due west from the coast. In between lay numerous airfields which threw up flak and interceptors.

"Bandits, dead ahead!" came the call as 15 to 18 Jap fighters confronted Buggsy Bayers' four lone Hellcats flying high cover to begin what Bayers would call 'Thirty Minutes over Tokyo.' "The roughest ride I ever hope to take. I had my entire division jettison bombs when I saw how things were shaping up, and it's just as well in view of what happened."

Scores of Jap fighters presented themselves—singly, in highside runs, from above—in an obvious effort to lure the four Cats away from their escorting position. But strict air discipline and a judicious use of the Thach weave kept the F6Fs locked on to the 14 bombers and 15 torpeckers.

Finally, the Japs ran out of patience and closed in for the kill. Said Bayers: "They positioned three Tojos about 2000 feet above us on the port side, and four Zekes directly above us about 2500 feet. There were from six to eight scattered planes directly astern of us at the same level. When the

planes astern closed for a no-deflection shot, we commenced our weave. Upon commencement of it, the planes positioned on the port and starboard would make highside runs.

"Another favorite tactic of the Jap fighters was to attack in a two-plane column, with approximately 2000 feet between planes. After the attack by the leading plane was warded off and an opposite scissors commenced, the second plane was beautifully set up for a shot. There was nothing wrong with the Jap tactics or with their gunnery. The great weakness of the Japs lay in the fact that they were not aggressive."

The green Japanese fliers seemed to know only the split-S maneuver, and that very well, but such evasive tactics did not win battles, and the four Hellcats pressed on to the target, only occasionally jockeyed off course to meet a fresh challenge. The Japs tried to steer them away from the coast and into Tokyo's heavy flak—but the flight was going there anyway.

In fact, using the two column device, the enemy badly shot up three of the four Hellcats and severed part of Frank Onion's finger and creased his leg, but he stayed in the weave, and Bayers' men shot down two attackers plus a probable before completing their mission and heading back out to sea.

Most importantly, the enemy fighters never got past Bayers' valiant four to molest the bombing planes, which "after what seemed an eternity" according to Topsy Turner, reached the target in relatively good formation between 10,000 and 12,000 feet. "Weather over Tokyo beautiful," reflected turret gunner John Dayton. "Mount Fujiyama stands out snowy and magnificent."

Attacking northwest to southwest, Charlie Crommelin's *Randolph* fighter-bombers went in first and gutted the main assembly area with well-placed rockets. Then torpeckers from a light carrier made their bomb runs, followed by VT-3, then VB-3, then other CVL planes. *York's* guys unleashed 30 thousand-pound bombs, 61 500-pounders, and many 250s, plus—to add insult to heavy injury—11,500 propaganda leaflets. They also dropped window, and the Jap gunners used their radar to lock on it with a few bursts.

The Tachigawa plant was literally blown apart, fires engulfing it as the planes rendezvoused to the southwest in the face of interceptors. An Oscar made a head-on run at a TBM, whereupon gunners Bob Brammer and Warren Boyer in two separate SB2Cs took it under fire. Brammer hit it before three fighters came up to finish it off. TBM turret gunner Al Raslowsky drilled lead into an attacking Zeke before it dived away with a Hellcat in hot pursuit. "Very pretty!" rejoiced John Dayton as he watched several Japs plummet earthward in flames.

More AA batteries contested the hundred planes as they passed outward over Sagami Wan, Tokyo's outer harbor, but without success. Unbelievably, no planes were lost during the day, though Charlie Turner remarked to his torpecker jockeys at the debriefing, "I don't know how you men felt up there, but my G-string was puckered!"

The Jap was getting it from all sides, at one point Alex Wilding's radar scope being "completely saturated with friendly air targets—a flight of B-29s heading from the Marianas to Japan, flying right over us." Lowering weather saved Tokyo from more carrier strikes, and TF 58 withdrew to the south. Admiral Mitscher proclaimed the two days as "an ignominious defeat for the enemy. The annals of naval history will record your deeds in bold letters."

Box score: some 341 Jap planes shot down—53 by Air Group Three—and perhaps 190 sitting ducks ruined on the ground. "Lots of fun!" concluded Pappy Dayton.

Commander Born composed the Plan of the Day, February 18, 1945, "We gave the Japs a stiff right punch to the jaw and we are still waiting for his reaction. Our attacks should have made him damn mad. Makes us wonder if it's not more than his skin that is yellow." Then he tempered his bravado, "We are not out here for any health treatment, nor should we go color blind. We are here to win this war regardless of how the Japs react. So it's on to the *next show* for us."

That "show" was the Iwo Jima landings, scheduled for the 19th, preceded the day before by strikes which kept Chichi Jima neutralized. Only the ubiquitous flak challenged these uneventful attacks by the *Yorktown* and her sisters. Dog Day, the 19th, was even quieter. The *York* received oil and replacement aircraft while the Marines stormed ashore at Iwo 85 miles away under the cover of other planes and ships. But Father Moody broadcasted grim news as it came in: heavy losses at the beaches.

Yorktown's contribution would be next day, and as sunset approached Coop Bright and Joe Bryan took a stroll on the flight deck. Navigator "Jesse" James spotted Skinhead from the pilot house and delivered a well-aimed shot: "Sunset! Darken Ship! Get that cap on!"

No sunlight would reflect off Chrome-dome or anywhere on Dog Plus One, the 20th, for the cloud ceiling dropped steadily all day. Before it reached down to 1000 feet in the afternoon, two support strikes were flown to Iwo, 95 miles away. There was no aerial opposition, and the pilots of all four squadrons used grid coordinates to bomb and rocket assigned targets. Virtually every projectile was on the mark.

Dwight Horner of VF-3: "Iwo Jima was practically 'blown off the map' by the heavy naval gunfire and air attacks. It seems impossible that anyone could survive the heavy shelling, but they did. It seems that this island is the most heavily fortified of any yet encountered. This island is completely surrounded by U.S. warships which shell every few minutes (each ship having a different color of shell burst to identify its hits) whenever a new enemy 'pill-box' is spotted. Overhead there are hundreds of fleet aircraft milling around waiting for target assignments or spotting naval gunfire. It is surprising that there aren't more mid-air collisions there are so many."

The Marines must flush out the Nips at ground level, where they were dug into an extensive network of caves.

Incoming bogeys bypassed the carriers to go after the assault forces, while Air Group Three visited Muko and Chichi Jimas to insure that no Jap planes staged through them. In the afternoon the screen chased a sub contact without result, and after dark a can attacked another contact just 6000 yards from the *York*. Ed Wallace recorded how the depth charges "scared everyone below deck and they came topside like rats."

One support strike hit Iwo on the 21st with bombs, rockets and napalm. "Our planes," dentist Smith observed, "have to fly so low in order to hit their targets that many come back with their own shell fragments in the fuselage."

One of the busiest officers on board was air ordnance boss John McCollow. With little sleep, only horsecock sandwiches to eat, and the resulting constipation, McCollow just lay down on the steel deck to catch a few winks until the call came to rearm planes. Disappearing for several minutes, he returned and declared, "Well, we're going to kill all the Japanese this time." He ran it well, and let off steam by foul streaks of profanity. Neither McCollow nor any of the crew got to shower during these intense operations and constant GQs;

Exhaustion, as airedales catch a few winks on the flight deck.

they all stank to high heaven.

Alex Wilding had to tend task force flagship radars through the noon hour and "couldn't leave CIC to go to the flag mess, so I worked right through lunch. I don't know how Adm. Radford knew it, but at 1300 his mess steward came in carrying a tray covered with a napkin. He set it down on the plotting board beside me, took off the napkin and handed it to me. There on the tray was the most delicious lunch, all served on the Admiral's good china and crystal. A beautifully broiled Filet Mignon, fresh frozen peas, escalloped potatoes and fresh frozen strawberries.

"I didn't care about the officers in CIC but the crew of enlisted men looked at that lunch and the service and I know everyone of them was thinking 'So that's how the other half lives.' As I ate I could see the men steal furtive glances at my lunch. When I was finished the steward mate took the tray and brought me in coffee and a cigar. I enjoyed the lunch but I felt guilty each time I took a bite. But I guess that's the way life really is."

Incoming bogeys chose to ignore the task force in favor of shipping nearer the beach, notably the

biggest target—the lumbering old *Saratoga.* Two zootsuiters crashed squarely into the big flattop, and three bombs as well. Soon after news of this calamity reached the *Yorktown,* an escort carrier— the *Bismarck Sea*—was sunk by the kamikazes. Casualties were heavy on both ships, but Sister Sara managed to limp away and even survive another bomb in the next attack at dusk. "Now that she's left the task force," Joe Bryan spoke for everyone, "they'll hit the *Essexes.*"

A wise observation. The sun set at 1828, and three minutes later *Yorktown* radars picked up a bogey 48 miles to the north and closing. A night fighter was rolled up to the catapult, but not quickly enough. Bogey—apparently a Betty—headed in at 200 knots oblivious to the flak thrown up by the screen.

It was four miles from the Fighting Lady when at 1846 she opened up: 5-inch, 40s, then 20s. Betty turned east and soon cleared the formation. When the 5-inchers quit, their concussion left the night Hellcat on the catapult and a TBM spotted aft utterly ruined—canopy glass shattered, skin fabric wrinkled and torn, ribs and rudders rent, and the VFN pilot

A division of *Yorktown* Hellcats strafes Japanese positions on Iwo Jima in support of the Marines on the beach, February 21, 1945. Amphibious craft stand offshore.

temporarily deafened and unnerved.

Four more single bogeys appeared on the radars during the action but none threatened until a fifth at 1916 registered 32 miles due east, closing. At four miles Earnshaw's 5-inch crews again opened up, when a lookout suddenly saw another one, a Betty, just 2000 yards out and close by the first. The 40s and 20s took this one under fire.

The moon was in its gibbous phase, bright and dangerous, but the *Randolph* had night fighters aloft. Bogey Number One dropped window to mess up radar images and cover its escape. In the midst of the excitement, a nervous Aerologists Mate Second Doug Davidson was buttoned up inside the chart room in the island with earphones on. He relayed ballistics data to the firing room as the bogeys were reported over the phones. Davidson and his equally young shipmates started jumping around when the guns opened up on the closing bogeys.

Curled up over in the corner of the room was Father Joe Moody, calmly reading a book about novelist Thomas Mann. He spoke to the excited kids, "Come over here. Sit down. If it's time for us to get it, it will happen—nothing we can do about it." Whereupon he started reading aloud to them from his book; his cool words succeeded in calming down everyone.

As for the enemy, noted Dwight Horner, "they gathered up enough courage, or whatever it takes, to make an attempted coordinated attack, but they turned back when they got within 3 miles and our heavy guns opened up. They did this three times and at 2000 they left. They were most likely from the Empire (650 miles).

"They did no damage to this task group and I doubt if they did any to anything. I was surprised to see the Japs take enough initiative to even fly down here. The operations plan has been changed and we are going back to the Empire."

When the excitement ended, the mechs got busy cannibalizing the two concussion-shattered airplanes prior to their being "surveyed"—pushed overboard. And a cartoonist sketched gun boss George Earnshaw admiring the two wrecks with the comment, "Three more and I'll be an ace!"

One close support strike to Iwo and an uneventful fighter sweep to Chichi Jima on the 22nd ended the *Yorktown's* role there, for the source of the fleet's trouble must be revisited—kamikaze bases in Japan. The fast carriers withdrew leaving the Marines in the hands of the amphibious shipping. Wrote Ed Brand, "There are 3500 men and 150 officers reported *killed* & 3000 wounded so far. Iwo Jima had 12 air raids last night. Those poor guys are catching Hell."

The new supply officer, Lieutenant Commander William J. Held, dished out "foo-foo" for gedunks—ice cream sundaes—as well as Cokes. Partakers could even remove their goodies from the fountain area—unless, warned the exec, they started throwing the cups overboard! It was a nice touch between battles.

"WE HAVE STARTED NORTH TO STRIKE AT JAPAN AGAIN. EVERY OFFICER AND MAN ON YOUR TOES. HEADS UP AND GIVE 'EM HELL!" Ben Born's battle cry was issued as the *Yorktown's* crew suffered a sleepless night from heavy seas, while the fliers spent much of February 24 in briefings for next day's strikes on Tokyo.

The Hellcats would carry napalm to hit the Asakusa rail center. The boys didn't like napalm, because they figured the Japs would give them no quarter if they were shot down and captured. Joe Bryan heard one remark, "I'm not worried. I'm an engineer. I'm too valuable for them to injure. They'll put me to work in the Mitsubishi factory."

"That's fine, chum, just fine!" replied another. "I'll think of you while I'm hanging by my balls."

The subject changed to the Imperial palace, terrestial Olympus for the celestial Hirohito. The ACIO answered a query about it as a target: "Well, there's nothing in the Op Plan that forbids an attack on the place, but it's important to bear three things in mind. First, the Son of Heaven will be below ground. Second, the palace is fireproof. Third, it's certain to be one of the most heavily defended places in the world. Now, has anyone any questions?"

"Yeah. When are we going home?" cracked someone.

Fritz Wolf took the floor with some stern orders and threats on air discipline. "When you're over water with a low overcast, it's rugged fighting, so stay together! I'll ground any man who breaks formation and goes chasing planes by himself. Further, I'll do my best to stop his awards. When you weave, weave by sections, and stay in there *tight*! If you get sucked behind, you'll get your ass kicked off."

With only the CAP up, air operations were minimal, releasing Cooper Bright to engage in some hi-jinks. He liked to stroll out of his office on the gallery deck and up to the flight deck for some fresh air. The journey took him past the radio shack, wherein he invariably saw fellow grabassers Pete Joers and Ray Knowlton Stuart bending over their radios, picking up and transmitting messages.

Of late, Coop had developed a new trick that was driving these guys up the bulkhead. A clipboard of top secret dispatches hung just inside the door, and when no one was looking Coop reached around, grabbed the clipboard, removed the dispatch on top, then replaced the board on its hook. "Where the hell is that dispatch?" and "What dispatch?" and "It was there" and "Well, it ain't there now!"—all music to his ears, as he chuckled scurrying up to the flight deck. Then, an hour or so later, he replaced it in the same clandestine manner and enjoyed the ensuing hoopla. The radio watch could never figure out what was going on.

On this day, just after lunch, this phantom decided to strike again. He reached around the door, grabbed the clipboard, and—Wham! A hand seized his wrist. It was Stuart, who pulled the rest of the culprit in, "It's you! You sonofabitch, *you're* the guy whose been taking these dispatches!''

Laughing, Skinhead and Stu grappled, rolling to the deck and knocking over chairs. After wrestling a few minutes, Coop broke away and ran out to the ladder. All of a sudden, he heard a familiar sound: *Frrrp!* Machine gun fire.

A *Randolph* fighter plane with engine trouble had been waved aboard the *Yorktown*, but the badly pitching deck suddenly lurched up and slammed into the Hellcat just as it caught the wire. The pilot, forgetting to put his guns on safety, sprayed the flight deck and island with perhaps 100 rounds. Worse, the jolt knocked the plane's belly tank off, and it flew into the spinning prop, igniting the gas.

As the flames erupted on the flight deck, Fire Quarters sounded and Barney Lally's men sprang into action with foam and hoses.

Meanwhile, Coop got to the top of the ladder to find an airedale lying there, writhing in pain, his intestines hanging out. Remembering the first aid lectures by the medicos, Coop obeyed their teachings: "Take your fist and stick it into the hole!" The exposed intestines began to bloat in the sunlight, so Bright covered them up to prevent them from exploding.

In so doing Coop saved the life of the kid, but on reflection he realized that R.K. Stuart had saved *his* life, for the young sailor had caught the slug which in all probability might have gotten Coop had he not been engaged in the brouhaha with Stuart in the radio shack. Stretcher bearers got the boy down to Sick Bay where the newly reported Dr. Glen Holmes performed a successful laparatomy, removing a large .50 cal. brass shell jacket.

"Bullets flew up the flight deck," Ed Wallace recorded, "near where I was standing and I dove between Mounts 1 and 3 twin 5-inch and escaped being hit." One bullet hit another swab in the hip, and more slugs sprayed the island half way up, mildly wounding five more enlisted men and riddling the island.

Some of the bullets, incendiaries, punched into the after cockpit of an SB2C which had just been loaded with two Torpex depth charges, starting a fire on the plane. With heads-up thinking, Ordnanceman Bill Schaffer immediately unloaded the two projectiles onto bomb skids and wheeled them to safety. Another Beast and three fighters were also damaged and a radio and a radar antenna knocked out.

The fire was extinguished in a phenomenally short five minutes after it had started.

News came in from Iwo. Alex Wilding: "Marines raised the American Flag on Mt. Suribachi today. Weather turning foul again—or maybe it's always foul near Japan.''

The task force churned northward, but the heavy seas impeded its progress. As darkness engulfed the ships, Jim Tippey's radios picked up Tokyo Rose; he relayed her message throughout the ship: The Fighting Lady would be sunk—"at all costs"—and Miss Rose had 40 suiciders waiting just for the *Yorktown*.

"ON TO TOKYO" was Ben Born's concise battle cry for Sunday, February 25, 1945. For Empty Evans' Air Department, awakened at 0400, the news was good and bad. The good news, according to Wilding: "Again made our run in undetected. How could they miss—the weather is so bad." Now the bad news; the force had not been able to buck the seas to reach the prearranged launch position during the night. The initial sweeps were delayed, but even so when they went at 0729—in murky daylight—Point Option was 217 miles from Tokyo, twice the hoped-for range.

Nevertheless, 32 fighters from the *York* and 16 from the *Randolph* made the flight and found Tsukuba airfield fairly clear of clouds. But two flights each of perhaps 16 Tojos, Zekes, Tonys and Oscars were seen orbiting over the field. These Nips were little better than others theretofore encountered. "Lucky" Leo Riley nailed a Tony, Jeeter Lindsay exploded a Tojo's left wing tank in a long head-on burst, and Sherm Olsen literally disintegrated another Tojo. When several bandits jumped Jim Haire's division, Haire dived after a Zeke and finally caused it to explode.

Johnny Schell shot down an Oscar at low altitude before heading over to Mito South field, where he saw three *Cabot* fighters trying to get a Topsy taking off. He dived down on it, guns blazing, but Topsy's engine didn't ignite until Johnny was almost on top of it. He nearly collided with it, so intent was he to get his fifth kill, but recovered under the Topsy at treetop level. His slipstream administered the *coup de grace,* and Topsy flipped over on its back and crashed. Schell was an ace.

Both Hellcats and Japs suffered damage, particularly Peking King's plane, badly enough that he had to ditch on the return flight, rescued being effected by a can. A Zeke made an overhead run on Ikey Hart and holed his fuselage, cutting rudder and tail wheel cables and hydraulic lines. Van Vanderhoof went after the Zeke and flamed it handily. But the flight now had a "sick chicken" and weaved defensively to protect Hart instead of dogfighting or strafing. Several pilots fired at one Zeke, but Earl Lankau finally blasted him at short range, and John Carmichael chased a Hamp at 8000 feet to register several hits until it exploded. Other planes strafed Konoike and Tsukuba airfields.

Admiral Mitscher cancelled further strikes in the face of worsening weather but ordered a fighter sweep to hit parked planes on the island of Hachijo Jima 175 miles south of Tokyo as the task force withdrew. In midafternoon Rider Moore of VBF-3 reached Hachijo with 32 Hellcats from the *York* and *Randy* in what he termed "probably the worst weather conditions the squadron has ever encountered over a target." Dodging a low ceiling into which two mountains towered, and in the face of heavy ack ack, the planes shot up ten Bettys on the airfield. Next day, Mitscher hoped to hit the city of Nagoya, but the weather made this impossible, and TF 58 headed for the barn, Ulithi.

The ensuing slack time led to the inevitable grabass on the *Yorktown*. Jovial Chaplain George Wright was the victim, aircraft maintenance officer Pat Haley and Doc Voris the culprits. The latter two worthies put together a Haley invention, the "Mark XIV Mod 5 Hotfoot"—an opened paper clip holding

As the Master-at-arms shoves culprits Pat Haley (center) and Doc Voris into the brig, Protestant Chaplain George Wright nurses his bandaged hot foot.

two pellets of powder from an airplane starter cartridge, wrapped in cotton and dabbed in shoe polish. When Haley discovered Wright sound asleep beneath a desk in Flight Deck Control, he quietly twisted the clip around Wright's shoe so that it couldn't be removed in *any* manner. He lighted it and ran, to a chorus of George's cries of pain and unchaplainlike curses.

Wright knew not the identities of his accosters but would spend several days investigating. When Haley slipped and betrayed his guilt, Wright had Pat and Voris locked up in the brig by the Chief Master-at-Arms. He had their pictures taken behind bars, then let them go.

Like their predecessors, the pilots of Air Group Three wondered if they would ever go home. Bob Rice found himself "starting to squeeze out my blackheads, which means I expect to be returning to the States in the near future."

The Group's scoreboard on the island structure now rivaled those of Five and One. The three days over Tokyo—February 16, 17 and 25—ended with 62 Jap planes shot down by the group and 31 sitting ducks burned on the ground. Japan lost at least 400 aircraft in these attacks by Task Force 58, and the kamikazes had left the force alone in order to concentrate on the shipping off Iwo Jima. Despite some successes there, they did not prevent the Marines from finally overwhelming Japanese resistance on the bloody island.

"We are going to Ulithi to rearm and resupply," said the Plan of the Day for the 27th simply. The air group rumor mill was so active, however, that the fliers issued a "Daily Scuttlebutt Summary," guessing that the *York* would next go either north to the Kuriles or south to Borneo or west to the coast of China or direct to the Jap fleet base at Sasebo or 14 other possibilities!

While the rest of Task Force 58 struck the Nansei Shoto Islands, particularly to get photos of Okinawa, on March 1, Radford's task group entered Ulithi. Leaning over the flag bridge on the *York,* Wellington Henderson and Joe Bryan were joined by the admiral, who remarked, "Nice trip."

"Yes, sir. Very nice."

The Admiral meant it and issued an all-hands message to TG 58.4: "It is the very definite beginning of the end for the Japanese and they know it. It gave me a deep feeling of personal satisfaction to take part in this strike and a great feeling of pride to have the honor to command such a splendid group. Well done."

Next day the Jap prisoner—by now known as "Little Tojo"—was transferred ashore against his will; wanting to stay with his new friends, he departed the ship, when Radford saw him, "sobbing."

Hangar deck movies and drinking parties at Mog Mog did not satisfy the fly-boys, whose only thought was to go home. Captain Combs, tired of being badgered by them, gave them the needle in a notice: "To kill all scuttlebutt, the shoot-downs of Air Group Three must be in excess of 102 prior to detachment." That was the record number Air

"WHEN THE LIGHTS GO ON AGAIN"...

Fighter pilot Bob Rice's thoughts of home, the caption taken from the popular wartime tune, "When the Lights Go On Again All Over the World." Courtesy of Robert S. Rice

Group One had rung up, and Three's count stood at only 90. The joke was not appreciated.

Sunday, March 4, saw the rest of Task Force 58 return to Ulithi and a fresh round of scuttlebutt to the *Yorktown*. "The word" filtered through the air group that it was going home; the next evening confirmed it when the ship's officers presented a farewell "Send Off" party for the group. The band played "California, Here I Come," and Chaplain Wright introduced the several characters of the group, and included "last but not the least, the man who sent a whole CAP off with the wrong dope, 'Buck' Bright." Theda Combs presented Jigger Lowe with a "Well Done Scroll," everyone sang "Auld Lang Syne," and a movie was shown, appropriately titled, "And Now Tomorrow."

"It was well done," concluded the VF-3 historians, "and left all hands with the feeling that they had done a good job and were now leaving the best damn ship in Uncle Sam's gargantuan Navy." The feeling was mutual. AA gunner Ed Wallace said it all in his diary, "They were good men." Next morning, the 6th, Jigger Lowe marched his pilots single file down the hangar deck where they dumped all their gear in a pile, without bothering to formally check in anything. After Admiral Radford presented them awards, they transferred to the *Lexington* for passage home; as they left the *Yorktown* they saw the crew giving their Lady a fresh paint job for the next battle.

Their fighter director, Alex Wilding, had just received orders transferring him to another admiral's staff as FDO. But Arthur Radford, knowing how long Wilding had been in combat, interceded on his behalf with Admiral Mitscher, and on the 9th Wilding got new orders. "Adm. Radford did it. It's goodbye *Yorktown*, goodbye Fleet and goodbye combat." Next day he packed "everything. I'll never be back." Next duty— Washington, D.C.

As Wilding prepared to leave the ship on the 11th, the phone rang in his room. It was Wellington Henderson of the staff "asking me to come up to Adm. Radford's quarters as he wanted to see me.

"I reported there on the double and the Admiral welcomed me and then said, 'Alex, I didn't want you to get away from here without my expressing to you my gratitude and thanks for the wonderful job you have done. The fact that my task group has not been damaged by air attacks is due directly to your outstanding ability as a Fighter Director Officer. I want you to know that I appreciate the long hours you have put in and your expertise. I am recommending you for a citation.'

"I thanked him and told him it was a pleasure working for him—and it was. He's a real gentleman. The task I was going to Washington for was the Number 1 priority project in the Navy—combating the kamikaze threat—and he had recommended me for the job in Washington because I was best qualified to work out a solution to the problem.

"He wished me well, said keep in touch, and he hoped we could serve together again at some time in the future—also if he could ever do anything for me to just let him know. We shook hands and I left."

Chapter XII
Bomb Sunday

"Think you're nice and safe at Ulithi, don't you, *Yorktown*," Tokyo Rose taunted her favorite target. "Well, we're fixing up a little surprise for you."

The men of the Fighting Lady had become pretty cynical about his yellow bitch, but still, one could never be sure.... Nerves *were* on edge and tempers short, a condition which Jap propaganda played on. So Commander Born offered some sound advice in the Plan of the Day for March 3, 1945: "If the strain of our present operation has given you a 'sour disposition,' give its effects to the Japs—not a shipmate. Guard against the hasty flow of ill-chosen words that not only cheapens you, but causes you to lose the friendship of a shipmate. Don't give the Japs the satisfaction of even giving us a sour disposition—it ain't worth it...."

"This climate!" wrote Joe Bryan of another irritant. "From the sheets that never dry out—from the prickly heat that never dries up—from the sourness of my clothes—from the torture of my razor, which leaves my face looking as if I'd massaged it with a nutmeg grater—from cramps—from the shirt that is stuck to my back two minutes after I've put it on—from short tempers—from lassitude—from all this, Good Lord deliver me!"

Boxing great Gene Tunney—head of naval aviation's athletic program—inspected the *Yorktown* on the 6th, the same day that the new air group reported aboard. Of all groups, it was Five's old nemesis, Air Group Nine of the *Essex*. After reforming, it had come back out to the *Lexington* and had lost its commander, Phil Torrey, in the strikes on Tokyo. It now inherited Air Group Three's F6F-5's, SB2C-4's and TBM-3's, most of them actually in pretty good shape. Empty Evans taught them the ropes, and fleet officers lectured on "escape and evasion" in China, with amplification by Lieutenant Harry "The Whorl" Worley of

VB-9 who had been raised there. Problem was, they weren't going to China!

The new air group commander, Herbert N. Houck, who had led Fighting 9 until Torrey's death, seemed more of a college professor type than fighter pilot—tall, lanky, knowledgeable, yet fond of cigars. Lieutenant Jack "Buster" Kitchen had moved up to command the hot VF-9, whose "star" performer was Lieutenant Eugene A. Valencia. An ace from shooting down three Jap planes at Rabaul, one at Tarawa and three more on the first Truk strike where 30 Zeros had ganged up on him, Valencia had gotten his own division in the re-formed squadron. He had handpicked its three best pilots to comprise his crack "Flying Circus." Gene had then made three more kills over Tokyo, giving him ten to date.

Bombing-Fighting 9 came under the command of an ex-Flying Tiger of China, Lieutenant Commander Frank L. Lawlor, a first cousin of Jigger Lowe. Lieutenant Tony F. Schneider led Bombing Nine in battle and softball games as an amiable and much-liked Missourian. VT-9's "quiet, capable" Lieutenant Commander Bryon E. Cooke, Annapolis '39, had been flying with the squadron in all of its battles.

These former *Essex* pilots had never conceded defeat to the rival *Yorktown* on their first war cruise; they still regarded the *York* with thinly-disguised disdain. This attitude was an open challenge to the ship's senior plankowner, Skinhead Bright, who teased them for not getting any mail from home. Overlooking the fact that their letters were still being routed to the *Lexington,* Bright held forth on the Air Plot teletype. They couldn't believe it.

"I HAVE JUST FINISHED READING THE FIRST OF THE TWELVE LETTERS I GOT FROM MY WIFE. SHE STARTS OFF, 'MY DEAREST, DEAREST

Air Group Nine's leaders study charts of the Japanese homeland: (L to R) Lieutenant Commanders Byron Cooke of VT-9 and Frank Lawlor of VBF-9, Lieutenant Tony Schneider of VB-9, Lieutenant Commander Houck, and Lieutenant Jack Kitchen of VF-9.

Herb Houck, skipper of Air Group Nine. Courtesy of Herbert N. Houck

COOPER.' I CAN'T TELL YOU ALL OF IT BECAUSE IT'S SO ROMANTIC. IT'S JUST FILLED WITH LOVE. I EVEN HAVE SOME MAIL FROM A GIRL BESIDES MY WIFE! I ASSUME YOU ALL HAVE YOUR MAIL BY NOW.''

The talkers in Air Plot roared as he dictated the message, especially when one passed the word, ''They're coming to get you!'' Several pilots burst into the room: ''Goddamn you! You *know* we didn't get our mail!''

''You didn't?? Gee, I didn't know that.''

When, finally, many days later, numerous bags of mail were delivered to the group on the ship, Bright struck again: ''I UNDERSTAND THAT WHEN YOU COUNTED ALL YOUR MAIL OUT, THEY WERE ALL FORM LETTERS, THAT NONE OF YOU EVEN GOT LETTERS FROM YOUR WIVES. YOU'RE SUCH SEX DUDS.'' By that time, however, they had learned to appreciate these antics, and they joined in the fun.

Air Group Nine's very first performance on the *Yorktown* occurred March 9, when the ship put to sea for a day of gunnery drill and a group grope. Earnshaw's gunners had lost none of their sharpness and shot down all five target sleeves, three immediately upon opening fire. After a well-executed mock attack on the ship, the fliers made generally ragged landings back aboard which embarrassed them before ship's comany. Recorded the VF-9 historian, they at least "had a few days ahead in which shore leave was possible and these were used to drown our sorrows."

Between beer parties at Mog Mog the crew labored long and hard preparing for the next operation. Thus, late on the afternoon of the 11th, a work detail began off-loading supplies from an LCM landing craft. At 1851 the sun went down over Ulithi—this haven from battle—and all lights were dimmed, the big steel curtains slammed shut, and the hangar rigged for movies. Anchored three-quarters of a mile on the port beam was the *Randolph*, also enjoying a taste of Hollywood while loading ammunition under the glare of a single cargo light. *Yorktown's* projector rolled.

After some 45 minutes of the movie, at 2011 the *York's* radios barked an alarm: "Air Flash Red. This is no drill!"

George Wille: "We heard, above the talking in the picture, the roar of a plane passing overhead at a fairly low altitude. Because there were planes flying patrols around the atolls all of the time, we paid no attention until a few seconds later; a muffled explosion was heard and a reddish-orange glow suddenly puffed up on the port beam. The glow grew brighter and practically everyone got to their feet, starting up in a blind movement, bordering on a mild panic.

"Chairs were upset, the movies flickered off and then the PA system belched forth in the urgent cacophony calling for battle stations. The ship was ordered blacked out except for the dull red glow of the battle lanterns, and in the dim light we groped our way out. The bugle had produced a steadying effect and every man knew what he was supposed to do."

"All special sea and up-anchoring details, man your stations!" barked the bullhorn.

"All boats, cast off and stand clear!" The landing barge alongside pushed away.

"General Quarters! All hands, stand by to get underway!!"

"Hoist in all boat booms and gangways! Boat crew, man your boats."

Coxswain Ted Rohrbaugh had seen the "whole sky and our ship lit up like daytime" the instant before the sound of the explosion. "It was a mad scramble to get to GQ stations in pitch darkness. I had forgot, I had the whale boat duty on the #2 whale boats which were hoisted up on the port side by an electric winch fastened under the flight deck. We were not allowed to use any light of any kind. We had to see that all lines and cables were straight by feeling them. This is hard to do in daylight, but it is a frightening thing to do at night."

A guy sitting on a bench next to Clyde Moneyhun got a bloody nose in the mad scramble, while Commander Lindsay of the admiral's staff jumped up to get a better view of the explosion only to be clipped from the rear as everyone near him hit the deck. "I don't know who did it," he said later, "but he's got a wonderful future as a blocking back with the Green Bay Packers."

AA gunner Ed Wallace thought "the impact sounded like a five-inch burst to me as if some ship was holding night battle practice off the port quarter. This ship had live ammo on the decks of all gun stations, my mount leaving 100 extra rounds on deck."

Like "most everybody" Jesse Bradley "thought we had been hit. The plane flew right over the bow of this ship about 500 ft. alt. I don't see how he missed us. A lot of fellows topside seen and heard the plane."

Wille: "Because of the darkness and conglomeration of men on the hangar deck, I had quite a job getting topside, but finally managed it by going forward to the vertical ladder leading to Radio 2 and from there to the flight deck. Getting up there, it was possible to see flames and explosions on a ship 1500 yards away. It was the *Randolph*.

"The plane we had heard passing over us a few minutes before"—a twin-engine Frances—"had crashed into her fantail, between the flight and hangar decks and started a fire which was consuming ready ammunition on the after 40mm mount and a couple of planes on the flight deck directly above. All of the other ships in the lagoon had blacked out, but we could make out the running lights of a couple of fleet tugs which were pulling alongside the burning ship to pick up survivors and put water on the blaze."

The *Yorktown* lighted all eight of her boilers in preparation for getting underway. A second kamikaze flew over but saw nothing and crashed into Mog Mog. A third apparently went into the drink nearby. Twenty-five men died on the *Randolph*, 106 were wounded. By 2100—less than an hour after the hit—her fires had been put out, and no more kamikazes appeared.

Wille: "This was our first experience with a zoot-suiter. Fortunately for the *Randolph*, he hit her in the stern rather than forward or amidships, and fortunately for us, he hit the 'R' rather than the 'Lucky Y.' "

Ben Born gazed through the "long glass" on the

signal bridge and remarked, "We can say a little prayer tonight for that bit of good fortune."

Amen. The brass, according to Jesse Bradley, "think maybe they came from Yap or one of those Jap islands around here. It was probably pieced together from scraps of other planes."

In fact, however, the Japs had sent two dozen of these suiciders all the way from Minami Daito Shima, 800 miles to the north. Apparently, only two or three of their pilots had known how to navigate. And an examination of the wreckage of the one on the *Randolph* showed the pilot to have been shackled into his cockpit! Tokyo Rose had meant business, but again, she had missed the Fighting Lady.

Ed Wallace recorded the scuttlebutt: "Radar reported bogies all along. Someone was sleeping on the job." FDO Alex Wilding had departed earlier that very day; this was a shattering initiation for his relief, Carl Ballinger. Ed Brand in CIC: "Whoever missed that interception will really catch hell. The easy going days are over here for a long time—Full Watches." Next morning revealed, in Brand's words, "the after end of the Randy's flight deck all crumpled up—burned planes—the entire fantail gutted."

Shortly after noon next day "Flash Red" alerted the ships at Ulithi again, and GQ sounded on the *Yorktown* for a bogey which proved to be a friendly. Then again, at 2200 that night, just as Dick Tripp and the new arresting gear officer Hank Reis were putting beer on ice in their room, GQ sounded. They and guest Joe Bryan scrambled to their battle stations. Wallace: "Four flares were dropped by our planes as a test for vigilance and we went to GQ when the last two were dropped. The first two were unobserved." The Secure sounded. Bryan: "When we got back to the room, the beer was cold."

Jitters mounted with another GQ at 0800 on the 13th. False alarm. At least there was some light relief in listening to a new Brooklynite bos'n on the bullhorn whom the boys nicknamed Babe Herman in honor of the great Dodger slugger. During movies on the 13th GQ again sent everyone scrambling. Bryan: "The harbor blacked out completely, but the stars were brilliant. The Big Dipper was hanging upside down on our port bow, close enough for you to shatter it with a club. We were pacing the flag bridge, waiting for developments, when the TBS suddenly broke the tension: 'Hello, Saniflush. This is Fairytale. A whaleboat is adrift 200 yards astern of us. Can you

recover it? We have no facilities.'' Ulithi had lost its sense of well-being.

These new dangers compounded fears during the preparations for what promised to be the toughest fight yet—support of a major landing in Japan's front yard: Okinawa. This key island in the Ryukyu chain lay fewer than 200 miles from the airfields on Kyushu, southernmost of Japan's four home islands. The distinct possibility of round-the-clock zootsuiters greatly narrowed the odds against the *Yorktown's* preserving her immunity from battle damage. L-Day, the landings, was scheduled for April 1, 1945.

With Japan now blockaded from outside supply, her surviving fleet units bottled up, her merchant marine nearly obliterated by U.S. subs, and with the Allies closing in, the struggle would be desperate. B-29s had begun devastating low-level fire bombing raids against Tokyo and had also commenced an aerial mining campaign of the harbors of Japan. The fast carriers would now round out this strangling air-sea encirclement of Nippon with continuous attacks on Japan proper. To record these dramatic events, war correspondents arrived in large numbers. Three of them, representing each of the wire services, joined the *Yorktown;* a fourth was Ralph Delahaye "Del" Paine, Jr., editor of *Fortune* magazine.

Vice Admiral Mitscher organized Task Force 58 into four task groups, each commanded by tried veterans, Rear Admirals Jocko Clark, 58.1; Dave Davison, 58.2; Ted Sherman, 58.3; and Arthur Radford, 58.4, the latter with the most muscle—no fewer than five flattops. In addition to the *Yorktown,* Radford had the *Enterprise,* the fleet's only available night carrier. Also, noted Bryan on the 13th, "they're giving us the luckless old *Intrepid.*" Navigator James: "There isn't a man in this task group who's not glad she'll be along. If any ship is going to get it, it's sure to be the Dry I"—"dry" because she had spent so much time in drydock getting repaired. In addition, TG 58.4 included light carriers *Langley* and *Independence;* battleships *Wisconsin* and *Missouri;* the fleet's only two "battle cruisers," *Guam* and *Alaska;* three light cruisers and fifteen destroyers.

The fleet needed all the experience available for this final push toward the Japanese homeland, reflected in more transfers. On the *Yorktown,* Captain Theda Combs—loved by many but regarded by others with indifference—had received his walking orders. Already selected for rear admiral, he was due to join the Seventh Fleet to

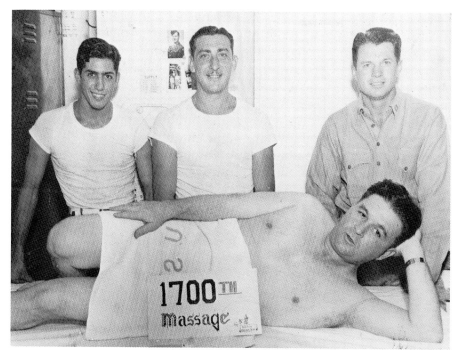

Ship's masseurs "celebrate" their 1700th massage on Commander Empty Evans. (L to R) Jack Gazarian, Doc DeWoskin, and Bill Lam, ship's athletic officer.

begin planning the invasion of Japan. His relief would be Captain Arnold J. "Buster" Isbell, a celebrated escort carrier skipper and U-boat killer from the Atlantic who now boarded the *Franklin* for "make-you-learn" exposure until he could relieve Combs later in the operation.

Commander M. T. Evans, though aptly nicknamed "Empty" by his detractors, endeared himself to others as, in the view of Pete Joers, "a rotund happy-go-lucky fellow of the 'Our Gang' comedian type." He was earmarked to replace Ben Born as executive officer. Evans' own pending relief as air officer now reported aboard—Commander R. A. "Sandy" Macpherson, Annapolis '33.

The reputation of the Fighting Lady as the pacesetter of the fast carrier forces was not lost on the crew. Some observers thought the men might even be getting a little cocky. Their enterprise remained undaunted, however, especially when they learned that $68,000 had been collected in the slot machines in the crew's mess and officers' wardroom. Some wanted a big party, whenever that might be possible. But the real brainstorm was for a nationwide beauty contest for a "Miss Fighting Lady." A committee drew up a letter for contestants and sent if off to *Life* magazine.

Life cooperated by printing the letter in its May 21 issue. Instead of a Petty or Varga-type pin-up gal, the men wanted "a typical American girl" of the teenaged Shirley Temple variety. The magazine agreed to accept photographs of entrants. Then, said the letter, "Upon the ship's arrival in the U.S. . . . .we hope to be allowed to give a ball" in her honor "at which time we shall pay our respects to our queen of the Fleet."

The realization of this dream was a long way off—how long was anybody's guess. Much depended on the outcome of Okinawa.

At 0555, March 14, 1945, Commander Jim Brady supervised the weighing of the 90 fathoms of anchor chain and 15-ton anchor from the "port chains," a platform just over the bow.

"Pilothouse says heave in, sir," the phone talker informed the First Lieutenant.

"Heave in!" Brady bellowed.

The anchor engine chugged, at first evenly then slower and louder as the slack was taken up by the big ascending chain links. "See how clean they are?" Socket-wrench remarked to the ever-present Joe Bryan. "That's because we've got a coral bottom. If this was a muddy bottom, the last 60 fathoms would be a goddamn mass of muck and slime. Now lean over here and look at the chain coming up. Vibrating like a harpstring, isn't it?"

When the vibration stopped, the engine speeded up, and Brady announced, "Anchors aweigh!"

"Anchors aweigh!" his talker repeated to the pilothouse, and one long bugle note followed. The hook rose out of the lagoon, and the *Yorktown* was underway. Time: 0620.

The Fighting Lady followed harbor minesweeps and her own destroyers through the lagoon's entrance and into an ocean filled with flying fish. Air Group Nine, anxious to make amends for its sorry showing five days earlier, landed, but with agonizingly long intervals, a process repeated next day. All Empty Evans could say was, "We are not discouraged!" But he was, and so were the pilots. Was it the tension—or just what—bringing ill fortune to the Lucky Y? On the 16th, during refueling, Ben Born gashed his head while walking under a wing, requiring a couple of stitches.

Task Group 58.4 was assigned to attack Japanese airfields on northern Kyushu, eastward almost to Kobe; all of Shikoku, the smallest of Japan's four home islands; and the Inland Sea, last refuge of the Imperial Fleet, along with adjacent northeastern Honshu. This would occur on March 18. The pilots were told nothing about succeeding days so that they would have nothing to reveal should they be shot down and captured.

The day before, the 17th, Theda Combs elaborated over the bullhorn, "All hands topside must have their steel helmets and protective clothing immediately available. Your gas masks must be ready for use." Gas! A new possible wrinkle which raised eyebrows. "This operation is very important. Its bearing on the future of the war will be great. All the strength we have in ships and planes will be needed as the action progresses. We intend to keep The Fighting Lady in it until the Nips are licked. It's up to us to do everything in our power to protect her. We must be alert for any emergency. That is all."

Frrp! The sound of machine gun fire pierced the normal noises of the busy ship moments after the captain stopped speaking. A mech had accidentally triggered two machine guns on a fighter being respotted on the flight deck. Since its wings were folded, the plane's guns were aimed down, and the bullets slammed through the flight deck, hitting six men working on an SB2C in the hangar and another man in Sick Bay on the third deck.

Thankfully, none of the injuries were serious, but Pat Patterson roared, "That damn Air Department! Minute your back's turned, they shoot at you!"

The Plan of the Day for the 18th insisted, "At General Quarters all hands above the Hangar Deck, exposed or not exposed, will put on Flash Burn Ointment ["a thick, gray cream; nasty looking" in Joe Bryan's opinion] and keep it on until secure. This procedure will be followed at all General Quarters on strike days. This ointment is called War Paint. The use of ointment is added protection along with Flash Proof Clothing. Exposed personnel must use both."

Shipfitter Ruben Kitchen tried a little experiment

with the goo by putting a match to it in a pan. When it erupted in flame, the startled sailor repeated the test for his divison boss, Lieutenant Fred Gary Weatherford. They decided that the alcohol in it was burning but that that would evaporate as the war paint dried on the skin. "What if," the men asked, "we get hit before the alcohol evaporates?!" Just another worry.

That night, as the carriers ran in to Japanese waters, that dreaded clang resounded through every space of the York: Bong! Bong! GQ!

"Damn those Japs!" Lieutenant Bob Lawrence, Radford's staff gunnery officer, griped to roomie Joe Bryan as he rolled out of bed, "Why the hell don't they stay home?"

"Look who's talking!" replied Joe.

"I know, but they started it!"

Yorktown's radar picked up the reported bogey at 30 miles, then a second one at 93 miles, but neither one closed, and at 2223 the Secure sounded. Half an hour later another contact rousted the gunners to their stations, but it too faded, and at midnight OOD Barney Lally passed the conn to the regular Navy, Lieutenant Thomas R. McClellan, Annapolis '43. An hour after midnight, the lookouts watched a bogey going down in flames off to the northwest—victim of an Enterprise night fighter.

March 18, 1945 was Passion Sunday, a week before Palm Sunday, two weeks before Easter Sunday. But before the day ended Yorktowners would rename it "Bomb Sunday." Seaman Stan Olter would remember it by keeping a one-day diary on the back of his copy of the Plan of the Day: "Today was the toughest we've ever had since being out here. We were under attack continuously day & night."

Heading north toward Point Option, Captain Combs kept the ship zigzagging amidst a windy, cloudy, wet, bone-chilling predawn blackness. Tom McClellan coolly executed course and speed changes, while CIC fed the bridge news about each bogey. At least the Intrepid was up ahead to draw the attention of the kamikazes, and the Big E's night fighters remained aloft. Astern lay Davison's TG 58.2 with the Hancock and Franklin.

Eight "raids" had been registered by the task force when finally at 0316 Combs recalled his gunners to Air Defense. Two minutes later Enterprise reported splashing one enemy plane, and soon the other raids faded from the radars. At 0330 Empty Evans roused the Air Department, and at 0345 Ben Born's reveille sounded for everyone else. Fifteen minutes after this McClellan passed the conn to

Japanese planes and hangars at Oita airfield on Kyushu, Japan, burn during attacks by *Yorktown* planes, March 18, 1945. Photo taken from a *York* aircraft.

Ensign Dick Drover. This lanky, soft-spoken peacetime architect from Arizona was one of Combs' veteran pros and would be kept at the conn all day long while the battle raged.

At 0410 a group of seven bogeys was picked up 60 miles to the west, but the contact was soon lost. At 0430 Flight Quarters sounded, and Herb Houck's air jockeys gathered in their ready rooms for the final briefing.

Two minutes before 0500 everyone topside saw firing by Davison's screen off the starboard quarter, and the ship went to GQ. Flares and gunfire now punctured the darkness off the port quarter. More and more raids were reported around the task force—though several were due to "window" being dropped, and several course changes had to be made. As the pilots manned their planes, the first glow of a cold dawn appeared in the east.

Chief Mueck of the admiral's staff prophesized gloomily to Bryan on the flag bridge, "We gonna get it today. Yessir, the old bucket's gonna take one. I saw it in the tea leaves. We gonna get it for sure!'' And to *Fortune* editor Del Paine he expressed his fear of dive bombers: ''I'd take ten torpedo attacks any day for one dive bombing. Those dive bombings they make me nervous.''

The first fighters were catapulted between 0529 and 0550, followed by the rest in a normal deck launch until 0558—in all 18 for the CAPs and 16 for the sweep. The latter proceeded to Saeki airfield in eastern Kyushu 150 miles to the northwest, found no air opposition and strafed. The first composite strike was sent off at 0658 to bomb, rocket and strafe Oita airfield on the Inland Sea coast, Herb Houck leading the flight but especially 16 Hellcats, Tony Schneider with ten 2Cs, and eleven torpeckers behind Byron Cooke. Forty-six planes from the *Intrepid* joined up on them. When they broke through the scattered clouds, they found no bandits but some 130 sitting ducks to strafe.

Rather than defending their own airfields, the Japanese apparently were sending their air strength against the fleet. So Admiral Mitscher ordered only VF-VBF sweeps against four airfields for the remainder of the day, and the VB and VT divisions stood down. The *York's* Hellcats shot down only one airborne bandit, a Val, but they lost one of their own to flak—Ensign Ardon Ives of VBF-9.

A relative quiet over the carriers at the 0612 sunrise—and a glorious one it was—led the *Yorktown* to modify the GQ half an hour later to Condition One Easy. The clouds that covered Kyushu did the same for much of TF 58, meaning that the kamikazes could hide from the CAP in the clouds until ready to commence their fatal plunges. All eyes topside strained to detect them.

''Bogey bearing 272, six miles, closing,'' reported CIC at 0715. It was coming in so low that radar had not seen it. GQ sounded.

Jesse Bradley: ''3 of our VF chased a plane across our bow believed to be a Judy. They went out a little ways and the Judy turned and came back down 000 degrees Rel. through the formation at about 200 ft. alt. And dropped a bomb on the forward end of the island of *Enterprise* about 2000 yards on our starboard beam.''

Before *Yorktown* could open fire, Judy's 600-pound bomb plummeted down but so low that it bounced off the Big E's Number One elevator. Joe Bryan saw flame spurt from her deck ''and we could see a plane swerving and weaving through spatters of smoke puffs. We waited for it to fall, but it vanished, still jinking. When we looked back

at the *Enterprise,* the fire was out.'' The fire had been the explosion of the bomb's detonator, broken off from the bomb to hit the island. This Judy had been a conventional bomber, not a zootsuiter, and it got away. George Wille: ''How he got in without making a contact on the radar no one knows. The nonchalance of it was revolting.''

Less than an hour later, an unannounced twin-engine Frances was spotted off the port quarter. When Bryan saw it over the destroyer *Melvin,* a passage from Melville's *Moby Dick* flashed through his mind: ''. . .My God, stand by me now!'' George Earnshaw's black mess stewards manning the 20mms aft responded on instinct. Del Paine witnessed the Frances passing through ''the fire of the ships to port at less than a thousand feet,'' where the mess boys exploded both engines with their very first burst. But Frances ''still headed directly for the carrier. The pilot was apparently dead. As the plane came on across the intervening space into the cone of tracers the tip of one wing started at last to disintegrate. That threw it into a steep bank . . . .''

George Wille: To ''this point he had flown a good course, but he swerved on being hit and paralleled our course for a few yards and then cut across our bow and in the general direction of the *Independence*. His altitude dropped and finally the plane went out of control and plunged in'' about 1500 yards on the starboard bow. It sank immediately.

''It was a beautifully terrifying sight to see—the plane with its flaming engines and its pilot trying to crash one and then another ship in its path.'' *Yorktown's* busy 5-inchers, however, had sprayed fragments over the *Melvin,* wounding two of her crew.

The time: 0801, and at 0803 the lookouts reported another plane 10 miles out, 090 degrees (T) and very high up, then another approaching from astern. The screen took the first one, a Frances, under fire as it headed toward the ''Decrepid'' 3000 yards to starboard. Jesse Bradley watched it ''hit so close that it started fires on her hangar and flight deck and caused some damage'' and one death. Poor *Intrepid*.

''Now comes up us,'' Chief Mueck snorted to Lieutenant Bryan. ''We couldn't get hit before the 'Decrepit' got it, but now's when it gets really rugged, and the bastards got all day to pour it on.'' Raids #35 and #37—single planes—now registered on the radar, closing.

All of a sudden, at 0822, several ships in the formation opened fire on a plane directly overhead, and five minutes later the *Yorktown* let go at it. The Earnshaw-Patterson teams scored again. Observed team member Bradley, "He lost control about half way down his dive and swerved off and crossed over and hit in the water on starboard bow."

But what kind of plane was it—a Hamp? As the victim burned in its plunge into the sea four miles away, the binoculars of the lookouts identified the stars of a Navy Hellcat. The realization was sickening.

Bradley: "A few minutes later a Jill dropped a bomb in the wake of a CVL on our port beam. He was shot down. This ship fired at it but does not claim it."

Another F6F—this from the *Yorktown*—now reported splashing a single-engine Myrt 20 miles out, one of three stopped by the CAP within moments.

The radar scopes cleared of unfriendly blips for the next four hours, allowing flight operations to proceed uninterrupted. Then, at 1237 came a fresh contact 44 miles to the east, followed by another 54 miles southeast.

1254: "General Quarters!"

"De-arm all planes on the double!" Pappy Harshman screamed over the bullhorn. "And jettison bombs and rockets!" No time to de-gas the planes ready for the next launch to Kyushu, but the airedales swiftly removed the heavy ordnance onto the bomb skids, pushed them to the edge of the deck and over the side—much to the horror of taxpaying *Fortune* editor Paine.

The destroyer screen opened fire all at once—along with the battleships, battle cruisers and light cruisers. It was 1306. One plane went down in flames, but three minutes later the other broke through. Plane captain Clyde "Goat" Moneyhun: "A Judy comes out of the clouds above us (the ceiling is around 5 or 6 hundred feet) and is on us before anything can open up. The twenties get to sling some lead before he pulls out of his dive. He drops a thousand lb. bomb (estimated to be that) and misses."

Paine: "The bomb sailed across the forward deck in plain view"—just clearing a 40mm mount on the port side—"and went into the water about sixty feet to port. It made a beautiful splash but failed to explode.

Joe Bryan, transfixed on the flag bridge, watched in awe "as a geyser of dirty brown foam spouted higher than our stack, about 75 feet on our port

beam [and splashed the flight deck]. The whole ship seemed to jump clear out of the water. The heavy steel hood of the compass leaped off its bracket, and the alidade was flung to the deck." The concussion knocked off Bryan's unstrapped steel helmet. Ed Wallace thought, "God was with us that time."

A minute later Judy finally succumbed to the *Yorktown's* guns and crashed into the sea 3000 yards off the port beam. The gunners let out a cheer, and the silence that followed was broken only by the empty 5-inch shell casings rolling around on the flight deck.

Now, without warning at 1317, the 20s and 40s opened up in thunderous rage, and all hands topside dropped flat to the deck. It was on the starboard bow now—another Judy at only 500 feet, sneaking in under the radar beam. Though hit by *Yorktown's* withering fire, she too dropped her bomb, which cascaded down close abeam on the starboard side near the gangway. The explosion shook and lifted the whole ship, momentarily tripping out the gyro compass down in the central damage control station five decks below the hangar.

For a full minute the men on the Bofors and Oerlikon guns followed Judy with their tracers as she passed parallel to the starboard side until she burst into flame, the tail blew off, and she plummeted into a watery grave 4000 yards off the starboard quarter. More cheers, and Admiral Radford ordered an emergency turn to prepare for the next onslaught. But these bogeys turned out to be friendlies.

"The gun team's really on the ball today," Chief Mueck rejoiced on the flag bridge, forgetting his dire earlier prediction of impending calamity. Others echoed him: "The Gunnery Department can eat at the head of our chow line any day of the week."

"I love 'em," signalman Red Jones announced. "I want to kiss every stinking son of a bitch on every stinking gun."

"Me too," Mueck agreed, "but I'd kiss 'em twice if they'd knock those bastards down *before* they dropped their eggs."

No-one topside liked bombing attacks. In the words of gunner Ed Spangler: "Every bomb you see released looks like you're gonna catch it. You think, 'This is it!'"

Though they couldn't see the falling bombs, everyone dogged down below shared this sentiment. In the ready rooms, pilots and aircrewmen played bridge with their flight gear on. They kept playing as the 5-inchers went off, and even the 40s didn't deter their game. But when the short-range 20s opened up, everybody dived under the steel tables.

The enlisted men down in the central station felt the same way. It was unnerving enough just to be trapped way down there, but the compartment beside them was the bomb magazine filled with 500-pounders, beneath them the gasoline, and above them another magazine stuffed with ammo. They appealed to talker Hank Bolden at Air Defense Forward to describe the action. In a slow Floridian drawl, he responded, "Well, things *is* gettin' a little excitin' up here."

By 1343 the radar screens were clear, and minutes later the fifth and final flight of the day took off—a dozen Hellcats to strike and photograph Kyushu and half a dozen more to fly a special rescue CAP to look for downed aviators. The last was off at 1358, and assistant LSO Lee Spaulding relieved Dick Tripp to bring aboard returning planes.

At 1420 Spaulding gave the cut to the first plane, then the second, but he waved off one plane whose tail hook was stuck in the up position. It was Gene Valencia in Fighter Number 57 who came around again and again and even a fourth time, but the tail hook stayed jammed. Captain Combs maneuvered the ship in preparation to let him make a barrier crash. As Air Group Nine's top ace, he was valuable property and rated special consideration.

In the midst of all this, the radio shack buzzed with a message from the radar picket destroyer *Heerman*: "Large group of bogeys, bearing 265 degrees True, distance 130 miles." Time enough to get Valencia aboard before this gang of Japs arrived, so *Yorktown* turned over formation guide to *Enterprise* and at 1456 began to line up for Valencia's crash landing. All ships now rang up battle speed of 25 knots.

The incredibly busy night and day had robbed everyone of sleep, so people grabbed a few winks whenever and wherever they could. Repair officer Fred Weatherford had a cup of coffee with dentist George Smith before checking on his men on the third deck. GQ trapped him below, so he stretched out on a bunk in the shipfitters shack. A popular guy, he was regarded by the men under him like a father.

Suddenly—at 1459—a cry from CIC: "Bogey, 045 degrees true, *eight* miles and closing!"

The gun directors swung the 5-inchers around, and they with the 40s and 20s erupted in a volcano of smoke, fire and thunder which rocked the ship and filled the sky. The time was exactly 1500, a

moment to be fixed in the minds of many a *Yorktowner* for eternity.

Marine First Lieutenant Barney Favaro was "back with the starboard Marine battery checking on the crew. I heard the 40mms open fire from the island batteries. I looked up and saw this big black bomb hurling out of the overcast." The release was under 1000 feet—a well executed attack.

Lieutenant Tom McClellan was at his station in charge of the Number One gun director as the plane, a Judy, "made his dive from nearly overhead, slightly starboard. He surprised us completely and I remember seeing the bomb release and float 'slowly' down barely missing the director and the bridge."

Lieutenant (jg) George Wille and two signalmen were on the starboard side of the signal bridge: "Again we all hit the deck, and this time the chief and I started for the hatch to get inside, Jim Johnston being one step ahead of us, and at that moment all three of us were tumbled over by a gust of air. The gunfire drowned everything else out."

The bomb hit the starboard side of the signal bridge—too close to Jesse Bradley for comfort—"on the deck above my head about 10 ft. behind me." Wille: "It passed right on through the deck at an angle, taking a squawk box, hatch door, and miscellaneous equipment with it." Obviously the bomb had a delay-action fuse as it did not detonate—yet. Instead, it left a 21" x 39" hole in the deck, the metal "punctured like a piece of soft cheese. The box was smashed in minute pieces and a ventilation duct was also severed."

Seamen First Elmer Jekel and Powell Barnette were firing away with the Number Seven 20mm battery as the bomb ricochetted off the incinerator smoke stack, slashing it and two steam pipes, then slammed through their splinter shield, leaving a 20" hole and passing through both men. Jekel's body was cut in half at the waist. He started to scream, but instantly blacked out with the trunk of his torso hanging from the gun into which he was strapped. Barnette had both legs severed at the knees, and he collapsed to the deck.

The bomb, having been deflected slightly away from the hull, detonated about 15 feet above the water and 30 feet outboard of the hangar deck at the shipfitters shack at Frame 121, having travelled about 150 feet from where it first struck the ship.

The blast blew a hole in the side of the hull, demolished the shipfitters shack, killed the sleeping Fred Weatherford there instantly, and sent shrapnel into the radar repair room just below the hangar, killing aviation radar technician Ed Sherman.

Another technician, Danny Carveth, had poked his head out of a porthole there just as the bomb ignited. The blast hit him full-face, bits of shrapnel digging into this face and eyes, and he was blown back, convulsed in searing agony. His shipmate Bob Lueck of the air group had both arms broken and his body peppered with shrapnel. A fire erupted in this space.

The flying shrapnel penetrated other spaces, wounding more men, but none quite so ignominiously as a little Russian they called "Rubles"—Seaman First John Gryshewich—hit on the knee by shrapnel while sitting in the head taking a crap.

The explosion occurred under the Number Seven quad 40mm mount and destroyed two of its guns. A foot-long five-and-a-half pound chunk of shrapnel struck Gunners Mate Bob Davis, fractured his left arm, tore open his guts, and caused his intestines to spew out eight or nine feet away from his body. But they were not severed. Pat Patterson, with

heads-up thinking, rushed over to the slight, blond-headed kid, carefully gathered up the intestines and piled them gently on top of the wound for the medicos to treat. Half of the piece of shrapnel stuck out of Davis' stomach.

At the same instant Davis was felled, ammo feeder Ted Johnson was blown several feet into the air backwards and came back down on top of the gun. But as one of the ship's pugilists, he was only bruised. "If I would have gone forward I would have went down 90 feet to the water. That made me wish I was home."

The adjacent Marines' 20mm gallery at the after end of the island was also devastated by the blast. The concussion flattened the gyrenes and wounded two. Hot shrapnel tore into the face of Private First Class Francis Morse and the leg of PFC Ed Sarkisian.

Gunners Mate Harold Brode held his breath as the shrapnel punctured the shell casings of the 40mm ammo at his gun, but the stuff did not explode. The crew quickly flooded several magazines, while ammo being passed up from the

Flames lick up the starboard side of the *Yorktown* just after the Jap bomb has detonated above the waterline just outside of the hull, March 18, 1945. The conical dome is a radar scanner to fill the overhead gap left by the other radars, installed at Bremerton. Courtesy of Peter D. Joers

storage areas in the bomb elevators was thrown over the side; thankfully, neither did any of it go off. Shrapnel ruptured the hydraulic lines of the Number Five after 5-inch mount, freezing it and igniting its oil.

Airedale Charlie Murray found the hangar deck above the third deck fire too hot to stand on, but the heat had activated the automatic sprinkler system which soon drenched the hangar and all its planes and mechs until the water was a couple of inches deep.

Terrified though the surviving gunners were, their training and instincts kept them blazing away at their assailant. Soon after they hit the Judy, it broke up on the pullout, whereupon its two occupants hit the silk. The enraged black stewards mates in the 20s aft took them under fire and succeeded in killing the gunner. The pilot, however, landed in the drink just after the wreckage of his plane and was soon picked up by a can.

Barney Lally's firemen took fewer than ten minutes to extinguish the fire, but most of the crew didn't even know whether or not the ship had been hit. Up on the bridge men groggily pulled themselves together, trying to comprehend what had happened.

After one look Chief Mueck came around the forward end of the flag bridge, drained of energy and hardly able to speak. Motioning toward what he had just seen on the gun mount below, he murmured to Joe Bryan, "Jesus Christ, sir, it looks like a butcher shop!"

"What do you mean?" demanded Joe, "Did we take one? Where?"

"Take one? *Take* one! You should see the mess. This guy's legs, and the blood, and—Jesus Christ Almighty!" And half to himself, "I knew we'd get it today! I knew it! I told 'em!"

The corpsmen of Battle Dressing Station Number Six had sprung into action, as had Father Joe Moody, whose battle station was above the shattered Repair 3 shack. Running onto the flight deck, he was drawn to screams around the corner of the island. It was PFC Morse, hands to blood-drenched eyes. When Moody identified himself, Morse cried, "Father, I am blind!" With three corpsmen and a stretcher, Moody hastened Morse forward to Battle Dressing One.

But en route a sailor yelled to him, pointing up to the stricken 20mm gun where the bomb had first struck, "Bad ones up there, Father! A lot of 'em!"

Leaving the corpsmen to tend to Morse, the historian-priest bolted up the ladder to a blood-covered gun platform and adjacent ammo-clipping room, where six men lay sprawled out, two without legs. As others brought stretchers, Moody leaned over the legless Elmer Jekel. "What is your religion, son?"

Jekel opened his eyes only long enough to whisper, "Jewish."

With his tall, strong frame Joe tenderly lifted the half-body of the boy onto the stretcher, and with three sailors bore him down to the nearest dressing station on the flight deck. There he found Dr. Benny Bond, Air Group Nine's flight surgeon, applying bandages to a wounded man's arm.

"Here's a bad case for you."

Bond took but one look, "He's gone. Put him aside."

The next stretcher down the ladder carried Powell Barnette, also minus legs but fully conscious. Barnette, a strong, tough individual, had told his rescuers, "Take care of the others. I'm alright." But he was not, and Moody also asked him his religion. Barnette answered that he was Protestant, and Moody, seeing Reverend George Wright helping Dr. Benny, patted Barnette on the shoulder, "Your chaplain's right ahead, son. Keep your chin up!"

Hastening up the ladder, Moody found the other four men lying amidst blood on the clipping room deck. The two most seriously wounded were Catholic, whereupon he anointed them then helped get them down the ladder in stretchers to Dr. Benny's station. The other two were able to walk there by themselves.

Most of the 23 dead and wounded had been brought into Bond's tiny first-aid center, leading him to appeal to Moody to help him get the men down to Sick Bay on the third deck, under the hangar. Moody ordered George Wright to collect stretchers and called up Pappy Harshman for permission to use the Number Three plane elevator. Granted. But with planes operating, fires being fought, and the ship at GQ under attack, the chaplains could only get six men to move the wounded below—themselves, two corpsmen and two volunteers. And there were 12 stretcher cases.

They must make four trips—two men to each basket-style litter—from the elevator, all the way forward to an open hatch in the fo'c'sle, then down two decks and all the way back aft to Sick Bay, undogging and redogging watertight doors in the GQ condition. Furthermore, they had to shelter their wounded from the sprinklers and crawl under the many planes, dragging and shoving the litters along the flooded hangar.

One of the first to go on the meandering journey was the badly-mauled Powell Barnette, his legs and a great deal of blood gone and he already being administered blood plasma. But who would hold up the bottle of plasma during the trip?

"Hand it to me," said Barnette himself, "I'll hold it!" Guts, pure and simple.

One of the first men into the gutted shipfitters shack was Eugene Murphy. Inadvertantly stopped from going there for idle chatter with a shipmate only minutes before the blast, he had narrowly escaped death. After Lieutenant Weatherford's body was taken out, Murphy found a hand lying in the corner which he was told to throw overboard, and did. Murphy's bunk had been demolished, the clothes in his locker soaked with saltwater. Luckily, Weatherford was the only fatality there.

Three men were dead and twenty others wounded, five critically. In addition to Barnette, Lueck and Carveth of the latter were Yeoman Third Alois Zacharewicz and Gunner Bob Davis.

Pharmacists Mate Third Carmine Pierro arrived at the damaged quad mount to find Davis' guts piled on his stomach and the hunk of shrapnel protruding out of it. Realizing Davis' life hung in the balance, Pierro decided to do emergency surgery himself right at the gun mount. Applying morphine and sulpha, he carefully removed the shrapnel and replaced the stomach organs, thereby saving Davis' life.

The steel deck of Sick Bay was smeared with blood as the surgeons got to work. Navy doctrine prescribed that the least wounded be treated first in order to be returned to duty as soon possible in order to fight again, but senior surgeon Jack Smith, being a humanitarian, bent the rules to try to save the worst hit first and ordered Drs. Glen Holmes and Harry Lenhardt and their corpsmen to do the same.

Topside, Pappy Harshman still had Gene Valencia orbiting in Fox 57 with a jammed tailhook and a handful of fighters he wanted to launch to help ward off the attackers. So he told Valencia to land in the water. Valencia obeyed and set his Cat down just ahead of the *Intrepid.* Destroyer *McNair* plucked him out of the drink within minutes.

Pandemonium reigned everywhere on the *Yorktown.* Fear had been a constant factor throughout the charmed life of the Lucky Y, but she was charmed no more, and the boys were scared—scared silly, scared shitless; words could not describe it. Harold Syfrett and the guys down in Central Control felt entombed. The gunners near the blast were frozen with terror. Dear God, dear God . . . .

Old timers among the crew took out their anger on whatever scapegoat they could find. On the signal bridge Red Jones railed at the battlewagons and battle cruisers over credit for splashing the Judy. "If anybody shot him down, you can be goddamn sure it was us! Those big bastards over there"—gesturing—"they couldn't hit a bull in the ass with a banjo, and I bet by God they claim it was them that did it all! You watch what I tell you!"

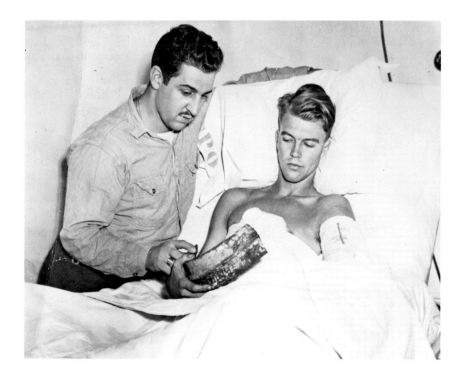

Gunners Mate Bob Davis looks at the 12 1/2-inch, 5 1/2-pound piece of bomb fragment that corpsman Carmine Pierro (Left) took out of his abdomen, then replaced his stomach organs, after the bomb hit, March 18, 1945. Courtesy of Carmine A. Pierro

While the other signalmen raged and bellyached in agreement, Red abruptly shouted, pointing up, "Bogey diving!"

Everyone on the bridge hit the deck—except Joe Bryan, who stared numbly, trying to see the newest attacker. In disbelief, he finally trusted his eyes—and voice: "That's no bogey. Look at it! It's a bird."

Geez! The men turned on Jones. "Now I know where I seen you before," one of them berated him, "you blind bastard! You umpired a game between the Nats and the Yanks....!"

Speaking of baseball, ex-chucker George Earnshaw remarked to Del Paine that these constant attacks seemed "like those days when I would throw 'em at Babe Ruth with all I had and Babe Ruth would knock 'em right back at me!"

The bogeys continued to appear on the radar screens, and Cyclops Ballinger directed the CAP to the intercepts. Pappy Harshman respotted his deck, and at 1556 he started catapulting more fighters. Half an hour later the *Intrepid* reported splashing a bogey, and at one minute before 1700 firing was observed astern by the *Franklin* and *Hancock* group.

As the sun dipped in the western sky, the last chickens were called in and began landing at 1722. A floating mine was reported just outside the formation, and the *McNair* scurried over to detonate it with gunfire. The last plane came aboard at 1808, and the sun set ten minutes after that—"in a soft haze of gray and gold" admired Bryan.

Chief Mueck had Bryan's ear: "I told 'em early this morning. I told 'em we'd take one. I knew it. I'm never wrong."

"How about tomorrow? Or can't you tell without your tea leaves?"

"Tomorrow? Hell, tomorrow'll be easy. That is, if we live through tonight's torpedo attack."

Jesse Bradley told his diary: "I don't guess we will get any sleep again tonight."

Yorktown didn't have long to wait. In the fading twilight, at 1844, CIC announced: "Bogey, 095 degrees True, eleven miles, very low." The next minute the cans off the port bow opened fire, and bogey did not close. Then at 1857 another came in from the opposite direction, also eleven miles out, and the screen on the starboard bow drove it off. And twenty minutes after that Davison's *Franklin* group on the starboard beam discouraged yet another.

Carl Ballinger reported the CIC radars clear of bogeys at 1930, and Captain Combs lost little time in going to One Easy to try to give the crew and

pilots some sleep. Finally at 2000, Ensign Dick Drover left the conn, which he had had for eighteen consecutive hours. The officers repaired to the wardroom for a sumptuous roast chicken dinner, some like Joe Bryan after a refreshing shower to wash off the "Elizabeth Arden" anti-flash facial goo, some like Cooper Bright without taking time to clean it off. "Hey, Skinhead," Cyclops greeted Bright, "where've you been all day—taking it easy? First time I ever saw you with any color in your cheeks!"

Padre Wright paid a visit to the stewards' compartment, where the excited men were trying to digest a quick meal before being called back to their guns. Their own preacher, "Brother" Davenport, had the Easter season in mind as he announced to them, "Chaplain Wright is down here to observe our Last Supper. Now, gentlemen, this may *be* your last supper, and them's the preachingest words I ever did say!"

An almost first quarter moon bathed the sea until midnight, and at 2226 lookouts at Air Defense Forward sighted gunfire on the horizon. It was Jocko Clark's *Hornet* group, which nailed another interloper. *Yorktown's* tired gunners returned to their posts, but all they saw were the exhausts of the *Enterprise* night fighters flying around.

Bomb Sunday ended with more gunfire in the distance, a day in which Earnshaw's and Patterson's gun crews had expended 123 rounds of 5-inch ammo, 2234 of 40mm and a phenomenal 6455 of 20mm—the latter so great because the bogeys had only been detected at short range. Jesse Bradley of the 40s: "CAP shot down 9 Japs and ships' AA got 6. This ship got 4 ½ . Three Judys, one Frances and part of a Jill. I fired about 100 rounds at the first two Judys and I believe I got some hits."

Bomb disposal officer Carl Obenauf retraced the course of the bomb, collected and inspected the large number of fragments, and deduced the projectile to have been a 250 kilogram (550 to 600 pound) semi-armor-piercing bomb with about a .025 second fuse. Later interrogation of the captured pilot revealed that the Judy had been one of 20 operating with the Japanese Navy's Fifth Air Fleet out of Kokobu, Kyushu, all day long to bomb then crash into the American carriers. He had done very well indeed and was given the decent kind of treatment on the destroyer *Heerman* that Pop Condit was *not* getting at Sumida.

Tiny Patterson should have been jubilant at the success of his gunners this day. Instead, he was grief-stricken over the death of his roommate, Fred

Weatherford. So were the men of Repair 1 Division and Weatherford's fellow Georgian and friend Yeoman Gene Braswell, the captain's writer. Patterson must inventory Weatherford's effects, soon mailed to his widow, but Pat overlooked one item: a camera Weatherford had stored at the Photo Lab.

When the camera was brought to the captain's office with a query as to its disposition, Yeoman Braswell volunteered to personally deliver it at the first opportunity when he went home to Georgia on leave. This he would do in December, returning for a visit to the family the following spring. At that time he saw a photo of Weatherford's sister Betty, which led him to look her up at college the next fall. They would fall in love and eventually be married. Tragedy in war was turned into a lifetime of happiness for two people and their offspring.

But there was only tragedy in Sick Bay this night of March 18/19, 1945. Holy Joes Moody and Wright tried to ignore the blood under their feet and the roar of the ammunition hoists as they assisted the corpsmen in giving blankets, water and cigarettes to the wounded. Both chaplains prayed with and for these brave boys, talked with them of home, and took down letters which might prove to be their last.

Powell Barnette, the legless tower of strength who had held the plasma flask on the long journey down to Sick Bay, told Moody of his folks at home as he lay on the operating table. But his body could not overcome its injuries, and a few minutes after midnight Barnette died. The priest administered last rites.

Joe turned his attention to Bob Lueck—whose first and middle names were for another great fighter, Robert Lee, though Lueck was from Akron, Ohio. The surgeons did not regard his two broken arms and abdominal shrapnel wounds as particularly dangerous, so they turned their attention to others in worse shape. But Lueck looked awful. The blood on his face had been dried by the smoke on top of the anti-flash ointment. Moody asked him, "Want a beauty treatment?"

"Sure," Lueck smiled.

As Joe began washing off the boy's face, Lueck asked, "Father, what are you spending so much time with me for?"

"Are you a Catholic?"

"Not too good a one."

"Well, we won't worry about that now."

"I'll tell you a funny thing, Father," Lueck remarked after a pause. "I'm glad this happened to me. I'm completely at peace with God for the first time in my life." Moody told him he would write to his mom and tell her her son was O.K.

The minutes passed, and after midnight Lueck repeated himself, "I'm glad this happened to me. It's made it easy for me to do what I've been wanting to do for a long time—be part of the church."

He lost consciousness, and the doctors discovered too late that he had been hit in the pancreas. The life within him slowly ebbed away as his body succumbed to shock. Robert Lee Lueck died at 0400—at peace with his Maker.

Five men were gone—Weatherford, Sherman, Jekel, Barnette and Lueck. Dr. Smith, an eye specialist, labored mightily on the eyes of Danny Carveth and Francis Morse but could partially save only one of Carveth's and not the injured one of Morse. Bob Davis, his entrails saved by Carmine Pierro's emergency treatment, was sewed up by the doctors and would be on a liquid diet again in three days. Similarly, the other 15 wounded men pulled through.

Repair crews spent the night making emergency repairs to the areas damaged by the bomb—from the island down to the evaporators in the engine room. The explosion had jarred loose a number of things there—and incidently destroyed the little still the men had had operating. The space reeked like a brewery!

Commander Born rushed an abbreviated Plan of the Day for March 19 into print for circulation, adding, "A WELL DONE TO THE GUNNERS. WE STRIKE AGAIN TODAY, IT MAY BE ANOTHER TOUGH DAY! HEADS UP! KEEP ALERT! USE YOUR HEAD!"

Captain Combs had fire marshal Barney Lally take the conn at midnight but told Dick Drover to sleep while he could and be ready for the duty at 0400. Drover had done such a helluva good job the day before that his reward would again be OOD another *full* day! The virtues of excellence.

The gunners tried to sleep at their mounts but were generally unsuccessful as bogeys kept reappearing on the screen; occasional flares were dropped by Jap snoopers to burn on the water; sporadic firing was observed in the distance; and possible surfaced submarine and surface ship contacts added to the confusion. Theda Combs ordered repeated course changes throughout the night, and

Lally had the ship's red truck lights switched on repeatedly to avoid collisions with other ships in the formation.

The exec's detailed Plan was scrapped from the first, for the crew was ordered to an 0230 steak breakfast—an hour early—so the men would have food in their stomachs should GQ be unexpectedly required. After that, only horsecock sandwiches would be possible during the day. Needless to say, the men failed to see the point of missing another hour's sleep, and the griping in the chow line was loud and long.

Sure enough, though, at 0332 the gunners were called to Air Defense as six to ten bogeys appeared 45 miles to the south. Tension reigned not only at the guns but, worse, in the buttoned-up spaces where no-one could see anything. Men fidgeted and smoked cigarettes in reluctant anticipation of an attack. Ensign Drover took the conn at 0400, and forty minutes later the *Enterprise* reported splashing a snooper. 0506—more flares fell, ten miles to the west.

"Pilots, man your planes!"

"Hello, Quebec. This is Russia," flag duty officer Joe Bryan called the task group on behalf of Admiral Radford, after putting the order to change course into shackle code. "Signals execute to follow, turn shackle Mike Charlie Baker unshackle. I say again, turn...," and repeated it. "Acknowledge."

Each ship in the group gave a "Wilco," and Bryan called again, "Hello, Quebec. This is Russia. Stand by.... Execute!"

Davison's TG 58.2 of *Franklin* and *Hancock* opened fire at snoopers at 0513, and six minutes after that the *Yorktown* went to GQ. At 0540 the first plane in a 16-plane fighter sweep was catapulted into the first traces of morning twilight. Bill May finished the catapult launches, then Junior Meyer waved the rest off the deck by 0600.

Targets were the airfields bordering the Inland Sea at Matsuyama and Saijo on Shikoku and Kure Naval base on Honshu, 225 miles to the northwest. They flew along the coast of Shikoku and over the heart of the Inland Sea to get there and back.

Yorktown planes bomb and strafe a Jap cargo ship southeast of Kure. One plane is recovering at the top of the picture after scoring a direct hit, while others approach in formation.

0610: "Sunrise! Light ship!" The light baffles came down, yet the steel battle ports went up as everyone braced for an attack, but it never came. As sailors shivvered at their stations, the bullhorn barked, "Now, secure from GQ. Set Condition One Easy and Material Condition Modified Affirm."

Pappy Harshman spotted Strike 1A to hit the Kure Naval Air depot and airfield—15 Hellcats, 11 Avengers and 9 Helldivers, all led by air group skipper Herb Houck. The first two planes were spotted on the cat, the rest in line for a powered launch.

Enemy planes were known to be in the vicinity but none within 20 miles of this task group. So Empty Evans gave the green light, at 0659 the first two planes were shot off, and a minute later the torpeckers started lumbering down the deck.

"*Enterprise* has opened fire!" a talker yelled from the flag bridge. "A bogey is diving on the formation from 260! Alert! Alert!"

As GQ sounded, the talker announced, "Bogey is an F4U!"—the U.S. Navy's gull-winged fighter now being introduced aboard the carriers. But he immediately pressed the earphones against his head, "What's that? Bogey 316, 12 miles?" It was 0707, and within seconds the tin cans on the port beam opened fire. Launching officer Meyer took no notice, and one by one the 2Cs followed the Turkeys into the air.

All eyes topside fixed on the *Franklin,* also launching planes as the zootsuiters roared in. George Wille: "We saw her group firing and black smoke blossomed up from a hit, followed by dense clouds of the stuff. All of her planes were gassed and bombed and they burned terribly—they were poised for a deckload launch.

"The whole thing looked like a fountain in Hell, and the ship was wracked by at least 30 explosions accompanied by great rolls of flame. We thought that her magazines and gas and oil went up, but apparently they did not."

Yorktown gun crews, signalmen, airedales and bridge personnel strained to get a better look at the conflagration on the *Franklin.* Bryan trained his binoculars on her and saw "a tremendous plume of black smoke rising from her deck. Every few seconds there was a gush of fire, and the whole ship quaked. I counted nine explosions before she fell astern, hull down over the horizon."

Airedale Joel Connell counted 35 explosions, dentist Smith estimated "about 30", plane captain Goat Moneyhun tallied 16 "big explosions," gunner Ed Wallace 21, Kenny Parkinson 26; no-one on the *Yorktown* could believe the *Franklin* would survive as she just seemed to "go up." Gunner Jesse Bradley: "It just about tore the island and all the flight deck off." Radar operator Ed Brand wrote, "She was completely gutted, and is just a floating hulk."

"That's all brother!" Red Jones exclaimed on the signal bridge. "We can tell 'Big Ben' goodbye. This'll be a different ship when the word gets around."

"What word?" Joe Bryan asked innocently.

"About losing the Big Ben. She's got Air Group 5 aboard, and we used to have 'em."

"That's right," Chief Mueck chimed in. "There ain't a man on the *Yorktown* who didn't have a friend on the Big Ben."

Air Group Five as *Yorktown's* charter air group had been the only one which the ship's company had gotten to know well, although this fight for survival was creating a close bond with Air Group Nine. Not only were several ex-*Yorktown* fliers killed or wounded on the *Franklin,* but among the more than 700 dead was Captain Buster Isbell, prospective commanding officer of the Fighting Lady. Captain Combs would have to stay on longer.

None of this was known on the *York* for some time, as the Big Ben disappeared over the horizon. Herb Houck's last fighters got off by 0716, and everyone waited for the zootsuiters to close on this task group. When they didn't come but continued to threaten Davison's exposed ships around the *Franklin,* Admiral Mitscher ordered Radford to transfer the *Enterprise* and some escorts from his task group to take the *Franklin's* place. They left the formation at 0910.

The Japs kept it up. One bomber planted a bomb on the *Wasp* in Jocko Clark's group, killing over 100 men. An *Independence* fighter shot down a Jill 38 miles from the group, and a *Langley* VF got another at 60. The kamikazes zeroed in on Davison's *Franklin* group the rest of the morning—and throughout the afternoon. But they failed to finish her off, while smart damage control succeeded in dousing the fires and saving Big Ben. George Wille spoke for the *Yorktown's* entire crew as he reflected, "Thank Heaven for looking after the ship, and I think that despite the bomb hit (yesterday), we are still very fortunate. We all hope and pray that our good luck will continue."

But it wasn't just luck that made the *Yorktown* a superior ship to the *Franklin,* as the men came to realize. The Fighting Lady was Number One for many concrete reasons. Unlike the *Franklin,* the

York never armed bombs and rockets on the hangar deck but only on the flight deck. *Yorktown* had been at GQ when she had been hit, while Big Ben had not. Many men killed on the *Franklin* had been in the chow line, whereas *Yorktown* had fed her crew at 0230; the men would never again gripe about early chow! And the Big Ben had a pompous martinet of a skipper, Leslie E. Gehres, who now tried to shift blame for *Franklin's* losses to some of his crew. Air Group Five's leading chief, P.P. Day, rated *Franklin* not even 30 percent as good as *Yorktown*; he now finagled a transfer.

The *Yorktown* and *Intrepid* provided CAP for the *Franklin* and *Enterprise,* still hurt from her hit the day before, as the two flattops crawled away toward Ulithi. So at 1535 battle cruisers *Guam* and *Alaska* pulled out of the task formation to accompany them back, leaving Radford's group without their many valuable anti-aircraft barrels. Yet this didn't bother the proud *Yorktown*ers. Joe Bryan even composed a ditty expressing his contempt for the heavies:

> *Wisconsin, Missouri, Alaska* and *Guam,*
> Sleep tight! The *Yorktown* will keep you from harm.

Red Jones agreed, "If it wasn't for *our* gunners—Jesus!"

Air Group Nine's airborne gunners and bombers were active all day too. The dawn fighter sweep, the first of three to Kure, ran into a surprisingly aggressive gang of Jap interceptors over the target and shot down three Zekes, a Frank and a Jack. But Lieutenant (jg) Dick Prior was shot down in flames over Saijo. The follow-up composite strike left anchored Japanese battleships and carriers at Kure to other squadrons and concentrated on the Kure air depot and Hiro airfield. The day ended with a flight of five Marine Corps F4U Corsairs from the *Franklin* being taken aboard—the first time this plane type had landed on the *York* in 14 months.

Withdrawing to refuel on March 20, the ship prepared for a late-morning funeral of its fallen shipmates. Read the Plan of the Day:

—OUR HONORED DEAD—
We pray to God that their loved ones will understand the real sacrifice they have made. Their loss is beyond the expression of words. They shall always be a part of each one of us and this ship we call "The Fighting Lady."

Just to be safe, Captain Combs kept Dick Drover at the conn for 12 more consecutive hours. A misidentified friendly brought the ship to GQ, which caused the last rites to be postponed to the afternoon. After lunch all crewmen who could be spared attended this first large burial at sea since the fire off Kwajalein 16 months before.

Both chaplains conducted the short service, which finished with "Taps" as the remains of Weatherford, Jekel, Barnette, Sherman and Lueck were committed to the deep. Another false bogey contact failed to interrupt the ceremony. Moments after it ended, however, firing was observed from Sherman's TG 58.3 off the port quarter, whereupon the ship returned to GQ.

The Japs were trying to complete their destruction of the crippled *Franklin, Wasp* and *Enterprise* as they retired and to inflict damage on Sherman's *Essex* group. Of 35 enemy planes which attacked during the afternoon, one scored another hit on the Big E, while Sherman's CAP repelled the rest some 40 miles northwest of the *Yorktown*. One zoot-suiter lunged at the *Hancock* in this group but just missed and smashed into the destroyer *Halsey Powell* alongside, causing heavy damage.

The excitement over by 1600, two cans moved up on either side of the *York* and threw across lines—the *Hazelwood* to deliver mail and the *Heerman* three Jap prisoners, two from the sunken fishing boat, the other the very same sonofabitch who had dropped the bomb on the *Yorktown*. The pilot came across first, suffering only from a torn shirt, but the sailors had been badly wounded and had to be hoisted across wrapped in blankets and basket litters.

Del Paine found the men on the fantail looking at them "curiously but with little comment. In the midst of the operation GQ sounded but the transfer went on. An officer on the destroyer insisted on getting back his blankets, as well as twenty-five gallons of ice cream. . .for the return of a pilot. The wounded prisoners were given a cabin by themselves in the crowded sick bay." Marine Eddie Murphy just shoved the pilot down the ladder to the brig.

The GQ was in response to a reported bogey spotted visually in a bright, sunny sky four miles to the west and very high up. *Hazelwood* cast off her lines just as Earnshaw's gun crews opened fire. *Heerman* waited until the POW transfer was completed before breaking her lines clear, and the guns pounded away, then stopped. Bogey turned out to be very high indeed—if not a star, probably the planet Venus in the unusually deep blue skies.

There was nothing funny about it. For at several 20mm and 40mm mounts near where the bomb had hit the ship two days before sat several young sailors, frozen with fear. The trauma of the bombing, plus watching the *Franklin* go up, had simply paralyzed their reflexes. An understanding Captain Combs lost no time in transferring them to other duties below decks—one all the way down to Central Damage Control, still a hotspot but out of sight of Jap bombers. Among the volunteers called for to man these exposed guns was Seaman First Ed Spangler. He would do anything to be topside when attacks were coming in, just to see what was going on.

As the sun set at 1811, Joe Bryan noted the anxiety coming over the flag bridge. Commander Andy Jackson complained about having to detach a can to deliver photos to Admiral Mitscher, pro-

bably for the press. And Chief Mueck figured that the clear skies which showed a star in daylight would do wonders for a first quarter moon; it was in the very same phase that had lit up the ship during the December 1943 retirement from Kwajalein, with moonset around 0100. This night would be no piece of candy—or pogey bait in Navy parlance. "Know what we are?" Mueck griped. "We're not cannon-fodder; we're *bogey* bait."

How right he was! Though the ship secured from GQ at 1912, Carl Ballinger picked up a bogey two hours later which brought the *York's* crewmen back to their battle stations. He designated it Raid One and began relaying the information to all interested parties—the ready rooms, the bridge, the flag bridge, gun control and the guns themselves, where the talkers repeated each report.

Kure's naval air station and adjacent industrial targets take Air Group Nine hits while two Jap carriers and a half-battleship (recently arrived from the South China Sea where Halsey had hunted it) are attacked by other groups in the harbor beyond, 19 March 1945.

2105: "Bogey 60 [miles], bearing 285 [degrees True]."

A pause of 17 minutes, then: "Bogey, bearing 215."

On the port beam, Del Paine noted activity by Sherman's ships: "Firing could be seen, sometimes in one spot, sometimes almost around the horizon. The moon shuttled in and out of the clouds and the night was warm enough to be pleasant." The screen opened fire.

"Bogey 25," a talker on the island announced bogey's withdrawal, "Son of a bitch is getting yellow—bearing 260!" Raid One opened the distance and fled.

2146: "Bogey 75, bearing 355."

Raid Two.

2216: "Bogey 20, bearing 325."

The destroyers on the starboard beam opened fire, followed by Sherman's group. Bogey opened, then closed, then opened again. Yellow.

Theda Combs zigzagged the ship, more raids appeared, and no-one got much sleep for the third night running.

2336: "Bogey 15, bearing 260."

Raid Six.

Joe Bryan: "The task group off to starboard started to fire heavily. Four flares blossomed in the sky to port"—the port bow on the horizon—"and suddenly the *Missouri* loosed four thunderclaps. When a nearby ship opens fire at night, the muzzle flash warns you to brace yourself for the *slam!*, but the 'Mighty Mo' was using flashless powder, and I jumped like a stung mule."

When one of the battleship's rounds erupted directly in front of the moon, George Earnshaw's voice boomed down from Air Defense Forward, "Sure as hell, they'll claim another plane shot down!"

Raid Six opened, the moon dipped lower in the west, and Combs made several emergency turns. Minutes after midnight Pappy Harshman catapulted two night fighters, control of which Admiral Radford passed to Admiral Clark in TG 58.1 and Jocko's FDO Charlie Ridgway. A good combination, for Ridgway picked up a bogey 35 miles due north at 0312 and directed *Yorktown*'s night fighter leader Lieutenant Dale Knopf to the intercept. Thirteen minutes later Knopf shot bogey out of the sky—a Betty.

But that ended the threat, and the men read a heartwarming message from Mitscher: "ALL HANDS IN THE TASK FORCE FOUGHT MAGNIFICENTLY AS ONLY VETERANS CAN. YOUR COUNTRY AND YOUR FAMILIES WILL BE PROUD OF THE BATTLE YOU HAVE JUST FOUGHT AGAINST HIROHITO'S POOR BEST."

"A nice commendation," Seaman Stan Olter wrote, "but the Japs are still giving us plenty of hell—and we're even 400 miles from Tokyo today. Where the hell are they coming from!?" From Kyushu, 300 miles away, for Bettys had that great range, forcing the task force to continue to cover the withdrawal of the cripples.

"Right now," March 21, gunner Wallace noticed, the crew was "pooped from lack of rest and sleep due to the continuous attacks night and day." Throughout the morning Radford's ships were only observers to the other task groups absorbing zoot-suiter attacks until 1300 when a *Yorktown* fighter on CAP registered the kill of a Peggy. When blips of many bandits began to fill *Yorktown*'s radars, the ship went to GQ and the mood among Radford's staff worsened.

"Flag bridge," a voice finally came from the tube. "Flag bridge, CIC has just reported that our fighters intercepted the raid and shot down 14 Bettys and four fighters, and the rest have beat it."

A cheer filled the room as the tension broke, and one exuberant swab exclaimed, "Them goddamn Japs, that'll teach 'em! What did I tell you?"

Chief Mueck cut him off acidly: "What did *you* tell us? You didn't tell us a goddamn thing, bud! You didn't need to tell us. Your goddamn teeth were chattering like a goddamn icebox. Your teeth told us plenty, but *you* didn't tell us a goddamn thing."

Radford's task group now broke away to cover the crippled *Halsey Powell* and to refuel. During the morning the oiler *Escalante* pumped across 425,000 gallons of fuel oil and 85,190 gallons of avgas. Admiral Mitscher offered Captain Combs the chance to return to Ulithi to make repairs, but according to George Smith, "We refused to leave the force, patching up the blasted areas temporarily."

"In the last four days," airedale Joel Connell told his diary, "we have had very little sleep. It's 2000 now and that's the earliest we have been secured in five days and nights."

March 22, the last chance for a breather, brought exciting news. In the words of Smith, "We have been notified that our scoreboard now displays one 'Oscar,' the Academy Award for our movie 'The Fighting Lady.'"

"Today," March 23, said the Plan of the Day, "we start on one of the most important phases of our present operations at sea. That is taking of the NANSEI-SHOTO [Ryukyu] Islands [principally Okinawa]. With these islands in our hands we will be able to control all the sea lanes across the Japanese Ill Begotten Empire. WE STRIKE AGAIN TODAY. GIVE 'EM HELL! HEADS UP! KEEP ALERT! USE YOUR HEAD!''

Just after midnight, Air Defense Forward saw "two distinct flashes which appeared to be explosions on port beam on same bearing as U.S.S. HAGGARD.'' This can had attacked and rammed a Jap sub it had forced to the surface with depth charges—the *RO-41*, which exploded and sank with all hands. The blast damaged the *Haggard* sufficiently to require her to return to Ulithi.

Then, just before dawn, with junior staff radio officer Lieutenant Harwell Proffitt on watch, a little Marine came running in from the bridge, yelling, "Mr. Proffitt, there's a submarine out there!'' Everyone looked, and sure enough a sub had surfaced between the *Yorktown* and the *Guam*, now back in the task group. The hatch in the conning tower opened, and a head popped up. Surprise!

The drawling Tennessean ordered a smoke flare thrown over the side to mark the spot—a stupid move, he later concluded, since it lighted up the ship. The sub dived as Proff called in the destroyers; *Guam* and *Yorktown* were both fearful that the other would fire on the diving sub and hit each other. Two cans zipped in and started flinging depth charges. Results negative. Sub contacts seemed to be everywhere.

At first light, from 205 miles southwest of Okinawa, the *Yorktown* sent off a deckload strike against AA positions and the airfield at Naha, Okinawa's capital. The low ceiling reached down to 800 feet, where the flak was so bad that strike leader Houck held back his bombing planes from making suicidal runs—a decision which led Admiral Mitscher to cancel all subsequent planned strikes for the day, and only the CAPs were launched. At least the overcast protected not only Okinawa but the carriers as well.

The morning quiet led to philosophical chatter on the flag bridge between Joe Bryan and Harwell Proffitt on the subject of battleship vs. carrier duty. Joe summed it up, "When you're in a battleship, you're in the Annapolis Navy. You feel that John Paul Jones and Admiral Dewey and Preble and Mahan and Farragut and all the rest of them are glaring at you, waiting to put you under hack because your shoe laces aren't tied with a false turk's-head knot, or some such nonsense.

"But when you're in a carrier, you're in the fighting Navy. Your ship is being run by and for a bunch of barn-storming youngsters who don't tie their shoes at all, if they don't feel like it . . . . Proff and I, we'll take the carrier duty.''

Rain lowered the cloud level at midday, which enabled a bogey to slip by the CAP. The ship went to GQ at 1244 with the bandit closing from 12 miles out. Pat Patterson bellowed over the "blow horn'' from Air Defense Aft on the island: "All Southerners, man yo' stations. All Northerners, take cover! Commence firing!'' Boy, this wasn't the Annapolis Navy—and Tiny went one further.

He held down the key on his squawk box to Air Plot, whereupon, noted Del Paine, "The after five-inch mounts opened with their muzzles . . . , relaying over the open circuit a blast so deafening that some thought the ship had been hit.'' Cooper Bright: "It sounded like every gun on the ship had moved into Air Plot. The exec came out of his chair like he'd sat on a tack. Telephones jumped out of their cradles. Pencils rolled off the desk. You couldn't hear yourself think.''

Near the horizon the *North Carolina* and *Guam* had joined in.

"You goddamned Yankees,'' Patterson yelled in the tube for Bright as the bogey bored in. "Come up here and see some shootin'. We're gonna knock his ass off!'' Figuring on getting a prisoner when they knocked bogey down, Tiny chided Skinhead, "When you bring him in, bring the body up here. I'll show you what gunnery is!''

Suddenly, everyone saw bogey—a single-engine torpecker. A TBM! "Cease firing! It's a friendly.''

The TBM had come back to the formation on the wrong heading and failed to turn on its IFF. Luckily, the plane was not hit, but the pilot and crew landed aboard their carrier pretty shaken up.

The opportunity was too perfect for Bright. He grabbed his bullhorn mike and broadcast a message to the assistant gunnery officer: "Patterson, this is Yankee Bright, talkin' to the Confederacy. I'd like to make a report on that enemy plane that just landed aboard. After a personal inspection, I found no holes in the fuselage, no holes in the wings, pilot uninjured.

"I interviewed the pilot. He said he was wondering what that smoke was way off in the distance. He felt he was in no danger and wanted to know if that was the best gunnery the *Yorktown* could do. He didn't need any heading to come in on. You couldn't shoot him down anyhow. This ship is defenseless!!''

Füming, Patterson bellowed back, "Can it, or we'll come down there and shoot *you!*"

By now everybody was laughing like hell, and the Bright-Patterson "war" began to ease some of the tension. Tiny was so chagrined he didn't even enter "ammunition expended" in the ship's log.

The wet weather postponed further air activity until next day, March 24, when two deckload strikes from the task group returned to Naha and its murderous ack ack. It hit the diving SB2C of Lieutenant (jg) Mitch Bailens of the first flight. One man parachuted before the plane crashed into the earth, but both Bailens and gunner Blackie Powell were lost. Otherwise, the bombing planes slammed Okinawa's AA gun positions with great accuracy. Also, at noon, a *Yorktown* CAP fighter splashed a torpedo-laden Jill just over the southern horizon.

Nearly continuous GQ brought on exhaustion to ship's company. This was no more apparent than in Air Plot, which had been a three-ring circus between flag ops officer Andy Jackson relaying frantic and confused orders from the flag and exec Ben Born keeping his battle station here to be close to his beloved aviation communications gear. He even had a pilot's ready room chair installed so he could fall asleep between attacks.

Over the past week, since the bomb hit, with everyone on edge, Coop Bright tried to relieve the anxiety by resurrecting his old taunt for Herman Rosenblatt. Using a piece of chalk, he drew a large circle on the deck and announced loudly: "The next target's going to go through there! Make out your last wills and testaments. We're all going to die. Target's gonna fly in here." And everyone chuckled.

Ben Born pretty much ignored all this and concentrated on the status board until one GQ when he came in to find a chalk circle drawn on his chair with the inscription: "2000# GP Japanese bomb."

"What the hell'd you do that for?" he inquired of Bright.

"You're gonna be dead. The next bomb's gonna go there!"

"Take that off!"

The big crowd of air operations officers and sailors stopped working to witness the exchange.

Bright: "I shouldn't take that off."

Born: "Take that OFF!"

"You're afraid it's gonna be right."

"The hell I am! I don't have any fear!"

"If you didn't have any fear, you'd be sitting in that chair. Commander, you're afraid to sit in that chair!"

"Goddamn you, you take that thing off!"

By now two rooting sections had formed. "Sit in the chair, Commander!" coaxed one group. "Take that the hell off of there!" rooted the other.

Bright: "If I erase that off, you'd become a coward where you're now a hero, in my estimation."

Born: "There's a thing in this Navy called the chain of command. Take that damned thing off!"

So Coop erased it, and in due course Born left the room to attend to other business—whereupon Coop drew it on again.

Born returned, took one look, exclaimed, "I ain't going through this thing again," grabbed a rag and wiped it off.

The story spread all through the ship in no time. Born would be on the flight deck, when someone remarked to him, "I understand you wouldn't sit in the chair."

"That damned Bright!"

The fatigue of constant GQ led all hands to grab sleep whenever and wherever they could, Bright among them. After one predawn launch, Skinhead flopped down on the night watch's bunk in CIC and fell asleep instantly.

He awoke with a yell. His foot was on fire! One of those infamous Pat Haley hot-foot devices was burning through his shoe on a wire, and his laces were too hot to handle. Finally, he got the shoe off but was left with a bad burn and huge blister. Ben Born just sat there in front of him, laughing like hell, "I don't mark 'em. I call 'em, boy!"

Air operations never seemed to let up, and during refueling on March 26 the ship's bakers fashioned a frosted cake for the 21,000th landing, though they complained to Joe Bryan that the blasts of the 5-inchers were flattening their sponge cakes in the ovens into pancakes, and the emergency turns of the ship tended to push the batter down to one end of the pans to produce cake unfit even for "a dogface" (soldier).

One baker said it all: "Whoever called this ocean 'Pacific'? It's about as pacific as a goddamn roller coaster!"

This Sunday was at least supposed to be pacific, and both Father Moody and Reverend Wright had their largest congregations ever. The Catholics and Mormons worshipped at 0900, the Protestants and Christian Scientists an hour later—and the Catholics again at 1645. Willie Davenport led the Negro Baptists too. Wright began his sermon with a sage observation, "Today is Palm Sunday. Last Sunday," when no services could be held, "was Bomb Sunday."

Chapter XIII
Zootsuiter Siege

"WAR IS HELL, BY

GEORGE! By Joers,'' read the title of the irrepressible radio officer's latest bit of humor, a funny essay which so impressed staff officer Bill Ogden that he sent it home for his peacetime office mates to share. That office happened to be the editorial room of the *The New York Times,* which found such antics on a warship slightly incredible but nevertheless fascinating enough to share with its readership though without mentioning names.

"Skippy" Evans, described as the "Wind Boss" and charter member of the "Lost Sheep Sector" (planes missing through navigational errors), felt the weight of Joers' barbs. Evans' life "is blighted by only three major obstacles—the Radio Officer (a handsome fellow, Pete Joers by name), the expansion of CIC [as the kamikaze menace grew] and their further encroachments on his spaces, and Andy Jackson." The latter, "the 'Silver Meteor' whose orbit is judged in ever-decreasing circles, solves 'Skippy's' problem of what to do with spare time. The frequent orders, all voiced in his typically calm mannerisms, for changing plans, giving them (sometimes the enemy) hell, all within the next few minutes are well known to 'M.T.' "

The exciteable Commander Jackson's notoriety for making up complex watch bills for Admiral Radford's staff became obvious even to Jackson himself when he added a sardonic note at the bottom of his watch bill for March 26, 1945: "Anyone who understands the system I use in this, please see me and explain it."

The campaign against Okinawa's zootsuiters *was* complex, as seen in Coop Bright's air operations plan the same day for *Yorktown's* planes alone: two fighter sweeps to the Ryukyu Island of Amami O Shima and its Koniya seaplane base, one to the airfield at nearby Kikai Wan, and two strikes to Okinawa, especially Naha's air base. Point Option

was 75 miles due east of Okinawa and 137 due south of Amami, where the carriers would generally stay until "Okie" was secured.

The strike schedule would be repeated daily for as many weeks as it took to support the invasion forces at Okinawa—set to land on April 1. But if the kamikazes were nearly as active as over recent days, Task Force 58 would be besieged by the Nips in an unprecedentedly long and hard fight.

"PILOTS, OFF YOUR DEAD ASSES" came Bright's order to man planes. Buster Kitchen led the predawn launch of fighters and dive bombers which clobbered Amami O Shima's boatyard, warehouses and barracks. Herb Houck then took 12 Hellcats and Bryon Cooke's 15 torpeckers to bomb, rocket and strafe gun positions, coastal boat revetments and buildings around Yontan and Kadena airfields on Okinawa—this under a cloud ceiling of 3500 feet and into the teeth of heavy flak.

Recovering from their second passes, two VBF-9 fighters miscalculated their positions and roared in directly on the port beam of the torpeckers. Fred Fox in one of the Hellcats headed straight toward Cooke's TBM, and just as Cooke banked sharply to avoid a collision, a burst of flak erupted beneath them, and Fox's F6 sheered off Cooke's starboard wing. Cooke's Turkey fell out of control in a spin and exploded on impact with the ground, instantly killing Cooke and crewmen Norm Brown and Matty Matthews. Fox's F6 also fell crazily, smoking, but Fox was able to right his plane just in time to make a crash landing in a flat area north of Yontan airfield. A few seconds later, however, the plane exploded.

Unknown to his comrades overhead, Fox was thrown clear of the wreckage and started running for cover. Fully aware that the Japs were close on his heels, he began making his way to the western shore of Okinawa. His luck and stealth enabled him to find a cave on the water there where he hid. Fox managed to steal a boat and waited for an opportunity to make contact with U.S. forces.

The flight continued its attack, now against Kadena, and got revenge for its leader's death by placing rockets and strings of bombs squarely into AA positions and an ammo dump. Command of Torpedo 9 fell to the exec, Lieutenant Tom Stetson, Williams College '40, and described as "a daring flier and inspiring leader."

The noon launch of 24 fighters and 15 bombers split up, with half of the fighters going north to Kikai Wan, the rest with Herb Houck west to work over Naha, Okinawa. The flak at the latter place licked up at the VF-9 strafers to destroy Tom Connor and wound Bob Finlayson. Another burst knocked the cockpit off Jack Greenwell's Beast, the cover hitting Greenie in the head, drawing a stream of blood, but he made it home.

At 1358 the last sweep of the day headed back to Amami O Shima to work over Koniya harbor. The eleven F6Fs of VBF-9 strafed patrol craft there, but Herb See's was shot down by flak in his run. Four men lost in one day threw a pall over Air Group Nine. During the night, the topside watch witnessed a Betty skyrocketing in flames from the work of Dale Knopf's night fighters.

Next day, March 27, with seasoned OOD Dick Drover at his usual 0400-0800 duty at the conn, 16 VF and 9 VB participated in a 96-plane raid on Amami which ravaged the sub base with relative ease, save for Ensign Ted Smyer of Fighting 9. As "tail-end Charlie," Smyer peeled off from 18,000 feet to drop his bomb, only to find a high-flying Zero rolling over right behind him. The Zeke opened fire and hit Smyer's Hellcat, starting a fire, but Smyer completed his dive, released his bomb and pulled out—when a burst of flak hit the plane, extinguishing the fire but the engine as well. He ditched within rifle range of the beach and swam away and was picked up by an approaching destroyer. In due course, when the officers of the can learned that Smyer was junior man in the squadron, they demanded 100 gallons of gedunk from the Yorktown instead of the usual reward of 50 for rescuing a flier. They were politely refused.

As amphibious forces occupied some of the outer islets, two Yorktown support strikes again socked the hot Kadena-Yontan area of Okinawa in the morning and two more in the afternoon. Most remarkable in all this was Pappy Harshman's flight deck which, including CAP fighters, at one time sent off 45 planes in a mere 12 minutes.

Commander Born issued a stern reminder for the exhausted crew of the York in his Plan of the Day for March 28: "You were informed before our leaving Ulithi that our estimate then of what we might expect from the Jap was an unknown quantity. Since then four carriers have been hit. Our days will be long—they will be tiring—they will be tough. While we all may be 'Dead Tired' let's not get 'dead' from being tired. WE MUST BE ALERT—WE MUST THINK AND WORK TOGETHER."

Not only did the ship refuel on this day but, for the very first time, took on ammunition while under way—bombs. Dentist Smith: "They came across by cable without mishap as everyone held his breath." This kind of logistical staying power enabled the fleet to sustain its operations without returning to Ulithi, a critical factor in the fight against Japan.

Then, momentous news—recorded by Smith, "We received word that the Jap Fleet was again moving out from the Inland Sea around the southern tip of the mainland" of Japan. Admiral Jocko Clark wanted to get going immediately and to have Commander Charlie Crommelin coordinate TG 58.1's attack on that fleet. But Charlie was over Okinawa when the news broke, and Jocko wanted him back in a hurry. The message went out, and Charlie asked to make one more photo run. Permission was granted, but in the run Crommelin collided with another photo plane and crashed to his death. Jocko Clark and the Yorktown alike were shaken by the loss of this fearless and loved leader.

Admiral Mitscher ordered the entire task force north in order to launch search-strikes along the coast of Kyushu at dawn of the 29th. "For us," declared Ben Born, "it's back deep into 'Indian Country'—the prize the Jap Fleet and shipping—a choice target—Heads up." To Radford's four-carrier flight the Yorktown contributed a deckload of 20 VF, 12 VBF, 11 VB and 15 VT. They swept the western coast of Kyushu for two hours but found nothing, whereupon Herb Houck shifted everybody to preassigned secondary targets, only to be frustrated by thick overcast over three airdromes. In all, the endeavor had been nothing but a wild goose chase.

With Jocko Clark's task group under attack by kamikazes all morning, Yorktown's CIC was primed for action, with Lieutenant John "Pistol Pete" Peterson directing the CAP over the screen and Cyclops Ballinger orchestrating the entire task group air defense. He remained a comical figure.

Fearing that CIC would take a bomb, he now wore a mask of a wet towel with a breathing tube through it. When an attack began, he periodically stepped out of CIC to wet the towel. He was no Alex Wilding; Radford was determined to get rid of him.

At 1400, just as the last sweep to Kyushu commenced its launch, Ballinger issued a warning: "Bogey 216 degrees, 16 miles and closing!"

Yorktown turned out of the wind and went to GQ, the other planes being struck below and the pilots ordered to scatter below decks. VF-9 ops officer Walt Klem was left standing on the flight deck where he and several mechs had been servicing the fighters: "As the ship swung from one side to the other with increasing speed, I found that the only ones left on the heeling flight deck were John Gresh, aviation chief ordnanceman, and myself."

Ship's radio now picked up a *Langley* CAP fighter pilot talking to his own ship: "You think bogey low on water?"

Langley's reply was garbled, save for its warning to the pilot: "Don't come too close."

Pilot: "Wilco—Tallyho! Bogey ten, course one forty!"

Langley: "Maybe friendly."

Pilot: "He's still climbing. I'm trying to get him. Looks like he's going to make a run. It's a bogey all right."

The screen opened fire.

Langley: "Keep clear of us. Keep clear of us."

Goat Moneyhun, off duty as a plane captain: "I go up on the catwalk by number 2 elevator to see what is coming in. All of a sudden I see 3 planes come out of the clouds real low on the starboard side headed our way. It looked like three Jap planes."

Klem: "When the [first] Jap went into his dive, I was running for the island, but Gresh wasn't following. I stopped and shouted at him, 'Take cover!'

"There stood Gresh, hands on hips, looking up at the diving Jap plane, and answering me with, 'Oh, Mr. Klem, I got to see this to tell my grandchildren about it.'" And he would.

Langley pilot: "Bogey hit by my fire. I see him burning."

Langley: "Orbit! Orbit!"

No response came as the F6 tried to pull up and was hit by flak. The Earnshaw-Patterson gun crews let fly at the zootsuiter.

Moneyhun: "Everything opens up. The one in front turns out to be a Judy. It comes right over

our radar, missing about five feet. As it came over my head it was so close to us I could feel the heat from it."

Gunner Jesse Bradley: "He dived from about 030 degrees (R), angle of dive about 35-40 degrees. The guns on this ship shot him down. He burst into flames while he was in his dive and passed over the after end of the island and over the flight deck, missing it about 6 feet."

Coxswain Ted Rohrbough: "The Jap plane missed the island structure by 10 or 15 feet, close enough for you to feel the heat, as the plane was on fire. The plane passed over Battery 10, close enough to singe the hair on the gun crew."

Dick Tripp watched in terror as Judy came toward him at the LSO platform. "The kamikaze had us boresighted but missed by a few yards just abeam the landing signal platform. I jumped into the net."

Del Paine: "Bursts from the guns of the pursuing Hellcat were spattering the water off the starboard bow; some thought it was the Judy trying to strafe us. Already blazing, the Judy took a direct hit from a five-inch shell . . . and plunged into the water sixty feet off the port side. It was so near that the after flight deck was showered with debris."

Bradley: Judy "crashed in the water about 20 yds. from the ship, port side aft. That plane was too damn close for comfort. When he hit the water he exploded—also his bomb, which he never had a chance to drop. He threw water and oil all over some of the fellows back there. Nobody was hit or killed. I fired 48 rounds at the Judy."

Tripp, lying in the LSO rescue net: "After the explosion a piece of cylinder from the Jap plane landed right next to me. Had the Jap hit us we would have been a carbon copy of the *Franklin* disaster."

Joe Bryan: " . . . .a thick column of mottled water spouted high in the air, 50 feet off our port quarter. The navigating bridge blotted most of my overhead view, but I caught a flash of the [second] plane . . . as it fled away—a low-mid-wing, single-engine monoplane, with tail assembly like an F6's . . . .

"Later: This plane was an F6."

Ship's log: "1414 Observed friendly fighter plane to crash into water 1000 yds. astern of the ship." It was the pursuing *Langley* fighter.

Paine: "He was hit again as he passed astern and was burning when he crashed. The other Hellcat was also hit by our AA but circled and came down low astern as if to make a water landing. At the last moment his nose went down and the plane spun end over end. Neither pilot was found."

A Judy misses the crowded flight deck by 15 feet; she is seen outlined against the hull a split second before striking the water. A direct hit among the *Yorktown's* planes would have caused a major conflagration as suffered by several of the *York's* sister ships. Photo is from battleship *New Jersey*, March 29, 1945.

Throughout the 45-second action, gun crews not well-placed to shoot at the Judy couldn't resist turning to look at it—but some were stunned by a firm swat on their helmets by George Earnshaw, patrolling behind them in his leather jacket and fur collar with a big billy club. "Watch your sector!" he bellowed, fearful of other incoming zooters. The *York* had splashed the 12th attacker of its career during its fourth close shave in the eleven days since Bomb Sunday.

Junior Meyer resumed waving the last sweep to Kyushu down the deck. All eyes continued to sweep the horizon for any more bogeys coming in under the radar beam. "In all the lather," noted Joe Bryan, "I forgot that we had been steaming through an archipelago of floating mines, until I saw a destroyer stop dead in the water and fire at one for what seemed ten minutes. No explosion."

It was the *Trathen,* and the mine was dead ahead of the *Yorktown,* which Theda Combs maneuvered to let the mine pass to starboard, which it did 75 yards abeam. *Thrathen* backed down then edged up toward the mine again. Cracked Wellington Henderson—Cooper Bright's "Man with the million-dollar name"—"Maybe he's desperate and is going to ram it."

As *Trathen* shot away at the mine, *McGowan* reported another, which *Monssen* went after. At 1449 the *Independence* sighted a mine, and *Melvin* proceeded hither. Six minutes after this, *Trathen* finally exploded her intruder, and at 1520 *Franks* chased yet another floater. Now *Melvin* detonated her prey, just as *Cushing* reported several more. *Colahan* joined her in disposing of them.

One by one the ubiquitous mines were eliminated, but the skipper kept Dick Drover at the conn at 1600 through this antimine battle. Jesse Bradley "saw three in the water at one time. One of them was only about 100 yds. away. If one of them things ever hit us it would blow a hell of a big hole in our side they say." By sundown, 1824, all mines seemed to have been destroyed, when one suddenly slipped by the *Guam.* Dr. Smith: "We progressed through dozens of floating mines during the night. At dusk several could be seen a matter of feet from our ship."

Thankfully, no more bogeys appeared at this inopportune time, and later Admiral Radford and Captain Combs transmitted their regrets to the *Langley* for the loss of her two pilots to *Yorktown's* guns. "They both should get Congressional Medals of Honor," Commander Evans repeated again and again at dinner in the wardroom. Unfortunately, concluded Del Paine, "nothing could blunt the tragedy. The ship felt sick about it."

At least some good news greeted the men of

A dramatic rescue and photo. Fred Fox of VBF-9 is seen wading out from the reef on March 29, 1945, after having spent three days hiding in a cave on Okinawa following his mid-air collision with Byron Cooke. The picture was taken from the float plane sent from the *San Francisco* to pick him up. In the background is the rowboat he stole and used to get out to the reef. Naval Historical Center

VBF-9. During the day their shipmate Fred Fox had come out of hiding from his cave on Okinawa's west coast at the sight of American frogmen swimming offshore to clear underwater obstacles for the coming landing. Climbing into the boat he had appropriated, he rowed out to the reef where a float plane from the *San Francisco* had landed to pick him up. He left his boat and waded out to the plane, but its pontoons had been too damaged to enable a takeoff. So it taxied out to the minesweeper *Heed*, which towed it to the cruiser *Birmingham*. Fox had spent three hair-raising days since his mid-air collision with Byron Cooke.

In another unusual incident, a lone zootsuiter had been seen to approach the formation, make no dive or run, but instead coast in for a very unhostilelike water landing several thousand yards from the *Yorktown*. Picked up by a can, the pilot was not transferred to the *Yorktown* until April 17, at which time he told interrogator Bill Kluss—in good English—that ,he had been a student at Cornell University before the war and had gone home to Japan to visit his family, but the war had caught him there.

His one desire since Pearl Harbor had been to get back to the U.S., finish his college work and become an American citizen. Which, he claimed, was why he joined the Kamikaze Corps as a pilot, so he could fly out to the American fleet, ditch in the water and be picked up by the Americans. So far, so good, but college would have to wait until after the war. To hasten its end, he told all he knew.

One bogey was splashed during the night, and just before dawn Goat Moneyhun climbed up onto Fox #27, the F6F for which he was responsible as a plane captain, and strapped in his pilot, the diminutive Ensign Ray Jehli of VBF-9, for a 14-fighter sweep against Tokuna airfield on Amami O Shima. The VF went off at 0550 and strafed and bombed against the usual flak.

One burst hit Jehli's plane in the wheel well. Moneyhun: "He made it back to the force OK but his landing gear wouldn't come down all the way, so they ordered him to hit the drink. He did so and was picked up" by the *Melvin* at 0830. Just five hours and ten minutes later Jehli was back on the *Yorktown* by bos'n's chair.

Air Group Nine hit Okinawa twice during the day and Amami and Kikai each once to keep the northern approaches to Okinawa neutralized. But no attacks were made on Radford's group this day. Lieutenant Joe Hachet, airborne radar officer in CIC, finally got his first opportunity in two weeks to write his family: "We've really been busy and frankly I'm 'pooped out.' I could sleep for a week now if they'd let me."

Saturday the 31st—the day before the main landings—opened with less promise. Greeted by a sparkling dawn sky, described by Joe Bryan as "fresh-scrubbed, fresh painted," the crew was jarred from its fatigue by the gruff bark of Pappy Harshman over the bullhorn: "Keep the area of the 5-inch mounts clear! They may have to fire across the deck!" The ship went to GQ, but the *Langley's* CAP splashed the bogey, an Oscar, 40 miles to the west.

Another GQ at 1104 responded to a bogey approaching ten miles to the west, but it ended immediately. According to the very poor teletyping of Coop Bright's ticker operator: "LAST,.1.,Q, XXXX GQ WAS DUE TO COZY PLANES RETURNING.,ON THE WRONG APPROACH PRODE, CEDURE. CAP THAT JUST LANDED HAD NO WAVEOFFS., ADVERAGE INTERVIL, 24 SECONDS. LANDING SIGNALS OFFICER SAYS 'VERY GODDL,'...SNACK SHOP ONE UNDER NEW MANAGEMENT—TRY ONE., OF MILLER'S HAM SNAWICH WITH MAN, YOMAISE.,..,."

Father Moody's afternoon broadcast impressed all hands. After discounting the absurd claims by Radio Tokyo of damage to the Fleet, he explained that on the morrow 1732 Allied vessels would descend on Okinawa in an operation surpassing the Normandy landings in size. The carriers would provide the defensive umbrella for the whole operation—the 12 of TF 58 and a dozen jeep carriers, with four British flattops covering the southern flank.

"2400. March went out like a lamb," recorded Joe Bryan. "But April came in like a lion."

During an 0130 GQ on April 1 a sailor hurried by Bryan, proclaiming, "I'm the only son of a bitch in the whole son-of-a-bitchin' fleet can put this sock on at a full gallop! And that ain't all, either...," but his voice faded down a passageway. The Betty that had interrupted everyone's precious slumber plummeted toward the horizon shortly afterwards in a ball of fire in full view of the flag bridge. "That'll teach him!" muttered Admiral Radford.

A predawn target CAP to Okinawa was followed shortly by Herb Houck with the first close support strike which encountered only light flak. Enemy opposition on the ground and in the air was minor, enabling the assault troops to move inland rapidly and take Yontan airfield. Goat Moneyhun captured the lazy mood on board the *York*: "We patrol around. We are about 30 to 40 miles from Okinawa. We can see the island but that is about all."

"Hey, Bright," Tiny Patterson yelled down from Air Defense Aft to Skinhead, standing on the flight deck during the afternoon, "Put on your cap! You're two-thirds naked!"

In Flag Plot things were so slow that Wellington Henderson and Joe Bryan whiled away their time playing April Fool's gags on unsuspecting victims. Their crowning ploy was to color the tips of several cigarette butts in the ashtray with red crayons when Captain Trapnell was out on the bridge. When he came back in, he looked, said nothing, in fact made no expression at all, but finally intoned, "Not mine." Trap was either terribly ensconced in thought about the battle, or he had mastered the fine art of a put-down for the pranksters.

Father Moody's report of the wonderful progress by the foot soldiers against minimal opposition added to a general guarded sense of well-being as the sun set. And Bryan was pleased to find a cake from his admiring baker friends when he returned to his room. "I guess it represents the thousandth time that Commander Jackson has landed on me." Indeed, Jackson was getting more exciteable with each passing day and sleepless night.

When a few zootsuiters concentrated on the landing ships on April 1 and 2, Ben Born told his crew, "The troops that landed on Okinawa depend on us to maintain control of the air. It will be done. HEADS UP! KEEP ALERT!" Unopposed at sea, the carriers easily launched their strikes on the 2nd, *Yorktown* fighters damaging a convoy and small landing craft at Amami and blasting its airstrips as well as Kikai Wan. The ship also sent three support missions to Okinawa, with only partial success due to faulty target assignments and lowering weather.

If air operations were dull for Air Group Nine, Coop Bright did his best to liven them up in the ready rooms. Today his target was John M. "Weasle" Wesolowski, a dark, bushy-haired VBF-9 pilot with a perennial five-o'clock-shadow who had flown with Smokey Stover at Guadalcanal. Weasle now disputed some of Coop's bulletins. "MY DARLING WEASEL, THE OBJECT IS TO EXECUTE THE INSTRUCTIONS AS ORDERED, OR THE FLAT OF MY FOOT ACROSS YOUR HAIRY PUSS. SIGNED, ONE WHO HATES YOU."

Progress ashore was good, Joe Moody's news being taken down by Jesse Bradley: "The Army at 1800 today reached the Eastern shore. They have got the airfield in operation. 3 of our CVEs sent all their planes over to the airfield. We now hold about 8 ½ miles of beach and an average of 2 ½ miles deep." The boys nicknamed captured Yontan airfield "Yorktown."

After supper, as Cooper Bright got up to leave the table, he remarked to Tiny Patterson, who had just taken a big bite of dessert, "Say, Pat, my grampaw told me the easiest part of the whole war was the march from Atlanta to the sea." As Pat gagged, Skinhead scurried out the door.

There was no humor in the weather though. A threatening typhoon thought to have died out, in the words of dentist Smith, "came into being again and we were caught in its outer area during the night." By dawn of the 3rd, the sea was so rough that the ships couldn't fuel until the late afternoon. But the high seas, whipped up by a 45-knot gale, stove in or bent catwalks and plates on the port bow and temporarily put two 5-inch guns and a 40mm mount on the port side out of commission.

The guns were not the only thing suddenly rendered inoperable. No fewer than 35 men had reported to Sick Bay with enlarged red tonsils, denoting acute tonsillitus, obviously an epidemic begun with three cases the day before. The blame was laid to the crowded sleeping compartments and lowered resistance due to lack of sleep and irregular meals.

At the urging of Dr. Jack Smith, Captain Combs ordered the alerts reduced if at all possible to give the crew a chance to rest. The weather front helped, but by Sick Call on the 4th Sick Bay was up to 55 tonsillitus cases.

Flight surgeon Benny Bond's basic remedy for any ills of the pilots—"Drink more whiskey"—didn't seem to fit this situation. Walt Klem called Bond's solution "an understandably rejuvenating and salutary prescription when it could be filled, but an exasperating and unsatisfactory approach on shipboard."

"The Yorktown bucked like a rogue stallion all night long," wrote Joe Bryan, and a huge wave at 0400 on April 4 knocked all hands in the pilothouse off their feet. "My God," Captain Combs roared to Harwell Proffitt as the skipper charged out of his sea cabin, "Are you sure that was a wave and not a *ship*?" It was and had stove in some side plating.

Now 120 miles off Okinawa, TG 58.4 was assigned to relieve the British carriers hitting the Sakishima Gunto and Japanese planes staging hence from Formosa. It was not an easy task, for the seas and wind were still heavy, and not only more oil but ammo were taken aboard in the midst of it on the morning of the 4th.

A 14-plane fighter sweep was virtually thrown into the sky by the pitching ship an hour before noon but proceeded to shoot up several planes on the ground and ships in the harbor at Miyako Jima in the Sakishimas. The fairly heavy flak claimed the life of Lieutenant (jg) Henry Hicks of VBF-9 and damaged several other planes. When the sweep returned, the Yorktown was receiving oil and gas from the Cimarron, battling parting hoses and lines in the process. Nevertheless, Theda Combs took up

the challenge and had all planes landed without interrupting fueling.

Before dawn on April 5 two night fighters heckling Miyako's airfield of Hirara shot down a Betty and two Irvings trying to land. Then the first of six flights took off to keep Hirara blanketed throughout the day. The 18 Hellcats went down through a 2000-foot ceiling, where the flak did its dirty work claiming the F6F of Ensign Howard Hudspeth of VF-9. But not the pilot, who was able to ditch south of the island though without his life raft.

The dawn composite strike had to go in under 1500 feet, where the AA found a mark in the engine of Lieutenant (jg) Ed Kemp's TBM. Kemp ditched just a thousand yards from Hudspeth. The four men floated around in their rafts—three more being dropped—for three hours, when a PBM "Dumbo" seaplane braved the 15-foot waves to set down and pick them up. It flew them back to newly-won Kerama Retto, whence they were flown to Yontan and then the York.

Three midday fighter sweeps and one composite strike struggled through an overcast that reached down to 200 feet to strike Miyara airfield on Ishigaki. But the flak knocked down the 2C of Lieutenant (jg) Bill May, who ditched just one mile offshore. After two and a half hours of being buffeted in their raft within gun range of the beach, May and his gunner welcomed a PBM. Though its pilot reported 20-foot waves and was ordered to return to base, he landed, picked them up, and took off again.

Ensign Eston Baden was not as fortunate. He ditched his stricken Hellcat 15 miles offshore, sans life raft but with dye marker, and was circled by the Rescue CAP until it lost sight of him. He was never seen again.

Only mines bothered Radford's task group during the day, and the tonsillitus epidemic was checked. Unfortunately, during the withdrawal to refuel, an ammo ship rammed a destroyer, which lost many men overboard, and much of the night was consumed looking for them.

April 6, 1945 began inauspiciously enough as the Yorktown refueled from the Lackawanna, passing over some of the wounded to her, and took on bombs from the ammunition ship Wrangell. In the midst of it a composite strike cratered the airfield at Minami Daito Shima without loss.

But the big news emanated from Radio Tokyo

as it warned its people that the landing at Okinawa was "the beginning of the end." Coop Bright celebrated to the ready rooms: "TOKYO BROADCAST JUST ANNOUNCED THAT.,THE CABNIT HAS RESIGNED. A 78 YEAR OLD., BLOKE & ALSO A RETIRED ADMIRAL HAS BEEN.,GIVEN THE NOD BY HIS ROYAL PANTS..,THE RUSSIANS HAVE CALLED OFF THERE NONAGGRESS . . .,ION PACT WITH THE NIPS. REASON GIVEN THAT., BECAUSE THE NIPS WERE AT WAR WITH UNCLE SMA., AND THE LIMIES—TO HELL WITH IT., CANT RUN THIS TELETYPE ANYWAY."

Dentist Smith: "Even though Russia is not supposed to attack for one year after revoking the treaty, she might lend a hand or give us opportunity to establish air bases and come at them from that side." Ed Wallace: "Here's hoping!"

Yet even more immediate news began to come into the radio shack during the afternoon that Jocko Clark's and Ted Sherman's task groups and the amphibious shipping off Okinawa were under a massive kamikaze attack. But their planes made quick work of the zootsuiters, and the *Yorktown* kept score of the shootdowns—over 150 planes. Ed Brand noted that "we are heading that way to give them a little help."

Jesse Bradley: "I hear they found some of the Jap fleet on the move again."

Eureka! Even as Clark's and Sherman's claims of 249 planes shot down were being added up, and damage to their carriers and destroyers from enemy hits and near-misses was being repaired, this intelligence from scouting subs at sunset meant a chance to go after the biggest prize of all—the 72,000-ton superbattleship *Yamato*, plus a cruiser or two and maybe ten destroyers!

Admiral Mitscher ordered Radford to steam north during the night in order to rendezvous at 0500 April 7 with Clark and Sherman. Radford's group must remain due east of Okinawa in order to assume the scheduled CAP over the island throughout the day. This would place it as the group furthest south of the *Yamato* force, reported to be proceeding south of Kyushu toward Okinawa, so Radford's strikes against the *Yamato* force would be longer than Clark's and Sherman's.

The two closer groups were to attack the *Yamato* itself, Radford's the cruiser, and everyone the cans after the heavies had been disposed of. Cooper Bright and Herb Houck worked out the air operations plan and set up a revised schedule in the hours before dawn of this memorable 7th of April. Houck would lead the 43 planes of Air Group

Nine's strike against the cruiser, nine Hellcats flying cover and strafing. Eight F6 fighter-bombers were each armed with a 500-pound general purpose bomb, and each of the 13 SB2Cs was getting two 1000-pounders, all but two of them semi-armor-piercing.

Bright's Air Plot ticker surprised everyone in the Torpedo 9 ready room: "LOAD WITH TORPEDOES."

The pilots let out a roar of approval, and as one of them chalked a picture of a "fish" on the blackboard, skipper Tom Stetson remarked, "Take a good look at it, fellows. That's a torpedo, remember? We haven't seen one in six months. Do you suppose you still know how to drop 'em?"

Admiral Mitscher wanted the fish to let the water in while the bombers let in air and started fires. "Stets" told his men to arm their wienies to run at a depth of ten feet, perfect for killing a cruiser.

The ticker continued, giving the total number of aircraft to be sent against the tiny Jap task force of a dozen or so ships: 386!! "The boys stared in amazement" at the massive planned strike, remembered ACIO Dick Montgomery, "then whooped and hollered."

"With that mass of planes," grunted Clyde "Ugh" Lee, "there probably won't be anything left for us to hit when we get there."

Lieutenant Thomas H. Stetson of Torpedo 9.
Courtesy of Floyd E. Bevill

Stets refreshed his men on the fine art of dropping torpedoes, Montgomery went over air-sea rescue procedures, and the pilots quietly put on their flight gear and waited—and waited.

As dawn broke with the customary overcast, the *Yorktown* sent a flight of fighters to patrol over Okinawa. Everyone figured the Jap warships would take advantage of the clouds to run south, and at half past eight the word came in from an *Essex* search plane just off the southwest coast of Kyushu. It was the *Yamato* alright, along with one 8500-ton *Agano*-class light cruiser—actually the *Yahagi*, plus eight tin cans. Two PBM Mariners began to shadow the force, and between 0915 and 1015 Clark and Sherman got off their strikes—some 300 planes.

At 1000 Herb Houck told Coop Bright, "Buck, we're ready to go. Let's get going."

"Herb, wait a minute," Skinhead answered. "Let me tell you something. I've been out here 20 months. I will bet you any amount of money that that contact is wrong."

"What do you mean?"

"Herb, if you come across a group with the *Yamato* coming down, you'd be astounded. The biggest ship in the world! So you see it. You get excited. Anybody would get excited. *I'd* get excited. My God, there's the prize! So you call it in. Do you really know your position? I've seen an awful lot of positions come back here to air operations, and they've been wrong. Including the Marianas Turkey Shoot. We stretched 'em out there till Alexatos was throwing away life preservers, charts, etc., to be light enough to get back. So wait. Wait!"

Houck was incredulous. "What do you mean, 'Wait'?"

"First of all," Coop argued, "everybody's going to launch—every ship will be launching on this thing. Go out and get the *Yamato!* They won't be armed exactly right, because we didn't expect to attack this big a ship. Are *you* sure you're all set?"

By now the bridge, Empty Evans, was yelling to Air Plot, "When are you going to be ready to launch aircraft?"

Houck: "Buck, we're gonna lose out!"

Bright: "We're the furthest ship from the *Yamato*." 260 miles away—a helluva long flight, *and* in poor weather. "Now, if they've got the wrong position, and you get up to that position, you can't make a search. You gotta come back."

Everyone was excited, including the captain, who knew Bright had made mistakes before. Combs summoned him to the bridge. Coop scrambled up the ladders from Air Plot and was puffing by the time he faced the skipper.

"Skinhead," said Theda Combs, "what the hell is going on?"

"Captain," Bright replied, "let me tell you what we're going to do." Between gasps, he related his reasoning to Combs.

"O.K., I'll buy it," Combs remarked finally, "but by God something's got to happen!"

At the same time, Admiral Radford was screaming from the flag bridge, "Why don't you launch?" Andy Jackson, no admirer of Bright, was practically having apoplexy.

All of a sudden, the shadowing PBM sent in a new position report. The *Yamato* had maneuvered 40 or so miles in another direction, hoping to elude what her commanders knew was coming. Bright was right! Air Plot transmitted the corrected position to the ready rooms.

"We're ready!" Coop informed Pri Fly and then dictated the electrifying word to the ready rooms: "PILOTS MAN YOUR PLANES. HUBBA! HUBBA! HUBBA!"

The torpecker jockeys bolted from their chairs, chanting in unison, "Hubba! Hubba! Hubba!"

An excited Tom Stetson, noticing a worried look on Dick Montgomery's face over Jap AA, waved back to his ACIO, "I'll bring you back a piece of the battleship."

At 1038 the *Yorktown* began launching her 43 planes—over half an hour behind the other groups. The *Intrepid's* deckload strike was waiting to lead the flight, and *Langley* and Independence each provided six torpeckers and eight fighters. Course was set at 350 degrees (T) for an estimated 225 miles.

By 1100 the 43 planes of Air Group Nine had passed out of sight of the ship, which settled down to lunch. It would be five or six hours before the planes returned, so no one was holding his breath. All hands were charged up, nevertheless.

"I wish Admiral Hokipoki, or whoever he is," Joe Bryan heard someone remark, "would head down this way, so we could get a look at 'em!"

"Me too," another chimed in. As for the *Yamato,* "I hear she looks like the Empire State [Building] with a foremast."

"Hell, if she's *that* big, maybe one of our BBs could hit her."

"Maybe. But she'd have to hold still." The carriermen had simply no love for the behemoths which never fired their big guns. Admiral Spruance,

Fifth Fleet commander, wanted nothing better than a gunnery duel between his BBs and theirs, but he had to agree with Admiral Mitscher that it would entail an unnecessary risk of lives. If his chickens, hawks and fish could do the job, it would be so much cleaner.

The first Target CAP had returned from the skies over Okinawa with four Vals under its belt, and the regular morning CAPs over the task force had also been recovered. Five minutes before noon the next CAP took off and directly intercepted and splashed a Judy approaching the carriers.

Suddenly, at ten past twelve, General Quarters!

As the crew raced to battle stations, a large column of smoke could be seen rising on the horizon. Men running across the flight deck paused to look at it.

"You men on the flight deck," the voice of Captain Combs boomed down from the bridge, "get your steel helmets!"

"Haven't got one, sir!" one called back.

"Well, goddamnit, *get* one!"

Presently, the word came in. It was the *Hancock* in Sherman's group. A zootsuiter had planted a bomb into her flight deck and followed it straight in, igniting parked planes and part of the hangar and inflicting over 150 casualties. By heroic damage control, however, *Hancock* had everything in hand by 1230.

The clouds broke away over the *Yorktown* to reveal a crystal blue sky, and an eerie silence enveloped the ship for several minutes.

The quiet was broken by returning planes, and One Easy was set. "Well," Chief Mueck sighed to Lieutenant Bryan, "one more year for Germany, two more years out here, and seven years to run the Yankees out of Texas, and we can secure this goddamn war!"

The ETA of the strike force at the target was about 1330, and at 1305 the planes of TG 58.4 in fact did arrive at the 1000 reported position of the Jap task force. No ships! Crap! Skinhead was right. Someone had erred. The strike made a course change to 270 degrees, figuring the *Yamato* had swung westward. The radar operators in the TBMs stayed glued to their scopes.

"Contact!"

At 1315 the radars showed blips on the surface twenty miles ahead. The flight pressed on and after ten minutes sighted the enemy ships, which had been under attack by Clark's and Sherman's planes for nearly an hour.

They were scattered but generally clustered into two main groups. Closest was the the *Yamato* and a screen of four destroyers. About five miles to the northwest of them was what appeared to be the battered hulk of a light cruiser (actually a destroyer). Five miles beyond that was the *Agano*-class light cruiser, attended by a can alongside. Actually, the *Yahagi* had been fatally damaged, and her admiral had called over the *Isokaze* in order to transfer his flag. The order to abandon *Yahagi* had already been given.

The *Intrepid* planes prepared to go in against the *Yamato*, which was running southwesterly at a brisk 20 knots in spite of the fact that she showed a fire amidships and was trailing oil from two bomb hits and a torpedo hit from Clark's and Sherman's planes. The *Yorktown*'s flight would tackle the cruiser, dead in the water, her stern visibly damaged from previous attacks and a vast oil slick spewing from her port side amidships.

The ceiling was still a low 2000 feet as the *Intrepid* planes peeled off in a wild, disorganized attack on the superbattleship. No order was possible at such a low altitude. *Langley*'s planes followed on the heels of *Intrepid*'s, while Herb Houck took *Yorktown*'s out to orbit beyond gun range and to look for possible other ships hiding under rain squalls. Houck had other concerns; his own F6F was having engine trouble and gas suction difficulties.

Finally, *Intrepid*'s leader radioed Houck, "We've hit the battleship pretty hard. A few more torpedoes should roll her over." At least five fish had hit squarely to slow down the *Yamato* to between 10 and 15 knots and had given her a list of ten degrees to port. Tom Stetson, leading his orbiting torpeckers, immediately asked Houck's permission to let his guys have a crack at her.

"Can you split your force?" Herb answered, "If so, put half against the battleship and half on the cruiser."

"Yes, sir!" came the emphatic reply.

"Then go ahead, and good luck!"

Stetson broke away his own six Avengers from the formation, while Houck searched for a hole in the clouds to lead his Hellcats, Helldivers and other seven TBMs for halfway decent dives on the cruiser. He found one and managed to get up to 4500 feet without losing sight of the target. Accurate and intense ack ack was being generated by both the *Yamato* and *Yahagi* groups.

On Houck's order, the eight fighters went screaming down first, at 1330, machine guns

The superbattleship *Yamato*, 72,000 tons and with 18.1 inch guns, reels under a bombing attack by Task Force 58 planes.

blazing away to try to suppress the flak for the following bomb and torpedo runs. The eight fighter-bombers came next; two of them scored direct hits with their 500-pounders, and all strafed after releasing.

Tony Schneider climbed with his 2Cs into the clouds to hide from the flak and to line up a fore-and-aft glide run on the *Yahagi*. She was a sitting duck. No-one should miss. Before reaching the attack position, however, Harry Worley suddenly broke away with his section and commenced diving on the port beam of the target. His bomb missed, as did those of Jack Bell and Bill Bowers, and they pulled out to head for the rendezvous.

Meanwhile, the remaining ten bombers had broken through the clouds in 40-to-50 degrees no-flap glides and in quick succession released their 1000-pounders. Perhaps eight scored direct hits from the 20 bombs unleased. Even as the last were still falling, "Admiral Ugh" Lee brought his seven

torpeckers through low cumulus clouds with a radar letdown in two lines abreast for full broad-side drops.

What a setup—a textbook attack! One by one the pilots pulled their release cords, though the torpedoes of Lee and Don Page did not release. The other fish dropped and ran "hot, straight and normal." Pilot Stew Bass looked back: "I suddenly saw all five torpedoes hit—bang! bang! bang! bang! bang! For a moment, nothing seemed to happen. Then she began erupting. Flames belched through holes in her deck, and great holes were blown in her portside."

Squirting jets of water shot up through the holes topside, and "in a matter of seconds the whole ship was enveloped in swirling clouds of smoke." The *Yahagi* made a sudden half-roll and plunged from sight, leaving a sea strewn with fiery bits of wreckage. Time: 1405.

Bombers and torpeckers recovered through a

At the beginning of Air Group Nine's attack southwest of Kyushu at 1330, April 7, 1945, the cruiser *Yahagi* lies dead in the water, streaming oil, while destroyer *Isokaze* hastens up to try to protect her.

The *Yahagi* rolls over following Ugh Lee's torpecker attack, and Hellcats are seen strafing and bombing to the left.

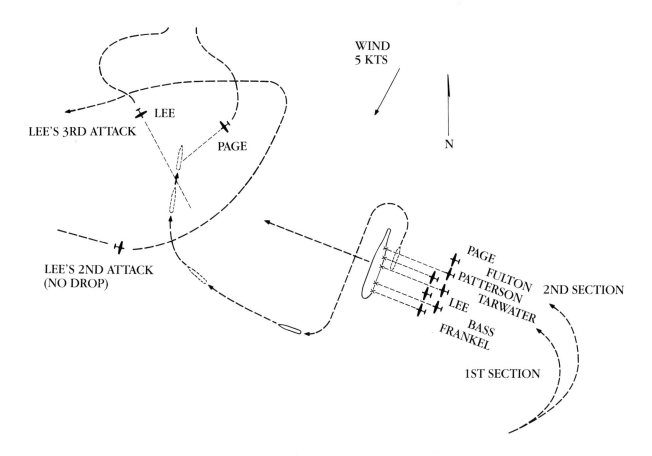

WIND
5 KTS

N

LEE

LEE'S 3RD ATTACK

PAGE

LEE'S 2ND ATTACK
(NO DROP)

PAGE
FULTON
PATTERSON
TARWATER
LEE
BASS
FRANKEL

2ND SECTION

1ST SECTION

Attack by Lt. (jg) Clyde J. Lee's division on *Yahagi* during Japanese fleet battle April 7, 1945, and subsequent attacks by Lee and Lt. (jg) John D. Page on the destroyer *Isokaze*. Graphics Courtesy of U.S. Naval Institute

cone of AA fire from the screening destroyer *Isokaze* which had followed them all the way down from the clouds. Lee and Page, still carrying fish, came around for second runs, but now against the can, plowing along at 25 knots. Neither man knew of the other's situation; each thought he was making a solo run. "This may be our neck," Page told his crew, "but we're going down after that can." Weighing heavily on him was the realization that this combat hop was his 13th and that he was in the No. 13 position in the squadron formation.

Ugh Lee beat him to it for a run "I'll never forget. The cruiser was bad enough, but then there had been seven of us and those Japs had to split their fire. But that can had me bore-sighted—and with nothing else to fire on. Once more I tried to release, but the torpedo wouldn't budge . . . .

"My heart sank when I realized I'd have to make still another run. As I flashed over the destroyer's bow, I could see the tracer spraying up, inching toward me. Just as it was about to intercept me, I'd jink a bit and dodge and twist. That would throw the gunners off for a moment, but then

they'd pick me up again."

At that moment Lee heard Don Page call for fighter cover and turned to see Page heading in at the *Isokaze's* bow, jinking so violently that Page's gunner Johnny Rodd "was bouncing around in that turret until I thought I'd be thrown clear out." Lee echoed Page's call for fighters and roared in for a simultaneous drop with Page. Both torpedoes plummeted free.

As the waterspouts rose, the destroyer tried to turn to comb them. Lee's fish missed by ten feet, but Page's smacked into the starboard quarter near the after gun mount. Both men looked back to see the flak being drawn away from them by their strafing pals.

In addition to the Hellcats, a Helldiver was boring straight into the *Isokaze's* ack ack, his 20mm cannon raking the destroyer's deck. It was Harry Worley. Bomber Jack Bell tried to join Worley, but his guns jammed, leaving "The Whorl" to absorb the Japs' fire alone.

Half way through his glide, Worley's Beast took a hit and started to stream smoke and flame. Harry

Oil and wreckage, including that of its
float plane, is all that remains of the
Yahagi after Air Group Nine's attack.
That, and survivors in the water.

Wracked by torpedoes from *Yorktown*
planes, the *Yahagi* turns turtle and
explodes.

Yorktown bombs bracket the Jap destroyer *Isokaze* standing by the doomed *Yahagi*. The can is nearly dead in the water. Courtesy of Floyd E. Bevill

pulled out of his glide but suddenly the plane lurched into a 60 degree dive toward the can. It did not recover but crashed off the starboard bow. Both Worley and gunner Earl Ward perished instantly; some of Harry's squadron mates believed he had been trying to make a suicide crash at the last moment. In any case, the *Isokaze* ground to a halt from Page's direct hit, so badly damaged from many hits she would have to be scuttled.

The loss of the popular Worley instilled fury in the hearts and minds of his pals. As they rendezvoused, they noticed a large whaleboat and many survivors floating in the spot vacated by the cruiser. The fighters and the bombers formed a strafing circle and began gunning down the survivors with their 50 cals. and 20mms. Ensign Bill Bowers, the newest replacement pilot in VB-9, was sickened by this act of barbarism. "I chose not to charge my guns, let alone fire them. I did not join in the pattern, kept my spacing and made dry runs."

Meanwhile, the giant *Yamato* was maneuvering frantically in a hard turn to port to avoid more attackers. The last *Intrepid/Langley* planes had planted three more bombs into her, and Tom Stetson passed the word to his division mates of their new target.

"Pilot to gunner," Bill Collins called over his intercom to Harvey Ewing, "We've been ordered to go in on the *Yamato*. Change the depth settings on the torpedo from a light cruiser to a battleship." As senior aviation ordnanceman in the flight, Ewing had the information on a pad strapped to his thigh and gave it to Collins: change the setting from ten to 20 to 22 feet. Collins relayed it to the other five planes.

Then, as Ewing remembered it, "I slid down from the turret, climbed over the back of the radioman, Jack Craven, and opened a small hatch to reach the bomb bay. Using a key like a roller-skate key, I felt for the lug and then made the necessary turns to make the fish run deeper. I then moved to the rear of the plane [in order to feed] 'window' out of the hatch as fast as I could while the radioman gave the pilot radar readings to help him maintain the proper altitude and course on the torpedo run.''

The same act was carried out on all six torpeckers as Stetson led them in a wide circling turn astern of the *Yamato* well outside of her AA gun range so he could survey his prey. Her reduced speed of eight knots and her ten-degree list to port thrilled him. ''One thought,'' Stets said later, ''ran through my mind: What a set-up for a starboard run!'' For the list had exposed the *Yamato's* starboard underbelly and massive armor belt for an ideal torpedo attack.

And yet, 'Old Stet' knew he couldn't make an orthodox approach, for the battlewagon's guns and those of her four escorting destroyers were throwing up a barrage of flak at the low clouds through which the planes must emerge in order to make their runs. He could not know that *Yamato's* admiral had just decided to abandon ship. As Stetson put it, ''I figured I'd better climb into the clouds until I got enough altitude, then come diving down at high speed, pop out, and make a hit-and-run attack.''

Continuing to watch the *Yamato*, which in fact had lost steering control from a torpedo hit in her rudder, he swung his division four and a half miles off her stern and then around to a position off her port beam where he took his planes up into the clouds to a point still four and half miles off her starboard bow. Ship and planes couldn't see each other, but the clouds were thin enough for the planes to see one another and thus maintain a tight formation.

At 4500 feet Stetson began his descent. The breakthrough at 2000 feet was some two miles from the *Yamato*—too far out. So the skipper pulled back on his stick, and his five teammates followed him back up into the overcast. They all came on again, planning for a line-abreast run by all six planes.

The return into the overcast, however, caused the formation to spread out a bit. When they let down into the clear again 2500 yards from the *Yamato*, only four of the torpeckers were still in rough line abreast—left to right Willie Collins, Stetson, Bill Gibson and John Kirwin. John Carter and Grady Jean trailed behind them.

A fighter pilot, watching from above, thought to himself, ''Jesus, they'll never get through that AA! It's murder! Jesus, there go those poor bastards, risking their lives to drop their fish, and the god-damn things won't run a hundred yards, because I've drunk all the alcohol out of them. Jesus!''

''Here we go'' Collins announced to crewmen Craven and Ewing, who was ''scared nearly out of my wits as we flew at a breathtaking 300 miles an hour toward the starboard side of the ship. I threw window into the slipstream as fast as I could'' to foul any radar-directed guns. ''In quick glances out the side windows, I could see bursts of anti-aircraft shells as they exploded closer and closer to our plane.''

Directly in front of the six Avengers, the mighty, awesome *Yamato*—largest warship in the world—turned hard to port, exposing the full length of her hull and underside.

''Hit her in the belly—now!'' Stetson commanded.

Pilot Collins and gunner Ewing felt they were ''flying straight toward the rising sun flag atop the superstructure'' when radio/radarman Craven, hunched over his scope, yelled, ''Fire torpedo!''

The four lead planes had accelerated from 220 to 280 knots in their descent, their pilots aiming to hit between the starboard bow and beam. Stetson's tactics were flawless, and at 100 yards from the target, from 800 feet up, Stets, Collins, Gibson and Kirwin dropped perfectly.

Each TBM lurched forward as the fish fell away. Willie Collins banked steeply, standing the plane on one wing directly over the stack of the *Yamato* for what seemed like an eternity.

''Move it! Move it!'' Harvey Ewing screamed, fearful that ''our torpedo bomber might slip right down into the gaping hole of the stack.'' Veering southward, the four Turkeys passed just 500 yards over the bow of the great battleship and between two destroyers.

Coming along behind them were John Carter and Grady Jean on individual runs. As they bored in, their eyes were greeted by three distinct explosions between amidships and the bow at the waterline; two of the fish struck so close together that they created a single blast.

Jean aimed his torpedo at *Yamato's* bow, and Carter swung toward the stern. Both released. Their fish ran hot and true. Jean's erupted at the bow, and Carter's cut across the battleships's wake to slam into the port quarter near the fantail. The time was 1417.

The *Yamato* pressed on, her batteries and three of her consorts blazing away at Stetson's division. Three of the six Turkeys were hit. In Collins', a 25mm shell rammed into the fuselage six inches

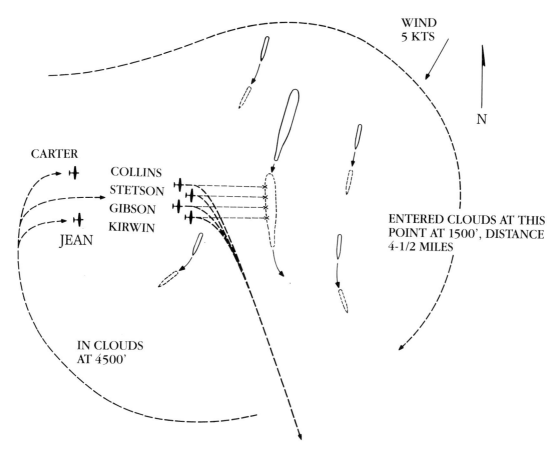

WIND
5 KTS

N

CARTER

COLLINS
STETSON
GIBSON
KIRWIN

JEAN

ENTERED CLOUDS AT THIS
POINT AT 1500', DISTANCE
4-1/2 MILES

IN CLOUDS
AT 4500'

Line-abreast attack on the *Yamato* by Lt. Thomas Stetson, Lt. (jg) William Collins, Lt. (jg) William Gibson and Lt. (jg) John Kirwin, with Lt. (jg) John Carter and Lt. (jg) Grady Jean coming in for an attack behind them. Solid outline of ships indicates their position at time of torpedo drop.

Graphics Courtesy of U.S. Naval Institute.

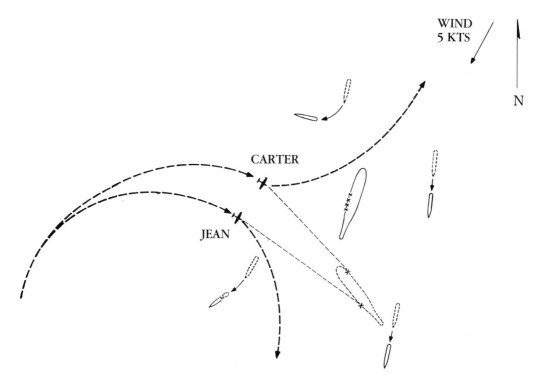

WIND
5 KTS

N

CARTER

JEAN

Attack by Lt. (jg) John W. Carter and Lt. (jg) Grady B. Jean on Japanese battleship *Yamato*, illustrating how *Yamato's* turn away from the attack caused Carter's torpedo to cross her wake and hit on the port quarter, close to the fantail. The solid line outline is position of ships at the time of the torpedo drops.

from the main gas tank but failed to detonate; it just stayed wedged in.

The men in the six Avengers looked back after getting out of AA range to behold the *Yamato* listing further to port, 20 degrees now, and she started to heel over on her beam ends. Abruptly, at 1423, some five or six minutes after taking the six fish, she rolled over on one side. A violent explosion tore her apart.

A column of flame shot straight up through the clouds, 2000 to 3000 feet in the sky, following by a billowing mushroom of smoke. Herb Houck rapidly snapped the shutters of his camera to record the death of the battleship—symbolically, too, of *all* battleships.

"God, look at that," Jack Craven gasped. "The most breathtaking sight I've ever seen," said Lieutenant (jg) Jean when it was over. "It made me tingle inside to know that I'd helped to do it. I felt as if I'd really done something in the war."

As the smoke cleared, no trace remained whatsoever of the world's largest warship—only a mammoth oil slick to mark her grave and that of over 3000 crewmen.

Houck collected his chickens, hawks and turkeys ten miles south of the remaining four Jap destroyers; the other four had gone down with the battleship and cruiser. The *Intrepid*'s planes had already departed, now followed by the *Yorktown*'s. Houck nursed his faulty engine all the way back, and his pilots conserved the last half of their gas supply.

Herb called the ship, which, however, had concerns of its own. The starboard catapult was out of order, so while the 1400 CAP of eight fighters was being launched on the port cat, puffs of flak appeared around the horizon from the screen and the other task groups.

"Bogey, 240, 16 miles!" and Theda Combs ordered, "Hard left!"

The last fighters went off and a spare was fastened to the cat, one wing folded to give room to the 5-inch starboard guns to fire. The ships on the horizon opened up again and splashed two bogeys, and many airedales—many still without helmets—ran toward the starboard bow for a look-see.

"Meyer!" Captain Combs bellowed down from the bridge. Junior looked up.

"Meyer, I want every man on that deck to wear a steel helmet! I've told them once today, and I'm going to hold you personally responsible! Either they wear helmets, or you put them on report!"

"'Aye, aye, sir!'"

All but one did, and he was castigated by a bark from Pappy Harshman over the horn.

It was now 1430 and soon word came that a *Yorktown* fighter had splashed a Frances near the formation.

At around 1500 Father Moody made an announcement on the loudspeaker, a bit earlier than his usual daily news broadcast: "Your attention, please! A flash report from one of our planes attacking the Jap fleet reports one battleship and one heavy cruiser definitely sunk, four destroyers smoking!"

No-one responded. No cheering. No excitement. Okinawa was an exhausting campaign. The *Yamato* fight was so far away. Everyone was pooped. "Roger," murmured a swab on the flag bridge.

Now, GQ again!

All hands sprang into action, but the bogey was knocked down some ten miles out. Secure.

The planes returned at 1630 with just enough fuel to stay in the landing circles, come aboard and taxi forward. The flight was logged in at 5.7 hours duration, and the torpeckers had but 12 to 32 gallons of gas left in each of their tanks.

Bill Gibson grinned as he led the torpedo pilots into the ready room: "We sank a battleship! Honest fellows! It blew up to the clouds!" The others were equally jubilant, especially when the photos confirmed everything they said. In the aircrewmen's ready room, someone asked Johnny Rodd, Don Page's gunner, what it felt like to see the *Yamato* blow. "Say," answered Rodd, "I wouldn't take a million bucks for what I saw."

Herb Houck ran up to Coop Bright with a confession, "Buck, I've had a lot of faith in you. We've gotten along, but I was on the verge of casting you aside. You were right!" The squadron CO's came in also and told Skinhead and their ACIOs how they took their time and then went in. "Bam! Bam! Bam! And then she went up!"

The bomber guys had mixed feelings, what with Harry Worley gone. Young Ensign Bill Bowers, still boiling with rage over the strafing of survivors, charged into the ready room, threw his helmet on the deck, and shouted, "Alright, who was the smart sonofabitch who thought it was cute to strafe survivors in the water?!"

Whereupon Lieutenant Commander Hank Pierson, liaison officer with the ship and ranking officer in VB-9, pulled Bowers aside and dressed him down, "If you know what's good for you, you'll keep your mouth shut!"

"Which I did," Bowers would recall thirty years

Yamato goes up into a mushroom cloud as her magazines ignite from VT-9 torpedo hits at about 1425. Three of her escorts mill around helplessly. National Archives

later after flying more missions over Korea and Vietnam, "to my everlasting regret." But what could a very junior boot-assed ensign do?

After all, war *is* hell, like General Sherman had said—and who can fairly judge the actions of men in battle?

A great victory had been won. It was *Yorktown*'s finest hour, and the ship's company showed its appreciation to the torpedo air crews. Eight of these boys were brought into a mess hall where hash was being served for dinner. Ewing: "The chow line was stopped and while a sizeable segment of the ship's crew waited, the cooks served us steak. It was a bit hairy dining that way while the hash was again dished out."

Wellington Henderson and Joe Bryan in Flag Plot were as tired as anyone to really celebrate. Hendy now sealed Bryan's despair with the remark, "Better sleep in your clothes tonight. I've got an idea the Bettys will be out."

ROOMS: ALERT YANKEES!! TODAY IS APPOMAT-TOX DAY. LET US EVER KEEP IN MIND THE EVENTS OF THAT SUCCESSFUL CAMPAIGN WHEN THE FLAG OF JEFF DAVIS WAS STOMPED IN THE DUST. WE MUST CONTINUE TO PRACTICE THE TACTICS AND TEACHINGS OF THAT GREAT GENERAL SHERMAN WHO GUIDED SO SUCCESSFULLY THE MARCH TO THE SEA. THE FAULTERING MOVEMENTS EMPLOYED AT GETTESBURG HAVE NO PLACE IN THIS WAR."

Bright sure knew his Civil War. Gettysburg *was* a Yankee victory, but since the winners did not capitalize on it to end the war immediately, that conflict had dragged on two more years until Lee's surrender at Appomattox 80 years ago this date.

The Bryans and Pattersons didn't take kindly to this typical insult, and someone posted a sign over the sofa in Skinhead's shop, "Lt. Cdr. Bright spun in here from a very low altitude."

Morning flights to Minami Daito Shima and

To the melody of a popular tune, Air Group Nine's squadrons celebrate the sinking of the *Yamato*; the whiskey-bottle throwing cat of VF-9, the Mexican fighting cock of VBF-9, the Hell's angel of VT-9, and Bugs Bunny of VB-9.

For once, the apprehensions were without foundation, and just about everyone got a decent night's sleep. Next day, April 8, one strike holed Tokuna airfield at Amami O Shima, two support strikes visited destruction on Okinawa, and a *Yorktown* CAP fighter splashed a Frances 15 miles out.

April 9 began for the ready rooms with a fresh tirade from the grabasser of Air Plot: "ALL READY

Amami expected no excitement, but flak over Minami scored a direct hit on a Hellcat of VBF-9, exploding its bomb and the whole plane. Lost was the squadron exec, Lieutenant Chad Jacobs, an Annapolis man and inspiring leader.

Shortly after noon a TBM was greeted aboard by the captain, navigator and air officer. The cargo was none other than Theda Combs's new relief, Captain W. Fred. Boone. Immediately referred to by the crew as "Dan'l," Boone had seen plenty of action in both oceans. A 1921 Academy grad and pilot since '26, he would ride in "makee-learn" status for two weeks before taking command of the Fighting Lady. Next day, during replenishment, Empty Evans quietly turned over his air officer duties to Commander Sandy Macpherson but remained on board to become executive officer as soon as Ben Born left.

Everything seemed to be such a dull anticlimax to the *Yamato* excitement. "While we may be tired," Born tried to enliven the crew in the Plan for April 11, "the Jap is damn miserable, and this is the way we must keep him. WE CAN'T AFFORD TO LET HIM GET A SECOND BREATH!"

Admiral Mitscher, for one, expected events on the 11th to show the Jap still full of fight. A talkative captured kamikaze pilot shot down by a *Hornet* plane on the 6th had bragged of a massive attack for this day. Mitscher cancelled all Okinawa support missions, and *Yorktown* concentrated on the northern approaches to the task force.

"At 1110," CIC's Ed Brand wrote in his diary, "a Kate reported our position and from then on things began to pop." The CAP chased Kate to 45 miles before nailing it at 1127. While strikes revisited Amami and Kikai Wan, the CAP over the task force began to knock down more incoming zootsuiters. Admiral Radford scrambled eight waiting *Yorktown* Hellcats at 1355. FDO Ballinger vectored them out to a fresh bogey contact 48 miles to the north. Watching the blips merge at 28 miles, he was surprised when the fighters reported no bogey.

Bogey, a Jill, had slipped by, coming in low off the starboard quarter. The fault lay in a downright faulty CAP-stationing procedure recently instituted by staff ops officer Jackson. Related Clyde Moneyhun, "He is real low, about 8 or ten foot off the water. Everything opens up. He seemed to be headed for *Intrepid* but didn't make it." Ed Wallace was one of the gunners firing away at her: "Under a heavy barrage she ducked in and out. After heading for us she turned and hedgehopped the *San Diego* and a can and dove into the battleship *Missouri.*

"My God!" exclaimed flag lieutenant Joe Hurley, "Right in one of the 20-millimeter batteries!" Damage was minimal, however; no casualties. This was the same Hurley who had conned the ship through her first night action off Kwajalein.

Four minutes later, at 1446, Earnshaw's gunners opened fire at another single-engine kamikaze 4000 yards away, "headed for us." Moneyhun: "The plane looked like he was going to make it. He tries to get in between the center of us and *Iowa*. Then we can't fire, and neither can they. But he is shot down about a hundred yards off our starboard quarter." The view from the bridge put it at 1800 yards.

The next object up the groove to land was neither a Turkey, hawk or chicken—but a seagull! Joe Bryan watched with the topside hands as it "lit on the flight deck, without so much as a flap of Dick Tripp's flags. It walked around a bit, then flew to the bow, perched again, ran a few steps, and took off. One of the signalmen called, 'Two-block Fox!' "

There was no humor aboard the *Enterprise,* just returned to battery after repairs from kamikaze damage. Within an hour of each other, two Judys plunged into her, while a near-miss killed several men on the *Essex,* and two destroyers got clobbered.

Late in the afternoon CAP fighters splashed four more suiciders, leaving Joe Bryan to admire a glorious sunset "out of Turner. A warm salmon light bathed the ships and flecked the seas. It was magnificent until a hack cartoonist rearranged things, poking a jagged hole in the cloud and pulling it across the sun so that its rays fanned out like a Japanese flag."

A fitting setting, for onto the darkening stage soon roared a Betty with two pursuers close behind. The Hellcats hit it, turning it into "a blob of flame" when Bryan saw it. George Wille: "He kept on coming, however, and we threw everything at him. In the darkness it was quite a sight—a veritable funnel of tracers streaking up and converging on the ball of fire that was our attacker. He finally went down [at 4000 yards], but he certainly took long enough." Ship's guns got partial credit, in spite of two malfunctioning guns.

Kenny Parkinson: "Thank God it is dark now." But the Japs countered by filling the night with parachute flares. Dentist Smith: "Thirty-five flares were counted at one time in the air" out of perhaps 80 in all. The snoopers also dropped loads of window which cluttered all the radars and enabled two of the zootsuiters to make runs on Radford's ships. The screen and battleships knocked them down before night fighters could close in.

Admiral Radford called Captain Boone on the squawk box, "How'd you enjoy your welcome

Eleven smashed Japanese planes are seen in this April 13, 1945 photo by a *Yorktown* plane over Tokuna airfield. Kept neutralized, this field could not help the defenders of Okinawa.

today?"

"Well, I'll tell you," replied Boone. "I'm like the old Southern mammy who used to say, 'When I sits down and begins to worry, I just falls asleep!' "

But the gun crews neither slept nor ate, for incessant bogeys and flares kept them at the ready all night long, though Radford's ships did no shooting. And next day the suiciders shifted to the shipping off Okinawa, where more than 150 were

destroyed. The *Yorktown* sent a Target CAP to Amami's Tokuna airfield where the Hellcats shot down three planes at the cost of Jim Kussmann's Cat. He ditched offshore, however, and was soon rescued by a float plane from a cruiser.

Aside from an early false alert, Friday the 13th was ushered in by an unhappy announcement over the bullhorn by Captain Combs: "Your attention, please. Word has just been received that President

Roosevelt died today of a cerebral hemorrhage."
Ed Wallace said it for the entire crew in his diary:
"The best leader we ever had and a 4.0 Navy man."
Ed Brand: "This certainly was a blow to everyone."
Next day the colors were dipped at half-mast for
a 30-day mourning period.

A single Myrt splashed by a *Yorktown* CAP
fighter on the 13th belied the true tactical situation
ashore. The Japanese were launching fanatical
counterattacks at American ground forces. Next
day's noontime CAP in short order splashed three
Bettys carrying manned suicide *"baka"* bombs. The
destroyer *Melvin* picked up three airmen from a
Jake float plane shot down during the night and
transferred them to the *York*.

When the Marine guards discovered that one of
them, an ensign, could understand some written
English, one of the gyrenes wrote on a pad, "My
name Richard. I am Marine. Why you fight us?"

The ensign scribbled, "I no win."

"You know B29?"

The ensign drew a fairly accurate sketch of one
and added, "Tokyo burn."

"We treat you good."

No comment.

Leaving the other task groups to deal with more
nocturnal bandits, Radford's group retired to
replenish on April 15. "AT 1200," Ben Born
pointed out, "THIS SHIP WILL BE TWO YEARS
OLD." "Seems a lot longer than that," Lieutenant
Joe Hachet, who had been on board with the radars
the whole time, reflected in a letter home. "We've
certainly covered a lot of territory in those two
years."

On the 16th, the kamikazes descended on the
picket destroyers while the carriers launched CAPs
and strikes. The can *Laffey* took five direct hits by
kamikazes and three by bombs but still managed
to shoot down eleven planes and sail away.
Yorktown's Target CAP splashed three bandits over
the island the boys called "Okie," where the
bombers attacked well-defended caves. Herb Houck
led a 275-mile sweep to blast parked planes at Izumi
and Kagoshima airfields on Kyushu, and Gene
Valencia splashed a Judy, his eleventh kill.

Just before noon, the suiciders reached the carriers, and *Yorktown's* CAP splashed four of them.
More came on at 1330. George Wille saw a plane
make "a run on the *Intrepid*, low-level. The Inter-
rogatory really opened up and stopped him cold
about 200 yards from home. They came down in
pairs. One tried for the *Missouri* again, a beautiful
dive. Set on fire about half way down and swerved
up again. He made a try for a can (the *Franks*, in
plane guard formation just forward of the *Missouri*)
which did some fancy maneuvering and blazed
away at him.

"The Jap's diving course looked just like the first
dip on a roller coaster: down steep, then up, then
down again for the destroyer. When they saw him
coming, hard left rudder was used, and the *Franks*
heeled way over in her turn. You could almost hear
the tires squeal!"

The zooter exploded on impact just off the stern

Assistant gun boss
George Earnshaw,
former pitcher for the
Philadelphia Athletics, is
flanked by Chief Gun-
ners Frans Nordling and
"Tiny" Pickett. They
pose before a 40mm
mount, April 15, 1945.

Courtesy of Mrs.
George A. Earnshaw

of the *Missouri*; "its bomb," related Joe Bryan, "blows a column of brown water higher than her foretop."

Task group gunners took a third diver under fire, and it crashed into the sea next to the destroyer *McDermut*. But a 5-inch shell from the Big Mo hit the can, causing casualties. More zootsuiters followed, still in pairs.

George Smith: "Two of them made a run on the *Intrepid*, one of which made a vertical dive, just missing the outboard elevator; the other hit in the vicinity of #3 elevator and its bomb exploded on the hangar deck." The Unlucky I burned again.

"Hard left!" Theda Combs barked as two more headed in at the *Yorktown*. Ed Wallace watched them come in high "across our stern at about 1100 yds. and the whole force opened fire. These planes got away hiding and streaking for the clouds. Those tin cans are really dishing it out."

"Poor 'Dry I!' Lucky *Yorktown*!" wrote Joe Bryan, summing up the combat records of the two flattops as he watched the *Intrepid* struggle to douse her fires for the next hour.

She succeeded, only to face three more single-engine zooters at 1515. Again, the entire formation opened fire, including the *York*. Two headed for the *Intrepid* and dropped their bombs to score near-misses. The first was then shot down, while the second recovered and flew across the stern of the *Yorktown* from starboard to port. Earnshaw's gunners knocked him out of the sky and chased the third away still carrying its bomb.

At 1730 the dusk CAP of two night fighters took off, and none too soon. As the sun went down an hour later, more bogeys appeared. Ted Sherman's gunners got a Frances, and Charlie Ridgway in Jocko Clark's group vectored little Johnny Orth of *Yorktown's* night team to a second one. At 1848 Orth splashed a Frances.

The nearly first-quarter moon brightened the night sky "and we had visitors." Wille: "The jerks dropped flares all around us and it looked like July Fourth. We expected at least one torpedo hit out of it but our night fighters got most of the attackers. Thanks to Johnny Orth, champ night fighter of the Navy" who shot down another, a twin-engine plane. "There is nothing more pleasant to watch than a nice big Betty get hit, burst into a flower of flame and then crash into the ocean. Cold hearted, yes, but it still looks good." More bogeys visited the other groups throughout the night as the damaged *Enterprise, Hancock* and *Intrepid* limped away for repairs.

Expecting the 17th to be a repeat performance by the Divine Wind Kamikaze Corps, the carriers operated only fighters for combat air patrols. Coop Bright assigned Gene Valencia's Flying Circus Division to circle north of the formation at angels 20—in the direction of the kamikaze fields at Kyushu—with Glenn Phillips' division below it at angels 18. Gene, with his eleven kills to date, did his usual 40 pushups before a hearty battle breakfast and manned his Hellcat alongside his mates Jim French, Harris Mitchell and Clint Smith. They took

George Earnshaw holds the cake for Hank Bolden as Air Defense Forward celebrates 12 1/2 shoot-downs by the ship's guns. Smiling at rear is Father Joe Moody. April 16, 1945. Courtesy of Henry E. Bolden

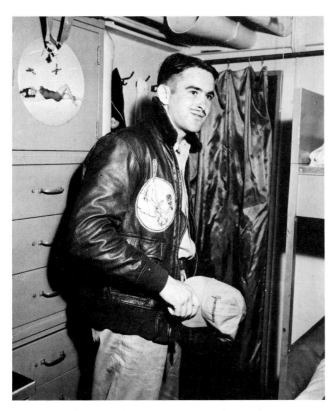

Gene Valencia in his stateroom on the *Yorktown* during the Okinawa campaign. The VF-9 emblem is a cat throwing an empty whiskey bottle down from a cloud. Courtesy of Joseph Kaelin

off at 0520 into the twilight—a fair morning broken only by low cumulus clouds—and assumed station. For two hours they saw nothing but a beautiful, empty blue sky.

Suddenly, at 0817, Ballinger's radars registered many blips, 78 miles, bearing 345 degrees (T)—right in Valencia's direction. The word was passed to Valencia, who, with his wingman Mitchell, searched the northern skies for the bogeys—as did French and Smith behind them. The *Yorktown* went to GQ.

"Tallyho! Bogeys! Three o'clock!" It was Smith.

The Flying Circus swung toward the dozen or so Jap planes approaching about ten miles ahead and 65 miles out from the carriers. Valencia now signaled section leader French to go in for the first dogfight. While French and Smith engaged, Valencia and Mitchell would fly top cover to protect them. Then the two sections would trade off. These were the tactics the Circus had been practicing for months. Now to try them out.

"Jeez," called French on the radio, "There must be fifty of 'em!" Zeros, Franks and Oscars—all single-engine planes headed toward the task force in many small V formations that were part of a larger one.

Valencia: "We came in high with the sun at our backs, and the green and brown camouflaged Japanese fighters with their big bright 'meatballs' were clearly visible. They weren't even aware of our presence. . . . We picked the top planes first." Mitchell: "I discovered the true meaning of anxiety, but when I looked over at Gene his expression was that of a young child who had just spotted his favorite toy under the Christmas tree."

Diving down on the bogeys at nearly 400 knots, French and Smith each picked out a Frank and opened fire. Both targets exploded! They were obviously zootsuiters carrying bombs; the fact that they refused to deviate from their straight course to defend themselves confirmed this. As these two pilots pulled up, Valencia and Mitchell roared in and detonated two more Franks.

The flight of kamikazes pressed on, the men in the ships gooped on their anti-flash mud, and the Flying Circus repeated its tactic—and each one of the Hellcats got another Frank, though Smitty couldn't confirm his kill. As Valencia turned left, a bandit filled his sights, and he fired but had to pull up to avoid ramming him—another probable. Seven down and two maybes in eight passes! Pretty good shooting.

But the big enemy formation was now nearing the task force, and it split up into tiny three-plane sections. "Break tactics!" Valencia ordered, "Select targets of opportunity." There was no time for the Circus' superlative system, for as many bandits as possible had to be prevented from reaching the ships—now visible in the distance.

At this moment, Glenn Phillips' division of VF-9 Hellcats appeared, and a number of the Japs started to parachute! Valencia came up behind another Frank, fired into it until smoke erupted, then it exploded. Simultaneously, French ignited his third Frank to keep pace with Valencia, who now swung in behind three Franks only to be startled by tracers from Mitchell's F6 zinging by him toward another prey.

Gene and wingman Mitchell scored again; smoke trailed from two Franks as a prelude, followed by the blasts when the bombs detonated. They pressed after the last plane in the trio until Valencia knocked that too out of the heavens. He had five now and a probable, but there were still so many left. French got one of them, as did Smith.

Valencia now zoomed over after a Jap who was on the tail of two Hellcats who in turn pursued another Jap. He opened fire, bogey exploded, and Valencia jerked away from the debris. Number Six!

As Gene surveyed the scene, the Jap survivors turned back with F6Fs in hot pursuit. Just then, a burning Jap passed by Valencia, who gave him an insurance burst but claimed no credit for this victim.

Low on fuel, Valencia and Mitchell headed for the rendezvous, but instead of French's section another Jap fighter appeared. Gene gave his throttle full juice, got in position, and squeezed the trigger. The guns did not respond. He was out of ammo—2400 rounds all used up on six kills and and a probable. This lucky Nip got away.

The Flying Circus "mowing machine" dropped down to land with 16 scores under its belt—Gene Valencia with six and a probable, giving him a total of 17 confirmed aerial victories to date; Harris Mitchell had three kills; Jim French four; and Clint Smith one and a probable. Valencia and Mitchell landed first.

"Bogey 050, 25, closing!" came a sudden announcement. The two other planes were waved off.

Independence fighters were vectored to the intercept and knocked down three Jills—just as a *Yorktown* CAP over the picket cans had eliminated two Oscars and two Tonys. Several more were scratched by other ships' fire.

Crewmen crowded around the jubilant Circus pilots as they left the flight deck. When the word filtered up to Captain Boone, he exulted, "How about that boy who just shot down six Japs? It wasn't so long ago that stuff like that was getting the Congressional Medal!"

Phillips' division also reported three kills—a Zeke, a Frank, and an Oscar, and Toby Larson intercepted and destroyed an approaching Frances eight miles out in the early afternoon, giving Fighting 9 22 definite kills for the day.

With the departure of the three stricken carriers. TG 58.4 was reshuffled to include the *Yorktown* as the only heavy amid three light carriers—*Independence, Langley* and *Bataan.* The far fewer anti-aircraft batteries of the CVLs placed a much heavier responsibility on the Earnshaw-Patterson crews. Number Two gun had alone nailed five bogeys, which meant a five-to-ten dollar bonus in each gunner's pay this month. But the round-the-clock hours hardly made the bonus worthwhile.

Joe Bryan dozed off at his desk in the evening and was glad of it after "seeing Pat Patterson at supper. The poor devil is really beat up. He's usually nimble with a knife and fork, but tonight he stared at his food, then shoved the plate away and put his head on the table and went to sleep."

The siege by the Okinawa zootsuiters dragged on. On April 18 *Yorktown* Helldivers and Avengers planted their bombs into buildings at "Okie's" heavily-defended Shuri Town and their rockets into nearby caves. Otherwise, the day passed without incident, enabling jovial Pete Joers to take a potshot at "Nude-noggin" Bright: "When you get home, Coop, don't go into any poolrooms. Don't even walk by the door, or somebody'll sure stick a cue in your ear!"

More support strikes on the 19th included napalm bombs and daisy cutters. And word was received that the beloved Ernie Pyle had been killed by a Jap machine gun on offshore Ie Shima. A sad statistic was also released, recorded by Ed Brand: "We have lost 150 planes & 130 pilots and crewmen since this ship was commissioned."

After refueling and rearming next day, the *Yorktown* rejoiced when another anticipated kamikaze deluge was snuffed out by a devastating B-29 raid on the zootsuiter bases of Kyushu. When word of this reached the *York*, Joe Bryan was pleased to see the crew unwind. "On the flight deck," where the gobs had knocked off bothering to wear war paint over recent days, "men are lounging in the sun; in the passageways, they're scuffling happily. It's about time they had a little rest."

But Coop Bright couldn't let *his* guard down, and again Pete Joers took aim at The Dome: "All I want to know is, how the hell did they put eyes in that stump?"

Gunner Ed Wallace had some mixed emotions about his own situation: "They put me in charge of Mt. 5 the twins, and today is my 27th birthday, also my worst. We are all in."

No suiciders appeared during daylight of the 21st, while a dozen bombers from the ship hit Okinawa. But at nightfall the *Yorktown* vectored night fighters to the destruction of three Bettys. The last went in just 15 miles away, and more than one lookout reported seeing a torpedo pass close to the stern.

Thanks to the Superforts again smacking Kyushu, the *Yorktown* could concentrate on supporting the embattled infantry on the island on April 22. As a dozen dive bombers worked over caves, division leader Ed "Wizzer" Wiezorek dropped his bomb but recovered so low—at 600 feet—that the blast sent shrapnel into his engine, stopping it. He glided to a coral ledge a few miles south of Yontan and made a neat shallow-water landing. When Wizzer and his gunner made their way onto the reef, a U.S.

Army ambulance simply drove out to them for a unique rescue!

A high-flying Myrt snooper tried to elude a VF-9 Hellcat after an 80-mile chase by diving away—only to have its wings pull off in the process! More *York* fighters shot down two more Myrts, a Judy and a Tony over the picket line. Then an enemy pilot was picked up in the water, having parachuted from one of the high-flying bogeys. Through an interpreter, he revealed that one of the planes shot down was one the CIC guys had dubbed "the Whip"—who had led the kamikazes to the force, watched their attack, then retired. This way, the Whip could make certain that no zootsuiter turned "chicken" and fled.

This pilot was angry. After the big ceremony the day before his scheduled one-way flight, he had been given a girl to sleep with. B-29 raids, however, had forced his flight to be postponed for many days, during which he had developed diarrhea from the whore. This made him furious at his superiors, so when the Whip got shot down, he figured to hell with it and had simply bailed out. No-one would be going back to squeal on him anyway.

On April 23, after Herb Houck escorted VT and VB to hit Tomui Town on Okinawa, the senior officers of the *Yorktown* and admiral's staff made their way to the flight deck for the brief change-of-command ceremony. Admiral Radford awarded Theda Combs with a Legion of Merit, and Commander Born presented him with his two-star flag. "You'll notice, sir, we've left plenty of room on it for your future stars." (He'd earn one more later.) At 1405 Combs and Freddie Boone read their orders, and it was over.

Joe Bryan observed that Combs and Ben Born "have made the *Yorktown* a happy ship. We hope to God that Captain Boone, our new skipper, can keep her so." Born later read a message over the bullhorn: "In losing Admiral Combs, we are saying farewell to a splendid skipper, who gave his time and efforts unceasingly to this ship, and who always had at heart the interest of every man in the crew. . . . We all unite in wishing our best to our departing skipper."

What kind of a captain would Boone be? Cooper Bright found out at once. With the afternoon strike returning from Okinawa, Bright called up the bridge, "Captain, we're ready to receive aircraft. Strike coming back."

Boone turned the ship—and consequently the entire task group—into the wind to receive the flight, whereupon the planes turned out to belong to another carrier. Boone was furious and summoned Bright to the bridge, "Didn't you report to me personally that you were ready to receive aircraft? What happened?"

"Captain, I made a mistake."

"You made a *mistake*?! Captain Combs told me you were the first one to know when your planes were coming back and that you were actually operating the whole task group."

The weary Bright replied, "You've got to work on averages, Captain. Every so often you drop the ball. You can't help it. I'm doing a hell of a lot of this through intuition, not through recognition of the planes. I missed it."

"Jesus! How many times has this occurred?"

"Well, this is the first time in months. And it'll happen again. But I'll tell you one thing. For the next 20 or 30 days, *I hope,* we're gonna be going down there looking real good—if the averages hold up."

Perplexed by this honest explanation, Boone accepted it. And Coop only had to hang on another month before his again-promised leave.

At least the day was a quiet one for ship's company. Wrote Ed Brand, "No Japs. Got a full night's sleep for a change & that was really a relief." And the next day the *York* received not only fuel and ammo but dry stores and food from a cargo ship—the first time fresh provisions had been delivered while underway.

They were welcome, for the flour had been turning bad, and the soup had left something to be desired of late. Gunner Ted Johnson: "Sometimes we had to pick the bugs out of the soup, so I wore dark glasses and just drank it one time." How times hadn't changed. Nelson's men at Trafalgar a century and a half before had complained of the same thing; lacking dark glasses, they had eaten at night.

Task Group 58.4 welcomed the battleship *Iowa* into the formation and exchanged the CVL *Bataan* for a brand new *Essex*-class carrier, the *Shangri-La.* Bryan: "The CV makes us happier than the BB does. The kamikazes' favorite targets are CVs. The *Yorktown* has been the only one in our task group [with three CVLs] for the past few days, so the *Shangri-La* should split the next attack."

And so it went, day after day, as strikes from a dozen fast carriers and more than a dozen jeep carriers besieged Okinawa's fanatical defenders—and as the zootsuiter corps besieged the Fifth Fleet and its flattops. In addition, the fast carriers sent daily strikes north to keep Tokuna and Kyushu neutralized. Veterans of many months were gradually transferred Stateside, and on April 28 Joe Bryan took his leave. Admiral Radford urged him, "Tell those people at ComAirPac they can't leave us here forever! That's the way they lost their carriers at Guadalcanal—keeping them in the same place too long."

Next day two *Yorktown* composite deckload strikes cratered the runways at Kikai and shot down five zooters there, part of a large afternoon flight heading south toward the carriers. At 1608 the radars picked up the rest at 70 miles out. GQ, and Pat Patterson rushed up to "Sky One" (Air Defense Forward) and uttered his favorite battle cry over the horn: "Rebels, man yo' guns! Yankees, take cover!" The call amused Captain Boone not at all.

Carl Ballinger vectored out two divisions of *Yorktown* Hellcats which splashed three Franks. A third CAP division roared down on four zootsuiters diving on the picket destroyers and managed to gun down a Zeke and a Judy. But the other two smashed into the *Hazelwood* and *Haggard*, causing great havoc.

Moments later another bogey suddenly appeared only ten miles to the east. No time for the CAP. The screen opened up, and Pat Patterson instinctively ordered, "Open fire!" Ed Wallace recounted how the *York's* guns concentrated "on one Zeke which was shot down in flames by one of our cans or battlewagons. The Zeke was upside down when it hit" off the port quarter of the *Wisconsin*.

Captain Boone was furious. He called Patterson to the bridge, "Now this ship has not been run correctly. *I* will give the orders when to open fire."

Patterson, who knew that an instantaneous order was essential to thwart low-flying zootsuiters, angrily replied, "Well, if you want to give the orders when to open fire—and little as you know about these kamikazes—you can get yourself another assistant gunnery officer, 'cause I'm not gonna let my boys die!"

At this moment, Admiral Radford sent a message to Boone and George Earnshaw, "That's the best shooting I've ever seen!" Boone said nothing. Earnshaw already had his orders to be transferred, which would make Patterson gun boss. Boone wouldn't have it and began the paperwork to have Patterson sent home too. Radford must concur, but for a different reason: at 42 Tiny was too old to keep up the difficult pace of running up through the island during GQ. He would get a medical discharge.

Come nighttime, no activity occurred until after midnight when night FDO Bob Haugh vectored the

two night fighters 40 miles to the north. Johnny Orth tallyhoed three snoopers there and shot down an Irving, then a Betty. The second one exploded directly in front of him, though, temporarily blinding him and allowing the third to escape, dropping window to foul the radar from tracking it.

All this took place in full view of the ship, with topside hands cheering as the two kills went down in flames off the starboard bow. Then the night lit up with tracers as the screen drove away three more bandits. The exhausted gunners fell asleep at their guns again as GQ remained in effect the rest of the night. At dawn the CAP shot down two bandits directly overhead.

As May began, the situation ashore was improving, the troops being assisted by Marine Corps F4U Corsair fighters operating out of Okinawa's Kadena field. While Air Group Nine pounded Japanese positions and revisited Amami on this May Day, the ship received a "may day" distress call at noon. Three patrolling Marine Corsairs from Kadena had been out at sea and blown off course by high altitude 100-plus-mph winds. Dangerously low on gas, they called for help. When the *Yorktown* answered them, the pilots reported that none of them had ever landed aboard a carrier.

"Do you have tailhooks?"

"We'll see. . . . Yes."

Air officer Sandy Macpherson obtained Captain Boone's permission to let them try, whereupon Jim "Hazy" Cozzens, Crash Two, manned a recently rigged radio on the LSO platform and "talked" the pilots into the landing pattern and up the groove while the new Crash One, Lee Spaulding, waved them aboard. All three landed safely, and as one climbed out of his cockpit he remarked to an airedale, "What was that man doing waving those paddles back there?"

"Brother, he's the Landing Signals Officer, and he was giving you a waveoff!"

While the Corsairs were refueled, the airedales painted little signs on them: "I shall return." The three gyrenes were catapulted off to return to Kadena, immensely proud of their achievement.

During replenishment next day a hospital ship briefly joined the task formation. Ed Brand reported that "some of the fellows got to see the nurses, but I didn't. The last woman I saw was about the 10th or 12th of July last year." The news from Europe was encouraging—Adolf Hitler reported dead and Berlin captured.

The kamikazes sank four picket ships off

Okinawa on May 3 then revisited Task Force 58 shortly after midnight of the new day. After a snooping Emily was splashed, Johnny Orth and Dale Knopf were catapulted. Locking on to a Betty with his airborne radar, Orth sent it down burning 58 miles north of the ship at 0345. The *Randolph* then directed him in the destruction of two more Bettys before dawn, making Orth a night ace. Knopf got one bandit. When they returned aboard, the airedales cheered Orth roundly, and Admiral Radford personally greeted him. But looking around Johnny said finally, "Where's the captain?" Boone was too busy on the bridge to be there.

Daylight of the 4th brought a swarm of zoot-suiters while the carrier planes worked over Okinawa and Kikai. Fighting 9 contributed to the massive CAP and in a half-hour's time splashed no fewer than 25 more suiciders. Gene Valencia's "mowing machine" Flying Circus claimed almost half of these, Gene himself getting four, which gave him a total of 21 kills. *Essex* planes accounted for 35 other kills of the total of 95 destroyed during the morning.

Successful as this interception had turned out, it had been accomplished in spite of the confused and complicated procedures and constant meddling of task group ops officer Commander Jackson. With the experienced FDO Wilding long departed, Jackson had unceasingly interfered with the work of Carl Ballinger. During a break in the action this day, May 4, Ballinger sent a handwritten note of thanks on fighter directing to the CIC on the *Langley* via a returning pilot. In it, he said, "The YORKTOWN has a bellyfull of being a flagship and my ulcer is in foul shape from arguments with guess who [Jackson]. Fortunately none of this has affected the group in the ultimate result which is a good job all around. . . ."

It had been so good in fact that the Japs were stopped for a few days, during which also, explained dentist George Smith, "some of our pilots returning after spending some time on the airfields report the marines having high praise for task force 58. Our aircraft and ships guns have knocked out gun emplacements and brought down many aircraft. They gripe about the slow moving army troops on the island and the poor army AA fire, stating that to date they [the army] have not brought down a single enemy!—only dropping flak into their forces.

"The latest Jap trick is to send attractive 'Geisha girls' into the marine lines at night with hidden explosives as well as brief cases filled with T.N.T.

Some women with babies in their arms have explosives which go off in the midst of our troops. Their own lives mean nothing."

"GERMANY SURRENDERS!" men wrote in their diaries on May 8 after the announcement and tumultuous cheering subsided. "Two down and one to go," observed Ed Wallace. "This sounds awful good" to Ed Brand, "Maybe the fellows will come over here & help us now. I think we could use it." Hard rain and wind caused flights to be cancelled, and Coxswain Ted Rohrbaugh was told "to check out the number 2 whale boat, hoisted up under the flight deck. When I lifted the boat's cover and looked inside, I found 2 gallons of some kind of home made wine cooling. I took the wine to the division gear locker, and we all had a drink to the end of the war in Europe."

Smith: "Fighting on Okinawa continues and slow gains are being made. We are afraid the German defeat will not be felt for several months out here. While people at home celebrate, have two-day holidays, raise hell in general, the marines, soldiers and sailors in the Pacific go on dying. It seems easy to forget a war so far away. The Japs seem to remember pretty well!"

May 9 dawned bright and clear, enabling *Yorktown* torpeckers to drop 2000-pound blockbusters and the bombers 1000-pounders to destroy a concrete barricade on Okinawa. Ugh Lee led the Avengers in glide bomb runs which touched off a gas or ammo dump. Unfortunately, on landing, a Hellcat pilot suffered a brain concussion when he rammed into the barrier. Worse, when Lee landed at midday and began folding his wings, he accidentally triggered his guns, strafing the plane handlers on the flight deck! The slugs, pointed down, struck Ensign John Battaile and 19 crewmen. Aviation Chief Machinist George Sieh of VT-9 had his right arm blown off, and two men were hit in the stomach. Ed Wallace and his mates were sickened at the sight of the wounded, with "guts and blood splattered all over them. A rotten bloody mess if I ever saw one." Ensign Battaile succumbed to his loss of blood two hours later, a rare tragedy of the operational variety in the life of the Fighting Lady. Thankfully, no-one else died.

Captain Freddie Boone aimed to put a stop to such growing carelessness. As rigidly professional and exact as the pencil-thin mustache painstakingly centered between his nose and upper lip, Boone intended to tighten up the *Yorktown* so that it could live up to its reputation as a first-class ship. In fact, he was proving to be as strong as Jocko

Landing Number 25,000 on the Fighting Lady, May 10, 1945, off Okinawa. (L to R) Captain Boone, pilot Pooch Maury of VBF-9, Baker Sid Allen, Lieutenant Commander Pappy Harshman, and Commander Ben Born.

The Flying Circus division of VF-9 celebrates its 50 kills off Okinawa and including Gene Valencia's previous scores. (L to R) Valencia (23 kills), Harris Mitchell (10), Clint Smith (6) and Jim French (11). The wartime censor has cut out their squadron patches on their jackets. National Archives

Clark ever was but without all the bombast. Every bit a polished gentleman, he was very hard to get close to.

Inasmuch as he could not tolerate mistakes, he meant to prevent them. His yeomen discovered what a punctilious s.o.b. he was when he insisted on such perfection in each written document, by always changing commas, that half of his messages didn't seem to ever get sent out. The men called him "Comma-Stop-Man" Boone behind his back. And of course, he was convinced that only Academy ringknockers could deliver this kind of quality. So when Pat Patterson started telling Texas stories to Boone, the captain cut him off. Tiny's drawl and inarticulate non-Academy manner added to Boone's decision to get rid of him.

Freddie—or "Dan '1'"—was obviously on the way up in his career to four stars and would get them by following the same book that Commander Andy Jackson followed. Unfortunately for everybody, Jackson now fell victim to the constant strain of Okinawa, as exhaustion overcame him, forcing his confinement for rest in Sick Bay. Luckily, he had the *Yorktown's* air ops people to cover for him, though they were none too happy about having their workload doubled. He should have been transferred ashore, but Radford had scheduled Jackson for greater things in the future.

Ensign Battaile was buried at sea with full honors on May 10 in the midst of five CAPs, two small support strikes to Okinawa, two Target CAPs to the Kikai-Amami area, and a late afternoon fighter strike to Minami Daito Shima. The B-29s kept the kamikazes away by continuing to pound Kyushu.

More of the same on the 11th—"57 DAYS AT SEA SO FAR" wrote Ed Wallace—with a dozen Hellcats patrolling over the picket line north of Okie at sunup. One of the destroyers vectored out Lieutenant Bert Eckard's division to a large incoming raid at its CAP sector 50 miles due west of Okinawa's northern tip. Eckard and wingman Ensign Joe Kaelin climbed to get above an estimated seven Zekes. At the same moment the second section of Emmett Lawrence and Al Honegger broke off and dived on other bandits below them, Lawrence splashing a Zeke and Honegger a Frank.

Suddenly Eckard and Kaelin realized that their "seven" Zekes were actually 35! Five were stacked in echelon to the right, small clusters comprised the van, and many stragglers brought up the rear. The two Hellcats waded into them from the port side and rear and burned at least two of the stragglers before being discovered by the rest.

The Japs, obviously unskilled in even the most elementary fighter tactics, either continued on course, dived down toward the deck, or turned about in acrobatic maneuvers. Eckard and Kaelin stayed together for their runs and recoveries between angels 17 and 20 in a general melee that lasted 20 minutes. Eckard easily destroyed five Zekes and Kaelin three plus a probable, after which they headed for the deck to find the others. Finding none, and low on ammo and gas, both men landed at Yontan.

Gene Valencia's Flying Circus and Marv Franger's division joined in the fracas, though the latter only encountered one Tony, Franger getting it for his ninth shoot-down of the war. Valencia's guys went after two nine-plane formations and had their by-now typical field day: two Tonys, two Oscars, a Frank, a Tojo, a Frances and two other single-engine planes. And Ace Valencia brought his grand total to 23—one of the highest scores of the war—while the Circus's aggregate was now 43 kills. Adding Gene's seven scores on his first cruise, the four men had a round 50 between them. Division mates Harris Mitchell, Jim French and Clint Smith were all aces as well.

Still, the energetic efforts of VF-9 and its sister squadrons from the other carriers weren't enough to stop the onslaught of these human guided missiles which smacked into two more destroyers and took on the fast carriers. With most of the *Yorktown's* Hellcats committed over Okie, the CAPs of the new *Shangri-La* and the *Langley* protected the *York*, which provided fighter direction.

While FDO Pete Peterson directed the destruction of three bogeys, topside hands witnessed smoking from a stricken carrier on the horizon. It was the *Bunker Hill,* flagship of Admiral Mitscher, who now transferred to the *Enterprise.* Two zootsuiters and their bombs had killed nearly 600 men. Dentist Smith watched the *Bunker Hill* "listing slightly to port and moving slowly, heading for safety. We passed by several scattered bodies floating in the area afterwards and destroyers moving about picking them up."

The Jap attack spent, after noon the *Yorktown* launched eight Helldivers to Okinawa, but Billy May's couldn't get enough airspeed and dribbled off the deck and into the drink off the starboard bow. He and gunner Abie Cohen got free, but Cohen swallowed too much of the Pacific, and May administered artificial respiration until a destroyer rescued them. May had saved Cohen's life. Then Jack Bell's engine failed during his takeoff, and the Beast plunged over the bow dead ahead. The ship just missed running over the plane, which however dragged Bell down with it. Gunner "Father John" Kirby, thrown free on impact, was picked up by a can.

The wearisome Okinawa campaign led Jocko Clark over in the *Hornet* to circulate a message throughout his task group: "See Hebrews 13, verse 8. No irreverence intended." A quick look at the reference drew universal agreement: "Jesus Christ, the same yesterday, and today, and forever." That was Okinawa.

But not forever, for good news changed everyone's mood on the *York:* retirement toward

Ulithi next day. After gunnery drill and simulated attacks on the ship during the withdrawal May 12, the crew gathered in the hangar in the evening for its first movie in a month. It was "Nothing But the Truth" starring Bob Hope. Laughter—just what the doctor ordered.

Next morning, Father Moody gave the crew some telling facts: The Fighting Lady had been at sea 61 days and steamed 35,000 miles. Of that time, 29 days had been spent under attack. Then, as the ship neared Ulithi the morning of the 14th, alarming news revealed that Jocko Clark's and Ted Sherman's task groups had been pounced on by more zoot-suiters, and one had crashed into the Big E, Mitscher's new flagship. The admiral again had to move, to the *Randolph,* while the *Enterprise* pulled out for repairs.

Little did anyone realize, however, that the siege of Task Force 58 was over. The zootsuiters had given up—at least for the present.

Returning from shore leave at Ulithi's Mog Mog. Cartoon by R.L. Streeter.

Chapter XIV
Bull Come

***"Truthfully,"* signal** officer George Wille told his diary, "we were all pretty jumpy" when the Fighting Lady led the ships of Task Group 58.4 in column into Ulithi lagoon at midday of May 14, 1945—for even Ulithi was no longer immune. Two Navy tugs eased the *Yorktown* alongside the repair ship *Jason* for a week of work on spaces damaged on Bomb Sunday and by the rough seas and to begin repainting the exterior of the ship a dark "Pacific" blue.

Chaplain George Wright edited the second anniversary issue of SEA-V-TEN (delayed from April 15) with the usual assortment of photos and gags, among them a rumor from the Torpedo 9 ready room that the "Lucky Lady" was homeward bound "for the sole purpose of picking up 500 WAVES!" Indeed, as Ed Brand recorded on the 15th, "There were 5 women on board today," four Red Cross workers and an Army nurse, "I didn't want to see them, so I stayed below decks." Presumably, the pain would have been too much for him. Predictably, the brass and fly-boys monopolized the ladies.

Mail, nightly movies, daily softball games and beer parties ashore at Mog Mog offered welcome diversions from the general housecleaning and loading of ammo. "A drenched crew" of fliers returned from their wing-ding, in Walt Klem's graphic description, "wetter with beer (inside) and salt water (outside) than most of us have ever been before or since." George Earnshaw and Cooper Bright manned the beer-filled reefers at the crew's party and were nearly crushed as the thirsty swabs stampeded. "My God," gasped Big George after escaping, "no-one will ever know that the greatest threat to my life wasn't the Japanese. It was almost being hit at the beer bust!"

On the evening of May 22 the *York* celebrated her belated second anniversary with one of Padre Wright's extravaganzas, built around the theme of what to do with the ship and her sisters after the war. Jeff Corey emceed the program, set in 1950, beginning with "Mr. Cooper Duper Bright" recommending "Club Yorktown" be established with name dance bands on each elevator, bathing beauties parading, and a three-ring circus on the hangar deck featuring bareback riding beauties and Pappy Harshman swinging from a trapeze. John Furlow, opposing the use of strong drink, preferred the ship becoming a health and body-building spa, while Texan Bob Eaton wanted her moved to his home state to become the "Big Bar Y" rodeo. A sailor planted in the audience closed the farce with a loud final solution for the veteran carriers: "Blow 'em all to hell!"

The joke was bittersweet. For while the men loved their Fighting Lady, they were sick and tired of combat. "Received a cholera shot today," the 23rd, snorted Ed Brand, "I don't know if they think we are going to China or going to sleep with the hogs." Especially caustic were the gripes of the pilots, who, like all the air groups before them, felt they had done as much as should have been expected of them.

A few *Yorktown*ers who had been in the Lady's battles far longer than Air Group Nine had did depart for home. Commander Ben Born turned over the exec's job to Empty Evans. Commander George Earnshaw handed over the reigns of gunnery to Pat Patterson. And Lieutenant Commander Jim Tippey relinquished the Communications Department to Lieutenant Pete Joers, the ship's most junior department head ever.

Lieutenant Commander Cooper Bright should have gone home, but Captain Boone wanted him to keep running air ops. A two-hour psycho-analytical session with the medicos straightened out a nervous twitch Coop had developed in his shoulder, but a letter from his wife Mary carried the only advice she had ever offered him about his work in the Navy. Enclosing a newspaper clipping of the battered *Franklin,* she wrote, "Get off that bucket of bolts and come home!"

To complete the Okinawa operation, Radford's, Jocko Clark's and Ted Sherman's task groups would resume their anti-kamikaze and close air support of the troops now pushing to victory on the hotly-contested island. But Admiral Pete Mitscher was not going to lead them. He and Admiral Spruance, in need of rest, again relinquished command to Bull Halsey and Slew McCain—a change welcomed by virtually no-one in the redesignated Third Fleet-Task Force 38. Halsey hoisted his flag in the battleship *Missouri* and McCain his in the *Shangri-La,* both part of Radford's task formation.

Underway again on the morning of May 24, the *Yorktown* received a distinguished visitor by high-line from a destroyer—Henry R. Luce, head of the *Time, Life* and *Fortune* magazine empire. He would observe first-hand what the since-departed *Fortune* editor Del Paine had already reported. Luce brought with him *Time* senior editor Roy Alexander, publisher Frank D. Schroth of the *Brooklyn Eagle,* and radio newscaster Cedric Foster of the Mutual network. Sneered Ed Brand in his diary, "The food will probably start improving now."

Unfortunately, Luce's introduction to the *Yorktown* began with a *faux pas* by Father Joe Moody who identified the famous journalist over the bullhorn only as "the husband of Claire Booth, who you will know as author of *The Women.*"

En route to Okinawa, VB-9 made simulated zoot-suiter runs, Tiny Patterson's gunners blazed away at target sleeves, paint brush-wielding crewmen finished camouflaging the flight deck dark blue between flights, and when the full moon lit up the formation one night, all the ships made smoke to hide them from possible snoopers.

That such elaborate anti-kamikaze measures were essential was borne out the moment the ships arrived on station at dawn May 28 when a bevy of zooters assaulted the picket line of cans. From the flight deck Joel Connell "saw one suicide bomber (Frances) hit a destroyer and sink it in thirty seconds." It was the *Drexler,* victim of actually two Franceses. Minutes later, VBF-9 intercepted eight to ten bandits 30 to 35 miles north of Yontan and splashed four.

Severe weather and fog forced a 16-plane CAP to land at Yontan and obscured Okie for four straight days, though Bombing 9 managed to seal up more caves. To break the tedium, Cooper Bright kept up his stream of outrageous messages to the ready rooms. But now, depressed at not going home, Herb Houck's heroes decided on action.

"Let's get him!" someone exclaimed, and Coop was able to escape from Air Ops just ahead of a gang of men coming down the passageway "like a herd of buffalo." He ran out on a sponson and up to the unbusy flight deck, planning to dash across it, go down the other side and lock himself in his room. But in the middle of the deck another group of pilots blocked his escape. The two waves of whooping, hollering pilots closed in on Skinhead, under the fascinated gaze of Admiral Radford from the flag bridge. The mob got him down, carried him below, and pinned him to the deck to taunts of "Let's give him the water treatment!" and "Cool him off!" and "Shut that teletype off!" They all cheered as the bucket was emptied over his bald pate. But even in defeat, a laughing Bright had gotten the pilots' minds off their work.

Admiral Radford wrote a letter to Coop's sis and Raddy's former colleague, Lieutenant Commander Joy Bright Hancock of the WAVES: "I saw your brother today. And he was charged on by two groups of commissioned officers, pilots of the United States Navy. He fought the best he could, but, poor soul, he went down in a sea of bodies. He did not win the battle."

In spite of the weather, Admiral Halsey wanted to hit the kamikaze fields on Kyushu before the enemy hit him, so during refueling on June 1 he called for several days of very long range strikes in support of the B-29s. Launched at the extreme range of 340 miles, only the Hellcats would be able to make the trip, each carrying an extra 55-gallon gas tank on the right bomb rack and a 250-pound fragmentation bomb on the left. Ever fearful of land-based air attacks on his carriers, Halsey in Radford's view was jeopardizing his pilots. "A round trip of 600 miles," Radford wrote many years later, left "scant leeway for errors in navigation and little allowance for time over the target or extra fuel in combat." But his recommendation to Halsey and McCain to move Point Option 100 miles closer went unheeded.

The first sweep at daylight on June 2 found thick weather and devastation caused by the Superforts at six airfields on southern Kyushu. In lieu of airborne bandits, the fighters faced only flak, but it claimed Ensign "Pop" Koeller's fighter-bomber. Koeller managed to ditch in rough seas, but lost his rubber boat, held onto his buoyant parachute until it became waterlogged and sank, and then grabbed onto an empty wing tank dropped by a division mate. The tank kept him afloat until a Dumbo rescued him in midmorning. Other pilots, as Radford feared, got lost and were never found. Beyond a swarm of three dozen front-line Jap fighters which tore up a dozen *Shangri-La* F6s keeping an eye on Koeller, the only threat to TG 38.4 was mines, which the destroyers exploded.

Virtually every available fighter in Task Force 38 headed for the six Kyushu fields on June 3, the 28 behind Herb Houck shooting down a Zeke and a Frank before dropping their frags from remarkably clear skies. But the day ended with bad meteorological news. In the words of a droll Ed Brand, "Typhoon on its way. We will probably go right through it; we always do." Yep!

During the morning of the 4th weatherguesser Bob Rapp detected radar signs of the possible typhoon working up about 250 miles south of the task group, confirmed at noon by Fleet Weather Central at Guam. Admiral Halsey cancelled all further flights. Not another typhoon for Bull Halsey! With Sherman's task group heading back to Ulithi, Halsey ordered the Clark's and Radford's groups to steam eastward during the night to avoid the storm. Radford opposed this decision and informed McCain he believed the new course would take the carriers into the path of the typhoon. For the second time he was ignored. The Fighting Lady rigged for heavy weather.

Unaccountably, as the day wore on, Halsey reconsidered his decision and decided on a different course change—to run northwestward ahead of and across the path of the rapidly-approaching storm, a tight and intense maelstrom. Arthur Radford was incredulous; "this seemed an even worse decision to me," and he sent repeated requests to McCain to order a clearing course. The *Yorktown's* log explained why: "Cyclonic storm increasing in intensity, barometer still falling, and true wind reaching velocities of 35 knots. The sea is rough and visibility is about 1000 yards."

Perhaps Radford's task group, with which Halsey and McCain were riding, would miss the worst of the typhoon by a few miles, but there was no such hope for Jocko Clark's group and the oilers with him to the south. When Lieutenant (jg) Dick Drover took the conn at 0400 on the 5th both carrier groups—on a heading of 000 degrees—were in the thick of the storm, the center of which lay 36 miles southeast of Radford's ships, heading directly at the carriers, Clark's first.

Finally, at 0505, Halsey allowed both groups to maneuver independently—too late for Clark, but Radford might yet have a chance to miss the eye. He immediately ordered course changes to the westward, and Captain Boone, navigator James and OOD Drover expertly maneuvered the *Yorktown* at 18 knots to keep the wind on the starboard quarter.

TG 38.4 shifted its track ever westward over the ensuing hour as a pale dawn revealed the mountainous seas. At 0600, the quartermaster wrote in the log: "Ship steaming in typhoon which is increasing in severity. Barometer 29.09 inches and falling. High winds from southeast to east increasing in intensity with gusts to 55 knots. Rain and spray reducing visiblity to approximately 800 yards. Ship rolling but not badly."

The maximum roll was only 17 degrees and the highest gust 57 knots as the course edged further to the west. By 0700, with the visibility improving, it was obvious that Radford's group had made it. The typhoon was passing astern, the wind remaining on the starboard quarter.

But not Jocko Clark's. At 0700 his group lay in the eye of the storm and was then pounded by the other half. The flight deck overhangs of the carriers *Hornet* and *Bennington* buckled under the fury of the winds and waves, and the entire bow of the heavy cruiser *Pittsburgh* tore off. Many of Clark's planes were wrecked and six of his sailors lost overboard. Worse, Clark soon reported the CVL *Belleau Wood* and several tin cans missing!

By the time Dick Drover relinquished the conn at 0800, visibility was up to 2500 yards, the barometer rising rapidly, and the *Yorktown* passing out of the storm. A flight of search planes was catapulted at 1052 to look for the missing ships, and soon spotted them—safe but shaken.

So Halsey had had his second typhoon. Thankfully, this time no ships had been lost. But Admiral Radford, angry as hell at Halsey, sent a dispatch directly to Washington criticizing him. And *Yorktown* poets got to work, poking fun at Halsey's hiding on a 16-inch gunned battlewagon and professing his well-known desire to ride Emperor Hirohito's white horse in Tokyo:

Ode to the BIG Wind
On a mighty Yankee Warship
On the broad Pacific Sea,
There's a guy with four stars sittin'
And a-thinking thoughts of glee.

Bull his name and bull his nature
    Bull his talk will always be.
But for me and many like me,
    He's a perfect S.O.B.

Typhoons never worry this guy,
    Though they come from north or
    south.
Typhoons, Bah, he has one every
    Time he opens his big mouth.

What if he should lose some pilots?
    War is war—the time is ripe!
Fifty more he'll sacrifice to
    Gain another inch of type.

Kamikazes, they're a nuisance—
    Shouts this hearty man with zeal.
Sure, he's behind that sixteen
    Inches of case-harden as steel.

He has uttered one desire to
    Mount Hirohito's steed,
And the peace parade in Nippon
    This bold warrior wants to lead.

He should be a mighty rider,
    For I tell you from my heart—
I consider him part equine,
    And I think you know which part.

While the screen fired at several mines, the *Yorktown* squared away in the aftermath of the storm, and Captain Boone used the breather to mete out punishment on lingering disciplinary cases and tighten up the laxity of recent weeks. The guests on the ship appreciated everything they witnessed aboard. While Cedric Foster made wire recordings to send home for nationwide broadcast and even substituted for Father Moody with the bullhorn news, the tireless Henry Luce rose early to watch all launches and to jaw with gobs about the course of world events. And Coop Bright won him over to the view that the Reserves were running 80 percent of the Pacific war; Luce had his *Time* staff do more features on the 90-day-wonders. A prescient observer, Luce also predicted that the war would end within two or three months.

In gratitude to his hosts, he thanked them in the Plan of the Day on the 5th. "I don't think," the highly knowledgeable editor admitted, "I have ever learned so much about so many things concerning which I was previously so ignorant. For example, I never knew before that a man could eat a full meal of soup, meat and potatoes, ice cream and all the extras, in 3 ½ minutes flat. The C.P.O. Mess taught me that. I never knew before that a man could sleep on a piece of iron with a 2000-horse-power engine

cooling each of his ear drums. But I've seen a hundred of you doing it—just as nice and quiet as a baby."

Among several individuals he singled out for special thanks was "Chief Aviation Storekeeper Score for inspiring me to crack out all the answers for all the national and international problems which I never did get figured out back in the old Time and Life Building.

"Thank you, Admiral Radford and Captain Boone, because we civilians can sit up on your bridge and talk to you as equals—equals under the Constitution of the United States. Thus you prove to us—and to all who serve under you—that America's greatest fighting men are also great civilians—the lovers of that human liberty for which they fight. This was the spirit in which George Washington fought for and won our first conclusive victory at Yorktown in 1783. You have carried that spirit and the name of Yorktown unsullied across half the world.

"Lastly, thank you, thank you one and all of the Fighting Lady for giving us the right to share a little, all the rest of our lives, in the reflected glory of those who sailed and fought the U.S.S. YORKTOWN CV10. To all of you we say in the language of our trade Ablest ABLEST Ablest."

Throughout June 6 seven CAPs and two support missions visited Okinawa, where the Jap defenders now reeled in retreat so rapidly that the pursuing troops required air drops of food, ammo and medical supplies from the carriers. In addition, *Yorktown's* last CAP over the island splashed four Tonys. And a new night carrier joined Jocko Clark's task group—the *Bon Homme Richard*. So the original name of CV-10 had arrived as the CV-31; she was immediately dubbed "the Big Dick."

On the 7th, after TBMs flew Henry Luce and his colleagues ashore to Yontan field, the *York* sent three strikes in support of the Marines, who advanced so fast that they overran the targets assigned to Tom Stetson's last torpecker strike. Tragedy struck, however, on VB-9's last hop when Ensign Billy Watson's Beast spun in on takeoff for lack of wind. The popular Watson was killed on impact, but rearseatman Gus Novesky swam clear and kept his pilot afloat, administering artificial respiration, unaware that Watson had expired. The equally likeable "Ski"—who had been VBF-3's Bob Rice's gunner in the Solomons—was lauded by the crew for his heroic efforts.

Task Force 58 struck Kyushu's big airdrome of Kanoya on June 8, with 44 Air Group 9 Hellcats taking part. Armed from frags, Houck's F6Fs demolished many sitting ducks there, and over Shibushu his photo division shot down two of five Zekes encountered. Organized resistance on Okinawa had ceased by sunrise of the 9th when all 14 dive bombers under Jack "Duno" Durio and ten torpeckers under Stetson used proximity-fused bombs to clobber AA positions on the island of Minami Daito Shima. Next day a dozen of Durio's bombers tried the VT-fuses there but with poor results, followed by devastating strikes by all four squadrons in the afternoon.

The Okinawa campaign was over. The fighting had also ended for the men of Air Group Nine— and they knew it as the ship headed for liberty at the new advanced base at Leyte in the Philippines. Homeward-bound Pat Patterson circulated a memo to Empty Evans—"Subj: Search Reconnaisance and Patrol Party, Establishment of." It requested special passes for "Commander R. MacPee [Macpherson], Wind Boss; Lieutenant Commander Splash Patterson, Gun Boss; Vice Lieutenant Flash Joers, Comm Boss." Objective: to be flown into Leyte ahead of the ship "to spread content among the natives and inspect WAC quarters and berthing assignments." Permission denied, said M.T.

Just after lunch on June 13, the *Yorktown* moved into Leyte Gulf, "the first real body of land" surrounding it, observed gunner Ed Wallace, "we have seen in 9 months. Some of the natives rowed out to the anchorage in their outriggers." Then a hundred or so officers headed for the beach to dive into some abominable Philippine imitation Scotch. Afterward, they had to be "poured" into the whaleboats then herded into cargo nets and hoisted aboard by the crane—Chaplain Wright among them—and simply dumped onto the flight deck. They had survived Okinawa.

All Admiral Radford could do was sleep, "almost 24 hours straight after our arrival," but upon awakening he did a humane thing. He had Father Moody arrange for all the Filipino boys in his task group to be specially delivered by destroyer or TBM to their families for visits. In addition, a Filipino bishop conducted a Catholic rite followed by a native feast for 100 Filipino sailors and select *Yorktown* guests. Otherwise, the liberty parties found Leyte dirty and uninviting.

Harwell Proffitt, now aide to Rear Admiral Theda Combs, had the unenviable task of bringing nurses ashore from a hospital ship through the surf on a landing boat for a party with Admiral Halsey and his staff, then taking the thoroughly inebriated lot back out to the flagship *Missouri* for dinner.

After the meal, one of the celebrants flipped a live cigarette in the wastebasket, which caught fire, whereupon an officer grabbed a CO_2 bottle, stuck the cone into the basket and quickly extinguished the flames. Then he pushed the nozzle up the dress of one of the nurses and squirted her between the legs. She let out a scream as the dry ice burned. Other schnockered officers grabbed CO_2 bottles and started chasing the nurses around the wardroom. Funny perhaps, but unthinkable behavior for the men Halsey had relieved—Spruance and Mitscher.

Maybe Halsey was trying to drown out thoughts over a very unpleasant piece of unfinished business—a court of inquiry over responsibility for the Fleet's recent encounter with the typhoon. He and McCain tried to put the blame on Jocko Clark. But Jock's flag secretary and defense counsel was still the shrewd Herman Rosenblatt, a peacetime attorney who exposed Halsey so badly during the hearing that the Court had no choice but to assign primary guilt to the Bull—a view shared completely by Admiral Radford.

Admiral Clark believed that the war had become too complex for the man who had saved Guadalcanal in the dark days of 1942. Privately, Clark and his staff officers wrote a parody screenplay of a dialogue between publicity-hound Halsey and his boss, Pacific Fleet commander Admiral Chester Nimitz, at Nimitz's advance headquarters on Guam.

WAS CHET CHECKMATED? or
WHAT TYPHOON?
A Halsey Productions Classic

Scene opens to disclose a [Guam native] Chamorran runner peering from the end of a jetty. As he observes a barge come into the frame he runs to a hut where a number of correspondents, wearing assorted hats, are busy polishing typewriters. He gasps out, "Bull come."

Correspondents rush across camera which discovers them lining up, and as the Bull drives past in a jeep they briskly present typewriters. The jeep halts and Halsey descends. Camera cuts back as Halsey makes his inspection. He discovers that all keys on the typewriters except the "I" key are dirty. He steps back, folds his face into a grimace, and chokes out, "In two weeks I'll have killed every yeller-bellied monkey-man in the entire goddamned monkey-man's Empire. Headline those quotes, goddamnit."

Camera fades and pans as Halsey walks into an office. Over his shoulder we see Chet at his desk.

Halsey, sitting, "Hi, Chet, I've got those yeller-bellied bastards on the run."

Chet: "That's fine, Bull, hope you're not having any trouble."

Bull: "Hell, no, Chet. You know me. Everything's fine. Just fine. Those yeller-bellied bastar—."

Chet, interrupting: "Yes, Bull. But I seem to remember that your current score of shot down 'yeller-bellies' is in the vicinity of minus two in combat and very much higher if we include operational losses."

Bull: "Aw, gee, Chet. You know how it is. You know how these young two stars and kids of captains get things fouled up. Don't seem to matter what plans I make to rub out these yeller-bellied little monkey-man bastards but that these kids of captains, dem damn two-stars—."

Chet, interrupting again: "Ray [Spruance] thinks they're all right."

Bull: "To hell with 'im. Who sunk the [giant battleship] *Musashi* anyway? [Halsey, at the Battle of Leyte Gulf] I'll show him how to kill yeller-bellies even if I have to do it with my own hands, where these captains won't screw my plans."

Chet: "Yes, Bull, maybe you'll get a chance. But didn't I hear something about a storm?"

Bull: "What storm?"

Chet: "Well! A typhoon."

Bull: "Which typhoon you talking about? I remember a lot of typhoons. Why last December three of those damn kids of captains went and deliberately sunk three cans to make me look small. I'll never forgive 'em."

Chet: "No, not that one, Bull. More recent."

Bull: "Recently. Oh, that bit of a blow. Nothing at all. Eye was flying next day."

Chet: "Were you? What about the *Pittsburgh*?" [The bow was torn off.]

Bull: "Gee Chet, I thought you'd know how it is."

Chet: "Can't say as I do, Bull."

Bull: "Aw hell, Chet. That's an easy one. Those kid designers. Just don't know about ships. Beats me how they ever got a bow to stay on at all."

Chet: "But you were flying next day, you say, sure."

Bull: "Well, I was. *I* wasn't in no storm. Goddamnit, I knew enough to keep out of typhoons."

Chet: "Seems the others don't have that much

sense. How'd they get into it?"

Bull: "They was joining up on me. I told 'em to. And when they goes and gets into the center of the storm and I tells 'em to use their discretion getting out, they foul up my orders. Goddamn kids of two-stars and captains. Bad as those yeller-bellied bast—. Just don't know what discretion means."

Chet: "Yes, Bull, I know. But did they fly next day?"

Bull: "Wasn't necessary. But next day they did."

Chet: "Tell me about that."

Bull: "Sure. Made another record. *Hornet* took off planes down wind."

Chet: "Down wind. What do you mean?"

Bull: "Over the stern."

Chet: "Over the stern. How come?"

Bull: "Damn kid fool of a captain. Guess he was backing down."

Chet: "Backing down! But why take off over the stern?"

Bull: "He claimed there was air turbulence over the bow. You know them *Essexes*. Always something wrong with them. Me, I'm all for the big battlewagons. Yeller bellies don't ever take a crack at them. *Essexes!* (Snorts contemptuously.) But say Chet, did I tell you my plans to ride that horse of the head yeller bellied monkey man? You see, I figgers it this way—."

Chet: "Hold up, Bull. How did the bow become a turbulent area? That's not always been the case. Or has it?"

Bull: "Sometimes they're all right. But I takes that horse."

Chet: "The bow, Bull, the bow."

Bull: "Oh that! (Surprised) Was just coming to that, Chet. Guess it was kinda weak and sorta folded down, sorta, if you know what I mean." [The flight deck overhangs of the *Hornet* and *Bennington* had buckled.]

Chet: "Not quite sure that I do, Bull. But there's a friend of yours would like to know. I'll get him."

End of first reel.

* * * * *

Second Reel.

"Return of the Thin Man."

Musical Accompaniment,

"You Ain't a Bull Big Boy.
Get Along Little Dogie, Get Goin'."

The "thin man" was Fleet Admiral Ernest J. King, the big boss in Washington, who found Halsey guilty of blundering into both typhoons,

December's and June's, and who, according to wishful thinkers, would relieve Halsey of command as punishment. This fate was not to be because of Halsey's considerable public image.

While Halsey and McCain retained command of the Third Fleet, only Arthur Radford retained task group command. Jocko Clark, after 26 months of uninterrupted sea duty since bringing the *Yorktown* into commission, handed over TG 38.1 to Tommy Sprague, while Ted Sherman was relieved by Gerry Bogan in TG 38.3. (38.2 had been dissolved.)

On the *Yorktown,* Captain Boone welcomed a sizeable number of new officers to the ship, notably Lieutenant Commander Daniel J. Carrison, late of the bowless cruiser *Pittsburgh,* as new gun boss for the departing—and embittered—Pat Patterson. Pappy Harshman also took his leave. "One of the best officers aboard here," in the opinion of airedale Joel Connell, "I really hated to see him go and he hated to leave too."

More exuberant about leaving was Cooper Bright. Coop packed his belongings in crates before performing one final chore—flying up to Manila Bay in a PBY to identify hulks sunk by *Yorktown* planes. Upon returning to the ship, he found all his gear unpacked and lying on his bed. When Freddie Boone failed to appear at Bright's farewell dinner, Coop knew Boone was the culprit. When Coop confronted the skipper, Boone confirmed the fact that he just couldn't afford to lose his experienced air operations officer just yet.

At least Skinhead was honored by departing Air Group Nine at its big farewell bash staged by Chaplain Wright the evening of June 16. The pilots got Bright up on the stage, presented him with a plastic helmet liner covered with glued-on hair obtained from the barber shop, and sang him "A 'Bright' Song" they had composed to the tune of "Home on the Range."

Oh Give Me a Dome, With some Hair I
    can Comb
Be it Red, Be it Black, Be it Gray

And, Before I'm Interred
Let Me Give Them The Bird
Who Make Sport of Me and My Toupee

Oh Give Me a Stand Of Those Filaments
    Grand
And Some Kreml to Give It a Sheen

I'd Burst Into Song
Comb That Hair All Day Long
And With Fitch's I'd Keep It-So-Clean

But I'm Cursed With A Mange
And My Fate Will Not Change
From Reflecting The Evening Sun's Ray

To My Back I Am Stirred
There to Dream I am Furred
So I'm Happy Until the Next Day

Dome, Dome With the Mange
Where The Dandruff and Cooties Won't
    Play
But In Spite of My Plight
Youth Will Never Take Flight
For My Bald Pate Will Never Turn Gray

Next morning the ship and pilots remembered their fallen comrades in special memorial services. Air Group Nine had lost fewer but destroyed more planes in the air than had its predecessors, largely because the untrained kamikaze pilots had offered no resistance. The number of aces was therefore high—including kills from the times spent on the *Essex* and *Lexington.* Gene Valencia had 23 (12 ½ while on the *Yorktown* alone), his Flying Circus teammates Jim French 11, Harris Mitchell 10 and Clint Smith 6. The other aces were Marv Franger 9; Bill Bonneau 8; Bert Eckard 7; Ed McGowan 6 ½; Johnny Orth 6, all at night; Les DeCew 6; and Herb Houck, Henry Champion and Howard Hudson 5 each.

At noon of the 17th ship's band struck up "California, Here I Come" as the group went over the side to the *Hornet* for passage home. Weary crewmen looked on with envy.

Japan was beaten; though its leaders didn't seem to want to admit it, and the kamikazes continued to fly down from Kyushu to pound Okinawa. Being developed as a new forward base and airdrome, Okinawa however began to strike back with its own land-based planes. The surest way to end the zoot-suiter attack, however, was to invade Kyushu— and ultimately the rest of the Japanese homeland. The invasion of Kyushu was therefore scheduled for November 1, 1945, to be preceded by fast carrier strikes across Japan commencing in July. The biggest operation of the war—the last—was about to unfold. How long it lasted depended entirely on the Japanese.

Air Group 88 reported aboard the Fighting Lady to replace Nine the very day it left, June 17. The enormously popular skipper, Commander Seth S. "Pete" Searcy, Jr., Annapolis '33, flew one of 37 brand new FG-1D Corsair fighter-bombers—the

Fighting 9 veterans celebrate their victories during the Okinawa campaign. (L to R) Gene Valencia, Herb Houck, Bert Eckard, and a listener. Courtesy of Herbert N. Houck

Goodyear version of the Chance Vought F4U—assigned to VBF-88. The introduction of this red hot airplane to the *Yorktown* greatly magnified the maintenance and spare parts requirements of the ship. The other squadrons inherited Nine's airplanes—the 36 F6F-5 Hellcat fighters, 15 SB2C-4 Helldiver bombers and 15 TBM-3 Avenger torpeckers. All received new coded markings painted on their tails—"RR," which immediately earned the group the nickname of "Radford's Raiders."

By the summer of '45 many veterans of the *Yorktown's* battles of 1943 and 1944 were returning to combat, like reformed Air Group One on the *Bennington,* its fighters led by the crack Boogie Hoffman, late of VF-5. The latter unit's Dick Newhafer was now writing his poems between hops from the *Hancock.* Former VT-5 jockeys Joe Kristufek and Roger Van Buren were on the repaired *Ticonderoga.* Air Group 88 even had a few returns—Torpedo 5 alums Boris Thurston, Tommy Quinn and "Judge" Harvey Reynolds, the former two now with VT-88, the latter as air group ACIO. Leading Fighting 88 was Lieutenant Commander Dick Crommelin, veteran of the Coral Sea and Midway and still mourning the loss of brother Charlie.

"Everyone was proud and glad to be aboard the ship," recorded the air group historian, not just because of her cinematic fame, "but also because she had a reputation as a happy ship, a clean ship, and a lucky ship."

Their first meeting in the wardroom, however,

was all business. Needing to be briefed on Air Plot procedures, they sat quietly and attentive when the serious-looking air ops officer strode in to address them. He introduced himself as Lieutenant Commander Bright. None of the newcomers had raised eyebrows over his full head of blond hair, since they were ignorant of his ways or his wig—which looked atrocious.

The 150 men sweated mightily in the non-air-conditioned wardroom as Bright lectured on. Finally, he said, "We're here to support the air group; that's what this ship is all about!" He paused, then observed, "Man, it's getting hot in here." Whereupon he matter-of-factly took out his handkerchief, lifted the wig, and patted his dome with the cloth. The men, sitting there in awe of their first day on a big carrier, were dumbstruck. Then they exploded with laughter. Coop had 'em in the palm of his hand from then on.

The *Yorktown* weighed anchor on June 27 to shake down the air group and conduct gunnery drills, but as the ship headed down the Leyte channel a tremendous explosion rocked it to its every frames. The OOD `rang the General Alarm, and pandemonium ensued over fears of a torpedo or mine hit. Then it was learned that John Dellenback's aviation ordnancemen had dumped some faulty 100-pound fragmentation bombs over the side, and they had gone off. Dellenback was chewed out by his boss Bright for this unusual display of carelessness by the crew.

Pete Searcy's fliers impressed air boss Sandy Mac-

Captain Freddie Boone inspects the crew. Note the scoreboard of planes and ships destroyed by *Yorktown* planes. Courtesy of Robert Hayes

pherson with a successful tactical group grope—that is until the recovery, when the Bombing 88 skipper coasted into the drink. Lieutenant Commander James S. Elkins, Jr., a 1940 Naval Academy graduate and well-liked guy, was easily retrieved by a can. Next day the ship returned to San Pedro Bay. "A Happy Hour" of skits, swing music and a movie gave the crew one last fling the evening of the 29th.

The day after that the *York* got the word, which Ed Wallace wrote down in his diary: "Tomorrow we get underway for a presumably 45-day operation in the Kuriles and will strike at Tokyo on the way north." Actually, the Kurile Islands lay to the north of Japan proper, which in fact would command all the attention of the Third Fleet—the home islands, south to north, of Kyushu, Shikoku, Honshu and Hokkaido. Final shore parties this last night toasted a last drink to old and new friends at the several bars, "I'll meet you at the O Club in Tokyo."

"July 1. Slipped from Leyte harbor early in the morning 'for colder climate,'" recorded *Yorktown's* newest diarist, turret gunner Ralph Morlan of VT-88. One of three task groups, Radford's 38.4 included the *Yorktown*; the new *Shangri-La*, with Admiral McCain embarked; night carrier *Bon Homme Richard;* CVLs *Independence* and *Cowpens*; the *Missouri,* wearing Admiral Halsey's flag, and two other battleships; four cruisers and no fewer than 22 cans.

Simulated zootsuiter attacks, constant gunnery, bombing of the sled, group gropes and combat air patrols occurred daily, a routine highlighted on July 2 when the ship fired a 17-gun salute for Assistant Secretary of the Navy for Air John L. Sullivan, flown aboard in a TBM for a short visit. A special Fourth of July feast did little to brighten spirits for a crew that believed Japan was already licked. "This routine is getting awful tiresome," griped Ed Brand.

Whereupon, next day, a Corsair slipped off the catapult during takeoff and went into the water, bursting its gas tank. The pilot swam clear, but when a smoke flare was tossed overboard to mark the survivor, it ignited the floating gas. The blaze went up the entire length of the starboard side and so badly burned the swimming pilot that he had to be sent home after being picked up.

Then, during the regular afternoon bullhorn news, Father Moody announced that three days hence the carriers would hit Tokyo!

Excitement mounted as the briefings got more detailed, and the high-speed run-in began on the afternoon of July 8 toward the Point Option, 200 miles from the Japanese capital. "Everyone talking about it, a few writing letters," Morlan observed on the 9th. "Tomorrow is the big day—God help us." Using voluminous intelligence on the twelve targeted airfields in the Tokyo area, Judge Reynolds told the pilots to concentrate on destroying aircraft—on the ground and in the air.

The pilots spent a restless night, with reveille for all hands this July 10, 1945 at 0230, which was first light in these northern latitudes. In the last-minute briefings, Torpedo 88 ACIO Earl Hudson reviewed the use of the proximity-fused fragmentation bombs on the Avengers designed to detonate between 50 and 100 feet above ground in order to shatter parked planes. Recalled the squadron historian (Hudson!), "One particularly obnoxious ensign insisted" that the talkative ACIO was "a 'mike hog'; another equally obnoxious lieutenant dubbed him 'Your Esso Reporter' with slight modifications to the word Esso. What some men will suffer for their country!"

"Today *OUR Group* 88 starts raising hell with the Japs," exec Empty Evans proclaimed in the Plan of the Day. With reassuring words for the pilots, he explained, "They are plenty good and we have to 'hump' to keep up with them; however we can do it by being on our toes all the time. Let's help them by keeping all planes flying—no dud bombs and all guns talking.

"Today there is a possibility that a few Indians (Kamikaze-Zoot Suiters) may be running loose so it behooves us to *keep alert* and scalp 'em as soon as they get within gun range. Remember that we have room for more scalps up on our score board. Kamikaze Boys try to attack individually, in groups of two, three, four or more so keep alert for every damn one of them. *Don't let the sleeper sneak in on us—nail him!!!*

"If the ship is under attack—DON'T BE A DILBERT BY EXPOSING YOURSELF UNLESS YOU ARE ENGAGED IN THE DEFENSE OF THE SHIP—REMEMBER TO SEEK SHELTER AND LIE PRONE ON THE DECK—KEEP SLEEVES ROLLED DOWN—WEAR FLASH PROOF CLOTHING, HELMETS AND LIFE JACKETS (If topside)."

After the predawn CAP went off at 0352 followed by Dick Crommelin's fighter sweep, the bombing pilots manned their planes for an 0730 launch into a warm and crystal clear morning. Watching from the bridge, Earl Hudson remembered loved ones going to the beach at Hyannis, where the group had trained. As he remembered later, "We were poles apart from that wonderful world so many thousands of miles away, but we all thanked God that this was the *Yorktown*, the *Lexington,* the *Bennington* and a host of other great *Essex* class carriers standing out a hundred miles or so from the Japanese coast, and not the *Hosho, Hayataka, Taiho* and other Jap CVs standing a hundred miles off New York, with a squat little Jap Fly One winding up Jap fighters and bombers for strikes against LaGuardia, Floyd Bennett, Newark Airport, with perhaps a second task group farther north smashing at Quonset Point, strafing parked planes at Westerly, Martha's Vineyard or Hyannis."

Pappy Harshman's relief Ed McCollon at *Yorktown's* Fly One gave the signal, and Bill Lam, Junior Meyer's replacement, waved them off. Flight by flight the planes of the fast carriers headed out to saturate Tokyo's air bases, but flight deck hazards never ceased. An airedale plane captain on the *York*, Seaman First Bob Miller, was blown into a whirling prop and mortally injured, dying two hours later.

The airmen were greeted over Tokyo by light but accurate flak. No bandits though—which meant the enemy either had been taken by complete surprise (true) or that he had shot his bolt at Okinawa (also true). And none took off during the day. The fighters striking Konoike and Katori fields in the first of four sweeps found that the cunning Japs had cleverly secreted their planes under camouflage, so the rockets and guns missed many sitting ducks. Valuable photos were obtained by the F6F of Marv Odom, filled full of shrapnel from many low-level passes, adventures described so graphically over the loudspeaker by Father Moody that the crew cheered Odom when he landed back aboard.

Among the Avengers catapulted in the afternoon was Dick Robinson's, with radioman Wally Stanton and gunner Ralph Morlan: "Toyko came in sight and we flew past up to Konoika. Flew over the coast and flak started coming up at '5 o'clock.' Started doing evasive action and dropped bombs on plane revetments. All bombs exploded, much fire and smoke."

This flight yielded up the group's first loss. Ensign Charles Emhoff's Corsair went down in flames, apparently the victim of AA, although some suspected that he had been destroyed by a bomb from the torpeckers, several of which exploded prematurely between 3000 and 1000 feet. This possibility made the pilots like the already suspect new proximity-fused bombs even less.

Dr. George Smith: "Over 1400 sorties were sent against airfields and aircraft" by the Fleet, 140 by the *York*, plus 46 on CAP. Morlan: "The sky was black with them, no Jap dared attack us." Damage proved exceedingly difficult to assess because of the camouflage, and what the Americans could not know was that the Japs, absolutely stripped of decent pilots, had decided to degas, dearm and disperse their planes until the invasion actually began, probably weeks or months in the future.

Third Fleet withdrew northeastward for a crack at cold rainy Hokkaido. In addition to submarine contacts, Ed Brand noted on the 11th, "We are in a mine field. The cans are blowing them up right & left." And next day, reported Ed Wallace: "Just before reveille this morning 2:45 four torpedo wakes came through this formation, the fourth being very close to this ship. We began some fast turns and zig zagging to have it cross our stern." No damage to any vessels, and the sub got clean away.

With a minimum of air operations, Cooper Bright

sharpened barbs for his fresh batch of characters who comprised Air Group 88, notably the bombers' sleepy South Carolinian administrative officer, Harry DePass. Learning that Lieutenant DePass was reading off intelligence reports in the ready room, Bright fed the ticker a Skinhead "pome" amidst the data: "THERE WAS A MAN NAMED DEPASS. HIS BALLS, THEY WERE MADE OUT OF GLASS. WHEN HE STRUCK THEM TOGETHER, THEY PLAYED 'STORMY WEATHER', AND LIGHTNING SHOT OUT OF HIS ASS!"

As the last line ended, Coop's talker listened closely to the ready room, then reported, "Commander, there must be a riot back there!"

The bomber pilots quickly committed this minor epic to memory and recited it in the wardroom at supper. DePass told Bright, "You've ruined me! I'll never live it down!"

Friday the 13th proved to be a lucky one for all hands. Cold rain and fog, zero visibility and the threat of a typhoon induced Admiral Halsey to cancel his plans to strike Hokkaido. But the fleet returned next day with fighter sweeps and a bombing strike under a 1200-foot ceiling for the first carrier attack against northern Japan. Lowering visibility hid all the airfields from view, however, and only Boris Thurston of the bombing planes broke through the mist to hit railroad facilities at a village on the south coast all alone; he flew straight back to the ship using his radar.

Formation flying was impossible, and vertigo gripped some pilots, but Dick Crommelin led the fighters down to 200 feet to strafe. Crossing over one another in a standard maneuver, he and Lieutenant (jg) Joe Sahloff suddenly collided; the fog was so thick that Sahloff couldn't even see Crommelin's plane crash into the sea. Joe managed to regain control of his Hellcat and carry out his attack. Later in the day four night fighters were catapulted to search for Crommelin, guiding on their radars.

Lacking aerial opposition, the afternoon strikes were diverted from targeted airfields to concentrate on shipping at Muroran and Hakodate harbors. When the skies suddenly cleared, the planes roared down to sink what appeared to be an old destroyer but was actually a brand new one, the *Tachibana*. Also hit and sunk or damaged were an assortment of destroyer escorts, freighters, luggers and escort boats. The rail line along the coast of Uchuin Bay yielded many locomotives, no fewer than 14 of which were destroyed by *Yorktown's* rockets and machine guns. Six bombs were seen to hit squarely on the Wanishi Iron Works at Muroran. Other planes plastered railroad ferries.

The Japanese contested this attack with a heavy volume of AA which hit several planes. The Hellcat of Ralph Koontz was so badly damaged that the pilot had to ditch ahead of the task group, to be picked up by a battleship moving in to bombard coastal factories at Kamaishi.

Airmen like Ralph Morlan were jubilant at their success. "We go on another strike tomorrow. Boy, I hope the weather is clear. I want to get those ships, coke ovens and steel plants. G. Whitehurst said he was strafing a town. He must be getting bloody thirsty. Ha!" (Torpecker radioman-gunner George William Whitehurst would in later years channel his energies into the Congress of the United States, from Virginia).

But deep gloom filled the VF-88 ready room. No trace was ever found of Dick Crommelin, who had followed brother Charlie into a fatal midair collision in combat. The third of the *Yorktown's* Crommelins, Captain John, was safe in California and Captain Henry in Washington, while Lieutenant Quentin Crommelin was heading west as a fighter-bomber pilot on the new *Antietam*. The Fighting 88 exec, Lieutenant Malcolm W. "Chris" Cagle, Annapolis '41, moved up to squadron command.

Dawn strikes on July 15 flew over 200 miles to hit shipping at Muroran, Hakodate and Otaru harbors in the midst of difficult fog which created a "flak trap" from shore batteries and small warships at Otaru. The ack ack struck three strafers fatally.

Ensign Heman Chase bailed out of his flaming Hellcat at low altitude, and Ensigns Maury Springer and Bob Shepherd rode their Corsairs into the drink. Chase was apparently near death in the water, making no effort to swim toward rafts dropped to him, but the other two climbed into their own. Two F6Fs and two FGs circled them for hours but finally had to leave as their fuel ran low. These Hellcats logged a remarkable 6 hours, 39 minutes on the hop, whereas the Corsairs set a phenomenal record of 7 hours, 35 minutes. But none of the three men was ever seen again.

Angry pilots of all four squadrons destroyed ten locomotives, radio and radar installations, powerhouses, luggers, trawlers, tugs and patrol craft to avenge their losses. Remembering Air Group Three's attacks on rolling stock at Formosa, the crew started calling these pilots "Train Busters." Ralph Morlan, in Robinson's TBM with four 500-pound bombs, told the torpecker story:

"We circled above the mountains for about ½ hour and went below and up the coast at 700 ft.

Saw a DD being attacked by F4Us by strafing. They quit and we took over and dive bombed it. The 'fish' from the *Independence* dove first. The first dive was a direct hit. You couldn't see the ship for smoke and water.

"It was sinking, but the blood thirsty pilots kept attacking it. We left it, broken in half and going down. We then strafed survivors in the water and lifeboats. There weren't many left when we left it. We then went along the coast and broke off and attacked houses on the beach, some small fishing boats, railroad bridges, and anything that moved.

"Robinson dropped a bomb on a fishing boat. It fell over and exploded in the water. If it hadn't a delayed fuse, we would have blown it to hell. It was a good near miss though. We then went in on a railroad bridge along a cliff.

"Robinson dropped his bomb directly on it. It really made a swell explosion. As we were going in after the bridge I strafed the beach. When we finished we had started three fires on the beach, mostly among the houses. F4U's were strafing the houses under us, they were really raising hell with that place. We had two bombs when we left and dropped them in the drink." Battleships added to the conflagration at Muroran.

During refueling on July 16 four British carriers joined the Fleet, their Seafire fighters flying overhead so the gun crews could learn to identify them. The Fleet then headed south for another shot at Tokyo on the 17th, aiming especially to sink the battleship *Nagato* anchored at Yokosuka near Tokyo, but a solid overcast frustrated the effort.

Dawn of the 18th proved equally dismal, so instead of strikes a flight of weather reconnaisance planes was sent. When these reported improving conditions over Tokyo, the three cancelled strikes were hurriedly armed for a noon launch. Two sweeps of Hellcats and Corsairs had difficulty pinpointing planes in revetments around four targeted airfields, while the heavy flak sent fighter-bombers Theron Gleason down in flames over Katori and Leon Christison off Kashima.

The anti-aircraft fire over Yokosuka, the worst yet encountered by American carrier planes in the entire war, threatened the afternoon strike of all 15 VB and 15 VT and eleven VF armed with 1000-pounders for the *Nagato*. The anchored and poorly camouflaged battleship hugged the shoreline as a very active flak boat, but as the planes began their high-speed dives from angels 12, aircraft from the *Shangri-La* suppressed or at least diverted the flak with well-placed frags.

Bombs rained down and around the *Nagato* for five to seven direct hits and two near-misses, though the resulting smoke obscured any fair evaluation. The boys knew very well, though, that the BB had not been sunk. "The axiom that you can't sink a capital ship with bombs still held true," according to the VT-88 historian. Even without torpedoes fired into her, however, the *Nagato* would never sortie again.

With three more locomotives destroyed and Yokosuka's naval facilities badly damaged, the Fighting Lady pulled out with the Third Fleet to replenish. The next several days turned out to be so peaceful that the *Yorktown* began having evening movies—off the Japanese coast, no less! Then, on the 23rd, electrifying news over the bullhorn from Father Moody, recorded by Ed Wallace: "We are making preparations to strike Kyushu, Kobe & Osaka. Our targets will mainly be the bulk of the Jap Navy. The battleship *Haruna*, many others along with cruisers, carriers, destroyers, drydocks, airfields, factories and other vital war interests. We expect some enemy opposition. Here's hoping we come through okay."

The big target was to be Kure. If hitting Tokyo was like New York, Kure on the Inland Sea was Japan's Alameda and San Francisco Bay—with the whole Pacific Fleet at anchor there. Photo intelligence showed not only the *Haruna* here, but the battleships-with-flight-decks *Ise* and *Hyuga*, two cruisers and several cans. This many warships meant intense flak. "Stay away from Kure," veterans of the March strikes had said.

Yorktown night fighters led by Freddie Sueyres must keep vigil in the evenings, and during one of them Coop Bright—acting as air officer for a bedridden Sandy Macpherson—was particularly angry and tired when Captain Boone suggested a change in the air ops plan. "Captain, we are trying to do the best we can," Coop tried to explain. Boone, realizing his old-timers were being pushed to the limit, put his hand on Coop's knee and reassured him in a manner most unusual for Boone, "Now, Buck, easy. I'm with you all the way."

In spite of poor early morning visibility from the eternal clouds, rain and mist, the first of four fighter sweeps this July 24 commenced launching at 0444 to neutralize six airfields around Kure. The 200-plus-mile trip over water and Shikoku island encountered such thick inland overcast that many planes preferred visible targets along the coast, destroying two locomotives and several boats. Hellcat and Corsair pilots were reluctant to strafe low because of both heavy flak coming up at them and proximity-fused bombs raining down from 4000 feet, but they did manage to add to the general destruction by Army planes from the Marianas, Iwo Jima and Okinawa.

At 0730 the first composite strike departed from the *Yorktown* to try to sink the *Haruna* and the cruiser *Tone,* but knowing the exact location of only the latter. En route Lieutenant Al Shefloe in his Corsair collided with a *Shangri-La* plane and spun 14,000 feet to his death. The others pressed on, as related by Ralph Morlan in Dick Robinson's TBM.

"Weather good with high scattered clouds. We had to go over 60 miles of land to get to the port. When within five miles of it we started getting flak. They shot colored tracers and everything they had. The heaviest barrage I have ever seen yet. We started doing evasive action and it was a 'free for all' for all pilots.

"Robby picked a battleship or heavy cruiser, one of the two sitting in a little bay." The heavy cruiser *Tone* was there as expected; the bonus was the light cruiser *Oyodo* near by. No sign of the *Haruna*. "We started diving, and it was the steepest dive yet on any raid. Flak was now bouncing us around quite a bit. We let our 4-500 lbs. bombs go and started pulling up. I saw our bombs hit . . . . Two direct hits.

"When we were pulling out and doing evasive action we got hit in the right wing by a 25mm. shell. It tore a big hole just in front of the flap. At the same time Wally was hit in the foot by shrapnel. He started rolling around on the floor and I got pretty scared.

"I got Robby and he said to do what I could for him, and we got the hell out of there. Stan[ton] put a leather strap around his leg and laid on the floor of the plane. We started back alone so we could get back faster, and a Jap plane started following us, so we rejoined formation."

Air Group 88 scored six direct hits on the *Tone* and eleven on the *Oyodo.* But, miraculously, neither one sank. The flak caused extensive damage to several planes. Ensign Ed Heck's Corsair went down for a water landing five miles off Kobe harbor, and a Dumbo was dispatched to rescue him, covered by eight fighters especially launched from the

The Jap heavy cruiser *Tone* reels under Air Group 88 bombs at Kure Naval Base, July 24, 1945.

Yorktown. Dumbo did the job. Two 2Cs also ditched near the picket line and one Corsair near the ship; all airmen were retrieved by cans.

Passing over the Bungo Strait after the rendezvous, planes from several carriers were jumped by twenty Georges—Japan's new superior fighters and flown by the enemy's best surviving pilots. It was the first air opposition Fighting 88 had encountered. Skipper Chris Cagle and wingman Ken Neyer engaged two, Cagle handily shooting down one and damaging the other, but Neyer was lost. Also, the Corsair of Ensign Frank Ritz was shot down.

Morlan: "We got one wave off and landed. They took Wally to sick bay and fixed his foot up. We had six shrapnel holes in the fuselage beside a two foot hole in the wing."

Ed Wallace: "The B-29s were over the formation and four enemy planes were shot down by CAP inside this group's formation, one splashing in the water dead ahead of us." *Yorktown* fighters got an assist from *Cabot* planes on an Oscar. "We made our 28,000th landing and went to GQ about five times today, but our luck held."

In the afternoon the second big strike returned looking for the *Haruna* and instead bombed an old target battleship hulk by mistake, their hits failing to sink it. Wallace: "Many of our planes had to land in darkness and had some pretty close calls."

Though planes from other carriers sank an escort carrier and heavily damaged two big flattops, Admiral Halsey was determined to finish off the Jap fleet and ordered more strikes for the 25th. Intelligence officers on the *Yorktown* regarded this as pretty stupid, since these ships would never sail again and more lives could be spent attacking them. It was the same bullheadedness that had taken Halsey into two typhoons, chasing a decoy force off Leyte Gulf the previous October, and looking for the two *Ises* in the South China Sea.

His old nemesis, the weather, frustrated him again, however, for Kure was socked in, and the one torpedo strike only hit rail yard facilities in southern Shikoku. Four fighter sweeps found good pickings at three Jap airfields, however, and shot up parked planes at Yonago and Miho on the west coast of Honshu. On one strafing run over Miho, Lieutenants (jg) Joe Sahloff and Maury Proctor followed Lieutenant Howard Harrison through the heavy flak.

Proctor: "The gunners got on Howdy as he pulled out of his strafing run. There were so many tracers sailing up past him that he could've lit a cigarette just by sticking it out of the cockpit. Then they connected. They hit the underside of his engine, and it put out a long black streamer of smoke and oil."

Harrison headed for the sea—west, to the Sea of Japan on the other side of Honshu. Recalled Sahloff: "Howdy's a wonderful pilot. He ditched about as smoothly as I could land on LaGuardia Field." Climbing into his life raft, Harrison spread green dye marker in the water, but his pals had to leave him because of their low fuel. "A sad sight," Harrison said later, "I hope I never have to feel that lonely again."

Harrison's position was radioed back, but distance and weather prevented its reception, so the gloom was deep when the men reported Howdy's loss after they landed. The weather was thickening, and no rescues of carrier pilots had ever been attempted on the west side of Japan.

Suddenly, the ticker brought a ray of hope from Air Plot: "8 VF(N) FROM QUAKER WILL ESCORT DUMBO TO RESCUE DOWNED PILOT."

"Like hell they will!" Maury Proctor blurted out. "*They'll* never find Howdy. But *we* saw right where he went down."

Proctor and Sahloff bolted for the door, clambered up ladder after ladder, and burst into Flag Plot to confront a surprised Captain Trapnell, chief of staff.

"Sir," gasped Proctor, winded from the climb, "wouldn't it be possible to send some of our own planes after Lieutenant Harrison?"

Trap frowned, "We've already launched planes from another carrier."

"But, sir, we saw where he went down—and, well, we just wouldn't come back without him."

The chief of staff thought a moment, then said, "You want to go yourself, don't you?"

"Yes, sir," Proctor smiled, "and may I take my wingman?"

"All right. Be ready in five minutes."

Down the ladders they went, and the whole task group swung into the wind to launch the two Hellcats. When Proctor reached his hastily regassed plane, the mechs were trying to repair his gyroscope. As Sahloff took off, Proctor dismissed the mechs and climbed into his cockpit. He uncaged his gyro, "It just laid down like a whipped dog." To hell with it; he'd follow Sahloff. And off he went.

The two joined up on the night fighters and Dumbo seaplane, this flown by one Lieutenant (jg) George Smith, who with his crew of ten only three weeks before had spent 38 hours in life rafts after trying to rescue an Army pilot. Not relishing a repeat performance, Smith had little enthusiasm for this first air-sea rescue attempt on the west side of Japan. Furthermore, the amphibian's engine was acting up, and the clouds were thick as soup. Neither Proctor nor Sahloff let on about their worries over navigating through it, yet they cheerfully reassured Smith he was right on course.

But Smith was dubious, and only by keeping the two Hellcats in sight could he counter the vertigo overtaking him. When his engine grew worse, he had the crew jettison everything movable. Nothing seemed to help.

Sahloff called Proctor, "We've got to do something to keep this guy from turning back. Any ideas?"

Maury didn't have any, but when Joe saw Smith looking over at him Sahloff had a brainstorm. With his free hand, he nonchalantly pulled out one of the big cigars he loved so much, lit up, puffed out blue smoke, cracked his canopy and flipped out the match, then settled back to enjoy the stogie. Smith watched this whole incredible performance and was quickly won ever. He thought, these guys must really know what they're doing!

Moments later, they broke into clear skies and bright sunlight. The night fighters were overhead, Miho lay below them, and now the flak came up. They headed for the sea, adroitly jinking.

Howdy Harrison had been dragging his parachute to keep from drifting from his original point of splash-down, but he figured he'd paddle to China if help didn't come soon. A Jap escort ship appeared on the horizon, but it was set afire by strafing planes. The silence afterward was mindboggling, especially as Howdy thought of home and his two infant children. In desperation, he burst into loud song on "God Bless America." It helped.

Now the rescuers and rescuee spotted each other, and Dumbo saw another pilot down several miles north of Howdy. The PBM coasted down and taxied over to Harrison. Grabbing the line thrown him, he was pulled aboard, soaking wet, whereupon he jubilantly hugged everyone within reach. Taxiing over to the other pilot, Dumbo picked him up too, and then the engines overcame their troubles to lift the big seaplane off after 45 minutes in the water.

Harrison climbed up into the top turret to watch his pals join up on Dumbo's wing When Proctor saw him, he thumbed his nose. Howdy could only laugh at these lovable guys who had saved his butt. Both fighters were ordered to hasten back to the ship rather than use up their gas to keep pace with the lumbering seaplane.

As the seas worsened, men lined the catwalks and flight deck of the *Yorktown* straining to spot the PBM, then a cheer erupted as she came into view. But trying to set down, Smith bounced off a big wave and gunned his tired engines to get back up until a battleship turned sharply, making a smooth slick of water on which Smith landed. A destroyer hurriedly took aboard Harrison, Smith and the Dumbo crew, then sank the plane since time and high waves made refueling it impossible. A quarter-of-a-million-dollar aircraft for a human life—a fair trade, something the Oriental mind could never have comprehended.

As Radford's task group withdrew during the night to replenish, it welcomed the *Wasp* to the formation and received mail from no fewer than 14 destroyers. Back to hapless Kure went Halsey on July 28, beginning with sweeps to Miho, Yonago and Hanshin (Osaka). Especially successful was Lieutenant (jg) Bob "Ripper" Hall who, according to Pete Searcy, "pin-pointed hidden and dispersed aircraft and analyzed AA positions so well that his flight was able to carry out its strafing attacks at low altitude and burn six aircraft at Hanshin and damage three, without loss to itself, as well as destroying 12 locomotives, 4 tank cars, a transformer station and other ground targets."

The morning strikes by *Yorktown* planes against the *Haruna* and cruiser *Oyodo* ran into horrendous flak which struck six planes, the 2C of Perry Mitchell and gunner Lou Fenton fatally; one of the men, as Ralph Morlan saw it, "bailed out and his chute was on fire. This is how war hits home, if there is such a place any more."

Five *Yorktown* 1000-pound bombs struck and four just missed the *Oyodo*, which rolled over on her side just after VF-88's bombs climaxed the group's attack. Other planes damaged the *Haruna* and returned again in thickening skies during the afternoon to score the last of seven direct hits on her. Part of her main deck was blown clean off, one gun knocked out of its turret, and the superstructure left a smoking mass of wreckage. She finally settled to the bottom of Kure harbor.

Planes from other carriers finally sank the half-battleships *Ise* and *Hyuga* along with two heavy cruisers and damaged a light cruiser, several destroyers, parked planes and rail facilities. By the time the day ended, the Japanese fleet was no more, its surviving battleship *Nagato,* three carriers and

The PBM Mariner "Dumbo" carrying Howdy Harrison returns to the task group after the long-distance rescue flight on July 25, 1945. Courtesy of Maurice Proctor

Maury Proctor (l) shakes hands with Howdy Harrison as the smiling Joe Sahloff enjoys the proceedings with a cigar. Courtesy of Maurice Proctor

three cruisers total wrecks. Next day brought a relaxing Ropeyarn Sunday, "our second since I came aboard here ten months ago," reflected Ed Wallace.

Predawn fighter sweeps on July 30 detoured around thick weather to reach the coastal area southwest of Tokyo where they discovered submarine nests as well as patrol craft and marus in hiding. Lacking bombs, they nevertheless sank a

small sub and four minor surface craft with their guns and rockets. The morning composite strike attacked shipping, the railroad and factories at Tsugara harbor and Maizuru on the west coast facing the Sea of Japan. Torpedo 88 skipper Lieutenant Commander Cliff Huddleston led the torpeckers which helped destroy four trains.

Light flak claimed the FG Corsair of Ensign Don Penn who ditched right in Maizuru harbor. An air-

The light cruiser *Oyodo* rolls over and sinks near Kure while planes from the Fighting Lady and other carriers finish her off. Photo by a *Cowpens* plane.

borne Army PBY Catalina from Iwo Jima hastened to the scene, escorted by four *Yorktown* night Hellcats. The pilot, 1st Lieutenant John Rairich, knew he'd eventually run out of gas and have to land at sea—and at night. As Rairich brought the seaplane down on the water near Penn, a Jap destroyer escort closed in, firing on them. The four night fighters strafed the can while Dumbo picked up Penn and took off.

Then the flak from the can hit the Hellcat of Lieutenant (jg) Hank O'Meara, who coasted into the harbor. So Rairich brought his PBY around, landed and rescued O'Meara, taking off while the other three night fighters smoked the can. Air-sea rescue at its best!

The absence of enemy interceptors or zootsuiters continued to bewilder the carriermen, but Admiral Halsey intended to capitalize on their absence and finish off the three derelict flattops at Sasebo and smack more airfields on August 2. A threatening typhoon on July 31 discouraged him, and he hightailed it out of there. The storm wound an erratic path toward the west coast of Japan and then Korea, forcing Halsey to further postpone then cancel altogether his Sasebo strikes.

Gunnery, group gropes, refueling, detonating mines, then another Ropeyarn Sunday ate up several

days; no one could figure out why the Fleet was stalling around and not going back to hit Japan, since the storm was well out of the way by the 4th. Then, dramatically, at 1930 on August 7 the mystery was cleared up as Pete Joers' radios picked up a broadcast from the States that set the crew abuzz.

Dr. Smith wrote it down: "Today President Truman announced a new weapon to the world which exceeds anything imaginable. It is an atomic bomb, which will wreck an area 15 miles square. One bomb of this kind could destroy the average city. One was dropped on a Jap naval base [Hiroshima] a few days ago [the 6th] and 17 hours later the damage could not be photographed due to smoke and [radioactive] dust eight miles up in the air. It is the most destructive weapon ever created, and the Japs have been notified to surrender within six days or be demolished by these bombs." Ed Brand: "Heard of the new bomb that had the striking power of 2000 B-29s." Ralph Morlan: "All hands very much thrilled about it. It will shorten the war tremendously." And the ship's scientifically-minded officers presented a special program on the theory of atomic energy.

Ed Wallace: "Meanwhile the war will continue its usual pace and we strike at dawn! Here's

Attack begins on the *Haruna* at Kure by *Yorktown* planes, July 28, 1945.

hoping."

With the target Chitose airfield, Hokkaido, on August 8, the planes warmed up until "a pea-soup fog blew in gusts across the flight deck," in Pete Searcy's words, and the engines had to be cut off. At least the CAP got off and shot down a snooper 35 miles out. Otherwise, the men learned more about the dawn of the Atomic Age from U.S. and Tokyo radio. At Hiroshima, 35,000 deaths were reported (in reality maybe three times that). Dr. Smith: "The heat was intense and bodies for some

miles were burned beyond recognition. A 'leukemia' develops in the individual going into the area. The Japs are shouting various names at us, calling us inhuman, uncivilized, barbaric. They still refuse to give up and so six more bombs will be dropped in a couple of days." (Mere hyperbole).

Halsey scratched the planned Hokkaido strikes in favor of a dozen airfields in central Honshu for August 9. As the pilots crowded into their ready rooms, they zipped into new skin-tight green nylon pressure suits to keep from blacking out on

"STAND BY FOR TARGET ASSIGNMENT"

Cartoon by Lieutenant Jack Stackpool, ACIO of Bombing 88.

pullouts—a recent invention—got the word, then filed out of the room.

"Give 'em hell," coaxed the men scheduled for the second sweep. "Pour it on 'em." "Burn 'em up." "Go fight those Japs!"

"I'm going!" came urgent replies. "Just don't push me!"

The Hellcats took off, the first of two *Yorktown* sweeps and four strikes to four airfields. With exceedingly light ack ack, Searcy's guns, bombs and rockets burned up 35 parked planes and struck at least an additional 40 which didn't burn, obviously degassed. Some went in so low that they surprised the flight deck crewmen by landing back aboard splattered with mud!

In the midst of it, Fighting 88 encountered bandits. Squadron exec Johnny Adams led his CAP division at them. Pilot Bob Appling gave this account: "We jumped two Graces at 18,000 feet. For no reason we could understand, one of them went into a spin. One of our pilots followed him down through a cloud layer and saw it splash. Meantime the rest of us took out after the other.

"It was a race. We used water injection and finally began pulling up after the Jap had dived and leveled off about 100 feet above the sea. I happened to have the fastest plane. Then Johnny pulled up. We took positions on either side and to the rear. I fired a burst over the Jap's cockpit to make him turn. It didn't make any difference which way he turned. Either Johnny or I would get him. He turned toward me. I fired four long bursts. Both wing tanks were burning as the plane crashed."

In midafternoon the sun began to break through the clouds, and soon Air Plot was picking up reports of the CAPs shooting down several bogeys beyond the formation, and a Val smashed into a picket destroyer, causing heavy loss of life. Ripper Hall's division got another Grace at angels 20, while Cy Gonzalez outran a Corsair in his Hellcat—most unusual—to nail an Irving way up at 34,000 feet. But other bandits eluded the fighters which chased them toward the carriers.

George Wille recorded that "It was quite warm and the sky had taken on an uncomfortably brassy look, with scattered low clusters of clouds. It was the type of day when it would be almost impossible to see the attacker before he was on top of the formation, and we [on the signal bridge] depended on the [gun] directors and the lay of the guns to ascertain the position of an attacker.

"At the first alert, all hands on the signal bridge donned helmets, flash clothing and gloves, and the extras sent below and then we sweated out something definite. The directors had all swung aft on a bearing off the port quarter, and all of the five inch mounts were pointing in that direction, accompanied by slight jockeyings as corrections kept feeding into the computers from the directors."

Ed Wallace "saw two planes high overhead go into the clouds, and about 3 minutes later we came under an air attack by two Jap Graces. I saw one dive beneath one F4U which fired on it and set its right wing afire and the Jap went into a gliding dive at the *Wasp* whose 5 in. and automatic weapons opened fire, along with us and two destroyers, and the Jap began burning like hell."

War correspondent Ira McCarty of the *Kansas City Star* was there too: "As the Jap nosed into an easy glide, still seeking a target, it began to smoke.... As the first shots broke around both planes the [Corsair] turned off. Then half a dozen ships opened fire. The 5-inch anti-aircraft guns of the [*Yorktown*] began shaking the ship as the Jap selected its victim and nosed into a vertical dive at about 3000 feet...."

Wille: "Down he came, headed directly for the *Wasp* in a dive which closely resembled the one which had put the *Intrepid* out of commission, months back. Because of our position in the formation, we were unable to keep up a steady fire for fear of hitting other ships, and so it was up to the *Wasp*.

"She threw up a tremendous barrage, and silhouetted against the brazen sky, she made a brave picture as her five-inch batteries blossomed forth again and again in great orange crashes of flame— the roar and rattle of her 20's and 40's became incessant as the target came lower. Half way down the plane began to show telltale signs of good gunnery and soon he was trailed by a smoky, flaming train. The hits were good enough to deflect him."

McCarty: "The [*Wasp*] was nearly obscured by the smoke of its guns. Huge flames flickered along the trailing edge of the wings of the diving plane. Fifty feet above the carrier the fire leaped out into two long streamers...."

Wallace: "As it passed over the *Wasp* it tried to crash dive the forward end of her flight deck but near missed (very close)." Wille: "...and he crashed into the water close aboard the *Wasp*'s starboard side."

Wallace: "The task force on our strbd quarter

opened fire on the other Jap and we tracked her out of range. This plane was shot down in flames by the C.A.P."

Though no one on the *Yorktown* suspected it, The Fighting Lady had just fired at her last zootsuiter.

While Radford's four cruisers bombarded coastal targets, Father Moody came on the bullhorn with his daily afternoon report, which was earthshaking. Dr. Smith: "RUSSIA DECLARES WAR. The big news is the declaration of war on Japan by Russia. She will fight them on the Manchuria battlefields where the Japs have a very strong, self sustaining force." "We were really surprised" by the declaration, according to Joel Connell.

There was more, summarized by dentist Smith: "Another 'atom bomb' was dropped today on the naval base of Nagasaki on Kyushu island. The Japanese are still shouting names at us for its use and admit damages more extensive than our own estimates." Ed Brand: "That must be a terrible thing. I'm certainly glad that it is in our hands. Rusha [*sic*] entered the war today. Maybe it won't be long now."

Ralph Morlan: "Our pickets were under attack. They are really out after us now. We strike tomorrow also. I wish we would get the hell out of here." Joel Connell: "A cruiser almost rammed us at sunset."

For the 10th, next day, Admiral Halsey scheduled not only a return to central Honshu, but he added targets in the southern Tokyo area. Unfortunately, the big fighter sweep had to go a distant 300 miles to hit Kisarazu and Yokosuka airdromes. Halsey liked to keep his distance. Extra fuel tanks reduced the ordnance the Corsairs could carry, so they were given rockets instead of bombs. Not enough fighters could make the journey to suppress the anticipated flak. And low fuel would not allow the planes sufficient time to hunt for camouflaged sitting ducks.

It was a dumb plan by the Bull, whose stupidity again cost lives. During the brief strafing at Kisarazu, nine VBF-88 FGs were badly peppered, two of them ditching offshore where a lifeguard sub picked up the pilots. Then Chris Cagle's bombless Hellcats braved flak to strafe shipping at Niigata harbor, where the murderous ack ack dug into seven fighters and a direct hit sent Bill Tuohimaa plummeting to his death. In sum, the planes burned four paltry boats and some 22 parked aircraft.

Among the men grieving over Tuohimaa's death was one of the younger pilots who, collapsing in his ready room chair, raged, "It was murder! Cold-blooded murder. We didn't have a chance. There are holes in nearly every plane!" He jumped out of his seat, brandishing his sheath knife, "I'm going to kill the ACI guy that assigned that target."

One of the older pilots blocked his way, "Tell me about it."

"We had a 3000-foot ceiling. We had to start our dives from 3000 feet. There was AA all over the place. They shot at us all the way in and all the way out. We had to make our turn right over the airfield with guns shooting at us every minute."

The veteran told him, "*We* had to go in at 500 feet at Tarawa. This is war." As he talked, the boy calmed down. ACIO Judge Reynolds was not to blame; it was the poor planning by the flag—and the damned weather.

Four other airfields felt the brunt of Jimmy Elkins' bombers and Cliff Huddleston's torpedo bombers, which did not fool with proximity-fused bombs as they demolished 20 revetted planes at clear, flakless Iwaki on the coast. Ralph Morlan was on this strike.

"We dropped 12 100 lbs with instantaneous fuses. We made two dives and dropped on planes camouflaged on the field. I then asked Robby to let me strafe. He said, 'it's all yours.' First we went over some houses and I gave them a burst.

"My gun then jammed, and I was working and sweating and cursing like hell to clear it. Robby kept asking if I had it cleared and that made me all the more angry. Both his guns were empty and there were no bombs left and it was a field day, so I had to get those guns cleared. He was sticking around just for me.

"I finally got the link ejector chute off and had to leave it off because that is the only way it would fire. Of course, links sprayed all over the turret, but I wasn't interested in that. We circled over water till I got to firing again.

"We then went down to 100 feet or less and I fired at buildings on the field. We then went over a barn filled with grain and I set it afire. After that we followed some railroad tracks and went down very low, about as high as the Jefferson High School [of Jefferson, Iowa] and I shot all the windows and doors out of the depot, and every time I'd hit a building a puff of smoke would come up. Wally [having recovered from his wound] was firing away at buildings also [with the stinger gun].

"We then turned toward a village that was burning very badly and I put a few shots into the houses that wasn't burning yet. We then went out to sea and rejoined. Robby was really good to his crewmen today. I got so worked up at trying to tear my gun apart and fix it that after it was all over I felt sick to my stomach."

The radio news from Father Moody informed the crew that the Russian army had already advanced over 100 miles into Manchuria, and the "Yorktown News" from the print shop carried details of the atomic bombs. "I wish," reflected Ed Brand, "we would get out of here. The atomic bomb can do a month's work in 1 second."

As the *York* retired to refuel, roommates George Wille of signals and Dave Case of the black gang hit the sack early, but "at 9:02 P.M. the peaceful quiet and darkness in Room 311 was shattered by the shrilling of the bosun's pipe over the loudspeaker and a voice. . . ."

"Stand by for a message from the Captain."

"This is the Captain speaking. Word has just been received that the Japs have notified the Swiss government that they are ready to agree to terms of unconditional surrender as discussed at the Potsdam Conference, provided they be allowed to keep Hirohito as emperor."

Wille: "It took a few minutes for this intelligence to sink in and then a stirring commenced in the top sack which culminated in a lamp being turned on and heavy-lidded eyes seeking to focus on a wristwatch dial. Then the full import struck home, and the figure craned over the side of the bunk: 'Hey, Case.' No answer. 'Case.'' No answer. 'Case.'

" 'Whaddyawant?'

" 'The Japs surrendered.'

" 'Who gives a damn? (groan) Shut that light off.'

"*Snap* went the switch, quiet settled down once more and thus was V-J day celebrated by the respective backbones of the engineering and communications departments."

"JAPAN SURRENDERS," penned Dr. George Franklin Smith in his diary. Ralph Morlan: "The whole ship went up in a roar." The VT-88 history: "Everyone on the ship was practically delirious with joy. Each shouted and smacked his mate on the back and shook hands with him. Parties were started in staterooms, ready rooms, anywhere handy." One guy even paraded through the passageways in a civilian business suit! In Joel Connell's compartment "did the guys jump to the overhead. We were really surprised to hear it. The war isn't over yet but it looks better now." "Boy-O'Boy," rejoiced Ed Brand, on watch in CIC, "We talked about it between ships [on the TBS]. Boy O-Boy, am I happy."

Ed Wallace: "Meanwhile we are still on the alert for Jap trickery and any attack they might try."

Next day, August 11, during refueling, all hands kept an ear to the radio—"a tense, questioning, expectant watch" Brand described the mood. The following morning a call went out for volunteers, ten percent of all crews, to form naval brigades to occupy Tokyo when the official word came. Wille: "Steps were taken to muster a blue jacket landing force, and even the Fleet Marine Force aboard began to learn the rudiments of deploying and how to rout snipers. The broad flight deck took on the appearance of a drill field with squads of sailors being initiated into the mysteries of close order drill and the handling of firearms."

Wallace: "We are still awaiting some kind of settlement to the surrender terms. The Allies rejected the Japanese conditions and defined more clearly that the emperor would not be harmed but would have to take his orders from the Supreme Commander." Dentist Smith: "The emperor will have no authority at all. It is believed they will accept it as it is a chance for a 'face saving' surrender."

"Meanwhile," noted a disappointed Wallace, "we are preparing to strike tomorrow if the Japs don't accept our final unconditional surrender offer. We are still hopeful of getting word soon. Otherwise we will blow up their biggest power station tomorrow."

Morlan: "We are supposed to strike tomorrow if nothing is settled. I surely hope and pray it is. I never want to fly again, at least in a military aircraft."

Halsey headed back toward the Japanese coast late in the afternoon for strikes on five Tokyo airfields and the big Tokyo Shibaura electronics plant. Foreboding Shibaura, reputedly ringed by 525 AA barrels, brought widespread disapproval; noted former *Yorktowner* Joe Kristufek, now on the *Ticonderoga,* "It seems like such a useless thing to do, and we feel pretty unhappy about it, especially after being shot at for so long and knowing that the war is just about over."

The first of four *Yorktown* sweeps and two strikes on August 13 found Shibaura socked in—to no-one's dismay—so the flight shot up some small boats and 21 sitting ducks. But the flak hit ten of the fighters and knocked off a wing of Lieutenant Wilson "Bull" Dozier's F6. He crashed into the sea to his death. Some surrender!

No fewer than 21 zootsuiters approached the carriers but were splashed by the CAP, one Irving by a *Yorktown* plane and one in full view of the ship. The screen opened up on another, but Captain Boone held *Yorktown's* fire— thankfully, as bogey turned out to be a friendly. Morlan: "We are supposed to get mail tomorrow. I hope the war is over by then."

Smith: "No word from Japan as yet." Wallace: "The men are pretty disappointed. But until we get some word about the Japs surrendering, we will keep on fighting, and it promises to be very rugged." On the 14th scuttlebutt about surrender was rampant. Ed Brand: "All hands still waiting on Japan. This is terrible; I wish Japan would make up their minds."

As the *Yorktown* refueled on August 14, the 45-day operation since leaving Leyte on July 1 was over, with Third Fleet now scheduled to withdraw to Eniwetok in the Marshalls in preparation for the sustained pre-invasion softening-up strikes on Japan. But the high command ordered the carriers instead to strike again on the morrow to keep the pressure on the Japs. So Radford's air group commanders from the *Shangri-La, Wasp, Cowpens* and *Independence* landed aboard to make hasty plans to strike Tokyo on the 15th and 17th. Pete Searcy would lead the composite strike groups.

Chapter XV

Last Tallyho

August 15, 1945 was a red-letter day for fire control repairman Bill Simpson, his 23rd birthday, and it also happened to be the first birthday of Air Group 88. Otherwise, it was another normal work day for the *Yorktown,* with Dick Drover at the conn for the 0215 reveille until relieved by Ensign Bill Miller of the hull gang at 0400. GQ came two minutes after this as the ship swung from course 300 degrees into the wind at 180 degrees, and Captain Boone increased speed from 18 to 26 knots.

To sweep Atsugi airfield, along with Corsairs from the *Shangri-La* and *Wasp,* eight Fighting 88 Hellcats were catapulted at 0415: cigar-puffing Joe Sahloff, energetic Maury Proctor, and the lovable guy they had saved just days before, Howdy Harrison, as well as Lieutenant (jg) Ted Hansen and Ensigns Gene Mandeberg and Wright Hobbs—the boys called this Hoosier boy "Hybrid" for his preoccupation with his native Indiana corn. Flight leader Harrison ordered the two others to orbit near the coast and relay messages to him during the attack.

Pete Searcy's bombing crews manned their planes as sunlight bathed the ship at 0453, while the Gunnery Department set Condition One Easy. At 0528 the first planes of the strike went off the cats, the rest making powered ascents until the last was clear by 0548. The fighters pressed on to Atsugi to rocket and strafe sitting ducks, and the strike headed again for the Tokyo Shibaura electronics plant, torpeckers loaded with 2000-pound blockbusters.

Searcy's flight ran into a low heavy cloud cover, forcing him to decide "if we should climb through the overcast or stay at about 1800 feet. I was sure that we would hit heavy anti-aircraft fire over and near Tokyo Bay if we went in low. If we climbed through I was doubtful that we would find a hole to come down through onto the target. I was really sweating this decision when I was called by the *Yorktown.*..." The time was 0645.

"All Bronco planes cease hostilities and return to base. The war is over." Unbelievable!!! They were instructed to dump their bombs into the sea.

Searcy: "I got an authentication on this message, called the fighter sweep and told them to return to the ship. I got an acknowledgement from them at which time I ordered the strike group to jettison ammo and return to their respective carriers."

Radio officers Pete Joers and Stu Stuart had received the electrifying message only moments before. It was a direct order from Admiral Nimitz, and Cooper Bright sent it straight to the ready rooms: "TIME 0634 15 AUG. 1945, . CEASE, XXXXXX, . ALL FLIGHT OPERATIONS ARE CANCELLED, . 11 MAGNOLIA IS BEING RETURNED TO BASE. . . ., THIS LOOKS GOOD TO US., DEPASS PACK YOUR BAGS. ., ., CLARK BULL HEDGPETH THIS MEANS YOU TO."

The addressees were the admin officers of each squadron—lazy Harry DePass of VB-88, Dex Clarke of VF-88, "John" Bull of VBF-88, and Sherwood Hedgpeth of VT-88—and the meaning was clear: we're *all* going home.

Airborne VT-88 skipper Cliff Huddleston: "All pandemonium broke loose. Radio silence was broken and bombs were falling all over the area accompanied by shouts, 'Hey, you so-and-so, your bomb almost hit me!' Some of the pilots in their exuberance forgot that there were formations of planes below them."

"Hurray!" was Ralph Morlan's reaction: "We had to drop our 2000 lb. bomb in the water. The war ended when I was on my way to Japan. We were all very happy. [Lieutenant John] Doran [leading the "Green Bananas" division of torpeckers] pretended like he was drinking when he flew wing on us going back. I really got a kick out of him.''

Howdy Harrison's six fighters were orbiting over Atsugi preparing to attack when they got Searcy's order. Keeping their wing tanks and rockets, they turned for home but got only five miles when Joe Sahloff called out, ''Tallyho! Many rats six o'clock high, diving!'' Over Tokorozawa airfield they were jumped by a swarm of bandits—15 to 20 Zekes, Franks, Jacks, Oscars and Georges! TALLYHO!!!

If the war was over, these monkeys seemed determined to finish it in style. What was more, they were good—in fact, the best Japan had left—and the last dogfight of the war turned into a wild one. The Japs dived from 8000 feet and behind, but Howdy turned his guys toward them, and the *Yorktown* pilots scratched four on the first pass.

The section of Maury Proctor and Ted Hansen wheeled around into the general free-for-all, and Hansen got his second and Proctor his first. They went after a Jack on Joe Sahloff's tail until Maury exploded it with a short burst. Joe's F6 was giving off smoke, so Maury told him to head for the water. Proctor intended to escort his stricken buddy, but a Frank got on Maury's tail, forcing him to go into evasive turns.

Hansen burned this Frank to save Proctor, but another Frank swung onto Maury's tail, and half a dozen others came at him dead ahead. As the front six pulled up, Maury turned his bullet-riddled Cat around and flamed his pursuer. The six came on again, but Maury headed into the clouds for refuge, jinking all the while. Jap slugs continued to pepper the rugged F6, leaving 28 holes in the fuselage and prop.

The bandits couldn't find him but wheeled back on Hobbs, Mandeberg, Harrison and Hansen, who continued to trade blows with Nippon's last. Jap and Yank fighters writhed and shuddered under the crunch of machine gun slugs and fell in flames for the last time in this long and bloody war.

One of the Hellcat pilots was forced to bail out. Though wounded, he reached terra firma safely, only to die of his wounds several days later.

As Proctor broke out of the clouds, he called his squadron mates but got an acknowledgement only from Hansen. Between them, they counted up nine bandits destroyed in the fracas—five Franks, three Jacks and an Oscar. Good shooting for Air Group 88's only big aerial battle, and not against zoot-suiters. But where were their friends who might be able to account for a few more scores? Heading back to the Fighting Lady, Maury and Ted looked especially for the crippled Joe Sahloff.

Yorktown Hellcats had fought the last aerial battle of the war, just as they had begun the first attack of the Pacific offensive at Marcus Island. Boogie Hoffman, who had been at Marcus with Fighting 5, now turned around his VF-1 and headed back to the *Bennington*. Lambchop Newhafer, another VF-5 alum now with *Hancock's* VF-6, felt that the recall order brought ''all the hope and unreasoning happiness that salvation can bring. It brought tears and laughter and a numb sense of unbelief.''

Joe Kristufek's flight returned to the *Ticonderoga* post haste ''and everyone in the ready room was singing and shouting. Someone put a pair of girl's pink panties on the bulletin board and wrote beside it, 'next target.' '' Celebrations on other ships matched this, but on the *Yorktown* there was apprehension and mixed emotions.

At 0742 a CAP was launched, and 16 minutes later Searcy's strike planes began coming aboard. Joers' radios crackled at 0803 in the midst of·the recovery, and Coop Bright spread the news to the airmen returning to their ready rooms: ''TRUMAN JUST ANNOUNCED THE SURRENDER., THE SURRENDER WAS UNCONDITIONAL. TIME 0812., IT TOOK AIR GROUP 88 TO GET THIS WAR OVER WITH, . , MACARTHUR WILL HEAD ARMY OF OCCUPATION. , .''

But Searcy and the others had a more immediate concern. ''We waited for the fighter sweep to get 'home.' In about a half hour a fighter returned, followed by another, both pretty well shot up, but they got aboard safely. We waited in vain for the other four. I was heartsick.''

Dear God Almighty, four shipmates had failed to make it back: Gene Mandeberg, Hybrid Hobbs, Joe Sahloff and the most popular of them all, Howdy Harrison, father of two, one of whom he never saw. All four men—gone forever.

''That damned Halsey!'' was the sentiment throughout Flag Plot and the ship. These losses could have been prevented, but old Bull had had to keep slugging away. *Yorktown's* CAP joined up on a Dumbo en route to Hokoda to search a lake for the missing four. When they got there, they saw instead three bomb-laden Myrts taking off and immediately shot them down—*Yorktown's* final air action of the war, though hardly a dogfight.

Captain Boone had been composing a surrender announcement message, and at 0950 he spoke into the bullhorn. ''This is the captain speaking.'' At the sound of his voice, the general pandemonium on the flight deck ceased. ''President Truman has announced that Japan has accepted the terms of the

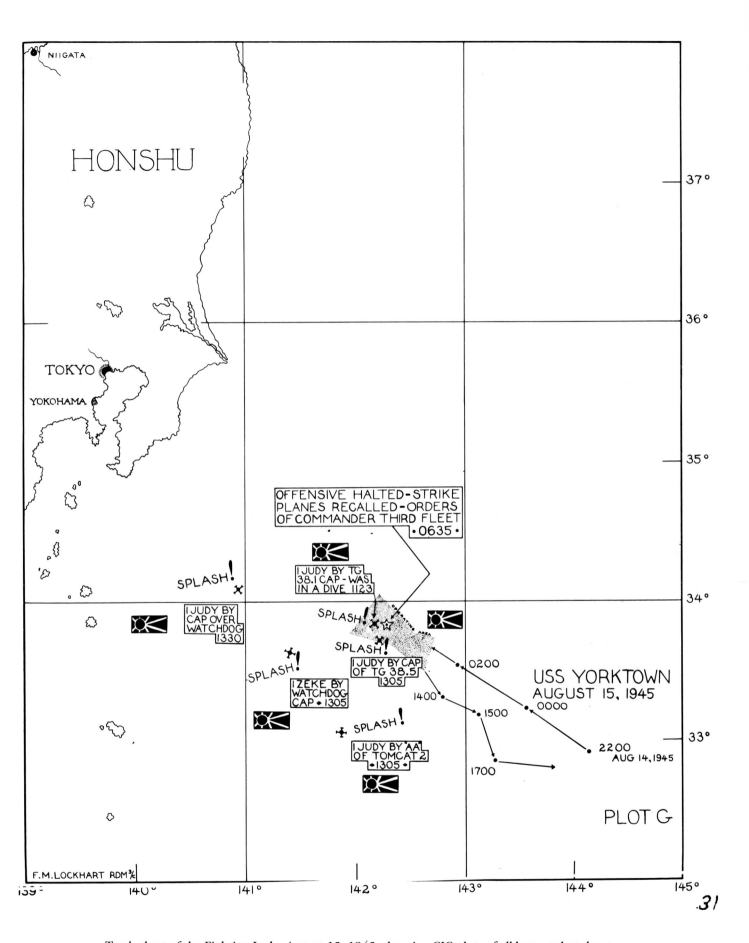

NIIGATA

HONSHU

37°

36°

TOKYO

YOKOHAMA

35°

OFFENSIVE HALTED-STRIKE
PLANES RECALLED-ORDERS
OF COMMANDER THIRD FLEET
•0635•

SPLASH! ✕

34°

I JUDY BY TG
38.1 CAP-WAS
IN A DIVE 1123

I JUDY BY
CAP OVER
WATCHDOG
1330

SPLASH!

SPLASH!

SPLASH!

I JUDY BY CAP
OF TG 38.5
1305

0200

USS YORKTOWN
AUGUST 15, 1945
0000

I ZEKE BY
WATCHDOG
CAP •1305

1400

1500

SPLASH!

33°

I JUDY BY AA
OF TOMCAT 2
•1305•

1700

2200
AUG 14, 1945

PLOT G

F.M.LOCKHART RDM³⁄c

139°   140°   141°   142°   143°   144°   145°

.31

Track chart of the Fighting Lady, August 15, 1945, showing CIC plots of all bogeys shot down.

surrender. . . . Our victory is a glorious one, in which every individual on board has had a personal and important part. We may be profoundly proud of the role played by our ship—our Fighting Lady—and by the air groups who have flown from her deck. But in our joyous relief that the fighting is over, let us not forget those gallant comrades who made the supreme sacrifice to make this victory possible. . . .''

"The biggest news of the century,'' in Ed Brand's opinion, was " 'The War is Over—The War is Over—The War is Over'—3 years 8 months & 7 days since Pearl Harbor.''

An hour later, the *Yorktown* hoisted her battle flag, but within minutes TG 38.1 reported splashing a zootsuiter, and *Yorktown's* gunners went to Air Defense. Brand: "A Judy was diving on the *Wasp*. The [can] *Uhlmann* was the first to open up & saved the day. Between the *Wasp* and the *Uhlmann* the Judy was hit and set afire. It hit the water about 50 yds. off the St. Bow of the *Wasp* at 1125.''

"At 1130 Adm. Halsey addressed all officers & men over the ship's radio. Well done, marvelous fighting force, etc. During his talk (which lasted about 45 minutes) 6 Zekes were splashed close by. In all 22 planes were splashed,'' but none penetrated the CAP or screen to test the Fighting Lady's guns one more time. At noon Dick Drover was summoned back to the conn, and the Emperor of Japan came on the radio telling his people it was all over.

Lieutenant Moe Sadler drilled the Marines and sailors on the flight deck for the initial landings, and the .30 cal. stinger guns were taken out of the TBMs and given to these police forces. Ed Wallace: "Later Hirohito spoke to his Jap nation and explained the reason for the surrender, and he was pretty slick with his words but admitted we whipped them good.''

The print shop immediately ran off the full text of the Emperor's remarks for next day's "Victory Roundup'' edition of the "Yorktown News.'' Said Hirohito in an ultimate expression of understatement,''. . .the war situation has developed not necessarily to Japan's advantage.'' Specifically, he blamed the defeat also on "a new and most cruel bomb,'' voicing an ominous warning for the future. The power of the A-Bomb "to do damage is indeed incalculable. . . .Should we continue to fight, it would not only result in the ultimate collapse and obliteration of the Japanese nation, but also it would lead to the total extinction of human civilization. . . .''

Wallace: "Father Moody held mass that night and everyone received communion. He said that if the war had lasted longer that the *Yorktown* and 3rd Fleet would have met with serious loss of life and destruction.

"Thank God it's over!''

Pop Condit began August 15, 1945 as his weekly day-off from his labors at Yokosuka's Sumida prison camp. He and his fellow POWs had known the end was coming from the increased bombings and the actions of the guards. Until the atomic bombing of Hiroshima on the 6th, the guards had just watched the B-29s go over, but after the A-Bomb, at the first sign of the Superforts they would run like hell, leaving the prisoners unattended. Then the head guard asked his charges to write him a letter of recommendation, and the guards in the prison hospital began to hoard all the American money they could get their hands on.

When the morning working parties returned from the railroad yard for the noon meal on the 15th, military policemen went around and told everyone to listen to the radio at noon, because the Emperor—for the first time ever—was going to speak to the people. This unprecedented news, coupled with the fact that they had seen no Jap planes over Tokyo yet that day, though they had heard bombing and shooting, led the prisoners to speculate that either the war was ending or that a big landing force was coming in. The Emperor would tell the people to fight or quit.

At noon the guards repaired to the camp commander's office, leaving the POWs all alone. They figured that if the guards returned and ordered them back to work, then a landing could be expected. Presently, the guards came back out, absolutely expressionless, and told the men to return to work. Condit went to this bunk and started getting his gear together to move, for the rail yard was sure to be hit.

But later the guards were called to a midday muster—most unusual—just as a group of prisoners came marching through the front gate, laughing and carrying on. Condit wondered what was up. Furthermore, these prisoners were not subjected to the usual search; they just walked in. They reported that the civilians had told them that the war was over and that they could all now be friends.

Still, the prisoners couldn't be certain, so they quizzed some of the guards, notably a Formosan conscript who had been learning to be an interpreter. He told them that indeed the war was over and that the guards had been ordered to stay in camp for fear that the civilians would kill them. Then other prisoners reported that they had heard the Emperor's broadcast and that they knew enough Japanese to understand the phrase, "The war is over."

A celebration dinner of "all dumpo"—gyp-corn and horse gut—was eaten, after which the camp commandant, known affectionately as "The Pig", told the prisoners to go to bed. When they tried to, though very excited, they complained that the bed bugs were too bad. The Pig got angry, not believing them, but came over to their huts in his nightshirt to see for himself. He took one look at

offshore ready to launch strikes should the surrender prove illusive; it was also waiting for landing forces to be brought up from Leyte or Okinawa. On the 16th the entire Third Fleet joined up in one massive formation 250 miles off the coast, though no hops were flown. Ralph Morlan "never saw so many warships in my life."

Father Moody reported next day that a hitch had developed in the surrender negotiations, which led to preparations for renewing hostilities. While the *Yorktown* put two strong radar pickets of 13 and 12 fighters into the air, Dan Carrison's gunners practiced on three target sleeves towed by TBMs. Ed Wallace: "We are still firing at floating mines which seem to be all over this area. This is our 49th

The only plankowning officers left aboard at the finish, photographed on August 18. (L to R) radar officer Jim Slater, signal officer Stu Stuart, Nick Nothstine of gunnery, pay clerk Joe Peascoe, Marine Moe Sadler, and "the Dome," Cooper Bright of air ops. Courtesy of R.K. Stuart

the bed bugs, jumping up and down, and left, saying not a word.

For several days Pop and his friends waited to be liberated and could not understand why the Navy just didn't land and take them out. One day their captors gave them a bucket of paint and told them to paint "PW" on the roof, something that should have been done long before, according to international law. The guards told them to do it because planes would be coming over at a certain day and time to drop supplies, and they'd need a marker.

The prisoners debated whether they should do the work, but they finally decided they would. Still, the whole long process mystified them.

The plain fact was that the occupation plans were still being worked out, and Third Fleet was standing

day from port. Pres. Truman said we are still standing by in case of treachery and will use more atomic bombs if necessary." (Though none were left in America's arsenal.) Morlan: "Scuttlebutt is going around that we are headed for the States. I sure hope so."

"With the ship," in the words of Ed Brand, "gradually converting itself to the peacetime Navy (no staying in compartment, field days, sunbathing hours, etc.)," Lieutenant Sadler's "Marine Landing Force" moved to an amphibious ship on Sunday the 19th as part of a 911-man unit. And the first of many hasty demobilization transfers began for men with the greatest number of discharge "points." A reshuffling of the task groups led to old friend *Essex* replacing the *Wasp* in TG 38.4 on the 20th. Two Augusts before, three of the flattops now in this very disposition—*Yorktown, Essex* and *Indpendence*—had started the Central Pacific offensive at Marcus.

Negotiations now progressed satisfactorily, as suggested by a frantic appeal from Halsey's staff for band music of the Russian national anthem to be played at the surrender ceremony. No ship had any, none, that is, except the Fighting Lady. First Class Musician Laiten "Prof" Weed, who had arranged and performed so much of the *Yorktown's* wonderful music throughout the war, remembered that Chief Shipfitter Anatole Koriakoff had been born in Russia. Koriakoff hummed the "Internationale" for Weed, who worked feverishly over one day and night orchestrating the piece for a standard 23-piece Navy band. Halsey had the music in time to impress the Reds.

Though replacement planes, bombs and rockets were taken aboard, they proved unnecessary. Japan was cooperating, and on the 22nd the *Yorktown* launched her 96 available planes for a massive flyby of 1200 carrier planes for picture taking.

Admiral Halsey pulled the *Missouri, Cowpens* and several escort ships out of Radford's task formation to proceed toward Tokyo Bay on the 23rd and sent the rest of the group to patrol 100 miles east of northern Honshu to cover the Fleet's entry into the Bay. The carriers were also ordered to prepare packets of food and medical supplies to drop to the POW camps on little parachutes.

The Bull had finally managed to bring the war to a finish, with no small help from the two A-bombs and the Russian attack and in spite of his own fumbling. Admiral Ted Sherman, now returning to the Fleet, agreed with a fellow admiral "that Halsey had not been thinking straight lately." He was simply worn out.

Yorktown's gunners spent August 24 knocking down target sleeves, and the fighters flew CAPs over the Fleet as it headed toward Tokyo Bay. When Torpedo 88 got word that "Dugout Doug" would land at Atsugi airfield in a few days, it decided on one final act of grabass. With the help of the parachute riggers it fashioned a large black banner with white letters to be dropped there and erected ahead of MacArthur's arrival: "WELCOME ARMY, 3-RD FLT."

Ralph Morlan was on the first flight to Tokyo at dawn of the 25th to drop supplies to the prisoners. There the fliers saw Jap planes all lined up with their props removed—as stipulated by the Allies. "It's hard to explain, you would have to see the sight for yourself to appreciate it. There was hardly anything left standing. The Superforts had actually wiped the city out.

"There was smoke one thousand feet high and it smelled awful, of smoke, of death, etc. We found our P.O.W.s along the bay area by a burnt out building. They waved frantically and we were so low we could see the expressions on their faces. We dropped food packages in the area. We put a message in one of our bundles we dropped, with Robby's, Wally's and my address inside wishing them good luck. . . .

"The streets were clean, but that was about all that was left of the place. People were getting off and on electric trains and buses. All they did was look up, but they didn't have to look very high because we were so low. Very few waved. We were so low we went between two chimneys of a factory and over a burnt out oil tank.

"There were aircraft all over the sky. We could see many air raid shelters, but no one used them when we came over. They knew the war was over. I saw many 'AA' guns, but they were not manned and had tarps thrown over them.

"I wish everyone in the U.S. could have seen what I saw today."

Ed Wallace: "The pilots claimed that Japanese street cars stopped when our planes zoomed over at about 100 ft. and the people got out and waved at them. Even groups of girls and people on the street did likewise. The Allied prisoners could not believe their eyes when our planes dropped the gear. They cheered, danced, climbed trees, and jumped into water after the packages." At Yokohama, Air Group 88 saw a big sign painted on a roof: "YORKTOWN THANKS."

Pop Condit and his comrades at Sumida heard the carrier planes on top of the morning overcast, and when the sun broke through in the afternoon they climbed up on the roof to see the planes flying off in the distance. Finally, one drifted over and spotted the "PW" on their roof. He was from the *York,* revealed when the planes roared over and dropped packets of goodies which included the latest issue of SEA-V-TEN. "That's my old ship," exclaimed Condit, "and there's somebody aboard that's going to know me."

He had an idea, namely, to paint his name on the roof, which a British officer helped him do. Presently, a photo plane came over. It was Bill Norris of Torpedo 88, whose skipper, Cliff Huddleston, had gone through carrier flight training with Pop before the war. The torpeckers also dropped their banner at Atsugi, and the Japs suitably

Surrendered Japanese planes line Komatsu airfield as *Yorktown* planes fly over, August 28, 1945.

erected it according to the attached instructions.

When the photo lab developed the pictures, two men in the air group virtually jumped for joy—Judge Reynolds and Boris Thurston, Pop's old shipmates who now assembled a special package for Pop of a survivor's kit, a letter from Pop's wife MaeBelle, and a note from Reynolds. Next day, a circling squadron of torpeckers jarred Pop out of his sleep, and soon a POW came running into the camp, hollering for Pop. He carried a package marked "Yorktown Air Mail."

Everyone sat down in a circle and broke out the gifts. "Here's a letter for you," said one. As Pop opened and read it he cried, and everyone started bawling with him. Then B-29s came over and started dropping supplies in 50-gallon drums—without parachutes! One fell on the guard house, demolishing half of it; one crashed into the outhouse; and one knocked over a telephone pole.

Everyone fled for cover.

Halsey planned to enter Tokyo Bay on the 26th, but two approaching typhoons ("They must be in style or something," joked Ed Brand) forced him to wait one more day. The carriers *Intrepid, Antietam* and *Cabot* joined the fleet east of Honshu, just in time to be socked by one of the storms; the "Unlucky I" was back! Wallace: "Our *rotten* luck in going back is still holding out. We have been at sea 56 days now and still going strong."

"Back in the U.S.," he went on, "commentator Cedric Foster announced to the world that the Fighting Lady was the U.S.S. YORKTOWN." This was particularly good news to over a thousand pretty lasses who had sent their photos into *Life* magazine for the "Miss Fighting Lady" contest. The winner would be selected as soon as the *York* got home.

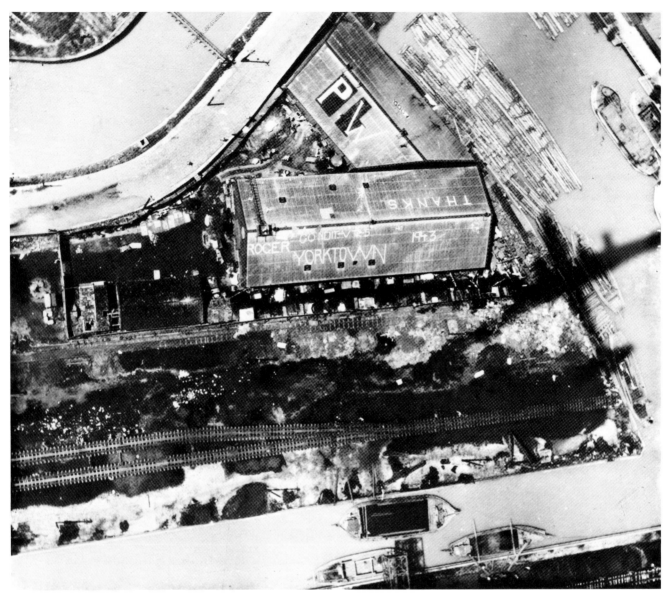

A B-29 Superfortress (shadow on ground) photographs Pop Condit's POW camp at Sumida, Japan, as the American planes drop supplies to the prisoners.

The health of the men was finally starting to break down after the long, arduous campaigns—notably the exec's. Empty Evans came down with a kidney ailment and had to be transferred on the 29th. Socket-wrench Brady replaced him—the first nonaviator to become executive officer of a U.S. flattop. A dearth of victuals did little to improve the physical condition of the men, due to the ship's not proceeding to Eniwetok as scheduled. The Supply Department, finally down to its last steak, auctioned it off for fifty bucks.

While Third Fleet units moved into Tokyo Bay on August 30, Admiral Halsey hoisted his flag at Yokosuka Naval Base. His flag secretary, Commander Harold Stassen, the boy wonder of

Republican politics, just walked into the POW camp at Sumida—much to the surprise of Pop Condit and his fellows—and told them that landing barges were waiting to take them out to the ships.

Gathering together their meager belongings, the men decided to march out in military style. After they passed out of the gate, they saw a TBM heading straight toward them, 50 feet off the deck. As the bomb bay door opened, they all broke and ran, and a 50-pound bag of sugar plunged down and exploded right where they had been! "Almost killed with kindness," in Pop's words. They formed up again and marched down to a canal where the barges were waiting to take them to a hospital ship for a cursory medical examination. They then

Pop Condit and his fellow POWs wave from the roof at low-flying VT-88 photographer. Courtesy of James Connaughton

transferred to a destroyer for their first good old American supper in a long time—the first of 19,000 POWs to come out.

On the last day of August, with the fast carriers in the open sea, *Yorktown's* George Smith observed, "We were in view of the Japanese mainland today for the first time. The long rugged coast line was our first sight of this target we have been hitting. Mt. Fujiyama was in view, her snow capped peak protruding above the low hanging clouds." Next day Vice Admiral Towers relieved McCain in command of the carriers, which moved even closer to Tokyo. In the evening Pop Condit was informed that he would be one of four liberated prisoners to represent the Navy at the surrender ceremony on board the *Missouri*.

Dawn of September 2, 1945—the official V-J Day—found the Fighting Lady steaming just 30 miles east of Sagami Wan with land on both sides. At 0710, the *Yorktown* launched a powerful 48-plane CAP over the ships in Tokyo Bay "to cover any threats of violence" as Ed Wallace put it. But there were none. These were joined by the rest of Air Group 88 for a massive thousand-plane fly-over of the *Missouri* at the ceremony's conclusion.

When Pop Condit went aboard that vessel, he met General Jimmy Doolittle whose bombers had been pounding Japan. Doolittle asked him where he'd been a prisoner. When Pop told him Sumida, the general remarked, "In a couple more weeks, we'd have finished that off!" The ceremony began

VICTORY DINNER
FOR
ALL HANDS

mixed olives

Cream of Tomato Soup
crackers

ROAST YOUNG TOM TURKEY
cranberry sauce

Giblet Gravy	Country Dressing
Whipped Potatoes	Buttered Peas
Orange Cake	Ice Cream

Parker House Rolls

Bread	Butter	Coffee
Cigars	Candy	Cigarettes

VICTORY PROGRAM
aboard
U. S. S. YORKTOWN, CV-10

Captain W. F. Boone, U. S. N.
Commanding Officer

Commander John W. Brady, U. S. N. R.
Executive Officer

At Sea   2 September 1945

Music by The Ship's Band

First Showing
of
"THE YORKTOWN REVIEW"
starring
You and *You* and *You!*

and

"Rhapsody In Blue" (Warner Bros.)
starring
Joan Leslie, Robert Alda
Alexis Smith, Charles Colbern

Mark 4.0

The Victory program of
September 2, 1945 showing
Emperor Hirohito.

-328-

The sun sets over Mt. Fujiyama and the silhouetted *Yorktown* in Tokyo Bay. The war is really over.

at 0930 and lasted for an hour. "The greatest sight I'd ever seen," Pop told a reporter afterward, "was the Japanese bowing down and signing the surrender papers." The proceedings were transmitted by TBS to all the ships; the *York's* crew heard them over the bullhorn.

The press conference afterward was broadcasted to the States, and Condit's wife and family—who had last heard him in an enemy broadcast in May—heard him say to the world that today was his wedding anniversary. Then he was ushered into Admiral Halsey's quarters to sit down for luncheon with the brass. When Halsey walked in, Pop rose and bowed low, half way down like the Japs had required. "You dumb bastard, stand up!" he thought to himself, but didn't think Halsey saw him.

Late in the afternoon, the *Yorktown* moved to within 16 miles of the coast. A "Victory Dinner" of turkey and trimmings and a "Victory Program" ended the day, with the ship otherwise darkened as the task force kept on its guard. Engineer George Crawford reported that the *Yorktown*, from its commissioning at noon of April 15, 1943 until noon of this day, had steamed 226,878 engine miles. Also, this day was the 64th at sea since leaving Leyte.

Daily CAPs continued to be flown over the next two weeks, while MacArthur's troops fanned out across Japan. Radford's task group—redesigned TG 58.1—became one of the two reduced groups keeping offshore vigil, to the keen disappointment of the crews, while other ships anchored in the Bay for liberty. Ed Brand: "This is almost heart breaking!"

But it was all over. On September 4 censorship regulations were lifted; another typhoon skirted the area; and the last morning GQ sounded on the 7th. On the evening of the 8th, Ed Wallace recorded a novel phenomenon in the life of the *Yorktown* crew and for those who had never served in the peacetime Navy: "Tonight the *lights went on again in the fleet* for the first time since the emergency began about five years ago."

As the *Yorktown's* cruise book put it: No sight "seemed stranger than to look out at night and see other ships lighted up, so that the Fleet looked like a city afloat. Peace meant that the hangar deck curtains could be up for the movies at night. It meant plain language instead of codes on the air, smoking on the upper decks at night, and a strange sense of something missing when the call came, 'Sunset'—lacking the familiar 'Darken Ship' which followed as inevitably as 'eggs' after 'ham.' It meant no general quarters each morning, and no censoring of mail. It didn't mean going home yet...."

Even if the threat of Japanese treachery was passing, the occupation forces could not get to all the POWs fast enough, and the carriers were needed to keep dropping supplies to them. To

Final awards for the Air Group 88 leaders (L to R) Chris Cagle of VF-88, Jimmy Elkins of VB-88, group commander Pete Searcy, Joe Hart of VBF-88, and Cliff Huddleston of VT-88. Gull-winged FG-1D Corsair fighter-bomber sits behind them. Courtesy of Robert N. Kelly

reward her crewmen who had never been up in a plane, the *Yorktown* allowed many to go in the TBMs for a look-see. Since not nearly enough hops could accommodate all 3100 officers and crewmen of the ship, air ops officer Cooper Bright gave precedence to those swabs who had been on board the longest.

The leading candidates, as a group, were the Negro mess stewards, many of whom had shot down several of *Yorktown's* assailants. These guys got a well-deserved kick out of these hops, and when some white Southern pilots protested to the captain, he—at the instigation of Father Moody—chased them off his bridge.

World War II brought an isolated American public face-to-face with alien cultures, and the flyovers of Japan were a beginning. Dr. George Smith marvelled at "the rugged beauty of the countryside. Mountains and green valleys are covered with rice fields, the steeper slopes are terraced in order to use all the land. Nearly every yard has several images, their shrine." The industry of the Japanese people—it seemed somehow inappropriate to call them "Japs" any longer—was impressive. Bomb disposal officer Carl Obenauf praised the rice fields of Nagoya, in which the "green water glistens like a silver mirror. Every available inch of land is cultivated, with irrigation ditches everywhere."

On September 15 Captain Boone informed the crew that it would have a closer look since the ship was going into Tokyo Bay next day, ending

Yorktown's longest cruise—78 days. Wallace: "As we steamed in, *Yorktown* led the long steady line of Uncle Sam's men-o-war. We dropped the hook at the outskirts of the Yokohama breakwater just forward of the British anchorage. We passed a few Jap sampans and fishing boats, and they all waved heartily at us—the rats." Ralph Morlan: "I think this was the day the whole ship was waiting for."

Freddie Boone offered Cooper Bright a direct flight home, the reward for his extraordinarily long service on board, but Coop told him, "For three years I've been trying to get to Japan. I'd like to get ashore and see what the hell that place looks like. Two more weeks won't made any damned difference after all this time. I'd like to stay." Boone happily agreed, and Bright joined several other long-term veterans in prolonging their tours to see the fruits of their labors.

"Japan and its people were utterly foreign and strange to most of the Americans," recounted the VF-88 history. "We had been fighting them for nearly four years, yet we knew very little about them." The first impression was one of shock. "Many thought that one trip to the beach was plenty. There was a certain characteristic odor in the Jap villages and cities that was nauseating. It was a rank combination of urine, fish, seaweed, and rotting debris. The Jap people appeared dirty and slovenly. Everyone was surprised that these people had lasted so long in the war. The general impression of those returning from liberty was that the Japs were thoroughly and decisively beaten; that the Japs were polite and considerate on the surface but treacherous and cruel beneath."

Or so it appeared to those who had but one day ashore. Little did they realize, like Pop Condit knew from experience, that the people had hated the military, but that in a modern dictatorship the will of the people could be totally suppressed. The men who spent some time shoreside got a better perspective, like George Wille:

"Regardless of the fact that a few short months before the people of this land were going to fanatical extremes to put their attackers out of commission, the natives whom we met on the streets and whose shoulders we rubbed in the shops and trains seemed to bear little malice towards us, the conquering horde, as it were. On the contrary, they were quite pleasant, eager to please and amazingly curious."

The liberty-hounds naturally bartered with the people, while more than one officer lost his heart to the lovely geisha girls they encountered. The plight of the children—the innocent victims of the carnage—tugged at everyone's heartstrings, and the *Yorktown's* Marine detachment, those toughest of the tough, threw a big party for the kids on board.

Afterward, Coop Bright was riding in one of the ship's jeeps through Tokyo with a Marine officer when a Japanese policeman suddenly shook his fist at them. The Marine remarked to Coop, "You know, I feel sorry for a guy that ignorant." The hatred was gone.

As the Fighting Lady remained in Tokyo Bay, the crew learned that a new sailing schedule would keep the ship there longer than less battle-worn vessels, which led to a near-mutiny. Freddie Boone sent Cooper Bright over to the *Missouri* to rectify this error, which Skinhead did with his usual aplomb—though he ruffled some feathers of Halsey's staff in the process. General cheering greeted the news when it was announced on the 20th.

The ship moved to a new anchorage by the *Nagato*, Admiral Radford relinquished command to Rear Admiral Donald B. Duncan, and paint brushes were broken out to spruce up the ship. History professor Father Joe Moody initiated classes on board "Yorktown University" to help prepare the younger men for peacetime careers, and after ten days the last sightseers were finally back aboard.

Trailing out a gigantic 600-foot-long homeward-bound pennant, held aloft by helium-filled weather balloons, the *Yorktown* weighed anchor on October 1 and headed for Okinawa to pick up

Marines and Seabees for passage home. During final flight operations and gunnery drills en route, the Fighting Lady recorded her 31,000th landing.

Equally memorable was the accidental landing of the skipper of VBF-88, Lieutenant Commander Joe Hart, on the *Hancock* instead of the *Yorktown*; the fact that his pilots did not forewarn him attested to his lack of popularity. Hart then had to spend the night on that ship and was further embarrassed returning next day to a crowded flight deck with welcoming banner and an elaborate ceremony in which Captain Boone presented him with a "brass medal."

Former *Yorktown* pilot Dick Newhafer on the *Hancock* gave his poetic touch to these final fast carrier operations of this great wartime armada.

> We've plotted our course for the
>   eastward,
> We're leaving the red Shinto shore;
> But shadows of great Fujiyama
> Grace scores of white crosses and more.

Taking two days to load passengers for this "Magic Carpet" ride, the *Yorktown* left Okinawa in company with other ships on October 6 for a 16-day direct voyage—5350 miles—to San Francisco. "Yorktown U." flourished for the 800 officers and men who attended regular classes, combat statistics were compiled, and final reports written. Stateside radio programs were picked up on the 15th.

After dawn on a misty, foggy October 20, the planes of Fighting 88 took off for the beach, while the other pilots and crew lined up in dress whites all around the edge of the flight deck, spelling out the words "YORKTOWN" and "FIGHTING LADY" as the Golden Gate came into view. A Navy blimp circled low with a big "Welcome Home" sign painted on it. And then the sun broke through, clearing the mist away to reveal a bright, sunny, almost cloudless day—unlike the dense, damp fog which had greeted most of the Third Fleet six days before.

Ed Brand: "Good old U.S.A.—Ha Ha—Boy, does it look good."

The *Yorktown* followed the *Bon Homme Richard* under the Golden Gate bridge. People lined its high span, waving and cheering, a thrilling sight for all hands, as 40 Navy fighters roared overhead before buzzing the deck. A small welcoming steamer fell in alongside with its whistles blowing, a band playing, and "loaded," noted George Wille,

The Fighting Lady enters San Francisco Bay flying her homeward-bound pennant (seen low, aft of the island), October 20, 1945.

"with local women who screamed and carried on at a great rate." Ships in the harbor blew their sirens and whistles, cars parked at the marina honked their horns, and spectators everywhere waved as the Fighting Lady headed into NAS Alameda and moored. She was home.

Two final pieces of business were hastily combined—selecting Miss Fighting Lady and holding a big victory celebration. The selection committee of 12 crewmen spent six hours eliminating the hundreds of entries received by *Life* magazine until they picked Betty Jo Copeland, a 19-year-old girl-next-door brunette from Fort Worth. Calling her long distance, the committee arranged her flight to Frisco to be crowned at the ship's party.

Father Joe Moody and Skinhead Bright rented the San Francisco Civic Auditorium for the celebrations. When its operators refused to allow the Negro stewards to attend, the two men went straight to the owners and turned that archaic policy around in short order. The other problem was finding girls for the sailors to dance with.

"We needed a thousand girls," Coop kidded later. "Did they come to me, the renowned Doctor of Love on the U.S.S. *Yorktown*? No, they went to Father Moody. The trouble is, he went out and *got* a thousand girls!"

After holding open house for some 19,000 visitors on Navy Day, October 27, the *Yorktown*

turned its attention to the party. The crew crowded into the Civic two nights later, crowned Miss Copeland, and nearly wore her out with endless jitterbugging and foxtrots. Next day the committee dined her at the St. Francis Hotel then returned her to the dance floor for a second party on the 30th. By the time she left for home next day—and ultimate immortality in a "*Life* Goes to a Party" story—many of the combat veterans had been discharged.

Their names shall ride high on the waters
And echo with each rolling swell;
When flying the glory road homeward,
We'll dip once our wings in farewell.

With tiers of bunks hastily welded onto the hangar deck, the *Yorktown* sailed on November 2 for Guam to pick up more returning servicemen on the "Magic Carpet," taking on a new captain when newly-promoted Rear Admiral Boone left at Guam. Another Magic Carpet cruise took Yule turkeys and Christmas trees to Manila, where the *York* picked up 4600 Army troops for transportation home.

En route, a final classic piece of hokum surfaced on board the Fighting Lady—a bogus Pacific Fleet directive which required naval personnel to "undergo an indoctrination course" before returning to civilian life. They were enjoined, upon leaving the service, "to make themselves as

Captain Boone dances with Miss Fighting Lady, Betty Jo Copeland, at the ship's big dance in San Francisco, October 29, 1945. Courtesy of Peter D. Joers

inconspicuous as possible,'' especially in eleven specific situations, to wit:

(a) In America there is a remarkable number of beautiful girls. These young girls *have not* been liberated and many are gainfully employed as stenographers, sales girls, and beauty operators or welders. Contrary to current practices, they should not be approached with ''How much?'' A proper greeting is ''Isn't it a love day?''or ''Have you ever been to Kansas City?'', then say, ''How much?''

(b) A guest in a private home is usually awakened in the morning by a light tapping on his door and an invitation to join the host at breakfast. It is proper to say, ''I'll be there shortly.'' Do not say, ''Blow it out your _____!''

(c) Very natural urges are apt to occur when in a crowd. If found necessary to defecate, one does not grab a shovel in one hand and paper in the other and run for the garden. At least 90 percent of American homes have one room called the ''bathroom'', i.e. a room that in most cases contains a bathtub, wash basin, medicine cabinet, and a toilet. It is the latter that you will use in this case.

Instructors should make sure that all personnel understand the operation of a toilet, particularly the lever or button arrangement that serves to prepare the device for re-use.

(d) Belching or passing wind in company is strictly frowned upon. If you should forget about it, however, and belch in the presence of others, a proper remark is ''Excuse me.'' Do not say, ''It must be the lousy chow we've been getting.''

(e) American dinners, in most cases, consist of several items, each served in a separate dish. The common practice of mixing various items, such as corned-beef and pudding, or lima beans and peaches to make it more palatable will be refrained from. In time the ''separate dish'' system will become very enjoyable.

(f) The returning sailor is apt to often find his opinions differ from those of his civilian associates. One should call upon his reserve for etiquette and correct his acquaintance with such remarks as, ''I believe you have made a mistake'', or ''I am afraid you are in error.'' Do not say, ''Brother, you're all f_____d up.'' This is considered impolite.

(g) Upon leaving a friend's home after a visit, one may find his hat misplaced. Frequently it has been placed in a closet. One should turn to one's host and say, ''I don't seem to have my hat; could you help me find it?'' Do not say, ''Don't anybody leave this room; some S.O.B. has stolen my hat!''

(h) In motion picture theaters, seats are provided. Benches are not required. It isn't considered good form to whistle every time a female over 8 and under 80 crosses the screen. If vision is impaired by the person in the seat in front, there are plenty of other seats which can be occupied. Do not hit him across the back of the head and say, ''Move your head, jerk; I can't see a damned thing through your thick skull.''

(i) It is not proper to go around hitting everyone of draft age in civilian clothes. He might have been released from service for medical reasons; ask for his credentials, and if he can't show them, then go ahead and slug him.

(j) Natural functions will continue. It may be necessary frequently to urinate. Toilets are provided in all public buildings for this purpose. Signs will read ''Ladies''— which, literally interpreted, means, ''Off limits to naval personnel.''

(k) Personnel attached to aircraft carriers

should make a special effort to restrain themselves while relating stories of actions with the enemy. Airmen should be exceptionally careful with their hands while explaining maneuvers of their aircraft while engaging Jap planes—you may gouge someone's eye out or goose the wrong party. Gun crews should refrain from making noises such as "brrrt-brrrt" and 'tat-aaatt-a-at-t-t" representing how they shot down a "zoot suiter." These gestures and sounds are unbecoming to naval personnel. It is permissible, however, for the airmen to use "zooms", and for the gun crews to say, "Bang, bang!" This should be limited to two "zooms" and three sets of "Bang-bangs" for each twenty minutes. The expression, "Splash!" may also be used sparingly . . . .
M.L.E. POST,
by direction.

Waiting for the ship upon its arrival at San Francisco on January 13, 1946 were orders to prepare her for mothballing. The country had no further need of her services. Moving to Bremerton, the *Yorktown* was gradually deactivated and relegated to reserve status in June, the same month she was awarded the prestigious and richly-deserved Presidential Unit Citation. The Fighting Lady was finally decommissioned on January 9, 1947.

In closing his diary, George Wille, one of the last men to leave, expressed feelings common to most of his shipmates in his final diary entry: "The Navy is now behind me, temporarily at least, and at this point I can frankly look back and say that it was a great experience. Although there were many times when things seemed pretty rough, seemingly endless days and nights at sea, with small breaks of liberty on smaller comfortable chunks of land, the spirit of every man—along with that spirit which helped keep the *Yorktown* out front—was founded on and bolstered up by companionship, loyalty to each other, and a willingness to give and take when necessary."

A world ended for the men as they left the ship they had grown to love, leaving only a few loose ends, some of which, however, would never allow that world to completely die as it should have— like Danny Carveth's blinded eyes from Bomb Sunday, Pop Condit's tortured body, and the pain of next-of-kin as they slowly realized that their missing loved ones weren't coming home. Of all the *Yorktown* airmen once listed as missing in action, only Condit and three aircrewmen survived.

In Smokey Stover's case, at least his executioners at Truk faced trial as war criminals. The two subalterns who had committed the act were given life imprisonment, and their captain who had given the order was executed at Guam in September 1947.

The last tallyho has been sounded,
The sea washes thick with the tears;
Remember the ranks of the fallen,
As memory fades with the years.

But many *Yorktown*ers refused to let the memory fade, notably Jim Bryan, former air ordnance boss. In April 1948 he convened a reunion in New York City at which 175 shipmates formed the Yorktown Association and decided to make the reunions annual. And so they have been ever since, many of them on board their old ship.

For she wasn't really very old when in 1953, as a new war raged in Korea, the Fighting Lady returned to active duty, though too late to see action there. She patrolled her old stomping grounds of the western Pacific as an attack carrier (CVA) for four years, then as an antisubmarine carrier (CVS). Her planes fought in the Vietnam War during the 1960s, and in 1968 the ship recovered the Apollo 8 astronauts returning from the first manned flight to the vicinity of the Moon. Shifting to the Atlantic, the Lady ended her long service with her final decommissioning in 1970.

Yet, the *Yorktown* still lived on, in body as well as in spirit, for five years later she was towed to Charleston, South Carolina, to form the nucleus of the Patriots Point Naval and Maritime Museum and to host the annual reunions of her veterans. In 1979, fittingly, the Fighting Lady became the nation's memorial to all its fallen carriermen. Then, five years after that, the Navy commissioned a brand new *Yorktown,* an Aegis guided missile cruiser (CG-48), the fifth United States warship to bear the name.

The impact of the Fighting Lady on the modern U.S. Navy is best illustrated perhaps by something a noncarrierman remarked to fellow officer Captain Cooper Bright several years after the war: "It's been a wonderful thing to meet you here in the Navy, Coop—to learn that I really didn't participate in the Navy in World War II at all, that anybody of importance was only on the *Yorktown*. You speak of 'Jocko', commander of the Seventh Fleet, and of 'Raddy' [Arthur Radford], Chairman of the Joint Chiefs of Staff, and of 'Andy' [George Anderson], Chief of Naval Operations. No-one else counted. The *Yorktown* won the whole war by itself!"

"You know," smiled Skinhead, his eye a-twinkle and his dome aglow, "you've *completely* got the picture!"

APPENDIX A

AA anti-aircraft fire

ace fighter pilot with at least five airborne kills to his credit

ACIO air combat intelligence officer

ack ack anti-aircraft fire

admin administrative

airedale enlisted flight deck crewman

Air Plot ship's space in which positions of friendly and enemy planes are plotted

angels one thousand feet altitude ("angels 15" = 15,000 feet)

AP armor-piercing bomb; enlisted "Aviation Pilot" (pre-1943)

avgas aviation fuel

bandit plane identified as enemy

BB battleship

barrier raised wires for trapping landing planes which miss the arresting cables

Bat team night fighters

black gang Engineering Department

blockbuster 2000-pound bomb

bogey unidentified plane, presumably enemy

BOQ bachelor officers quarters

bos'n, bosun boatswain's mate (worked with rigging, anchors, ship's boats, etc.)

Boys Town Junior Officers' Bunk Room

BuAer Bureau of Aeronautics

bulkhead wall on a ship

bullhorn ship's loudspeaker system

CA heavy cruiser

can destroyer

CAP combat air patrol of fighters

cat catapult

Cat F6F Hellcat

CBI China-Burma-India theater of war

ceiling maximum altitude for flying (base of the cloud cover)

Charlie order to land planes

CIC Combat Information Center (Radar Plot)

chicken fighter

CL light cruiser

CO commanding officer

CO₂ bottle carbon dioxide fire extinguisher

ComAirPac Commander Air Force Pacific Fleet

composite strike attack force of fighters, bombers and torpedo planes

CPO chief petty officer

"Crash One, Two" landing signal officers

cumshaw purloining needed equipment surreptitiously

the cut LSO hand signal for pilot to land

CV aircraft carrier

CVE escort carrier

CVL light carrier

daisy cutter anti-personnel fused bomb

dam con damage control

DD destroyer

DE destroyer escort

deckload strike maximum number of planes to fit on the flight deck for one continuous launch, about 45

deflection shots fighter plane leading his airborne target by firing from a particular angle

dogfight aerial battle between two or more fighter planes

exec executive officer (second-in-command)

fantail after end of the ship above the stern, hangar deck level

FDO fighter director officer

fish torpedo; torpedo plane

Flag Plot admiral's working spaces

flak burst of anti-aircraft fire

flash gear protective clothes and ointment to prevent burns from the blast of bomb explosions

flattop aircraft carrier

fo'c'sle forecastle (front part of the ship behind the bow)

4F draftee rejected for being physically unfit

frag fragmentation explosives

gedunk ice cream

gig small power boat

gob sailor

GP general purpose (bomb)

GQ General Quarters (man your battle stations)

grabass low humor

in the groove plane approaching the ship astern to land

group grope training flight comprised of the entire air group

gyrene U.S. Marine

hawk dive bomber

HF high-frequency radio

hit the silk to parachute

Holy Joe chaplain

the hook anchor

IFF airplane's identification friend-or-foe radio signal

island superstructure rising from the starboard side of the carrier

jamoke coffee

jinking evasive airplane maneuver

JO junior officer

JOOD junior officer of the deck

joy stick pilot's control rod for flying the plane and firing its machine guns

kt. knot (speed at one nautical mile per hour or 1.15 statute miles per hour)

Lieutenant (jg) lieutenant (junior grade)

LSO landing signal(s) officer ("Crash One"; Assistant LSO-"Crash Two")

Mae West inflatable life jacket named for the buxom movie star

main comm main communications station

maru Japanese cargo ship

mech mechanic

mule flight deck tractor for pulling planes

napalm jellied gasoline that clings to an object after it hits and ignites

NAS naval air station

NASKA Naval Air Station Kahalui on Maui, Hawaiian Islands

Nips Japanese; Nippon is the native word for Japan

O Club officers club

OOD officer of the deck

op, ops operation, operations

pancake time time to land

pig boat submarine

plane captain enlisted airedale assisting the pilot

pogey bait candy

Point Option geographical position of launching carrier strike planes for combat

pollywog uninitiated person who has never crossed the Equator

portside left side

POW/PW prisoner-of-war

Prep Charlie prepare to land order

Pri Fly primary fly control station on the island

probable an enemy plane likely to have been destroyed in aerial combat, but not confirmed

quals carrier landing and takeoff qualifications

(R) Relative; bearing of an object relative to the direction the ship is moving, as opposed to (T) True

Radar Plot CIC; ship's space in which positions of all ships and planes are plotted and from which defensive fighters are vectored out

ready room squadron briefing and lounging space on the ship

respot the deck park the planes

Ropeyarn Sunday a day to relax and mend socks, not necessarily a Sunday

SAP semi-armor piercing (bomb)
scramble hurried launch of planes
scuttlebutt drinking fountain; rumor (drinking fountain conversation)
Sick Bay ship's hospital spaces
hit the silk to parachute
sitting ducks parked planes, exposed to air attack
Sky One Air Defense Forward on the island
snooper enemy reconnaisance plane
sock towed target sleeve
sortie a ship leaving port for battle; a plane taking off for battle
sponson platform extended outboard of the hull, usually for anti-aircraft guns
spot the deck park the aircraft
squawk box ship's intercom speaker-receiver
starboard side right side
star shell shells fired to illuminate the surface of the sea
strafe to fire plane's machine guns at ground targets in a low-level pass
swab, swabbie sailor
sweep attack by fighter planes to eliminate airborne enemy fighters, to sweep the skies of them
(T) True; actual bearing on the compass, as opposed to (R) Relative
tail-end Charlie last plane in a formation
TBS Talk-Between-Ships radio
TF Task Force
TG Task Group

tin can destroyer
top off refuel to capacity
torpecker torpedo-bomber
torpedo juice alcohol strained from the torpedoes for making booze
Torpex explosive composed of T.N.T. and cyclonite; 1.5 times more explosive force than T.N.T.
tracer visible bullets; every third round fired from airplane and anti-aircraft guns
Two-block Fox launch aircraft signal
VB dive bomber; carrier bombing squadron
VBF fighter-bomber; carrier bombing-fighting squadron
to vector direct a fighter to intercept an enemy plane
Very pistol for firing rescue flares to attract attention
VF fighter plane; carrier fighting squadron
VFN/VF(N) night fighter; night fighting squadron
VHF very-high-frequency radio
V-J Victory over Japan
VT torpedo-bomber; carrier torpedo squadron
waveoff LSO instructing a pilot to go around the landing circle again before trying to land
WAC Women's Army Corps
WAVES Women Accepted for Voluntary Emergency Services in the U.S. Navy
weatherguesser aerologist
window aluminum foil strips, dropped from planes to foul radar scopes in making fixes
wing root where the wing joins the fuselage of an airplane
zootsuiter Japanese kamikaze suicide plane

APPENDIX B

AIRPLANE NAMES
(All carrier planes are single-engine)

United States
Navy

F4F/FM Grumman Wildcat fighter
F6F Grumman Hellcat fighter and fighter-bomber; "F6" "Cat"
F4U/FG Chance Vought Corsair fighter and fighter-bomber
TBF/TBM Grumman Avenger torpedo-bomber; "Turkey"
SBD Douglas Dauntless dive bomber
SB2C Curtiss Helldiver dive bomber; "Beast" "2C"
PBY Consolidated Catalina twin-engine patrol-bomber flying boat
PBM Martin Mariner twin-engine patrol-bomber flying boat; "Dumbo"
PB4Y Privateer (Navy version of Army B-24)
SNJ North American Texan single-engine scout trainer

Army

P-38 Lockheed Lightning twin-engine fighter
B-24 Convair Liberator four-engine heavy bomber
B-25 North American Mitchell twin-engine medium bomber
B-29 Boeing Superfortress four-engine heavy bomber
L-5 Vultee-Stinson Sentinel single-engine reconnaissance plane

Japanese

(Code names assigned by Allies)
Betty Army and Navy twin-engine land-based medium and torpedo bomber
Dinah Army twin-engine reconnaissance plane
Emily Navy four-engine flying boat

Frances Navy twin-engine land-based light and torpedo bomber
Frank Army single-engine fighter
George Navy carrier fighter
Grace Navy carrier bomber
Hamp Navy carrier fighter
Helen Army twin-engine medium bomber
Irving Army twin-engine fighter-reconnaissance plane
Jack Navy carrier fighter
Jake Navy single-engine reconnaissance float plane
Jill Navy carrier torpedo-bomber
Judy Navy carrier dive bomber
Kate Navy carrier torpedo-bomber
Mavis Navy four-engine patrol-bomber flying boat
Myrt Navy carrier scout
Nate Army single-engine fighter
Nell Navy and Army twin-engine land-based medium bomber
Nick Army twin-engine fighter
Oscar Army single-engine fighter
Peggy Army twin-engine heavy bomber
Pete Navy single-engine reconnaissance float plane
Rufe Navy single-engine float fighter
Sally Army twin-engine medium bomber
Tojo Army single-engine fighter
Tony Army and Navy single-engine fighter
Topsy Army and Navy twin-engine land-based transport
Val Navy carrier dive bomber
Zeke/Zero Navy and Army single-engine fighter, carrier- and land-based

APPENDIX C

SENIOR OFFICERS OF THE *YORKTOWN* (April 15, 1943 to September 30, 1945. Highest rank while on board)

Commanding Officer
Captain Joseph J. Clark — April 1943-February 1944
Captain Ralph E. Jennings — February 1944-September 1944
Captain Thomas S. Combs — September 1944-April 1945
Captain W. Frederick Boone — April 1945-November 1945

Executive Officer
Commander Raymond R. Waller — April 1943-November 1943
Commander Cameron Briggs — November 1943-June 1944
Commander Arthur S. Born — June 1944-May 1945
Commander Myron T. Evans — May 1945-August 1945
Commander John W. Brady — August 1945-September 1945

Navigator
Commander George W. Anderson, Jr. — April 1943-October 1943
Commander Raymond N. Sharp — November 1943-May 1944
Commander Alfred R. Matter — May 1944-September 1944
Commander Elliott L. James — September 1944-September 1945

Air Officer
Commander Henry L. Dozier — April 1943-March 1944
Commander Arthur S. Born — March 1944-June 1944
Commander Myron T. Evans — June 1944-April 1945
Commander Robert A. Macpherson — April 1945-September 1945

Chief Engineer
Commander James A. McNally — April 1943-December 1943
Commander Walter T. Hart, Jr. — December 1943-August 1944
Commander George A. Crawford — August 1944-September 1945

Head, Gunnery Department
Commander Cecil L. Blackwell — April 1943-February 1944
Commander George A. Earnshaw — February 1944-May 1945
Lt. Commander Thomas J. Patterson — May 1945-June 1945
Lt. Commander Daniel J. Carrison — June 1945-September 1945

First Lieutenant/Head, Hull Department/Head, Construction and Repair Department
Commander Daniel J. Sweeney — April 1943-May 1944
Commander John W. Brady — May 1944-August 1945
Lt. Commander Worth C. Sherrill — August 1945-September 1945

Head, Communciations Department
Commander James A. Morrison — April 1943-March 1944
Lt. Commander James M. Tippey — March 1944-May 1945
Lieutenant Peter D. Joers — May 1945-September 1945

Head, Medical Department
Captain Clifton A. Young — April 1943-April 1944
Commander John T. Smith — April 1944-May 1945
Commander Earle E. Metcalf — May 1945-September 1945

Head, Supply Department
Commander William L. Patten — April 1943-March 1944
Commander William E. Moring — March 1944-Janauary 1945
Commander William J. Held — January 1945-September 1945

Air Group Five
Commander James H. Flatley, Jr. — February-September 1943
Commander Charles L. Crommelin — September-November 1943
Lietutenant Commander Edgar E. Stebbins — November 1943-May 1944

VF-5
Commander Charles L. Crommelin — February-September 1943
Lieutenant Commander Edward C. Owen — September 1943-March 1944
Lieutenant Robert C. Jones — March-May 1944

VB-5
Lieutenant Commander Robert M. Milner — January-September 1943

Lieutenant Commander Edgar E. Stebbins — September-November 1943
Lieutenant Daniel J. Harrington, III — November 1943-May 1944

VT-5
Lieutenant Commander Richard Upson — February 1943-April 1944
Lieutenant Andrew C. Lett — April-May 1944

Air Group One
Commander James M. Peters — November 1943-August 1944

VF-1
Commander Bernard M. Strean — May 1943-August 1944

VB-1
Lieutenant Commander Joseph W. Runyan — December 1943-August 1944

VT-1
Commander, Walter F. Henry — May 1943-August 1944

Air Group Three
Commander Macpherson B. Williams — September-December 1944
Commander John T. Lowe, Jr. — December 1944-March 1945

VF-3
Lieutenant Commander William L. Lamberson — August 1944-January 1945
Lieutenant Commander Edward H. Bayers — February-March 1945

VBF-3
Lieutenant Commander F.E. Wolf — February-March 1945

VB-3
Commander John T. Lowe, Jr. — September 1943-December 1944
Lieutenant Raymond S. Osterhoudt — December 1944-March 1945

VT-3
Commander Charles H. Turner — September 1943-March 1945

Air Group Nine
Lieutenant Commander Herbert N. Houck — February-July 1945

VF-9
Lieutenant Jack S. Kitchen — February-July 1945

VBF-9
Lieutenant Commander Frank L. Lawlor — January-July 1945

VB-9
Lieutenant Tony F. Schneider — September 1944-July 1945

VT-9
Lieutenant Commander Bryon E. Cooke — April 1944-March 1945
Lieutenant Thomas H. Stetson — March-July 1945

Air Group 88
Commander Seth S. Searcy, Jr. — August 1944-October 1945

VF-88
Lieutenant Commander Richard G. Crommelin — August 1944-July 1945
Lieutenant Malcolm W. Cagle — July-October 1945

VBF-88
Lieutenant Commander Joseph E. Hart — January-October 1945

VB-88
Lieutenant Commander James S. Elkins, Jr. — January 1944-October 1945

VT-88
Lieutenant Commander J. Clifford Huddleston — August 1944-October 1945

SOURCES

The men of the Fighting Lady have made this book possible, especially their active help in telling their stories to the writer, beginning with letters to him as a three-year-old kid from his uncle Bob Reynolds in 1943 and culminating in the stories at the reunions and numerous letters through 1985. As ghostwriter, I helped Admiral Jocko Clark write his autobiography, *Carrier Admiral* (New York: David McKay, 1967), and doctoral research at Duke University led to the book *The Fast Carriers: The Forging of an Air Navy* (New York: McGraw-Hill, 1968; reprinted by Robert Krieger, 1978), which focused on the same period covered in the present work. For my short account of carrier warfare between 1903 and 1945, see *The Carrier War* (Alexandria, Va.: Time-Life Books, 1981).

Most of the active research and writing of this particular book was undertaken with the generous support of the U.S.S. Yorktown CV-10 Association, Inc., notably its leaders and benefactors James T. Bryan, Jr., and Peter Dierks Joers. The support of the Patriots Point Development Authority, which employed me as curator and historian of the ship, was also instrumental in the completion of the book. The typing of the long and often undecipherable manuscript was done by my tireless wife Connie.

Credit for providing the action reports, air group and squadron histories, ship's musters and miscellaneous official documents belongs to Dr. Dean C. Allard and his very helpful staff of the Operational Archives Branch, Naval Historical Center, Washington Navy Yard. The log and war diary of the *Yorktown* are located at the National Archives, and documents relating to the construction and physical changes to the ship are deposited in Boxes 892 to 896, Record Group 19, Bureau of Ships General Correspondence 1940-1945, at the National Federal Records Center, Suitland, Maryland. The official U.S. Navy photographs were provided by the Naval Historical Center, National Archives, the Edward Steichen collection at the U.S. Naval Academy (Alice Creighton, archivist), and by many former *Yorktown*ers. Lieutenant Charles W. Kerlee took the majority of them. The paintings from the U.S. Navy Art Collection were generously made available by John Barnett. The color photographs were made available by Charles Haberlein of the Photographic Section, Curator Branch, Naval Historical Center.

The unique items utilized herein were made available through the generosity of the veterans or their widows who have saved them over the years: plans of the day, ready room ticker tapes, dispatches, snapshots, cartoons, ship's newspapers, flight logs, the daily Radio Press News, miscellaneous shipboard and personal documents (official and otherwise), diaries and scrapbooks.

All the former officers and crewmen who helped are simply too numerous to list, although many are mentioned in the text. Special thanks are due the following individuals for their diaries and letters as well as general reminiscences: Charles H. Ambellan; George M. Bernard; Jesse Bradley; Edward A. Brand; James T. Bryan, Jr.; Edwin H. Buickerood; James H. Campbell; Joe E. Chambliss; Joel R. Connell; John R. Dayton; Norman D. Duberstein; Robert A. Frink; Raymond F. Gard; Harry W. Harrison; Dwight C. Horner; Oliver Jensen; Joseph R. Kristufek; J.T. Lowe, Jr.; Jack MacDade; Clyde A. Moneyhun; Ralph L. Morlan; Kenneth Parkinson; James W. A. Pickard; Trueman A. Place; Russell L. Reiserer; Robert W. Rice; Charles D. Ridgway, III; George Franklin Smith; Bernard Swanson; C. Roger Van Buren; Edward N. Wallace; A. L. Wenger, Jr.; Alexander Wilding, Jr.; George A. F. Wille; Macpherson B. Williams; Tony Yankovich; and Robert K. Yount.

Thanks go also to Benjamin S. Stover for the use of his brother E. T. Stover's diary, the first part of which was edited by me as *The Saga of Smokey Stover* (Charleston: Tradd Street Press, 1978); to Ralston Gray for his son John's exquisite diary; to Thomas LeBoutillier III for the use of his brother John's letters; and to the family of Marshall S. Hopp for its booklet memorial to their son which includes his diary. J. Bryan, III kindly gave permission to quote from his diary, published as *Aircraft Carrier* (New York: Ballantine, 1954), as did Frederica B. Newhafer from her husband Richard L. Newhafer's *Poems 1942-1945* (privately published).

In addition to the above, the following individuals provided unusual amounts of time and effort to recall their wartime experiences for the writer: Arthur Abramson; Robert L. Alexander; George W. Anderson, Jr.; Cooper B. Bright; J.J. Clark; James W. Condit; John G. Crommelin, Jr.; Robert W. Duncan; Robert W. Eaton; Bernard J. Favaro; Dorothy Flatley; Truman J. Hedding; Peter D. Joers; Ernest B. Kelly; Raleigh A. Lancaster; George J. Largess; Dwight S. Long; Frank J. Losey, Jr.; Carl F. Luedemann; Edward J. McCarten; Douglas A. McCrary; John E. Montgomery; Joseph N. Moody; H. S. Moore; Thomas J. Patterson; Douglas Petty; Maurice A. Proctor; Carness F. Ramey; F. Robert Reynolds; Jesse Rodriguez; Theodore H. Rohrbaugh; Raymond N. Sharp; Charles A. Sims; Edgar E. Stebbins; Richard C. Tripp; Joseph L. Tucker; John R. Wadleigh; and Raymond R. Waller. Also, Ruben P. Kitchen Jr., generously made available his father's reminiscences and sources collected for use in his own book about the ship which covers all 27 years of its service: *Pacific Carrier* (New York: Zebra, 1980).

For overall background of naval warfare in this century, reference of U.S. flag officers, and the carrier war, I used my own three works, *Command of the Sea: The History and Strategy of Maritime Empires* (New York: William Morow, 1974), *Famous American Admirals* (New York: Van Nostrand Reinhold, 1978), and *The Fast Carriers*. For the context of World War II, in spite of many errors, the standard source remains Samuel Eliot Morison, *History of United States Naval Operations in World War II*, 15 volumes (Boston: Little, Brown, 1947-62).

The most valuable published sources were those written by on-board observers. In addition to Jocko Clark's *Carrier Admiral* and Joe Bryan's *Aircraft Carrier*, they are Oliver Jensen, *Carrier War* (New York: Simon and Schuster, 1945); Max Miller, *Daybreak for Our Carrier* (New York: Whittlesey House, 1944); and Ralph D. Paine, Jr., "Carrier Notebook," *Fortune*, XXXII, no.1 (July 1945), 152-153, 186-196, also the fictionalized account by Richard L. Newhafer, *The Last Tallyho* (New York: G. P. Putnam's Sons, 1964). The ship's cruise book, *Into the Wind*, edited by Lieutenant Robert L. Brandt and printed privately, was useful only as a reference for the 1945 period.

Published works used mostly for reference and an occasional story were:

Alexander, Jack. "They Sparked the Carrier Revolution," *Saturday Evening Post* (September 16, 1944).

Belote, James H. and William M. Belote. *Titans of the Seas*. New York: Harper & Row, 1975.

Blair, Clay, Jr. *Silent Victory*. New York: Lippincott, 1975.

Boyington, Gregory "Pappy." *Baa Baa Black Sheep*. New York: Putnam, 1958.

Bryan, Joseph, III and Philip Reed. *Mission Beyond Darkness*. New York: Duell, Sloan and Pearce, 1945.

Bryan, J., III. "A Couple of Lollipops," *Liberty*, XXII, no. 2 (June 2, 1945).

Clark, Blake, and Paul W. Kearney. " 'Pete' Mitscher, Boss of Task Force 58," *Reader's Digest*, XLVII (July 1945).

Clayton, Kenneth. "Iwo Never Was a Pushover," *Flying* (June 1945).

Draper, William F. "Painting History in the Pacific," *National Geographic*, LXXXVI, no. 4 (October 1944).

Earle, Sylvia A. "Life Springs from Death in Truk Lagoon," *National Geographic*, 149, no. 5 (May 1976).

Flying Special Issue: "U.S. Naval Aviation at War," 35, no. 4 (October 1944).

Friedman, Norman, Arnold S. Lott, and Robert F. Sumrall. *USS Yorktown (CV-10): Ship's Data 7*. Annapolis: Leeward Publications, 1977.

Hancock, Joy Bright, *Lady in the Navy*. Annapolis: Naval Institute Press, 1972.

Hara, Captain Tameichi, IJN *et al.*, *Japanese Destroyer Captain*. New York: Ballantine, 1961.

Hipple, William, in *Newsweek* (April 17, 1944).

Johnston, Stanley. *The Grim Reapers*. Philadelphia: Blakiston, 1943.

Karig, Walter, *et al. Battle Report*, V. *Victory in the Pacific*. New York: Rinehard, 1949.

Maloney, Tom. " 'The Fighting Lady' and 'Power in the Pacific,' " *U.S. Camera*, VIII, no. 2 (March 1945).

Markey, Morris. *Well Done!* New York: D. Appleton-Century, 1945.

Monsarrat, John, *Angel on the Yardarm: The Beginnings of Fleet Radar Defense and the Kamikaze Threat*. Newport: Naval War College Press, 1985.

Montgomery, Richard K. "We Watched a Battleship Die," *Liberty* (September 1, 1945).

Morrissey, Thomas L. *Odyssey of Fighting Two*. (Private, 1945).

Newport News Shipbuilding and Dry Dock Company. "Second *Yorktown* Launched," *Shipyard Bulletin*, VIII, no. 9 (January-February 1943).

O'Kane, Richard H. *Clear the Bridge!* New York: Rand, 1977.

Pratt, Fletcher. *Fleet Against Japan*. New York: Harper & Brothers, 1946.

_____. *The Navy's War*. New York: Harper & Brothers, 1944.

Radford, Arthur, W. (Stephen Jurika, ed.) *From Pearl Harbor to Vietnam: Memoirs*. Stanford: Hoover Institution Press, 1980.

Sakai, Saburo, *et al. Samurai*. New York: E.P. Dutton, 1957.

Sakaida, Henry. "The Last Dogfights of World War II," *Naval Aviation Museum Foundation*, VI, no. 1 (Spring 1985), 27-34.

Sims, Edward H. *Greatest Fighter Missions*. New York: Ballantine, 1962.

Spurr, Russell. *A Glorious Way to Die*. New York: Newmarket Press, 1981.

Steichen, Edward. *The Blue Ghost*. New York: Harcourt, Brace, 1947.

Tillman, Barrett A. *Hellcat*. Annapolis: Naval Institute Press, 1979.

_____. "Coaching the Fighters." *U.S. Naval Institute Proceedings*, 106, no. 1 (January 1980).

"USS Yorktown CV-10," *Our Navy* (June 1, 1950).

Walker, S.P. "Operation Dumbo," *Our Navy* (March 1, 1946).

Y'Blood, William T. *Red Sun Setting*. Annapolis: Naval Institute Press. 1981.

" 'Yorktown' Picks Miss Fighting Lady," *Life* (November 12, 1945).

The action reports utilized at the Navy's Operational Archives Branch were:

Yorktown Serial 1042 of 6 September 1943. "Air Attack on Marcus Island on 31 August 1943."

Commander Air Group Five Serial 016 of 3 September 1943.

C.A. Pownall no serial of 4 September 1943 and Serial 005 of 22 September 1943.

Yorktown Serial 1056 of 10 October 1943. "Air Attack on Wake Island on 5 and 6 October 1943."

Yorktown Serial 1069 of 1 December 1943. "Operation GALVANIC, 19 November to 27 November 1943."

Yorktown Serial 1074 of 12 December 1943. "Post Galvanic Operations, Attacks on Kwajalein and Wotje Atolls, 4 December 1943."

Commander Air Group Five Serial 001 of 4 February 1944. "Air Group Commander's Combat Report of Attacks on Maloelap and Kwajalein Atolls, 29 January 1944-3 February 1944."

Yorktown Serial 008 of 18 February 1944. "CATCHPOLE Operations, Truk Islands, 16 and 17 February 1944."

Commander Air Group Five Serial 003 of 23 February 1944. "Air Group Commander's Combat Record of Attacks on Saipan and Tinian Islands, 22 February 1944."

Yorktown Serial 0013 of 6 April 1944. "Operations against the Palau Islands and Woleai Atoll; 30 March to 1 April 1944."

Yorktown Serial 0015 of 2 May 1944. "Operations in Support of the Occupation of the Hollandia area, New Guinea, 21 April to 27 April 1944."

Yorktown Serial 0016 of 5 May 1944. "Operation against the Truk Islands, 29 and 30 April 1944."

Yorktown Serial 0020 of 29 June 1944. "Operations in Support of the Occupation of Saipan and against Major Units of the Enemy Fleet, from 11 June 1944 to 24 June 1944."

Additional sources for reconstructing the events of the night of June 20, 1944 were the action reports of CTG 58.1 (Serial 0052 of 14 July 1944), CTG 58.2 (Serial 00223 of 10 July 1944), and CTG 58.3 (Serial 00116 of 16 July 1944) and the ships' logs of the *Yorktown, Hornet, Bataan, Lexington, Wasp, Essex, Bunker Hill, Belleau Wood, Enterprise, Oakland, Boston, Reno, Santa Fe, Baltimore, Canberra* and *San Juan*, and a letter from Admiral J. W. Reeves, Jr., to the writer, January 8, 1962.

Yorktown Serial 0028 of 29 July 1944. "Operations in Support of the Occupation of the Marianas Islands, from 30 June to 21 July 1944."

Yorktown Serial 0029 of 29 July 1944. "Operations against Yap Islands, Ngulu Atoll and Ulithi Atoll, from 25 through 28 July 1944."

Yorktown Serial 0250 of 20 November 1944. "Operations Against Enemy Shipping in the Philippine Islands Area, from 11 November to 15 November 1944."

Yorktown Serial 0258 of 23 November 1944. "Operations against Enemy Airfields in Central Philippines, 19 November 1944."

Yorktown Serial 0287 of 25 December 1944. "Operations against enemy airfields on Luzon in support of landings on Mindoro, from 14 to 16 December 1944."

Yorktown Serial 036 of 26 January 1945. "Report of Actions during the period 30 December 1944 to 23 January 1945."

Yorktown Serial 075 of 2 March 1945. "Report of Actions during the period 10 February to 27 February 1945."

Yorktown Serial 0205 of 17 May 1945. "Actions in preparation for and support of occupation of Okinawa from 14 March to 11 May 1945."

Air Group Commander Serial 0138 of 13 May 1945. "Comments on Air Operations covering occupation of Okinawa, Nansei Shoto, Period 18 March-11 May 1945."

Yorktown Serial 0242 of 15 June 1945. "Actions in Support of occupation of Okinawa, including strikes against Southern Kyushu, from 24 May to 13 June 1945."

Yorktown Serial 0441 of 6 September 1945. "Actions Covering Attacks on Aircraft, Shipping, and Strategic Targets on

Northern Kyushu, Shikoku, Tokyo Plain area, Northern Honshu, and Southern Hokkaido from 2 July 1945 to 15 August 1945."

"Action Report of Commander, Air Group Eighty-Eight, Air Operations against Shikoku, Honshu and Hokkaido, aboard U.S.S. *Yorktown* - Period 1 July to 15 August 1945."

Yorktown Serial 0447 of 12 September 1945. "Operations from 15 August to 2 September 1945 which consisted of airfield surveillance and searches for prisoner of war camps during initial occupation phases."

Yorktown no serial of 3 January 1946. "Supplementary Historical Report, from 2 September 1945 to 1 January 1946."

Information on treatment and fate of American prisoners of war is from Commander Marianas to Chief, Bureau of Naval Personnel, Serial 10916 of 27 August 1946, and "Final Report of Navy War Crimes Program (1 December 1949), "II, App. A and B.

All but one of the air unit histories are unpublished and most are deposited at the Naval Historical Center:

Jensen, Oliver, to Assistant Secretary of the Navy for Air, 3 May 1944: "Air Group Five (USS *Yorktown*)."

Duncan, Robert W. "History of Fighting Squadron Five."

"The History of Bombing Squadron Five."

"A Brief History of Torpedo Squadron Five."

"Air Group One History," 2 August 1944.

"Fighting Squadron One History," 2 August 1944.

"History of Bombing Squadron One."

"This Is It: The Story of Bombing Squadron One."

"Torpedo Squadron One."

"The Story of Torpedo Squadron One."

"History of Air Group Three."

"Air Group 3."

"Fighting Squadron Three History."

"Narrative History of Bombing-Fighting Squadron Three."

"History of Bombing Squadron Three."

"Torpedo Squadron Three."

"History of Carrier Air Group Nine."

Air Group Nine Second Pacific Cruise.

"Unit History of VF-9."

"Squadron History, Bombing Squadron Nine."

"History Torpedo Squadron Nine."

"Torpedo Squadron Nine 1944-45."

"History of Carrier Air Group Eighty-Eight."

"History of Fighting Squadron Eighty-Eight."

"The Story of Air Group 88," including chapters on VF-88, VBF-88, VB-88 and VT-88.

"Martha's Vineyard to Tokyo: A Historical Report of VT-88."

Newspaper clippings were utilized from *The New York Times,* New York *Herald Tribune,* San Diego *Evening Tribune,* Scripps-Howard Ernie Pyle columns, *The Honolulu Advertiser,* Iowa City *Press-Citizen,* Green Bay *News-Chronicle,* and miscellaneous unidentifiable journals in veterans' scrapbooks. The five issues of SEA-V-TEN were especially helpful.

The motion pictures "The Fighting Lady" and "Wing and a Prayer", both filmed on board the *Yorktown,* provided excellent visual confirmation of the printed record, as did a private half-hour "home movie" made by Maurice A. Proctor of VF-88 during the summer of 1945.

INDEX

An F6F-3 clears the deck of the *Yorktown* late in 1943.

Fighting 5 F6F-3 Hellcat lands
aboard.

Crew stands at attention as the flag goes up during the *Yorktown*'s commissioning at Norfolk Navy Yard, April
15, 1943.

"GENERAL QUARTERS"

"A SHIP FEIGNS SLEEP"

"DONE IN"

"READY ROOM"
VT-5: Bennie Benson (standing), (L to R) Dick Upson, Bill Laliberte, Joe Kristufek, Tommy Quinn.

-349-

"REPAIRING TBF'S"

"COMMUNION"

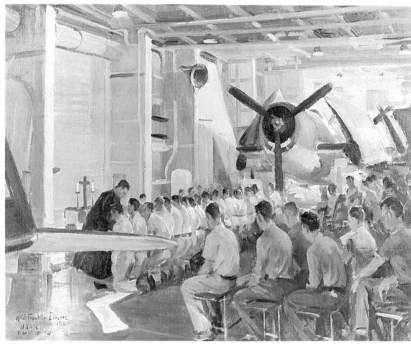

"AMMUNITION COMES
ABOARD"

"PRE-DAWN
LAUNCHING"

"OVER PALAU"

"CRASH LANDING"

"NIGHT ATTACK"

"PLANES RETURN"

"UP TO THE FLIGHT
DECK"

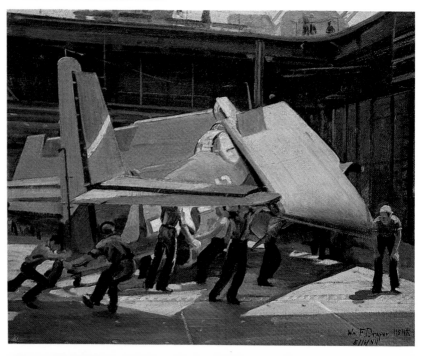

"JAPS FEEL THE STING OF OUR AA"

Signal flags fly from port side halyards during the Wake raid, October 1943.

Yorktown airedales service a Grumman TBF Avenger torpedo-bomber, late-1943.

Screening destroyers are seen from a twin 40mm mount on the *Yorktown.*

A Grumman TBF Avenger clears the deck, heading out over the escorting heavy cruiser *New Orleans* late in 1943.

En route from Panama to Pearl Harbor, the *York* kicks up a huge bow wave, July 1943. Lieutenant Charlie Kerlee, ship's photographer, climbed out on a lowered radio antenna to capture this dramatic picture.

Signalmen hoisting flags on the Fighting Lady.

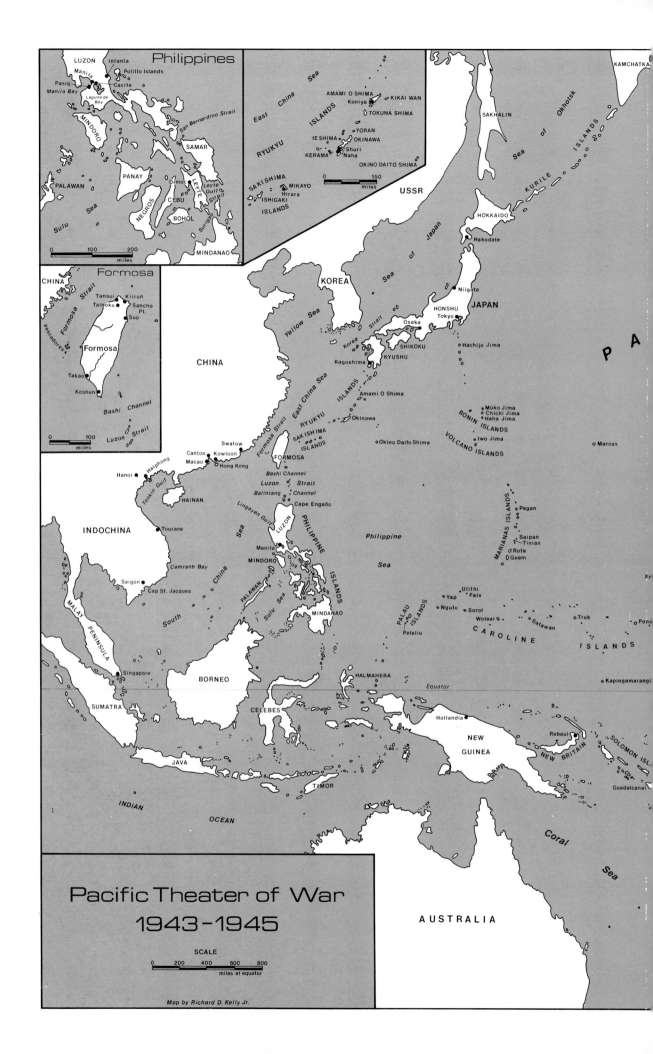

Philippines

LUZON
Infanta
Manila
Polillo Islands
Pasig
Cavite
Manila Bay
Laguna de Bay
MINDORO
San Bernardino Strait
SAMAR
PALAWAN
PANAY
Ormoc
Leyte Gulf
LEYTE
Sulu Sea
NEGROS
CEBU
Leyte Strait
BOHOL
Surigao
MINDANAO

0 100 200
miles

East China Sea
ISLANDS
RYUKYU
AMAMI O SHIMA
Koniya
KIKAI WAN
TOKUNA SHIMA
YORAN
IE SHIMA
OKINAWA
KERAMA
Shuri
Naha
OKINO DAITO SHIMA
SAKISHIMA
MIKAYO
Hirara
ISHIGAKI
ISLANDS

0 150
miles

Formosa

CHINA
Formosa Strait
Tansui
Kiirun
Taihoku
Sancho Pt.
Suo
Pescadores
Formosa
Takao
Koshun
Bashi Channel
Luzon Strait

0 100
miles

KAMCHATKA

Sea of Okhotsk

SAKHALIN

KURILE ISLANDS

USSR

KOREA
Sea of Japan
HOKKAIDO
Hakodate

HONSHU
Niigata
JAPAN
Osaka
Tokyo
Korea Strait
SHIKOKU
Hachijo Jima
Kagoshima
KYUSHU
Amami O Shima

East China Sea
RYUKYU
ISLANDS
Okinawa
SAKISHIMA
ISLANDS
Okino Daito Shima

Muko Jima
Chichi Jima
Haha Jima
BONIN ISLANDS
Iwo Jima
VOLCANO ISLANDS

Marcus

P A

Swatow
Canton
Kowloon
Macao
Hong Kong
Hanoi
Haiphong
Tonkin Gulf
FORMOSA
Bashi Channel
Luzon Strait
Channel
Balintang Channel
Cape Engaño

CHINA

HAINAN

INDOCHINA
Tourane

Camranh Bay
Saigon
Cap St. Jacques

MALAY PENINSULA

Singapore

SUMATRA

South China Sea

Lingayen Gulf
LUZON
Manila
MINDORO
PALAWAN
PHILIPPINE ISLANDS
Sulu Sea
MINDANAO

MARIANAS ISLANDS
Pagan
Saipan
Tinian
Rota
Guam

Ulithi
Fais
Yap
Ngulu
Sorol
Woleai
Satawan
Truk
Pona

PALAU ISLANDS
Peleliu

CAROLINE ISLANDS

Philippine Sea

Fr

Kapingamarangi

BORNEO

Equator

CELEBES

HALMAHERA

Hollandia

NEW GUINEA

NEW BRITAIN
Rabaul

SOLOMON ISL.

JAVA

TIMOR

INDIAN OCEAN

Coral Sea

Guadalcanal

Pacific Theater of War
1943-1945

SCALE
0 200 400 600 800
miles at equator

Map by Richard D. Kelly Jr.